Social Archaeology of
Funerary Remains

SOCIAL ARCHAEOLOGY OF FUNERARY REMAINS

Edited by
Rebecca Gowland and Christopher Knüsel

Oxbow Books

Published by
Oxbow Books, Oxford, UK

ISBN 978-1-84217-365-7

A CIP record of this book is available from the British Library

This book is available direct from

Oxbow Books, Oxford, UK
(Phone: 01865-241249; Fax: 01865-794449)

and

The David Brown Book Company
PO Box 511, Oakville, CT 06779, USA
(Phone: 860-945-9329; Fax: 860-945-9468)

or from our website

www.oxbowbooks.com

Cover image: X-Ray, French Vogue, Paris 1994
© The Helmut Newton Estate/TDR

Printed in Great Britain by
Short Run Press
Exeter

Contents

List of Contributors

PETER ANDREWS, Department of Palaeontology, The Natural History Museum, Cromwell Road, London, SW7 5BD, UK

JESSICA BECKETT, Department of Archaeology, University of Cambridge, Downing Street, Cambridge, CB2 3DZ, UK

SILVIA BELLO, Department of Palaeontology, The Natural History Museum, Cromwell Road, London, SW7 5BD, UK

JULIE BOND, Department of Archaeological Sciences, University of Bradford, Bradford, West Yorkshire, BD7 1DP, UK

HENRI DUDAY, Directeur de Recherche au CNRS et Directeur d'Etudes à l'EPHE, UMR 5199, Laboratoire d'Anthropologie des Populations du Passé, Université Bordeaux 1, Avenue des Facultés, 33405 – TALENCE CEDEX, France

JANE EVANS, NERC Isotope Geosciences Laboratory, BGS, Keyworth, Nottingham, United Kingdom, NG12 5GG, UK

ISLA FAY, School of History, University of East Anglia, Norwich, Norfolk, NR4 7TJ, UK

PAMELA GELLER, Department of Anthropology, American University, Battelle-Tompkins, Room T21, 4400 Massachusetts Ave., NW Washington, DC 20016-8003, USA

REBECCA GOWLAND, St John's College, Cambridge, CB2 1TP, UK

CHRISTOPHER J. KNÜSEL, Biological Anthropology Research Centre (BARC), Department of Archaeological Sciences, University of Bradford, Bradford, West Yorkshire, BD7 1DP, UK

JOHATHAN D. LE HURAY, Department of Archaeological Sciences, University of Bradford, Bradford, West Yorkshire, BD7 1DP, UK

SIMON MAYS, Senior Scientific Officer, Ancient Monuments Laboratory, English Heritage Centre for Archaeology, Fort Cumberland, Eastney, Portsmouth, PO4 9LD, UK

JACQUELINE I. MCKINLEY, Wessex Archaeology, Portway House, Old Sarum Park, Salisbury, Wiltshire, SP4 6EB, UK

JANET MONTGOMERY, Department of Archaeological Sciences, University of Bradford, Bradford, West Yorkshire, BD7 1DP, UK

SHANNON NOVAK, Department of Anthropology, Campus Box 8005, Idaho State University, Pocatello, Idaho, 84105, USA

ALAN K. OUTRAM, Department of Archaeology, School of Geography, Archaeology, and Earth Resources, University of Exeter, Laver Building, North Park Road, Exeter, EX4 4QE, UK

PAUL. B. PETTITT, Department of Archaeology, University of Sheffield, Northgate House, West Street, Sheffield, S1 4ET, UK

MIKE RICHARDS, Department of Human Evolution, Max Plank Institute for Evolutionary Anthropology, Deutscher Platz 604103, Leipzig, Germany

JOHN ROBB, Department of Archaeology, University of Cambridge, Downing Street, Cambridge, CB2 3DZ, UK

RICK SCHULTING, School of Geography, Archaeology and Palaeoecology, Queen's University, Belfast, Northern Ireland, BT7 1NN, UK

HOLGER SCHUTKOWSKI, Biological Anthropology Research Centre (BARC), Department of Archaeological Sciences, University of Bradford, Bradford, West Yorkshire, BD7 1DP, UK

JOANNA R. SOFAER, Department of Archaeology, University of Southampton, Avenue Campus, Highfield, Southampton, SO17 1BF, UK

PAMELA K. STONE, School of Natural Science, Hampshire College, Amherst, MA 01002, USA

DANA WALRATH, University of Vermont, Department of Medicine, 371 Pearl Street, Burlington, VT 05401, USA

FAY WORLEY, Department of Archaeological Sciences, University of Bradford, Bradford, West Yorkshire, BD7 1DP, UK

Acknowledgements

We thank the following reviewers for their efforts on behalf of those contributing to this volume. Although they are not responsible for the final form of the contributions, each gave their time and expertise to making this volume better.

Anthea Boylston (Biological Anthropology Research Centre, Department of Archaeological Sciences, University of Bradford), Megan Brickley (Institute of Archaeology and Antiquity, University of Birmingham), Andrew Chamberlain (Department of Archaeology, University of Sheffield), Elizabeth DeMarrais (Department of Archaeology, University of Cambridge), Clive Gamble (Department of Geography, Royal Holloway, University of London), Roberta Gilchrist (Department of Archaeology, University of Reading), Dawn Hadley (Department of Archaeology, University of Sheffield), Anthony Harding (Department of Archaeology, University of Exeter), Catherine Hills (Department of Archaeology, University of Cambridge), Mary Lewis (Department of Archaeology, University of Reading), Sam Lucy (Cambridge Archaeological Unit, Department of Archaeology, University of Cambridge), Simon Mays (English Heritage, Portsmouth), Andrew Millard (Department of Archaeology, Durham University), Jacqueline McKinley (Trust for Wessex Archaeology), John Moreland (Department of Archaeology, University of Sheffield), Janet Montgomery (Department of Archaeological Sciences, University of Bradford), Gundula Mülder (Department of Archaeology, University of Reading), Shannon Novak (Department of Anthropology, Idaho State University), Terry O'Connor (Department of Archaeology, University of York), Carol Palmer (Department of Archaeology, University of Sheffield), Carole Rawcliffe (School of History, University of East Anglia), John Robb (Department of Archaeology, University of Cambridge), Rick Schulting (School of Geography, Archaeology and Palaeoecology, Queen's University, Belfast), Holger Schutkowski (Biological Anthropology Research Centre, Department of Archaeological Sciences, University of Bradford), James Steele (Department of Archaeology, University of Southampton), Robert Tague (Department of Geography and Anthropology, Louisiana State University), Tim Taylor (Department of Archaeological Sciences, University of Bradford), Tim Thompson (Unit of Anatomy and Forensic Anthropology, School of Life Sciences Research Biocentre, University of Dundee), John W. Verano (Department of Anthropology, Tulane University), Alasdair Whittle (School of History and Archaeology, Cardiff University), Lori Wright (Department of Anthropology, Texas A & M University)

We also acknowledge the discussions during and after a session entitled, "The Social Archaeology of Funerary Remains", co-organised by the editors and Lola Bonnabel (Institut National de Recherches Archéologiques Préventives (Inrap), France) and Liv Nilsson Stutz (Department of Archaeology and Ancient History, Lund University) for the European Association of Archaeologists meeting in Lyon, France (8–9 September 2004), where early versions of some of the papers in this volume were aired.

Introduction

Rebecca Gowland and Christopher J. Knüsel

Human bones are the most tangible and direct form of evidence for understanding how people lived in the past, who they were, and where they came from. The human skeleton is not a universal, static entity; it is a unique repository for social information concerning the lifestyles and lifeways of past peoples, shedding light on, amongst other things, craft and occupational activities, diet, living conditions and health, migration and mobility, and social inter-actions. As a result, human skeletal remains must rank as one of the (if not *the*) most information-rich sources of archaeological evidence. On a micro-level, skeletal remains can often provide intimate information concerning individuals *(e.g.* they smoked a clay pipe) that simply cannot be accessed by any other archaeological means, but, equally, one can 'zoom out' and discover answers to population level questions *(e.g.* impact of changing subsistence strategies on population health). Few forms of archaeological evidence have this investigational versatility.

Given their evident importance, it is surprising that, for many years, the potential of skeletal material for answering important archaeological questions was overlooked. Human skeletal remains only began to play a part in archaeological interpretation from the 1960s; prior to this they were only deemed relevant for answering specific questions concerning 'race', or when medical curiosity was peaked by the unearthing of a particularly abnormal specimen. Even during the theoretical developments of New Archaeology and Processualism, when archaeology was given a scientific make-over, studies of human skeletal material remained on the periphery. Quite why this was so, when environmental evidence, such as animal bones, carbonised plant remains and pollen, were at the forefront of these developments is unclear.

Key initiators in the field of human skeletal analysis, Calvin Wells and Don Brothwell in the UK and Lawrence Angel in the US, continued to highlight the social relevance of the skeleton in their publications. However, despite these efforts, studies of human remains continued to be marginalised, usually confined to cemetery reports, often in the appendices or microfiche (which invariably went missing). Osteological data in cemetery reports still tend to be reduced to a series of summary tables of demographic and palaeopathological statistics. Often linking this information to individual skeletons can be difficult or impossible and the data presented in formats incompatible with those from other cemeteries.

As a consequence of this, there continues to be a distinct lack of a synthetic treatment of human remains and their burial context, even today, with unprecedented numbers of trained osteologists in the field. Human skeletal analysis is still not fully incorporated into social archaeology – the dominant theme of much of archaeological research today. For example, we frequently find comments such as these: "In spite of several analyses of human osteological material from the area of the Danube Gorges, there has been little integration of the results from physical anthropology and the archaeological context of the burials" (Borić and Stefanović, 2004). Later, in the same treatment, these authors note that: "Although isotopic measurements were analysed for ten children from Lepenski Vir and 7 from Vlasac… it is not possible to relate palaeodietary results to particular individuals as information on what skeletons were analysed was not published in the… report" (p.527). This type of oversight is not as uncommon as one might hope and attempting to link burial cuts with individuals, burial inclusions and position within a particular site, let alone a description of the burial position, perhaps accompanied with an *in situ* photograph are labours of some difficulty when dealing with many published reports.

Larsen (1997), in his introduction to *Bioarchaeology*, also laments the fact that many archaeologists in the United States (generally believed to be a few steps ahead of the UK when it comes to the integration of skeletal analysis) are actually unaware of the potentials and limitations of osteological evidence for contributing to debates concerning aspects of social organisation and identity. Why should this be when these are the remains of the people who inhabited the past, who farmed the animals, made the pots, built the houses, etc., and whose very lives we are trying to access?

Science/theory divide

Human skeletal analysis has been conceptualised as a purely scientific undertaking, contributing to the arsenal of archaeological evidence, but not fundamental to social analysis. This perception appears to be derived from the insidious belief that the skeleton is a universal, fixed biological entity. This is untenable: the skeleton is more than a series of biological facts; it is the remains of an individual who interacted within a social as well as physical environment in a dynamic way. Where people lived, what they ate, their experiences, all affected their bodies in a particular way. Even adverse *psychological* experiences can leave their mark on the developing skeleton in the form of dental enamel defects. In turn, the (culture-laden) physical appearance of an individual will also have affected the way in which they were perceived within a particular society. As Michael Sims (2003, 4) observed: 'Through your body the world touches you' and *vice versa*. There is a dialectic between the physical and the social body, and it becomes very difficult to tease one apart from the other (see Sofaer, this volume).

There is, however, a strong divide in archaeology between those engaged in the scientific aspects of enquiry and those involved in what Jones' (2002) refers to as interpretive archaeologies. For many years, since the inception of post-processual archaeology, archaeological research falling under the umbrella of 'science' was considered decidedly untrendy and empiricist – human remains analysis included. The emphasis was instead very much on the subjective and relativist nature of archaeological interpretation; the past, in some respects, became a more intangible, less 'knowable' and even 'foreign' place. While much of this research was very important for the way in which archaeologists approached the past, an unfortunate initial side-effect was that concepts associated with scientific archaeological techniques (*e.g.* objectivity, immutability, *etc.*) became antithetical to this new theoretical framework and the divide between science and social theory further compounded.

This situation has recently been addressed by Jones (2002) who, quoting C.P. Snow, refers to the divisive effect that these 'two cultures' have on archaeological interpretation. There has, at times, been an almost antagonistic lack of communication across this science/ social theory divide, resulting in the bewildering situation whereby researchers in one 'camp' were actually answering some of the questions posed in the other without either fully realising their mutual and complementary interest. This lack of communication has also meant that there has been a misuse/abuse of osteological evidence by those that do not fully understand its limitations. For example, Tyrrell (2000) discusses this position with regard to the pervasive use of non-metric traits, particularly in studies of Anglo-Saxon cemeteries, observing that: 'Many studies have treated trait frequencies as if they were an archaeological typology, using a mix and match approach to determine if skeletons in a cemetery belonged to related individuals, or to determine the 'ethnic' group to which an individual skeleton belonged. This is unacceptable since not only does it lead to misleading conclusions, but also promises to access information which morphological studies cannot at present ascertain'. However, as Beckett

and Robb (this volume) point out, in many respects this is a two-way street, with osteologists also guilty of failing to fully engage with the broader social and theoretical implications of their findings.

One of the key aims of this book is to stress that *context* is of paramount importance to skeletal analysis. Information derived from the skeleton is highly culturally contingent and may have variable meanings through time and space depending on social context. A thorough knowledge of the archaeological context not only informs the skeletal analysis, but also ensures that the information gained from the skeleton can feed back and aid the interpretation of the site. The paper by Knüsel and Outram (this volume) on cannibalism highlights this, in particular. They demonstrate the way in which subtle differences in depositional context, in addition to the appearance of the bone, helps to establish the presence of cannibalistic activity, while this skeletal information, in turn, provides a better understanding of the nature/usage of the archaeological site.

Preservation and taphonomy

Archaeological research occurs at many scales, be they site specific, regional, or global, as well as many temporal scales from the single event to long-term sequences. The resolution of these scalar qualities is influenced by the quality of the research design and its completeness, the intensity of research at a site or in a region, and by the relative resilience of material to taphonomic and decay processes. Hodder (2000, 21) observes: 'From many periods and areas, few sites survive or few have been excavated with modern scientific techniques. Thus, there is little choice but to talk of the large scale, the generalised, the gross patterning'. Archaeological research designs have all too often left out or underplayed the importance of human remains and thus contributed to their often inadequate recovery and disassociation from their archaeological context.

Because they appear and ossify at different rates, the number of bones in the human body rises from the roughly 270 of the neonate, to about 940 due to the appearance of secondary centres (epiphyses) of ossification in children, to the adult total of 206, when the epiphyses fuse. Unless these and the place of burial are excavated with appropriate procedure and expertise, a wealth of information is lost. The presence of trained people in the field is vital to ensure that the maximum amount of contextual information is available for later analysis and interpretation. As Duday emphasises in his contribution to this volume the relationship of the skeleton to the grave and its inclusions has much to contribute to a fuller and more refined appreciation of mortuary variability, especially with regard to the once organic features of burials. Many of the sites currently being investigated have developed important new strategies to deal with co-mingled and fragmented remains and, building on techniques like those used for forensic contexts, make it likely that even these remains can be used to address research questions that have, at their core, the understanding of how the material came to be deposited (see, for example, Knüsel and Outram 2004, Sutherland 2000, McKinley 1997, Bond 1996). Insights gained from the study of funerary remains also have the potential to feed back into not only archaeological studies but also those related to medico-legal interests, especially where ethical constraints prevent experimentation, a pertinent point made by Henri Duday in this volume.

With this in mind, the opening papers of this book seek to elucidate and characterise the social and taphonomic factors governing the survival of human bone; this is essential for subsequent interpretations of skeletal assemblages. Bello and Andrews observe that while detailed taphonomic studies of animal bones abound, very few studies have examined the variables governing the survival of human bone. They analyse the differential survival of skeletal elements and the differences in patterns of preservation between different age and sex classes. Importantly, they also discuss the repercussions of their findings for subsequent social interpretations of the burial assemblage. The following paper by Andrews and Bello also focuses on taphonomy, this time characterising the different patterns of skeletal element survival associated with particular burial practices (*e.g.* primary, secondary, disturbance, *etc.*). By looking at the way in which particular funerary rites differentially affect the skeletal element composition of an assemblage, they have produced criteria that can be used to aid in the identification of specific types of cultural activity within the funerary domain.

Beckett and Robb's study of Neolithic monuments in Ireland also focuses on taphonomy as well as the effects of cultural activity on assemblages of human remains. They highlight the lack of research on osteological assemblages from these mortuary contexts and contrast this with the abundance of theoretical interpretations mooted concerning the ideology of the burial population. Once again, this provides a clear example of archaeologists trying to reconstruct past societies and yet overlooking the remains of the people that constituted them. Beckett and Robb argue that this situation stems from a lack of dialogue between osteologists and archaeologists concerned with social theory. Their paper goes on to develop an innovative simulation model in order to analyse the effects of both cultural burial practices and natural processes on the bone assemblages over time. These findings have important implications for current interpretations of social practice from skeletal assemblages from Neolithic tombs.

One could argue that the ultimate form of bodily modification in the funerary context is the practice of cremation. McKinley reviews the social context for cremation in the UK and dispels the myth that it was practiced as a 'cheap option', as one might anticipate from the modern adoption of this funerary rite. Staying with the theme of cremation, Bond and Worley look at the evidence for animal remains burnt alongside or simply included afterwards in the burials of cremated individuals from Anglo-Saxon and Viking England. They highlight the significance of different species of animals, finding that not all inclusions were the result of feasting, some species having a totemic symbolism, whilst others may have been companions during life. This paper leads on to the following section, which focuses on the interpretations of skeletal remains within the grave, moving away from the previous emphasis on objects and towards a contextualisation of the anthropology of the deceased.

The skeleton in the grave

Much research in the funerary domain has centred on the relationship between skeletons and objects (usually within a grave). Although various methods of analysis have been championed, most have seen the relationship between the body of the deceased and the grave and its contents as separate sets of data, created by separate sets of researchers, using separate and unrelated recording systems, one in the field and a second, in the laboratory. As discussed previously, this results in an unsynthesised archive that more often than not reveals that these separate groups do not address themselves to the same questions and any synthesis that is attempted is rather inadequate, superficial at best, or at its worst, leaves the reader wondering at the motivations for excavation in the first place.

Furthermore, there has been a long tradition in funerary archaeology of overlooking the skeletal evidence and privileging the objects as the focus of analysis. Up until very recently, for example, cemetery reports either relied on objects entirely for establishing aspects of identity such as sex, or, when skeletal and artefactual evidence were apparently 'contradictory' (*e.g.* female weapon burial), more often than not the skeletal data was disregarded. Over more recent years, despite theoretical developments that have seen a rise in the importance of the 'body' as an integral part of social identity (Shilling 1997, 65), skeletal remains continue to be marginalised. Shilling (1993, 1997) argues that social constructionism, whereby aspects of social identity are perceived not to be biologically determined, but subject to culturally specific interpretation, has led to an increased marginalisation of the physical body. As Duday notes in this volume one often gets the impression that the deceased was placed as an offering to a ceramic vessel, rather than the other way around. The large numbers of human remains that have not been analysed or received inadequate treatment are a grim reminder of the consequence of an object-centred approach.

The current theoretical climate within the social sciences now questions the existing dichotomy between science and social theory. The primary strength of many of the papers in this book is that they connect the biological aspects of the human remains more strongly and thoroughly with their burial context. There are a number of practical and heuristic, as well as social reasons, for adopting such a body-centred approach. With specific reference to funerary remains, Byrd and Monahan (1995, 257–260) note, "Archaeology frequently suffers from the lack of a standardized, consistent body of terminology." One of the most nagging problems to affect archaeology is the rather cavalier use of terminology that it often borrows from other disciplines. Funerary studies are especially adversely affected by an incomplete understanding of the specific meaning of anatomical terms. In order to standardise the use of anatomical terms and orientations, the position of skeletal elements with respect to each other, researchers should use standard anatomical position for the body. Although this standard did not exist until comparatively recently and does not necessarily reflect emic understandings of the body of past peoples, it relies on the fact that the body and its constituent parts have not changed their basic organisation for at least the past five million years since the advent of bipedal australopithecines.

In archaeological contexts, the human body can thus act as a datum point due to its standard anatomical description that does not change with changes in body position. In fact, since the body occasioned the deposition and proportions of the burial feature, it should act as the reference for all other features of burial. In other words, the body's standard anatomy could be used to avoid referents for objects that are interpretative identifiers, such as, for example, calling objects 'ear-rings', even if they do not occur anywhere near the temporal bone of the interred individual but simply because they resemble more recent objects. Here, one might invoke the confusion caused by the metal weaving battens or the numerous, but differently shaped objects referred to as 'keys' or 'cosmetic brush cases' in post-Roman burials (Knüsel and Ripley 2000) or 'mirrors' in Iron Age ones, which confuses or disguises symbolic and ceremonial importance or ascribes to them a potentially anachronistic function. Such objects may resemble Roman keys but that does not necessarily mean they retained this function or, furthermore, explain why such objects were placed in burials. The positioning of objects with respect to the body reveals behaviours that took place at death, after death and during burial and should not be confused with the identification of how the items functioned.

As discussed above, the impetus for this book was a desire to marry these cultural aspects of burial with the anthropology of the deceased so as to include a comprehensive perspective on the human, faunal, and artefactual aspects of burial of past societies, their practices, beliefs, and social organisation. The over-arching guide here is one that encourages researchers to control for the taphonomic and biological manifestations of the funerary record before invoking the social and cultural, and this principle is implicit in the ordering of the contributions. Progressing on from the earlier papers that have dealt primarily with taphonomic aspects of the burial domain are two papers (Le Huray and Montgomery and co-authors) that examine stable isotope evidence and seek to address important social questions, including 'ethnic' identities and 'sensory' experiences of the people buried. Stable isotope studies are currently making pivotal contributions to archaeological debates concerning diet and the movement of peoples. Le Huray and colleagues' analysis of carbon and nitrogen isotopes in skeletons dating to the La Tène period in Bohemia illustrates not only practical aspects of the diet (*e.g.* millet cultivation), but also, intriguingly, dietary differences based on grave good associations; those buried with weapons exhibit a distinctive isotopic signature. These findings have some parallels with dietary isotope work carried out by Privat and O'Connell (2002) on the Anglo-Saxon site of Berinsfield, Oxfordshire, where some dietary differences were, again, noted among the weapon burial group. Montgomery and Evans' paper examines strontium and lead isotopes in combination with funerary evidence from sites in the Outer Hebrides in relation to social differentiation and movement of peoples over time. Research such as this is proving extremely important for examining and often challenging previously held perceptions concerning population movement. When used in conjunction with grave good analysis, these studies frequently indicate that the straightforward associations between 'ethnicity' and grave goods usually made by archaeologists are misleading, and instead a much more complex pattern emerges concerning both the 'ethnicity' of these people and the dynamics of group identity.

Indeed, the complexity of patterns of grave good deposition are also discussed in the following paper by Gowland which focuses on age as an aspect of social identity in Anglo-Saxon England. Gowland examines how the ageing body was understood culturally in fifth to sixth century England, demonstrating the fluid and dynamic way in which age interacts with other social facets such as gender and status, throughout the life course. Sofaer also touches upon age in her discussion of the plasticity of the human body as it develops, the extent to which it may be affected and moulded by cultural activities and the implications for studies of sex and gender in bio-archaeology. This distinction between sex and gender has been the subject of considerable discussion over the last few decades and Sofaer's paper provides an osteological perspective to this debate and highlights some of the tensions in the way that such terms are applied to the funerary domain. Gender is the focus of the following paper by Stone and Walrath who critique the emphasis placed on 'obstetrical hazard' as an explanation for female mortality in the past. They argue that, instead, skeletal and biocultural information must be linked for a more systematic and less cavalier understanding of female morbidity and mortality in the past.

Health in the past is also the focus of the two following papers, both concentrating on medieval England and both integrating historical evidence. The first paper by Mays questions the relationship between gluttonous monks and DISH, a condition that has been used to support this Late Medieval literary equation (*cf.* Geoffrey Chaucer's monk). In this instance the biological data may suggest that this image of the corpulent monastic was as much a political ploy to exploit the wealth controlled by the monasteries, a situation that eventually presaged the Dissolution. The second paper, by Fay, looks at the burial treatment accorded individuals in Medieval Norwich with disfiguring infectious diseases (*e.g.* leprosy, treponemal disease), with the aim of understanding the social implications of these diseases for the sufferers. Historical evidence indicates that diseases such as these were thought to reflect a moral and spiritual, as opposed to simply a physical, contagion and one would expect their burial rites to reflect this stigma.

Knüsel's paper also integrates historical evidence, using the Investiture Contest as a model for interpreting funerary rites at those times when succession to leadership was uncertain and power more likely to be contested. This model is well illustrated by the contrasting burials of the Merovingian leaders Childéric and his eldest son and successor, Clovis. Knüsel notes that, unfortunately, while the skeletal remains of the former are said to be well-preserved, almost no information about them is available; again the objects prevail over the individual who actually occasioned their presence.

Continuing with the subject of power and the contesting thereof, the following three papers examine trauma in the past; the first two of these look at inter-personal violence (Schulting and Novak). Schulting discusses the range of skeletal evidence for interpersonal violence and the various social contexts of violence dating to the Mesolithic/ Neolithic transition in Europe. The archaeological study of violence has become a key topic of study over recent years and the integration of human skeletal evidence of trauma should be central to such research, providing as it does the most direct verification. Novak's study of inter-personal violence specifically relates to that occurring within the domestic context. Drawing upon a large sample of hospital medical records, Novak compares the types of trauma associated with accidental injury with those occurring as a result of domestic violence, applying her findings to the patterns of trauma observed in an archaeological sample from the prehistoric Great Basin. Finally, Knüsel and Outram look at another type of trauma altogether – the identification of cannibalistic activities through the presence of peri- and post-mortem cut marks and bone modification. The authors bring together an immense and disparate body of evidence to comprehensively review and identify the evidence for cannibalism stemming from a variety of different social contexts and motivations behind the act itself (*e.g.* funerary ritual, exerting power over enemies, survival).

The following paper by Geller also deals with trauma, but of a different sort – bodily modification. Geller examines dental modification in an assemblage of archaeological human remains from northwestern Belize, contextualising this with both material and ethnohistoric evidence and noting that frequently such analyses fail to adequately consider social context. She discusses this type of bodily alteration as a means of imprinting the body, producing, as it were, an 'embodied text' towards the construction of particular social identities. Geller also focuses on the significance of the 'performative' aspect of this rite within a ritual setting. Continuing with the theme of bodily decoration, the final paper in this volume, by Pettitt, examines embodiment in Upper Palaeolithic Europe. Pettitt's chapter suggests that ochre found covering skeletal remains likely came from decorated objects, such as masks, or from body coverings using this red pigment. This contrasts with a recent paper by Wadley *et al.* (2004, 661) on residue analysis for the use of ochre in hafting of stone projectiles where we read: 'There is, however, no way of testing whether ancient people in Africa practised body painting'. Pettitt's paper also highlights some fascinating parallels between the presentation of the bodies in the graves of the Upper Palaeolithic and the Venus figurines, linking the use of the body through ornamentation to the emerging social complexity during this time.

In summary, the papers in this book take an incomplete funerary analysis that is a major part of the focus of standard archaeological enquiry, recombines it with the skeletal report that is often a separate and incompletely synthesised addendum, and replaces people (the dead) as a focus rather than as an adjunct to the material remains of their lives and activities. In doing so, they reveal not only the interpretative strength of such an approach but also, importantly, the thought processes that researchers adopt to link what have been two separate realms of concern. The skeleton is not simply a clothes-horse for cultural symbolism and, as these papers demonstrate, the skeleton and its context need to be fully integrated as part of a more holistic and meaningful component of archaeological and anthropological research.

References

Bond, J. M. (1996) Burnt offerings: animal bone in Anglo-Saxon cremations. *World Archaeology* 28(1), 76–88.

Borić, D. and Stefanović, S. (2004) Birth and death: infant burials from Vlasac and Lepenski Vir. *Antiquity* 78, 526–546.

Byrd, B. F. and Monahan, C. M. (1995) Death, ritual, and Natufian social structure. *Journal of Anthropological Archaeology* 14, 251–287.

Hodder, I. (2000) Agency and individuals in long-term processes. In M.-A. Dobres and J. E. Robb (eds.) *Agency in Archaeology*, 21–33. London and New York, Routledge.

Jones, A. (2002) *Archaeological Theory and Scientific Practice*. Cambridge, Cambridge University Press.

Knüsel, C. J. and Outram, A. K. (2004) Fragmentation: the zonation method applied to fragmented human remains from archaeological and forensic contexts. *Environmental Archaeology: The Journal of Human Palaeoecology* 9(1), 85–97.

Knüsel, C. J. and Ripley, K. M. (2000) The Man-Woman or 'Berdache' in Anglo-Saxon England and Post-Roman Europe. In W. Frazer and A. Tyrrell (eds.) *Social Identity in Early Medieval Britain*, 157–191. Leicester, Leicester University Press.

Larsen, C. S. (1997) *Bioarchaeology: Interpreting Human Behavior from the Human Skeleton*. Cambridge, Cambridge University Press.

McKinley, J. I. (1997) Bronze Age 'Barrows' and Funerary Rites and Rituals of Cremation. *Proceedings of the Prehistoric Society* 63, 129–145.

Privat, K. L. and O'Connell, T. C. (2002) Stable isotope analysis of human and faunal remains from the Anglo-Saxon cemetery at Berinsfield, Oxfordshire: dietary and social implications. *Journal of Archaeological Science* 29, 779–790.

Shilling, C. (1997) The body and difference. In K. Woodward (ed.) *Identity and Difference*, 63–120. London, Sage.

Sims, M. (2003) *Adam's Navel: A Natural and Cultural History of the Human Body*. London, Penguin.

Sutherland, T. (2000) Recording the grave. In V. Fiorato, A. Boylston, and C. J. Knüsel (eds.) *Blood Red Roses: the archaeology of a mass grave from Towton, A.D.* 1461, 36–44. Oxford, Oxbow Books.

Tyrrell, A. (2000) Skeletal non-metric traits and the assessment of inter- and intra-population diversity: past problems and future potential. In M. Cox and S. Mays (eds.) *Human Osteology in Archaeological and Forensic Science*, 289–306. London, Greenwich Medical Media.

Wadley, L., Williamson, B., and Lombard, M. (2004) Ochre in hafting in Middle Stone Age southern Africa: a practical role. *Antiquity* 78, 661–675.

1. The Intrinsic Pattern of Preservation of Human Skeletons and its Influence on the Interpretation of Funerary Behaviours

Silvia Bello and Peter Andrews

Introduction

From at least Upper Palaeolithic times, we may suppose that the main agents responsible for assemblages of human bones are humans themselves. But, how did humans treat their dead? From an archaeological point of view, this question corresponds to understanding if an unequal representation of bones or individual subgroups in the human assemblage is the manifestation of human behaviour or the result of natural/taphonomic process. In order to optimise information on health and environmental conditions gained from the bones of historic and prehistoric skeletal populations, it is necessary to increase the understanding of processes affecting their preservation.

In recent years there has been much research on the factors modifying bones in the process of becoming fossilised. This is the science of taphonomy, defined as all those processes affecting bones in the transition from the biosphere to the lithosphere (Efremov 1940). While in the strictest sense of the word, taphonomy is devoted to the analysis of post-mortem processes affecting organic remains, it has often been used in palaeoecological and palaeobiogeographical contexts (Gifford 1981). Taphonomic processes and artificial human modifications related to funerary practices, grave typologies, excavation and storage techniques may determine a differential state of preservation and representation of osseous remains. Since 1950, the tendency has been to focus on the fossil record in terms of how well it reflects the actual palaeoecology of the biotic community (Clark and Kietzke 1967), and on the selective processes that determine the constitution of a fossil assemblage (Johnson 1960). Even in palaeo-anthropological studies the palaeoecological focus takes the lead, and research on hominids as taphonomic agents has aimed to uncover bio-cultural activity in past populations (Dart 1949, 1956, 1960; Behrensmeyer 1975;

Binford 1981). At present, the notion of human taphonomy finds a new dimension in forensic anthropology, where the term refers to the use of taphonomic models, approaches and analyses in forensic contexts, to estimate the time since death, reconstruct the circumstances before and after deposition, and discriminate the products of human behaviour from those created by earth's biological, physical, chemical and geological subsystems (Haglund and Sorg eds. 1997; Haglund and Sorg eds. 2002).

Since at least the middle of the twentieth century, archaeologists have been trying to perfect methods to explain why some portions of animal carcasses are abundant and other portions are rare at sites (Lyman 1996). In a palaeoanthropological context, variation in frequencies of animal skeletal parts has been associated with variable strategies in human use of food sources (*e.g.* Shipman *et al.* 1984; Potts 1986; Bunn 1981; Blumenschine 1986). In funerary archaeology, the absence of specific human remains from a burial site (single bones, individuals or specific subgroup of individual according to their biological or social status) has been ascribed to cultural and/or social practices (*e.g.* Duday and Masset eds. 1987; Crubézy *et al.* eds. 1990; Crubézy *et al.* eds. 2000).

When considering frequencies of human skeletal parts in burials and of human categories according to age and sex criteria, it is important to distinguish between the secondary effects of the funerary ritual and the preservation patterns linked to the anatomical structure of the bones. Thus, absence or under-representation of specific human remains from funerary sites may be ascribed to cultural and/or social behaviour, but it could also reflect characteristic preservation patterns of the skeleton due to inherent structural properties of the bone. What would be the consequences for research if a differential state of preservation of bony remains is due to taphonomic processes dependant on anatomical, age and/or sex features?

This work aims to increase understanding of the burial domain by identifying preservation patterns of specific bones and sex and age categories. Improving our recognition of the combined effects of burial practices and anatomical/individual characteristics on the state of preservation of human remains will enhance the information that can be gained from key osteological collections.

Material and methods

Three medieval and three post-medieval collections were analysed in order to determine specific anatomical patterns of preservation: St. Estève Le Pont, Hauture, St. Maximin, Fédons, Observance and Spitalfields. The preservation pattern according to individual sex and age has been evaluated on the Spitalfields sample where legible coffin plates give details of name, age, and date of death for 369 individuals (Table 1.1).

This sample of over nine hundred skeletons from the six osteological series has been analysed using an "Anatomical Preservation Index" (API) and the "Bone Representation Index" (BRI). The Anatomical Preservation Index (API) is a preservation score assessing the quantity of osseous material present. It is an elaboration of a previous index proposed by Dutour (1989) and expresses the ratio between the score of preservation (*i.e.* the percentage of bone preserved) for each single bone

SITE	PERIOD	LOCATION	NOTES	NO. INDIVIDUALS	REFERENCES
St. Estève Le Pont	8th century	Berre L'Etang, Bouches-du-Rhône, France.	cemetery	*84 individuals*: 32 subadults 52 adults *20 males, 29 females 3 sex-undetermined*	Bello et al., 1999; Thomann et al., 1999; Bello et al., 2000; Thomann et al., 2005
Hauture	11th–12th centuries	Fos-sur-Mer, Bouches-du-Rhône, France.	cemetery	*112 individuals*: 1 fœtus, 53 subadults 58 adults *17 males, 15 females 26 sex undetermined*	Signoli et al., in press a
St. Maximin	12th–13th centuries	St. Maximin, Var, France	cemetery	*68 individuals* 3 foeti 33 subadults 32 adults *14 females, 12 males 6 sex undetermined*	Signoli et al., 1999; Signoli et al., in press b.
Fédons	1590	Lambesc, Bouches-du-Rhône, France.	bubonic plague cemetery	*133 individuals* 72 subadults, 61 adults *29 males 32 females*	Reynaud, 1996; Castex, 1996; Bizot et al., eds. 2005
Observance	1722	Marseilles, Bouches-du-Rhône, France	bubonic plague mass grave	*179 individuals*: 51 subadults 128 adult *59 males, 58 females 11 sex-undetermined*	Dutour et al., 1994; Signoli et al., 1997 Signoli et al., 1998
Spitalfields	1729–1857	London, UK.	crypt	*369 individuals*: 87 subadults *48 males, 37 females 2 sex-undetermined* 282 adult *139 males, 139 females 4 sex-undetermined*	Reeve and Adams, 1993; Molleson and Cox, 1993.

Table 1.1. Details of the three medieval and three post-medieval Christian cemeteries coming from the South of the France (Bouches-du-Rhône).

and the skeleton's total anatomical number of bones. The preservation scores were arranged in six classes:

- class 1, bone not preserved (0% of bone preserved);
- class 2, 1–24 % of bone preserved;
- class 3, 25–49% of bone preserved;
- class 4, 50–74% of bone preserved;
- class 5, 75–99% of bone preserved;
- class 6, bone completely preserved (100% of bone preserved).

We defined well-preserved bones (WPB) as those having a preservation score of more than 50% (classes 4, 5 and 6), and well-preserved skeletons (WPS) as those having more than 50% of their bones well preserved (Bello *et al.* 2006).

Intra-observer and inter-observer errors were tested using the t-test for paired observations. The scores of preservation were estimated by one of the authors and a different researcher on 34 osseous remains of a single skeleton. Both the intra- and the interobserver errors produced a t-score very closed to 1, meaning that there were neither significant errors between two measurements taken at both times by the same observer, nor between the measurements taken on the same example by two different observers.

The "Bone Representation Index" (BRI; Dodson and Wexlar 1979) expresses the frequency of each bone in a sample. It is the ratio between the actual number of bones excavated (Number of observed bones, No. obs.) and the number of bones that should have been present according to the Minimum Number of Individuals (MNI) of the sample (Theoretical total number of bones, No. Theor.): BRI = 100 x Σ (No. obs. / No. theor.). The Minimum Number of Individuals has been defined on the basis of the most common bone in the assemblage for subadult and adult individuals (Bökönyi 1970).

We defined well-represented bones (WRB) as those being present in the sample at more than 50%, and well represented skeletons (WRS) as those having more than 50% of their bones present (Bello *et al.* 2006).

Results

Anatomical preservation

The BRI values were evaluated for the adult and subadult individuals of the three medieval (St. Estève le Pont, Hauture and St. Maximin) and the three post-medieval (Fédons, Observance and Spitalfields) cemeteries. Figure 1.1 and Table 1.2 show the differing preservation patterns of skeletal elements at these six sites. The joining of the BRI values by lines has no mathematical significance, but it allows a better visual comprehension. The relative abundance of the teeth in the Hauture and St. Maximin collections and the mandibles in the case of the Fédons collection has not been evaluated since these pieces were partially or completely unavailable at the time of observation.

The **cranium** is generally well represented in the six collections, with BRI values largely greater than 50%. In the five studied collections, lower values were generally evaluated for facial bones. The state of preservation of the frontal bone was often related to that of the facial bones, especially in the area of the supra-orbital margin, which could explain the poorer state of preservation of the frontal compared to the other bones of the cranium. Parietal bones were generally well represented. The good state of preservation of these bones is probably related to their relatively high bone density (Boaz and Behrensmeyer 1976). However, due to high fragmentation, parietal bones become difficult to identify and include in the evaluation of the Minimum Number of Individuals (MNI;

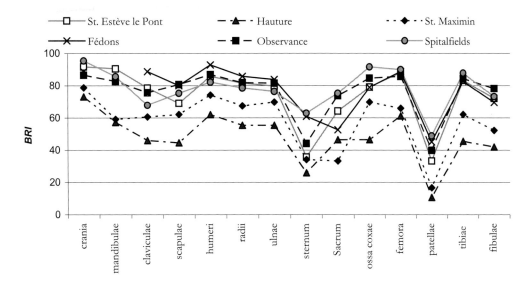

Figure 1.1. BRI values observed for the whole sample (subadult and adult individuals) of St. Estève le Pont, Hauture, St. Maximin, Fédons, Observance and Spitalfields sites.

	St. Maximin	St. Estève	Hauture	Fédons	Observance	Spitalfields
Crania	78.8	91.7	73.2	88.8	86.6	95.4
Mandibulae	59.1	90.5	57.1		82.7	85.6
claviculae	60.6	78.6	46.0	88.7	75.7	67.9
scapulae	62.1	69.0	44.6	80.1	80.7	75.3
humeri	74.2	85.7	62.1	92.9	86.9	82.2
radii	67.4	81.5	55.4	85.7	81.8	78.6
ulnae	69.7	79.8	55.4	83.8	81.6	76.4
sterna	34.2	35.7	25.9	60.9	44.1	62.9
Sacrum	33.3	64.3	46.4	52.6	73.7	75.3
ossa coxae	69.7	79.2	46.4	78.9	84.6	91.6
femora	65.9	88.1	61.2	88.7	85.8	90.0
patellae	16.7	33.3	10.7	45.1	39.9	48.9
tibiae	62.1	83.3	45.5	82.7	84.4	87.8
fibulae	52.3	72.0	42.0	69.5	78.2	73.2

Table 1.2. BRI values observed for the whole sample of St. Maximin, St. Estève le Pont, Hauture, Fedons, Observance and Spitalfields sites.

Russell 1987). Temporal bones were also generally abundant elements of the cranium. The mastoid process, the petrous portion, the temporal portion of the zygomatic process and the upper portion of the external auditory meatus were all generally well-preserved and abundant in the six osteological samples observed. The occipital bone was also present in high frequencies: the internal occipital protuberance, the occipital condyles and the posterior border of the foramen magnum were particularly well preserved and easy to recognise (Bello 2001).

The **mandible** was one of the better preserved elements of the skeleton in the six osteoarchaeological samples observed. This observation has previously been made both for archaeozoological and for human bones assemblages (*e.g.* Bouchud 1977; Badgley 1986; Grayson 1989; Klein 1989; Kreutzer 1992; Lyman 1996; Tattersall 1995). In the six observed samples, the body of the mandible, especially in the area between the two mental foramina, was generally better preserved than the rami. The better preservation of this portion of the mandible has also been attested at other sites where it was used in the MNI evaluations (Brézillon 1963).

Moving to the post-cranial skeleton, **claviculae** were reasonably abundant in all the samples observed, especially the middle portion of the diaphysis. The **scapula** has been generally considered a poorly preserved bone because of the fragility of the sub-scapular fossa (Russell 1987). Nevertheless, five of the six collections observed show BRI values higher than 50%, comparable to those of the clavicle. This relative abundance of scapulae is mainly due to the good preservation of the acromion process, the coracoid process and the lateral border by the infraglenoid tubercle, all of which have high bone density.

In the six collections observed, the BRI of **long bones** appeared to be related either to their size, such that the bigger the long bone, the greater the abundance in the sample, or to their position, with proximal limb elements

being better preserved than distal elements. Thus, humeri were better represented than radii and ulnae, and femora were better represented than tibiae and fibulae. The poorer state of preservation of the fibula is often due to severe fragmentation, perhaps because of its far greater length than width. Even when long bones were fragmented, the diaphysis was the best preserved portion. This preservation pattern is consistent with the bone density: higher density is found in the midshaft of the diaphysis, while lower density may be seen in the proximal and distal epiphyses (Galloway *et al.* 1997; Willey *et al.* 1997).

Patellae were often under-represented in the observed osteological samples, but they were almost complete when present. This under-representation could be the result of excavation bias, but since the patella can easily be removed from its articulation during body decomposition its under-representation can also depend on animal scavenging activities.

The **sacrum**, was often fragmented and poorly preserved in the observed collections. The portions most resistant to taphonomic processes were the median sacral crest and the promontory of the first sacral vertebra. The poor preservation of this element is associated with its low bone density and high proportion of cancellous bone (Boaz and Behrensmeyer, 1976).

The **sternum** was also often fragmented in the six observed collections, again due to its low bone density. The manubrium was better preserved and more abundant than the body, as seen at other sites (Brézillon 1963; Waldron 1987).

In the case of the **ossa coxae**, five of the six collections observed show BRI values higher than 50%, despite the strong fragmentation of this element. The acetabulum and the sciatic notch were the best represented element.

The detailed analyses of the representation of single teeth and ribs have not been obtained for this work.

The **vertebral column** is generally abundant in osteological collections. The detailed evaluation of the mean BRI values for each vertebra of adult individuals at St. Estève le Pont, Hauture, St. Maximin, Fédons and Observance collections showed a generally better representation of cervical and lumbar vertebrae (Fig. 1.2). The good preservation of lumbar vertebrae is probably associated with their shape and structural robusticity while that of cervical vertebrae, especially C1 and C2, could be due to the protection afforded by the cranium when the skeleton is articulated. The poorer state of preservation of thoracic vertebrae has been ascribed to their low bone density (Willey *et al.* 1997). In the five collections observed, the best preserved portion of the vertebrae were the facet of the dens of the axis and the dens itself. Even in very fragmentary collections (Bello *et al.* 2003a) and in cremated samples (Duday 1989) these are well represented. The lamina and the spinous processes were also generally well preserved, but they were frequently fragmented. Thus in case of isolated spinous processes, these elements are poorly identifiable (Grayson 1989). The vertebral body was the poorest preserved portion due to its high proportion of cancellous bone (Münzel 1988).

The small bones of the **hands** and **feet** were generally poorly represented in the six observed osteoarchaeological collections, but they tend to be well preserved and almost complete when present. The good state of preservation of the hand and foot bones has been associated with the reduction of the medullary cavity (Guthrie 1967), which facilitates the complete preservation of these bones even in very fragmented and damaged collections (Defleur *et al.* 1993). In the observed samples, hand bones were generally more abundant than foot bones. The detailed evaluation of the mean BRI values for each single bone of the hands and feet of the adult individuals of the St. Estève

le Pont and Observance collections showed different relative abundances according to the shape and dimensions of bones (Fig. 1.3). Metacarpals and metatarsals were generally more abundant than carpal and tarsal bones. The frequency of phalanges, of both hand and foot, was directly related to their dimensions, with proximal phalanges being more abundant than middle phalanges, and middle phalanges more abundant than distal ones. This observation could suggest a consistent relationship between size and survival (Bouchud 1977) as well as reflecting the size and recovery relationship of human anatomical remains (Ubelaker 1981; Henderson 1987).

Individual preservation

It has already been observed that subadult individuals generally had skeletons less well preserved and less well represented than adults in osteological series (Angel 1969; Walker *et al.* 1988; Guy and Masset 1997; Guy *et al* 1997; Buckberry 2000; Bello *et al.* 2006). Also in the six observed samples the lower frequencies of well-preserved skeletons and well-represented skeletons have been evaluated for subadults (Table 1.3).

We extend the analyses to specific subgroups of individuals in the case of Spitalfields, since for this sample the sex and age diagnoses were directly derived from coffin plates and confirmed, where possible, by cross-checking baptism dates and burial registers (Molleson and Cox 1993). The analysis of age and sex differences in the state of preservation which has been applied to this collection had, therefore, the purpose of avoiding the circularity of previous work in which the age and sex of the skeletons were estimated from morphological observations.

It has been suggested by Guy and co-authors (1997,

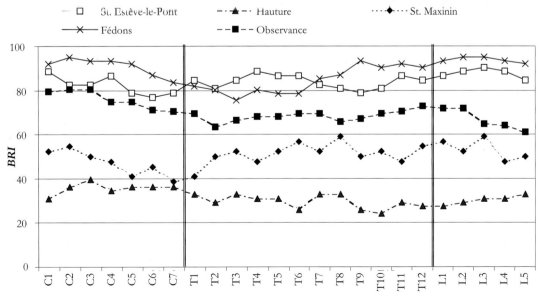

Figure 1.2. BRI values observed for the vertebrae of the whole sample of St. Estève le Pont, Hauture, St. Maximin, Fedons and Observance sites.

226) that there is a threshold separating two types of human remains: an infant type, with soft ill-structured bones, rich in interstitial water, poorly protected against chemical or mechanical degradation, and a more robust adult type. However, in the case of the Spitalfields sample, the patterns of preservation appear more continuous than has been proposed by Guy and co-authors. By considering the percentage of bones for each class of preservation (API scores of preservation), subadults aged 5–19 years at Spitalfields had a pattern of preservation with intermediate characteristics between the younger subadults and the adults (Fig. 1.4). Subadults aged 0–4 years were mainly characterised by a poor state of preservation with high frequencies of API class 1. The percentages of bones per class of preservation progressively decrease and the lowest values were evaluated for API class 6 (bones completely preserved). Conversely, the frequencies of bones per class of

preservation increased proportionally with increase in API preservation scores in the case of adults. These last were generally characterised by lower percentage of API class 1 and higher percentages of API classes 5 and 6. The anomaly for the API class 5, for which subadults aged 0–4 years were scored with a higher percentage than adults, can be explained by the generally good state of preservation of Spitalfields remains. Remains of subadults at Spitalfields were generally well preserved when present (*cf.* exclusion of API class 1), most of them being preserved more than 75% (classes 5 and 6). Nevertheless, the epiphyses of long bones were generally absent or poorly preserved in the case of subadults aged 0–4 years, and thus their long bones scored class 5. Only 6 long bones (0.23% of all long bones of subadults aged 0–4 years) were complete and scored class 6. The long bones of subadults aged 5–19 years and adults were generally well preserved with comparable frequencies for API classes 5 and 6.

These results suggest that human remains cannot be separated into only two age classes of preservation. It is likely that the state of preservation of osseous remains increases proportionally with individual age (*cf.* Table 1.4). Unfortunately, the reduced number of subadults for the age class 5–19 years at Spitalfields does not allow a definitive conclusion.

Taking into consideration the sex of subadult individuals, subadult females were less well preserved than subadult males. The patterns of preservation (frequencies of bone per class of preservation, API) were generally similar with main differences for the age class 0–4 years (Fig. 1.5). For this age class, females had a higher percentage of bone not preserved (API class 1: Chi^2 = 5.391, p = 0.0202) and a lower percentage of well preserved bones (API class 5: Chi^2 = 5.14, p = 0.0233) than subadult males of the same age class.

By considering the frequency of well preserved bones, females aged less than 1 year and females aged 1–4 years had frequencies of well preserved skeletons at 35.7% and 38.5%. Conversely, this low frequency was only observable for males aged less than 1 year: 36.8% for the age class 0–1 year and 56.5% for the age class 1–4 years. These results suggest that the threshold between poorer and better states of preservation should be set around 1

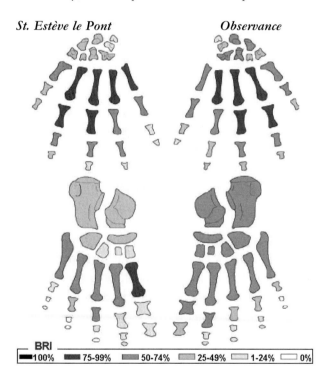

St. Estève le Pont   **Observance**

BRI
■100% ▦75-99% ▨50-74% ▦25-49% ▢1-24% ▢0%

Figure 1.3. BRI average values of the hands and feet bones of adult individuals of St. Estève le Pont and Observance collections. Darker grey means more abundant bones.

	St. Estève le Pont	Hauture	St. Maximin	Fédons	Observance	Spitalfields
% WPS						
Subadults	15.6	16.7	40.0	25.0	56.9	51.1
Adults	75.0	24.1	47.7	98.4	75.0	76.6
% WRS						
Subadults	46.9	51.9	62.9	62.5	68.7	63.4
Adults	96.2	37.9	63.6	100	87.5	51.4

Table 1.3. Percentage of well-preserved skeletons (WPS) and well represented skeletons (WRS) in the six observed samples according to the individual groups of age.

year for males and around 4 years for females (Table 1.4). A similar pattern with generally higher values was also evident for the frequency of well represented skeletons. In the case of females, the classes of less than 1 year and 1–4 years had frequencies of well preserved skeletons of 50.0% and 53.8%. In the case of males, a lower frequency was observable for individuals aged less than 1 year (57.9%), while a higher percentage was achieved for the age class 1–4 years (73.9%). Nevertheless, the limited number of individuals for smaller subclasses of age (*e.g.* only 2 females and 2 males aged 3–4 years) might have introduced a bias in these analyses. Consequently, these results should be treated with caution.

Discussion

Humans are the only living species which pays and paid great attention to death. They treat their dead according to the criteria and cultural expression of the period, going beyond the mere necessity of simply disposing of the bodies and manifested by a burial often rich in symbolic and ritual connotations. Although, on a functional level, the intention may have been to protect the bodies of the dead from animal and weathering damage, the action taken during the funerary ritual could involuntarily or deliberately have contributed to the destruction and/or the disappearance of all or part of the body/skeleton. Particular

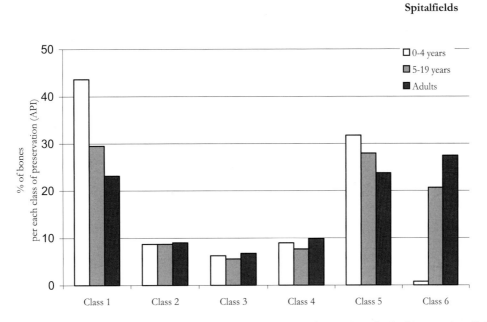

Figure 1.4. Percentage of bones per each class of preservation (API) according to the individuals' age in Spitalfields sample.

Age	No. of Individuals		API						BRI				
			No. of WPS		% of WPS			No. of WRS		% of WRS			
	F	M	F	M	F	M	TOT.	F	M	F	M	TOT.
< 1 year old	14	19	5	7	35.7	36.8	40.0	7	11	50.0	57.8	48.6
1–2 years	11	16	4	11	36.4	68.8	55.6	11	16	45.5	68.8	59.3
3–4 years	2	7	1	2	50.0	28.6	55.6	2	7	100	68.8	77.8
1–4 years old	*13*	*23*	*5*	*13*	*38.5*	*56.5*	*55.6*	*7*	*17*	*53.8*	*73.9*	*66.7*
0–4 years old	27	42	10	20	37.0	47.6	47.9	14	28	51.9	66.7	57.7
5–9 years old	0	2		1		50	33.3		1		50	33.3
10–14 years old	3	1	2	1	66.7	100	100	2	1	66.7	100	75.0
15–19 years old	7	3	5	2	71.4	66.7	60.0	7	3	100	100	100
5–19 years old	*10*	*6*	*7*	*4*	*70*	*66.7*	*64.7*	*9*	*5*	*90.0*	*83.3*	*82.4*
Subadults	*37*	*48*	*17*	*24*	*45.9*	*50*	*51.1*	*23*	*33*	*62.2*	*68.8*	*63.4*
Females		139		107			77.0		120			86.3
Males		139		106			76.3		123			88.5
Adults		*282*		*210*			*76.6*		*246*			*51.4*

Table 1.4. Number and Percentage of well preserved skeletons (WPS) and well represented skeletons (WRS) according to the individuals' age and sex at the Spitalfields site.

funerary practices may result in the unequal representation of specific anatomical elements or entire skeletons (see Andrews and Bello; Beckett and Robb, this volume).

The unequal representation of bones

Analysis of the skeletal part profiles (*e.g.* the relative frequency of a bone in the sample, Lyman 1996) is one of the major fields of taphonomic research in archaeo-zoology. The goal of this research is to identify the taphonomic agent (fluvial, animal or human agent) responsible for the constitution of the assemblage. The application of archaeozoological methods to the study of human skeletal remains allows researchers to assess the influence of funerary practices and natural taphonomic processes on the abundance of human bone. As pointed

out by Willey and co-authors (1997), the absence of certain elements, where bone mineral density is low, should be expected where environmental conditions are particularly destructive. Conversely, the absence of more densely constructed bones suggests a form of selection process, perhaps opportunistic scavenging or deliberate human modification of the remains, such as mortuary processing or suspected acts of cannibalism.

In the case of assemblages, the unequal representation of specific bones can be the result of funeral practices that involved voluntary or involuntary destruction and/or disappearance of specific anatomical components. In the case of secondary burials, the remains are displaced from their first place of deposition (primary burial) into a new, often final, place of deposition (secondary burial).

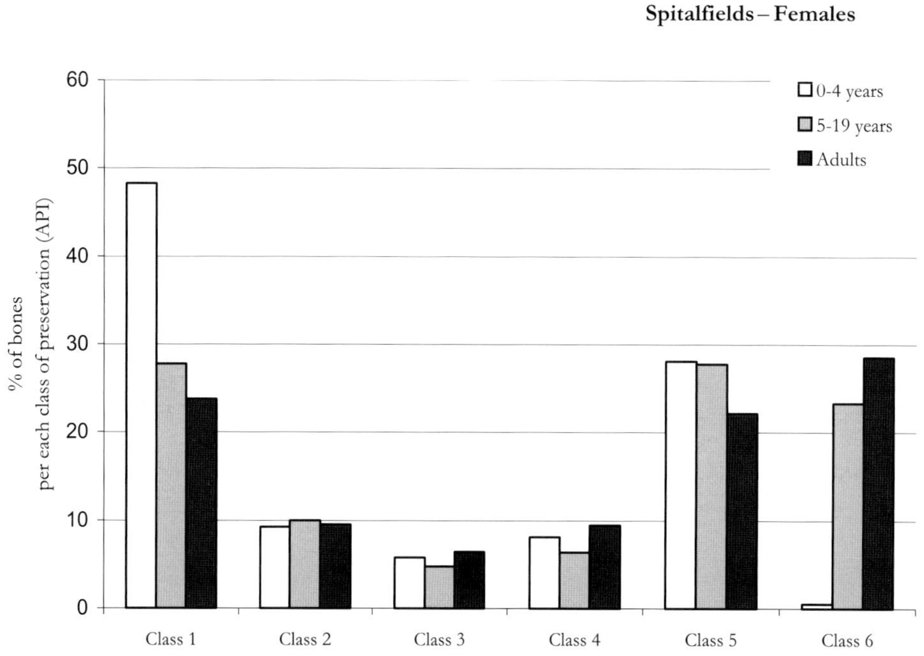

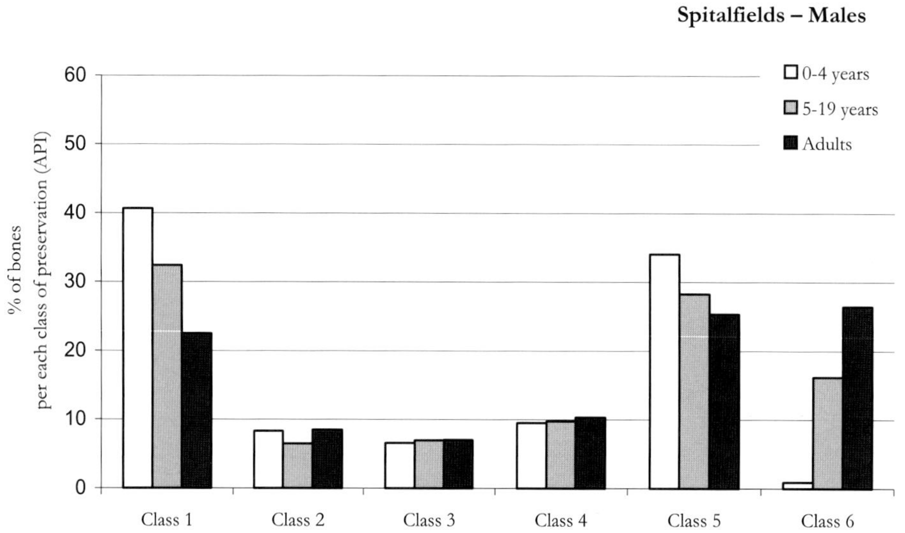

Figure 1.5. Percentage of bones per each class of preservation (API) according to the individuals' age and sex (Spitalfields sample).

This transfer can involve some or all of the body, and it can involve either a time element or a spatial element, or both (Andrews *et al.* 2005). When the intention is to bury only specific bones after initial exposure/interment elsewhere, there will be a better representation of these elements in the secondary burial. The cranium has being considered the most significant skeletal element in different populations and its high representation has been documented for several sites (*e.g.* Duday 1986a, 1986b; Boës and Sears 1996; Baills and Chaddaoui 1996; Malone, 1996; Andrews and Bello, this volume). The same has been observed for femora (Garland *et al.* 1988; Andrews and Bello, this volume), for example, one of the multiple burials at the Neolithic site of Çatalhöyük consists of the remains of four individuals represented mainly by skulls and femora (Andrews *et al.*, 2005).

When the ritual involves the spatial movement of a body from its primary to its secondary burial, it is possible that the original intention was to transfer all the elements. However, some of these, most often the smaller and distal elements of the skeleton (*e.g.* bones of the hands and feet, hyoid, patellae) can be involuntarily lost during the transfer of the remains (*e.g.* Duday 1986a, 1986b; Masset 1986; Duday and Sellier 1990; Gambier and Le Mort 1996; Lambot *et al.* 1996; Masset 2000). The same phenomenon may also be seen when secondary burial is delayed for ritualistic or ceremonial reasons, for unless the body is protected in some way, many of the smaller elements may be lost. We wish to emphasize, however, that the over-representation of specific bones, such as the cranium, and the under-representation of others (*e.g.* phalanges) are not of themselves sufficient indication of secondary burial. This interpretation must be mediated by the preservation patterns linked to the anatomical structure of human bones.

At the majority of medieval and post-medieval Christian cemeteries interments were made as complete corpses, without the intervention of rituals leading to the alteration or disappearance of selected portions of the skeleton. In the present study, where the re-use of grave plots was evident, remains from these graves were excluded from the analysis. Therefore, the absence of bones was likely to be associated with natural taphonomic processes taking place in the sediment and differences in the relative frequency of osseous remains in the assemblages were more likely to depend on the structural features of bones (shape, dimension, density) given the same taphonomic processes. The frequencies of skeletal parts observed in the six medieval and post-medieval collections described earlier, where we supposed that complete bodies were buried without the intervention of rituals leading to the disappearance of selected portions of the skeleton, are very similar to each other. Moreover, the frequencies observed for the French cemeteries (earthen burials) are also similar to those observed at the Spitalfields site. At this site, the bodies were buried in coffins and deposited in a crypt, and it could be predicted,

therefore, that the skeletons should retain most elements as there would have been less opportunity for the small bones to have become separated from their parent skeletons. The degree of similarity between such disparate forms of interment suggests that human bones have a common pattern of preservation, regardless of the characteristics of the site. This pattern of preservation has a major influence on the relative abundance of the bones at a site, and it is characterised by higher frequencies for more robust and dense bones and lower frequencies for smaller and more cancellous elements. In this sense the better representation of the skull in human assemblages could be related to the better preservation of this bone or of some portions of this bone, as well as to the easier identifiability of its fragments compared to other bones. The temporal bone, for instance, is frequently used in the calculation of Minimum Number of Individuals in cases of very fragmentary collections or cremated samples (Duday 1989; Bello *et al.* 2002a and 2003a).

The absence of the smaller bones of the hands and feet could also be related to the structural characteristics of these bones, the rates of decay being inversely proportional to bone size (Bouchud 1977; Von Endt and Ortner 1984; Lambert *et al.* 1985). Smaller size constitutes a disadvantage for bone preservation, not only in terms of vulnerability to decay but also of retrieval during excavation.

The analysis of the frequencies of skeletal parts suggests that in order to better understand funerary practices, it is necessary to recognise the pattern of preservation and representation of bones. The comparison of the skeletal part profile of a collective burial with the frequencies of human remains from medieval and post-medieval Christian burials (characterised by similar environmental, climatic and sedimentological features), can offer a new interpretative tool for the comprehension of human collective burial formation (for some examples of comparisons between skeletal part profile, refer to Bello *et al.* 2002a and Bello *et al.* 2003b).

The unequal representation of skeletons

Palaeodemographical reconstruction from the analysis of human skeletons is based on the assumption that the sex and age distribution of a skeletal sample reflects the constitution of the original population. In order to justify this assumption, three suppositions must be confirmed. First, the osteological sample must allow the correct determination of the age and sex of the buried individuals (Bocquet-Appel and Masset 1982, 1985; Buikstra and Konigsberg 1985; Greene *et al.* 1986; Usher 2002). Second, all individuals (irrespective of age or sex) must have had the same chance of being represented at the site (Lovejoy 1971; Piontek and Henneberg 1981; Milner *et al.* 1989; Hoppa 1996; Paine and Harpending 1998). Third, any bias that may affect the data must be detectable and taken into account (Ubelaker 1989; Bello *et al.* 2003b).

With regard to the first point, it has been recognised that no method of establishing sex and age in an archaeological sample guarantees 100% reliable results (Lovejoy *et al.* 1985). The age-at-death is usually biased in the direction of the age distribution of whatever reference sample was used to generate the individual estimates in the first place (Holman *et al.* 2002).

Concerning the second and third hypothesis, Bocquet-Appel and Masset (1977) emphasise that palaeo-demographical studies will never be able to prove that the exhumed sample represents the total number of dead individuals from the original, living population, both for archaeological and ethnological reasons. On the one hand, skeletal features used in age and sex determination have different patterns of preservation (Walker *et al.* 1988; Walker 1995; Bello 2001; Bello *et al.* 2002b). On the other hand, funeral and burial practices may focus on a portion of the population according to biological (sex, age or family relations) and/or social criteria (*e.g.* Masset 1986; Tillier and Duday 1990; Sansilbano-Collilieux 1990). The exclusion of the new-born and the old, who may not be recognised as active members of the community, is well evidenced in different historical periods (Dedet *et al.* 1991; Perrin 2000; Tranoy 2000). People with infectious diseases (leprosy, tuberculosis, treponematosis and plague victims) were often excluded from the mortuary space of the rest of the community (Lorans 2000; Dutour *et al.* 1998). Moreover, different types of funerary structures (*e.g.* burials in the ground, wood or lead coffins, stone or metal sarcophagi) do not provide the same environment for preservation (Mant 1987; Bello 2001). Selective burial or non-burial of all, or parts, of individuals, as well as the use of different burial structures for subjects of different biological or social status produce a bias in the palaeo-demographic reconstruction of the original population.

As stated earlier, it is important to ascertain if the absence of specific groups of individuals is due to selective/cultural exclusions or to natural/taphonomic processes. The preservation and representation of bones according to age and sex in the Christ Church, Spitalfields, suggests the following:

- Subadult skeletons are less well preserved and skeletal elements were less well represented than those of adult skeletons. This pattern has also been observed in cemeteries where individuals were buried in the ground (Angel 1969; Walker *et al.* 1988; Buckberry 2000; Bello *et al.* 2002b).
- The state of preservation of osseous remains increases proportionally with the individual age.
- Among subadults, female skeletons are generally less well preserved and with bones less well represented than male skeletons, the main differences being observed in the age class of 0–4 years.

Whether this pattern of preservation holds true for every osteoarchaeological sample or not, we would expect subadults in general to be less well-preserved and with bones less well-represented than those of adult individuals, and subadult females to be less well preserved and their bones less well represented than subadult males, irrespective of the characteristics of the site. Experimental work (Bouchud 1977; Von Endt and Ortner 1984; Lambert *et al.* 1985) has shown that rates of decay are inversely proportional to bone size. It is conceivable that the generally smaller size of subadult bones would lead to poor preservation. Moreover, since the relative volume of bones is related to the individuals' age, it is probable that the bones of the younger infants would be even more affected than the bones of older subadults. It has also been shown that bone mineral density (defined as mass of mineral per unit area) decreases in the first month after birth followed by a rapid increase during the next two years and slower changes thereafter (Rauch and Schoenau 2001).

It is easy to understand the impact of this statement on the interpretation of burial practices and palaeo-demographical reconstruction. The absence of young subadults and specifically females from sites, generally associated with ritual exclusion of non-active members of the community, could instead be the result of a natural process of decomposition and disappearance of immature osseous material.

Conclusion

Both taphonomic processes and artificial human modifications related to funerary practices may determine the state of preservation and survival of osseous remains. The study of human remains from medieval and post-medieval Christian cemeteries, where we supposed that complete bodies were buried, enabled us to identify the most likely profile of bone representation when only the first of these, taphonomic processes, was operational. The absence or under-representation of specific human remains from these funerary sites thus reflects only the characteristic preservation patterns of the skeleton due to inherent structural properties of bone. The comparison of skeletal bone frequencies for these sites with those of assemblages where funerary practices selecting specific osseous elements are suspected offers a new interpretative tool in the understanding of human collective burial formation.

The analysis of the Spitalfields sample, where individuals' age and sex were derived directly from a coffin-plate, shows that the state of preservation and representation of bones are age and possibly sex-dependent. The state of preservation of osseous material according to the specific age and sex groups may determine the relative frequency of these groups in the sample. In terms of palaeodemographical reconstruction, the analysis of the Spitalfields sample suggests that female skeletons aged 0–4 years and male skeletons aged less than 1-year represent the main source of bias because they have the lowest chance of survival. This would mean that the under-representation of infants in collective burials could be the result of a natural process of decomposition and preservation and not necessarily an indication of past population behaviour.

Acknowledgements

We thank Professor Olivier Dutour, Dr Michel Signoli, Ms Aminte Thomann and Mr Alain Genot for the support in the analysis of the French collections and Dr Louise Humphrey for the assistance at the Natural History Museum (London). We are grateful to the editors, Dr. Christopher Knüsel and Dr. Rebecca Gowland, and the three anonymous reviewers for valuable comments on an earlier version of this paper. A Marie Curie Individual Fellowship (contract n° HPMF-CT-2002-01667) supported the analysis of the Spitalfields collection.

References

Andrews, P., Molleson, T. and Boz, B. (2005) The human burials at Çatalhöyük. In I. Hodder (ed.) *Inhabiting Çatalhöyük: reports from the 1995–99 seasons*, Cambridge, McDonald Institute Monographs, 261–278.

Angel, J. L. (1969) The bases of paleodemography. *American Journal of Physical Anthropology* 30, 427–435.

Badgley, C. (1986) Taphonomy of mammalian fossil remains from Sivalik rock of Pakista. *Paleobiology* 12(2), 119–142.

Baills, H. and Chaddaoui, L. (1996) La sépulture collective de Can-Pey (Pyrénées-Orientales): étude des pratiques funéraires. *Bulletins et Mémoires de la Société d'Anthropologie de Paris* 8(3–4), 245–260.

Behrensmeyer, A. K. (1975) Taphonomy and Paleoecology in the Hominid Fossil Record. *Yearbook of Physical Anthropology* 19, 36–50.

Bello, S. (2001) *Taphonomie des Restes Osseux Humains. Effet des Processus de Conservation du Squelette sur les Paramètres Anthropologiques.* Unpublished Thesis, University of Florence and University of Medicine La Timone of Marseilles.

Bello, S., Thomann, A., Adalian, P., Ardagna, Y., Gibert, M., Maczel, M., Vergonzanne, L., Signoli, M. and Dutour, O. (1999) *Etude anthropologique des Sépultures du Cimetière de Saint Estève Le Pont (Berre L'Etang, Bouches-du-Rhône). Opération de Sauvetage du 1ᵉʳ au 19 février 1999.* Unpublished Report, University of Medicine La Timone of Marseilles.

Bello, S., Lalys, L., Thomann, A., Adalian, P., Ardagna, Y., Gibert, M., Maczel, M., Vergonzanne, L., Boule, E., Dagnas, G., Genot, A., Signoli, M. and Dutour, O. (2000) *Etude Anthropologiques des Sépultures du Cimetière de Saint-Estève-le Pont (Berre L'Etang, Bouches-du-Rhône). Opération de Sauvetage du 21 au 16 juillet 2000.* Unpublished Report, University of Medicine La Timone of Marseilles.

Bello, S., Thomann, A., Signoli, M., Rabino Massa, E. and Dutour O. (2002a) La conservation différentielle des os humains et le "Profil théorique de survie osseuse. *Archéologie et Préhistoire* 113, 105–120.

Bello, S., Signoli, M., Rabino Massa, E. and Dutour, O. (2002b) Les processus de conservation différentielle du squelette des individus immatures. Implications sur les reconstitutions paléodémographiques. *Bulletins et Mémoires de la Société d'Anthropologie de Paris* 14(3–4), 245–262.

Bello, S., Thomann, A., Lalys, L., Signoli, M., Rabino-Massa, E. and Dutour, O. (2003a) Calcul du "Profil théorique de survie osseuse la plus probable" et son utilisation dans l'interprétation des processus taphonomiques pouvant déterminer la formation d'un échantillon ostéologique humain. *British Archaeological Reports,* S1145, 21–30

Bello, S., Thomann, A., Rabino Massa E. and Dutour, O. (2003b) Quantification de l'Etat de conservation des colections ostéoarchéologiques et ses champs d'application en anthropologie. *Antropo* 5, 21–37. *www.didac.ehu.es/antropo*

Bello, S., Thomann, A., Signolli, M., Dutour, O. and Andrews, P. (2006) Age and sex bias in the reconstruction of past population structures. *American Journal of Physical Anthropology* 129(1), 24–38.

Binford, L. R. (1981) *Bones: Ancient Men and Modern Myths.* New York, Academic Press.

Bizot, B., Castex, D., Reynaud, P., Signoli, M., eds. (2005) *La Saison d'une Peste (avril-septembre 1590): le Cimetière des Fédons à Lambesc.* Valbonne, Monographies du C.R.A. de Valbonne, CNRS.

Blumenschine, R. J. (1986) Carcass consumption sequences and the archaeological distinction of scavenging and hunting. *Journal of Human Evolution* 15(8), 639–659.

Boaz, N. T. and Behrensmeyer, A. K. (1976) Hominid taphonomy: transport of Human skeletal parts in an Artificial Fluviatile Environment. *American Journal of Physical Anthropology* 45(1), 53–60.

Bocquet-Appel, J.P. and Masset, C. (1977) Estimateurs en paléodémographie. *L'Homme* XVII(4), 65–90.

Bocquet-Appel, J. P. and Masset, C. (1982) Farewell to palaeodemography. *Journal of Human Evolution* 11, 321–333.

Bocquet-Appel, J. P. and Masset, C. (1985) Palaeodemography: resurrection or ghost? *Journal of Human Evolution* 14, 107–111.

Boës, E. and Sears, S. (1996) Les crânes trophées marquisiens (XVIIIᵉ et XIXᵉ siècles). Interprétation des interventions anthropiques. *Bulletins et Mémoires de la Société d'Anthropologie de Paris* 8(3–4), 245–260.

Bökönyi, S. (1970) A new method for the determination of the number of individuals in animal bone material. *American Journal of Archaeology* 74(3), 291–292.

Bouchud, J. (1977) Etude de la conservation différentielle des os des dents. *Bulletin de l'Association Française pour l'Etude du Quaternaire* Supplément 47, 69–73.

Brezillon, M. (1963) L'Hypogée des Mournouards. Démographie. *Gallia Préhistorica* V(1), 50–63.

Buckberry, J. (2000) Missing presumed buried? Bone diagenesis and the under-representation of Anglo-Saxon children. *Assemblage* 5, http://www.shef.ac.uk/~assem/5/buckberr.html

Buikstra, J. E. and Konigsberg, L. W. (1985) Palaeodemography: critiques and controversies. *American Anthropologist* 87, 316–334.

Bunn, H. T. (1981) Archaeological evidence for meat-eating by Plio-Pleistocene hominids from Koobi Fora and Olduvai Gorge. *Nature* 291, 574–577.

Castex, D. (1996) Etude paléodémographique du cimetière Fédons. In P. Raynaud (ed.) *Les Fédons (Lambesc).* Marseilles: Anthropological Rapport, AFAN.

Clark J. and Kietzke K. K. (1967) Paleoecology of the Lower Nodular Zone, Brule Formation, in the Big Badlands of South Dakota. In J. Clark, J. R. Beerbower and K. K. Keitzke (eds.) *Oligocene Sedimentation Stratigraphy, Paleoecology and Paleoclimatology in the Big Badlands of South Dakota,* n° 5, 111–137. Fieldiana, Geology Memoir.

Crubézy, E., Duday, H., Sellier, P. and Tillier, A. M., eds. (1990) *Anthropologie et Archéologie Dialogue sur les Ensembles Funéraires.*

Bulletins et Mémoires de la Société d'Anthropologie de Paris, Paris.

Crubézy, E., Masset, C., Lorans, E., Perrin E. and Tranoy, L., eds. (2000) *Archéologie Funéraire*. Paris, Editions Errance.

Dart, R. (1949) The predatory implemental technique of the australopithecines. *American Journal of Physical Anthropology* 7, 1–16

Dart, R. (1956) Myth of the bone-accumulating hyena. *American Anthropologist* 58, 40–62

Dart, R. (1960) The bone tools manufacturing ability of *Australopithecus prometheus*. *American Anthropologist* 62, 134–138

Dedet, B., Duday, H. and Tillier, A. M. (1991) Inhumation de fœtus, nouveau-nés et nourrissons dans les habitats protohistoriques du Languedoc: l'exemple de Gailhan (Gard). *Gallia* 48, 59–108.

Defleur, A., Dutour, O. and Valladas, H. (1993) Cannibals among the Neanderthals? *Nature* 362, 214.

Dodson, P., and Wexlar, D. (1979) Taphonomic investigations of owl pellets. *Paleobiology* 5, 279–284.

Duday, H. (1986a) Organisation et fonctionnement d'une sépulture collective néolithique. L'Aven de la Boucle à Corconne (Gard). In H. Duday and C. Masset (eds.) *Anthropologie Physique et Archéologie*, 89–97. Paris, Ed. CNRS.

Duday, H. (1986b) Contribution des observations ostéologiques à la chronologie interne des sépultures collectives. In H. Duday and C. Masset (eds.) *Anthropologie Physique et Archéologie*, 51–54. Paris, Ed. CNRS.

Duday, H. (1989) La nécropole du Peyrou à Agde (Hérault). Etude anthropologique. *Revue Archéologique de Narbonnaise* suppl. 19, 459–471.

Duday, H. and Masset, C., eds. (1987) *Anthropologie Physique et Archéologie*. Paris, Ed. CNRS.

Duday, H. and Sellier, P. (1990) L'archéologie des gestes funéraires et la taphonomie. *Les Nouvelles de l'Archéologie* 40, 12–14.

Dutour, O. (1989) *Hommes Fossiles du Sahara: Peuplements Holocènes du Mali Septentrional*. Paris, Edition du CNRS.

Dutour, O., Signoli, M., Georgeon, E. and Da Silva, J. (1994) Le charnier de la Grande Peste de Marseille (1720–1722) de la rue Leca: données de la fouille de la partie centrale et premiers résultats anthropologiques. *Préhistoire et Anthropologie Méditerranéennes* III, 191–203.

Dutour, O., Signoli, M., Bello, S. and Palfi, Gy (1998) Paleoepidemiology of infectious disease: New challenges. *Homo* 49/Suppl., 21.

Efremov, I. A. (1940) Taphonomy: a new branch of paleontology. *Pan-American Geologist* 74, 81–93.

Galloway, A., Willey P. and Snyder L. (1997) Human bone mineral densities and survival of bone elements: a contemporarary sample. In W. D. Haglund and M. H. Sorg (eds.) *Forensic Taphonomy: the Postmortem Fate of Human Remains*, 295–317. Boca Raton, CRC Press.

Gambier, D. and Le Mort, F. (1996) Modifications artificielles et séries anciennes: possibilités et limites de l'interprétation paléoéthnologique. *Bulletins et Mémoires de la Société d'Anthropologie de Paris* 8(3–4), 245–260.

Garland, A. N., Janaway, R. C. and Roberts, C. A. (1988) A study of the decay processes of human skeletal remains from the parish church of the Holy Trinity, Rothwell, Northamptonshire. *Oxford Journal of Archaeology* 7(2), 235–252

Gifford, D. P. (1981) Taphonomy and paleoecology: a critical review of archaeology's sister disciplines. In M.B. Schiffer (ed.) *Advances in Archaeological Method and Theory*, vol. 4, 365–438. New York, Academic Press.

Grayson, D. K. (1989) Bone transport, bone destruction, and reverse utility curves. *Journal of Archaeological Science* 16, 473–652.

Greene, D. L., Van Gerven, D. P. and Armelagos, G. J. (1986) Life and death in ancient populations: bones of contention in palaeodemography. *Human Evolution* 1, 193–207.

Guthrie, R. D. (1967) Differential preservation and recovery of Pleistocene large mammal remains in Alaska. *Journal of Paleontology* 41, 243–246.

Guy, H., and Masset, C. (1997) Particularités taphonomiques des os d'enfants. In L. Buchet (ed.) *L'enfant son corps, son histoire*, 35–43. Paris, Edition APDCA.

Guy, H., Masset, C. and Baud, C. A. (1997) Infant taphonomy. *International Journal of Osteoarchaeology* 7, 221–229.

Haglund, W. D. and Sorg M. H., eds. (1997) *Forensic Taphonomy: the Postmortem Fate of Human Remains*. Boca Raton, CRC Press.

Haglund, W. D. and Sorg, M. H., eds. (2002) *Advances in Forensic Taphonomy: Method, Theory and Archaeological Perspectives*. Boca Raton, CRC Press.

Henderson, J. (1987) Factors determining the state of preservation of human remains. In A. Boddington, A. N Garland. and R. C. Janaway (eds.) *Approaches to Archaeology and Forensic Science*, 43–54. Manchester, Manchester University Press.

Holman, D. J., Wood, J. W. and O'Connor, K. A. (2002) Estimating age-at-death distributions from skeletal samples: multivariate latent-trait approach. In R. D. Hoppa and J. W. Vaupel (eds.) *Paleodemography. Age distributions from Skeletal Samples*, 193–221. Cambridge, Cambridge University Press.

Hoppa, R. D. (1996) *Representativeness and Bias in Cemetery Samples: Implications for Palaeodemographic Reconstructions of Past Populations*. Unpublished thesis, McMaster University.

Johnson, R. C. (1960) Models and methods of analysis of the mode of formation of fossil assemblages. *Geological Society of American*, 73, 1075–1086.

Klein, R. G. (1989) Why does skeletal part representation differ between smaller and larger bovids at Klasies River Mouth and other Archeological Sites? *Journal of Archaeological Science* 6, 363–381.

Kreutzer, L. A. (1992) Bison and deer bone mineral densities: comparisons and implications for the interpretation of archaeological faunas. *Journal of Archaeological Science* 19, 271–294.

Lambert, J. B., Simpson, S. V., Weiner, J. G. and Buikstra, J. E. (1985) Induced metal-ion exchange in excavated human bone. *Journal of Archaeological Science* 12, 85–92.

Lambot, B., Meniel, P. and Metzler, J. (1996) A propos des rites funéraires à la fin de l'âge du fer dans le nord-est de la Gaule. *Bulletins et Mémoires de la Société d'Anthropologie de Paris* 8(3–4), 245–260.

Lorans, E. (2000) Le monde des morts de l'Antiquité tardive à l'époque moderne (IVe – XIXe S.). In E. Crubézy, C. Masset, E. Lorans, F. Perrin and L. Tranoy (eds.) *Archéologie funéraire*, 155–197. Paris, Edition Errance.

Lovejoy, C. O. (1971) Methods for the detection of census error in palaeodemography. *American Anthropologist* 73, 101–109.

Lovejoy, C. O., Meidl, R. S., Mensforth, R. P. and Barton, T. (1985) Multifactorial determination of skeletal age at death: a method and blind test of its accuracy. *American Journal of Physical Anthropology* 68, 1–14.

Lyman, R. L. (1996) *Vertebrate Taphonomy*. Cambridge, Cambridge University Press.

Malone, C. (1996) *Avebury*. London, B.T. Batsford Ltd / English Heritage.

Mant, A. K. (1987) Knowledge acquired from post-war excavations. In A. Boddington, A. N. Garland and R. C. Janaway (eds.)

Approaches to Archaeology and Forensic Science, 65–78. Manchester, Manchester University Press.

Masset, C. (1986) Le "recrutement" d'un ensemble funéraire. In H. Duday and C. Masset (eds.) *Anthropologie Physique et Archéologie*, 109–134. Paris, Edition CNRS.

Masset, C. (2000) La mort aux périodes préhistoriques et protohistoriques (-1 000 000 à -750). In E. Crubézy, C. Masset, E. Lorans, E. Perrin and L. Tranoy (eds.), *Archéologie Funéraire*, 55–85. Paris, Editions Errance.

Milner, G. R., Humpf, D. A. and Harpending, H. C. (1989) Pattern matching of age-at-death distribution in paleodemographic analysis. *American Journal of Physical Anthropology* 83, 349–357.

Münzel, S. C. (1988) Quantitative analysis and archaeological site interpretation. *Archaeozoologia* II/1(2), 93–110.

Molleson, T. and Cox, M. (1993) *The Spitalfields Project. Volume 2 – The Anthropology*. York, The Middling Sort, CBA Research Report 86, Council for British Archaeology.

Paine, R. R. and Harpenting, H. C. (1998) Assessing the reliability of palaeodemographic fertility estimators using simulated skeletal distributions. *American Anthropologist* 101, 151–160.

Perrin, F. (2000) Le mort et la mort en Gaule à l'âge du fer (VIIIe–Ier S. av.J.-C.). In E. Crubézy, C. Masset, E. Lorans, F. Perrin and L. Tranoy (eds.) *Archéologie Funéraire*, 86–104. Paris, Edition Errance.

Piontek, J. and Henneberg, M. (1981) Mortality changes in a Polish rural community (1350–1972), and estimation of their evolutionary significance. *American Journal of Physical Anthropology* 54, 129–138.

Potts, R. (1986) Temporal span of bone accumulation at Olduvai Gorge and implications for early hominid foraging behaviour. *Paleobiology* 12(1), 25–31.

Rauch, F. and Schoenau, E. (2001) Changes in bone density during childhood and adolescence: An approach based on bone's biological organization. *Journal of Bone and Mineral Research* 90(4), 597–604.

Reeve, J. and Adams, M. (1993) *The Spitalfields Project. Volume 1 – The Archaeology*. York, Across the Styx, CBA Research Report 85, Council for British Archaeology.

Reynaud, P. (1996) Présentation du site des Fédons. In Raynaud P. (ed.) *Les Fédons (Lambesc). Anthropological Rapport*, 4–7. Marseilles, AFAN.

Russell, M. D. (1987) Bone breakage in the Krapina hominid collection. *American Journal of Physical Anthropology* 72, 373–379.

Sansilbano-Collilieux, M. (1990) Les caractère discrets et le "recrutement" de deux nécropoles du Haut Moyen Âge à Poitiers. *Bulletins et Mémoires de la Société d'Anthropologie de Paris* 2, 179–184.

Shipman, P., Foster, G. and Schoeninger, M. (1984) Burnt bones and teeth: an experimental study of color, morphology, crystal structure and shrinkage. *Journal of Archaeological Science* 2, 307–325.

Signoli, M., Leonetti, G. and Dutour, O. (1997) The Great Plague of Marseilles (1720–1722): new anthropological data. *Acta Biologica* 42, 123–133.

Signoli, M., Bello, S. and Dutour, O. (1998) La rechute épidémique de la Grande Peste de Marseille (Mai-Juillet 1722): le charnier de l'Observance. *Médecine Tropicale* 58, 7–13.

Signoli, M., Bello, S. and Dutour, O. (1999) – *Etude Anthropologique des Sépultures de Cimetière de la Basilique Sainte-Marie-Madeleine (Saint Maximin, Bouches-du-Rhône)*. Unpublished Report, University of Medicine La Timone of Marseilles.

Signoli, M., Adalian, P., Ardagna, Y., Bedoui, H., Bello, S., Lagrue, J. P., Lalys, L., Maczel, M., Tatilon, C., Thomann, A. and Dutour, O. (in press-a) La Nécropole de Saint-Sauveur de l'Hauture (Fos-sur-Mer, Bouches-du-Rhône): données archéologiques et anthropologiques. In G. Boetsch, O. Dutour, H. Pagezy, M. Signoli (eds), *Actes du XXXVème Colloque du GALF 2001*, July 16–18, 2001. Faculté de Médécine de Marseille, Marseilles, France.

Signoli, M., Adalian, P., Ardagna, Y., Bello, S., Carraze, F., Guyon, J., Fixot, M., Lalys, L., Maczel, M., Tatilon, C., Thomann, A. and Dutour, O. (in press-b) Les sepultures médiévales du cimetière de la Basilique Saint-Marie-Madeleine (Saint Maximin, Var): données archéologiques et anthropologiques. In G. Boetsch, O. Dutour, H. Pagezy, M. Signoli (eds), *Actes du XXXVème Colloque du GALF 2001*, July 16–18, 2001. Faculté de Médécine de Marseille, Marseilles, France.

Tattersall, I. (1995) *The Fossil Trail*. Oxford, Oxford University Press.

Thomann, A., Lalys, L., Bello, S., Adalian, P., Ardagna, Y., Gibert, M., Signoli, M. and Dutour, O. (1999) *Etude anthropologiques des sépultures du cimetière de Saint-Estève-le Pont (Berre L'Etang, Bouches-du-Rhône). Opération de sauvetage du 13 au 18 mars 1999*. Unpublished Report, University of Medicine La Timone of Marseilles.

Thomann, A., Bello, S., Lalys, L., Adalian, P., Ardagna, Y., Devriendt, W., Gibert, M., Maczel, M., Genot, A., Dutour, O. and Signoli, M. (2005) Etude anthropologique du cimetière médiéval de Saint-Estève-le-Pont (Berre l'Etang, Bouches-du-Rhône). *British Archaeological Reports*, S1355: 31–39.

Tillier, A. M. and Duday, H. (1990) Les enfants morts en période périnatale. *Bulletins et Mémoires de la Société d'Anthropologie de Paris* 2, 89–98.

Tranoy, L. (2000) La mort en Gaule romaine. In E. Crubézy, C. Masset, E. Lorans, F. Perrin, L. Tranoy (eds.) *Archéologie funéraire*, 105–154. Paris, Edition Errance.

Ubelaker, D. H. (1981) Approaches to demographic problems in the Northeast. In D.R. Snow (ed.) *Foundations of Northeast Archaeology*. New York, Academic Press.

Ubelaker, D. H. (1989) *Human Skeletal Remains: Excavation, Analysis and Interpretation, 2nd edn*. Washington, Manuals on Archaeology 2, Smithsonian Institution.

Usher, B. M. (2002) Reference samples: the first step in linking biology and age in the human skeleton. In R. D. Hoppa and J. W. Vaupel (eds.) *Paleodemography. Age Distributions from Skeletal Samples*, 29–47. Cambridge, Cambridge University Press.

Von Endt, D. W. and Ortner, D. J. (1984) Experimental effects of bone size and temperature on bone diagenesis. *Journal of Archaeological Science* 11, 247–253.

Waldron, T. (1987) The relative survival of the human skeleton: implications for palaeopathology. In A. Boddington, A. N. Garland and R. C. Janaway (eds.) *Approaches to Archaeology and Forensic Science*, 55–64. Manchester, Manchester University Press.

Walker, P.L. (1995) Problems of preservation and sexism in sexing: some lessons from historical collections for palaeo-demographers. In S. R. Saunders and A. Herring (eds.) *Grave reflections, Portraying the Past through Cemetery Studies*, 31–47. Toronto, Canadian Scholars' Press.

Walker, P. L., Johnson, J. R. and Lambert, P. M. (1988) Age and sex biases in the preservation of human skeletal remains. *American Journal of Physical Anthropology* 76, 183–188.

Willey, P., Galloway, A. and Snyder, L. (1997) Bone Mineral Density and Survival of Elements and Element Portions in the Bones of the Crow Creek Massacre Victims. *American Journal of Physical Anthropology* 104, 513–528.

2. Pattern in Human Burial Practice

Peter Andrews and Silvia Bello

Introduction

Prehistoric burial practices are diverse, but they serve to tell us much about the life of the communities practising them. Humans are the only species that pay attention to their dead, acting in accordance with the criteria and cultural expression of the period, which goes beyond the mere necessity of simply getting rid of the bodies. This interest is seen in the treatment of the dead, frequently manifested by the voluntary burial of bodies often rich in symbolic and ritual connotations. Remains may be found in cemeteries, in funerary structures, under floors of houses or as scavenged discards; they may be complete skeletons, broken remains, or burnt cremation residues. Much of this variability comes as a result of human activity, but some also results from post-mortem changes depending on the nature of the soil, the type of interment, and post-depositional factors such as burrowing animals, pressure from overlying rocks or sediment, or even disturbance by later humans. On the one hand, human intervention may be seen to protect the bodies from animal and weathering damage and to limit the dispersion produced by natural agents, but on the other hand, burial practices could involuntarily contribute to the destruction and/or the disappearance of all or some part of the body/skeleton. We will be concerned here to evaluate how far human funerary practice alters human skeletal assemblages and what this tells us about past human behaviour, drawing on evidence of the human burials from Çatalhöyük (Andrews *et al.* 2005).

Funerary practices can affect human remains at different stages. Damage to single anatomical elements may be seen in the form of cut marks, slicing or scraping marks, percussion marks and breakage as a result of ritual activity or cannibalism. Damage to entire skeletons may occur as a result of lime treatment, or disturbance by later burials in the same graves. Secondary burial can produce patterned loss of skeletal elements such as the distal limb elements, but it can also positively select elements of special significance such as crania and femora. Funerary practice may also select parts of the population according to biological criteria such as sex, age or family relations or according to social criteria.

The earliest known cases of human burials are of Neandertal burials, which may have had a ritual significance or just a matter of convenience to remove dead bodies from habitation areas (Klein 1999). At issue here is the establishment of criteria by which intentional inhumations are accepted (Leclerc 1990; Duarte 2002). Identification of a burial pit is of first importance, as is the presence of a body with the bones in articulation, although in cases of secondary or disturbed burials skeletons may be disarticulated. The presence of grave goods, ornaments or ochre are good evidence of intentional burial, although their absence in early graves may not be significant.

There are up to 20 possible cases of Neandertal burials (Harrold 1980), all tightly flexed, and the best case for ritual treatment is the burial at Grotta Guattari (Stringer 1986; but see White and Toth 1991). It has been claimed that the human remains from Krapina also show the result of ritual activity in the cut marks present, but it is likely that the great majority of the supposed cut marks are, in fact, the result of trampling, and the few genuine cut marks could be the result of cannibalism or possibly of secondary burial (Russell 1987). The general consensus is that there is no firm evidence for ritual burial in the Middle Palaeolithic (Gargett 1989), but intentional burial is well authenticated (*e.g.* at Saint-Cesaire [Leveque and Vandermeersch 1980] and Kebara [Bar-Yosef *et al.* 1986]).

Burials in the Upper Palaeolithic are both more common and have abundant evidence of ritual activity and collective burial. A young woman and two males were buried together at Dolní Vestonice in the Czech Republic (Klíma 1987), and at Predmostí a multiple grave contained remains of 18 individuals (Smith 1982). Even richer cemeteries have been found in younger deposits (15–10 ky) such as at Taforalt (Klein 1999). The Sunghir grave contained the extended skeletons of two children placed head to head, with evidence of clothing and large numbers of beads (White 1993).

There is also an indication of secondary burial in the Upper Palaeolithic and earlier. At Abri Pataud the skull of a young woman was separated from the rest of her skeleton (Movius 1975); the Krapina remains mentioned above, for which Russell (1987) suggests the skeletons were disarticulated at their joints and bundled together before burial; and at Gough's Cave there is good evidence of human cannibalism and the deposit of several individuals in the cave (Andrews and Fernandez-Jalvo 2003). In the last case, several human skeletons were found mixed in with animal bones, both sets having cut marks indicating similar processing of the bodies. By inference, if the animals were being butchered for food, so also were the humans. The child burial at Lagar Vehlo (Duarte 2002) was in a shallow pit, and although it was not certain if the pit was natural or intentional, the presence of red ochre and evidence of burning wood beneath the body like the Sungér burial (Binant, 1991) indicate the latter. This skeleton was lying in an extended position on its back, an unusual position (see below).

With the establishment of permanent settlements in the Neolithic, burial under the floors of houses became common practice. At first there may have been little difference between people living in caves and burying their dead in the floor of the caves, and house burials, but with the increase in population that went along with development of agriculture there was much greater call for space to be used efficiently. At Abu Hureyra 2, the remains of 102 individuals were found, with the majority of burials under the floors of houses but some in shallow pits in the yards outside. Graves contained either single individuals, buried in tightly flexed position, or groups of individuals apparently interred together (Moore and Molleson 2000), but both were frequently incomplete and had often been placed in a bag or on a mat. Separation of skulls from skeletons was commonplace. Two of the group assemblages had different age structures, burial pit 144 having mainly older children, adolescents and young adults, and the charnel house having mainly adults. Infants and neonate burials were almost absent in the houses, although some were recovered from open spaces between buildings, and it is concluded that they were deemed too young to be full members of society (Moore and Molleson 2000). Individuals found in the charnel house were buried towards the middle of the rooms, not around the edges, and it is suggested that they were placed there to decay, waiting for later removal (Moore and Molleson 2000). The majority of burials, however, were placed either in a corner of the room or to the side, and only two graves were found towards the centre of the room. The collective burial in pit 144 has some related individuals (Molleson 2000), but the number of people is said to be too great for them all to have lived in the one house. There was a 2:1 ratio of women to men.

Burial in houses continued in to the Roman period, at least for infants, for example at Sallèles d'Aude in the south of France (Duday *et al.* 1995). One level at this site had 12 burials of infants and foetuses placed irregularly around the perimeter of the room, with no preferred orientation but mostly crouched except for three lying on the back, one prone and one extended. There was no obvious preference to one part of the house other than the fact that all burials were close to the walls, a general pattern for Roman infant burials.

The evidence from Çatalhöyük

The sample from Çatalhöyük has 94 individuals from 49 graves excavated during 1995–1999 (Andrews *et al.* 2005). Most of the human remains consist of complete skeletons or parts of skeletons, generally very well preserved and buried beneath the floors of buildings (Table 2.1). One burial only was found in midden deposits in an open area, and one was found in fill deposits beneath an oven, so that the available sample was reduced to 92. These numbers compare with the 216 adults and 72 infants and children available for study from Mellaart's earlier excavations at the same site (Mellaart 1962, 1963; Angel 1971). The distribution of graves with respect to buildings, spaces, floors, features are detailed in Andrews *et al.* (2005), where four kinds of grave were recognized at Çatalhöyük. These are graves with single primary burials, graves with possibly double burials, graves with secondary burials, and graves with many disturbed skeletons. They were defined on the basis of their contents rather than their structure, or what kind of body and how many were present in each feature. These issues have been found to be partly independent of the grave structures (depth, manner of cutting, size relative to bodies, number of floors sealing the tops of the graves, nature of the fill).

Most graves at Çatalhöyük were under the floors of the houses and mostly around the edges of the houses but concentrated beneath platforms, the function of which is unclear (Andrews *et al.* 2005). No preferred alignment of either the graves or the bodies was found, either with respect to the room or to points of the compass. Most burials were more or less tightly flexed, some with evidence of binding or placement in a bag or on a mat, but a few skeletons were found supine, prone, or sitting upright. No evidence was found of any body having been buried in an extended position. There was total recovery of bone from the excavation.

We will concentrate here on the evidence from two buildings, Building 1 in North Area (Cessford, in press) and Building 6 in South Area (Farid, in press). There were 62 individuals identified from Building 1, some of which were articulated skeletons, and the assignment to individual of incomplete remains was based on three criteria: firstly there was sometimes a degree of association and/or articulation of elements during excavation; secondly, there was similarity in age and size of elements;

and thirdly, evidence specific to individuals such as task-related wear or pathologies was taken into account. This is not a standard calculation of MNI, and when all recovered elements from all individuals are combined, and the numbers compared with those expected from 62 individuals, it can be seen from Figure 2.1 that there is only 15–35% representation of most elements (Fig. 2.1). Some of this can be attributed to secondary action, with some elements never reaching the burial place, some may be due to post-depositional damage due to recent mammal

and invertebrate burrowing, and some of it is probably due to mixing of bones between graves. When bones are moved from one grave to another, it is difficult to restore all parts of the skeletons to their original position, and in this event it is inevitable that the numbers of individuals estimated by MNI would be under-estimated. The best represented element is the cranium at 60%, although deliberate removal of the cranium from certain skeletons is known to have occurred at Çatalhöyük (Mellaart, 1967 and see below). In South Area on the other hand, there is

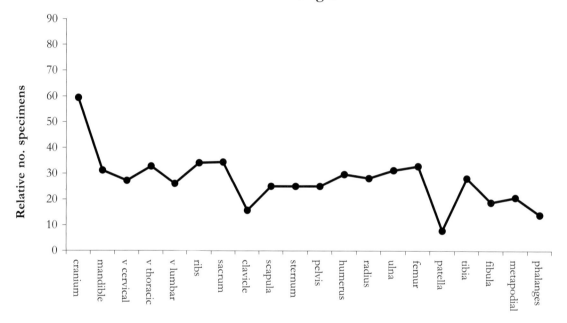

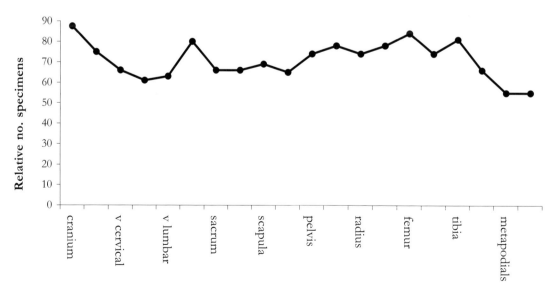

Figure 2.1. Distribution of skeletal elements at Çatalhöyük for all burials sin Building 1 (N = 62) and all buildings in South Area (N = 30). Relative numbers of specimens is based on the actual number divided by the expected number for that element ×100.

much higher representation of skeletal elements, 60 to 80% for most elements, for most of the 32 graves contain undisturbed primary burials (Fig. 2.1).

The questions we will be considering here mostly relate to Çatalhöyük, for example, how may different burial types can be identified? What is the significance of primary vs secondary burials? Different ages? Different sexes? Depth of grave cuts? Differences in grave goods? Differences in locations? What are the reasons for delayed burials – seasonality, people travelling off site, people being brought to the site? What is the nature of disturbed burials? Since there is no evidence of cremation or cannibalism at Çatalhöyük, we will draw on evidence from other sites to discuss these activities, but there is some evidence of ritual activity which will be briefly discussed.

Definitions of burial types

Primary burials are interments of one or more individuals in graves cut for their use alone. Where there is more than one individual in the grave, they were buried at the same time, and disturbance is limited to within-grave collapse due to decay of soft tissues. This is the case with plague sites (Bello *et al.*, 2002), for example, multiple burials (2 to 4 individuals) in the Fédons cemetery, (1590 epidemic Lambesc, France), in a huge plague pit at Observance (1722, Marseille, France) and in another plague cemetery in Délos composed of parallel trenches (1720, Martigues, France). In these last two cases, the delay between successive burials was very short or absent. But this is also the case at catastrophic sites like Pompeii or battlefields (*e.g.* Arnaud 2002).

Criteria for identifying a burial as primary are based on completeness of the skeletal remains and the maintenance of articulation in those parts of the skeleton that disarticulate most quickly, namely those of the neck, hands and toes, as well as the fragile scapulo-thoracic and costo-sternal joints. The basic requirement is for all bones to be present, including 'floating' bones such as the hyoid in the throat region and the patella. All or most phalanges should also be present, and the requirement here is for the terminal phalanges to be present (Bello *et al.* 2002). Some phalanges may be missed in even the best of excavations, but the presence of the terminal phalanges indicates no loss of fingers or toes.

Secondary burial is the process of intentional (or socially sanctioned [Metcalfe and Huntington 1991]) rearrangement of human remains by human action, and it has two components, movement and delay. The first entails the movement of some or all parts of bodies from a temporary place of burial or exposure to their present resting place. This may entail loss of certain skeletal elements, particularly distal limb elements, retention of specific elements held to have some significance, such as crania (rarely complete skulls) and femora, and evidence of secondary action may also include cut marks on some bones where bodies have been defleshed, and surface modifications on bones in cases of prior exposure.

The second component of secondary burial entails a period of time between death and final burial. The delay may be days, weeks or years, and it might occur for several different reasons, for example, death away from home, delay while the necessary finance or material is accumulated, delay while waiting for a communal burial, or delay for reasons of hygiene, waiting for the flesh to decay (Miles 1965; Carr and Knüsel 1997). Clearly, the identification of the reasons for delay, or the nature of the initial burial/exposure of the bodies, would provide insights into the social structure of the populations concerned.

It has been suggested that delayed burial has a distinctive three-stage structure (Moore and Molleson 2000), each accompanied by ceremony and ritual. First, there is a ceremony at the time of death; the period of decay while the corpse is being defleshed is an intermediate period that may have an importance of its own (van Gennep 1909); and finally, the bones are reburied with a second ceremony. Reburial does not always follow immediately on decay of the flesh and might be postponed for many years.

We also recognize here as secondary action the removal of body parts such as the cranium from a primary burial. In this case the primary interment of a body remains in place, but after a period of time to allow for decay of soft tissues, the grave is reopened and the cranium (or other body part) removed. It may be that the body is positioned in a certain way to allow this to be done more easily, for example, if the body is in supine or prone position rather than on its side.

Disturbance of burials is the process of movement of human remains as a result of some later activity unconnected with these remains, such as another burial in the same grave, digging a post hole or building works. This is activity that is incidental to the skeleton already in place in a grave. The results of such disturbance, such as loss of skeletal elements, partial or complete dis-articulation, and breakage of bones, are often difficult to separate from secondary action, and a distinction is made here based on intention. In secondary activity, a body is disturbed as a result of human action directed at that particular individual; in disturbed burials, later human disturbance is incidental to the individual being disturbed, the intention being directed at some other event, such as another burial in the same grave. Disturbance of a grave can occur at any stage after initial burial, but secondary burial has a discrete timetable, depending on the cultural development of the society.

Disturbance can also be caused by non-human agencies, such as rodents or invertebrate burrowing. It can produce similar effects, and again it is incidental to the individuals being disturbed (Armour-Chelu and Andrews 1994). It is usually possible both to identify the agent of disturbance (*e.g.* animal burrows) and to identify the original nature of the burial.

Cremation is the process of disposing of a body by burning (McKinley 1998), and it almost always produces extensive loss of skeletal elements. The original source may be a complete body, a secondary interment, or disturbed remains, and these may sometimes be identified by degrees of completeness of the cremated skeletons. Thus, cremated deposits can be primary or secondary, and individual or collective.

Cannibalism is the practice of eating one's own kind. It may be identified by the presence of cut marks or other evidence of human action on skeletal elements related to butchery, loss of specific skeletal elements, or patterns of preservation comparable with those of associated non-human bones identified as the butchered remains of animals. Where human bones are associated with animal bones, and both exhibit the same distribution and degree of cut marks and breakage, evidence for cannibalism as distinct from ritual defleshing and cleaning of the bone is strong (Andrews and Fernandez-Jalvo 2003).

Non-human action may occur where human remains are accumulated and preserved without the intervention of human activity. In this case they may form part of the general palaeontological fauna, subject to whatever taphonomic and sedimentological framework is present at the fossil site. In this event, the expectation is that the human remains would be similar in modification and preservation to those of the rest of the fauna, taking into account differential properties of the bones.

Evidence for burial types

In order to provide some level of consistency into the evidence of different burial types, a **Taphonomic Index** has been devised based on differences in preservation of the human skeletons. This is based on four aspects of taphonomy, using a scale of 1 to 10 for each, grading from poor preservation (score = 1) to maximum preservation (score = 10). The four aspects are as follows:

- skeleton completeness
- breakage of bones
- disarticulation
- surface modification

For skeleton completeness, a single bone or part of a bone scores 1 while a complete skeleton scores 10, with all stages in between based on bone counts in units of 20. Breakage is scored 1 where all bones are broken, up to 10 where all bones are complete, based on proportions of the skeleton that were intact. Disarticulation is scored 1 for total disarticulation, up to 10 for a completely articulated skeleton, including such easily moved bones as the patellae and hyoid. In this case, because disarticulation does not occur at a regular rate, arbitrary scores were assigned, for example, one articulated upper or lower limb was given a score of 3, an articulated axial skeleton was given a score of 5–7 depending on numbers of bones preserved, and so on. Surface modification was scored mainly on the degree of black fungal staining of the bones, for there were few other forms of modification at Çatalhöyük, although in other circumstances evidence of carnivore chewing, weathering, human-derived cut marks, trampling, and root marks could be incorporated into the index. The scale for surface modification ranges from heavy modification scoring 1 and little or none scoring 10, and in the specific case of Çatalhöyük the scores are based on the proportions of bones covered by the fungal staining. After the four values were assigned for each individual or skeleton, they were added together to provide a single score for the taphonomic index. The index derived in this way has a maximum score of 40 and a minimum score of 4, but it should be noted that it is an ordinal system that reflects the degree of modification and the different burial types within Çatalhöyük, but scaling may be different for different sites. The scores for all skeletons at Çatalhöyük are provided in Table 2.1.

Primary burials

Important issues for primary burials involve their distribution in space and time and any indications of special treatment such as grave goods, textiles, mats, bags *etc*. Differences between primary burials may provide evidence of ritual activity associated with burial of the dead, but even when complete, as defined above, the possibility always exists that what appears to be a primary burial may, in fact, be secondary. For example, initial exposure of a body in a bag (which might be hung from a tree out of reach of scavengers) or on a mat in a charnel house, might preserve the skeleton intact for reburial. One requirement in this event, as far as tightly flexed burials are concerned, would be for the bodies to be bound in the flexed position, for this position could not be achieved after partial or complete decay.

The spatial distributions of graves in Building 1 (Fig. 2.2) and Building 6 (Fig. 2.3) at Çatalhöyük are very different. In Building 1 most of the graves are in groups around the outside of the room beneath platforms, with only a few early graves under the floor of the room (Cessford, in press). In Building 6, there were 10 burials cut into the fill of Building 17 below, with only one under a platform and showing no particular spacing in the room, other than being concentrated in the central-eastern part (Farid, in press). All except one of the graves contained single primary inhumations, but in most cases the bodies had suffered some post-mortem disturbance.

Individuals in primary burials are mainly the very young and the old, and the distribution of ages of individuals in the primary burials shows the pattern that would be expected for normal attritional mortality of a human population. Infant mortality would have been high, with mortality dropping in adults and only rising again in old adult individuals. The same pattern exists for primary burials both in single graves and as the last to be interred in collective burials (except that no neonates have been

Ind	Building	Phase	Burial	Skeleton	Maturity	Complete	Break	Surface	Artic.	Index
North Area										
1	1	4	28	1378	old	10	10	8	10	38
2	1	4	29	1466	adult	9	10	8	10	37
3	1	4	29	1364.3, 1467	adolescent	5	5	5	1	16
5	1	4	213	1928.2+3	old	2	5	1	1	9
7	1	2C	213	1949, 1968	adult	6	6	8	7	27
8	1	2B	29	1949, 1963	old	7	7	5	7	26
9	1	2B	384	1978 1364.2	adult	2	1	2	1	6
11	1	4	29	1364.1 1928.3	old	2	1	2	1	6
12	1	4	29	1364.4	adult	2	1	2	1	6
15	1	2B	30	1424	old	10	8	8	10	36
17	1	2B	30	1425.1	adolescent	2	4	3	1	10
18	1	2B	30	1425.2+3	adult	3	4	4	2	13
20	1	2B	30	1425.4	adult	1	2	1	1	5
21	1	2B	30	1426	infant	3	2	4	1	10
21	1	2B	210	2510	infant					
22	1	2B	30	1450	infant	10	6	10	10	36
23	1	2B	30	1464	adult	1	1	1	1	4
25	1	2B	31	1481, 1489, 1934	old	7	7	8	7	29
26	1	2B	31	1481.1, 1491	adolescent	4	6	6	7	23
27	1	2B	31	1498	infant	9	9	8	10	36
28	1	2B	31	1481, 1483	adult	5	7	8	7	27
29	1	2B	31	1481, 1482	juvenile	6	5	7	7	25
32	1	4	35	1913	juvenile	10	8	6	10	34
33	1	2C	36	1495	juvenile	10	9	9	10	38
34	1	2B	38	1923, 1448.1	juvenile	4	8	2	1	15
35	1	2B	38	1937, 1926.4	juvenile	4	5	2	1	12
36	1	2B	38	1448.2	old	2	7	2	1	12
37	1	2B	38	1926.5	adult	1	6	2	1	10
38	1	2B	38	1496	infant	1	5	2	1	9
39	1	2B	38	1922, 1939	juvenile	7	8	5	8	25
40	1	2B	38	1925, 1938.3	juvenile	7	7	5	7	23
41	1	2B	38	1493, 1926.2	juvenile	4	5	2	1	12
43	1	2B	38	1938.2	adolescent	6	5	2	7	20
44	1	2B	38	1924	old	10	10	8	10	38
45	1	2B	38	1478, 1926.1	juvenile	3	4	2	1	10
48	1	2B	38	1926.3, 1938.1	juvenile	4	5	2	1	12
49	1	2B	375	2520	juvenile	4	8	2	1	15
50	1	2B	40	1912	juvenile	8	7	8	10	33
51	1	2B	40	1950	infant	9	9	9	10	36
52	1	2C	41	1916	infant	10	7	8	10	35
53	1	2B	42	1484, 1961, 1989	juvenile	5	8	4	1	18
54	1	2C	44	1935	infant	3	5	4	1	13
55	1	2C	44	1959	juvenile	9	8	7	10	34
56	1	2B	45	1992	infant	9	9	9	10	37
57	1	2B	47	2125, 1955.3	infant	9	9	9	7	34
58	1	2B	204	2195, 1955.2	juvenile	3	2	3	1	9
59	1	2B	47	2126, 2168	juvenile	7	5	4	5	21
60	1	2B	204	1955.1, 2506	old	8	8	8	7	31
61	1	2C	49	1995	adult	7	10	10	8	35
62	1	2C	44	1960	infant	9	8	7	9	33
67	1	2B	200	2115	old	10	10	7	10	37
68	1	2B	202	2105	infant	9	9	6	10	34

Table 2.1. Summary of burials at Çatalhöyük. From left to right are shown individual numbers of skeletons, the building number, the phase of occupation, the burial number, the skeleton number, the age class (maturity) of the individual, and then five columns relating to the taphonomic index: degree of completeness of the skeletons, the degree of breakage, the presence of surface modifications, and the degree of articulation of the skeletons; in all cases the scores range from lowest, score of 1, to highest, score of 10, and the individual scores are added together to make up the taphonomic index, which has a maximum score of 40 for intact, fully articulated skeletons with no broken bones and no surface modifications, and a minimum score of 4 for a skeleton represented by a single broken bone with heavy surface modifications.

Ind	Building	Phase	Burial	Skeleton	Maturity	Complete	Break	Surface	Artic.	Index
North Area										
69	1	2B	204	2169	adult	10	10	8	10	38
70	1	1B	205	2181, 2199	neonate	9	10	6	10	35
71	1	1B	206	2197	neonate	9	9	9	6	33
72	1	2B	207	2141	infant	6	5	4	7	22
73	1	1B	208	2515	neonate	9	10	9	8	36
74	1	1B	209	2529	old	10	10	8	10	38
75	1	1B	211	2527	adult	10	9	10	10	39
76	1	1B	211	2532	neonate	8	8	9	10	35
77	1	2B	212	2119	juvenile	10	10	7	10	37
South Area										
100	112	VII	83	1884	juvenile	9	9	7	9	34
101	112	VII	84	1885	juvenile	8	9	8	9	34
102	112	VII	84	2033	juvenile	8	9	6	8	31
103	112	VII	89	2056	old	10	9	9	10	38
104	112	VII	89	2058	old	8	8	5	7	28
105	112	VII	251	2362	neonate	9	9	8	7	33
106	112	VII	258	2728	infant	9	9	9	9	36
107	109	VII	264	2772	neonate	8	9	9	7	33
108	112	VII	265	2779	neonate	6	2	2	4	14
109	112	VII	fill	2017	neonate	4	2	3	3	12
110	112	VII	274	2842	infant	9	7	6	8	30
111	112	VII	277	2886	adult	10	10	8	10	38
112	115	VII	285	3368	adult	9	9	7	9	34
113	6	VIII	487	4438	neonate	9	9	10	9	37
114	6	VIII	494	4458	infant	10	9	9	8	36
115	18	X	493	4555	neonate	10	10	8	7	33
116	6	VIII	492	4593	adult	9	10	10	10	39
117	6	VIII	513	4615	adult	10	10	7	10	37
118	6	XII	525	4828	neonate	9	8	8	10	35
119	23	X	543	4853	neonate	9	9	8	10	36
120	23	X	544	4861	infant	9	9	9	8	35
121	6	VIII	537	4927	neonate	9	10	6	10	35
122	17	IX	4604	5022	adult	1	4	2	1	8
123	17	IX	564	5177	infant	9	8	7	10	34
124	17	IX	576	5357	infant	10	10	6	10	36
125	17	IX	563	5169	old	10	9	7	10	36
126	6	VIII	417	4215	infant	8	9	5	10	32
127	6	VIII	442	4328	neonate	10	10	5	10	35
128	6	VIII	460	4394	adolescent	10	10	4	10	34
129	6	VIII	464	4406	infant	10	10	10	8	38
130	6	VIII	475	4424	infant	10	9	5	9	33
131	6	VIII	476	4427	infant	9	10	10	9	38

Table 2.1. continued.

found in collective graves). This distribution of ages is distinct from that seen in the secondary burials at Çatalhöyük (see next section and Fig. 2.4), and it suggests that few of the fully intact bodies could have resulted from secondary burial.

Twenty seven of the 62 graves in Building 1 at Çatalhöyük contained primary burials (44%) compared with 29 out of 32 in the buildings in South Area (91%). Building 6 contained 100% primary burials. The degree of preservation was notably greater than other burial types, with average taphonomic scores of 35.7 for Building 1 and 34.8 for South Area (see Table 2.1 for data). These high scores are based on the overall completeness of the skeletons, the lack of breakage of the bones and their lack of surface alteration, and the fact that they were all generally in articulation. Where disturbance occurred, the cause could be attributed to post-depositional factors such as rodent burrowing.

Secondary burials

The evidence for secondary burial may sometimes be confused with disturbance when based on the lack of

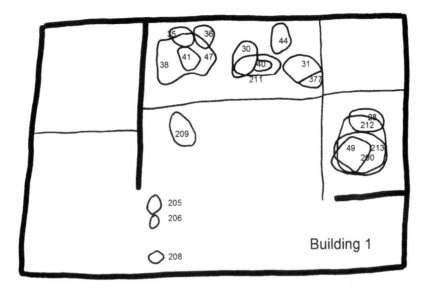

Figure 2.2. Plan of Building 1, Çatalhöyük showing the locations of the graves. The numbers on the plan refer to grave (feature) numbers.

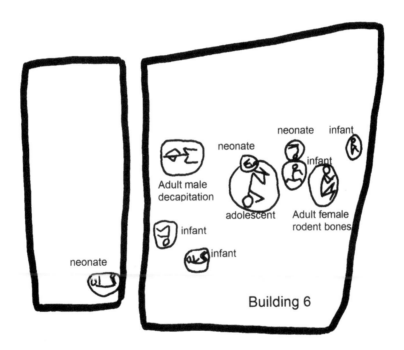

Figure 2.3. Plan of Building 6, Çatalhöyük showing the locations of the graves and the disposition of the burials, all primary, in the graves. The numbers on the plan refer to grave (feature) numbers.

completeness of the burials. In the excavations at Çatalhöyük, the burials that are identified here as due to secondary action are from grave 31, possibly from grave 30, and two headless skeletons (Fig. 2.5).

The headless burials both have cut marks preserved on bones, in the first case on a bone tentatively identified as the broken styloid process of the missing cranium, and in the second case on the first cervical vertebra, the atlas (Fig. 2.6). In both cases, the skeletons are complete and in articulation, and the only body part missing is the skull and atlas in the first case and the skull only in the second; and in both cases, the mandible was removed with the cranium, although in cases where crania have been found in niches or on platforms at Çatalhöyük the mandible has not been present (Mellaart 1967). The identification of secondary action in these two cases depends on whether the skulls were removed before or after burial. Evidence favouring removal of the intact head before burial is that in both cases the top of the vertebral column was up against the edge of the grave cut (Fig. 2.5), leaving little room for the head. If the head had not been removed before burial, it would have had to have been bent up

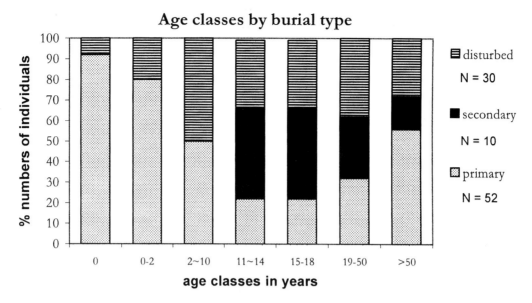

Figure 2.4. Age distribution of all burials in the 1995–1999 excavation seasons at Çatalhöyük, including both North and South areas (N = 92).

Figure 2.5. Skeleton 1466 in process of excavation under a platform in Building 1 at Çatalhöyük.

against the chest, and this might have produced distortion of the upper neck vertebrae. Similarly, the removal of the skull after burial could have caused the upper vertebrae to have become detached from the rest of the vertebral column, or at least displaced. Finally, there was no evidence of a later cut in the region of the skull, although this might not be evident during excavation (Farid, in press). Evidence favouring post-burial removal of the skull is the extreme difficulty in severing the joint between atlas vertebra and skull in one case, or between atlas and axis in the other, a process difficult enough on a modern operating table with modern tools. It would be much easier to separate the head from the body after decay has set in. There is also the matter that both headless burials were lying on their backs, the only bodies at Çatalhöyük buried in this position, and it is possible that they were

placed like this to enable the skull to be removed at a later date. Moreover, one of the skeletons was covered by a rough plank of wood across the thorax and abdomen (Farid, in press; Andrews *et al.*, 2005), again the only instance of this kind at Çatalhöyük, and this may also be connected with the intention of later removal of the skull.

The most positive identification of secondary action at Çatalhöyük has been made for grave 31. The presence of four axial skeletons, with limb bones greatly under-represented and few distal limb elements, indicates a strongly selective action that is consistent with prior exposure and subsequent transfer of the remaining bones to grave 31. The four axial skeletons were all oriented approximately east-west and were lying very close to floor level. The four axial skeletons are as follows:

– *Individual 25,* A skull and distorted cervical vertebrae (1489) associated with the rest of the vertebral column (1934) of an old individual;
– *Individual 26,* five thoracic and one lumbar vertebrae in articulation of an adolescent;
– *Individual 28,* articulated ribs and vertebrae (1483) from an adult;
– *Individual 29,* articulated vertebral column with several limb bones allocated to this individual because of its distinctive age.

Little can be said of where and for how long the bones were previously exposed, but there is evidence of trampling that suggests that they were exposed on the ground. No evidence of carnivore chewing has been found, so that they must have been protected from scavenging animals. There is one proximal humerus that has two deep gouges with splinters of bone embedded into the head of the humerus (Andrews *et al.* 2005). These may be cut marks in the head, apparently for the purpose of disarticulating the shoulder joint, but it is possible also that this is due to post-depositional processes. No other cut marks were found despite intensive searching. No evidence of weathering (Behrensmeyer 1978; Andrews 1990) was seen, not surprising since the ribs and vertebrae were still in articulation, indicating a period of, at the most, a few months' exposure.

The relative abundances of skeletal elements for grave 31 are shown in Figure 2.7. This shows the strong representation of vertebrae and ribs and the poor representation of limb elements. Hand and foot bones are extremely poorly represented. This pattern is very different from that of the general element distribution (Fig. 2.1), and although it indicates extensive bone loss, this has taken place in the context of the vertebral columns still being articulated. It would appear from this that the bodies were first placed elsewhere, and they were moved to their present burial position when most of their limbs had disarticulated, but their ribs and vertebrae were still together. It is likely that all four axial skeletons were placed in the grave together, all lined up in approximately the same orientation.

The pattern of skeletal abundance in grave 30 is different from that of grave 31, but it is again suggestive of secondary action (Fig. 2.7). There are seven individuals present, four of which were in a single bone bundle numbered 1425 containing two adult and two late adolescent individuals. The bones assigned to the 1425 bundle of long bones were greyish brown to dark reddish brown in colour, with dispersed black fungal staining, and compact surfaces with extensive surface modifications. The fragments of ribs, teeth and hand bones are light orange brown in colour with patches of black staining, probably the result of fungal attack. The ends of the bones have suffered some loss of tissue. There is also a fifth individual represented by a single adult femur, which is separated from the bone bundle and which is slightly less modified. The extent of modification in these disarticulated bones contrasts with that seen in the two primary burials found beneath the bone bundle, and in general bones that are clearly disturbed at Çatalhöyük show much greater degrees of surface modification than do bones from primary burials. There were seven femora present in the bone bundle, including the isolated femur, no upper limb bones at all, and few other elements except for three crania. This combination of crania and femora has been documented in several archaeological sites (although not exclusively femora) (*e.g.* Duday 1986a, 1986b; Boës and Sears 1996; Baills and Chaddaoui 1996; Malone 1996). It is possible that this is a skull and crossed bones effect, with the femora and skulls being considered the most significant skeletal elements, and therefore the elements selected for reburial, as for instance in the Medieval belief "that the skull and thigh bones were the minimum physical remains essential for resurrection on the Day of Judgement" (Garland *et al.*, 1988). The forelimb of most mammal species is more easily detached from the rest of the skeleton than is the hindlimb, so that the natural disarticulation process entails the loss of the forelimbs before any other body part (Hill 1979). In this case it is inferred that reburial of the five individuals took place after the disarticulation and removal by scavengers of the upper limb bones and many of the other bones of the five skeletons, and the remaining bones, including particularly the cranium and femora, were moved to Building 1 and buried in grave 30.

Most of the graves at Çatalhöyük for which secondary action is identified are beneath floors rather than platforms. This is the case for grave 31, which has the strongest evidence for secondary burial, and it is also the case for grave 30 and the headless burial in Building 6. Only the decapitation burial in grave 29 is buried below a platform.

While the disturbed nature of so many of the burials does not of itself imply secondary burial, a disturbed burial for which there is no other agent of disturbance could be attributed to secondary action. For example, in grave 49, there is an adult female lacking both lower limbs and part of one upper limb, but otherwise the skeleton is complete and in articulation, including the hyoid and skull. There is no indication that any of the later burial pits were made as deep as this skeleton's, and so the loss of these bones could have occurred before burial (*i.e.* as a result of delayed burial).

When the numbers of secondary burials are analysed, it becomes very clear that there is a major disproportion of ages compared with primary burials (Fig. 2.4). It is seen, for instance, that most secondary burials are adolescents or adults, and in fact the age category used for adolescents obscures the fact that half the number of individuals are aged 15 or over, 15 being the biological age of maturity identified for the Çatalhöyük population (Molleson *et al.* 2005). This emphasizes what is already evident from Figure 2.4, that secondary burials are largely restricted to adults. This remains the case even when less certain secondary burials, such as from graves 30 and 49, are included in the analysis. The absence of infants and juveniles suggests that the emphasis on secondary burial was towards delayed burial of individuals who died away from Çatalhöyük. Adults and adolescents are the individuals most likely to leave the town for protracted periods of time, herding, collecting firewood, tending crops, hunting etc., and it is likely that if they died away from the town, their final burial was delayed until they could be brought back.

The secondary burials have more variable scores as reflected by the Taphonomic Index, depending on the nature of the secondary process. Thus, the four skeletons in grave 31 have intermediate scores, reflecting the presence of partially articulated skeletons (index values 23–29), whereas the two decapitation burials have values similar to those of primary burials, since they are essentially unmodified except for the loss of the skull (Table 2.1). On the other hand, the four individuals comprising the bone

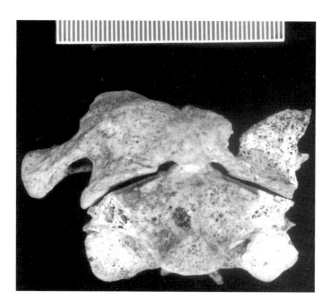

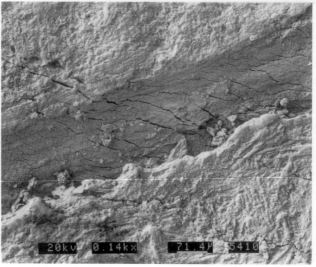

Figure 2.6. Atlas and axis of skeleton 4593 buried under the floor of Building 6 at Çatalhöyük, with scanning electron microscope images of the cut marks shown below.

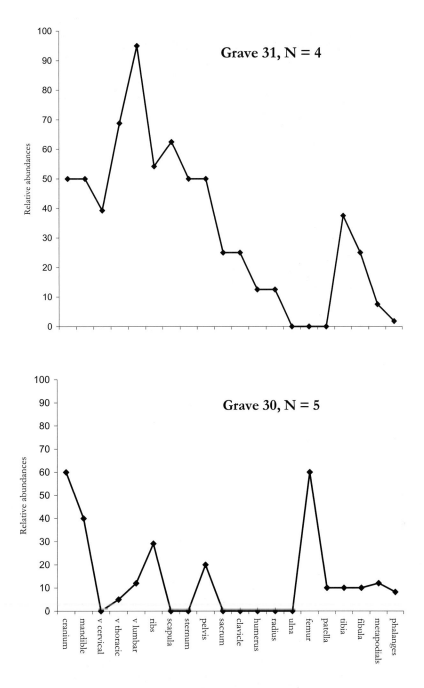

Figure 2.7. Distribution of skeletal elements for two graves at Çatalhöyük, above in grave 31 (N = 4); below in grave 30 (N = 5). Relative numbers of specimens is based on the actual number divided by the expected number for that element ×100. V signifies vertebra.

bundle in grave 30 have index values of 4–13, similar to values found for disturbed burials (Table 2.1). Burial 49 has an intermediate score of 15 (Table 2.1).

One other feature of secondary burials is that, at least in grave 31, the grave was very shallow, only just below floor level. None of the primary graves were as shallow as this one, and neither were the other putative secondary graves such as grave 49. The disturbed bones in grave 30 were also close to floor level. It could be that the secondary burial of bones already cleaned of most of the soft tissues

could be buried less deeply than whole bodies because the smell or danger of infection would not be as great, but this is speculation based on only a single grave. Further evidence is needed to corroborate this.

In summary, there is evidence from Çatalhöyük of element removal (the two skulls in the headless burials), of element selection (the femora and skulls in grave 30), and selective element loss (the loss of most limb elements from grave 31), all examples of intentional secondary interment of bodies or skeletons.

Disturbed burials

The distinction between disturbed and undisturbed burials in one way is very clear. At Çatalhöyük there is only one case of an isolated burial of a single individual that shows obvious signs of disturbance (skeleton 2017 in fill deposits – see Table 2.1). This is the incomplete remains of a neonate buried beneath or within an oven. All other disturbance can be attributed to post-depositional movement or loss of bones, either as a result of human action, with collective burials within single grave complexes, or by animal burrows that are recorded within the area of the excavation. All graves with disturbed skeletons at Çatalhöyük (*i.e.* with loss of skeletal elements, disarticulated bones etc.) are without exception found in collective burials with up to 12 individuals in a single grave. On this basis alone, the indications are that the disturbance of earlier burials is the result of re-opening of graves to bury additional bodies, and this can be seen to involve the unintentional movement of bones to make way for another individual(s). In most collective burials at Çatalhöyük, however, there is usually a single individual in the grave that is undisturbed. This is inferred to be the last burial in the complex, the one that disturbs the earlier burials but is undisturbed itself. The single grave lacking such a final primary burial is grave 31, which has four definite secondary burials. Grave 30 may be another case in point, for the primary burials in this grave were deeper than the disturbed burials, and it is possible in this case that they were earlier than the disturbed secondary burials.

It has been noted above that the percentage distribution of human ages of disturbed burials at Çatalhöyük has a pattern distinct from either primary or secondary burials. It is quite possible that the disturbed burials of adults are disturbed secondary burials, and those of infants and neonates (and some old individuals

perhaps) are disturbed primary burials, but on present evidence it is not possible to verify this. The bones in disturbed burials show greater surface modification than is present in primary burials. This implies greater exposure to air, oxygen and moisture specifically (Goffer 1980), which is what would be expected of disturbed burials.

The disturbed burials in Building 1 (50% of the total in Building 1) and 3 disturbed burials in the South Area buildings (9% of the total) are all characterized by low and highly variable values of the taphonomic index. Means for Building 1: 14.4; and for South Area, 11.3. These reflect both greater loss of elements (with greater degrees of modifications to the bones) and the variable nature of the modification processes that produced the change.

There is one positive outcome of disturbance by later burials. It is often possible to relate sequence of burial to the degree of disarticulation, completeness, breakage and surface modification of the skeletons, the four taphonomic processes that have been used to compile the taphonomic index (Andrews *et al.* 2004). An example is shown here (Fig. 2.8) from grave 38 at Çatalhöyük where the inferred order of burial for the five individuals for which there was reliable excavation data, and four of which are disturbed, is plotted against the taphonomic index, showing a strong relationship between them.

Cremation

No evidence of cremation has been found at Çatalhöyük, although the first cases of incineration/cremation date to the Mesolithic period (Cauwe 2001). They are more widespread during the Neolithic period (*e.g.* Masset 1997; Guilaine 1998; Thomas 2003), becoming a general phenomenon around 200 BC (Perrin 2000), and finally diminishing after the introduction of Christianity (Lorans 2002).

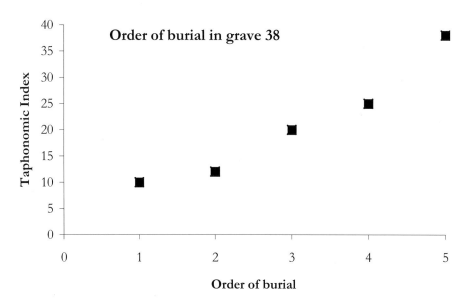

Figure 2.8. Order of burial in grave 38 at Çatalhöyük compared with the taphonomic index (Andrews et al. 2005).

According to Kurzawki and colleagues (Kurzawki *et al.* 1986) the word incineration should be employed in cases of assemblages composed of ashes or very small fragments of bone, all that remains after lengthy burning, while in the case of assemblages where ash is mixed with bigger fragments of bone or complete bones, and there has been less destruction, cremation should be used. The process of burning can involve fleshed or defleshed bodies. In this second case there are two consecutive secondary treatments of the dead, with a process of defleshing that can be active or passive (Grévin *et al.* 1990). The distinction between the cremation of fleshed and defleshed bones is generally obtained by the analysis of the fractures of the bones, the diagnosis being more precise in case of remains treated at very high temperatures (Guillon 1986).

Cremations could be practised in different ways: in the case of primary cremation, the fire, the *bustum*, is built over or inside the grave room (Duday and Sellier 1990; Thuillier 2000). In secondary cremations, the dead are burnt on the *ustrium* (primary deposition) and then the remains are collected and deposited in the final secondary burial (Duday and Sellier 1990; Tranoy 2000). As in the case of secondary burial, in secondary cremations bones could be partially lost during this process (Duday 1990). Furthermore, cremations may be individual or collective cremations based on the number of bodies burnt on the pyre. In the case of collective cremations the main problem is to understand if the cremation of the remains was simultaneous (multiple cremations; Duday 1990) or if primary or secondary cremations have been disturbed by the deposition in the same grave of another successive cremation (collective cremations; Tranoy 2000). In both cases the cremation can involve fleshed and/or defleshed bodies.

Cannibalism

The effects of cannibalism are akin to natural processes of predation but differ in detail. Breakage patterns for instance show preference for the most nutritious parts of bones (Turner 1983), which may be too robust for access by carnivores, and there may be selection of certain body parts. These patterns of butchery should be similar on both animal and human remains and should show similar butchering marks, such as the frequency, location and type of cut marks (see Knüsel and Outram, this volume). In the case of ritual defleshing, these patterns would be different (Villa *et al.* 1986). There may be evidence of cooking, and again this should be similar on both animals and human remains.

No evidence of butchery has been seen at Çatalhöyük, for the cut marks seen on the human bones described above are distinct from the marks seen on animal bones (Russell and Martin 2005). They indicate removal of the skull, presumably for ritual purposes. On the other hand, the Upper Palaeolithic fossil assemblage at Gough's cave in Somerset shows convincing evidence of cannibalism (Andrews and Fernandez-Jalvo 2003). There were extensive butchering marks on both animal and the remains of at least six human individuals, and the pattern of marks was similar on both (Table 2.2). Most cut marks on the long bones of both were located on areas of muscle attachment or articular surfaces, indicating dismembering activities, and there were extensive cut marks and chop marks on the ribs, in some cases with percussion marks coinciding on adjacent ribs (Andrews and Fernandez-Jalvo 2003).

Non-human activities

These may form part of the general palaeontological

		equid	cervid	human
Cranial	Dismembering	x	x	x
	Filleting	x	x	x
	Tongue extraction	x		x
	Skinning			x
Axial	Dismembering	x	x	x
	Filleting	x		x
	Marrow extraction			
	Skinning	x	x	x
Limbs	Dismembering	x	x	x
	Filleting			
	Marrow extraction	x	x	x
	Skinning	x		x
Cranial	Dismembering	x	x	x
	Marrow extraction	x		

Table 2.2. Butchery activities at Gough's Cave, Somerset (Andrews and Fernandez-Jalvo 2003).

fauna, subject to whatever taphonomic framework is present at the fossil site. There is an extensive literature on taphonomic modifications by non-human activities which will not be documented here. They may affect human burials, *e.g.* scavenging (Sutcliffe 1970), not seen at Çatalhöyük, or animal burrowing, which is common at Çatalhöyük and which has caused extensive bone loss. Humans have also been subjected to predation in the not so distant past (Patterson 1931; Brain 1981) and there is an extensive forensic anthropological literature where natural processes have been documented (Haglund and Sorg 1997, 2002; Andrews and Armour-Chelu 1998).

Conclusions

This review of burial practice has been applied mainly to the Neolithic human population from Çatalhöyük. The majority of burials were in graves beneath the floors of houses, and over half the number have been shown to be primary and undisturbed, even including some in collective burials, where they are inferred to have been the last interments in those graves. Several burials were identified as resulting from secondary action, *i.e.* burial/ exposure elsewhere for a period of time and then moved to their present resting place. This identification was based on specific patterns of skeletal element loss, but it is not known where or for how long the bodies had been deposited before they were placed in graves at Çatalhöyük. In a special case, there were two decapitation burials from which the skull had been removed and which had evidence of cut marks on remaining bones (hyoid bone in one case and the atlas vertebra in the other). Finally, many of the graves had disturbed multiple burials, up to 12 in one case, and the disturbance of earlier burials was caused by the later interments (except for the final burial in each case, as mentioned above). The age structure of primary, secondary and disturbed burials was found to differ, and both their distribution within Çatalhöyük and their distribution within buildings also had some points of difference, although these conclusions are tentative because sample sizes are limited. No evidence of cremation, cannibalism, or gnawing by scavenging animals was found.

Acknowledgements

We gratefully acknowledge help at Çatalhöyük from Basak Boz, Craig Cessford, Shahina Farid, Ian Hodder and Theya Molleson. We are also grateful to the three anonymous referees, and to the editors both for the invitation to contribute to this book and for their extremely detailed and helpful comments on the text.

References

Andrews, P. (1990) *Owls, Caves and Fossils.* London, Natural History Museum and University of Chicago Press.

Andrews, P. and Armour-Chelu, M. (1998) Taphonomic observations on a surface bone assemblage in a temperate environment. *Bulletin de la Société Géologique de France* 169, 433–442.

Andrews, P. and Fernandez-Jalvo, Y. (2003) Cannibalism in Britain: taphonomy of the Creswellian (Pleistocene) faunal and human remains from Gough's Cave (Somerset, England). *Bulletin of the British Museum (Natural History) Geology Series* 58, 59–81.

Andrews, P., Molleson, T. and Boz, B. (2005) The human burials at Çatalhöyük. In I. Hodder (ed.) *Inhabiting Çatalhöyük: Reports from the 1995–1999 seasons* volume 4 (British Institute of Archaeology in Ankara Monograph.

Angel, J. L. (1971) Early Neolithic skeletons from Çatalhöyük: demography and pathology. *Anatolian Studies* 21, 77–98.

Armour-Chelu, M. and Andrews, P. (1994) Some effects of bioturbation by earthworms (Oligochaeta) on archaeological sites. *Journal of Archaeological Science* 21, 433–443.

Arnaud B. (2002) Vilnius and the Ghosts of the Grande Armée. In P. Bahn (ed.) *Written in the Bones. How human remains unlock the secrets of the dead*, 72–77. London, David and Charles.

Baills, H. and Chaddaouil, L. (1996) La sépulture collective de Can-Pey (Pyrénées-Orientales): étude des pratiques funéraires. In D. Castex, P. Courtaud, P. Sellier, H. Duday and J. Bruzek (eds.) *Les ensemble funéraires du terrain à l'interprétation.* Numéro spécial de *Bulletin et Mémoires de la Société d'Anthropologie de Paris* 8, 365–371.

Bar-Yosef, O. (1986) New data on the origin of modern man in the Levant. *Current Anthropology* 27, 63–64.

Behrensmeyer, A. K. (1978) Taphonomic and ecological information from bone weathering. *Paleobiology* 4, 150–162.

Bello, S., Thomann, A., Signoli, M., Rabino Massa, E. and Dutour, O. (2002) La conservation différentielle des os humains et le "Profil théorique de survie osseuse. *Archéologie et Préhistoire* 113, 105–120.

Binant, P. (1991) *Les Sépultures du Paléolithique.* Paris: Editions Errance.

Boës, E. and Sears, S. (1996) Les crânes trophées marquisiens (XVIIIᵉ et XIXᵉ siècles). Interprétation des interventions anthropiques. *In* D. Castex, P. Courtaud, P. Sellier, H.

Brain, C. K. (1981) *The Hunters or the Hunted.* Chicago, University of Chicago Press.

Duday, J. Bruzek, (eds.). Les ensemble funéraires du terrain à l'interprétation. Numéro spécial de *Bulletin et Mémoires de la Société d'Anthropologie de Paris* 8, 275–288.

Carr, G. and Knüsel, C. (1997) The ritual framework of excarnation by exposure as the mortuary practice of the early and middle Iron Ages of central southern Britain. In A. Gwilt and C. Haselgrove (eds.). *Reconstructing Iron Age Societies*, 167–173. Oxford, Oxbow Monograph 71, Oxbow Books.

Cauwe, N. (2001). *L'Héritage des chasseursrs-cueilleurs dans le Nord-Ouest de l'Europe (10,000–3,000 avant notre èra).* Paris, Edition Errance.

Cessford, C. in press. Neolithic excavations in the North Area. In I. Hodder (ed.) *Excavating Çatalhöyük: South, North and KOPAL Area reports from the 1995–1999 seasons* volume 3. British Institute of Archaeology in Ankara Mongraph.

Duarte, C. (2002) The burial taphonomy and ritual. In J. Zilhao and E. Trinkaus (eds), *Portrait of the Artist as a Child,* 187–202. Portugal, Instituto Portugues de Arqueologia.

Duday, H. (1986a) Organisation et fonctionnement d'une sépulture collective néolithique. L'Aven de la Boucle à Corconne (Gard). In H. Duday and C. Masset (eds.) *Anthropologie physique et Archéologie*, 89–97. Paris, CNRS.

Duday, H. (1986b) Contribution des observations ostéologiques à la chronologie interne des sépultures collectives. In H. Duday and C. Masset (eds.) *Anthropologie physique et Archéologie*, 51–54. Paris, CNRS.

Duday, H. (1990) L'étude anthropologique des sépultures à incinérations. *Les Nouvelles de l'Archéologie* 40, 27.

Duday, H. and Sellier, P. (1990) L'archéologie des gestes funéraires et la taphonomie. *Les Nouvelles de l'Archéologie* 40,12–14.

Duday, H., Laubenheimer, F. and Tillier, A. (1995) *Sallèles d'Aude: Nouveau-Nés et Nourrissons Gallo-Romains*. Paris, CNRS.

Farid, S. (in press) South Area excavations. In I. Hodder (ed.) *Excavating Çatalhöyük: South, North and KOPAL Area reports from the 1995–1999 seasons* volume 3. British Institute of Archaeology in Ankara Monograph.

Gargett, R. H. (1989) Grave shortcomings: the evidence for Neandertal burial. *Current Anthropology* 30, 157–177.

Garland, A. N., Janaway, R, C. and Roberts, C. A, (1988) A study of the decay processes of human skeletal remains from the parish church of the Holy Trinity, Rothwell, Northamptonshire. *Oxford Journal of Archaeology* 7, 235–252.

Van Gennep, A. (1909) *Les Rites de Passage*. Paris, Emile Nourry.

Goffer, Z. (1980) *Archaeological Chemistry*. London, Wiley.

Grévin, G., Baud, C. A. and Susini, A. (1990) Etude anthropologique et paléopathologique d'un adulte inhumé puis incinéré provenant du site de Pincevent (Seine-et-Marne). In E. Crubézy, H. Duday, P. Sellier and A.-M. Tillier, (eds.) Anthropologie et Archéologie: Dialogue sur les ensembles funéraires. Numéro spécial des *Bulletins et Mémoires de la Société d'Anthropologie de Paris*. 2, 77–88.

Guilaine J. (1998) *Sépulture d'Occident et genèse des mégalithismes (9000 – 35000 avant notre èra)*. Paris, Editions Errance.

Guillon, F. (1986) Brulés frais ou brulés secs? In H. Duday and C. Masset (eds.) *Anthropologie physique et Archéologie*, 191–195. Paris, CNRS.

Haglund, W. D. and Sorg, M. H. (eds) (1997) *Forensic taphonomy: the postmortem remains*. Boca Raton, CRC Press.

Haglund, W. D. and Sorg, M. H. (eds) (2002) *Advances in forensic taphonomy: method, theory and archaeological perspectives*. Boca Raton, CRC Press.

Harrold, F. B. (1980) A comparative analysis of Eurasian Paleolithic burials. *World Archaeology* 12, 195–211.

Hill, A. (1979) Butchery and natural disarticulation: an investigatory technique. *American Antiquity* 44, 739–744.

Klein, R. (1999) *The Human Career*. Chicago, University of Chicago Press.

Klíma, B. (1987) A triple burial from the Upper Paleolithic of Dolní Vestonice. *Journal of Human Evolution* 16, 831–835.

Kurzawski, V. Bouville ,C. Totoyan,C. (1986) Fouille d'un ensemble de sépultures à crémation à Martigues (Bouches-du-Rhône). In H. Duday and C. Masset (eds.) *Anthropologie physique et Archéologie*, 67–72. Paris, CNRS.

Leclerc, J. (1990) La notion de sépulture. *Bullétins et Mémoires de la Société d'Anthropologie de Paris* 2(3–4), 13–18.

Lévêque, F. and Vandermeersch, B. (1980) Découverte des reste humains dans un niveau castelperronean à Saint Césaire. *Comptes Rendus des Séances de l'Academie des Sciences*, D 291, 187–189.

Lorans, E. (2000) Le monde des morts de l'Antiquité tardive à l'époque moderne (IVe – XIXe S.). In E. Crubézy, C. Masset, E. Lorans, F. Perrin and L. Tranoy (eds.) *Archéologie funéraire*, 155–197. Paris, Edition Errance.

Malone, C. (1996) *Avebury*. B.T. London, Batsford Ltd, English Heritage.h.

Masset, C. (1997) *Les dolmens. Sociétés néolithiques et pratiques funéraires*. Paris, Edition Errance, Paris.

McKinley, J. I. (1998) Archaeological manifestations of cremation. *The Archaeologist* 33, 18–21.

Mellaart, J. (1962) Excavations at Çatalhöyük, first preliminary report. *Anatolian Studies* 12, 41–65.

Mellaart, J. (1963) Excavations at Çatalhöyük, second preliminary report. *Anatolian Studies* 13, 43–103.

Mellaart, J. (1967) *Çatalhöyük*. London, Thames and Hudson.

Metcalf, P. and Huntington, R. (1991) *Celebrations of Death: the Anthropology of Mortuary Ritual*. Cambridge, Cambridge University Press.

Miles, D. (1965) Socio-economic aspects of secondary burial. *Oceania* 35, 161–174.

Molleson, T., Andrews, P. and Boz, B. (2005) The Neolithic people of Çatalhöyük. In I. Hodder (ed.). *Inhabiting Çatalhöyük: Reports from the 1995–1999 seasons* volume 4 British Institute of Archaeology in Ankara Monograph.

Molleson, T. and Moore, A. M. T. (2000) The people of Abu Hureyra. In A. M. T. Moore, G. C. Hillman and A. J. Legge, eds), *Village on the Euphrates: from Foraging to Farming at Abu Hureyra*, 301–324. Oxford, Oxford University Press

Movius, H. L. (1975) *Excavation of the Abri Pataud, les Eyzies (Dordogne)*. Cambridge, Peabody Museum.

Patterson, (1907) *The Man-eaters of Tsavo*. London, Macmillan.

Perrin F. (2000) Le mort et la mort en Gaule à l'âge du fer (VIIIe-Ier S. av.J.-C.). In E. Crubézy, C. Masset, E. Lorans, F. Perrin and L. Tranoy (eds.) *Archéologie funéraire*, 86–104. Paris, Edition Errance.

Russell, M. D. (1987) Mortuary practices at the Krapina Neanderthal site. *American Journal of Physical Anthropology* 72, 381–398.

Russell, N. and Martin, L. (2004) The Çatalhöyük mammal remains. In I. Hodder (ed.) *Inhabiting Çatalhöyük: Reports from the 1995–1999 seasons* volume 4. London, British Institute of Archaeology in Ankara Monograph.

Smith, F. H. (1982) Upper Pleistocene hominid evolution in south-central Europe. *Current Anthropology* 23, 667–703.

Stringer, C. (1986) Ice age relation. *Geographical Magazine* 58, 6562–65.

Sutcliffe, A. (1970) Spotted hyaena: hunter, gnawer, digester and collector of bones. *Nature* 227, 1110–1113

Thomas, J. (2003) *Understanding the Neolithic*. Second edition. London, Routledge.

Thuillier, F. (2000) Les incinérations primaires de la nécropole Gallo-Romaine des "oblets" à Thérouanne (Pas-de-Calais). In E. Crubézy, C. Masset, E. Lorans, F. Perrin and L. Tranoy (eds.) *Archéologie funéraire*, 130–133. Paris, Edition Errance.

Tranoy, L. (2000) La mort en Gaule romaine. In E. Crubézy, C. Masset, E. Lorans, F. Perrin and L. Tranoy (eds.) *Archéologie funéraire*, 105–154. Paris, Edition Errance.

Turner, C. G. (1993) Cannibalism in Chaco Canyon. *American Journal of Physical Anthropology* 91, 421–439.

Villa, P., Bouville, C., Courtin, J., Helmer, D., Mahieu, E., Shipman, P., Belluomini, G. and Branca, M. (1986) Cannibalism in the Neolithic. *Science* 233, 431–437.

White, R. (1993) Technological and social dimension of Aurignacian-age body ornaments across Europe. In H. Knecht, A. Pike-Tay and R. White (eds) *Before Lascaux*, 277–299. Boca Raton, CRC Press.

White, T. and Toth, N. (1991) The question of ritual cannibalism at Grotta Guattari. *Current Anthropology* 32, 118–124.

3. L'archéothanatologie ou l'archéologie de la mort (Archaeothanatology or the Archaeology of Death)

Henri Duday

Translated from the French by Christopher J. Knüsel

The improvements in archaeological techniques and interpretations that have developed over the last few decades have concentrated, for the most part, on settlements. It is far rarer to see the same insights applied to burial deposits. The excavation of burials was – and remains – all too often dependent on the work of archaeologists more accustomed to reading stratigraphic sequences and with a knowledge of grave inclusions or architectural features than with the anatomy of the human skeleton and, as a consequence, their reports only reflect what they have been trained to observe. If one evaluates the respective place of the diverse elements that make up a burial as a function of the number of written lines an author devotes to them in a publication, one often has the unfortunate impression that the deceased had been placed as an offering to a ceramic vessel or to a flint projectile point, rather than the other way around.

All too often, as well, the anthropologist (*i.e.* the skeletal biologist or osteoarchaeologist), when they are consulted, limits their input to morphological study only – mostly palaeopathological interests – of osseous material deprived of all cultural context. Therefore, they develop this discourse within a restricted disciplinary interest only, without addressing themselves to any site information other than the number, age, and sex of the dead. These analyses, though, represent the only tangible testimony derived from the cadaver, which was, without doubt, the *raison d'être* of the grave and the central focus around which the funerary rites were organised. The attempt to reconstruct such rites, the goal of funerary archaeology, without considering the data provided by the human remains constitutes a flagrant epistemological aberration. One must admit, however, that the discipline was erected on such studies and that similar studies continue to the present day.

For the anthropologist, like the archaeologist, it is essential that the study of burials begins in the field. The care that one takes in the exposure of the bones and the recording of these data conditions, to a large extent, their

potential and the validity of further study of them (Duday 1978, 1981, 1987a and b; Masset 1987; Duday *et al.* 1990a). The excavator of the remains (the 'field' anthropologist) must assure the precise identification of each bone element or fragment of an element *in situ*, record the exact position of each, its anatomical orientation, and relation to other bone elements. They must also document the relationship between the skeletal elements and all of the other parts of the grave, such as the grave architecture, grave furniture and other funerary objects, as well as make a provisional record of osteological measurements, the number of individuals, and the age and sex of the deceased, features that can be determined later in the laboratory if the preservation of the remains permits it (Figs. 3.1a, 3.1b, 3.1c, 3.1d and Table 3.1 – see p. 53). It is rarely possible to reconstitute this information afterwards if it is not noted in the field, no matter what the quality and abundance of the excavation archives. Furthermore, the factors which must be taken into account in interpretations are generally anatomical details that the draftsman or photographer would not think to detail in their plan or photograph without understanding the importance attaching to them.

One must demonstrate the intentionality of a deposit to confirm its funerary character (Leclerc 1990), but one must not presuppose a funerary context of all such deposits because certain intentional deposits of human remains have nothing to do with burial, for example, those deposits of individuals said to be "discarded, bodies dismembered after a murder, denigrated corpses, cadavers or parts of cadavers included as trophies, sacrificial bodies or individuals who 'accompany' the dead" (Thomas 1980). Even if it plays an undeniable role for the living, the burial is, at least in part, prepared for the deceased, and this function brings with it an interpretive context.

Of course, such considerations are often hard to establish, especially for the earliest periods. Happily, they are demonstrated in the majority of cases, the laying out of the body resulting – without doubt – from a voluntary

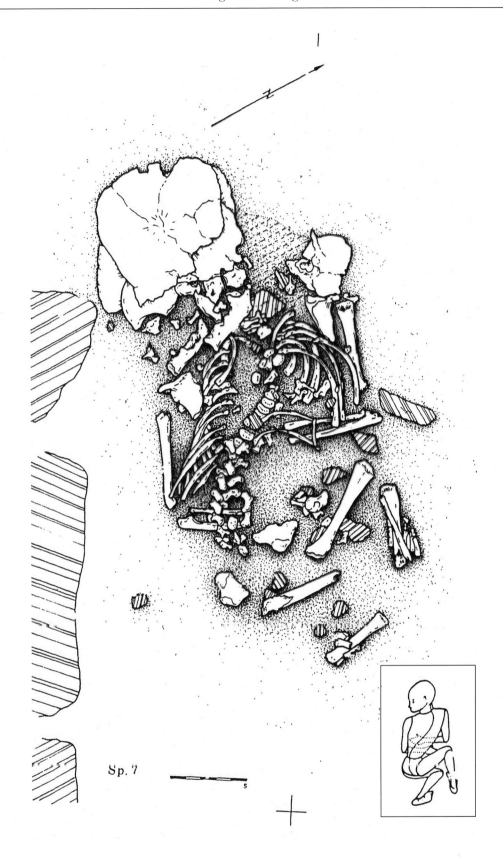

Figure 3.1. A composite drawing (3.1a, see above) of one of the burials of a newborn discovered in a Gallo-Roman pottery workshop from Sallèles-d'Aude (Aude, France), and the reconstruction of the original position of the body. This image was obtained by the super-imposition of successive drawings corresponding to three consecutive cleanings (3.1b, 3.1c, 3.1d, overleaf) reproduced at a scale of 1/2 and rotated through 90 degrees. Each osseous element was drawn, inventorie by specific number and its depth and anatomical orientation recorded (See Table 3.1). (Excavations of H. Duday, F. Laubenheimer and A. M. Tillier; drawing: H. Duday).

Figure 3.1. continued.

action and the overall context clearly oriented towards a funerary display (one thinks here of cemeteries surrounding a cult centre, for example). It is important, therefore, to determine those observations for each burial that translate directly into funerary practices: preparatory practices or pre-burial treatments of the corpse (before deposition), funerary practices (such as the structure of the grave, the position of the body and of the funerary material), post-burial practices (re-opening of the grave, manipulation of the bones, dismemberment, and secondary burial). These processes must be differentiated from taphonomic effects that occur during the decomposition of the corpse and through the intervention of natural agents (erosion, water action, compaction, physico-chemical alteration, the action of micro-organisms and burrowing animals). The nature of these processes is not as obvious as they might first appear because they depend, to a large extent, on the structure of the grave and its 'functioning' (the manner in which the body is affected is conditioned by the size of the animals which feed on it, for example). These features of the burial carry precious and unique information about burial practices.

This type of approach is, in its essence, a dynamic one because it is based on the interaction between funerary practices and the distorting influences of taphonomic factors precipitated by the initial construction of the grave. This approach is not known to be specific for any one period or to a particular geographic area; it is identical from the Palaeolithic to the modern period, even if it is sometimes necessary to adapt it to the conditions of archaeological excavation – to the means and with regard to the objectives of each excavation (for example, in rescue archaeology on sites likely to be destroyed within the short term). The discussion here is limited only to osteo-archaeological findings. It is hoped that, in due course, this type of consideration will also be applied to the archaeothanatology of mummified corpses, both natural and artificial. It is likely, though, that these principles will differ little from those developed for skeletonised remains, and both draw on techniques derived directly from biological and medical sciences.

This contribution begins with concepts that seem most fundamental, those founded on the analysis of isolated primary burials. It addresses the relative timing of the loss of integrity of the various articulations and the transformation of the micro-environment related to the organic fluids produced during decomposition, the reconstruction of the original position of the corpse, and the disposition of the burial decoration or costume, the analysis of the relationship between grave architecture and funerary trappings, and even some considerations of palaeopathology. Subsequently, it moves on to address more complex problems, such as those of multiple burials characterised by simultaneous deposition, and secondary burials, the dismemberment of the corpse and manipulation of the bones. It finishes with the most complex possibility – that of the collective burial.

Primary individual deposits

In archaeology, a primary deposit is defined as the placement of a 'fresh' body in a final resting place, where the entire process of decomposition takes place. Since funerary rites generally follow a short time after death, the body's anatomical integrity is preserved, at least from the perspective of macroscopic change.

The characteristics of primary burials

Anatomical articulations: unstable (labile) and persistent articulations

The characterisation of primary burial deposits rests principally on the observation of anatomical articulations. In effect, it is necessary to demonstrate that when the body was placed in the grave, the organic support structures that maintained the articulations (skin, tendons and especially fibrous aponeuroses, and ligaments) were still present and sufficiently intact to prevent the disarticulation of two contiguous bones. In a 'fresh' cadaver all osseous elements are found in proper anatomical position – they conform to the architecture of the human skeleton. Ideally, one could imagine observing the retention of these relationships as decomposition proceeded within the protected space afforded by the grave.

From this perspective, the most pertinent indicators involve those joints which lose their anatomical connection most rapidly *(unstable or labile articulations)* because their maintenance in anatomical position implicitly demonstrates the integrity of the cadaver, contrary to those that resist the processes of decomposition for a longer time *(persistent articulations)*. The time required for the complete destruction of these soft tissue support structures and the order in which these articulations lose their integrity varies as a function of the funerary treatment and with the environment in which the body is found – between the nearly immediate and simultaneous destruction (cremations in modern crematoria, cadavers abandoned by large carnivores such as hyenas) and the complete preservation for several millennia that one observes in certain cases of mummification (by cold, drying, salt water or even the acidic environments of bogs or, moreover, by a pre-burial treatment), all intermediaries being possible. These variations mean that it is not possible to create a timetable of decomposition that would cover all burials.

However, in 'average' conditions (a temperate humid region in which an inhumed cadaver is protected from carnivores and omnivores), it appears that the time necessary for the natural disarticulation is never less than some weeks, which fixes the limit on discriminating between a true, primary burial and a different type of deposit. Generally, unstable articulations involve bones of small size (those of the cervical region of the vertebral column, the hands, and distal parts of the feet) or fragile ones (such as the scapulo-thoracic joint, this anatomical relationship being one of anatomical placement only, *i.e.*

one not maintained by osseous articulations). These are the ones that require meticulous excavation. On the other hand, persistent articulations consist of elements placed under substantial biomechanical constraints, those which require the presence of thick and powerful ligaments (like the atlanto-occipital articulation, the lumbar segment of the vertebral column, the lumbo-sacral joint, the sacro-iliac articulations, the knees, the ankles and tarsal bones of the foot). Larger bones and/or more solid ones – those that are more easily recovered in assemblages and, therefore, those most visible in excavation – are, un-fortunately, the least informative.

If the preservation of anatomical articulations of joints reputed to be unstable seems to be necessary to demon-strate the primary nature of a burial deposit, the inverse type of reasoning has no validity. Let us imagine, for example, a body which had been placed in a closed space on a slightly raised platform above ground-level or on wooden funerary bier. Soft tissue putrefaction would leave the skeleton in proper anatomical position on its support until that support, in its turn, decomposed, after which the disarticulated bones would collapse onto the soil. It is very unlikely that this sort of endogenous disturbance, even if sufficiently late, would preserve any anatomical connections, even in an undisturbed primary burial. In this case, the absence of all anatomical connections might lead one to believe that these were not the remains of a primary burial. In order to demonstrate that it is, in fact, not a primary burial, though, it would be necessary to show the unlikelihood of the occurrence of either intrinsic changes within the deposit or that disturbances of an extrinsic origin had affected the burial. As this example shows, such disturbances are difficult to invoke or even completely illusory. Here, then, is a fundamental element of reasoning in funerary archaeology that has, never-theless, escaped the notice of numerous authors. How many publications have interpreted secondary burial deposits based on the simple argument that the bones were 'in disorder' (this form of words signifying, in fact, that the excavators could not observe anatomical connections), forgetting the essential role of the most universal of taphonomic agents – the law of gravity.

Decomposition fluids and the decomposition of the burial environment

The putrefaction of the cadaver produces organic fluids ('liquors') that infiltrate the surrounding sediments. The nature of these sediments will thus be modified, and it is often possible to detect these signs. Moreover, enriched organic matter works on a trophic level for earthworms which concentrate in the vicinity of the corpse; they can leave calcareous spherules in the sediment which one can find in great numbers. Furthermore, earthworms and sacrophagous insects draw numerous predators (insec-tivores such as moles, shrews, batrachians (frogs, toads and newts), and reptiles), the bones of which one often finds in the area of a burial. Certain terrestrial gastropods

also feed on these invertebrates, for example, one type of shelled slug, *Testacella* sp., is a specific predator on earthworms, and they possess a vestigial shell on their tails and lay calcified eggs. If found in abundance and in close proximity to human bones they demonstrate that earthworms were particularly active in the grave, and this observation argues strongly in favour of a primary deposit. If the decomposition had taken place in another location (an area of putrefaction or 'rotting place', see below), the contribution of already defleshed bones would have had little chance of encouraging an influx of sacrophagous insects.

It is even often possible to reveal the chemical action of decomposition fluids on certain geological substrates. At Villedubert (Aude, France), the author and colleagues were able to show that the calcareous deposits from an alluvial terrace of the Aude had been attacked by phosphoric acid coming from cadavers. This had precipitated the formation of calcium phosphate crystals in the cleavage planes that resulted in surface alterations (desquamation).

The displacement of bones within the cadaver in the course of decomposition

As is so obviously perceptible within the funerary space, gravity also influences changes within the original internal space of the body. To a limited extent, the disappearance of the soft tissues frees empty spaces within which skeletal elements can become displaced as soon as the supporting ligaments have, in their turn, decayed. Naturally, these movements vary considerably based on the original position of the cadaver. But it seems worthwhile to present here some often-encountered examples:

– **The flattening of the rib cage:** the ribs in their original anatomical position deviate inferiorly and this inferior deviation has a tendency to become accentuated after the rupture of the intercostal, costo-sternal, and costo-vertebral attachments; this process results in a major reduction of thoracic volume. In fact, it seems that the costo-transverse articulations are the last to decay, in that the lowering of the body of the rib is accompanied by the raising of its head to a position about half way up the vertebra above it. The determination of the level of the ribs in the field is often confused as a result of this process because, for reasons of ease, one often refers to the vertebral level to keep track of the costo-transverse relationships, although these are barely or not at all visible when the subject is lying on their back. As a consequence, there is a tendency to consider only the relations between the head of the rib and the vertebral body, a relationship which is thus systematically altered in the process of decomposition.

When the individual is lying on their side, the flattened ribs on the bottom of the grave are held in place by friction and the bones leaning on them from above. The increased angulation only affects the contra-lateral hemi-thorax such that one observes a gap between the anterior ends of the right and left ribs from the same vertebral level.

The descent of the sternum (in particular, the gladiolus) and elements which were originally placed on the anterior surface of the thorax or abdomen, for example, parts of the funerary costume or the hands, follows the subsidence of the ribs and the disappearance of the viscera. It is thus common to find the bones of the wrist, the metacarpals and the phalanges dispersed in the abdomen on either side of the vertebral column.

– *The partial dislocation of the vertebral column:* in excavation, the vertebrae often appear to be divided into sub-sections composed of several vertebrae (generally from two to five) in full articulation, between which one notes disjunctures due to rotation, through movement or angulation of elements. These movements take place as soon as there is an asymmetrical relationship in the ligaments by which the spine is articulated. When decomposition progresses to destruction of ligaments at the intervertebral level, a slight displacement is produced and the segments immediately above and below experience differential forces that lead to their dislocation. The vertebrae involved then stay in perfect articulation until the stage when another rupture occurs and there is another displacement linked to other constraints.

– *The collapse of the pelvic girdle:* the sacrum is situated like a wedge between the two iliac blades; the destruction of the sacro-iliac ligaments leads naturally to the migration of the sacrum towards the front, into the space liberated by the decay of the pelvic viscera. If the subject is lying on their side, the *os coxae* situated upper-most will fall into the interior of the pelvic cavity. Alternatively, if the subject is lying on their back, the displacement is more limited, the two *ossa coxae* fall towards the rear in the direction of the space created by the destruction of the muscle masses of the buttocks.

No matter how much the archaeological literature makes reference to the exceptional state of preservation of the remains, there are always differences between the original position of the skeleton and the one observed at excavation. Bone movements obey relatively simple and logical rules which are dictated by the relative timing of the destruction of the various articulations and by the action of gravity, both of which vary with the varying positions of the body. It is the absence of all disturbances that can, in certain cases, carry significant information about funerary behaviour. But the fact that these movements take place is, itself, independent of the unstable or persistent character of the articulations. The lumbar region of the vertebral column and the sacro-iliac joints are nearly always disturbed, although they can be counted among the most persistent structures of the body; they decay very late, but they always complete the process of decay as bones found generally in a disordered situation (except in cases of mummification). They displace themselves due to the effects of gravity. To affirm that one has found a primary deposit, it is thus not necessary to observe the preservation of all of the anatomical articulations, even in exceptional cases when the grave had not been altered in the process of decomposition. It is sufficient in these instances to note the maintenance of the unstable articulations.

The original position of the body
Reconstructing the original position of the body is obviously an essential step in funerary archaeology. All

excavators, even if they have only a limited familiarity with osteology, are certainly capable of determining the general traits of burials. It is somewhat different, though, for the extremities, especially the hands, or for burials of children who died at a young age. For these, a developed anatomical knowledge and a very meticulous recovery are required. Their analysis must take into consideration natural movements, the importance of which requires further emphasis, and also diverse phenomena which precede this step in decomposition. There are many relatively complex typologies established to describe the placement of the hands with regard to the trunk, which do not consider the not insubstantial factors relating not only to the initial placement of the body, but also to the flattening of the thorax, the swelling of the abdomen and oftentimes its explosion and then collapse, all of these phenomena being linked directly with putrefaction.

Another very important example concerns the rotation of the head, which can relate to funerary practices (*i.e.* the determination of the direction the deceased was facing) and, as such, constitutes evidence that must be discussed. This orientation can change as a result of the weight of the cranium when the decay of the cranio-vertebral attachments places it in an unstable position (for example in cases when the occipital rests on a flat surface).

In the living person or fresh cadaver, rotation of the head also involves the cervical vertebrae (Kapandji 1975, 206–213), the degree of movement being much more extreme between the first two vertebrae (the atlanto-axial articulation) than for the remainder of the more inferior articulations (at the cervical level the posterior amphi-arthrodial joints between the bodies of the vertebrae are locked by the superior and inferior articular processes). Upon decomposition, initial disarticulation often affects the intervertebral space between the atlas and axis, but more often at the joint between the axis and third cervical vertebra, and sometimes between the third and fourth cervical vertebrae (see Fig. 3.5) or, alternatively, the fourth and fifth. It is, therefore, crucial to observe the respective position of the superior-most cervical vertebrae. Continuity amongst them will attest to the original rotation of the head, at each level the degree of rotation conforming to biomechanical givens. On the contrary, a limited dislocation at a single intervertebral space, and that which surpasses that permitted by the morphology of the skeleton and the adhering ligaments, will act to indicate rotation due to taphonomic processes. It is thus essential to conduct a detailed examination of this region after lifting the cranium and the mandible when these structures block the view of the superior part of the cervical column. In the absence of systematic recording, these positions will not be discerned through the application of existing grave typologies that will, as a result, act to disguise the fact that the original position of the cephalic extremity of the vertebral column was very different from that observed at excavation.

In the same vein, one can sometimes resort to the relative position of the cranio-facial region and the mandible when the latter is displaced to one side (for example, in front of the cervical region of the vertebral column) and the former in another direction, there is a strong chance that this disjunction attests to rotation of the cranium that takes place during decomposition. It appears often that the release of the temporo-mandibular attachments (in this case there is the disassociation of two osseous elements, the mandibular condyle of the mandible from the mandibular fossa of the temporal bone that leaves the mouth in an open position) may occur some time before those of the cervical spine or it may occur afterwards. In the case of the latter, displacement involves the two parts (*i.e.* the cranium and mandible) that remain in a more or less close articulation, even though the (whole) skull was originally in an axial position.

Beyond these considerations, it is necessary to be conscious of the inherent limits to this approach. Meticulous recording of the osteological observations in the field, in most cases, permits one to discern the original posture of the body, but it is necessary to ask if the characteristics which have been observed relate to the actual funerary rite or if they attest only to a chance event. In the positioning of the body, not every aspect necessarily has a codified symbolism. In order to distinguish the significant elements from those of only anecdotal value, it is useful to consult the literature to determine if the same observations made in one burial can be found in many others from the same chronological and/or cultural context. Only the repetition of the same features is a means to demonstrate their intentional character. Inferring ritual positioning from a single burial, as one reads about all too often, constitutes, without doubt, an unacceptable abuse of the data. That the burial had been excavated well and that the position of the respective skeletal elements had been recorded in a particularly detailed manner do not in themselves confer a more rich ritual significance; one can document in a very precise way an observation that is purely fortuitous.

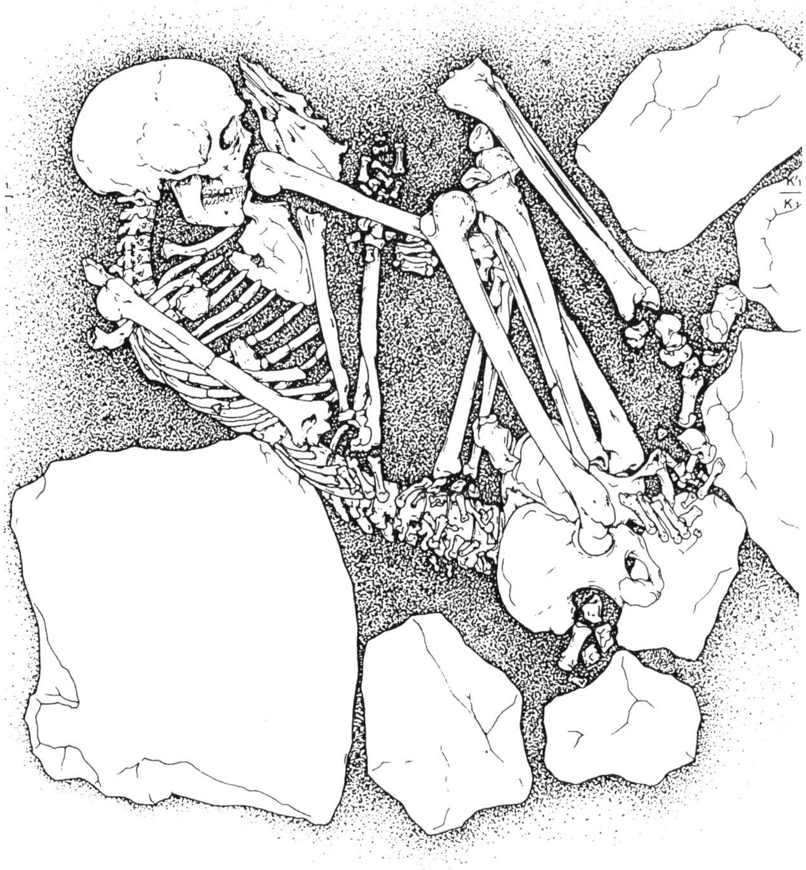

Grotte Gazel

Sépulture 1

25 cm.

Figure 3.2. An Early Neolithic burial discovered at Gazel cave at Salèles-Cabardès (Aude, France). The body of a male adult lies in a contracted position in a grave-cut partially surrounded by stones. The cranium of a young pig had been placed in front of the face of the deceased, near the right hand, the bones of which lie beneath the left axilla. (Excavations of J. Guilaine and H. Duday; drawing: H. Duday).

The disposition of accompanying funerary objects

The typological analysis of the accompanying burial material constitutes one of the most discussed subjects in the literature devoted to funerary archaeology. It relates, in effect, to objects – many times prestigious – that are generally better preserved in comparison to the residues accumulated in refuse or abandoned in settlements. As elsewhere, individual burials represent the type specimen of 'closed assemblages' (*i.e.* sealed contexts), so it is logical that archaeologists have regularly used them as a foundation for their chronological sequences.

Poorer is the information on the relative placement of this or that object with respect to the deceased (Fig. 3.2). These data can also be used to construct seriations that carry a chronological or ritual significance. This point is particularly evident for material coming from pieces of clothing or jewellery. However, it is not an unlikely occurrence that an excavator discovers a ring and takes the precaution during excavation of isolating the phalanx upon which it had been worn; this laudable, *a priori* precaution is, however, illusory because it is difficult to determine the ray (that is to say the finger) from an isolated phalanx and more so if it is eroded or if it comes from an intermediate or distal phalanx. The method chosen in these instances is inadequate to the purpose the archaeologist hoped to attain. In this case, it is indispensable to know 'to read' the precise position on the hand in the field and to identify each finger in the process of excavation in a veritable work of dissection (Fig. 3.3).

Finally, it is necessary to take into account the transformations linked to taphonomy. Pieces of jewellery or clothing are often involved in the processes of displacement that affects the skeleton, to an extent that the reconstruction of their original placement demands an understanding of the mechanisms that govern the decomposition of the cadaver (Fig. 3.4).

The decomposition process of the cadaver, or field anthropology in the quest of referents

From the foregoing, it is clear that the order in which the various articulations decay constitutes one of the fundamental bases of consideration in studies of the funerary context. Unfortunately, there are few detailed studies that exist on this sequence or on the speed of decomposition as it relates to the environment, and one must make reference to older works (Orfila and Lesueur 1831, although the research undertaken on the 'body farm' by William Bass and colleagues is a rich source of information, this is geared to medico-legal rather than archaeological investigation). One can easily perceive that ethical constraints and the sensibilities of modern people prohibits experimentation in this area. It is thus through the multiplication of archaeological observations that one can hope to establish a body of referents. With each favourable occasion it is thus essential to know to record

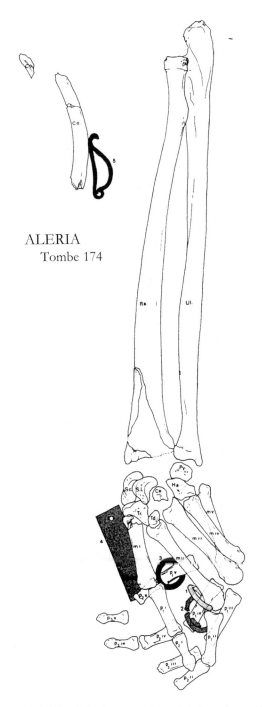

ALERIA
Tombe 174

Figure 3.3. The skeletal remains of an adult from the protohistoric burial site of Aléria (Corsica, France). The remains were protected by blocks of unfired clay that had fallen on the floor of the funerary chamber when looters of the burial broke down the wall which sealed the chamber. Beside two rib fragments, one notes a bronze brooch which seems to have been worn about half-way up the thorax, an observation which can be verified in other burials from the same site (see Fig. 3.6). There is a drilled rectangular bronze plaque and three rings (two on the proximal phalanx of the fourth digit and one on the proximal phalanx of the fifth). (Excavations of H. Duday and J. Jehasse; drawing: H. Duday).

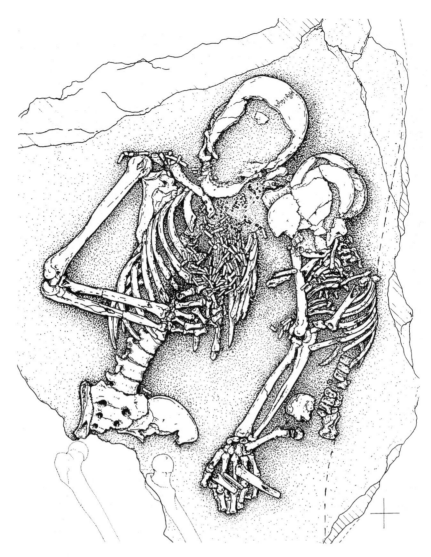

Figure 3.4. *An Early Neolithic double burial discovered at La Chapelle-Saint-Mesmin (Loiret, France). A young woman of twenty years of age and an infant of about 18 months were deposited in a grave-cut accompanied by rich inclusions. The infant wears a necklace of teeth, the woman a complex adornment of numerous teeth and discoid jet beads. These elements had fallen into the axial and peri-axial region of the thorax in a space freed by the subsidence of the sternum and the costo-sternal cartilages. The absence of all other elements of the costume on the opposite part of the thorax excludes a hypothetical 'breastplate' and suggests a deposit of bead and tooth necklaces instead. (Excavations of H. Duday, G. Richard and C. Verjux; drawing: H. Duday).*

the information that promises to enrich our understanding of these processes.

A human skeleton brought to light in a 6th-century B.C. context, found near the ancient town of Lattes (Hérault, France), provides a point of departure for consideration. The burial was located about 1.5 m below the level of the ground water; it seems not to have been an intentional burial, but instead resulted from an 'unknown occurrence' (drowning, accident… ?), as a result of which the archaeological interest in the discovery would seem limited. The body of an aged female was lying in a prone position, and for the most part the articulations were in close approximation, most notably the preserved hands, including the sesamoids (Fig. 3.5). From these observations, it is clear that decomposition occurred *in situ*. Excavation demonstrated many apparently paradoxical disarticulations: the cranio-facial region was not found as an extension of the vertebral column, which had been disarticulated at the fourth cervical vertebra; the atlas had been placed against the inferior aspect of the occipital, in the immediate vicinity of the second and third cervical vertebrae which were oriented to reveal their superior aspect in plan, although the right lateral aspect of the first cervical vertebra was visible in the same orientation as the remains of the cranial skeleton. The left hemi-thorax was equally disturbed with certain ribs disassociated, the fourth and the fifth having passed behind the thoracic region of the vertebral column. The left shoulder was raised to the level of the fourth cervical vertebra, but the clavicle, the scapula, and the humeral head had remained

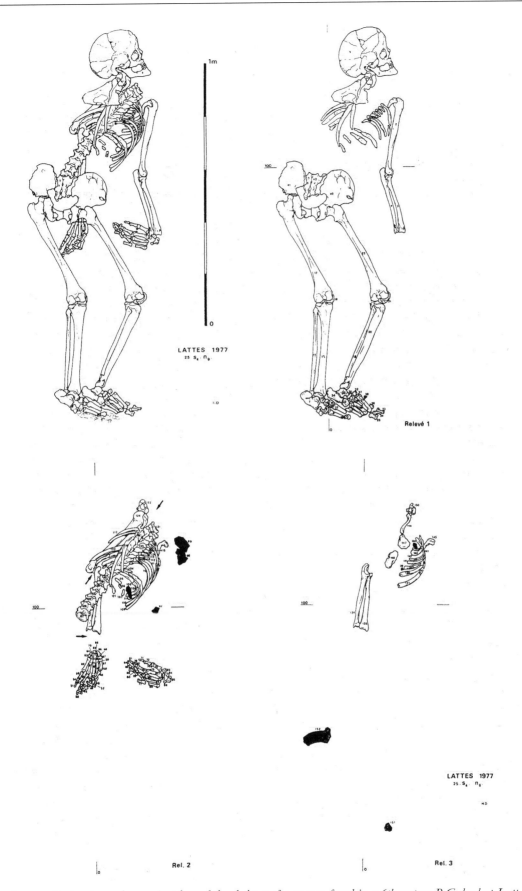

Figure 3.5. A composite drawing and successive plans of the skeleton of a woman found in a 6th century B.C. level at Lattes (Hérault, France) (arrows indicate areas of skeletal displacement described in the text). (Excavations of H. Duday and H. Prades; drawing: H. Duday).

in close articulation. The left elbow was also amongst the preserved remains, but the olecranon process was located in front of the distal extremity of the humerus. Finally, the anatomical relationships of the various bones of the left hand were perfectly respected, even though there was a gap of 7 cm between the proximal row of carpals and the distal extremity of the forearm.

It seems that these displacements must have taken place in a water-logged environment, with the effect of drawing the cervical region to a left lateral position and, in the process, precipitating the toppling of the cranial skeleton and the raising of the left shoulder. It is difficult in this occurrence to estimate the time interval that passed between the decay of soft tissue and this re-arrangement of skeletal elements, especially given the very unusual preservation conditions. In retrospect, one could affirm that at the moment when the disturbances were produced, certain ligaments had ensured the maintenance of osseous articulations – mandible-cranium-atlas, clavicle-scapula-humerus, axis-third cervical vertebra – with others being further advanced in the process of decay, resulting in the bones concerned having been displaced from anatomical alignment and the introduction of anomalies of position or orientation- atlas-axis, elbow. Still other articulations were completely decayed, which explains the very clear disjunction between the third and fourth cervical vertebrae and especially that of the left hand. When the superior portion of the left limb was drawn upward, nothing survived of the attachments between the forearm and the hand, and, as a result, the left hand remained in its original position. One can easily understand the interest in such a discovery with regard to the relative chronology of the destruction of the different articulations.

As a biological discipline in which particular views are deprived of facts established by true experimentation, archaeothanatology is obliged to establish foundations for its own discourse at the same time that it contributes to the understanding of funerary assemblages. The field must then give way to the laboratory, the excavation to the experiment. It is essential that archaeologists who direct field campaigns are aware of their incumbent responsibilities – an observation can be of minor importance for understanding the study site, but will have an enormous importance for understanding the process of decomposition and thus for the interpretation of other funerary deposits. The most compelling example of this 'experimental' archaeology is, doubtless, represented by the recent study of a funerary deposit of 21 French soldiers and officers who, having perished at the front, were buried on 22 September 1914 (Boura *et al.*, 1992, *cf.* below, Fig. 3.15).

The contribution of osteological observations to the reconstruction of funerary architecture

Osteological field data often permit one to identify the environment within which the body decomposed. As such, these data contribute to the appreciation of burial architecture, especially when the containers do not leave directly observable remains.

The decomposition of the body in an empty space

Decomposition in an empty space is, in certain cases, evident because of the peculiarities of grave architecture (for example, a sealed sarcophagus empty of all sediment) or because the skeleton lies on the surface of the soil in a natural cavity. Such evidence suffices to refute the hypothesis that a once buried body had been disinterred after burial by natural means or by humans.

This argument is subtler when, upon discovery, the bones are covered by sediment. The reasoning that one is tempted to apply to such contexts is as follows: the destruction of the articular attachments progressively liberates bony elements which, as a result, become mobile and, if decomposition has progressed far enough, areas once occupied by soft tissues leave empty spaces, into which certain bones may fall, after having left the original body cavities under the effect of gravity or another factor and come to reside in the empty spaces. In order for the observation to be completely convincing, it is necessary to eliminate the eventuality of later interventions which would have had the effect of 'opening' an empty space in an initially filled grave (by the actions of burrowing animals, or the digging of another grave-cut, for example).

When they are due to gravity, these movements still depend on the original position of the body; the only bones susceptible to entering or falling into the area external to the body are those that decomposition frees, and these are found in anatomical disorder with regard to other bone elements. Although certain postures are relatively commonly encountered, one quite regularly finds other patterns that require additional explanation:

– When the subject is lying on their back, the opening of the pelvic girdle may proceed until the *ossa coxae* lie flat, with the complete separation of the pubic symphysis. As the *ossa coxae* fall laterally, the femoral heads are pushed into the acetabula, which is precipitated by the lateral rotation of the femora, which also causes the patellae to fall to the outside of the knees. This last indication is easy to spot – it constitutes an important argument in favour of the decomposition occurring in an empty space (although one must be aware that sometimes bones have been placed in correct anatomical position in the field in order to take photographs).

– On the other hand, if the body is lying on its side, a scapula and an *os coxae* can topple over in back of the trunk and can be found on edge.

In the course of excavation, one is often confronted with graves in which the sacrum, the sternum, the ribs, and several vertebrae (principally the cervical vertebrae, but also the inferior lumbar vertebrae) and, many times, the cranio-facial region have undergone displacement to a considerable degree. The fact that skeletal elements of a small volume are involved suggests a cause other than the mere weight of elements as responsible for these displacements. In such instances, it is possible to demonstrate that these graves were those more susceptible to inundation from a rising water table, and it is likely, then, that these bones floated. Whatever the cause, though, it is clear that movements of such an extent could only have been produced in the presence of an empty space.

Other displacements are due to the collapse of the floor or the lateral walls of a burial. Mordant (1987) has also emphasised information that can derive from the fragmentation of bones when linked to these events; here, as well, the reconstruction of the grave architecture benefits from observations linked to the skeleton.

Original empty space / secondary empty space

It is important to distinguish original empty spaces, those which characterise the grave at the moment of deposition, from those that one could call secondary empty spaces, the latter appearing in the space outside of the body after a relatively long time. They result from the disappearance of architectural elements or funerary inclusions made of perishable material, the decomposition of which is slower than that of the cadaver. Some bone already disarticulated by putrefaction can also slip into a pre-existing cavity, until then inaccessible or one entirely 'newly formed'. These can provide paradoxical perspectives that are often difficult to interpret.

Moreover, the coffin may have been raised with stones (which will still be in place at the moment of excavation) or on blocks of wood (which will have disappeared), the floor of which, impregnated with the products issuing from the decomposition of the cadaver, will eventually collapse, and certain bones can then fall to the bottom of the grave-cut, as can easily be discerned by systematic recording of each layer (Duday *et al.* 1990b). In the same vein, the secondary disappearance of a support which raises the head (a head support in wood or a cushion) produces the tell-tale signs of a complete dislocation of the cranium (which the atlas generally follows), the mandible and the superior cervical vertebrae (Fig. 3.6). These are signs that are easy to recover and interpret. It is hoped, then, that they can soon be taken into account in archaeological burial typologies, since they concern an element of the funerary trappings that totally disappears but of which the field anthropologist has the ability to demonstrate the existence of or, indeed, its absence.

The decomposition in a filled space (in an earth grave)

The procedure is founded on the same principles for a filled space as for an empty one, but the reasoning is diametrically opposite. When a bone freed by the disappearance of soft tissues is found in a situation of instability with respect to the space external to the cadaver, it will normally fall into this space. If this displacement does not occur, then there was no empty space (Fig. 3.7). This negative determination often demonstrates the existence of a *wall* effect, and the subsequent discussion must thus address the nature of this wall. Naturally, it can relate to the limit of a grave-cut or of a funerary chamber,

or of a perishable wall situated at a distance from the latter (for example, the lateral board of a coffin), but also of the earth with which the grave has been filled as soon as the corpse was in place, or at least before the disarticulation(s) of skeletal elements. The discrimination between these diverse possibilities relies on arguments which relate to general archaeological methods and not only on osteological observations: definitions of stratigraphic units between underlying rock and earth fill, the arrangement of coffin nails and wood residues *etc.*

It is thus contended here that the characterisation of the environment in which the body decomposes relies on the observation of the relations between the various elements of the skeleton and the external dimensions of the cadaver. But it is also often the case that they draw on other useful information that will now be addressed.

The in-filling of the internal space of the cadaver

It is surprising to see to what extent the archaeological literature remains silent on an essential taphonomic event- the (in)filling of the space freed by the disappearance of the soft tissues. For most burials (except those in hermetically sealed vaults) the main difference between the time of deposition and the time of excavation lies in the fact that the muscles, the viscera, and the adipose tissue have been replaced by interstitial sediment.

Differential in-filling and progressive in-filling

The decomposition of the soft tissues creates empty spaces in which the bones, once they are freed by the destruction of ligaments, are susceptible to displacement under the effect of gravity. This mechanism was invoked above to explain the differences between the original position of the skeleton and that which one observes at excavation. Movements of skeletal elements are obviously only possible because these empty spaces occur within the original space occupied by the body. They have an important impact on the appearance of the burial because in-filling with earth prevents all subsequent displacement, but this process does not immediately follow the disappearance of the flesh, but rather one speaks of differential in-filling.

Contrarily, if the bones have been maintained in their initial position, and they were in disarray with regard to the internal space of the body, it is necessary to conclude that in-filling was progressive; the surrounding sediment replaced the perishable parts of the cadaver as they gradually disappeared (Figs. 3.8, 3.9, and 3.10). In all cases that the author has observed personally, this situation occurs in contexts characterised by particularly fluid sediments (fine sand, powdery ash) that have infiltrated by percolation (and thus under the action of gravity), a mechanism that one might describe as an 'hour-glass effect'. This phenomenon can only be produced if the sediment is in immediate contact with the body; this appearance, then, constitutes an indirect but irrefutable demonstration of a deposit made in the bare earth.

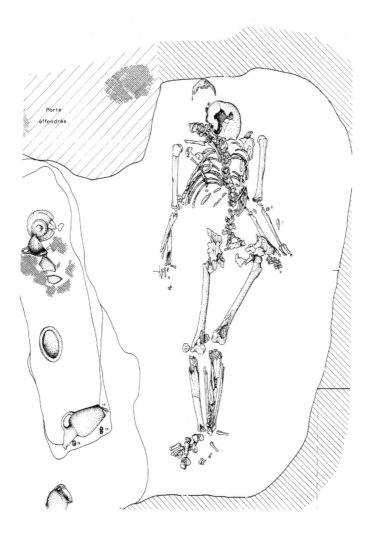

Figure 3.6. Drawing of part of grave 175 at the pre-Roman burial ground at Aléria (Corsica, France). Within the funerary chamber there is a central pit with accumulated offerings between two benches on which the bodies of two adults had been placed. One of the two (depicted here) shows a dislocation of the cranium (with the atlas in articulation beneath the occipital), the mandible, and the cervical region of the vertebral column completely in agreement with there having once been a perishable object supporting the head. (Excavations of H. Duday and J. Jehasse; drawing: H. Duday).

The mechanisms of in-filling of the space liberated by the disappearance of soft tissues

Diverse mechanisms play their parts in the in-filling of the internal space of the cadaver: the collapse of the overlying sediment under the effect of gravity, the swelling of the earth by water ('proliferation' of clay), and especially the action of biological agents among which worms play a prominent role – the enrichment of the soil by putrefactive organic matter attracts them in great numbers and their excreta accumulate in proximity to and in the interior of the skeleton. The knowledge of such phenomena is essential in funerary archaeology; 'black' or 'organic' earth of burials does not necessarily correspond closely with the filling of the grave by humans; it can simply indicate the zone where the action of earthworms had been most intense, which relates to the validity of certain deductions with regard to the limits of grave-cuts.

In order to demonstrate the veracity of this remark, it suffices to follow the excavation after the lifting of the skeleton. One is very often surprised to realise that the "more brown, more aerated, more lumpy – in a word 'organic'" – fill that excavators consider as characteristic of the fill of graves is often found some centimetres below a level on which the cadaver has decomposed. Certainly, it is possible that the latter has been raised by an organic support above the level of the bottom of the grave-cut (for example, in the case of a coffin lying on wedging stones, see above), but also, in general, when this perceived difference in excavation is not marked by the distinction between the surrounding sediment and the fill of the grave-cut, but rather between the sediment of the fill and the zone where the activity of worms had been particularly intense. The instances of this interpretive error become most important when considering the re-cutting of graves,

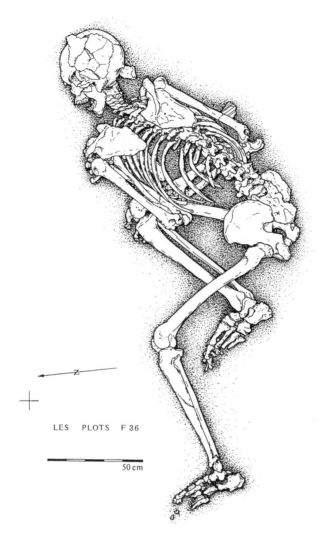

LES PLOTS F 36

50 cm

Figure 3.7. A Middle Neolithic burial in a storage pit at Berriac (Aude, France). The body lies in a prone position. The right hand is placed on the right knee such that the distal phalanges of the fingers appear in front of the knee vertically in the soil. After the disappearance of the interphalangeal articular attachments, which are particularly unstable, these elements were in an unstable situation with regard to the external space of the cadaver. They would have fallen, then, into this space; their maintenance in their original position demonstrates the existence of a wall effect. Because this area is found at some distance from the limits of the grave-cut, and there is no obvious limit on the left side of the body, it is likely that this effect occurred with the immediate filling of the grave, soon after the cadaver had been deposited (a burial in the 'bare earth'). (Excavations of H. Duday and J. Vaquer; drawing: H. Duday).

free spaces between graves and also the relations between the decomposing body and the walls of the grave-cut.

The evidence for constraint effects: the effect of the container on the organisation of the skeleton

Even the form of the container plays an essential role on the position of the body. The container also conditions taphonomic changes of the body. Some classic examples, which have sometimes given rise to erroneous interpretations, are discussed here.

When the deceased is lying on bare earth in a contracted position the peripheral pressure of the sediment can induce the progressive closure of the angles between limb segments, the degree of flexion of the joints being augmented progressively with the decay of the muscle masses. The discovery of a 'hypercontracted' skeleton, of which the large long bones of the limbs are in contact with one another (Fig. 3.11), does not imply that the body had undergone a pre-burial defleshing, nor that it had been tightly bound or placed in a sack.

One can also examine transverse compression phenomena when the body lies on its back in a narrow container (in a tied shroud, for example, but also in a narrow coffin or a pit grave).

– At the level of the shoulders, this constriction usually induces a 'verticalisation' of the clavicles; such that the lateral extremity of the shoulder is, in effect, raised and projected forward due to restrictions imposed by the container; at the same time, the humeri undergo a medial rotation which exposes their lateral or even their postero-lateral aspect and

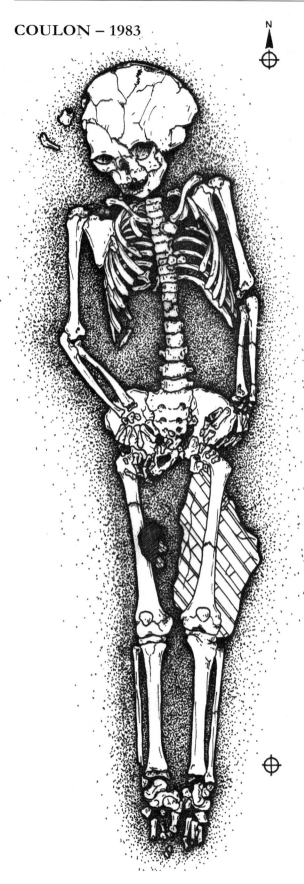

COULON – 1983

N

Le Coteau de Montigné - P9

25 cm

the scapulae – as a consequence found in a very oblique position – present their antero-lateral aspect. Contrarily, the medial extremity of the clavicles is inferiorly pulled towards the manubrium which, in turn, usually follows the movement of the first ribs when the rib cage is flattened. It is due to these two joint phenomena that the clavicles have a tendency to become almost parallel with the axis of the vertebral column (Fig. 3.12).

At the level of the pelvic girdle, a similar effect (which is similar to a wall effect) can prevent the flattening of the *ossa coxae*, even if there is an empty space.

Pit burial can at the same time cause the raising of the head and of the feet. In all cases, the discussion of such burials must take into account the relative depth of all the osseous elements. This is why the recording of data in field anthropology depends on systematic recording of a large number of levels, both in plan but also with regard to the depth of excavated remains (see Table 3.1). It is often necessary to make plans of the same bone from many perspectives (cranium, scapulae, *ossa coxae*, major long bones *etc.*) in a manner that permits the reconstruction of the exact disposition of the 'soil' into which the body has been deposited.

In many instances, a general understanding of taphonomic processes permits the recovery of anomalies with regard to 'normal' changes of the cadaver. An excavated burial in which the normal phenomenon of the flattening of the ribs does not take place has added importance. The greater part of these cases relate, in fact, to analogous circumstances; the subject is crouched on their back in grave-cuts with a flat bottom in which the central part is over-dug to form a pit. The upper limbs are pulled into abduction and lean on the side walls at a distance from the rib cage, such that the ribs are supported for nearly their full length by the walls of the pit and are thus held as if in a corset (Fig. 3.13). In such instances, the thorax retains its original volume.

Palaeopathological information

Palaeopathology is principally a laboratory discipline as applied to diagnosing anomalies observed in human

Figure 3.8 (left). The protohistoric burial of a child of 8 to 10 years of age at death in a circular funerary enclosure at Coulon (Deux-Sèvres, France). A burrowing animal had displaced two small pieces of the cranial base. Except for this exogenous re-organisation, the skeleton has retained its original position; the thoracic space is nearly completely preserved, the ossa coxae, *composed of three separate elements, the ilium, ischium, and pubis, separated by cartilagenous plates, have been maintained in place, despite the disappearance of the abdominal viscera and the muscle masses of the buttocks. The hands, placed in front of the abdomen and against the left buttock, have also remained in position. It is thus evident that the destruction of the soft tissues did not succeed in producing a temporary empty space, which demonstrates the process of progressive in-filling of the freed space as the cadaver decomposed. (Excavations of H. Duday and J.P. Pautreau; drawing: H. Duday).*

ABRI PENDIMOUN
Sépulture 1

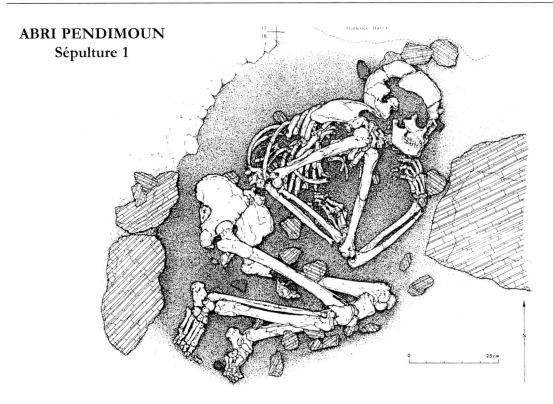

Figure 3.9. An Early Neolithic burial from the Abri Pendimoun at Castellar (Alpes-Maritimes, France). The right scapula, on edge, and the bones of the left hand have been maintained in their original position, although they are in a position of instability with regard to the external space of the cadaver (wall effects linked to the immediate filling of the grave-cut). Furthermore, the left foot leans almost vertically against the wall of the grave-cut; there is a difference in height of 15 cm between the distal extremity of the hallux and the posterior aspect of the calcaneus. This observation demonstrates that the space freed by the disappearance of the fleshy parts of the plantar surface of the foot had been filled soon afterwards by very fine sediment in such a way that the phalanges and sesamoids have remained in place. (Excavations of H. Duday and D. Binder; drawing: H. Duday).

remains from archaeological sites, and the interpretations of the state of health of populations, and the history of illnesses and medico-surgical techniques. Palaeopathological study can nevertheless benefit from observations obtained during excavation.

Certain unusual postures often constitute an indispensable element to aid diagnosis. For example, a pre-Neolithic skeleton from Bonifacio (Corsica, France) possessed a very peculiar position of the left hand that reproduced very exactly the classic 'claw-grip' which characterises ulnar nerve paralysis (Duday 1975). The same subject also presented with old (*i.e.* well-healed) traumatic lesions that had damaged the nerve and produced the usual sequelae of motor deficit (ankylosis and demineralisation). The first element of the diagnosis is indicated in this example by the position of the hand that only a meticulous excavation would recover.

Equally, the precise placement of biological calcifications (calculi, pleural plaques, cysts, tumours *etc.*) with respect to the skeleton can be a precious indicator for their identification because their placement also indicates the health status of the viscera concerned (Baud and Kramar 1990).

Finally, the systematic notation of the altered areas on the skeleton *in situ* often helps to make the distinction between taphonomic changes, arising *post-mortem*, and true pathological lesions resulting from *intra vitam* bone reactions that affect the skeleton before burial.

Secondary deposits: secondary burials and apparent funerary practices

In secondary deposits, 'dry' bones are transported to the place of their final deposition. This practice, then, is preceded by a period of defleshing (active or passive), the duration of which is variable and generally takes place in the context of a temporary deposit (one often refers to these places explicitly as 'rotting places').

The most obvious example concerns cremations on an *ustrinum* placed at a distance from the grave. These secondary burials correspond to what ethnologists refer to as 'double funerals'. They have often been cited in the archaeological literature on the basis of arguments that warrant discussion:

– Many times researchers emphasise cutmarks that attest to the active defleshing of the cadaver, but the same marks have

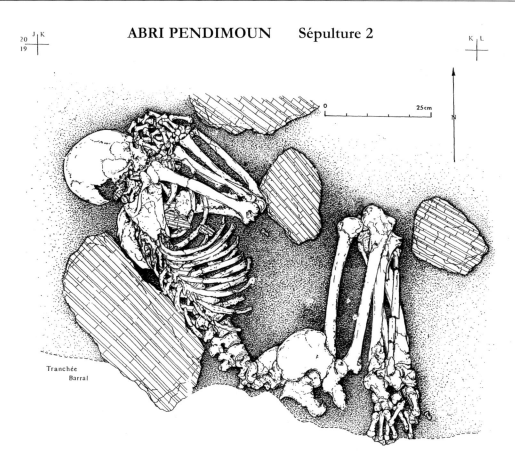

Figure 3.10. An Early Neolithic burial in the l'Abri Pendimoun at Castellar (Alpes-Maritimes, France). One can observe a very marked effect of constraint on the anterior aspects of the lower limbs and dorsum of the feet. The sesamoids of the right and left first metatarsals have been maintained in their original position, despite a very strong inclination linked to the rising of the end of the grave-cut (3.5 cm between the distal and proximal extremities of the left first metatarsal). It is certain that here again the ashy sediment has progressively filled the spaces liberated by the decomposition of the plantar soft tissues, which demonstrates a deposit in a filled-in space. (Excavations of H. Duday and D. Binder; drawing H. Duday).

been used to advance hypotheses of cannibalism or surgical practices as well. The discussion of them, then, must be supported and critiqued in order to have real significance (see Knüsel and Outram, this volume).

– Researchers often explain the incompleteness of certain skeletons by the voluntary selection of bones destined for the final resting place, and equally by the 'forgotten', lost, or destroyed small bones of the skeleton that remain at the place where defleshing was performed or during transport from them. This determination certainly has value, on the condition, however, that one can separate all destruction due to taphonomic processes (differential preservation), and that one is certain that the missing elements have not been tumbled into inaccessible fissures or crevices and, furthermore, that they have not been left at the site by a careless excavator.

– As noted above, one often observes an apparent 'disorder' in the placement of human remains (with respect to the original order of a skeleton in proper anatomical alignment), but this does not necessarily correspond to a secondary deposit. It is necessary to know (or be able) to eliminate the hypothesis of a re-organisation that occurs after the decay of articulations.

The diagnostic feature of a secondary burial lies, then, principally, on negative arguments. This is why *bona fide*

cases are necessarily rare, much more rare than for primary burials, the recognition of which relies on positive observations such as the preservation of unstable articulations and, more accessibly, the diagenesis of the burial environment linked to the fluids of putrefaction. For twice-deposited remains, the interpretation demands the refutation of all later intervention that would not have been part of the funerary ritual 'programme'. The use of the same cemetery for many centuries necessarily occasions the accidental re-cutting of older graves, the bones which are thus exhumed are not, in general, treated as 'neutral' remains in that they often contribute to secondary deposits in an ossuary or 'communal' deposit. This respectful *a posteriori* management must obviously not be held to be characteristic of funerary practices from the period during which the individuals concerned lived and died. It informs us only about the considerations of the grave-diggers who made the burials, and possibly about the religious thoughts of the population to whom they are related. Moreover, the absolute dating that one obtains from the displaced bones has nothing to tell us about when the secondary deposit was made.

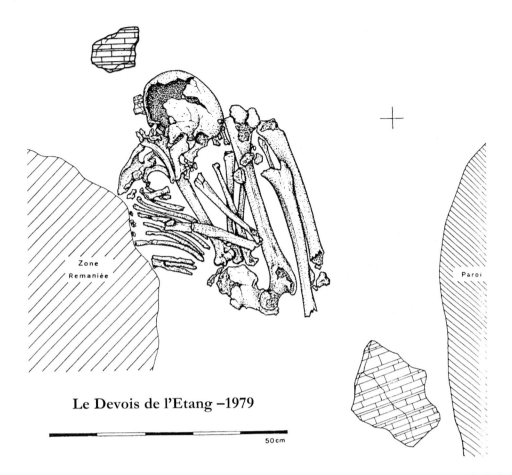

Le Devois de l'Etang –1979

50 cm

Figure 3.11. One of the Chalcolithic burials from the hypogeum of Devois de l'Etang at Tresques (Gard, France). The body lies on its left side: the hypercontracted appearance of the skeleton is, in part, due to closing of the inter-segmental angles. Under the pressure of surrounding sediments, the large long bones of the limbs have come in contact with one another as the muscular masses decomposed. (Excavations of A. Colomer, J. Coularou, H. Duday, X. Guther_q and A. Raux; drawing H. Duday).

Furthermore, however, anatomical connections can survive in truly secondary burials if the defleshing has been incomplete when the remains of the deceased were transferred to the final resting place. Generally, this means that the persistent articulations had not yet been lost through decay. It is the same as in cases where the unstable articulations are involved, and these are so numerous that the archaeological interpretation – especially if historical or ethnographic textual references are not available – must logically conclude that it is a primary deposit. A particularly poignant example has been reported by Ubelaker (1974) with regard to the Indians of the Potomac (US), dated to the 16th and 17th centuries. The historical documentation indicates that these relate to veritable collective and simultaneous secondary burials performed at regular intervals such that the stage of decomposition attained by each individual at the moment of burial could be determined. In such a case, the bodies of the most recently deceased subjects were only slightly disarticulated, which gave the impression of them being primary interments.

This example again illustrates the interpretive limits of our considerations; all that can be determined with any precision is the stage of decomposition that the corpse had attained when it was manipulated. In the absence of other data, there is nothing that permits us to understand what significance ancient peoples accorded to this state, nor even if they accorded the process one at all. The funerary practices are only the material translation of funerary ritual, and only the practices are accessible to us.

These interpretive limits render the distinction between a true secondary burial and the reduction of the corpse a very delicate one. The latter corresponds to the bundling together of bones of an individual – or at least of portion of them – inside a space that accommodated the primary deposit (*i.e.* where decomposition took place). Such a deposition is particularly frequent in sarcophagi when the inclusion of another deceased person necessitates 'making room' for it. One must also, perhaps, consider the same process of re-arrangement in the interpretations of the large collective tombs of the Late Neolithic. In this case, the bones of many individuals are gathered together in well-delimited areas (bundles of long bones and of ribs and crania placed along walls), in such a manner that it is sometimes possible to suggest a partition of the chamber

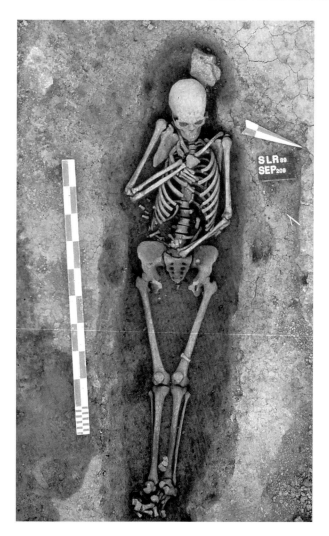

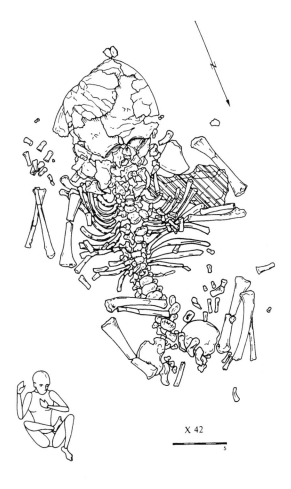

Figure 3.12. An overhead photographic view of burial 209 from the burial ground of Serris (Seine et Marne, France) (Early Middle Ages). The oblique position of the clavicles is due to constriction of the grave-cut and the sharp rise at the bottom of the immediate surroundings of the head niche; the shoulders are thus projecting anteriorly and superiorly, a mechanism equivalent to that produced when the cadaver is constrained in a container that is too narrow and very tight at the level of the shoulders. (Excavations of F. Blaizot and H. Guy, Photograph by F. Gentili).

Figure 3.13. A composite drawing of the burial of a neonate from the protohistoric oppidum *of Gailhan (Gard, France). The body lies in a supine position, the upper right limb and the left upper arm lean against banks that border a deep and relatively narrow central pit. This disposition permits good preservation of the thoracic space; the difference in depth between the sternal extremity and the heads of the middle ribs is 5 cm. One notes here, too, the disposition of the ribs in a 'fan' shape, the superior ribs have fallen in a cranial direction. This observation, the norm for dead neo-natal infants, is less common in subjects of a greater age at death, the obliquity of the ribs inferiorly and anteriorly being the natural tendency that is exaggerated in the process of decomposition. (Excavations of H. Duday and B. Dedet; drawing H. Duday).*

into differentiated functional zones (Duday 1987a). But it remains impossible to know if such assemblages can be associated with simple body reduction, or if they relate to true secondary burials – whether or not they can provide information on the manner with which this subdivision of funerary space was perceived by prehistoric peoples.

The intentional removal of bones after disarticulation of the cadaver pre-supposes the re-opening of the grave and implies, in general, the existence of an empty space. The disturbances can be inferred from the bones that remain in the grave, which depend, naturally, on the state of the cadaver at the moment of disturbance. The

elements recovered can be considered 'relics', but they can also have been re-interred at a distance or transported to another funerary location in a manner that the same individual can simultaneously be found to have been the subject of an incomplete primary deposition (which can then retain its funerary importance or simply become profane) and a partial secondary burial (see Vigneron 1985, with respect to the Marae Ta'ata of Tahiti).

Multiple and collective burials

Up to this point, this treatment has been essentially pre-

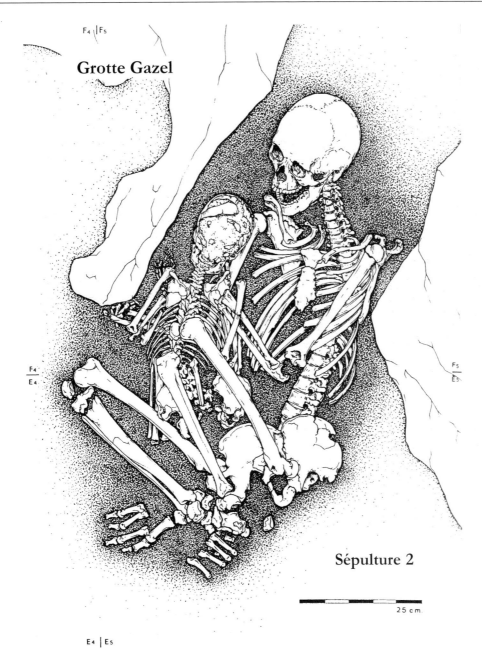

Figure 3.14. An Early Neolithic double burial from Gazel cave at Sallèles-Cabardès (Aude, France). A woman holds the body of a child of about five years of age at death. The intermingling of the two skeletons (the child covered by the upper right limb of the woman, whose left knee covers the trunk of the child, and whose the left hand is held beneath the child's axilla) demonstrates that these are simultaneous burials. (Excavations of J. Guilaine and H. Duday; drawing H. Duday).

occupied with individual burials. Interpretation becomes more delicate when many bodies are grouped in a limited space, but if the excavation and the reading of the remains are more difficult, the means of analysis remains, for the most part, identical to those examples already addressed. There are cases, however, that necessitate recourse to specific methods.

The chronology of deposits in primary multiple burials
To the problematical study of individual primary burials

one can add a new type of inquiry – that of the relative chronology of deposits. The classic archaeological methods (stratigraphy, dating of grave inclusions *etc.*) are of obvious importance, but the osteological data are a great help here as well. If the formation of the funerary assemblage covers a relatively long period, one must consider the re-organisation linked to the placing of each new cadaver in direct contact with bodies whose articulations have already been disturbed. Conversely, if the deceased individuals had been deposited simultaneously, these displacements

Figure 3.15. Overhead photographic view of the grave-cut in which 21 French officers and soldiers, killed at the front at Saint-Rémi-la-Calonne (Meuse, France), were interred on the 22nd of September 1914. This exhumation, which was carried out for non-archaeological reasons, considerably enriched the referents for the taphonomy of the cadaver. (Excavations of F. Adam and F. Boura, Photograph by H. Paitier).

should be absent (Fig. 3.14). One can easily comprehend that here, again, the unstable articulations are more pertinent than the persistent ones. But the essential limits of this approach appear at once – it is not possible to differentiate among deposits when the period that separates them is less than the time necessary for the disarticulation of the unstable articulations.

Furthermore, one can observe in mass burials – those that correspond to crises that produce high mortality (also referred to as catastrophic burial assemblages) – movements due to synchronous decay of the piled cadavers (Fig. 3.15) and, in their decomposition, soft tissues of those individuals lying more inferiorly creating, in effect, empty spaces which, in part, dictate the effects of settling and which, on the other hand, attract disarticulated bones from those individuals lying above.

Collective burials and their contribution to osteological relations of the second order

Up to this point, the discussion has consistently made reference to the fundamental notion of anatomical articulations and has systematically sought to understand the conditions that permit the preservation of articular relations (and from that moment to draw out information that follows from it, notably that which concerns the initial position of the body), or, on the contrary, to explain the mechanisms which led to their displacement. This approach presupposes that one can identify the entirety or at least a portion of the same skeleton in the field,

whatever the complexity of the context. This condition is implicitly filled at the moment that one can confirm the reality of anatomical articulations, because they can only occur between bones of the same individual. This particular type of relationship is referred to as a 'relationship of the first order' – that is to say, a relationship that is perceptible at the time of excavation (Duday 1987b).

However, certain funerary assemblages are uncovered as enormous accumulations of several dozens of individuals (Figs. 16 and 17), even many hundreds of individuals. In these collective burials, of which the second half of the Neolithic provides some of the most significant examples in Western Europe, the osseous remains are, for the most part, disarticulated and are many times fragmented in the extreme. The articulations, when they survive at all, do not involve more than a tiny part of the bones, with the result that the key to their interpretation becomes practically inoperable following the precepts discussed so far. In order to understand the dynamics of the composition of such assemblages, it again becomes indispensable to recognise bones of the same individual in order to analyse their distribution in the site in the same way that one does usually for scattered fragments of the same pot or of flint flakes deriving from the same core (see Beckett and Robb, this volume). Each individual is composed of, in effect, an ideal example of what one usually calls a 'closed assemblage', all elements that make it up (and notably all of the elements of the skeleton) are, on all evidence, very closely contemporaneous. This data,

Figures 3.16 and 3.17. A general (16) and detailed (17) view of the Chalcolithic funerary layer of the Dolmen des Peirières at Villedubert (Aude, France). These photographs provide an excellent example of the density and complexity of the fill of Neolithic collective burials, as well as the fragmentation of the remains (Photographs: H. Duday).

though, is no more directly accessible in the field, and only anthropological study in the laboratory will be capable of furnishing the necessary information. It is thus suitable to direct systematic research to *relationships of the second order*, which can be defined as:

– Those related by conjoined fragments: if one joins two fragments of a femur, then they belong to the same bone and, therefore, to the same individual.

– Those related by contiguous articulations: certain articulations have such a complex morphology that they generally permit one to recognise contiguous bones of the same individual. This is the case for interdigitated cranial sutures, but also, for example, with the sacro-iliac joint.

– Those related by stage of development: when the site contains no more than a single deceased individual from the peri-natal period, it is clear that all the bones corresponding to that stage of ossification could be related to the same individual. In this case, the efficacy of this approach depends on the size of the series as it becomes obviously null and void as soon as one finds the remains of two subjects of ages that are relatively close together.

– Those related by belonging to the same pathological assemblage in the case of a localised lesion (a monoarticular arthrosis, for example), or a more extensive one (such as diffuse lesions of the vertebral column), or indeed one of a systemic disease. In a collective Neolithic burial from Corconne (Gard, France), one could observe more than sixty remains (without duplicating any single bone element) that showed signs of a hyperostotic disease that Arnautou (cited in Duday 1987a) linked to Paget's disease.

– Finally and especially, those related by matching symmetrical bones: although no individual is completely symmetrical (an effect of laterality), one can easily understand that, for example, a first left metacarpal of an individual will more often resemble the right one of the same individual than it will that of another.

These are all examples of positive relationships. Conversely, one could, with greater reservation, make further associations by taking account of pathological dysmorphies or establish negative relations which rest on affirmations of exclusion, for example, the dissimilarity or discordance between two paired or contiguous elements such that they could in no way belong to the same skeleton. These types of determinations are often essential in assessing the number of deceased individuals.

The results of relationships of the second order should be exploited in archaeological analyses because they constitute, in most cases, a unique interpretive key to the funerary proceedings that determined the composition of the deposit. In order to assure that the archaeological analysis which follows is pertinent, it is essential that one knows with sufficient precision the position of bones related to the same individual in the grave. Otherwise, nothing will permit one to predict *a priori* which remains are connected to one another. In the case of matching, the elements which provide the best 'scores' seem to be the patellae and the little bones of the extremities (carpals, tarsals, metacarpals and metatarsals). The understanding of large collective burials depends, then, to a large extent on information from bones that are not immediately and obviously important in physical anthropology and that excavators frequently neglect to observe in deference to more 'noble' elements (crania, mandibulae, and large long bones of the limbs).

Conclusions and perspectives

Archaeothanatology (field anthropology) participates in archaeological analyses of funerary assemblages in a decisive fashion whether in the study of funerary practices or in the internal (*i.e.* relative) chronology of deposits. It appears at the present time to be one of the most favourable routes to understanding in funerary archaeology. Accountable in its methods and in its perspectives, it needs to identify the kinds of observations necessary for the resolution of diverse problems that arise in the interpretation of structures brought to light of day by archaeological excavation, among them strategies for intervention in the field, notably for rescue excavations, that could not be defined without taking into account the observations under discussion in this contribution.

The objectives and the methods of this new discipline are, in their essence, independent of chronological and cultural divisions. Further experience from each site will refine future analyses and broaden the influence of its contributions. Only these repeated occurrences will develop the necessary body of specialised researchers with training in the general methods of archaeology but also possessing deeper understandings of human osteology. It is only then that our understanding of ancient burials will progress. Field anthropology has yet to fully define its methods and to determine its operational procedures. However, it is through its systematic application to large funerary assemblages emerging today, and with the appearance of the first synthetic publications founded on its parameters, that this nascent science will truly acquire its full historical importance.

References

Baud C. A. and Kramar C. (1990) Les calcifications biologiques en archéologie. *Bulletins et Mémoires de la Société d'Anthropologie de Paris* 2, 163–170.

Boura F., Adam F., Duday H., Hervet P. and Piechaud S. (1992) Fouille archéologique d'une sépulture militaire de 1914: la sépulture collective de Saint-Rémy-la-Calonne (Meuse). *Les Nouvelles de l'Archéologie* 48–49, 56–70.

Duday H. (1975) Le sujet de la sépulture prénéolithique de Bonifacio (Corse). *Cahiers d'Anthropologie*, 1. Paris: LA 220 du CNRS/ Laboratoire d'Anatomie des Saints-Pères.

Duday H. (1978) Archéologie funéraire et anthropologie. Application des relevés et de l'étude ostéologique à l'interprétation de quelques sépultures pré- et protohistoriques du midi de la France. *Cahiers d'Anthropologie* 1: 55–101.

Duday, H. (1981) La place de l'anthropologie dans l'étude des sépultures anciennes. *Cahiers d'Anthropologie* 1: 27–42.

Duday H. (1987a) Organisation et fonctionnement d'une sépulture collective néolithique: l'Aven de la Boucle à Corconne (Gard). In H. Duday and C. Masset (eds.), *Anthropologie Physique et Archéologie. Méthodes d'Etude des Sépultures*, 89–104. Paris, CNRS.

Duday H. (1987b) Contribution des observations ostéologiques à la chronologie interne des sépultures collectives. In H. Duday and C. Masset (eds.), *Anthropologie Physique et Archéologie. Méthodes d'Etude des Sépultures*, 51–59. Paris, CNRS.

Duday H., Lambach F. and Plouin S. (1990a) Contribution de l'anthropologie de terrain à l'interprétation architecturale d'un ensemble funéraire : la tombe 12 du tumulus 2A à Nordhouse (Bas-Rhin). *Les Nouvelles de l'Archéologie* 40: 15–18.

Duday H., Courtaud P., Crubézy E., Sellier P. and Tillier A. M. (1990b) L'anthropologie «de terrain» : reconnaissance et interprétation des gestes funéraires. *Bulletins et Mémoires de la Société d'Anthropologie de Paris* 2: 29–50.

Kapandji I. A. (1975) *Physiologie Articulaire. Schémas Commentés de Mécanique Humaine. Tome 3 : Tronc et Rachis.* Maloine, Paris.

Leclerc, J. (1990) La notion de sépulture. *Bulletin de la Société d'Anthropologie de Paris.* n.s. 2(3–4): 13–18.

Masset C. (1987) Le «recrutement» d'un ensemble funéraire. In H. Duday and C. Masset (eds.), *Anthropologie Physique et Archéologie. Méthodes d'Etude des Sépultures*, 111–134. Paris, CNRS.

Mordant C. (1987) Des inhumations «en pleine terre» ? L'exemple de la Petite-Seine. In H. Duday and C. Masset (eds.), *Anthropologie Physique et Archéologie. Méthodes d'Etude des Sépultures*, 155–165. Paris, CNRS.

Orfila M. and Lesueur M.O. (1831) *Traité des Exhumations Juridiques, et Considérations sur les Changements Physiques que les Cadavres Éprouvent en se Pourrissant dans la Terre, dans l'Eau, dans les Fosses d'Aisance et dans le Fumier.* 2 vol., Béchet Jeune, Paris.

Thomas, L. V. 1980. *Le Cadavre. De la Biologie à l'Anthropologie.* Brussels, Édition Complexes.

Ubelaker D.H. (1974) *Reconstruction of Demographic Profiles from Ossuary Skeletal Samples. A Case Study from the Tidewater Potomac.* Smithsonian Contribution to Anthropology 18. Washington D.C., Smithsonian Institution Press.

Vigneron E. (1985) *Recherches sur l'Histoire des Attitudes devant la Mort en Polynésie Française.* Unpublished Ph.D. Thesis, Toulouse, École des Hautes Études en Sciences Sociales.

N°	Figure	Side	Exposed Aspect	Depth from Arbitrary Datum (cm)
	3.1a			
	No elements removed			
	3.1b			
1	Metatarsal I	L	disturbed	29.0
2	Calcaneus	L	disturbed	29.0
3	Metatarsal II	L	proximo-lateral	29.0
4	Tibia	L	disto-postero-lateral	28.0 distal/31.5 proximal
5	Fibula	L	disto-postero-lateral	28.0 distal/31.5 proximal
6	Ilium	L	infero-medial	30.0 inferior/31.5 superior
7	Femur	L	anterior	32.0
8	Ischium	R	lateral	33.5
9	Femur	R	antero-latero-distal	31.5 distal/32.5 proximal
10	Fibula	R	proximo-lateral	31.0 proximal/32.5 distal
11	Tibia	R	proximo-postero-lateral	31.0 proximal/32.5 distal
12	Ilium	R	infero-lateral	33.0
13	Rib fragment		inferior ?	32.0
14	Vertebral neural hemi-arch T1? (T2)	L	inferior	31.5
15	Vertebral neural hemi-arch T1? (T2)	R	postero-lateral	31.5
16	Cranial Fragment		endocranial	32.0
17	Vertebral neural hemi-arch (T3)	R	medial	31.5
18	Proximal hand phalanx		palmar (head to West)	32.5
19	Parietal	L	ectocranial	31.0 boss/32.0 sutures
20	Greater wing of sphenoid	L	posterior	31.0/32.0
21	Maxillary fragment?		disturbed	32.5
22	Maxillary fragment?			31.5
23	Hemi-mandible	L	posterior	31.5
24	2nd rib	L	superior	33.0
25	Middle rib	R	inferior	33.5
26	Humerus	R	lateral	33.0 proximal/34.0 distal
27	Temporal	L	lateral (and postero-inferior)	33.0
28	Thoracic vertebra centrum (T2, T3?)		superior? (anterior to East)	33.5
29	Scapula	L	infero-postero-medial	31.5 medial/33.0 lateral
30	Inferior rib	R	inferior (head to South)	34.0
31	Vertebral neural hemi-arch S1? (S3)	L	disturbed	33.0
32	Vertebral neural hemi-arch S1? (S3)	R	disturbed	33.5
33	Sacral Vertebral neural hemi-arch (S3)		postero-lateral	33.0

Table 3.1. Field and laboratory recording forms for figure 3.1b, 3.1c, and 3.1d. Figure 3.1a is a composite of all three. Numbers refer to the indicated elements in three successive cleanings and removal of layers associated with a single infant burial. Parentheses indicate original field identifications before cleaning and laboratory identifications after cleaning of the skeletal remains had been undertaken.

N°	3.1b	Side	Exposed Aspect	Depth from Arbitrary Datum (cm)
34	Vertebral neural hemi-arch L5? (S1)	L	posterior	33.0
35	Vertebral neural hemi-arch L4? (L5)	L	posterior	33.0
36	Vertebral neural hemi-arch L3? (L4)	L	postero-superior	33.0
37	Vertebral neural hemi-arch L2? (L3)	L	postero-superior	33.0
38	Vertebral neural hemi-arch L1? (L2)	L	postero-superior	33.0
39	Vertebral neural hemi-arch T12? (L1)	L	postero-lateral	33.0
40	Vertebral neural hemi-arch T10? (T11)	L	postero-lateral	33.0
41	Vertebral neural hemi-arch T10? (T12)	R	postero-lateral	33.5
42	Vertebral neural hemi-arch T11? (T12)	L	postero-lateral	33.5
43	Vertebral neural hemi-arch T11? (L1)	R	inferior	33.5
44	Vertebral neural hemi-arch (L2)	R	postero-inferior	33.5
45	Vertebral neural hemi-arch (L3)	R	infero-postero-lateral	33.5
46	Lumbar vertebra centrum (L5)		antero-superior	33.0
47	Sacral vertebra centrum (S2)		superior	32.5
48	Humerus	R	medial	33.0
49	12th rib	L	ventral	33.5
50	11th rib	L	postero-lateral	33.0/34.0
51	10th rib	L	infero-postero-lateral	33.0/34.0
52	9th rib	L	infero-posterior	33.5/34.5
53	8th rib	L	postero-lateral	33.5/34.5

N°	3.1c	Side	Exposed Aspect	Depth from Arbitrary Datum (cm)
54	Proximal phalanx of the hallux	R	dorsal (distal to the West)	33.5
55	Metatarsal I	R	dorso-medial (distal to the West)	33.5
56	Metatarsal II	R	dorsal (distal to the West)	33.5
57	Proximal foot phalanx	R	proximo-dorsal (distal to the West)	33.5
58	Proximal foot phalanx	R	disturbed	33.5
59	Proximal foot phalanx	R	disturbed	33.5
60	Metatarsal III	R	proximo-dorso-medial	33.5
61	Metatarsal IV	R	proximo-dorsal	33.5
62	Metatarsal V	R	proximo-dorso-lateral	33.5
63	Pubis	R	anterior	33.0
64	Proximal hand phalanx	(L)	dorsal (distal to the North)	34.0
65	Vertebral neural hemi-arch S1? (S2)	R	posterior	33.5
66	Vertebral neural hemi-arch L4? (L4)	R	antero-supero-medial	34.0
67	Vertebral neural hemi-arch L5? (L5 and S1)	R	antero-supero-medial	34.0
68	Ulna	R	proximo-medial	33.0 proximal/33.5 distal
69	Centrum L4		inferior (anterior to South-East)	33.5
70	Centrum L3		posterior	33.5
71	Centrum L2		posterior	33.5
72	Centrum L1		postero-supero-lateral left	33.5
73	Centrum T12		posterior	34.0

N°	3.1c	Side	Exposed Aspect	Depth from Arbitrary Datum(cm)
74	Centrum T11		posterior (and inferior)	34.0
75	Centrum T10		posterior	34.5
76	Vertebral neural hemi-arch (T11)	R	superior	33.0
77	Vertebral neural hemi-arch (T10)	R	superior	33.5
78	Centrum T9		posterior	34.0
79	Centrum T8		posterior (and left lateral)	34.0
80	Inferior rib	R	inferior (head to the South)	33.0
81	Centrum T7		posterior	34.0
82	Centrum T6		left lateral	34.0
83	Centrum T5		postero-superior	34.0
84	Proximal hand phalanx (middle)		disto-palmar (head to the South)	34.0
85	Proximal hand phalanx		disturbed	34.0
86	7th rib	L	inferior	33.0
87	6th rib	L	inferior	33.0
88	Vertebral neural hemi-arch (T5)	L	lateral	33.0
89	5th rib	L	inferior	33.0
90	4th rib	L	inferior	33.0
91	3rd rib	L	inferior	33.0
92	1st rib	L	inferior	33.0
93	Vertebral neural hemi-arch (T9)	R	medial	34.0
94	Vertebral neural hemi-arch (T5)	R	superior	33.5
95	Thoracic vertebral centrum (C7)		flat (superior or inferior) (anterior to the East)	34.0
96	Clavicle	R	posterior	33.0
97	7th rib	R	inferior	33.0
98	2nd rib	R	inferior	33.0
99	1st rib	R	inferior	33.0
100	6th rib	R	infero-anterior	32.5 anterior/33.5 posterior
101	5th rib	R	inferior	32.5 anterior/33.5 posterior
102	Ulna	R	medial	33.5
103	Radius	R	antero-distal	33.5 distal/34.0 proximal
104	Vertebral neural hemi-arch (T7?)	L	inferior	33.5
105	Vertebral neural hemi-arch C7? (T1)	R	inferior	33.5
106	Vertebral neural hemi-arch C6? (C7)	R	antero-medial	33.5
107	Scapula	R	postero-medial	32.5 medial/33.5 lateral
108	Manubrium		disturbed	33.5
109	Vertebral neural hemi-arch (T4)	R	postero-infero-lateral	33.5
110	Vertebral neural hemi-arch (T10)	L	infero-postero-lateral	33.0
111	Vertebral neural hemi-arch (T9)	L	inferior	33.0
112	Vertebral neural hemi-arch C4? (C5)	L	postero-lateral	33.0
113	Vertebral neural hemi-arch C5? (C6)	L	postero-lateral	33.0
114	Vertebral neural hemi-arch C6? (C7)	L	postero-lateral	33.5
115	Vertebral neural hemi-arch C7? (T1)	L	postero-lateral	33.5

N°	3.1c	Side	Exposed Aspect	Depth from Arbitrary Datum(cm)
116	Zygomatic	L	postero-lateral	32.0
117	Hemi-frontal	L	lateral	30.5 boss/32.5 sutures
118	Cervical vertebra neural hemi-arch (C4)	L	disturbed	33.5
119	Ex-occipital (Pars lateralis)	L	superior	33.5
120	Hemi-mandible	R	antero-medial	32.5 anterior/33.5 posterior
121	Metacarpal II? (V)	L	dorsal (distal to North-East)	34.5
122	Metacarpal III? (IV)	L	medial (distal to North)	34.5
123	Metacarpal IV? (III)	L	dorsal (distal to North-West)	34.5
124	Vertebral neural hemi-arch (T8)	R	postero-inferior	33.5
125	Occipital squama		posterior (lambda to North)	32.0 centre/33.0 sutures
126	Greater wing of sphenoid	R	postero-supero-lateral	31.5 superior/32.5 inferior
127	Body of sphenoid		inferior (posterior to South)	32.5

N°	3.1d	Side	Exposed Aspect	Depth from Arbitrary Datum(cm)
128	Radius	L	antero-medial	33.5
129	Vertebral neural hemi-arch (T4)	L	superior	33.0
130	Clavicle	L	posterior	33.0
131	Cervical vertebra centrum (C6?)		flat (superior or inferior)	33.5
132	Cervical vertebra centrum (C3)		disturbed	33.5
133	Cervical vertebra centrum (C2)		flat (superior or inferior)	33.5
134	Cervical vertebra centrum (C4)		flat (superior or inferior)	33.5
135	Vertebral neural hemi-arch (T7)	R		33.5
136	Vertebral neural hemi-arch (T6)	R		33.5
137	Vertebral neural hemi-arch (T6)	L		33.5
138	Metacarpal I	R	palmo-lateral (distal to the East)	34.5
139	3rd rib	R	inferior	33.0
140	4th rib	R	inferior	33.0
141	Vertebral neural hemi-arch (C5)	R	medial	33.5
142	Vertebral neural hemi-arch (C4)	R	superior	33.5
143	Vertebral neural hemi-arch (C3)	R	superior	33.5
144	Ex-occipital (Pars lateralis)	R	on edge (superior to the West)	33.5
145	Incus			33.5
146	Malleus			33.5
147	Basi-occipital		postero-superior	33.0 posterior/33.5 anterior
148	Petrous	R	medial	32.5 medial/33.3 lateral
149	Hemi-atlas	L	superior	33.5
150	Sternebra ?			34.0
151	Parietal	R	endocranial	30.0 sutures/33.5 boss
152	Palatine		disturbed	33.5
153	Hemi-frontal	R	postero-medial	31.5 coronal/33.5 zygomatic process
154	*Testacella* sp. shell		concave	33.5

4. Neolithic burial taphonomy, ritual, and interpretation in Britain and Ireland: a review

Jessica Beckett and John Robb

Osteology and the theoretical interpretation of Neolithic burials

Burial rites are a mainstay of interpretations of Neolithic society, particularly in Britain where the Neolithic record is dominated by funerary and ritual monuments. British Neolithic burials are of interest to archaeologists working in other periods and areas as well; much like French cave art for Upper Palaeolithic symbolism or Mesoamerica for early states, they have provided the paradigm case for important bodies of theory. The British Neolithic is characterised by varied and colourful funerary rites taking place at barrows, causewayed enclosures or other impressive monuments. Neolithic people, it is often argued, had a complex burial programme combining rites such as primary burial, secondary burial, excarnation, and the ceremonial manipulation of bones. In general, archaeologists have interpreted these funerary rites either as expressions of territoriality or of social inequality (Renfrew 1976, 1979; Chapman 1981, 1995), ideological masks for inequality (Shanks and Tilley 1982; Hodder 1984), ethnicity (Sherratt 1990), or, more recently, ritual ways of understanding and experiencing landscapes (Richards 1993; Tilley 1994; Bender 1998) and of creating relationships between the living, the dead, and places (Whittle 1996; Bradley 1998; Thomas 1999, 2000; Whittle *et al.* 1999).

There has been surprisingly little actual osteological research to support this grand theoretical edifice. Until the 1990s, the argument rested entirely on impressionistic anecdotes, supported by a handful of poorly excavated and published sites such as West Kennet long barrow. Over the last two decades, several excellent studies with new data and analysis have been published (Mercer 1980; Saville *et al.* 1990; Whittle and Wysocki 1998), but these have had little impact as yet on theoretical writings, which often remain facile generalisations. The osteology-theory nexus remains a street poorly travelled in both directions; osteologists need dialogue with theoretically-minded archaeologists to spur them to try to answer new questions creatively.

This chapter has several goals. We first review the current state of knowledge concerning the osteology and taphonomy of Neolithic burials in Britain. We then present two case studies illustrating different ways forward towards interpreting Neolithic burials. Finally, in light of the assembled evidence and these new studies, we revisit questions about burial ritual of Neolithic people.

A review of Neolithic burial research

The earliest real consideration of Neolithic burial taphonomy we possess is Keith's study of the human remains from Ward's excavation of the St. Nicholas chambered tomb, Glamorgan in 1916 (Keith 1916; Ward 1916). With a surprisingly modern line of reasoning, Keith discussed the type of fragmentation found, the colour and accretions on bones. He concluded that due to the unweathered surfaces of the bones, their decayed and chalky appearance, and the lack of scratches and cut marks, mostly complete burials had been made, with each burial disturbing previous ones. However, other antiquarians and archaeologists did not follow up this direction, and several decades passed before further serious investigation of burial ritual using taphonomy was considered. By the 1970s, it was commonly acknowledged that the jumbled and scrappy bones found in Neolithic tombs were evidence of collective burial, or at least of serial primary inhumation with each new inhumation disturbing earlier burials. Interpretations of excarnation, secondary burial, and manipulation of skulls and long bones had also been raised.

Appendix 4.1 contains a summary of taphonomic and burial findings for Neolithic sites with human remains in Britain and Ireland, though we do not claim it is an exhaustive list. Although over 137 Neolithic sites with human bone have been excavated and published for Britain and Ireland, the nature of the data remains disheartening. Most taphonomic judgements are cursory pronouncements without much supporting data. There are reliable contextual data and published illustrations for very few sites; for most collections, there is no published study by a trained osteologist, and astonishingly few collections have been studied for palaeopathological data. For the reconstruction of burial programmes, a serious limitation is the lack of attention to "stray" bone, isolated and sporadic fragments found in contexts not obviously tomb-like. It is no surprise, therefore, that much of what we know comes from a very few well-analysed sites.

Stonehenge and environs (Cleal et al. 1995; McKinley 1995)

Like Avebury, the Stonehenge area contains several distinct forms of funerary behaviour which may have been related to form a ceremonial landscape. While Stonehenge has often been considered a monument of life, in contrast to tombs as monuments of death, recent re-study and synthesis has made clear the substantial presence of funerary remains at the site, a fact obscured by some of the less fortunate aspects of its archaeological history. In particular, while the Post-Roman inhumation (Pitts *et al.* 2002) and the famous Beaker period man (Evans *et al.* 1984) – probably killed on the spot with arrow shots – are later, numerous cremations were deposited during the Neolithic, principally in the Aubrey holes and the bank and ditch. Some scattered disarticulated bone is found around the monument; it is unclear if this is disturbed or was deposited in this condition.

West Kennet Long Barrow, Windmill Hill, and the Avebury area (Piggott 1962; Thomas and Whittle 1986; Wells 1962; Whittle et al. 1999)

West Kennet long barrow, outside Avebury, was excavated by Piggott after a long history of disturbance; his report and Wells' skeletal report were subsequently reanalysed by Thomas and Whittle. Taphonomic interpretation relies primarily upon disarticulation and skeletal element representation. The basic rite appears to have been successive inhumation of fleshed corpses, with some excarnation and the removal and circulation of bone. Interestingly, access to the tomb was probably restricted and bones appear to have been re-arranged and sorted among the chambers of the tomb; it is interpreted as an arena for ritual practices reproducing the structural components of the group and its solidarity.

West Kennet long barrow illustrates one form of funerary behaviour in the Avebury area; human remains are also found at other locations such as the causewayed enclosure at Windmill Hill. As Smith (1965) reported, Windmill Hill received much attention from the 1920s until the 1950s, having been excavated by both Kendall and Keiller. It contained the remains of at least 10 individuals, both subadults and adults. Some mixed burial occurred with at least one child inhumed in a flexed position (Smith 1965, 136), and the rest found scattered and fragmented. The interpretation of burial practice relied on observations made during excavation and

Brothwell's description of the bones. Smith (1965, 137) notes that it is possible that this site saw the dismemberment and circulation of bones that originated from nearby long barrows.

Hambledon Hill (Mercer 1980)

Mercer excavated the Hambledon Hill landscape from 1974 to 1980, investigating over 15, 000 sq. metres, including a causewayed enclosure, long barrow and outworks. In the causewayed enclosure several pits and deposits of ceramics, flint, axes, antler and human remains were found. During one phase of ditch use deliberate placements of fragmented human remains occurred, including crania which were probably primary deposits, two child burials inhumed in crouched positions, and the bones of the trunk of a young man. Other fragmented human remains were also deposited in other phases, possibly disturbed from earlier placements. The long barrow contained the remains of at least one individual. Based upon the fragmented condition of the remains, missing skeletal elements, animal gnawing marks on the young man's skeleton, and the mandibles and cervical vertebrae missing from the crania, Mercer concluded that that the enclosure probably was used as an exposure area with remains subsequently going into long barrows following exposure.

Wayland's Smithy (Atkinson 1965; Brothwell and Cullen 1969; Mays 1998; Whittle 1991); Fussell's Lodge (Ashbee 1966; Mays 1998)

Wayland's Smithy is a long barrow in Oxfordshire excavated by Atkinson and Piggott; the original skeletal report by Brothwell has been reanalysed both by Mays and by Whittle. Whittle argues for both the primary burial of complete bodies and the secondary deposition of bodies exposed elsewhere, based on high levels of disarticulation and fragmentation and the absence of small hand and foot bones. Mays, however, argued that hand and foot bones were adequately represented and the principal rite was sequential primary inhumation within the tomb. In contrast, in the long barrow of Fussell's Lodge in Wiltshire, Mays argues that the extreme lack of small and fragile bones implies the secondary redeposition of bodies originally decaying elsewhere.

Hazleton North (Saville et al. 1990)

Hazleton North provides one of the flagship analyses for Neolithic ritual taphonomy. In this Cotswold-Severn tomb, skeletal remains were analysed through piece plotting, re-fitting, element distribution, weathering and fragmentation. Collective burial rites were carried out with the successive interment of intact corpses at the north entrance of the tomb; cremation was also used. Skeletons were disturbed by new interments, with the re-arrangement of crania. There is no evidence for secondary interment or exposure of corpses.

Ascott-under-Wychwood (Chesterman 1977; Benson and Clegg 1978; Baxter 2001)

In the Ascott-under-Wychwood long barrow, both Chesterman's original study and Baxter's re-discussion highlight the general disarticulation and fragmentation of the bones, as well as the intentional re-arrangement of some. However, Chesterman argued that excarnation was a common rite, based on the severe weathering and bleaching of bones; Baxter argues that this was not the case.

Parc Le Breos (Whittle and Wysocki 1998)

Parc Le Breos is an early fourth millennium collective tomb where the remains of at least 40 individuals were excavated. Whittle and Wysocki carried out explicit taphonomic study of burial rites. They concluded that the assemblage was formed through a mixture of burial rites, including primary inhumation and secondary burial of bodies originally exposed elsewhere; the latter was responsible for weathering and scavenging marks on bones. They related mortuary patterning both to symbolic oppositions and to a dispersed, mobile way of life with reliance on hunting and herding.

Haddenham and Giant's Hill 2 (Hodder and Shand 1988; Evans and Simpson 1991)

Although the Giant's Hill 2 long barrow was a rescue excavation, it nevertheless provided a substantial amount of detailed taphonomic information on bone weathering and fragmentation, disarticulation, re-fitting, and carnivore damage. Evans and Simpson found that bones had not moved after their deposition, and hence cut marks, animal gnawing, weathering and disarticulation had occurred during the ritual process. Almost all of the bone showed animal gnawing, suggesting the exposure of bodies, and anomalies in skeletal element representation suggest the selection of some bones and the omission of others. At Haddenham long barrow as well there was evidence for selective burial, with bodies being buried complete and then subsequently re-arranged within the tomb (Baxter 1999).

Orkney: Ibister, Quanterness and Point of Cott (Chesterman 1979, 1983; Richards 1988; Barber 1997; Baxter 2001)

In the chambered tomb of Ibister, Chesterman argued for excarnation, based on the bleaching, weathering and general lack of carpals and tarsals. Baxter, however, criticised this interpretation, emphasising sequential primary burial instead. Likewise, at Quanterness Chesterman argued again for secondary burial with excarnation and intentional fracturing of bones, before burning; however, Baxter again saw a mixture of primary and secondary burial for this site. Barber (1997) carried out a parallel analysis for the stalled cairn tomb at Point of Cott. Using element representation, fragmentation, and articulation, Barber argued against excarnation, citing a lack of weathering and carnivore gnawing, and suggested that bodies were deposited complete and then damaged either by later burials or by differential preservation within tomb microenvironments. Richards (1993) has argued that skeletal elements were circulated among tombs and social groups on Orkney.

As an increasing number of sites are studied in this way, we can make some general statements about Neolithic human biology and ritual practices.

Demography, stature, palaeopathology and mobility

As the sites discussed above and those listed in Table 4.1 demonstrate, males and females were deposited in most Neolithic sites, even through a particular tomb may have an imbalance. Similarly, many sites (at least 52 of the 137 in Table 4.1) include sub-adults. Without concrete statistics, this nevertheless suggests no striking age or sex bias in who was selected for burial in the excavated tombs. Unfortunately, there has been no real attempt at palaeo-demography, whether through skeletal remains or through other sources (as in Scarre's recent study of Brittany (Scarre 2001)). Pooled stature estimates from the small samples available show an average stature of 165 cm for males and 157 cm for females (Roberts and Cox 2003).

Although British Neolithic skeletal samples are normally small, commingled and highly fragmented, a critical mass of data on health and disease has accumulated. The reader is directed to the recent comprehensive synthesis by Roberts and Cox (2003). This reveals a fairly typical picture of palaeopathological conditions, with some prevalence of cribra orbitalia, enamel hypoplasia, and non-specific infections, a number of trauma cases and congenital conditions, and, interestingly, five cases of trepanation. It should be noted that many conditions identified as "pathologies" would have had few symptoms or visible signs in life (*e.g.* spina bifida occulta and anomalies of cranial fusion at West Kennet (Wells 1962)). Dental disease, the only quantifiable condition, shows a prevalence comparable to most Neolithic populations (Brothwell 1963; Roberts and Cox 2003). This is interesting to examine in relation with recent stable isotope and residue evidence which shows a decline in marine resources but also a marked variability in diet, with some dairying and with animal protein much more important in some areas than in others (Richards and Hedges 1999; Copley *et al.* 2003). Since dental disease reflects the carbohydrate component of the diet while stable isotope evidence reflects the importance of different protein sources, one possibility is that most protein came from a variable range of animal or marine sources with plants contributing especially cariogenic foods such as wild fruits.

Some of the most high-profile recent work on Neolithic skeletons has focused on personal mobility, using stable isotopes of strontium and lead to try to identify people whose chemical composition is unusual for the area in which they were buried. Four skeletons from Monkton-up-Wimbourne in Dorset had moved during their lifetimes, in one case coming from at least 80 km away (Montgomery *et al.* 2000). The "Boscombe Bowmen", six burials found together at Amesbury, near Stonehenge, have chemical profiles typical of Wales. Since the bluestones at Stonehenge itself are thought to have originated in the Preseli Mountains of South Wales, the burials were immediately presented in the national press as the "original family" which brought the megaliths from Wales to Wiltshire. Similar analysis has been used to claim that the Beaker period "Amesbury Archer" originated in Central Europe or the Alps (Wessex_Archaeology, 2004).

Burial rites

The above reveals a substantial, if patchy, body of evidence for Neolithic funerary ritual. While there is much we do not know, some general lines of interpretation are clear.

As this review shows, the most commonly identified rite is primary inhumation. Primary inhumation is well attested through complete skeletons in many of the tombs discussed, and is also suggested by commingled remains containing small and fragile bones. However, complete, articulated skeletons are rare; it was normal to disturb and damage skeletons during later burials, and in some cases, bones were clearly re-arranged and manipulated.

Other rites are more contentious. Secondary burial will presumably be denoted by biases of element representation, and is commonly cited to explain a lack of hand and foot bones and other small or fragile parts. However, this can also be explained through differential destruction (see below), and we are on more solid ground when bones are evidently re-arranged. Similarly, given how prominent excarnation has been in archaeological reconstruction, it is remarkably elusive in the skeletal record, with very few cases upon which all analysts agree. For both secondary burial and excarnation, the collective tomb evidence is often rather indeterminate. The best evidence is likely to come from finds of human bone on non-tomb sites and from the combination of multiple lines of taphonomic inquiry rather than simple reliance only upon element representation.

One of the most important conclusions of this review of the evidence is that Neolithic burial programmes sometimes involved multiple rites at several locations. In addition to tombs, burial programmes at times demonstrably involved ditches at causewayed enclosures

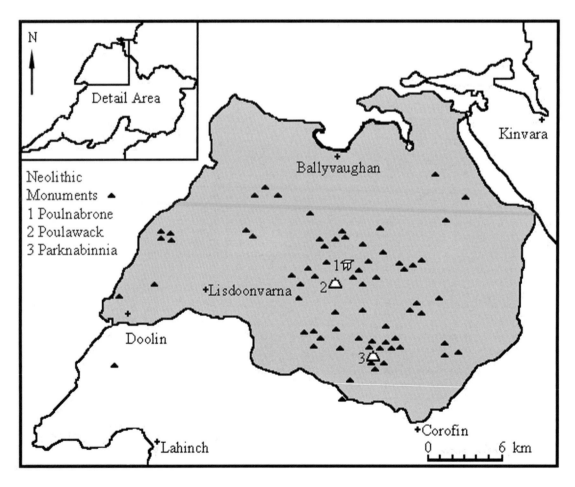

Figure 4.1. Neolithic monuments on the Burren, Ireland, (after Jones, 2003; Waddell, 1992).

(Windmill Hill, Hambledon Hill) and ritual sites such as the Wessex henges. Archaeologically, causewayed enclosures and long barrows are more common in the earlier Neolithic, with a gradual shift towards more elaborate ritual landscapes of henges and cursuses. It is hard to correlate taphonomic evidence with such broad portraits; for example, the best-documented cases of excarnation come from the earlier Neolithic, but this may simply be because it is easier to discern this practice most clearly in causewayed enclosures which are earlier in date than henge monuments. Given the undeniable evidence for multiple practices going on contemporaneously within all regions which have been subjected to intensive study, and often within single sites as well, it seems best not to generalise chronologically.

Case study: GIS analysis of collective burials in Neolithic Ireland

The studies above are normally limited by the available data, particularly for re-analysis of older collections. Here, we discuss a case study which illustrates some avenues of research available when taphonomic analysis is integrated into excavation from the start.

The Burren, a limestone upland in western Ireland, is a rich archaeological landscape, including hundreds of megalithic monuments (Jones 1998). Three sites are presented in this case study, Poulnabrone, Poulawack, and Parknabinnia (Fig. 4.1). Poulnabrone (Lynch 1994; Lynch and O'Donnabhain 1994) is a classic single-chambered portal tomb dating to between 3800–3200 cal. BC (Fig. 4.2). The burials are collective and disarticulated. The site contained both male and female adults and sub-adult remains. Adult bones displayed little evidence of palaeopathology, though osteoarthritis, fractures, heavy dental wear, and violent injuries were present (Waddell 1998).

Poulawack is a Linkardstown grave monument excavated in 1934 by Hencken (1935) with eight graves identified (Fig. 4.3). The Neolithic dates range between 3,614–3,373 cal BC with further burial in the Bronze Age (Brindley and Lanting 1991/92). Both adults and sub-adults were buried in all phases, with an equal number of males and females. There were signs of osteoarthritis, periodontal disease, trauma and severe dental wear.

Parknabinnia (Fig. 4.4) is a chamber tomb with a rounded cairn, a narrow forecourt, and two chambers. It dates from 3,600 cal BC to 2,800 cal BC.[1] Again, there were male and female adults and sub-adults buried here. The bones show few pathologies, though there is some osteoarthritis, periodontal disease, and a few small fractures, as well as other vertebral traumatic injuries.

Comparative taphonomic analysis of the three sites

A taphonomic analysis was carried out of all three sites, including skeletal element representation, fragmentation and completeness, colouration, weathering and modifi-

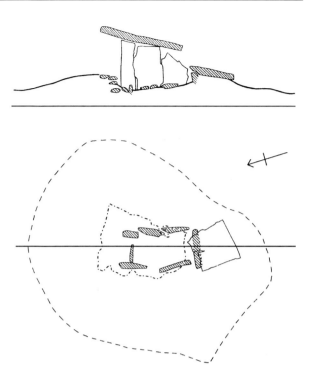

Figure 4.2. Plan of Poulnabrone (after de Valera and O'Nualain, 1961).

cation (see Buikstra and Ubelaker (1994) for methodology; also Saville *et al.* 1990; Whittle 1991; Mays 1998; Whittle and Wysocki 1998; Baxter 2001). Finally, the Parknabinnia tomb was analysed through a re-fitting study and GIS. While re-fitting studies are often used for lithics; they have only been carried out in a few burial contexts, notably White's (1992) study of Mancos Canyon. In British Neolithic sites, they have been carried out for Hazleton North (Saville *et al.* 1990) and Point of Cott (Barber 1997). A re-fitting study can help to show patterns of fragmentation and particularly how bones were moved around. GIS, to our knowledge, has not been applied to tomb assemblages. However, GIS potentially has two specific advantages for taphonomic studies. As a spatial technology (Wheatley and Gillings 2002), it allows us to visualise and present spatial arrangements such as distributions of bones and the location of conjoined elements or articulations. Secondly, GIS analyses can help us identify patterns too subtle to be immediately apparent in the data. GIS could be applied to the Parknabinnia assemblage because each bone fragment in this assemblage (n = 20,532) had been point-plotted during excavation.

Table 4.1 describes the basic taphonomic patterns of the three sites. All three assemblages are highly fragmented, Parknabinnia to the greatest degree. Only Poulawack displays animal modification (with seven rodent-gnawed specimens). These differences may reflect microenvironmental factors between the sites.

The most informative differences come from skeletal element representation, here presented as the proportion

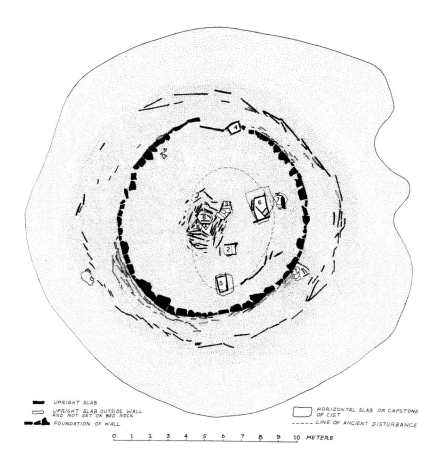

UPRIGHT SLAB

UPRIGHT SLAB OUTSIDE WALL
AND NOT SET ON BED ROCK

FOUNDATION OF WALL

HORIZONTAL SLAB OR CAPSTONE
OF CIST

LINE OF ANCIENT DISTURBANCE

0 1 2 3 4 5 6 7 8 9 10 METERS

Figure 4.3. Plan of Poulawack (after Brindley and Lanting, 1991/92; Hencken, 1935).

Parknabinnia CL 153

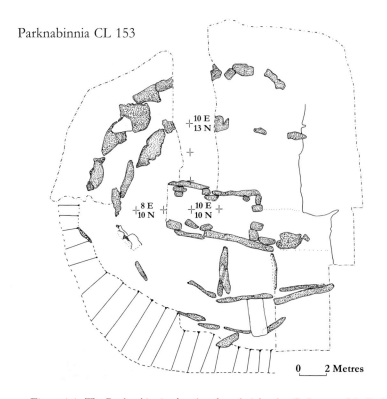

10 E
13 N

8 E
10 N

10 E
10 N

0 ___ 2 Metres

Figure 4.4. The Parknabinnia chambered tomb (plan by C. Jones and J. Beckett).

	Poulnabrone	Poulawack	Parknabinnia
Identified human bones (NISP)	4,755	2,648	6,084
Unidentified bones	68%	59%	70%
MNI	22	19	20
% under 5cm in size	90%	91%	91%
% <1/2 complete	87%	88%	92%
Articulations	4 articulated bone groups	14 of 19 reported as individuals	26 articulated bone groups
Burnt human bones	1.7%	20%	1.6%
Weathering (cracked and split bones)	71%	77%	82%
Slight exfoliation	56%	54%	77%
Plant/ root etching	50%	2%	4%
Rodent gnawing	0	.2%	0

Table 4.1. Taphonomic characteristics of the three burial assemblages analysed.

of an element present compared with what would be expected if each of the MNI were a complete skeleton (Fig. 4.5). At Parknabinnia all skeletal elements are present but robust bones are generally well-represented, fragile bones poorly so. This common pattern probably results predominantly from primary inhumation with successive interments; this interpretation is consistent with the contextual archaeology, which shows repeated, sealed deposition levels within the chambers. At Poulnabrone, in contrast, less than 50% of almost all skeletal elements are present, but carpals and tarsals are over-represented; remarkably, the MNI was calculated from the scaphoid bone. This is an unusual and informative anomaly (see simulation study below). There are also discrepancies between elements from the upper body and elements from the lower body, particularly for the long bones. This site most likely represents secondary burial, perhaps with the removal of crania and major bones for use elsewhere, leaving residuals of small bones. Contextually, more recent bones were found below older bones, stuffed down into crevices of the bedrock (Cooney 2000). It is possible that this represents collection of remains from other tombs, or later robbing of the tomb. Poulawack shows a third pattern. The skeletal representation for Grave 8, the Neolithic primary burials (Hencken 1935), reveals good preservation of fragile bones such as scapulae, pelves, and vertebrae, but very low representation of small bones. There is also slight over-representation of crania. Combined with the contextual archaeology, this suggests that the remains of at least five well-preserved skeletons

were collected together, placed into the central cist of the cairn, sealed and left undisturbed.

GIS and re-fitting studies of Parknabinnia

GIS and re-fitting studies were used for Parknabinnia to depict the distributions of bones within the tomb and to track bone movement. For example, GIS plotting (Fig. 4.6) can show that there are spatial distinctions where different types of bone are located, or alternatively confirm that no real patterning exists. A second use of plotting spatial distributions is to identify bone clusters. Visually, besides the few articulations noted, there were no apparent groups or arrangements of bones. However, when particular elements were plotted, clusters of bones could be spotted (for example, clusters of cervical, thoracic and lumbar vertebrae) (Fig. 4.7). While in some cases these represent articulations noted *in situ*, in other cases they are disarticulated remains, which still retain some general proximity.

Re-fitting was used to study whether or not bones were moved around within the site. Following White's (1992) example, bones were laid out by element and side, then tested against each other systematically. This yielded a total of 118 bone groups (Fig. 4.8).[2] GIS analysis of point-plotted proveniences was used to track how far bones had travelled. This showed interesting differences among elements; while most re-fit groups (77 out of 118) moved less than 30 cm, long bones moved further, with an average distance in the 50–60 cm range (Fig. 4.9 gives an example, tibiae). This helps us picture people moving disarticulated

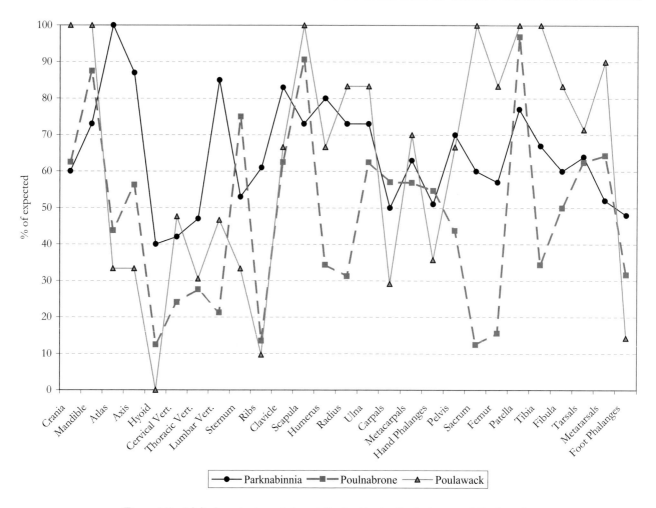

Figure 4.5. Adult element representation at Parknabinnia, Poulnabrone and Poulawack.

bones around in episodes of tomb cleaning, "paving" to seal levels, and further depositions. Larger and more substantial bones were moved more; smaller bones tended to stay closer to where they were originally deposited.

As this case study suggests, even using current methods, there is much we can still learn by pursuing taphonomy, by integrating it fully with excavation, and particularly by using statistical and GIS techniques to analyse taphonomic data. One of the fascinating implications of this study is observing three quite distinct burial programmes – cist burial of individuals, successive primary inhumations punctuated by tomb clearing and sealing levels, and secondary deposition of collected remains – were used in three more or less contemporary sites within three kilometres of each other.

Case study: the "virtual tomb" for testing taphonomic interpretation

Taphonomic interpretation is notoriously difficult to test critically. Forensic investigations of taphonomic processes such as carnivore scavenging and weathering typically are confined to short time-spans, rather than the centuries or

millennia which we must consider in prehistory. On the other hand, studies of the actual sites themselves are limited because we normally do not know key information such as how many people were actually buried at a site before taphonomic processes influenced their remains. This lack of critical testing contributes to situations as reviewed above, where a site can be interpreted by different analysts as demonstrating primary burial, secondary burial or excarnation.

To address this dilemma, we have used simulation; as used here, simulation is a heuristic tool useful in modelling processes systematically rather than an attempt to reproduce reality in all its complexity. We have simulated burial in a virtual Neolithic "tomb." This relatively simple program, designed in the Stella 7.0 modelling package, tabulates bone assemblages in a hypothetical collective tomb. With each new burial, new bones are added to the assemblage; however, in doing so, a certain proportion of the existing assemblage is destroyed (*e.g.* subtracted from the assemblage). As time passes, too, some of the existing assemblage is destroyed due to natural processes such as microbial and fungal attack and soil pressure. Both destructive processes can be set to affect fragile bones

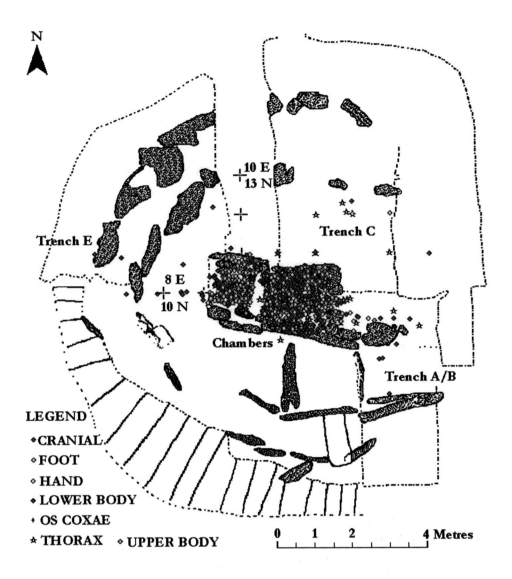

Figure 4.6. Distribution of human remains within Parknabinnia.

more severely than robust bones, and, to model secondary burial or excarnation, the part representation of bodies being deposited in the tomb can be varied. At the end of the tomb's pre-set use-life, burial ceases. From that time on, until excavation in the present, bones are destroyed only by *in situ* natural processes. At the end of the simulation run, skeletal element representation curves and the final MNI based on the best-represented skeletal element are calculated.

Like any simulation, the "virtual tomb" experiment relies on its model architecture and parameters for realistic results, and much relevant information is unknown in any quantifiable form. Degradation rates for undisturbed bone can be estimated from studies such as Waldron's West Tenter Street report (1987) or Mays' Blackfriars study (1998), but such rates will, of course, vary from environment to environment. Similarly, although Caffell's (2001) study of breakage in osteological collections used

for teaching shows that handling dry bone repeatedly can have quite destructive effects, we have no real basis for estimating the destructive effect of subsequent burials, which in any case is likely to vary from situation to situation. Nevertheless, general results from the simulation casts interesting light on several classic interpretations.

Why do collective tombs have the number of burials they do, which is normally small? It is rare to reach more than a few dozen burials (*cf.* Table 4.1) and the excavated population never reaches a fraction of what the population of a local area must have been. Here we have run the simulation many times with different levels of bone destruction and with different population levels. Figure 4.10 shows a typical result. Here both destruction from subsequent burials and *in situ* decomposition are set to 1% per burial episode or time interval. To model this bone destruction, each time a new burial is deposited in

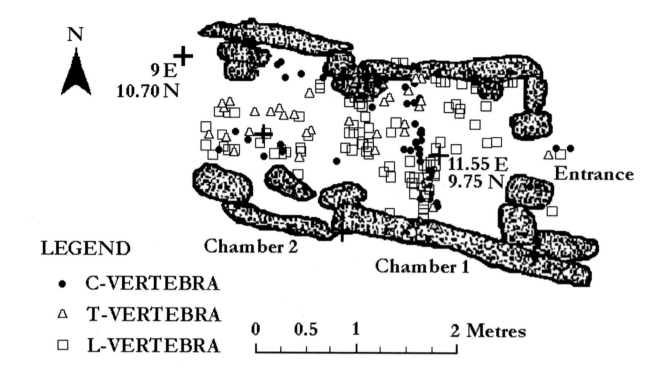

Figure 4.7. GIS plot of vertebrae; note clustered groups of particular segments.

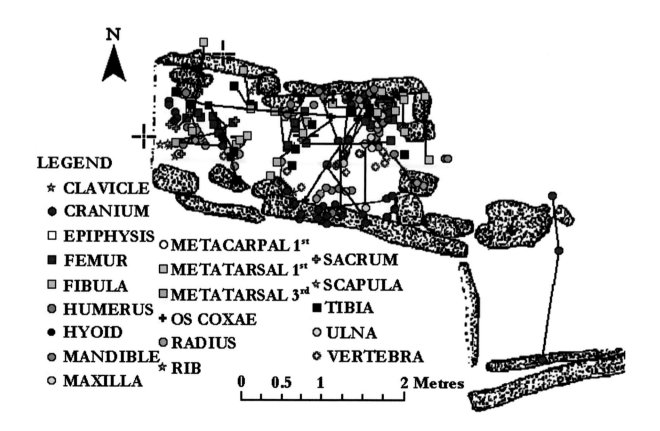

Figure 4.8. Distribution of re-fitted specimens.

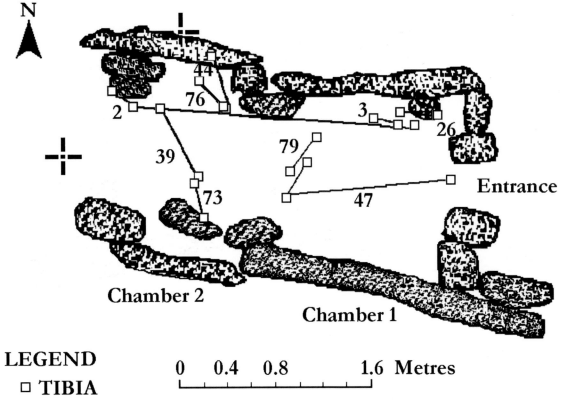

Figure 4.9. Re-fitted tibiae in Chambers 1 and 2.

the tomb, the program simply reduces the count of each element in the assemblage by 1%; this represents formerly identifiable elements which have now been reduced to the "unidentifiable" category. Likewise, with each century that passes, the MNE is similarly reduced by 1% to represent bone being rendered unidentifiable by processes of *in situ* decomposition. It should be noted that reliable statistics nowhere exist for either of these rates, nor for whether processes such as long-term *in situ* decomposition of bone proceed linearly or at variable rates. However, the level of 1% used here is less than a level calculated from either the West Tenter Street or the Blackfriars samples, and represents a cautious estimate. Without claiming that it is particularly accurate, we do think that it provides a useful cautionary example of the cumulative effect of gradual, often invisible processes over long time spans.

As this demonstrates, as long as there is an appreciable level of on-going bone destruction, the tomb MNI quickly converges upon a ceiling. Regardless of whether 100 or 1000 people are originally buried in the "tomb", and regardless of whether bone loss per episode is .05% or 5%, the MNI excavated never gets above 100, and often converges upon some far lower figure. More detailed modelling shows that the principal cause is destruction of prior burials when a new body is buried, which can cumulatively destroy 95–99% of an assemblage. Hence,

low numbers of people in excavated tombs do not necessarily imply that only elites were buried in tombs, nor that the missing bodies must have been buried during other kinds of rites elsewhere.

What about skeletal element representation? Element representation curves with over-representation of crania and/or long bones are often cited as evidence of secondary burial or excarnation. Here we have run the "virtual tomb" simulation with three different forms of burial: primary inhumation of complete bodies, secondary burial and/or excarnation with under-representation of small and fragile bones, and residual bone (*e.g.* with some crania and long bones removed for rites elsewhere). Each of these was modelled simply by altering the numbers of each kind of bone added to the tomb assemblage when a new "deposition" occurred. For each of these three modes of burial, the simulation was run several times to illustrate differential preservational conditions: with equal destruction of all bones, greater destruction of flat bones (such as the pelvis, scapula and sternum), vertebrae, and small bones, and with or without preferential curation of skulls. These were modelled by setting the rates of bone destruction differently for each category of bone. For example, in the version with greater destruction of flat bones, vertebrae and small bones, when the destruction rate for crania and long bones was set to 1%, these more fragile bones were destroyed at a rate of 2%. As noted

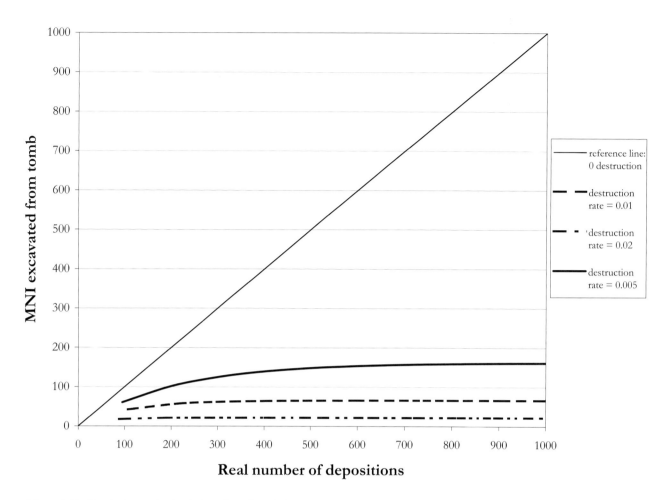

Figure 4.10. Simulation results for the hypothetical Neolithic chamber tomb. Starting 5000 years ago and running to the present, the "tomb" is used for 1000 years and then left undisturbed. Each line shows how the MNI changes over time with different rates of burial, from 10 per century to 100 per century (horizontal axis), and with different rates of bone destruction.

above, in the absence of real destruction rates available from the taphonomic literature, these destruction rates should be understood as plausible guesstimates for purposes of modelling a thought experiment.

The results are complex and informative. The most striking result is that, as long as flat bones, vertebrae, and small bones are more vulnerable to destruction than long bones and crania, the element representation curves for primary burial and secondary burial/excarnation will not be clearly distinguishable; both will show a marked deficit of these bones. Figure 4.11 shows the results for the runs with differential bone destruction of more resistant and more fragile elements (Fig. 4.11). This throws into question the most commonly cited plank in the argument for secondary burial. On the other hand, if we find *over-representation* of small or fragile bones, it is likely to reflect a genuine ritual pattern such as removal of crania and long bones (the Poulnabrone tomb discussed above may provide an archaeological illustration of this). Thirdly, crania curation or the deposition of isolated crania will

not be apparent in comparing element representation curves generally, as crania tend to preserve better than small or fragile bones anyway. However, skull curation is likely to be manifest itself as an imbalance between crania and major long bones.

The "virtual tomb" suggests that we should shift the basis for interpretation from single lines of evidence, particularly skeletal element representation, that can display identical patterns for primary and secondary burial depending on preservational circumstances. Instead, we should look for taphonomic anomalies among multiple lines of evidence, with particular attention to contextual archaeological detail. In a more philosophical sense, it also suggests that, though the distinction between natural processes and cultural behaviour is a cornerstone of traditional taphonomy, it is theoretically suspect. In the MNI example, the major factor in destroying burials was human action. There is no reason to suppose that this was unconscious; people moving bones to make space for a new inhumation would have known about the

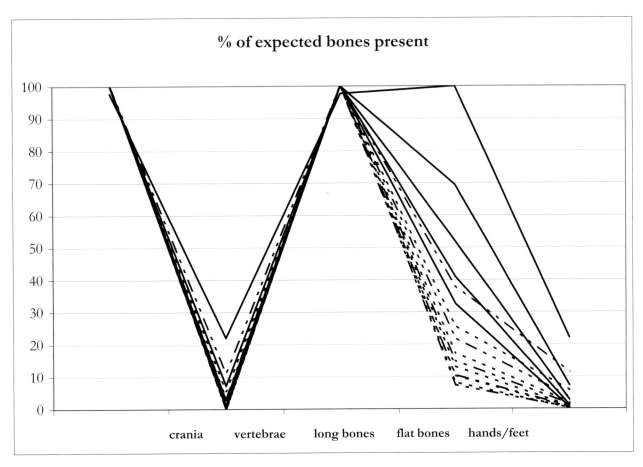

Figure 4.11. Part representation following deposition of complete bodies (dotted lines), "secondary" bodies (dashed lines) and "residual" bodies (solid lines); each is run at five levels of bone destruction. Note general similarity between primary and secondary burial; residual deposition is visible as over-representation of flat bones and hands/feet.

commingling and breakage they were causing. If it was considered important to maintain the integrity of the dead body, they could presumably have done so (for instance, by having separate individual burials or by carefully collecting and setting aside the bones of each body). It follows that "natural" processes are culturally understood, and are channelled or allowed to happen the way they do in accordance with their cultural interpretation. In some way, the destruction of bone must have been understood as, if not purposeful or desirable, at least normal, expected, or inevitable, part of the process of disintegrating and forgetting individuals to create generalised group history. Neolithic collective tombs, thus, should perhaps be considered not as faulty machines for preserving bone but rather as efficient, slow-acting machines for destroying it in a socially acceptable way.

Conclusions

After more than a century of study, some of the basic outlines of Neolithic burial are clear. The commonest rite, attested at almost all burial sites, particularly in the later Neolithic, is to repeatedly bury complete bodies in collective tombs, with each one disturbing earlier depositions. Cremation is found at a surprising number of sites and seems not to constitute an opposed rite to inhumation so much as a particular focus or moment in a complex burial programme. Secondary burial, excarnation, and manipulation of bones can be clearly demonstrated much less frequently, though they did occur sometimes. There was also much variety, even within very small regions; demonstrating or disproving a rite at one tomb does not mandate it or rule it out at other sites, even just a few kilometres away.

This review has two important methodological implications. First, we need to investigate Neolithic burial sites using broad and integrated taphonomic studies rather than relying on one or two methods. We should be particularly wary about making inferences principally based upon skeletal element representation, as differential natural destruction and secondary burial can leave very similar patterns. In contrast, contextually observed details such as the arrangement of bones and the structuring of deposits are likely to be informative and reliable. Secondly, as both the Stonehenge and Avebury landscapes and the Irish example above show, different sites may have formed complementary parts of a dispersed burial programme. Thus, to understand Neolithic burial, we must move from focusing on sites to focusing on broader landscapes.

Notes

1   Dates courtesy of Scottish Universities Research and Reactor Center, 2003.
2   Re-fitting also provided a corrected MNE which altered element representation curves noticeably; this reinforces that it is important to carry out an integrated suite of taphonomic studies rather than focussing narrowly on one or two methods.

Acknowledgments

We are grateful to Becky Gowland, Chris Knüsel, and an anonymous reviewer for helpful comments on the manuscript of this article.

References

Ashbee, P. (1966) The Fussell's Lodge Long Barrow, Excavations 1957. *Archaeologia* 100, 1–80.

Ashbee, P. (1970) *The Earthen Long Barrow in Britain.* London, James L. Dent and Sons Ltd.

Atkinson, R. J. (1965) Wayland's Smithy. *Antiquity* 39, 126–133.

Barber, J. (1997) *The Excavation of a Stalled Cairn at Point of Cott, Westray, Orkney.* Edinburgh, Scottish Trust for Archaeological Research.

Baxter, M. (1999) Dancing with the dead in a mass grave. *British Archaeology* 50.

Baxter, M. (2001) *Human Remains from the British Neolithic: a taphonomic perspective.* PhD, University of Cambridge.

Bender, B. (1998) *Stonehenge: Making Space.* Oxford, Blackwell.

Benson, D., and Clegg, I. (1978) Cotswold Burial Rites? *Man* 13, 134–137.

Bergh, S. (1995) *Landscape of the Monuments.* Stockholm, Riksantikvarieambet Arkeologiska Undersoknigar.

Bradley, R. (1984) *The Social Foundations of Prehistoric Britain.* London, Longmans.

Bradley, R. (1992) The excavation of an oval barrow beside the Abingdon causewayed enclosure, Oxfordshire. *Proceedings of the Prehistoric Society* 58, 127–42.

Bradley, R. (1998) *The Significance of Monuments: on the Shaping of Human Experience in Neolithic and Bronze Age Europe.* London, Routledge.

Bradley, R., and Holgate, R. (1984) The Neolithic sequence in the Upper Thames Valley. In R. J. Bradley and J. Gardner (ed.), *Neolithic studies,* vol. 133. 107–35. Oxford, British Archaeological Reports.

Brindley, A. L., and Lanting, J. N. (1991/92) Radiocarbon dates from the cemetery at Poulawack, Co. Clare. *Journal of Irish Archaeology* 6, 13–17.

Britnell, W., and Savory, H. (1984) *Gwernvale and Penywyrold: Two Neolithic Long Cairns in the Black Mountains of Brecknock.* Cardiff, Cambrian Archaeological Association.

Brothwell, D. (1963) The macroscopic dental pathology of some earlier human populations. In D. Brothwell (ed.), *Dental Anthropology,* 271–287. Oxford, Pergamon.

Brothwell, D., and Cullen, R. (1969) Wayland's Smithy, Oxfordshire: the human bone. *Proceedings of the Prehistoric Society* 57, 72–80.

Buikstra, J., and Ubelaker, D. H. (1994) *Standards for Data Collection from Human Skeletal Remains.* Fayetteville, Arkansas Archaeological Survey.

Bulleid, A. (1941) Notes on some chambered long barrows in north Somerset. *Proceedings of the Somerset Archaeology and Natural History Society* 87, 56–71.

Caffell, A. (2001) The effect of handling on human skeletal remains. *British Association for Biological Anthropology and Osteoarchaeology Annual Review* 2, 6–8.

Case, H. J. (1982) Cassington, 1950–52: late Neolithic pits and the big enclosure. In H. Case and A. Whittle (ed.), *Settlement Patterns in the Oxford Region,* 118–51. London, Council for British Archaeology.

Chapman, R. (1995) Ten years after – megaliths, mortuary practices, and the territorial model. In L. A. Beck (ed.), *Regional approaches to mortuary analysis,* 29–51. New York, Plenum.

Chapman, R. W. (1981) The emergence of formal disposal areas and the 'problem' of megalithic tombs in prehistoric Europe. In R. W. Chapman, I. Kinnes, and K. Randsborg (ed.), *The archaeology of death,* 71–81. New York, Cambridge University Press.

Chesterman, J. T. (1977) Burial rites in a Cotswold long barrow. *Man* 12, 22–32.

Chesterman, J. T. (1979) Investigations of the human bone from Quanterness. In A. C. Renfrew (ed.), *Investigations in Orkney,* 97–111. London, Society of Antiquaries.

Chesterman, J. T. (1983) The Human skeletal remains from Ibister. In J. Hedges (ed.), *Ibister, a Chambered Tomb, Orkney,* vol. 115, 73–133. Oxford, British Archaeological Reports.

Cleal, R., Walker, K., and Montague, R. (1995) *Stonehenge in its landscape: Twentieth century excavations.* London, English Heritage.

Clifford, E. M. (1936) Notgrove long barrow, Gloucestershire. *Archaeologia* 86, 119–62.

Clifford, E. M. (1938) The excavation of Nympsfield long barrow. *Proceedings of the Prehistoric Society* 4, 188–213.

Clifford, E. M., and Daniel, G. (1940) The Rodmarton and Avening portholes. *Proceedings of the Prehistoric Society* 6, 133–65.

Collins, A. E. P. (1954) The excavation of a double horned cairn at Audleystown. *Ulster Journal of Archaeology* 17, 7–56.

Collins, A. E. P. (1976) Dooey's Cairn, Ballymacaldrack, Co. Antrim. *Ulster Journal of Archaeology* 39, 1–7.

Collins, A. E. P., and Waterman, D. M. (1955) *Millin Bay, a Late Neolithic Cairn in Co. Down.* Belfast, HMSO.

Conwell, E. A. (1866) On ancient sepulchral cairns on the Loughcrew Hills. *Proceedings of the Royal Institute of Archaeology* 9, 355–79.

Cooney, G. (2000) *Landscapes of Neolithic Ireland.* London, Routledge.

Copley, M., Berstan, R., Dudd, S., Docherty, G., Mukherjee, A., Straker, V., Payne, S., and Evershed, R. (2003) Direct chemical evidence for widespread dairying in prehistoric Britain. *Proceedings of the National Academy of Sciences (USA)* 100, 1524–1529.

Corcoran, J. W. X. P. (1970) The Giant's Cave Luckington (WIL2). *Wiltshire Archaeological Magazine* 65, 39–63.

Crawford, O. G. S. (1925) *The Long Barrows of the Cotswolds.* Gloucester, John Bellows.

Cunnington, M. E. (1929) *Woodhenge.* Devizes, Simpson.

de Valera, R., and O'Nualain, S. (1961) *Survey of the Megalithic Tombs of Ireland, vol.1, Co. Clare.* Dublin, Stationary Office.

Dixon, P. (1988) The Neolithic settlements on Crickley Hill. In C. Burgess, P. Topping, C. Mordant, and M. Madison (ed.), *Enclosures and Defences in the Neolithic of Western Europe,* vol. 403, 750–788. Oxford, British Archaeological Reports.

Donovan, H. E. (1938) Adlestrop Hill barrow, Gloucestershire.

Transactions of the Bristol and Gloucester Archaeological Society 60, 152–164.

Drew, C. D., and Piggott, S. (1936) Excavation of Long Barrow 163a on Thickthorn Down, Dorset. *Proceedings of the Prehistoric Society* 2, 77–96.

Drewett, P. (1975) The excavation of an oval burial mound of the third millennium BC at Alfriston, East Sussex. *Proceedings of the Prehistoric Society* 41, 119–52.

Eogan, G. (1984) *Excavations at Knowth 1*. Dublin, Royal Irish Academy.

Evans, E. E. (1938) Dooey's Cairn, Dunloy, Co. Antrim. *Ulster Journal of Archaeology* 1, 59–78.

Evans, J. G., Atkinson, R. J. C., O'Connor, T., and Green, H. S. (1984) Stonehenge – the environment in the Late Neolithic and Early Bronze Age and a Beaker-Age burial. *Wiltshire Archaeological and Natural History Magazine* 78, 7–30.

Evans, J. G., and Simpson, D. D. A. (1991) Giant's Hills 2 long barrow, Skendleby, Lincolnshire. *Archaeologia* 109, 1–45.

Greenwell, W. (1877) *British Barrows*. Oxford, Clarendon Press.

Grimes, W. F. (1939) The excavation of the Ty Isaf long cairn, Breconshire. *Proceedings of the Prehistoric Society* 5, 119–42.

Grimes, W. F. (1960) *Excavation of Defense Sites, Vol.1: Neolithic/Bronze Age*. London, HMSO.

Harding, P., and Gringell, C. (1986) The excavation of two long barrows by F. de M. and HFWL. Vatcher. *Wiltshire Archaeological Magazine* 80, 7–22.

Hartnett, P. J. (1957) Excavation of a passage grave at Fourknocks, Co. Meath. *Proceedings of the Royal Irish Academy* 71C, 35–89.

Hencken, H. O. N. (1935) A cairn at Poulawack, Co. Clare. *Journal of the Royal Society of Antiquaries Ireland* 65, 191–222.

Hoare, R. C. (1812) *The Ancient History of Wiltshire*. London, Duckworth.

Hoare, R. C. (1821) An account of a stone barrow in the parish of Wellow at Stoney Littleton. *Archaeologia* 19, 43–8.

Hodder, I. (1984) Burials, houses, women and men in the European Neolithic. In D. Miller and C. Tilley (ed.), *Ideology, Power, and Prehistory*, 51–68. Cambridge, Cambridge University Press.

Hodder, I., and Shand, P. (1988) The Haddenham Long Barrow: an interim statement. *Antiquity* 62, 349–353.

Houlder, C. (1968) The henge monuments at Llandegai. *Antiquity* 42, 216–31.

Jones, C. (1998) The discovery and dating of the prehistoric landscape of Roughan Hill in Co. Clare. *The Journal of Irish Archaeology* 9, 27–43.

Jones, C. (2003) Fourth Millennium Beginnings on Roughan Hill and the Burren. In E. N. I. Armit E. Murphy and D. D. A. Simpson (ed.), *Neolithic Settlement in Ireland and western Britain*, 188–94. Oxford, Oxbow.

Keiller, A., and Piggott, S. (1938) Excavation of an untouched chamber in the Lanhill long barrow. *Proceedings of the Prehistoric Society* 4, 122–50.

Keith, A. (1916) The Human Remains. *Archaeologia Cambrensis* 16, 268.

Kinnes, I. (1992) *Non-megalithic long barrows and allied structures in the British Neolithic*. London, British Museum.

Kinnes, I., Schadla-Hall, T., Chadwick, P., and Dean, P. (1983) Duggleby Howe reconsidered. *Archaeological Journal* 140, 83–108.

Lynch, A. (1988) Poulnabrone, a stone in time. *Archaeology Ireland* 5, 105–7.

Lynch, A. (1994) Poulnabrone portal tomb. *Burren, Co. Clare, Irish Association for Quaternary Studies Field Guide* 18, 18–20.

Lynch, A., and O'Donnabhain, B. (1994) Poulnabrone, Co. Clare.

The Other Clare 18, 5–7.

Manby, T. G. (1963) The excavation of the Willerby Wold Long Barrow. *Proceedings of the Prehistoric Society* 29, 173–205.

Manby, T. G. (1976) The excavation of Kilham long barrow, East Riding of Yorkshire. *Proceedings of the Prehistoric Society* 42, 111–60.

Manning, C. (1985) A Neolithic burial mound at Ashleypark, Co. Tipperary. *Proceedings of the Royal Irish Academy* 85C, 61–100.

Masters, L. (1973) The Lochhill long cairn. *Antiquity* 47, 96–100.

Masters, L. (1983) Chambered tombs and non-megalithic barrows in Britain. In C. Renfrew (ed.), *The Megalithic Monuments of Western Europe*, 97–112. London, Thames and Hudson.

Mays, S. (1998) *The Archaeology of Human Bones*. London, Routledge.

McKinley, J. I. (1995) The human bone. In R. Cleal, K. Walker, and R. Montague (ed.), *Stone___ ___ its Landscape: Twentieth-Century Excavations*, 451–461. London, English Heritage.

Mercer, R. J. (1980) *Hambledon Hill: A Neolithic Landscape*. Edinburgh, Edinburgh University Press.

Montgomery, J., Budd, P., and Evans, J. (2000) Reconstructing the lifetime movements of ancient people: a Neolithic case study from southern England. *European Journal of Archaeology* 3, 370–385.

Mortimer, J. R. (1905) *Forty Years Researchers in British and Saxon Burial Mounds of East Yorkshire*. London, A. Brown and Sons.

O'Kelly, M. J. (1983) The excavation. In M. J. O'Kelly, R. Clearly, and D. Lehane (ed.), *Newgrange, Co. Meath Ireland: The Late Neolithic/Beaker Period Settlement*, 1–57 vol. 190. Oxford, British Archaeological Reports.

O'Neil, H. E. (1966) Sale's Lot long barrow, Withington, Glos. *Transactions of the Bristol and Gloucester Archaeological Society* 85, 5–35.

O'Riordan, S. P. (1954) Lough Gur excavations: Neolithic and Bronze Age houses on Knockadoon. *Proceedings of the Royal Irish Academy* 56C, 297–459.

Passmore, A. D. (1938) Gatcombe Lodge. *Proceedings of the Prehistoric Society* 4, 124.

Piggott, S. (1931) The Neolithic pottery of the British Isles. *Archaeological Journal* 88, 67–158.

Piggott, S. (1936) Handley Hill, Dorset – a Neolithic bowl and the date of the entrenchment. *Proceedings of the Prehistoric Society* 2, 229–30.

Piggott, S. (1962) *The West Kennet Long Barrow Excavations 1955 56*. London, HMSO.

Piggott, S. (1966) Unchambered long barrows in Neolithic Britain. *Paleohistoria* 12, 381–93.

Piggott, S., and Piggott, C. M. (1944) The excavation of barrows on Crichel and Lauceston Downs. *Archaeologia* 90, 47–80.

Pitts, M., Bayliss, A., McKinley, J., Boylston, A., Budd, P., Evans, J., Chenery, C., Reynolds, A. and Semple, S. (2002) An Anglo-Saxon decapitation and burial at Stonehenge. *Wiltshire Archaeological and Natural History Magazine* 95, 131–146.

Pitt-Rivers, A. L. F. (1898) *Excavations in Cranbourne Chase near Rushmore, on the Borders of Dorset and Wilts, Vol. IV*. Privately Printed.

Powell, T. G. E. (1938) Excavation of a megalithic tomb at Ballynamona Lower, Co. Waterford. *Journal of the Royal Society of Antiquaries of Ireland* 68, 260–71.

Proudfoot, E. (1965) Bishop's Cannings, Roughridge Hill. *Wiltshire Archaeological Magazine* 60, 133.

Renfrew, C. (1976) Megaliths, territories and populations. In S. De Laet (ed.), *Acculturation and continuity in Atlantic Europe*. 198–220. Brugge, De Tempel.

Renfrew, C. (1979) *Before Civilisation*. New York, Cambridge

University Press.

Richards, C. (1988) Altered images: a re-examination of Neolithic mortuary practices in Orkney. In J. Barrett and I. Kinnes (ed.), *The Archaeology of Context in the Neolithic and Bronze Age*, 42–56. Sheffield, Sheffield Academic Press.

Richards, C. (1993) Monumental choreography: architecture and spatial representation in Late Neolithic Orkney. In C. Tilley (ed.), *Interpretive Archaeology*, 143–180. Oxford, Berg.

Richards, J. (1990) *The Stonehenge Environs Project*. London, English Heritage.

Richards, M., and Hedges, R. (1999) A Neolithic revolution? new evidence of diet in the British Neolithic. *Antiquity* 73, 891–897.

Roberts, C., and Cox, M. (2003) *Health and Disease in Britain: from Prehistory to the Present Day*. Stroud, Sutton.

Rolleston, G. (1876) On the people of the long barrow period. *Journal of the Anthropological Institute* 5, 120–75.

Saville, A., Hall, E., and Hoyle, J. (1990) *Hazleton North: The Excavation of a Neolithic Long Cairn of the Cotswold-Severn Group*. London, English Heritage.

Savory, H. N. (1956) The excavation of Pipton long cairn, Breconshire. *Archaeologia Cambrensis*, 7–48.

Scarre, C. (2001) Modeling prehistoric populations: the case of Neolithic Brittany. *Journal of Anthropological Archaeology* 20, 285–313.

Shanks, M., and Tilley, C. (1982) Ideology, symbolic power and ritual communication: a reinterpretation of neolithic mortuary practices. In I. Hodder (ed.), *Symbolic and structural archaeology*, 129–154. Cambridge, Cambridge University Press.

Sherratt, A. (1990) The genesis of megaliths: monumentality, ethnicity and social complexity in Neolithic north-west Europe. *World Archaeology* 22, 147–167.

Smith, I. (1965) *Windmill Hill and Avebury: Excavations by Alexander Keiller 1925–1939*. Oxford, Clarendon Press.

Thomas, J. (1999) *Understanding the Neolithic*. London, Routledge.

Thomas, J. (2000) Death, identity, and the body in Neolithic Britain. *Journal of the Royal Anthropological Institute* 6, 653–668.

Thomas, J., and Whittle, A. (1986) Anatomy of a tomb – West Kennet revisited. *Oxford Journal of Archaeology* 5, 129–156.

Thurnam, J. (1857) On a cromleck-tumulus called Lugbury, near Littleton Drew. *Wiltshire Archaeological Magazine* 6, 164–73.

Thurnam, J. (1869) On ancient British barrows, especially those of Wiltshire and the adjoining counties (part 1, long barrows). *Archaeologia* 42, 161–244.

Tilley, C. (1994) *A Phenomenology of Landscape: Places, Paths and Monuments*. Oxford, Berg.

Waddell, J. (1992) The First People; The Neolithic Burren. In J. W. Connell and A. Korff (ed.), *The Book of the Burren*, 59–76. Galway, Tir Eolas.

Waddell, J. (1998) *The Prehistoric Archaeology of Ireland*. Galway, Galway University Press.

Waldron, T. (1987) The relative survival of the human skeleton: implications for palaeopathology. In A. Boddington, A. Garland, and R. Janaway (ed.), *Death, Decay and Reconstruction: Approaches to Archaeology and Forensic Science*, 149–162. Manchester, Manchester University Press.

Ward, J. (1916) The St. Nicholas chambered tombs, Glamorgan. *Archaeologia Cambrensis* 16, 239–267.

Waterman, D. M. (1965) The Court Cairn at Annaghmare, Co. Armagh. *Ulster Journal of Archaeology* 28, 3–46.

Wells, L. H. (1962) Report on the inhumation burials from the West Kennet barrow. In S. Piggott (ed.), *The West Kennet Long Barrow: excavations 1955–56*, 79–89. London, HMSO.

Wessex_Archaeology (2004) http://www.wessexarch.co.uk/projects/wiltshire/boscombe/bowmen/index.html, and http://www.wessexarch.co.uk/projects/amesbury/analyses.html. Accessed 24 September 2004.

West, S. E. (1990) *West Stow: The Prehistoric and Romano-British occupations*. Vol. 48. Bury St. Edmunds, East Anglian Archaeology.

Wheatley, D., and Gillings, M. (2002) *Spatial Technology and Archaeology: the Archaeological Applications of GIS*. London, Taylor and Francis.

Wheeler, R. E. M. (1943) *Maiden Castle, Dorset*. London, Society of Antiquaries.

White, T. (1992) *Prehistoric Cannibalism at Mancos 5MTUTR-2346*. Princeton, Princeton University Press.

Whittle, A. (1991) Wayland's Smithy, Oxfordshire: Excavations at the Neolithic Tomb in 1962–63 by R.J.C. Atkinson and S. Piggott. *Proceedings of the Prehistoric Society* 57, 61–101.

Whittle, A. (1994) Excavations at Millbarrow chambered tomb, Winterbourne Monkton, North Wiltshire. *Wiltshire Archaeological Magazine* 87, 1–53.

Whittle, A. (1996) *Europe in the Neolithic: the Creation of New Worlds*. Cambridge, Cambridge University Press.

Whittle, A., Pollard, J., and Grigson, C. (1999) *The Harmony of Symbols: The Windmill Hill Causewayed Enclosure*. Oxford, Oxbow.

Whittle, A., and Wysocki, M. (1998) Parc le Breos, Gowen, transepted long cairn, west Glamorgan: date, contents and context. *Proceedings of the Prehistoric Society* 64, 139–182.

Witts, G. B. (1881) Description of the long barrow called West Tump in the parish of Brimpsfield, Gloucestershire. *Transactions of the Bristol and Gloucester Archaeological Society* 5, 201–211.

Witts, G. B. (1883) Randwick long barrow. *Proceedings of the Cotswold Naturalists Field Club* 8, 156–60.

SITE	LOCATION	TYPE	MNI	DEMOGRAPHY	METHODS	CREMATION	INHUMATION	REPORTED PRACTICES	REFERENCES
ENGLAND									
Stoney Littleton	Avon	cts-svrm	~8	?	O,C	Y	Y	INTERMENT OF WHOLE BODIES + CREMATION	(Hoare, 1821)
Gwernvale	Brecknockshire	cts-svrm	?	?	?	Y	N	?	(Britnell and Savory, 1984)
Haddenham	Cambridgeshire	lb	5-6	ADULTS + SUBADULTS	O,T	N	Y	PRIMARY ARTICULATED + SECONDARY, DISMEMBERMENT, SELECTION, RE-ARRANGE + ROBBING	(Baxter, 1999; Hodder and Shand, 1988)
Launceston Down, b13	Cornwall	single/cremation	1	?	O	?	?	CROUCHED BURIAL.	(Piggott and Piggott, 1944)
Wor barrow	Cranbourne Chase Wiltshire	lb	6	MALES + 1 SUBADULT	O?	N	Y	COMPLETE BURIAL WITH COLLECTION OF BONES	(Pitt-Rivers, 1898)
Dorchester	Dorset	single/cremation	?	?	?	?	?	TRADITION OF SINGLE BURIALS	(Bradley and Holgate, 1984)
Hambledon Hill	Dorset	causeway	1	?	O, M, DPTH	?	?	EXPOSURE SITE	(Mercer, 1980)
Mere 13d	Dorset	single/cremation	1	?	O	Y	N	?	(Piggott, 1931)
Pentridge	Dorset	lb	?	?	?	?	?	?	(Bradley, 1984)
Handley, barrow 26	Dorset	barrow	1	1 ADULT	O	?	?	RECOVERED REMAINS LATER	(Piggott, 1936; Pitt-Rivers, 1898);
Handley, barrow 27	Dorset	barrow	1	1 ADULT	O	?	?	RECOVERED REMAINS LATER	(Piggott, 1936; Pitt-Rivers, 1898)
Maiden Castle	Dorset	barrow	6	1ADULT + 5 SUBADULTS	O	N	Y	PIT BURIAL, CROUCHED, SPECIAL INDIVIDUALS	(Wheeler, 1943)
Thickthorn Down	Dorset	lb	> 4	1 FEMALE + 1SUBADULT	O	?	Y	?	(Drew and Piggott, 1936)
Therfield Heath	Cambridgeshire	barrow	1	?	?	N	Y	ARTICULATED REMAINS	(Ashbee, 1970)
Whiteleaf	Buckinghamshire	barrow	2	?	?	N	Y	DISARTICULATED REMAINS - SECOND INHUMATION	(Ashbee, 1970)
Alfriston	East Sussex	single/cremation	1	1 FEMALE	O, S, PTH	N	Y	CROUCHED BURIAL	(Drewett, 1975)
Windmill Hill	Wiltshire	causeway	10	4 ADULTS + 6 SUBADULTS	O, M, DPTH	N	Y	DISMEMBERMENT OF SKELE, CIRCULATION OF BONES	(Smith, 1965)
Adlestrop Hill	Gloucestershire	cts-svrm	7	2 ADULTS + 5 SUBADULTS	O, C	N	Y	PARTIAL ARTICULATED + DISARTICULATED SKELES	(Donovan, 1938)

Appendix 4.1 (continued on pages 74–80). British and Irish Neolithic sites with human remains: a taphonomic catalogue. Note that burial practices are listed as reported in sources.

								PRIMARY BURIAL + SECONDARY, SACRIFICIAL VICTIMS	
Belas Knap	Gloucestershire	lb	36	7 MALES + 2 FEMALES + 5 SUBADULTS	?	?	Y	PRIMARY BURIAL + SECONDARY, SACRIFICIAL VICTIMS	(Crawford, 1925)
Bisley	Gloucestershire	lb	3	1 MALE + 1 SUBADULT	?	N	Y	?	(Crawford, 1925)
Bown Hill	Gloucestershire	lb	6	2 MALES + 2 FEMALES + 2 SUBADULTS	?	N	Y	SCATTERED BONES	(Crawford, 1925).
Burn Ground	Gloucestershire	cts-svrn	~7	1 SUBADULT	O, C	?	?	?	(Grimes, 1960)
Camp	Gloucestershire	lb	SEV	1 SUBADULT	?	N	Y	CROUCHED POSITIONS OF BODIES	(Crawford, 1925)
Carn Goch	Gloucestershire	lb	?	?	?	?	?	?	(Crawford, 1925)
Coberley	Gloucestershire	lb	1?	?	?	N	Y	?	(Crawford, 1925)
Cow Common	Gloucestershire	cts-svrn	5	3 MALES + 2 FEMALES	O, C, S	?	?	ARRANGEMENT OF SKULLS	(Rolleston, 1876)
Crickley barrow	Gloucestershire	lb	?	?	?	?	?		(Dixon, 1988)
Crippets	Gloucestershire	lb	1	?	?	N	Y	?	(Crawford, 1925)
Eyford, Swell vi	Gloucestershire	cts-svrn	19	12 ADULTS (2 MALES + 3 FEMALES) + 7 SUBADULTS	O, C	Y	Y	SKULLS CLUSTERED	(Rolleston, 1876)
Ffostyll	Gloucestershire	lb	?	?	?	?	?	?	(Crawford, 1925)
Gatcome Lodge	Gloucestershire	cts-svrn	1	1 FEMALE	O, C	?	Y	?	(Passmore, 1938)
Hazelton North	Gloucestershire	cts-svrn	41	22 ADULTS (3 FEMALES + 11 MALES) + 19 SUBADULTS	O, P, DISTRI PAIRED AND ARTIC, PRES, AN, ABRAS	Y	Y	PRIMARY + SUCESSIVE BURIALS, CLUSTER OF BONES	(Saville et al, 1990)
Hetty Pegler's Tump	Gloucestershire	lb	6	1 FEMALE	?	N	Y	?	(Crawford, 1925)
Norn's Tump	Gloucestershire	lb	?	?	?	?	?	?	(Crawford, 1925)
Norgrove	Gloucestershire	cts-svrn	2	?	O	?	Y	PARTIAL + COMPLETE ARTICULATED SKELES	(Clifford, 1936)
Nympsfield	Gloucestershire	cts-svrn	16	ADULTS + SUBADULT	O, C	Y	Y	CREMATION WITH CHILDREN IN SEPERATE CISTS	(Clifford, 1938)
Pinkwell	Gloucestershire	lb	3	?	?	N	Y	?	(Crawford, 1925)
Pole's Wood East	Gloucestershire	cts-svrn	12	?	O	?	Y	SECONDARY, STORAGE FIRST, DISPLACE OLDER DEPOSITS, ARRANGEMENT OF SKULLS	(Greenwell, 1877)
Querns	Gloucestershire	lb	?	?	?	?	?	?	(Crawford, 1925)

Site	County	Type	No.	MNI breakdown	Codes			Description	Reference
Randwick	Gloucestershire	cts-svrn	~4	?	O	?	?	SECONDARY, SCARCITY OF SKULLS AND FEMURS	(Witts, 1883)
Rodmarton	Gloucestershire	cts-svrn	13	?	O, C	Y	Y	?	(Clifford and Daniel, 1940)
Sale's Lot	Gloucestershire	cts-svrn	21	8 ADULTS (2 MALES + 2 FEMALES) + 6 SUBADULTS	O	Y	Y	FRAGMENTED	(O'Neil, 1966)
Salway Barn	Gloucestershire	cts-svrn	?	?	?	?	?	?	(Grimes, 1960)
Snowshill	Gloucestershire	lb	1	1 MALE	?	N	Y	THOUGHT TO BE BRONZE AGE BURIAL	(Crawford, 1925; Greenwell, 1877)
Througham	Gloucestershire	lb	1	?	?	N	Y	?	(Crawford, 1925)
Uley	Gloucestershire	cts-svrn	~9	9 ADULTS (1 FEMALE)	O, PTH, C	NO	Y	SITTING/SQUATTING BURIALS, HEAPS OF BONES	(Crawford, 1925)
West Barrow	Gloucestershire	lb	20	1 FEMALE + 1 SUBADULT	?	?	Y	"HONORARY BURIAL OF CHIEFTAINESS"	(Crawford, 1925; Witts, 1881)
West Tump	Gloucestershire	cts-svrn	4	?	O, C	?	?	?	(Witts, 1881)
Willersey	Gloucestershire	lb	?	?	?	?	?	?	(Crawford, 1925)
Woodbarrow	Gloucestershire	lb	?	?	?	?	?	?	(Crawford, 1925)
Barton Saucey	Hampshire	barrow	1	?	?	N	Y	PROBABLY ARTICULATED SINGLE SKELETON	(Ashbee, 1970)
Moody's Down	Hampshire	lb	?	?	?	?	?	?	(Grimes, 1960)
Nutbane	Hampshire	lb	4	ADULTS + SUBADULTS	O	N	Y	ARTICULATED SKELES, DIFF DEPOSITS BASED ON AGE	(Piggott, 1966)
Giant's Hill	Lincolnshire	lb	3	1 MALE + 1 AMBIGUOUS + 1 SUBADULT	O, W, AN	N	Y	ARTIC, DISARTIC, MIXED, SECONDARY, EXPOSURE	(Evans and Simpson, 1991)
Ascott-under-Wychwood	Oxfordshire	cts-svrn	46–49	13 MALES + 15 FEMALES + 8 SUBADULTS	O, T	Y	Y	PRIMARY INHUM, SELECT PARTS, RE-ARRANGE, GROUP SKULLS, SEGREGAT BASED ON AGE	(Baxter, 2001; Benson and Clegg, 1978; Chesterman, 1977)
Barrow Hills, Radley	Oxfordshire	lb	2	1 MALE + 1 FEMALE	O, P	N	Y	SOME ARTICULATIONS	(Bradley, 1992)
Crawley	Oxfordshire	lb	SEV	?	?	N	Y	SOME SECONDARY BURIAL	(Crawford, 1925)
Lyneham	Oxfordshire	lb	SEV	?	?	N	Y	WITH SECONDARY	(Crawford, 1925)
North Stoke	Oxfordshire	lb	1	?	?	N	Y	CENTRAL INHUMATION	(Case, 1982)
Spatepits Copse	Oxfordshire	lb	?	?	?	?	?	?	(Crawford, 1925)
Wayland's Smithy	Oxfordshire	lb	14	10 MALES + 3 FEMALES + 1 SUBADULT	O, PTH, C, S, %C	N	Y	ARRANGED IN PILES, REWORKING, CIRCULATION	(Atkinson, 1965; Brothwell and Cullen, 1969; Mays, 1998; Whittle, 1991)

Site	County	Monument	No.	Demographics				Description	Reference
Whispering Knights	Oxfordshire	lb	?	?	?	?	?	?	(Crawford, 1925)
Nempnett Thrubwell	Somerset	cts-svrn	?	?	?	?	?	MULTIPLE BURIALS	(Bulleid, 1941)
Streethouse	W. Yorkshire	lb	SEV	ADULTS + 1 SUBADULT	O	Y	Y	DISARTICULATED WITH SELECTION + CREMATION	(Kinnes, 1992)
Crosby Garrett	Westmorland	barrow	6	?	?	Y	N	BURNED DISARTICULATED	(Ashbee, 1970)
Amesbury 42	Wiltshire	lb	2	?	O	N	Y	PROBABLY SECONDARY INHUMATIONS	(Richards, 1990)
Avebury	Wiltshire	henge/circle	~5	4 MALES + 1 ADOLESCENT MALE	O	N	Y	TAKEN FROM LB, LIKE WINDMILL, RITUAL/MAGIC	(Smith, 1965)
Bishops Cannings 62a	Wiltshire	barrow	2	?	?	Y	N	?	(Proudfoot, 1965)
Bishops Cannings 65	Wiltshire	barrow	4	2 MALES + 2 SUBADULTS	?	N	Y	DISARTICULATED REMAINS	(Ashbee, 1970)
Boyton 1	Wiltshire	barrow	9	7 ADULTS + 1 SUBADULT	?	N	Y	ARTICUATED SKELETONS + SECOND INHUMATION	(Ashbee, 1970)
Bratton 1	Wiltshire	barrow	1	?	?	Y	N	BURNED, DISARTICULATED, POSS. SECONDARY	(Ashbee, 1970)
Calne-Cherhill	Wiltshire	barrow	3	1 MALE + 2 FEMALES	?	N	Y	ARTICULATED REMAINS	(Ashbee, 1970)
Chute 1	Wiltshire	barrow	?	?	?	N	Y	DISARTICULATED REMAINS	(Ashbee, 1970)
Coneybury	Wiltshire	henge/circle	?	?	?	?	Y	?	(Richards, 1990)
Durrington Down	Wiltshire	barrow	5	1 MALE + 1 SUBADULT	O, P, S, M	Y	Y	MIXED BURIAL RITES	(Richards, 1990)
Edington 7	Wiltshire	barrow	?	?	?	N	Y	DISARTICULATED REMAINS	(Ashbee, 1970)
Figheldean 31	Wiltshire	barrow	2	?	?	N	Y	DISARTICULATED REMAINS + SECOND INHUMATION	(Ashbee, 1970)
Fittleton 5	Wiltshire	barrow	?	?	?	N	Y	DISARTICULATED REMAINS	(Ashbee, 1970)
Fussell's Lodge	Wiltshire	lb	53–57	15 MALES + 16 FEMALES + 22–24 SUBADULTS	O	Y	Y	DISARTICULATION, GROUPS, PARTS REMOVED	(Ashbee, 1966; Mays, 1998)
Heddington 3	Wiltshire	barrow	1	?	?	N	Y	ARTICULATED SINGLE CROUCHED SKELETON	(Ashbee, 1970)
Heytesbury 1	Wiltshire	barrow	14	?	?	N	Y	DISARTICULATED REMAINS	(Ashbee, 1970)
Heytesbury 4	Wiltshire	barrow	?	?	?	N	Y	DISARTICULATED REMAINS	(Ashbee, 1970)
Knook 2	Wiltshire	barrow	7	?	?	Y	N	BURNED, DISARTICULATED	(Ashbee, 1970)

Site	County	Context	No.	Demographics				Description	Reference
Knook 5	Wiltshire	barrow	4	1 ADULT	?	N	Y	ARTICUATED SKELETONS	(Ashbee, 1970)
Lanhill	Wiltshire	cts-svrn	11	?	O, C	?	Y	SUCCESSIVE PRIMARY, CLUSTERS OF LONG BONES	(Keiller and Piggott, 1938)
Luckington	Wiltshire	cts-svrn	1	1 FEMALE	O	Y	Y	PRIMARY CREMATION	(Corcoran, 1970)
Lugbury	Wiltshire	cts-svrn	27	1 MALE + SUBADULTS	O	?	Y	DISTINCTIVE BURIALS, CROUCHED	(Thurnam, 1857)
Maiden Bradbury	Wiltshire	barrow	?	?	?	N	Y	DISARTICULATED REMAINS	(Ashbee, 1970)
Millbarrow	Wiltshire	cts-svrn	14	8 ADULTS + 6 SUBADULTS	O, PTH	Y	Y	?	(Whittle, 1994)
Milton Lilbourne 7	Wiltshire	barrow	3	?	?	N	Y	DISARTICULATED REMAINS	(Ashbee, 1970; Richards, 1990)
Netheravon Bake	Wiltshire	barrow	1	?	?	N	Y	DISARTICULATED REMAINS	(Ashbee, 1970)
Norton Bavant	Wiltshire	barrow	18	?	?	N	Y	DISARTICULATED REMAINS	(Ashbee, 1970)
Stockton 1	Wiltshire	barrow	3	?	?	N	Y	PRIMARY ARTICUATED SKELETONS	(Ashbee, 1970)
Stonehenge (Aubrey holes)	Wiltshire	holes	200	?	?	y	n		(Cleal et al., 1995; McKinley, 1995)
Tilshead 1	Wiltshire	barrow	?	?	?	Y	N	BURNED, DISARTICULATED	(Ashbee, 1970; Thurnam, 1869)
Tilshead 2	Wiltshire	barrow	5	?	?	?	Y	ARTICULATED AND DISARTICULATED	(Ashbee, 1970; Thurnam, 1869)
Tilshead 5	Wiltshire	barrow	2	?	?	N	Y	ARTICULATED SKELETONS	(Ashbee, 1970; Thurnam, 1869)
Tilshead Old Ditch	Wiltshire	lb	4	FEMALES	O	?	?	ARTICULATED SINGLE BURIAL	(Ashbee, 1970)
Tilshead 7	Wiltshire	barrow	8	3 MALES + 3 FEMALES + 2 SUBADULTS	?	N	Y	DISARTICULATED REMAINS	(Ashbee, 1970)
Warminster 1	Wiltshire	barrow	3	?	?	N	Y	DISARTICULATED REMAINS	(Ashbee, 1970)
Warminster 6	Wiltshire	barrow	1	?	?	N	Y	ARTICULATED REMAINS	(Ashbee, 1970)
West Kennet	Wiltshire	lb	40	30 ADULTS + 10 SUBADULTS	O, PTH, S	Y	Y	COMP/PARTIAL ARTIC, POSS EXCARN + SUCC. INTER	(Piggott, 1962; Thomas and Whittle, 1986; Wells, 1962; Whittle et al., 1999)
Westbury 7	Wiltshire	single/cremation	?	?	?	?	?	DISARTICULATED REMAINS	(Hoare, 1812)
Wexcombe Tow	Wiltshire	barrow	1	?	?	N	Y	DISARTICULATED REMAINS	(Ashbee, 1970)
Wilsford 3	Wiltshire	barrow	?	?	?	N	Y	DISARTICULATED REMAINS	(Ashbee, 1970)
Wilsford 30	Wiltshire	barrow	4	?	?	N	Y	ARTICUATED SKELETONS	(Ashbee, 1970)

Site	County	Type	Count	Demographics				Description	Reference
Winterbourn Stoke	Wiltshire	single/cremation	1	?	O	?	Y	PRIMARY AND SECONDARY	(Thurnam, 1869)
Winterbourne Stoke 1	Wiltshire	barrow	6	?	?	N	Y	SECONDARY INHUMATIONS	(Ashbee, 1970)
Woodford G2	Wiltshire	lb	1	1 MALE	O	Y	Y	LIKE WAYLANDS SMITHY	(Harding and Gringell, 1986)
Woodhenge	Wiltshire	single/cremation	1	POSSIBLE CHILD	O	Y	?	SPECIAL DEPOSITS OF DISARTICULATED BITS	(Cunnington, 1929)
Cropton	Yorkshire	barrow	2	2 ADULTS	?	N	Y	ARTICULATED REMAINS	(Ashbee, 1970)
Duggleby Howe	Yorkshire	single/cremation	28	?	O, C	Y	Y	?	(Kinnes et al, 1983; Mortimer, 1905)
Ebberston	Yorkshire	barrow	14	?	?	Y	N	BURNED DISARTICULATED	(Ashbee, 1970)
Hanging Grimston	Yorkshire	lb	1	?	?	N	Y	?	(Mortimer, 1905)
Kilburn	Yorkshire	barrow	SEV	?	?	Y	N	BURNED DISARTICULATED	(Ashbee, 1970)
Kilham	Yorkshire	barrow	9	1 FEMALE + 1 SUBADULT MALE	O?	Y	Y	PRIMARY ARTICULATED SKELETONS + SECONDARY INHUMATIONS	(Manby, 1976)
Market Weighton	Yorkshire	barrow	26	?	?	Y	N	BURNED, DISARTICULATED	(Ashbee, 1970)
Over Silton	Yorkshire	barrow	5	?	?	N	Y	DISARTICULATED REMAINS	(Ashbee, 1970)
Pickering	Yorkshire	barrow	3	?	?	N	Y	ARTICULATED REMAINS	(Ashbee, 1970)
Rudstone	Yorkshire	barrow	?	?	?	Y	N	BURNED, DISARTICULATED	(Ashbee, 1970)
Weststow	Yorkshire	barrow	11	2 MALES + 2 FEMALES + 1 AMBIGUOUS + 2 SUBADULTS	?	Y	Y	BURNED ARTIC + DISARTIC, 4 SECONDARY INHUMED	(Ashbee, 1970; West, 1990)
Willerby Wold	Yorkshire	Lb	4	MALES	O	Y	Y	ARTIC + DISARTIC, BURNING, SECONDARY INHUM	(Manby, 1963)
IRELAND									
Audleystown	Co, Down	courtt	31–33	9 MALES + 5 FEMALES + 6 AMBIGUOUS + 2 SUBADULTS	O	Y	Y	COLLECTIVE, SINGLE BURIAL WITH GROUPING OF BONE	(Collins, 1954)
Dooey's Cairn	Co. Antrim	courtt	5	ADULTS	O	Y	N		(Collins, 1976; Evans, 1938)
Annaghmare	Co. Armagh	courtt	5	1 FEMALE + 1 CHILD	O	Y	Y	?	(Waterman, 1965)
Poulawack	Co. Clare	linkard	19	ADULTS + SUBADULTS	O	Y	Y	SINGLE, MIXED BURIAL	(Hencken, 1935)

Site	County	Type	MNI	Demography	PRELIM O/T				Interpretation	Reference
Poulnabrone	Co. Clare	portalt	22	16 ADULTS + 6 SUBADULTS		Y		Y	COLLECTIVE, MIX, SINGLE	(Lynch, 1988; Lynch, 1994; Lynch and O'Donnabhain, 1994)
Milin Bay	Co. Down	cist	16	5 ADULTS + 11 SUBADULT	O	Y		Y	COLLECTIVE INHUMATION WITH SUBADULTS	(Collins and Waterman, 1955)
Lough Gur	Co. Limerick	settl	4	1 FEMALE + SUBADULTS	O	N		Y	BURIAL PROBABLY BASED ON AGE	(O'Riordan, 1954)
Fourknocks I	Co. Meath	passagt	65	ADULTS + 10 SUBADULTS	O	Y		Y	PART SELECT, DIFF RITES/AREAS BY AGE, CREM ADULTS	(Hartnett, 1957)
Fourknocks II	Co. Meath	passagt	17	6 ADULTS + 11 SUBADULTS	O	Y		Y	ADULT CREM, CHILD IN PASSAGE	(Hartnett, 1957)
Knowth	Co. Meath	passagt	30	14 ADULTS + 19 SUBADULTS	O	Y		Y	SUCESSIVE AND PRIMARY, WITH SOME GROUPING	(Eogan, 1984)
Loughcrew	Co. Meath	cemetery	SEV	?	?	Y		?		(Conwell, 1866)
Newgrange	Co. Meath	passagt	5	?	O, S, F, DENT	Y		Y	SINGLE COLLECTIVE DEPOSIT, SPECIAL PLACEMENT	(O'Kelly, 1983)
Carrowmore no.4	Co. Sligo	cemetery	3	1 MALE + 1 FEMALE	O	Y		Y		(Bergh, 1995)
Carrowmore no.7	Co. Sligo	cemetery	7	2 FEMALES	O	Y		?		(Bergh, 1995)
AshleyPark	Co. Tipperary	linkard	3	1 MALE + 2 SUBADULTS	O	N		Y	CELEBRATE INDIVIDUAL	(Manning, 1985)
Ballynamona	Co. Waterford	Court	1	?	?	Y		N	CREMATED REMAINS MIXED WITH CHARCOAL	(Powell, 1938)
SCOTLAND										
Lochill	Ayrshire	lb	~1	?	O?	Y		?	COMPLETE BURIAL + SCATTERED, DISARTICULATED PILES	(Masters, 1973)
Slewcairn	Dumfries and Galloway	lb	?	?	?	Y		?	COMPLETE BURIAL + SCATTERED, DISARTICULATED PILES	(Masters, 1983)
Ibister	Orkney	cairn	341	ADULTS + SUBADULTS	O, T	?		?	INCLUSIVE BURIAL WITH PARTS SELECTED	(Baxter, 2001; Chesterman, 1983)
Point of Cott	Orkney	cairn	13	5 ADULTS + 7 SUBADULTS	O, ARTIC, PRES, W, PTH, REP	N		Y	COMPLETE BURIAL WITH SUCCESSIVE DISTURBANCE	(Barber, 1997)
Quanterness	Orkney	cairn	165	ADULTS + SUBADULTS	O, T	?		?	3 PRIMARY BURIALS + SECONDARY, ALL INCLUSIVE	(Baxter, 2001; Chesterman, 1979)

WALES									
Pipton	Breconshire	cts-svrn	11	7 MALES + 1 FEMALE + 1 SUBADULT	O, C, BIOAR	?	Y	DISCRETE GROUPS OF BONES	(Savory, 1956)
Ty Isaf	Breconshire	cts-svrn	33	ADULTS + 4 SUBADULTS	O, S, C, PTH	Y	Y	DISARTICULATED	(Grimes, 1939)
Tinkinswood	Glamorgan	cts-svrn	~50	MORE FEMALES + 4 SUBADULTS	O, C, REPB	Y	Y	SECONDARY, DISTURBANCE, + SUCCESSIVE BURIALS	(Keith, 1916; Ward, 1916)
Parc Le Breos	Gower	cts-svrn	40	ADULTS + SUBADULTS	O, PTH, T, DIET	Y	Y	EXPOSED FIRST, AGE CRITERIA WHERE PLACED	(Whittle and Wysocki, 1998)
Llandegai, Henge A, B	Gwynedd	single/cremation	SEV	?	O	Y	N	CONCENTRATION OF CREMATIONS, SUCCESSIVE BURIAL	(Houlder, 1968)
Heston Brake	Monmouthshire	lb	1	?	?	N	N	?	(Crawford, 1925)
Penywyrlod	Powys	cts-svrn	6	6 ADULTS (5 MALES + 1 FEMALE) + SUBADULT	O, BIOAR	N	Y	OSSUARY, LONG BONES, SKULLS ARRANGED	(Britnell and Savory, 1984)

KEY

O	OSTEOLOGY
S	STATURE
C	CRANIAL
M	METRICS
PTH	PATHOLOGY
D OR DENT	DENTAL
DIET	DIETARY STUDY
T	TAPHONOMY
F	FRAGMENTATION
N	

W	WEATHERING
PRES	PRESERVATION
AN	ANIMAL
%C	% COMPOSITION
DISTRI	DISTRIBUTION
REPB	REPRESENTATION OF BONES
REP	REPRESENTATION OF PARTS
BIOAR	BIOARCHAEOLOGICAL DATA
ARTIC	ARTICULATION
	STUDY

KEY

LB	LONG BARROW
CTS-SVRN	COTSWOLD SEVERN TOMB
PASAGT	PASSAGE TOMB
PORTT	PORTAL TOMB
COURTT	COURT TOMB
LINKARDT	LINKARDSTOWN TOMB
CAUSEWAY	CAUSEWAYED ENCLOSURE
SETTL	SETTLEMENT SITE
SINGLE/CREMATION	SINGLE OR CREMATION BURIAL

5. Cremation ... the cheap option?

Jacqueline I. McKinley

Introduction

Cremation is cleaner, '...a necessary sanitary precaution against the propagation of disease...' (Thompson 1889, 1–2); cheaper, '...the cost of funerals during the year 1884 in England and Wales was ...nearly five millions sterling. One-third of this sum would amply suffice for cremation ...' (*ibid.* 63), and the resulting burial takes up far less space than one by inhumation – '...thousands of acres ...might be restored to better uses than that of storing decaying bodies...'(*ibid.* 61–62). Thompson was a leading advocate for the re-introduction of cremation to Britain in the late 19th century after a gap *c.*1000 years. This modern Western attitude to cremation leaves it devoid of any directly related briefs, stripped of 'ritual' and reduced to a utilitarian means of disposing of the dead. Characteristics of the rite which do survive from the past include transformation, admittedly seen as a 'sanitary measure' rather than a 'ritual (probably viewed as magical) process', and the major focus on cremation rather than burial '...when no desire is manifested to preserve the relics of the departed, and no urn or casket is sought to contain them, they may be safely spread abroad the soil ...' (*ibid.* 65).

Cremation may now represent the 'cheaper option' in the mechanised West, but such is not the case in other contemporary cultures (*e.g.* Metcalf and Huntington 1991, 141–143; Downes 1999), nor would it necessarily have been in earlier phases of its use within the British Isles, the archaeological evidence for which forms the focus of this paper. Until relatively recently there was often a tendency to regard archaeological cremation burials as something of a 'poor relation', particularly within periods noted for their artefact-rich inhumation burials, such as the early Anglo-Saxon period. The common failure to analyse the cremated remains from archaeological contexts frequently led to the range and quantity of pyre goods being underestimated (McKinley 1989, 244; 1994a, 86–100; Lucy and Reynolds 2002, 9), and, by focusing on

the artefactual inclusions within the burial, evidence for the multifaceted nature of the mortuary rite as a whole tended to be overlooked. The mortuary rite was complex in its concept, including transformation by cremation and subsequent closure by burial, and expensive in terms of the time expended in its undertaking and the required (fuel) and additional commodities (pyre and/or grave goods). While not all aspects of the rite are represented archaeologically, historical, cultural (contemporaneous poetry and art), ethnographic and anthropological data may illustrate some of the missing components or enable them to be deduced. This paper aims to highlight those parts of the rite for which there is evidence, and tries to understand the motivation and beliefs behind the actions.

The primary rite – cremation

Liminalisation of the dead is illustrated in the positioning of graves and cemeteries relative to settlements (*e.g.* Bradley 1990, 131; Parker Pearson 1999, 124–141). Practical factors and ritual issues may have affected the length of time between death and the removal of the deceased from the vicinity of the living for, or to await, cremation, and the positioning of the body in the intervening period.

In the British Isles, the climate will have been a determining factor in when cremation could be undertaken; pyres will not burn in torrential rain or if the wood is soaked. The latter would have been well understood and prepared for by those for whom wood was a precious source of power. The use of the powerful life-sustaining force of fire being used as a means of transporting the dead from this world to the next may in itself have held symbolic significance. The weather could not be controlled, and it may have been necessary to await a relatively dry day on which to undertake a cremation which, particularly at certain times of year and in certain localities, may have extended to several weeks. This occasional need to wait on the weather is illustrated in contemporary cultures; if it is raining too hard to undertake cremation, the Kol of India may bury the corpse until 'after the harvest'; otherwise the corpse is buried for a short while for ritual reasons to assist the soul to 'find its way to the [underground] home of the dead' (van Gennep 1977, 151).

Time may have been required to make preparations for cremation. In his account of the cremation of a Rus chieftain in 922 AD, Ibn Fadlan tells how the deceased was buried in an earth-cut grave for ten days to allow time for the preparation of his funeral clothes (Brøndsted 1960, 301–2). There are ethnographic references to similar practices in parts of contemporary Asia, to allow the deceased's family sufficient time to save or prepare for the funeral. Here, too, the body is first buried and later exhumed for cremation (Metcalf and Huntington 1991, 101, 141–2; McKinley 1994a, 79; Downes 1999, 22). Since there is no reference to their re-use as permanent graves, these temporary resting-places would presumably leave empty features of grave-like form and size. Archaeological inhumation cemeteries from across the temporal range in the British Isles occasionally include one or more empty graves but, although some comprised mixed-rite cemeteries, more often these are single rite grave groups and such features are likely to represent cenotaphs rather than temporarily occupied graves (Toynbee 1971, 54; McKinley 2003, 13; 2004, 30); though the latter remains a possibility.

Other delays to cremation may carry more ritual connotations. The Roman upper classes had a period of up to seven days lying-in-state (Toynbee 1971, 45), the less exalted generally being cremated within two days of death (Noy 2005). A 10th century account of a Baltic cremation tells how the dead may remain '...at home with relatives and friends for a month, or more...' dependant on how wealthy they were (the wealthy remaining above ground longer; from *Old English Orosius*, cited in Swanton 1975, 34). An account of 19th-century cremation within the Thai royal family tells of six to twelve months of rituals prior to cremation (Leonowens 1988, 205–206).

Delays between death and cremation clearly varied widely. In the intervening period the corpse sometimes resided with the living while in others, even if the duration between death and cremation were short, it was seen as necessary for practical (*e.g.* smell and appearance) or ritual reasons (*e.g.* the corpse viewed as potentially 'dangerous') to 'remove' the dead from the sphere of the living. Specific mortuary structures could have provided an alternative 'liminal' space to temporary graves; possible British examples of such structures have been found in several inhumation cemeteries (*e.g.* Fitzpatrick 1997, 194–5). Four-post structures found in Anglo-Saxon cemeteries in the south of England have been interpreted as 'houses' for cremation burials made above ground (Evison 1988, 35–36; Down and Welch 1990, 25–33; Lucy 2000, 118–119; McKinley 2003, 15–18); an alternative interpretation may be that some of the larger ones, at least, were mortuary structures used to house the deceased prior to cremation.

Nonetheless, much of the available evidence suggests that cremation was undertaken shortly after death and in some temporal/geographic groups undue delays may have been seen as undesirable. Where cremation was seen to effect 'immediate' transformation, thereby affording entry to the other world, it is unlikely that it was seen as helpful to the dead (or the living) to keep them in this world longer than was necessary. In the *Iliad* Patroclus' ghost beseeches Achilles; '...Bury [*cremate*] me instantly and let me pass the Gates of Hades. I am kept out by the disembodied spirits of the dead ... for once you have passed me through the flames I shall never come back again ...' (Book 33, Lines 70–78). Although the stuff of epic poetry, Homer, writing in the early part of the last millennium BC (Rieu 1950, 14–15), will have been expressing the beliefs of his time (*ibid.*). Patroclus' 'spirit' was trapped in his un-transformed corpse unable to enter the realm of the dead. Reasons for not delaying cremation in contemporary cultures include: preventing the soul from re-entering the body (Northern India; Crooke 1926 in Barber 1990), or the deceased from becoming a vampire (19th century Bulgaria; Jiracek 1891 in Barber 1990), freeing the spirit (Gräslund 1994), or facilitating entry to 'the land of souls' (Caribs; van Gennep 1977, 148).

Materials cremated and/or buried with the dead offer insights into beliefs in the nature of the afterworld and the point of entry to it (Gräslund 1994, 19–20). Material types generally fall into two main categories which may be described as Intrinsic – personal items 'worn' by the deceased, linked to dress and display – and Extrinsic – food offerings and other practical or 'personal' items the deceased may require for their journey to and/or in the afterworld. Other goods may have represented gifts or mementoes from friends or relatives, or ritual offerings not pertaining directly to the deceased (Gräslund 1994, 15–16; McKinley 1994a, 90). Although grave goods were deposited at the time of burial in some periods within the British Isles (see below), the majority of goods were placed on the pyre: they were transformed with the body and simultaneously sent to the other world. Written sources for such practices are numerous. The offerings on Patroclus' pyre included sheep and cattle, jars of honey and oil, horses and two of his nine pet dogs (*Iliad* Book 23, Lines 170–180). Pliny tells of a boy whose pets – horses, dogs, nightingales, parrots and blackbirds – were slaughtered to be cremated with him (Toynbee 1971, 291). A Roman testator's will instructed his hunting equipment, sailing boat and best clothes be cremated with him (*ibid.*, 63; see also Alcock 1980, 62). The Rus chieftain, dressed in his funeral clothes, was furnished with food (fruit, aromatic plants, bread, meat and onions), his weapons, a dog, two horses, two cows, a cock and a hen (Brøndsted 1960, 303).

Not all items placed on a pyre will show visual signs of

heating; steel requires temperatures (1350°C; Northover and Montague 1997, 91) well in excess of those which would have been attained by pyres (*c.*1000–1100°C; McKinley 1997a, 134; *pers. obs.*) to effect any visual changes; items with lower melting points such as glass and copper-alloy will have been affected by their position on the pyre relative to the heat source (McKinley 1994a, 90–1; Northover and Montague 1997, 90). Conversely, much that went on the pyre will have been organic – most clothing, items of wood, horn and basket-work, food-stuffs and materials such as amber – evidence for which rarely survives (Kreuz 2000). In addition, since not all the human remains from a cremation were subjected to burial, it is highly likely that surviving pyre goods were accidentally or deliberately excluded from the burial (McKinley 1994a, 88; Polfer 1993; 2000). The archaeologist sees only the minimum, but the picture which emerges from this data is not of a rite less palpably wealthy than that seen in disposal by inhumation.

Clothing is generally represented by items used as fastenings, the materials for which changed over time. Jewellery is closely associated with dress, as may be items which would have been contained in pouches or bags suspended from the neck or waist. Fragments of worked bone pin are a common find in British Bronze Age burials, whilst those of the Iron Age frequently contain metal items (*e.g.* brooches, bracelets and knives, of copper-alloy, iron and silver) in varying heat-altered states (Northover and Montague 1997; Fitzpatrick 1997, plate 22). Romano-British burials contain a similar variety of items but with a wider range of types (including buckles, necklaces and hobnails) and materials (*e.g.* glass, semi-precious stones and worked bone). In general, the items seen throughout these periods are similar to those seen in contemporaneous inhumation graves.

Cremations of the early Anglo-Saxon period, with its rich array of metal brooches and glass necklaces in the female graves and items (*e.g.* combs, playing pieces, bag rings) of worked bone/ivory (which do not always survive in inhumation graves where the human bone may also be lost, most often due to high soil acidity), also bear close similarities to the inhumation burials, but there are striking differences. There were apparently no 'weapon cremations' in the way there were 'weapon burials'. Were the males in the major cremating areas of Anglo-Saxon England, if one is to judge from their pyre/graves goods, more interested in maintaining their personal appearance (with shears, razors, tweezers, combs and toilet sets; McKinley 1994a, 89–90) than brandishing weapons, or did their ethnic identity/social structures/lifestyle negate the need for the latter? (*e.g.* as discussed by Carver for later barrow burials; 2003, 135). Weapons were sometimes placed on pyres (Brøndsted 1960, 303; Gräslund 1994, 21). Tacitus, in his *Germania*, describes how the deceased's arms and sometimes his horse were placed on the pyre (Chapter 27, para.1). Beowulf was cremated on a mound hung about with '…shining mail-coats and shields

of war and helmets …' (Lines 3140–2); his armour was there but not physically on the pyre. Physical transformation of these large metal items would be difficult (see above; Gräslund 1994, 22) and none – sword, shield boss or helmet – would fit into one of the urned burials characteristic of the rite within the English northern and Anglian regions. If the presence of the goods was required at the time of transformation to ensure their passage into the next world with the deceased, it may not have been necessary to include them in the burial; some large inorganic items may have been disposed of elsewhere or destroyed by melting the metal down, possibly even for re-use.

Evidence for extrinsic pyre goods such as containers, food offerings, other personal possessions (see below for animal remains) in British cremations is most apparent in the Romano-British period, where fragments of bone veneers, believed to be attached to funeral biers or caskets, have been recovered in large quantities from some cemeteries (*e.g.* Cool 2004, 274–282, figs. 4.108, 4.166 and 4.215). Fragments of glass vessel have also been found in Iron Age (Fitzpatrick 1997) and Romano-British burials (Cool 2004, 365–366), while evidence of burning to some Anglo-Saxon pot fragments recovered from burials indicates they were placed on the pyre (McKinley 1994a, 89).

Cremated animal bone has been recovered from burials of all periods in the British Isles with varying frequency, quantity and range of species (Table 5.1). In most periods the quantities are small (a few grams), the species limited and the remains generally represented are joints of meat (Bond 1994; 1996; McKinley *et al.* 1997; Bond and Worley 2004); food for the dead to sustain them in their journey to or within the afterworld. The inclusion of 'utility' animals or 'pets' on the pyre is also indicated in written sources from Homer to Ibn Fadlan (see above), but not until the Romano-British period in Britain do we have supportive archaeological evidence. The small bird bones recovered from some of the burials in the East London cemeteries may have been pet birds or food (Barber and Bowsher 2000, 72–73). The horse and dog bones commonly recovered from Anglo-Saxon burials (Bond 1994, 123–126 and 132–134; 1996; McKinley 1994a, 92–100), and recently from the late Romano-British cemetery at Brougham, Cumbria (Bond and Worley 2004, 325–326; McKinley 2004a, 332) are less ambiguous (often in large quantities of several 100 grams and elements indicative of whole animals); utility, pet or both, these species are amongst those with which humans can have close relationships and affinities (Bond and Worley, this volume). The Anglo-Saxon burials also contain wild species not seen in other periods, including bear and raptor claws, fox, deer and beaver. Some of these animals may be linked to hunting for food, but others are more ambiguous, apparently carrying amuletic qualities (Bond 1994; 1996; McKinley 1994a, 97; Bond and Worley, this volume).

Period	Frequency (variations between cemeteries)	Quantities	No. species	Common species
Neolithic	c. 4%	few grams	single	sheep/sheep/size
Bronze Age	c. 16%	few grams	single	immature pig/sheep and bird
Iron Age	c. 22%	few grams	1–2	domestic fowl and pig (often immature)
Romano-British	c. 10–50%	few grams	1–2	pig/sheep (often immature) and bird
Anglo-Saxon	c. 23–44%	often several 100g	1–5	horses, sheep, cattle, pig

Table 5.1. Frequency and range of animal species commonly observed in British cremation burials (from a multi-period sample of c.5000 *burials from* c. *200 sites examined by the writer).*

Pyre construction appears to have remained relatively consistent throughout time (Holck 1986, fig. 2; McKinley 1994a, 80–83; 1997a figs. 1 and 2, 132–144). The optimum form varied only in volume, depending on the size and status of the individual and the amount of goods to be burnt with the deceased. The funeral pyres depicted on Roman *sestertii* (Toynbee 1971, fig 15–16, 60–61) show massive four or five tiered structures for the cremation of emperors while amongst the Rus '...if the dead man is poor they make a little ship, put him in it, and burn it ...' (Brøndsted 1960, 301). The wood used for fuel generally comprised what was most effectively to hand; in England, oak, hazel, ash, *Pomoidaea* and *Prunus* spp. are the most common species recovered (*e.g.* Murphy 1994; Gale 1997 81–83; Campbell 2004, 267–271). In Scotland, pine is common in pyre debris and peat also appears to have been used in the north and west. The choice of fuel may have been influenced by the age and sex of the deceased (Tacitus, *Germania*, Chapter 17, para.1, Campbell 2004, 270; Cool 2004, 441), but this may be due to practical considerations – those undertaking the cremation understanding the strengths of different fuels – rather than anything symbolic (*ibid.*; Holck 1986, table 6). Other forms of symbolism related to the individual (*e.g.* status, achievements) or attitudes to death may have influenced some fuels used in the pyre (Kreuz 2000, 47–50).

Cremation is effected by interaction between three basic requirements: sufficient temperature to ensure the body will burn; sufficient time for the body tissues to be oxidised; and sufficient oxygen supply (McKinley 1994a, 72–81; 2000a). The complete skeleton, the majority in a recognisable form irrespective of the age of the individual, survives even full oxidation, albeit in a heat-altered state (McKinley 1994a, 72–81). Full oxidation of the organic components of the body is largely a modern Western health and safely requirement; if it is the 'magic' of transformation that is required rather than 'sanitary disposal', then full oxidation of the organic components of the body is not necessarily a prerequisite of the rite and is not viewed as such in some contemporary cultures

(Barber 1990, 381–3; Perrin 1998). Although most British archaeological cremation burials appear to contain well oxidised remains (predominantly white in colour; Holden *et al.* 1985a; 1985b), there are commonly minor and occasional major variations demonstrating incomplete oxidation (McKinley 1994a, 85; 2004b, 294; 2000b, 39). Charred soft tissues, indicative of incomplete combustion, have occasionally been recovered from burials (McKinley 1994a, 83–4; 2000c, 269). There are rare cases of partial Romano-British cremations (*e.g.* McKinley 1991; 2000b, 39) from urban cemeteries (where cremations are more likely to have been undertaken by professional *ustores* than members of the deceased's family/friends) in which curtailment of the process is indicated. The burial of these half charred bodies – supposedly undesirable since it was believed to affect the deceased's ability to enter the underworld (Noy 2005) – suggests that full oxidation was perhaps no great matter, at least in the provinces, and/or that contrary to the Roman tradition of relatives collecting the remains for burial (Toynbee 1971, 50), none were on hand in these instances to see the deed committed. Inevitably, the poor, unable to afford sufficient fuel, appear to have been less well cremated than the better-off (Morris 1992, 43); a problem still experienced in contemporary cultures (Barber 1990, 380).

In contrast to the 'hidden' transformation which occurs on decomposition of inhumation burials, the 'immediate' transformation effected by cremation is witnessed and leaves material evidence of its occurrence. Undertaking a cremation in the dark, however, would undoubtedly have added to the spectacle and perhaps increased the magic of the transformation. Written evidence for the timing of cremations presents a varied picture and although some were apparently proscribed, the reasons are not clear. Patroclus' pyre was constructed in the afternoon and lit towards sunset, continuing to burn through the night (*Iliad* Book 23, Lines 162 and 212–218). Roman funerals in the years BC were normally undertaken at night, a practice continued for children and the poor in the years AD, while others' pyres were lit in the morning (Toynbee

1971, 46; Noy 2005). The cremation of the Rus chieftain appears to have been undertaken in the afternoon (Brøndsted 1960, 304). Cremation takes several hours to complete (Barber 1990, 379; McKinley 1994a, 80–81; 1997a, 134; Downes 1999, 23; Noy 2005). Consequently, since the recovery of the cremated bone is better effected in the daylight, where a pyre was lit late in the day, collection of the remains is likely to have been undertaken the day, or several days, after cremation (*Iliad*, Book 23, Lines 227–431; McKinley 1994a, 80).

Both the Rus funeral and that of Patroclus included human sacrifices, the former of a slave girl 'to accompany her master' and the latter of ten Trojan prisoners (Brøndsted 1960, 301; *Iliad* Book 23, Lines 180–2). However, most multiple cremations – *c*.5% of cremation burials include the remains of two individuals and a small proportion may contain more (from a sample of *c*. 4000 multi-period burials from *c*.200 sites) – were probably of individuals who had been close in life and died within a short time of each other. They most commonly include a subadult (13–18yr) or adult, of either sex, with an immature (<18yr) individual, and in most instances the evidence implies dual cremation on a single pyre (McKinley 1994a, 100–102; 1997a, 142). However, there is also archaeological and written evidence indicative of the remains from two or more cremations being added to an urn prior to burial (McKinley 2000d, 116). The *Iliad* refers to both the mingling and addition of bones from three separate cremations in one urn (Book 24, Lines 73–76). Roman sources indicate that soldiers killed in battle may have been cremated communally (Toynbee 1971, 55) and the poor subjected to 'mass cremation' (Morris 1992, 42), otherwise dual cremation occurred only if the individuals were closely connected (Noy 2005). In most archaeological cases the data imply a parent and child cremated together, occasionally possibly siblings, though some burials may have included comrades or close friends as well as relatives. There are some records of infants being buried with unrelated adults in inhumation cemeteries from the early Anglo-Saxon period (Stoodley 2003, 115); in small prehistoric communities using the same cemeteries, however, most individuals will probably at least have been known to each other.

There are numerous references to pyres being 'put out', 'drenched' or quenched with wine or water at the end of cremation (*Iliad* Book 23, Lines 239–240; Toynbee 1971, 50 and 63; Perrin 1998; Downes 1999, 23; Noy 2005). In addition to symbolically marking the end of the cremation this would serve to cool the bone on/in the upper levels so they could be collected. Due to the usual position of the body on top of the pyre and the way in which the pyre collapses the (generally white) cremated bone is easily visible at the end of cremation, and even individual sets of bones (animal or human) are easily distinguished (McKinley 1994a, 79–80; 1997a, 134–5; 2000b, 39). That such differences between remains were recognisable and acted upon is suggested by a passage in the *Iliad* (Book 23,

Lines 141–144) where Achilles instructs '... we must collect my lord Patroclus' bones, being careful to distinguish them, though that will not be difficult, as he lay in the centre of the pyre, separate from the rest, who were burnt on the verge of it, horses and men together ...'. The apparent deliberate exclusion here of the pyre goods is in contrast with what is commonly observed in cremation burials from the British Isles (see above) and may suggest an individual or cultural variation, but also indicates that the goods had served their purpose on the pyre and were not required for burial.

Collection of the bone, as with lighting of the pyre, generally seems to have been undertaken by relatives or friends of the deceased, even in Roman towns where cremation was undertaken by professionals (Toynbee 1971, 50; McKinley 1994a, 80; Downes 1999, 23; Noy 2005). Bone was chiefly recovered by hand, some collection may have included raking and winnowing, or the use of tongs and shovels (Alcock 1980, 61; McKinley 1997a, 136; 1997b, 68; 2004b, 300–301). The task of recovering all the bone individually by hand would have been relatively time-consuming, estimated at up to four person-hours (McKinley 1997b, 68); it is clear, however, that rarely, if ever, were the entire cremated remains collected for burial as a standard characteristic of the rite.

The secondary rite – burial

The quantity of bone recovered from burials varies greatly, with a weight range of 57–3000g recorded from *c*.5000 British multi-period burials; some of the lower weights (<100g) may represent remains within cenotaphs rather than 'burials' (McKinley 1997b, 71–72; 2000b, 42–43; 2003, 13–15; 2004b, 306–7). Intrinsic factors affecting the weights of bone recovered ought to include the age of the individual (immature as opposed to adult), but even this is not consistent; the sex of the individual is of no significance. Extrinsic factors related to bone survival include levels of disturbance, soil type and mode of burial (*e.g.* unurned or urned and inclusions/exclusion of pyre debris in the grave fill; McKinley 1993; 1997b, 69). On average *c*.40–60% of the expected bone weight is recovered from adult burials (McKinley 1993; 1994b), and the four main areas of the body (skull, axial skeleton, upper and lower limbs) are generally represented to some degree. Currently, there are few clear patterns evident in the variable weights recovered other than the consistently high weights from primary burials associated with Bronze Age barrows (McKinley 1997a, 142). The variations may reflect the individuals' status translated into the length of time people were willing to expend on collecting bone for burial; a wealthy, popular or much admired individual may warrant a greater expenditure of time than someone who was disliked or who had no living relatives.

Most of the rest of the bone remained amongst the pyre debris, which has been found in a variety of deposit and feature types (McKinley 1997a, 137–139; 2000b, 41–42; Polfer 1993; 2000). There is evidence to suggest that some of the bone may also have been disposed of in other ways (McKinley 1997a, 138); some may have been distributed to relatives or friends (Hiatt 1969, 105), some or most may have been dispatched for burial elsewhere (Oestigaard 1999; McKinley 2004b, 306–7); some scattered on the land/water as in some contemporary cultures (Metcalf and Huntington 1991, 102; Perrin 1998; Downes 1999, 23).

The inclusion of pyre debris in many graves suggests not only the proximity of the pyre site, but that burial occurred shortly after cremation; bone for burial may be curated and transported, but it is unlikely that pyre debris would be too. However, cremated bone placed in ceramic vessels is particularly storable and portable. Some of the Anglian Anglo-Saxon cemeteries served wide areas with cremation probably being undertaken at the deceased's settlement and the urns carried to the cemetery for burial (McKinley 1994a, 70–71). The transportation of cremated remains in urns from the place of death to the deceased's birthplace has been discussed by Oestigaard (1999) for multi-period Scandinavian material. There is evidence that members of the Roman military who died away from home were cremated where they died and their remains transported back for burial (Oestigaard 1999; McKinley 2004a, 306–8; Noy 2005). The Indian Kol hang the urn containing the deceased's bones from a post at his/her house prior to burial, which takes place in the village of his/her ancestors (van Gennep 1977, 152).

Pyre goods were often included in the burial but there is evidence to suggest deliberate exclusion of certain items within some periods (Polfer 1993; 2000). In the British Isles, grave goods (included only at the time of burial) are mostly found in burials of Iron Age and Roman-British date, and to a lesser extent in the Anglo-Saxon period. The most common forms of grave goods recovered from Iron Age and Romano-British graves include unburnt animal remains (Barber and Bowsher 2000, 71–76; Bond and Worely 2004) and ceramic vessels, though a wide range of materials have been recorded in Britain and elsewhere (Toynbee 1971, 52–3). The predominant inclusion of dining and serving vessels may be linked with the practice of relatives eating funerary meals at the tombs (Toynbee 1971, 51), although there is relatively little evidence for libation holes or pipes from graves in Britain (Toynbee 1971, 52, plate 14; Crummy 1993, 265–6). The common recovery of pig remains amongst both pyre and grave good from Romano-British graves may be related to the need to sacrifice one of these animals at Roman gravesides to make the grave legal (Toynbee 1971, 50).

Concluding remarks

There is no single answer as to why some groups of people elected to cremate their dead. Beliefs clearly varied/vary temporally and geographically, but the speedy trans-formation effected by burning the body – freeing the spirit to enter the 'otherworld' or another body (reincarnation), or for reasons of hygiene – is a recurrent theme throughout much of the use of the rite.

Homer's Hades was populated by disembodied souls and cremation was required to free the spirit '... once the life-force has departed from our white bones, all is consumed by the fierce heat of the blazing fire, and the soul slips away like a dream ...' (*Odyssey* Book XI, Lines 221–2). The Romans apparently had a ritual-free attitude to cremation, seeing it as an excuse to put on a good show whilst rendering inert a corpse which would otherwise putrefy and could potentially be subjected to desecration and, in the process, providing a more convenient 'package' for final disposal (Noy 2005). The Romans believed the soul left the body with the final breath (Toynbee 1971, 43). Would cremation of the corpse stop it returning, as is believed in modern European cultures? (Barber 1990, 385–7). In *Beowulf* '...Heaven swallowed the smoke ...' (Line 3154) and presumably the soul of the deceased with it. Perhaps the best known and most expressive view comes from the 10th century Rus observer at his chieftains' cremation: '...You ...are foolish ...because you throw those you love and honour to the ground where the earth and the maggots and fields devour them, whereas we...burn them up quickly and they go to Paradise that very moment ...' (Brøndsted 1960, 304). Looking at contemporaneous evidence from Europe, Barber (1999, 385–387) found cremation typically used where the corpse was seen as 'dangerous', fire being used to ward-off evil spirits and rendering the corpse inert – emphasising the power of rapid visible transformation. Contemporary Eastern cultures view fire as a purifying element (Downes 1999, 28), cremation freeing the spirit (*ibid.* 23).

The majority of archaeological cremation burials are, characteristically, 'token' – only the size of the token varies. This exemplifies the secondary nature of the burial within the overall rite; but why bother to 'bury' anything? Obviously, burial may not always have occurred, and it would be difficult to recognise deliberately scattered cremated bone if it survived at all. Similarly, bone deposited in rivers, lakes or the sea would rarely figure in the archaeological record.

Returning material to the earth and creating a 'place' in which the dead may be seen to rest helps create a sense of 'closure' and is a well understood territorial statement (*e.g.* Bradley 1990, 131). There may also be links with the 'earth' and the idea of the 'underworld', though this concept is not common to all belief systems and graves were not always earth-cut (*e.g.* Roman *columbaria*, though very few such burial places have been found in Britain). Burial was important to the Romans since other modes of deposition were considered deliberate desecration (Noy 2005); yet often only a small proportion of the cremated bone was included in the burial, the rest being dumped with the other pyre debris. Are we seeing a difference between Rome and the provinces, or between written 'theory' and 'practice', or was the burial really just 'symbolic'? Why bury pyre debris? Was this merely a 'cleaning-up' process as is suggested by the surface deposits in some Romano-British cemeteries (Barber and Bowsher 2000, 63–65), or part of the 'closure' suggested by the secondary part of the rite.

The inclusion of grave goods in cremation graves from the late prehistoric period onwards suggests the soul may have been viewed as multifaceted (Gräslund 1994, 18). Why provide goods for the deceased at the time of burial if the soul has already departed? (*ibid.* 19). It may be at this stage that the items are not necessarily related to the dead individual but with the living and their interaction with the 'place' in which the dead are seen to rest.

The 'wealth' and 'cost' of the mortuary rite of cremation in archaeological contexts needs to be measured in more than the material remains contained within the burial, including the time and effort involved in its undertaking. Though not easily accessible or comprehensible, data pertaining to this broader view has the potential to provide a wider understanding of the rite.

Acknowledgements

Thanks to Stephen Morgan for his Latin translations and to Michael Heaton and annonymous referees for their comments on the text.

References

Alcock, J. P. (1980) Classical religious beliefs and burial practice in Roman Britain. *Archaeological Journal* 137, 50–85.

Anon. (1973) *Beowulf.* Translated by M. Alexander. Harmondsworth, Penguin.

Barber, B. and Bowsher, D. (2000) *The Eastern Cemetery of Roman London.* London, Museum of London Archaeological Services Monograph 5.

Barber, P. T. (1990) Cremation. *The Journal of Indo-European Studies* 18 (3–4), 379–88.

Bond, J. M. (1994) The cremated animal bone. In J. I. McKinley *The Anglo-Saxon cemetery at Spong Hill, North Elmham Part VIII: The Cremations.* East Dereham, Norfolk, East Anglian Archaeology No. 69, 121–135.

Bond, J. M. (1996) Burnt offerings: animal bone in Anglo-Saxon cremations. *World Archaeology* 28 (1), 76–88.

Bond, J. and Worley, F. (2004) The animal bone. In H. Cool *The Roman Cemetery at Brougham, Cumbria.* Britannia Monograph Series 21, 311–331.

Bradley, R. (1990) *The Passage of Arms.* Cambridge, Cambridge University Press.

Bröndsted, J. (1960) *The Vikings.* Harmondsworth, Penguin.

Campbell, G. (2004) Charcoal and other charred plant remains. In H. Cool *The Roman Cemetery at Brougham, Cumbria.* London, Britannia Monograph Series 21, 267–271.

Carver, M. (2003) Reflections on the meaning of Anglo-Saxon barrows. In S. Lucy and A. Reynolds (eds.) *Burial in Early Medieval England and Wales.* Society for Medieval Archaeology Monograph 17, 132–143.

Cool, H. (2004) *The Roman Cemetery at Brougham, Cumbria.* London,

Britannia Monograph Series 21.

Crummy, P. (1993) The cemeteries of Roman Colchester. In N. Crummy, P. Crummy and C. Crossan *Colchester Archaeological Report 9: Excavations of Roman and Later Cemeteries, Churches and Monastic Sites in Colchester, 1971–88,* 257–275. Colchester, Colchester Archaeological Trust Ltd.

Down, A. and Welch, M. (1990) *Chichester Excavations 7, Apple Down and the Mardens.* Chichester, Chichester District Council.

Downes, J. (1999) Cremation: a spectacle and a journey. In J. Downes and T. Pollard (eds.) *The Loved Body's Corruption,* 19–29. Glasgow, Cruithne Press.

Evison, V. (1988) *An Anglo-Saxon Cemetery at Alton, Hampshire.* Hampshire Field Club Monograph 4.

Fitzpatrick. A. P. (1997) *Archaeological Excavations on the Route of the A27 Westhampnett Bypass, West Sussex, 1992 Volume 2.* Salisbury, Wessex Archaeology Report No. 12.

Gale, R. (1997) Charcoal. In A. P. Fitzpatrick *Archaeological Excavations on the Route of the A27 Westhampnett Bypass, West Sussex, 1992 Vol 2.* Salisbury, Wessex Archaeology Report No. 12, 77–82.

Gräslund, B. (1994) Prehistoric soul beliefs in Northern Europe. *Proceedings of the Prehistoric Society* 60, 15–26.

Hiatt, B. (1969) Cremation in Aboriginal Australia. *Mankind* 7(2), 104–120.

Holden, J. L., Phakley, P. P. and Clement, J. G. (1995a) Scanning electron microscope observations of incinerated human femoral bone: a case study. *Forensic Science International* 74, 17–28.

Holden, J. L., Phakley, P. P. and Clement, J.G. (1995b) Scanning electron microscope observations of heat-treated human bone. *Forensic Science International* 74, 29–45.

Holck, P. (1986) *Cremated Bones. A Medical-Anthropological Study of an Archaeological Material on Cremation Burials.* Anthropologiske skrifter 1 Anatomisk institutt. Oslo, University of Oslo.

Homer (1950) *The Iliad.* Translated by E. V. Rieu. Harmondsworth, Penguin.

Homer (1946) *The Odyssey.* Translated by E. V. Rieu. Harmondsworth, Penguin.

Kreuz, A. (2000) Functional and conceptual archaeobotanical data from Roman cremations. In M. Millett, J. Pearce, and M. Struck (eds.) *Burial, Society and Context in the Roman World,* 45–51. Oxford, Oxbow Books.

Leonowens, A. (1988) *The English Governess at the Siamese Court* Oxford, Oxford University Press.

Lucy, S. (2000) *The Anglo-Saxon Way of Death; Burial Rites in Early England.* Stroud, Sutton.

Lucy, S. and Reynolds, A. (2003) 'Burial in Early Medieval England and Wales: past, present and future' in S. Lucy and A. Reynolds (eds.) *Burial in Early Medieval England and Wales* Society for Medieval Archaeology Monograph 17, 1–23.

McKinley, J. I. (1989) Spong Hill. Anglo-Saxon cremation cemetery. In C. A. Roberts, F. Lee and J. Bintliff (eds.) *Burial Archaeology Current Research, Methods and Developments.* Oxford, British Archaeological Reports (British Series) 211, 241–248.

McKinley, J. I. (unpublished) Cremated Bone from the Area 15 cemetery, Baldock, Hertfordshire. (Report for G. Burliegh, Letchworth Museum).

McKinley, J. I. (1993) Bone fragment size and weights of bone from modern British cremations and its implications for the interpretation of archaeological cremations. *International Journal of Osteoarchaeology* 3, 283–287.

McKinley, J. I. (1994a) *Spong Hill Part VIII: The Cremations.* East Dereham, Norfolk, East Anglian Archaeology 69.

McKinley, J. I. (1994b) Bone fragment size in British cremation burials and its implications for pyre technology and ritual. *Journal of Archaeological Science* 21, 339–342.

McKinley, J. I. (1997a) Bronze Age 'barrows' and funerary rites and rituals of cremation. *Proceedings of the Prehistoric Society* 63, 129–145.

McKinley, J. I. (1997b) The cremated human bone from burial and cremation-related contexts. In A. P. Fitzpatrick *Archaeological Excavations on the Route of the A27 Westhampnett Bypass, West Sussex, 1992 Volume 2*. Salisbury, Wessex Archaeology Report No. 12, 55–73.

McKinley, J. I. (2000a) The analysis of cremated bone. In M. Cox and S. Mays (eds.) *Human Osteology*, 403–421. London, Greenwich Medical Media.

McKinley, J. I. (2000b) Phoenix rising; aspects of cremation in Roman Britain. In M. Millett, J. Pearce and M. Struck (eds.) *Burial, Society and Context in the Roman World*, 38–44. Oxford, Oxbow Books.

McKinley, J. I. (2000c) Cremation burials. In B. Barber and D. Bowsher *The Eastern Cemetery of Roman London*. London, Museum of London Archaeological Services Monograph 5, 264–277.

McKinley, J. I. (2000d) Human bone and funerary deposits. In K.E. Walker and D. E. Farwell *Twyford Down, Hampshire Archaeological Investigations on the M3 Motorway from Bar End to Compton 1990–93*. Hampshire Field Club Monograph 9, 85–119.

McKinley. J. I. (2003) The Early Saxon cemetery at Park Lane, Croydon. *Surrey Archaeological Collections* 90, 1–116.

McKinley, J. I. (2004a) Aspects of the cremation ritual as evidenced by the animal bones. In H. Cool *The Roman Cemetery at Brougham, Cumbria*. London, Britannia Monograph Series 21, 331–2.

McKinley, J. I. (2004b) The human remains and aspects of pyre technology and cremation rituals. In H. Cool *The Roman Cemetery at Brougham, Cumbria*. London, Britannia Monograph Series 21, 283–309.

McKinley, J. I. (2004) Archaeological investigations at The Bostle, Bronze Age and Anglo-Saxon barrow cemeteries, Balsdean, East Sussex: 1997. *Sussex Archaeological Collections*, 142, 25–44.

McKinley, J. I., Smith, P. and Fitzpatrick, A. P. (1997) Cremated animal bone from burials and other cremation-related contexts. In A. P. Fitzpatrick *Archaeological Excavations on the Route of the A27 Westhampnett Bypass, West Sussex, 1992 Volume 2*. Salisbury, Wessex Archaeology Report No. 12, 253.

Metcalf, P. and Huntington, R. (1991) *Celebrations of Death*. (Second Edition) Cambridge, Cambridge University Press.

Morris, I. (1992) *Death-Ritual and Social Structure in Classical Antiquity*. Cambridge, Cambridge University Press.

Murphy, P. (1994) The carbonised plant remains from the cremations. In J. I. McKinley *Spong Hill Part VIII: The* Cremations. East Dereham, Norfolk, East Anglian Archaeology 69, microfiche.

Northover, P. and Montague, R. (1997) Heat-altered metal. In A. P. Fitzpatrick. *Archaeological Excavations on the Route of the A27 Westhampnett Bypass, West Sussex, 1992 Volume 2*. Salisbury, Wessex Archaeology Report No. 12, 90–91.

Noy, D. (2005) Romans. In D. Davies (ed.) *Encyclopaedia of Cremation*. Aldershot, Ashgate, Hampshire.

Oestigaard, T. (1999) Cremations as transformations: when the dual cultural hypothesis was cremated and carried away in urns. *European Journal of Archaeology* 2(3), 345–364.

Parker Pearson, M. (1999) *The Archaeology of Death and Burial*. Stroud, Sutton.

Perrin, J. (1998) 'Great Goddess Ganges' *The Daily Telegraph; Travel* 31.1.1998, 1–2

Polfer, M. (1993) 'La nécrople gallo-romaine de Septfontaines-Deckt (Grand-Duché de Luxembourg) et son ustrinum central: analyse comparative du matériel archéologique. In A. Ferdière (ed.) *Monde des Morts, Monde des Vivants en Gaule Rurale*, 173–176. Tours, Actes du Colloque AGER/ARCHEA.

Polfer, M. (2000) Reconstructing funerary rituals: the evidence of *ustrina* and related archaeological structures. In M. Millett, J. Pearce, and M. Struck (eds.) *Burial, Society and Context in the Roman World*, 30–37. Oxford, Oxbow Books.

Rieu, E.V. (1950) Introduction. *The Iliad*. Translated by E. V. Rieu. Harmondsworth, Penguin.

Stoodley, N. (2003) Multiple burials, multiple meanings? Interpreting the early Anglo-Saxon multiple interment. In S. Lucy and A. Reynolds (eds.) *Burial in Early Medieval England and Wales* Society for Medieval Archaeology Monograph 17, 103–121.

Swanton, M. (1975) *Anglo-Saxon Prose*. London, Dent.

Tacitus. *Germania*. 1975 edition, translated by H. Mattingly and S. A. Handford. London: Penguin.

Thompson, H. (1889) *Modern Cremation Its History and Practice*. London, Kegan Paul, Trench & Co.

Toynbee, J. M. C. (1971) *Death and Burial in the Roman World*. London, Johns Hopkins University Press.

van Gennep, A. (1977) *The Rites of Passage*. London, Routledge.

6.   Companions in Death: The Roles of Animals in Anglo-Saxon and Viking Cremation Rituals in Britain

Julie M. Bond and Fay L. Worley

Introduction

It has long been known that the Anglo-Saxon people interred in urns in southern and eastern England took animals or parts of animals onto the pyre with them. Previous writings on Anglo-Saxon cremations have assumed that the animal bones identified in the burials represent the remains of food offerings for the dead or funeral feasts which actually took place at the cremation site (Vierck 1971). This paper draws on the most comprehensive studies of the osteological material available and, with the benefit of new taphonomic research, aims to show that the animal remains represent a wide range of offering types and that some animals played more complex roles in the funerary ritual. Some animals may have been food offerings, but others may have been put on the pyre as skins, tokens or charms. Yet others can be demonstrated to be the remains of whole animals – cattle, sheep, horses and dogs. These were living animals chosen for some reason to go with the dead human to the pyre – to be companions in death.

This paper will attempt to look at the range of animal offerings from both the Anglo-Saxon and the Viking period in Britain, not only in terms of their final resting place in the grave, but also in the context of the cremation ritual which preceded it. Some animals may have been companion animals (*e.g.* horses, dogs), others indicators of wealth or status, whilst the burial context of a few remains suggests a possible totemic function. In order to investigate the role of animals in these rituals, it is necessary to employ an holistic approach and to assess the place of animals in the Early Medieval universe, using not just the bones from graves and settlements but other aspects of the culture.

Animals and the Anglo-Saxon and Viking world-view

Archaeozoologists rarely take art and artefacts into account when assessing a bone assemblage, yet the Germanic art which is found in North-west Europe from the fifth century AD strongly suggests (as the osteological remains cannot) that animals were central to the world-view of these societies (*e.g.* Leigh 1984). In Salin Style I and II, animals are seen both as recognisable forms and also transformed into complex interlace patterns. Sometimes human faces are visible in these designs, such as that incorporated into the leg of the bird of prey from the Sutton Hoo shield, where it forms part of a composite design along with a dragon's head (Care Evans 1994, Illus. 35). Men, either wearing animal skins or in transition between man and animal, are seen on objects such as the sixth-century dies from Torslunda, Sweden. Animals are everywhere; the helmet from mound 1 at Sutton Hoo had a face mask partly composed of a winged creature, whilst a dragon-like animal draped itself protectively along the helmet's crest. Faces of men and animals, side by side, decorated the drinking flasks, whilst horses ran around the edge of the shield boss. Amongst the other treasures from the mound, boars draped across the shoulder clasps, the purse was decorated with birds of prey and men entwined with pairs of beasts; snakes, birds and unidentifiable creatures were twisted together on the belt buckle, a stag sat aloft the whetstone sceptre and cattle heads topped the wrought iron standard (*ibid.*).

Archaeologists have linked the Germanic animal style both with exclusive 'warrior elites' (see *e.g.* Kristofferson 1995; Høilund Nielsen 1997; Price 2002; Hedeager 2003) and with shamanistic beliefs. The appearance of animal motifs on objects such as pottery suggests, however, that the ideas were not confined strictly to one part of society, and may have been much more widespread (Capelle 1987). Hedeager (2003, 133, 134) has expressed most succinctly the kind of mindset which might be associated with a shamanistic model of Anglo-Saxon society;

The animals originally laid down the order and design of human social existence and were ultimately responsible for its continuation (Ingold 1994, 11–12) … Animals are not just *like* people, they *are* people, and the boundary between man and beast is a cultural construction.

Animals in Anglo-Saxon and Viking cremations: the osteological evidence

Large cremation cemeteries of the pagan Anglo-Saxons are found mainly in Eastern England, and date from the early fifth to the mid seventh centuries AD or a little later. Very few of these cemeteries have been studied by archaeozoologists and yet most have produced some evidence of animal offerings. Once Christianity began to gain a hold, both the practice of cremation and of animal offerings disappeared in Britain, although in pagan Scandinavia the tradition continued certainly into the tenth century. Although occasional Viking Age cremations have been found in Britain, only one cremation cemetery is known: at Heath Wood, Ingleby, Derbyshire (Posnansky 1955, 1956; Richards *et al.* 1995; Richards *et al.* 2004).

There has been little specialist archaeozoological work on the animal bone in cremation cemeteries found in Britain. Apart from the work of Gejvall (1969, 1975), the authors of this paper (Bond 1993, 1994, 1996, Bond forthcoming; Bond and Worley 2004; Richards *et al.* 2004) and a few recent publications such as the eastern cemetery of Roman London (Barber and Bowsher 2000), most identifications have been by human osteologists in the course of their own investigations. The problems of identification of cremated animal bone are very great; aside from taphonomic considerations (which show that bones of different animals, and different elements of the same animal, survive to varying degrees and that all of these may be influenced by variable factors in the cremation pyre itself), the degree of fragmentation can affect the identifiability of the bone fragment. Fragmentation can be affected not only by initial cremation and by the size and type of animal cremated, but also by subsequent treatment of the bone during collection and burial, by conditions in the ground and by the means of excavation (Bond 1996; Worley forthcoming; references in McKinley and Bond 2001). In brief, studies have shown a bias in favour of the survival of more readily identifiable bone fragments of smaller mammals such as sheep over larger mammals such as horse and cattle, so the reliability of non-specialist identifications must be viewed with some caution. Some older site reports will undoubtedly have missed or misrecorded animal bone remains, and for this reason the authors are basing this paper mostly on data from their own work: the sites of Spong Hill, Norfolk, Sancton I, Humberside, Sutton Hoo mounds 5, 6 and 7, and Heath Wood, Ingleby (Bond 1993, 1994, 2005; Richards *et al.* 2004).

As more than one commentator has noted, although animals are present in inhumations of the Anglo-Saxon period in Britain, they do not appear in the same frequency as in the cremation burials (Filmer-Sankey and Pestell 2001, 231–2; Williams 2001). Moreover, sites such as Spong Hill and Sancton show a range of taxa and numbers of animals not duplicated in inhumations (Bond 1993, 1994). This suggests that cremations and inhumations were not simply alternative rites, dependent perhaps on availability of fuel or other considerations, but represented different attitudes to death and to the rituals necessary to guarantee a successful passage to the afterlife. The presence of animals in the funerary rite and during the transition from recognisable corpse to fleshless bone seems to have been more important to those who were cremated than to those who were inhumed.

That the animals in cremations were not a simple reflection of their place in everyday life may seem obvious but perhaps needs restating. It is illustrated by comparison of the frequency of domestic taxa from the cremation burials at Spong Hill and the settlement site of West Stow. The two sites are both in East Anglia and broadly comparable in date; the bone assemblage from the Spong Hill settlement is too small to be useful (Bond 1995). West Stow (Crabtree 1989) is one of the best assemblages of animal bone from a settlement of the period, whilst Spong Hill is the largest published animal bone assemblage from a cremation cemetery. There is very little correlation between the two data sets; at West Stow sheep/goat dominated the domestic food animals, with cattle and then pig as the least common animal. In the Spong Hill cremations sheep/goat were again the most common 'food' animal, but cattle were much more rare. Of the 'non-food' domesticates, horse and dog were quite rare at West Stow, a fact Crabtree commented on when comparing the settlement to Continental counterparts such as Feddersen-Wierde (Crabtree 1989, 13). In complete contrast, dogs were relatively common in the Spong Hill cemetery and horses were actually the most common animal, found in 23% of the cremations which contained animal bone (Bond 1994; McKinley 1994, 92).

The Anglo-Saxon and Viking cemeteries studied

Spong Hill had possibly 2384 burials in total; of these, 44% contained animal bone. Most of the burials were in pottery urns, with animal and human bone mixed together, whilst in the larger cremations occasionally there were two urns, one of which contained virtually all human bone and one virtually all animal; McKinley has termed these 'animal accessory vessels' (McKinley 1994, 93). The amount of animal bone in the burials varied greatly – some had over a kilogram, whilst in others just a few grams were present. The urns themselves show evidence for the importance of animals in Anglo-Saxon society, with animal stamp motifs and one, possibly unique, urn which has a hunting scene with deer and dogs incised around its shoulder (Bond 1994; Hills *et al.* 1994, tables 8–10; and Hills *et al.* 1987 fig. 73). The smaller cemetery at Sancton I in Humberside had approximately 300 recoverable cremations, of which 48% contained animal bone (Bond 1993). Both of these cemeteries had not only a high proportion of cremations containing animal bone, but there was a wide range of animals represented. The main domestic animals, horse, cattle, sheep or goat and pig, were the most common, but there were other domesticates – dogs, domestic fowl and goose, as well as a range of wild animals or animal parts – beaver, fox, red deer, roe deer, bear and hare.

The site of Sutton Hoo is also a pagan Anglo-Saxon cemetery but a rather different one. It is most famous for the excavation of the impressive ship in mound 1 in the late 1930s and again in 1965–70 and the treasures recovered from it (Bruce-Mitford 1975). This work included a report on some fragments of cremated human and animal bone found in two other burials, mounds 3 and 4 (Gejvall 1975). The site was again the subject of investigation from 1983 by Carver, whose excavations included mounds 5, 6, and 7, dating from the early seventh century AD; these excavations also recovered cremated animal bone (Carver 1998; Carver 2005; Bond 2005).

The Viking barrow cemetery in Heath Wood is located close to the village of Ingleby, in Derbyshire. The cemetery is located on high ground overlooking Repton, the site of a Viking Great Army encampment, used, according to the *Anglo-Saxon Chronicles*, over the winter AD 873–4 (trans. Swanton, 2000; Winchester Manuscript (A) 874 [873], Peterborough MS (E) 874 [873]). It has therefore been suggested that the cemetery may be the burial ground for dead from a section of that army. The cemetery consists of 59 mounds clustered into four groups and spread over approximately three hectares (Richards *et al.* 2004).

The animals represented

As might be expected, the majority of animals in these early Medieval cremations were domestic; potential food species such as cattle, sheep or goats and pigs (both meat-age and suckling pig), occasionally domestic fowl and goose, but also non-food animals such as horses and dogs. Wild animals are also represented in the cremations, but oddly, few of these seem likely to represent food offerings; two hare bones from Spong Hill might be from a meat offering, but beaver and fox seem unlikely to be food. Only the terminal phalanges (claws) of bear have ever been identified from cremations and, although both red and roe deer have been identified at Spong Hill and elsewhere, only unworked antler fragments have been found; there is no evidence for joints of venison. Other explanations must therefore be sought for the roles of these animals in the cremations. In order to try to understand these roles taphonomic information, butchery evidence, age at death and evidence of the age and sex of the associated human will be used.

It is, perhaps, simplest to start by examining the traditional explanation for animals in cremations, the idea that they represented food offerings. The commonest possible food animal at Spong Hill and Sancton (and the commonest animal overall in other cremation cemeteries) is the sheep (more correctly, sheep/goat, although no goat bones have been positively identified from cremations). At Spong Hill 170 burials out of 1019 with animal bone (16.7%) had some sheep bone in them. The ageing data suggests animals were killed at a range of ages with a majority in the 'prime meat' range of between one and three and a half years.

The sheep show the highest percentage of butchery marks of all the animals. Almost all are associated with dismemberment, suggesting the sheep went to the pyre either as joints or dismembered carcasses. There are many instances at both Spong Hill and Sancton I where sheep are represented by a single long bone or even just a few ribs; approximately one third of the 170 cremations containing sheep contained no other bone, suggesting that only a joint of meat was present, presumably a food offering. However, four other cremations from Spong Hill have a range of bone fragments from all parts of the skeleton, suggesting that a whole animal was present on the pyre. In two instances these whole sheep are with demonstrably 'richer' cremations. For example, individual 1488 was a mature adult female whose other goods included iron and copper alloy objects, glass beads, a comb and fragments of an ivory bag-ring, whilst two urns, 1725 and 1726, contained cremated remains of the same adult, unsexed, whose other goods included a horse and two dogs (McKinley 1994, table 2; Bond 1994, 130, 132 and microfiche). Similar evidence for whole sheep has been found from Mounds 6 and 7 at Sutton Hoo, again with multiple other animals (Bond 2005).

Cattle occurred in 80 cremations at Spong Hill. The majority of the animals were younger than three and a half years, as one might expect if they were killed for meat, with only three animals demonstrably older than this. There was little butchery on the cattle bones and what little there was suggested dismemberment. Cranial fragments were present in many contexts and this, together with the overall distribution of body parts, suggests that many of these records represent whole cattle carcasses. Again, whole animals seem to be associated with 'wealthier' burials; burial 1818/1838, the grave of a younger mature female, contained a horse, a cattle carcase, a whole or half sheep, an unidentified bird and a copper alloy object. Cremation 2672, a young/mature adult (unsexed) had, as well as a cattle carcase, a horse, sheep ribs, a glass vessel, amber, crystal, and another glass object. At least seven of the Spong Hill graves contained sufficient identifiable body parts to say with certainty that whole cattle carcasses were present, and these graves tended also to be ones with multiple animal offerings, including horses and a range of pyre goods. Often the animal bones were in an 'animal accessory' vessel (Bond 1994 and microfiche; McKinley 1994, table 2). At Sutton Hoo, the cremation in Mound 7 included, probably, a whole cattle carcase as well as a horse, probably a whole sheep, and a joint of pork (Bond 2005).

Pigs are a less common domestic animal at Spong Hill, present in just 8.5% of the cremations where animal bone was present. There were no identifiable instances of entire pig carcasses being cremated; indeed in many cases only a single bone or a very few identifiable bones were present. Although it could be argued that this is a result of taphonomic processes, it is in complete contrast to the data for sheep or cattle, suggesting a difference in use. Ageing data indicates that all the animals save one were under three years of age, the usual profile for killing pigs as meat. Five animals were neonates, perhaps 'suckling pigs' prepared whole as a delicacy; there was no correlation of these young animals with a particular human age or sex. Butchery was consistent with all the animals, save the neonates, being prepared as meat joints.

It would seem, therefore, that at least two different roles can be discerned for these domesticates; pigs always seem to have been present as 'food', either as joints of meat or young suckling pig. Sheep may also be present as joints of meat, but also sometimes as whole animals. Cattle mostly seem to have been present as whole animals; perhaps these whole sheep and cattle represent 'portable wealth' rather than food offerings.

There is another possible role for the whole cattle carcasses, if literary evidence is taken into account. Bede's *Ecclesiastical History of the English People* includes a letter said to have been sent by Pope Gregory in AD 601, in which he mentions that the English 'have a custom of sacrificing many oxen to demons' (I.30). It may be that cattle represented not only the dead person's wealth but also acted as a powerful propitiatory sacrifice, carried out as part of the cremation ritual.

When horses have been found in Anglo-Saxon *inhumations* they seem to have been associated with male burials with weapons and an inference has been drawn that these are 'warrior burials'. Among the most recently excavated of these burials are those of a man and horse from Sutton Hoo (O'Connor 1994), one from Laken-heath, a decapitated horse from the cemetery at West Heslerton (Powlesland *et al.* 1986, 163; though in this case there is no mention of an accompanying human) and a horse's head from a 20–30 year old animal, complete with bit and harness, found in a boat burial with sword, shield and spears at Snape (Filmer-Sankey and Pestell 2001, 102–111; Davis 2001, 231–2). Horses in cremations seem to be different; not only are they more common than in inhumation cemeteries (as are animals in general), but they do not seem to be associated exclusively with male weapon burials.

At Spong Hill, horse was by far the most common animal in the cremation graves; at least 227 individuals in 23% of the graves which contained animal bone. This is a high percentage of horses compared to most other cremation cemeteries in Britain, but comparable to Sancton I and to a cemetery at Elsham, Humberside (Richards 1987). Horse was found in Mounds 3 and 4 at

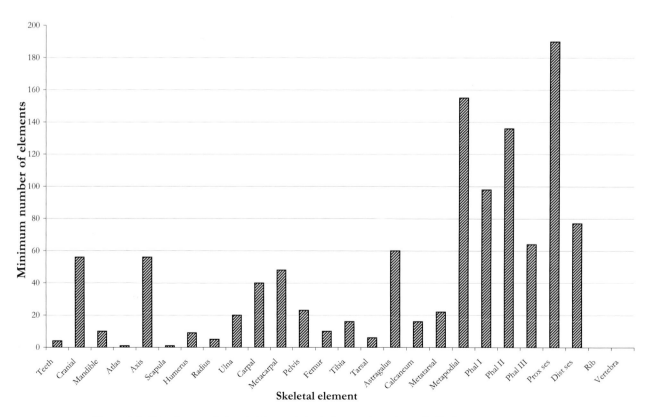

Figure 6.1. Distribution of identified horse skeletal elements from Spong Hill. Data from Bond 1994.

Sutton Hoo (Gejvall 1975) and was identified in Mounds 5 and 7, and probably 6, during the more recent excavations (Bond 2005). As argued elsewhere (Bond 1996) it is probable that horse (and cattle) bones are underrepresented in older studies because the bones of larger mammals tend to break up into small fragments, difficult to identify. It has also been suggested that the identified horse bones indicate that only head and hoof elements were present, suggesting either a ritual of 'head and hoof' burial, or that only skins were cremated. However taphonomic studies have shown that the smaller, denser elements of the head (*e.g.* occipital, mastoid, tooth root) and of the lower leg (*e.g.* distal sesamoids, carpals and tarsals, the articular surfaces of the phalanges) are among those most likely to survive cremation and burial. Moreover, personal experience has shown that they are also the most likely to be amenable to identification (Bond 1994, 121–2; Worley forthcoming).

Figure 6.1 shows that at Spong Hill, elements from all the major skeletal areas of horse were identified, though the proportions are skewed by the factors noted above. The number of individual cremations at Spong Hill containing elements from all parts of the body (together with a lack of butchery marks on the horse bones) also indicates that most, if not all, of the horses were whole animals. One animal from Sancton I does, however, show dramatic evidence of butchery; a fragment of a second

cervical vertebra (axis) of a horse had a massive chop mark, showing that part of the odontoid process had been severed by the blow separating the head of the horse from the body. This enormous blow, presumably from an axe or similarly heavy blade, must have come slightly from above whilst the horse was on the ground; other marks show that at least three previous attempts had been made. The similarity with the Snape horse head and the decapitated horse from Heslerton is striking; however the rest of the bone in this cremation (210) suggests that subsequently the whole horse was placed on the pyre. The burial also contained the right side of a young pig as well as ribs and thoracic vertebrae from a sheep.

The horses from the cremations at Spong Hill and Sancton I, unlike those seen in inhumation burials, do not seem to be exclusively associated with male humans. Table 6.1 shows details of the age and sex of the 174 human cremations which could be associated with horses. Of the 54 humans to whom a sex could definitely or probably be assigned, 31 (17.8%) were male and 23 (13.2%) were female. Though there seems to be a bias towards males, there is still a substantial proportion of these horses linked to female burials, and so a straightforward explanation such as the cremation of a warrior with his horse does not seem to be the whole answer.

At Spong Hill, the presence of pathological traits was noted on some horse metapodials. These exostoses have

Age & Sex	No. of cremations	%
Infant/juvenile (unsexed)	*1*	*0.6*
Juvenile (unsexed)	*4*	*2.3*
Young subadult (unsexed)	*3*	*1.7*
Young male	10	5.7
Young female	11	6.3
Young unsexed	*61*	*35.1*
Mature male	15	8.6
Mature female	10	5.7
Mature unsexed	*38*	*21.8*
Older male	6	3.4
Older female	2	1.1
Older unsexed	*13*	*7.5*
TOTAL	**174**	

Age class	No. of cremations	%
Infant/juvenile	1	0.6
Juvenile	4	2.3
Young subadult	3	1.7
Young adult	82	47.1
Mature adult	63	36.2
Older adult	21	12.1
TOTAL	**174**	

Sex	No. of cremations	%
All male	31	17.8
All female	23	13.2
All unsexed	120	69
TOTAL	**174**	

Table 6.1. Cremations with horses at Spong Hill, classified by i) age and sex, ii) age class only, iii) sex only; data from Bond 1994. Human age classes based on McKinley 1994, table 1:

Infant/juvenile; infant 0–4 yr, juvenile 5–12yr.
Juvenile; 5–12 yr.
Young subadult; 13–15 yr.
Young adult; 19–25 yr.
Mature adult; 26–40 yr.
Older adult; 40+ yr.

been suggested to be particularly common in draught animals; possibly the females at Spong Hill and Sancton had wagons or carriages in which to ride. Some of the Viking period horse burials at Birka have also been interpreted in this way; harness for draught animals have been found there, sometimes in double graves of a male and female human (Gräslund 1980, 43). Price (2002) has recently drawn attention to other Viking period wagon burials from Scandinavia, of which eleven are female and three of indeterminate sex, as well as a ninth-century cremation of a woman from Aska, Östergötland, which included a quantity of animal bone (unidentified) and harness for four horses. Price (2002) also notes a rune-stone from Gotland which, instead of showing a man riding into the next world, appears to show a woman driving a wagon there, accompanied by her dog and possibly her husband as passenger (Price 2002, 150–8, fig. 3.25). A Viking period female from Heath Wood, Derbyshire, was also cremated with a horse.

If these horses are not part of the trappings of a warrior, what else might they be? Certainly they represent a major investment in the cremation ritual. A horse will not be broken to riding or work until it is several years old; in 'wealth' terms this is an expensive item. Is it possible to see the sacrifice of horses in terms of a shamanistic cult? In an interesting paper, Williams (2001) has suggested that:

> the cremation of sacrificed beasts served to transform animals, and mingle or confuse their forms with those of people…the aim seems to have been to regard the animals either as integral parts of the deceased's new identity or as agents for the transformation of that identity… Their bones were retrieved, combined and buried in the same urns, almost as if the identity of the dead…incorporated elements of both human and animal. Furthermore, animal accessory vessels have been identified at both Spong Hill and Sancton… Here, horse is predominant but usually combined with other species (McKinley 1994, 93). It seems as if the analogy of person and animal is taken one step further in this case. Faunal remains are accorded the same respect as the human occupant of the grave and given their own cinerary urn.

Whilst a war-pony might seem an apt identity for a warrior's transformation into the next world, a cart-horse is a rather duller counterpart for his female consort. The question of the animal accessory vessels as somehow transforming the animals into 'human' equivalents, however, is an interesting one. Closer examination of the Spong Hill data shows that animal accessory vessels are only present when the cremation has been a large one, involving a horse and usually other animals such as a cow or sheep. A more prosaic explanation may be that such a large quantity of bone would not fit into a single urn – and indeed, sometimes the bone is not in a second urn, but simply placed in the grave pit. However, what the accessory vessels do show, and what Williams' paper highlights, is that it was important for *all* the bone, animal as well as human, to be collected as far as possible *and*

placed in the same grave. Where accessory vessels are present, it seems as if there was separation of human and animal bone (though some mingling inevitably occurred), and the fact that this was possible suggests that animals and humans may have been placed in separate positions on the pyre.

The human age groups with which horses are found also throws light on how the animals were viewed. It has been said (*e.g.* Williams 2001) that young adult males in particular are associated with animal remains. However, the evidence from the horses, the biggest group of animals at Spong Hill and West Stow, does not seem to bear this out; there is little sex-related difference in this age group (Table 6.1). What is apparent is that the vast majority of the horses are to be found with young adults (*c*.19–25 years old) whether male, female or with no attributed sex. Over 47% of the horses are found with this age group, compared to 36% associated with the 26–40 year age group. Even given a slight peak in mortality at this point in the cemetery as a whole, this seems significant. Moreover, four juveniles (*c*.5–12 years old) and one infant/juvenile (*c*.3–7 years old) were also cremated with horses. This suggests that the role of horses in this group's identity was not a simple personal identification of the warrior with (his) trusty mount. The horse might signify the social grouping to which the child belonged, as has been suggested for the 'weapon burials' (although in the weapon burials there is also a strong correlation with males; *e.g.* Härke 1992). Although there is undoubtedly the possibility that some of these horses may be seen almost as companions – animals with which the owner has strongly identified, and which may even be seen as the dead person's transport, shamanistic or otherwise symbolic, into the afterlife – we would suggest that they can also be viewed as signifiers of status or wealth.

It might be thought that dogs, even more than horses, were most likely to have been companions or personal possessions. Although well-bred and well-trained hunting or working dogs are (and presumably always were) themselves valuable, the nature of the dog/human relationship is such that it is often hard for successful transference of ownership to take place and so their value as commodities is lessened. Dogs are occasionally found in Anglo-Saxon inhumations (Wilson 1992, 100). Twenty-six deposits of dog bone were found at Spong Hill, and three at Sancton I; Spong Hill forms the largest collection of dog cremations in Britain. The Spong Hill dogs ranged in size from a large wolf-type animal to small terrier-sized ones, suggesting a variety of functions from working dogs to lap-dogs. Where sufficient evidence exists, it seems that these are whole animals rather than token body parts or specific bones. One cremation (1725/1726) of an unsexed adult at Spong Hill had two dogs of slightly different sizes, as well as a horse and a whole sheep. Examination of the age and sex of humans cremated with dogs at Spong Hill (Table 6.2) shows an interesting pattern. Once again, there is no real difference between male and female cremations, but over half of the animals were with young adults, with a spread through the other age classes. Could this pattern be seen as representing true 'companion' animals, working dogs or personal possessions, killed with their owners?

Wild animals in cremations

Analysis of the animals in cremations has mostly centred on the more numerous domestic taxa (*e.g.* Williams 2001), but there is another, more ambiguous class of animal remains found in cremations; wild animals, either whole bodies or animal parts. Oddly, these do not seem to represent food; for example, the authors know of no instance where the presence of a haunch of venison could be inferred. Some may be the remains of animal skins, but even these examples seem ambiguous. For example, three fox mandibles were found in cremations at Spong Hill, as well as another probable fox mandible and a fragment of probable fox atlas. One cremation from Sancton I had several bones of fox, suggesting a whole animal. Of the animals from Spong Hill, three were from the burials of young females, the other two with unsexed individuals. At Spong Hill there was also the cremation of an adult

female with the distal humerus (and possibly a radius fragment) of a beaver. It is hard to see all these animal parts as the remains of conventionally prepared skins or even, for the most part, as single bone elements used as amulets. Unworked antler from red and roe deer has also been found in cremations with no other identified body parts. It has been suggested that these antlers could have been used in shamanic practices (Wilson 1992, 136–7). There is no particular sex or age bias obvious in the Spong Hill examples; one was from a female adult cremation, the others could not be sexed. Other examples have been found in male cremations, such as that from Lackford, Suffolk (Lethbridge 1951).

The terminal phalanges of brown bear are recorded in cremations from all over Europe from the Iron Age onwards, and there are inhumations of both men and women with bearskins from the Scandinavian Iron Age (see *e.g.* Kühl 1984; Price 2002, 374). In Britain they have been recovered from just three cremation cemeteries; two cremations from Elsham Wold (Harman 1989), six at Spong Hill and two at Sancton I. No bones other than claws have been identified in cremations, and the usual interpretation is that they are the remains of skins, perhaps used as cloaks. Bear bones are extremely rare from this

Age & Sex of human	No. of cremations Spong Hill
Infant/juvenile (unsexed)	*1*
Juvenile (unsexed)	*2*
Young subadult (unsexed)	*1*
Young male	2
Young female	3*
Young unsexed	*6*
Mature male	1
Mature female	
Mature unsexed	*3*
Older male	1
Older female	
Older unsexed	*1*
TOTAL	**21***

*one is identified only as dog/fox

Age class of human	No. of cremations Spong Hill
Infant/juvenile	1
Juvenile	2
Young subadult	1
Young adult	11
Mature adult	4
Older adult	2
TOTAL	**21**

Sex	No. of cremations Spong Hill
All male	4
All female	3
All unsexed	14
TOTAL	**21**

Table 6.2. Cremations with dogs at Spong Hill; data from Bond 1994. Human age classes based on McKinley 1994, table 1:

Infant/juvenile; infant 0–4 yr, juvenile 5–12yr.
Juvenile; 5–12 yr.
Young subadult; 13–15 yr.
Young adult; 19–25 yr.
Mature adult; 26–40 yr.
Older adult; 40+ yr.

period in Britain; probably no more than a handful of other instances are known, all possibly from skins, and none have been found in inhumations. The archaeological and historical evidence suggests that bears were rare if not actually extinct in Britain by this time. These skins, therefore, are likely to be imports from the Continent and given the effort required to capture the animals and then transport the dressed skins, they are unlikely to have been common items and this is reflected in their rarity in the cemeteries.

One might assume that such prestigious items would be found in the richest of graves and perhaps with the wealthiest cremations, but this does not appear to be the case, although both the Sancton I cremations also contained a horse. At Spong Hill, all the bears were with young or mature adults; only one could be sexed, and that was a young/mature adult female. Two others were with young adults and two with mature adults. Only two occurred with horses. These burials were not conspicuously rich in grave goods. It seems odd that these prestige items are also conspicuously absent from the 'royal' cremations at Sutton Hoo (though this may perhaps be accounted for by the level of disturbance and the level of recovery in the earlier excavations). There is, however, an odd pairing with one of the other 'wild' animals; cremation MS202 at Sancton I contained not only a horse and the body of a fox, but also two bear claws. Cremation 2890 at Spong Hill, the burial of a young/mature adult female, contained both bear claws and a fox mandible. Given the rarity of both these animals, their occurrence

together looks significant.

Bears and bearskins have been strongly associated with ideas of shamanism in Viking and earlier society; the battle-frenzied *berserkir* of the sagas have been interpreted as either literally clad in bearskins, or merely bare-chested but with animal aspects to their strength and ferocity (see *e.g.* Price 2002, 366–74 for detailed discussion). If we are to interpret the bearskins in Anglo-Saxon cremations in this way, there is an obvious problem in that, as with Scandinavian inhumations, at least one has been found with a woman. However the other factors detailed above do suggest that a bearskin is somewhat out of the ordinary as a cremation offering, and shamanic practices are not confined to men. Bears have a special place in shamanic beliefs both in Europe and North America, and transformation between bear and human is a common theme. Bears are both hunters and hunted; they are omnivores with forward-facing eyes, able to walk on all fours, but also to stand upright. Skeletally, their bones and especially their paws bear many resemblances to the human skeleton. Their tracks are said to resemble those of a short, broad-footed man – albeit one with claws. The boundary between man and bear is perhaps not always an entirely clear one. We would suggest that all these 'wild' animals represent possible shamanistic elements in the cremations. Speculation on the exact symbolism of these offerings is probably fruitless, and the intent unknowable, but they are probably the strongest archaeozoological evidence we have that animals were central to these people's worldview.

Spong Hill (Anglo-Saxon)	Sancton I (Anglo-Saxon)	Sutton Hoo (Anglo-Saxon)	Heath Wood, Ingleby (Viking)
Domestic animals			
Horse	Horse	Horse	Horse
Cattle	Cattle	Cattle	Cattle
Sheep/goat	Sheep/goat	Sheep/goat	Sheep/goat
Pig	Pig	Pig	Pig
Dog	Dog	Dog	Dog
Domestic fowl	Domestic fowl	--------	--------
?Domestic goose	--------	--------	--------
Non-domestic animals			
Red deer (antler only)	Red deer (antler only)	Red deer (antler only)	--------
Roe deer (antler only)	--------	--------	--------
Bear (terminal phalanges only)	Bear (terminal phalanges only)	--------	--------
Beaver (humerus)	--------	--------	--------
Fox (mandible & other parts)	Fox (mandibles only)	--------	--------
Hare	--------	--------	--------
--------	Small bird	--------	--------
Fish	--------	--------	--------

Table 6.3. Comparison of the animals found in cremations in the four cemeteries studied. Data from Bond 1993, 1994, Bond 2005, Bond & Worley 2004.

Conclusion

From the Judeo-Christian cultural tradition, where the division between animal and human is fixed and definite, it can be difficult to envisage a world in which people and animals, and sometimes the objects made from those animals, form a continuum. Within the Anglo-Saxon cremations there are also animal tokens and amulets made from barely-altered animal parts – antler tines and burr rings, sheep calcanea, a pierced raptor claw found at Spong Hill – which may also have been considered to hold the essence of the animal. There is not space here to consider them, but they also need to be seen as part of the whole. Identification of cremated animal bone is not easy and a better understanding of the taphonomic processes involved have led us to believe that not only have all animal taxa been under-identified in many early studies, but that the larger mammals, specifically horses and cattle, have probably been grossly under-identified. Yet unless we look at the evidence as a whole and study the animals these people chose (or were given by others) to take with them into death, we are missing not just a small part of the cremation rite, a funeral feast for the mourners or food for the dead on their journey; we are ignoring the way in which they saw themselves. They went to the pyre with foodstuffs, with evidence of their wealth and social standing in herds or flocks, and also with the animals closest to them in life and those with which they somehow saw themselves linked – spirit helpers or alter egos, all companions in death.

References

Barber, B. and Bowsher D. (2000) *The Eastern Cemetery of Roman London. Excavations 1983–1990*. London, Museum of London Archaeology Service Monograph no. 4.

Bede (1968). *A History of the English Church and People*. Trans. Sherley-Price L. and R.E. Latham. London, Penguin Books

Bond, J. M. (1993) Cremated animal bone. In J. Timby, Sancton I Anglo-Saxon cemetery: excavations carried out between 1976 and 1980. *Archaeological Journal*, 150, 300–308.

Bond, J. M. (1994) The cremated animal bone. In J. McKinley *The Anglo-Saxon Cemetery at Spong Hill, North Elmham, part VII: the Cremations*. East Anglian Archaeology 69, Dereham, Norfolk Museums Service.

Bond, J. M. (1995) Animal bone from early Saxon sunken-featured buildings and pits. In R. Rickett (ed.) *Spong Hill part VII: the Iron Age, Roman and Early Saxon settlement*, 142–146. East Anglian Archaeology 73, Dereham, Norfolk Museums Service.

Bond, J. M. (1996) Burnt offerings: animal bone in Anglo-Saxon cremations. *World Archaeology* 28, 76–88.

Bond, J. M. 2005. The cremated animal bone. In M. O. H. Carver *Sutton Hoo, a seventh century princely burial ground and its context*. British Museum Press, London, 275–80.

Bond, J. M. and Worley, F. L. (2004) The animal bone. In H. E. M. Cool (ed.) *The Roman cemetery at Brougham, Cumbria*. Britannia Monograph Series 21, 311–332.

Bruce-Mitford, R. (1975) *The Sutton Hoo Ship Burial, volume 1. Excavations, Background, the Ship, Dating and Inventory*. London, British Museum Press.

Capelle, T. (1987) Animal stamps and animal figures on Anglo-Saxon and Anglian pottery. *Medieval archaeology* 31, 94–5.

Care Evans A. 1994. *The Sutton Hoo Ship Burial* (Revised edition). London, British Museum Press.

Carver, M. O. H. (1998) *Sutton Hoo: Burial Ground of Kings?* London, British Museum Press.

Carver, M. O. H. (2005) *Sutton Hoo, a seventh century princely burial ground and its context*. British Museum Press, London.

Crabtree, P. J. (1989) *West Stow, Suffolk: Early Anglo-Saxon Animal Husbandry*. East Anglian Archaeology 47, Dereham, Norfolk Museums Service.

Davis, S. (2001). The horse head from Grave 47. In W. Filmer-Sankey and T. Pestell (eds.), *Snape Anglo-Saxon Cemetery: Excavations and Surveys 1824–1992*. East Anglian Archaeology Report 95, 231–2. Ipswich, Suffolk County Council Archaeological Service.

Filmer-Sankey, W. and Pestell, T (eds.) (2001) *Snape Anglo-Saxon Cemetery: Excavations and Surveys 1824–1992*. East Anglian Archaeology Report 95. Ipswich, Suffolk County Council Archaeological Service.

Gejvall, N.G. (1969) Cremations. In D. Brothwell and E. Higgs (eds), *Science in Archaeology* (2nd edition), 468–479. London, Thames and Hudson.

Gejvall, N. G. (1975). Osteological investigations of cremated bone from a funeral urn from Sutton Hoo, 1938. In R. Bruce-Mitford (ed.), *The Sutton Hoo Ship Burial, Vvolume 1. Excavations, Background, the Ship, Dating and Inventory*. London, British Museum Publications.

Gräslund, A.-S. (1980) *Birka IV, the Burial Customs*. Kungl. Vitterhets Historie och Antikvitets Akademien, Stockholm.

Harman, M. (1989) Cremations. In A. G. Kinsley, *The Anglo-Saxon Cemetery at Millgate, Newark-on-Trent, Nottinghamshire*, 23–25. Nottingham Archaeological monographs 2, University of Nottingham.

Härke, H. (1992) Changing symbols in a changing society; the Anglo-Saxon weapon burial rite in the seventh century. In M. Carver (ed.) *The Age of Sutton Hoo*, 149–165. Woodbridge, Boydell Press,

Hedeager, L. (2003) Beyond mortality – Scandinavian animal style AD 400 – 1200. In J. Downes and A. Ritchie (eds.), *Sea change: Orkney and Northern Europe in the Later Iron Age AD 300–800*, 127–136. Balgavies, Angus, Pinkfoot Press.

Hills C., Penn K. and Rickett R. (1987). *The Anglo-Saxon cemetery at Spong Hill, North Elmham, Part IV: Catalogue of Cremations*. East Anglian Archaeology 34. Dereham, Norfolk Archaeological Unit/Norfolk Museums Service.

Hills, C., Penn, K. and Rickett R. (1994) *The Anglo-Saxon Cemetery at Spong Hill, North Elmham, Part V: Catalogue of Cremations*. East Anglian Archaeology 67, Dereham, Norfolk Museums Service.

Høilund Nielsen, K. (1997) Animal art and the weapon burial rite – a political badge? In C. Kjeld Jensen and K. Høilund Nielsen (eds.) *Burial and Society: the Chronological and Social Analysis of Archaeological Burial* Data, 129–148. Aarhus, Aarhus University Press.

Ingold, T. (1994) Introduction, In T. Ingold, (ed.) *What is an Animal?* One World Archaeology vol 1, 1–16. London, Routledge.

Kühl, I. (1984) Animal remains in cremations from the Bronze Age to the Viking period in Schleswig-Holstein, North Germany. In C. Grigson and J. Clutton-Brock (eds.) *Animals and Archaeology 4: Husbandry in Europe*, 209–219. British Archaeological Reports International Series 227, Oxford.

Kristofferson, S. (1995) Transformation in Migration Period animal art. *Norwegian Archaeological Review* 28(1), 1–17.

Leigh, D. (1984) Ambiguity in Anglo-Saxon Style I art. *Antiquaries Journal* 64, 34–42.

Lethbridge, T. C. (1951) *A Cemetery at Lackford, Suffolk: Report of the Excavation of a Cemetery of the Pagan Anglo-Saxon Period in 1947.* Cambridge Antiquarian Society Quarto Publications, New Series, 5.

McKinley J. I. (1994) *The Anglo-Saxon cemetery at Spong Hill, North Elmham, part VIII: the cremations.* East Anglian Archaeology 69, Dereham, Norfolk Museums Service,

McKinley, J. and Bond, J. M. (2001) Cremated bone. In D. Brothwell and A. M. Pollard (eds.) *Handbook of Archaeological Sciences*, 281–292. Chichester, Wiley and Sons Ltd.

O'Connor, T. P. (1994) A horse skeleton from Sutton Hoo, Suffolk, UK. *Archaeozoologia* VII/I, 29–37.

Posnansky, M. (1955) The pagan Danish barrow cemetery at Heath Wood, Ingleby: a preliminary excavation report. *Derbyshire Archaeological Journal* 75, 140–4.

Posnansky, M. (1956) The pagan Danish barrow cemetery at Heath Wood, Ingleby: 1955 excavations. *Derbyshire Archaeological Journal* 76, 40–56.

Powlesland, D., Haughton, C. and Hanson, J. (1986) Excavations at Heslerton, North Yorkshire 1978–82. *Archaeological Journal* 143, 53–173.

Price, N. S. (2002) *The Viking way. Religion and War in Late Iron Age Scandinavia.* Aun 31, Department of Archaeology and Ancient History, Uppsala, University of Uppsala.

Richards J.D. (1987) *The Significance of Form and Decoration of Anglo-Saxon Cremation Urns.* Oxford, British Archaeological Reports (British Series) 166

Richards, J., Beswick, P., Bond, J. M., Jecock, M., McKinley, J., Rowland, S. and Worley, F. (2004) Excavations at the Viking barrow cemetery at Heath Wood, Ingleby, Derbyshire. *The Antiquaries Journal* 84, 23–116.

Richards, J. D., Jecock, M., Richmond, L. and Tuck, C. (1995) The Viking barrow cemetery at Heath Wood, Ingleby, Derbyshire. *Medieval Archaeology* 34, 51–69.

Rieu, E. V. (1950) (trans.). *The Iliad.* Middlesex, Penguin Books Ltd.

Swanton M (trans.) (2000). *The Anglo-Saxon Chronicles* (Revised edition). Phoenix Press, London.

Vierck, H. (1971) Pferdegräber im Angelsächsischen England. *Berichten van de Rijksdienst voor het Oudheidkundig Bodemonderzoek* 20–1, 189–98.

Williams, H. (2001) An ideology of transformation: cremation rites and animal sacrifice in early Anglo-Saxon England. In N. Price (ed.) *The Archaeology of Shamanism,* 193–212. London, Routledge.

Wilson, D. (1992) *Anglo-Saxon Paganism.* London, Routledge.

Worley, F. L. (forthcoming) *Taken to the Grave. An Archaeozoological Approach Assessing the Role of Animals as Crematory Offerings in First Millennium AD Britain.* Unpublished PhD thesis, University of Bradford.

7.   La Tène Dietary Variation in Central Europe: A Stable Isotope Study of Human Skeletal Remains from Bohemia

Jonathan D. Le Huray, Holger Schutkowski and Michael P. Richards

Introduction

Carbon and nitrogen stable isotope analysis of bone collagen is now an almost routine method in the study of prehistoric diet. Unlike more traditional methods, such as the analysis of faunal and floral remains, the study of pottery residues and the identification of pollen finds, stable isotope analysis reflects direct consumption at the level of the individual. This means that as well as examining practical aspects of diet at the larger population and regional levels, similarities and differences in the diet of individuals within a single population and group can be examined. As a result, inferences can be made regarding some of the more social aspects of prehistoric diet by correlating observed dietary differences with other indicators of the social lives of prehistoric populations, such as the age and sex of an individual, the form and construction of a grave, and the type and quantity of grave goods. This paper outlines the underlying principles and method involved in isotopic dietary reconstruction and presents some of the data obtained from an ongoing study of dietary variation during the La Tène period in Bohemia and surrounding regions of central Europe. The potential of sulphur isotope analysis for migration studies is also highlighted and initial data from a series of La Tène period cemeteries in Bohemia, Moravia and Slovakia are presented.

What are atoms, ions and isotopes?

An atom is defined by the number of protons in its nucleus (see Fig 7.1); for example a carbon atom has six protons, while a nitrogen atom has seven and an oxygen atom has eight. The overall charge of an atom is determined by the balance of the positively charged protons in the atom's nucleus and the negatively charged electrons in the outer shells of the atom. A positively or negatively charged atom (ion) is produced by the addition or removal of electrons

through a process termed ionisation. The mass of an atom is determined by the sum of the protons and neutrons, each having a mass of one atomic mass unit (amu). The mass of an electron is negligible and does not contribute to the overall mass of an atom. Therefore, a carbon-12 atom, with an atomic mass of 12, has a nucleus containing six protons and six neutrons, with six electrons surrounding the nucleus of the atom. Variation in the number of neutrons in the nucleus of an atom produces atoms of the same element which differ by mass; these are known as isotopes. Isotopes can be either stable, such as ^{12}C, ^{13}C, ^{14}N and ^{15}N, or radiogenic, such as ^{14}C. Radiogenic isotopes decay at a set rate and, as a result, measurement of the $^{14}C/^{12}C$ ratio is the underlying

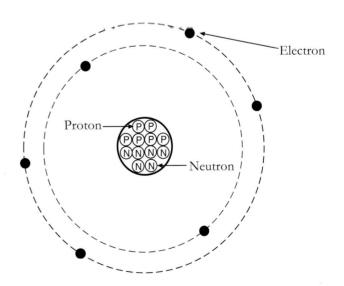

Figure 7.1. Schematic diagram of a carbon-12 atom, showing the 6 protons and 6 neutrons in the nucleus of the atom which is surrounded by 6 electrons in the outer rings.

principle behind radiocarbon dating, since the original isotopic ratio and the rate of decay are known constants. For dietary reconstruction, it is the stable isotopes that are of interest, since the relative quantities of the stable isotopes do not change over time and, as a result, stable isotope ratios in archaeological bone will reflect the stable isotope ratio at the time of death, providing that diagenetic alteration has not taken place.

What is fractionation?

Chemically, all isotopes will react in the same way, whether stable or radiogenic, however the difference in mass between the isotopes means that sometimes chemical reactions and physical processes will discriminate against the heavier isotope in an attempt to preserve energy; this process is termed fractionation. An example of this can be seen in the evaporation and precipitation of water (H_2O) that results in changes in the isotopic ratio of oxygen ($^{18}O/^{16}O$) at different stages in the water cycle. During evaporation, the lighter oxygen isotope (^{16}O) will be the first to be incorporated into the water vapour cloud, meaning that the oxygen stable isotope ratio of rainwater differs from that of ocean water. This process of fractionation also occurs in biological systems, meaning that ratios of the stable isotopes of carbon ($^{13}C/^{12}C$) and nitrogen ($^{15}N/^{14}N$) will vary between plants, animals, humans and other members of a local dietary system. These principles form the foundation of dietary reconstruction using stable isotope analysis.

Stable isotope ratios are presented as delta (δ) values in parts per thousand (‰) relative to an international standard reference material according to the formula below:

$$\delta\ (‰) = \left[\frac{R_{sample} - R_{standard}}{R_{standard}} \right] \times 1000$$

R = stable isotope ratios (e.g. $^{13}C/^{12}C$ or $^{15}N/^{14}N$)

For carbon stable isotope analysis, this standard is a marine carbonate, PeeDee Belemnite (PDB); for nitrogen stable isotope analysis, the standard is atmospheric nitrogen (AIR); and for sulphur isotope analysis, the standard is a meteoric standard, Canyon Diablo Troilite (CDT). Therefore, a sample with a reported $\delta^{13}C$ (PDB) value of 0‰ indicates a sample that has a stable isotope ratio identical to that observed in the PDB standard. This system makes small differences in isotopic ratios between samples much easier to identify and quantify.

Stable isotopes, bone collagen and diet

Feeding experiments have shown that $\delta^{13}C$ and $\delta^{15}N$ values in the organic protein portion of bone (collagen) are directly related to dietary intake and can be used to examine the contribution of specific dietary components (Ambrose 1993; DeNiro and Epstein 1978, 1981; Schoeninger and DeNiro 1984). These $\delta^{13}C$ and $\delta^{15}N$ values are passed along the food chain in a relatively predictable pattern and by determining the $\delta^{13}C$ and $\delta^{15}N$ values of archaeological human and animal bone collagen, local dietary systems can be reconstructed, and interpretations can be made about human diet and subsistence patterns. Differences in carbon stable isotope values can be used to examine the importance of what is termed C_3 and C_4 plant food species (see Fig. 7.2). This categorisation refers to the production of either a three- or four-chain carbon molecule during the initial stages of photosynthesis. C_3 plants, with more negative $\delta^{13}C$ values, include the temperate species, such as the native European species of wheat, barley and oats, while C_4 plants, with more positive $\delta^{13}C$ values, are adapted to more tropical environments and include some of the imported domesticated species such as maize, millet and sorghum. As a result of these differences in isotopic signals, stable isotope analysis has been used successfully to trace the emergence of maize agriculture in the northeastern United States (see Fig. 7.3) (*e.g.* Bender *et al.* 1981; Buikstra and Milner 1991; Katzenberg *et al.* 1993; van der Merwe and Vogel 1978; Vogel and van der Merwe 1977). Dual analysis of $\delta^{13}C$ and $\delta^{15}N$ values enables an examination of the role of marine foods in diet, since marine ecosystems have more positive $\delta^{13}C$ and $\delta^{15}N$ values than terrestrial ecosystems (Chisholm *et al.* 1982; Schoeninger *et al.* 1983). Any contribution from marine foods in an individual's diet, would therefore result in an increase in both the $\delta^{13}C$ and $\delta^{15}N$ values of bone collagen. Stable isotope ratios can also be used to examine trophic level, since there is a shift of approximately +2–4‰ in nitrogen and +0.5–1‰ in carbon between the bone collagen of an organism and its consumer. As a result, both $\delta^{13}C$ and $\delta^{15}N$ values gradually increase along the food chain from plant species with low $\delta^{13}C$ and $\delta^{15}N$ values though to herbivores, carnivores and super-carnivores with increasingly more positive $\delta^{13}C$ and $\delta^{15}N$ values. This trophic level effect can also be seen in human infants during pregnancy, breast-feeding and weaning. While in the womb, a foetus will obtain its dietary protein directly from the mother's diet, meaning that $\delta^{15}N$ values in the bone collagen of the foetus and mother will be identical and will reflect the $\delta^{15}N$ value of the mother's diet (see Fig. 7.4a). When breast-feeding, however, an infant is essentially feeding on the body protein of the mother and, as a result, the bone collagen $\delta^{15}N$ value of the infant will increase to reflect this change in diet (see Fig. 7.4b). Once an infant is then weaned onto a solid diet, the $\delta^{15}N$ value of bone collagen will begin to decrease at a rate reflecting the rate of weaning (see Fig. 7.4c) before levelling out to reflect the $\delta^{15}N$ value of this new solid diet (see Fig. 7.4d). Attempts can therefore be made to examine the age and rate of weaning of infants within a population, providing

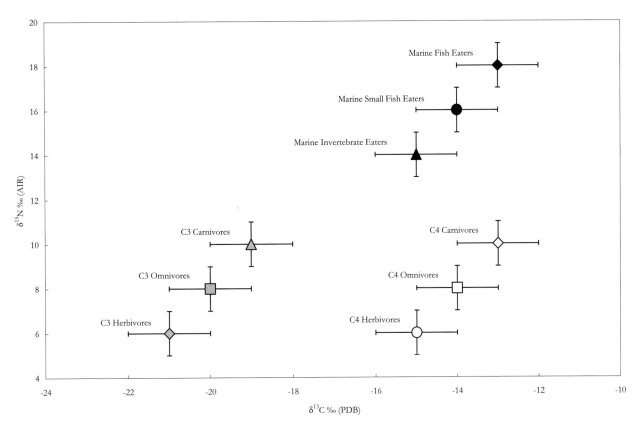

Figure 7.2. Example of a stable isotope bi-variate plot showing theoretical data points for specific diets.

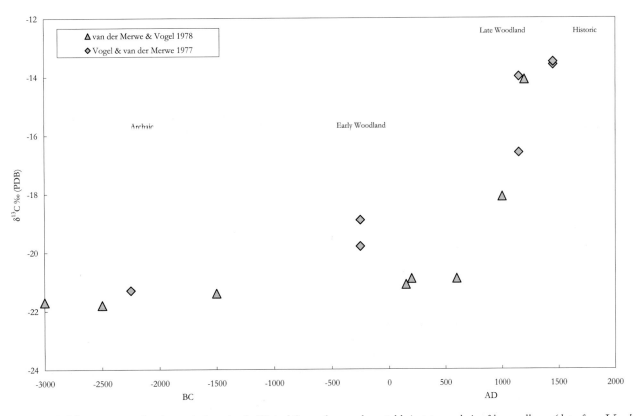

Figure 7.3. The emergence of maize agriculture in the United States from carbon stable isotope analysis of bone collagen (data from Vogel and van der Merwe 1977; van der Merwe and Vogel 1978).

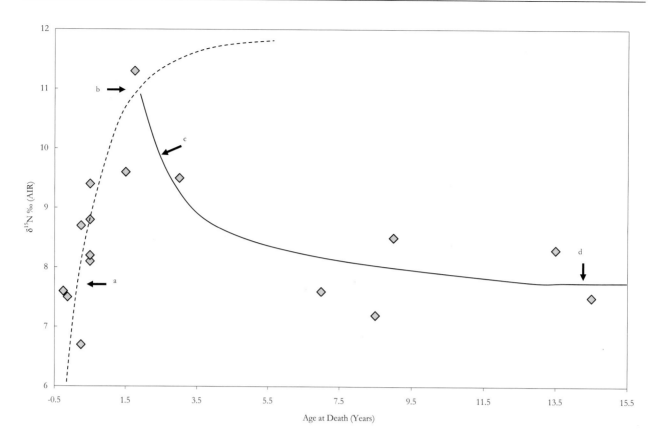

Figure 7.4. The effects of breast-feeding and weaning on nitrogen stable isotope ratios in infant bone collagen (adapted from Schurr 1997). See text for explanation of points a-d.

there are sufficient infant skeletal remains of identifiable age at death (*e.g.* Fuller *et al.* 2003; Katzenberg *et al.* 1996; Mays *et al.* 2002; Schurr 1997; Wright and Schwarcz 1999).

La Tène Bohemia

The La Tène period in Central Europe is characterised by the abandonment of the large Hallstatt period hilltop settlements and the emergence of a settlement system of small self-sufficient units (*e.g.* Kuna 1990). The burial evidence changes from the use of rich tumulus and chariot inhumation burials, and the use of cremation burial, to a system of flat inhumation burials, with little or no obvious differences in the wealth of individual graves. Systems of production and trade become focussed on the small-scale production of objects and goods for local use, with the disappearance of imported goods from the Mediterranean and the abandonment of specialised sites, such as the amber processing site at Poříčany (Čtverák 1986). The provision of grave goods becomes based on an almost standard set of objects with distinctive local designs characteristic of the La Tène period. Male burials include items of bronze and iron jewellery (such as bracelets, brooches and finger rings) and occasionally items of iron weaponry which may include a sword, a shield and/or a spear. Female burials include items of bronze and iron

jewellery, including bracelets, brooches, finger rings, ankle rings, and torcs. Bodies are laid extended and supine, often in a wooden coffin, in graves that are aligned N-S with the head to the north. The lack of any obvious differences in wealth between graves, and the poor preservation of many La Tène skeletons, means that stable isotope analysis will provide additional data that can aid in the interpretation of both diet and social stratification, since the availability of specific dietary components may be based on social factors.

Materials and methods

Human skeletal remains from the La Tène period sites of Soběsuky, Tišice, Jinonice, Ruzyně and Makotrasy in Bohemia were examined at the National Museum in Prague for demographic and pathological data. The location of these sites can be seen in Figure 7.5 and background information on the archaeology of these sites has been published elsewhere (Čižmář 1978; Holodňak 1991; Turek 1997; Velemínský and Dobisiková 1998; Waldhauser 2001). Bone samples of approximately 0.5g were taken from either the rib or long bone elements for collagen extraction and isotopic analysis. A selection of animal bone samples were also taken from La Tène period contexts at the settlement site of Soběsuky for use as comparative data. Bone samples were cleaned using air abrasion with an aluminium oxide powder to remove soil and other adhering particles and then subjected to a modified Longin (1971) collagen extraction method. Cleaned bone samples were demineralised in 0.5M HCl at 2–5°C for up to 14 days, and then gelatinised at 72°C for 48 hours in sealed tubes of de-ionised water adjusted to pH 3 with 0.5M HCl. The resulting solutions were filtered using 5-8μm Ezee filter separators (Elkay Laboratory Products, Basingstoke) to remove insoluble materials and then concentrated using Amicon® Ultra-4 centrifugal filters fitted with Biomax-30 membranes (Millipore) to remove components lower than 30,000 NMWL (Brown *et al.* 1988). Resulting solutions were lyophilised for 48 hours before a sub-sample of 1.0mg ± 0.1mg was combusted and analysed by Isotope Ratio Mass Spectrometry (Europa 20-20). In order to examine the accuracy and precision of analytical methods, a Methionine standard reference material, with known $\delta^{13}C$ (-26.6‰) and $\delta^{15}N$ (-3.0‰) values (Elemental Microanalysis, Devon, UK), and a Bovine Liver standard reference material (NIST SRM 1577b), with known $\delta^{13}C$ (-21.6‰) and $\delta^{15}N$ (7.6‰) values (National Institute of Standards and Technology, Gaithersburg, MD, USA), were analysed in tandem with samples of bone collagen. Analytical error was defined as one standard deviation of multiple analyses of these standards and was 0.2‰ for both carbon and nitrogen. Collagen yield, the percentages of carbon and nitrogen, and the C:N ratio were determined to examine whether samples were affected by diagenetic processes (Ambrose 1993). Data from the Kutná Hora – Karlov, Radovesice and Hallstatt Austria samples analysed as part of this project have been published elsewhere (Le Huray and Schutkowski 2005).

Collagen integrity

Preservation of collagen can potentially be assessed by an examination of the amino acid profile of the collagen sample and a comparison with expected patterns (*e.g.* Grupe *et al.* 2000). However, the standard method (Ambrose 1993) is a consideration of the amount of collagen recovered from a bone sample (collagen yield), as well as the amount of total carbon and total nitrogen (and the C:N atomic ratio) in the extracted collagen. Modern bone is approximately 20% collagen by weight and archaeological bone will have anywhere between 0 and 20% collagen. Ambrose (1990) found that collagen samples with a total yield of over 3.5% represented well-preserved collagen, while van Klinken (1999) found that

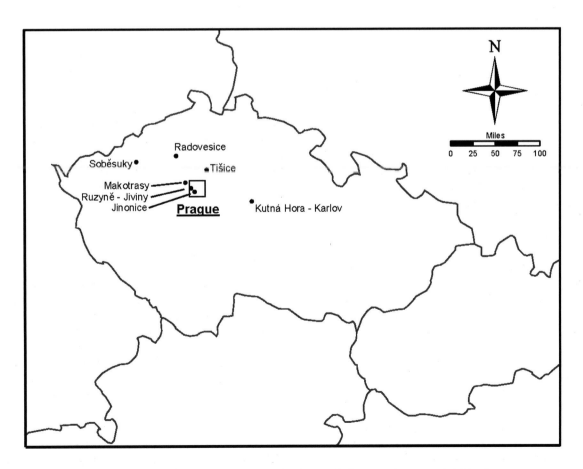

Figure 7.5. Map of the modern Czech Republic showing the location of sites mentioned in the text.

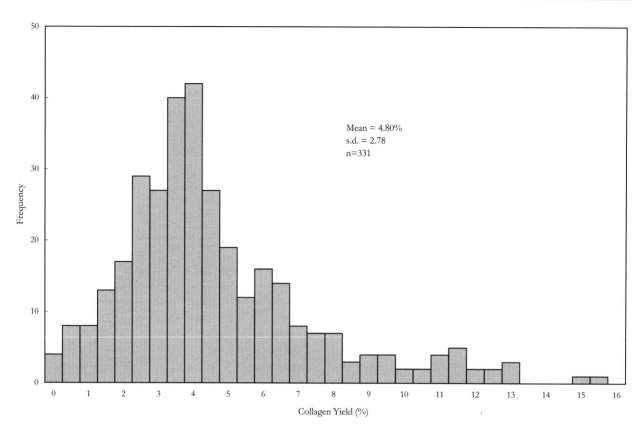

Figure 7.6. Percentage collagen yield for all bone samples processed for isotopic analysis. Included is data from Kutná Hora – Karlov, Radovesice and Hallstatt Austria from Le Huray and Schutkowski (2005).

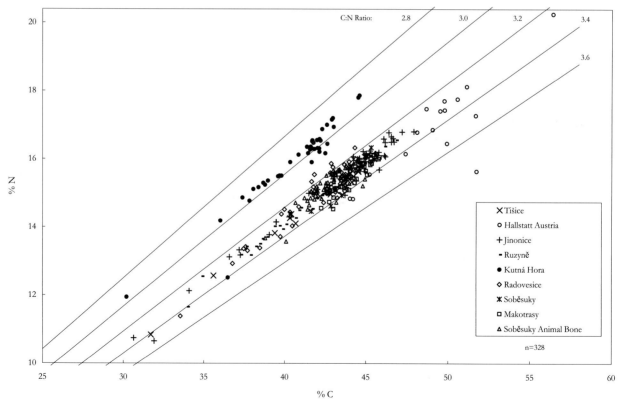

Figure 7.7. Percentages of carbon and nitrogen in all collagen samples analysed to date, with various C:N ratio lines marked. Included is data from Kutná Hora – Karlov, Radovesice and Hallstatt Austria from Le Huray and Schutkowski (2005).

collagen was well preserved in samples with a collagen yield as low as 0.5%. The addition of an ultrafiltration step in the method used in this study lowers the collagen yield by removing contaminants and fragmented collagen below a molecular weight of 30,000 units. As a result, any comparison of collagen yields obtained in this study with previously published work should take this into consideration. The collagen yields obtained in this study can be seen in Figure 7.6 and Tables 7.1–8 in the appendix. A total of 331 bone samples were processed with three producing insufficient collagen for analysis and a further one having a collagen yield below 0.5%, suggesting that stable isotope data from this sample should be considered suspect. The percentage of carbon in the samples analysed (see Fig. 7.7) ranged from 30.2% to 56.4% (mean 42.8%, $\sigma = 3.1\%$). These values are slightly higher than the mean values observed by the Oxford Radiocarbon Accelerator Unit ($34.8\% \pm 8.8$, n=2146) (van Klinken 1999, 691) but well within the range accepted as representing collagen. The percentage of nitrogen in the collagen samples analysed (see Fig. 7.7 and Tables 7.1–8 in the appendix) ranged from 10.7% to 20.2% (mean 15.3%, $\sigma = 1.1\%$), a figure comparable to the 11–16% observed by van Klinken (1999, 691). The percentage of carbon and nitrogen in a collagen sample can be used to obtain the C:N atomic ratio for each sample (see Fig. 7.7 and Tables 7.1–8 in the appendix). Theoretically, collagen will have a

C:N atomic ratio of 3.23, however, the range observed in modern bone, and therefore the range used as representing collagen free from contamination, is 2.8–3.6 (Ambrose 1990, 1993). Of the 328 samples analysed for carbon and nitrogen stable isotope ratios, only one from Hallstatt Austria (HA 5795) had a C:N atomic ratio outside of the acceptable range of 2.8–3.6. This elevated C:N ratio may suggest contamination of this sample with organic carbon. As a result, data from this sample were discarded from the analysis. Final data for Sobĕsuky, Tišice, Jinonice, Ruzynĕ and Makotrasy are presented in Tables 7.1–8 in the appendix.

Stable isotope data from Sobĕsuky

The stable isotope data from animal bone samples from the La Tène period settlement site at Sobĕsuky can be seen in Figures 7.8 and 7.9 and Tables 7.1–2 in the appendix. The data obtained can be used to establish the isotopic baselines of the local environment and its inhabitants and, when compared with the human bone data, can be used to make interpretations about human diet. The isotopic data obtained suggests that the diet of the horse and cow species is terrestrial and herbivorous in nature, as would be expected. The cow sample with a more positive $\delta^{15}N$ value (SOBA 25) is an adult tooth dentine sample and may reflect a delayed suckling signal,

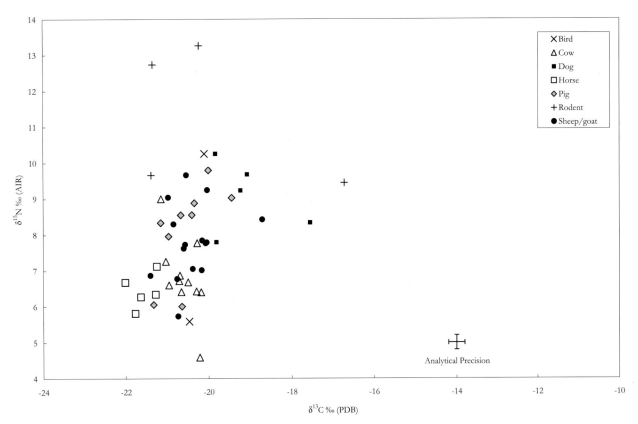

Figure 7.8. Carbon and nitrogen stable isotope data from animal bone samples recovered from the La Tène period settlement site at Sobĕsuky, Czech Republic.

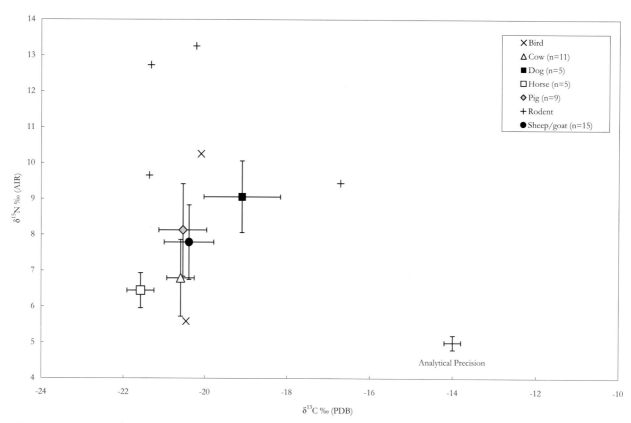

Figure 7.9. Mean carbon and nitrogen stable isotope data (±1σ) from the animal bone samples recovered from the La Tène period settlement site at Soběsuky, Czech Republic.

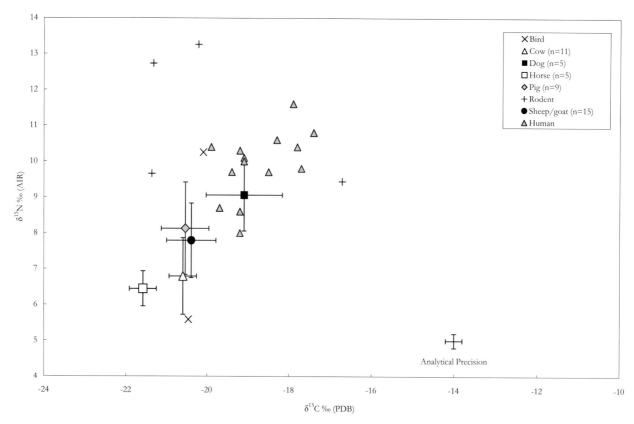

Figure 7.10. Carbon and nitrogen stable isotope data from animal and human bone samples recovered from the La Tène period settlement and cemetery at Soběsuky, Czech Republic.

since the turnover of dentine collagen may be slower than bone collagen (*e.g.* Fuller *et al.* 2003). The large differences in $\delta^{15}N$ values in the rodent and bird samples most likely reflects the presence of both carnivorous and herbivorous rodent and bird species. Unfortunately, these samples could not be assigned to a specific species to confirm this. The more positive $\delta^{15}N$ values of the majority of the pig samples suggests an omnivorous diet, while the two pig samples with apparently herbivorous $\delta^{15}N$ values may, in fact, reflect the presence of wild boar, since these animals could be expected to have a more herbivorous diet than domesticated pigs who would be consuming both plant and animal remains provided by the human population. Further isotopic studies on domestic pig and wild boar are required to confirm this. The dog stable isotope data appears to be largely carnivorous in nature, as would be expected, although two individuals do have lower $\delta^{15}N$ values than would be expected, and one has a more positive $\delta^{13}C$ value suggesting the presence of C_4 plant foods, probably millet, either in the diet of the dog or, more likely, in the diet of the animal species consumed by the dog. The sheep/goat samples are a little more puzzling since the large range in $\delta^{15}N$ values is unusual and suggests either the presence of juvenile sheep/goat with elevated $\delta^{15}N$ values due to suckling, or the consumption of an as yet unidentified plant species with more positive $\delta^{15}N$ values. Samples were not taken from any obvious juvenile

animal bones and elevated $\delta^{15}N$ values as a result of a suckling signal should be negligible.

When the human bone data are examined in relation to the animal bone data (see Fig. 7.10), a local dietary system is produced with the data from the human bone samples indicating a diet based on terrestrial C_3 plant foods and animal protein.

Carbon Stable Isotopes and Millet Consumption

Previously published stable isotope data from a Hallstatt period cemetery at Magdalenska gora in Slovenia (Murray and Schoeninger 1988) has shown that Broomcorn millet (*Panicum miliaceum*) played a major role in the diet of this population (see Fig. 7.11). Since millet is the only C_4 plant food known to be present in prehistoric Europe, variations in $\delta^{13}C$ values observed in human bone collagen may reflect the relative importance of millet in the diet of populations and individuals. Where available, animal bone samples should be taken to examine whether millet signals are the result of direct consumption of millet by the human population, or instead a reflection of the consumption of animals fed on millet. At Magdalenska gora, animal bone samples were unavailable and, as a result, were taken from a similar site at Altdorf in Bavaria. In this case, the authors did note that animal bone data may not always be directly comparable between sites and

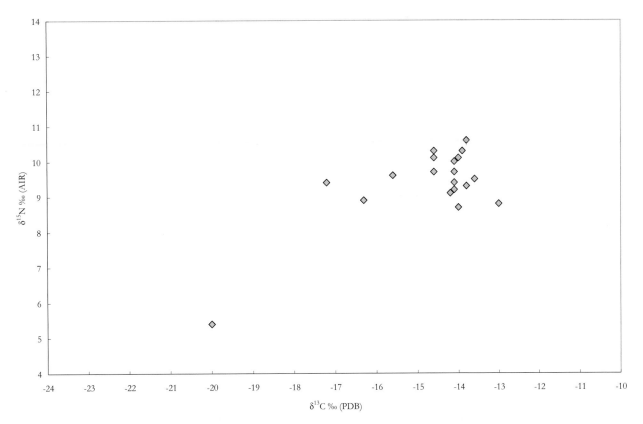

Figure 7.11. Carbon and nitrogen stable isotope data from the Hallstatt period cemetery at Magdalenska gora in Slovenia (Murray and Schoeninger 1988).

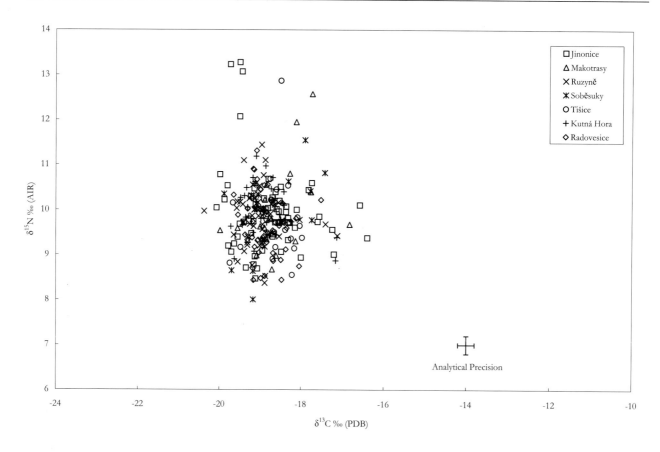

Figure 7.12. Carbon and nitrogen stable isotope data of human bone samples from the La Tène period cemeteries of Soběsuky, Tišice, Jinonice, Ruzyně, Makotrasy, Kutná Hora and Radovesice in the Czech Republic (Data from Kutná Hora and Radovesice from Le Huray and Schutkowski, 2005).

regions, especially when interpretations are to be made on whether millet played a major role in human diet, in animal diet, or both. However, by combining human and animal bone data from various sites across prehistoric Europe, it may be possible to trace the spread of millet as a major dietary component in the same way that maize agriculture has been examined in the north-eastern United States. At the La Tène period sites in Bohemia, the stable isotope data suggests that overall human diet is based on C_3 plant foods and animal protein, although some of the more positive $\delta^{13}C$ values (*i.e.* greater than -18‰) may reflect at least some contribution from millet as a major dietary component (see Fig. 7.12). Archaeological evidence, in the form of carbonised plant material, indicates that millet was present in the modern Czech Republic from the early Bronze Age (Zohary and Hopf 2000, 220), however, the low quantities observed do not suggest a large-scale system of cultivation, a view supported by the isotopic data.

Nitrogen stable isotopes and "warrior" status

Previous stable isotope studies (*e.g.* Ambrose *et al.* 2003; Richards *et al.* 1998; Schutkowki *et al.* 1999) have

attempted to relate diet to aspects of social status and social stratification through a comparison of stable isotope data with archaeological evidence (such as grave form and structure, and the type and quantity of grave goods) and biological features of the dead (such as age-at-death and sex). These interpretations are based on the hypothesis that the consumption of specific dietary components within a population may be based on factors other than simple availability. Murray and Schoeninger's study of the Hallstatt period tumulus burials at Magdalenska gora suggested that the smaller range of variation in the isotope data of female burials may reflect a more restricted and homogenous diet in females than in males, although the small number of female samples was recognised as a possible contributing factor (Murray and Schoeninger 1988, 164). Differences in $\delta^{15}N$ values between younger and older males also suggested that the younger males consumed more animal protein than the older males and females (Murray and Schoeninger 1988, 166), although this pattern was not statistically significant. No correlations were observed between social status as revealed through grave goods and diet, suggesting that there was no relationship between 'wealth' and diet. An examination of the isotopic data from the La Tène period cemeteries in Bohemia appears to shows the opposite pattern; although no correlation was observed between the sex/age of an individual and diet, within the male group at both Tišice and Makotrasy, there appears to be a relationship between more positive δ^{15}N values and the presence of items of iron weaponry in the grave (Fig. 7.13 and 7.14), suggesting differences in the consumption of animal products, such as meat and/or dairy produce, between these individuals. This pattern is more readily observable in the data from Tišice than in the data from Makotrasy, where there is some overlap between status groups, and mean values are within analytical error. However, this is a pattern that was also observed in the isotopic data from Kutná Hora (see Fig. 7.15) and, to a lesser extent, in the isotopic data from Radovesice (see Fig. 7.16) where again there is a degree of overlap between status groups and mean values are within analytical error of each other (Le Huray and Schutkowski 2005). However, the underlying pattern is that males buried with weapons do generally have more positive δ^{15}N values than the remaining male population, suggesting that a dietary distinction may have existed during the La Tène period in Bohemia that was based on the "warrior" status of an individual as expressed through the provision of items of weaponry in the grave.

Nitrogen stable isotopes and weaning

At the La Tène cemetery sites in Bohemia, the small population numbers means that often only one or two infants are identified in each population and, as a result, determinations of weaning age within a single population are not possible. At Soběsuky (see Fig. 7.17), three infants aged between 0–6 months and an infant aged between 0–12 months have more positive δ^{15}N values, almost certainly as a result of this breast-feeding signal. A similar situation can be seen at Makotrasy (see Fig. 7.18), with an infant, two 4-year-olds and a 6-year-old having decreasing δ^{15}N values respectively, most likely reflecting the effect of weaning on δ^{15}N values. A 2-year-old infant from Tišice (see Fig. 7.19) and an 18-month-old infant from Ruzyně (see Fig. 7.20) both have more positive δ^{15}N values than their adult counterparts, again almost certainly a result of a breast-feeding signal. By combining this data, it may be possible to examine the age of weaning at a regional level. This approach must be used with caution since the assumption is that there are no major dietary or environmental differences that may result in differences in δ^{15}N values between populations and that weaning ages are similar between populations. An additional assumption is that infants who died during breast-feeding or weaning

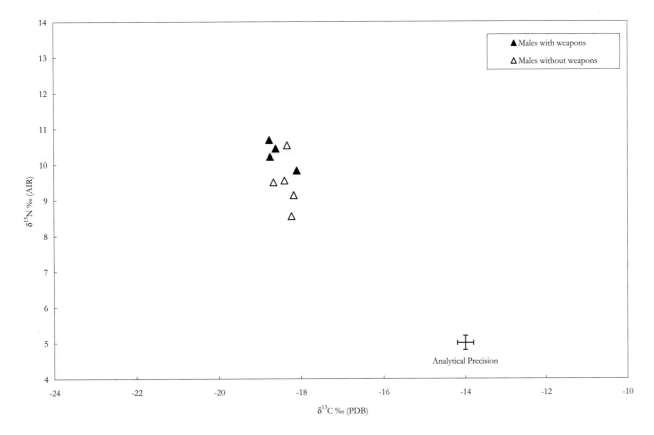

Figure 7.13. Carbon and nitrogen stable isotope data from males buried with and without iron weaponry at the La Tène period cemetery at Tišice, Czech Republic.

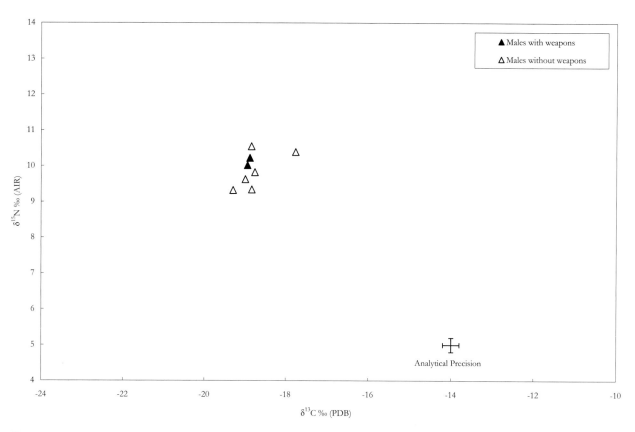

Figure 7.14. Carbon and nitrogen stable isotope data from males buried with and without iron weaponry at the La Tène period cemetery at Makotrasy, Czech Republic.

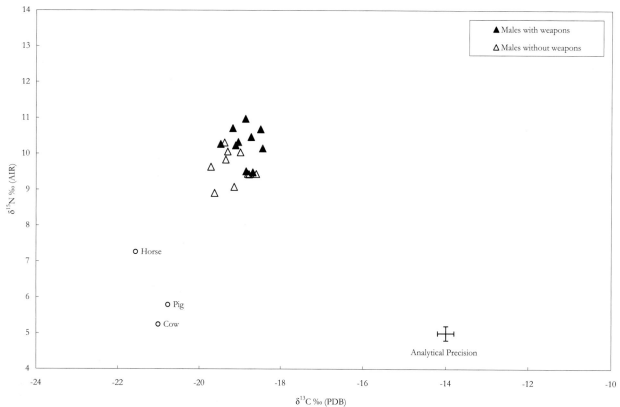

Figure 7.15. Carbon and nitrogen stable isotope data from males buried with and without iron weaponry at the La Tène period cemetery at Kutná Hora – Karlov, Czech Republic (Le Huray and Schutkowski, 2005).

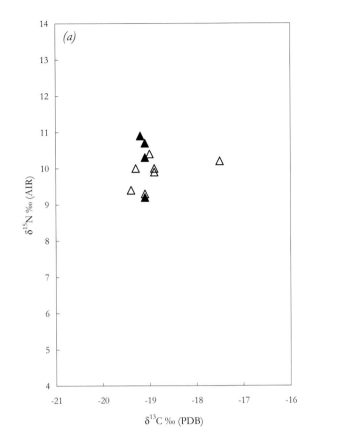
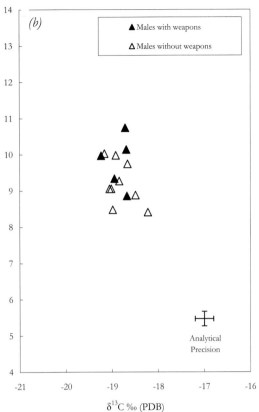

Figure 7.16. Carbon and nitrogen stable isotope data from males buried with and without iron weaponry at the La Tène period cemetery at (a) Radovesice 1 and (b) Radovesice 2, Czech Republic (Le Huray and Schutkowski, 2005).

were not fed different diets or died of malnutrition, since this has been shown to affect $\delta^{15}N$ values (Hobson *et al.* 1993). The collated stable isotope data from the La Tène period cemeteries sampled as a part of this study appear to suggest that by the age of 2 years infants continued to be breast-fed (see Fig. 7.19), by the age of 4 years, weaning had begun and was completed by the age of 6 years (see Fig. 7.18).

Sulphur isotope analysis and migration

Stable isotope studies are not limited only to dietary studies using carbon and nitrogen isotopes; strontium and lead isotope ratios in human dental enamel have been used to examine prehistoric migration patterns (*e.g.* Montgomery *et al.* 2005; Schweissing and Grupe 2003; Montgomery and Evans, this volume) since the strontium and lead isotope ratios observed in enamel will reflect the underlying geology of an individual's habitat. More recently, studies of the ratios of oxygen isotopes within the phosphate (PO_4) portion of both dental enamel and bone apatite have been used in dietary analyses as well as in climate reconstruction (*e.g.* Sponheimer and Lee-Thorp 1999; White *et al.* 2004). An additional element of recent interest is sulphur (*e.g.* Richards *et al.* 2001, 2003), which is present in the mineral phase of bone as calcium sulphate ($CaSO_4$) and the organic bone collagen as methionine

(Richards *et al.* 2003, 38). The isotopic ratio of sulphur ($\delta^{34}S$) in human and animal bone collagen is a reflection of dietary sulphur that originates from a combination of geological sulphur, atmospheric SO_2 and aquatic sulphate (SO_4^-). As a result, variations in the $\delta^{34}S$ values of a local food web will depend on the form and age of the local geology, as well as distance from the coast and the contribution of marine foods in diet. Initial data from modern animal-feeding experiments and archaeological bone collagen and hair keratin (*e.g.* Richards *et al.* 2001; Macko *et al.* 1999; Leach *et al.* 1996) appears to suggest that sulphur isotope analysis will be of benefit when used in combination with carbon and nitrogen isotope analysis to provide additional dietary information and reveal patterns relating to prehistoric migration (see Fig. 7.21).

Analysis of some of the initial human bone collagen $\delta^{34}S$ values from the La Tène period inhumation cemeteries in Bohemia, Moravia and Slovakia (see Fig. 7.22) indicates that although a wide range of $\delta^{34}S$ values are observed, there does appear to be a degree of site-specific clustering that suggests micro-regional variations in $\delta^{34}S$ values may exist in this area. These findings support the hypothesis that sulphur isotope analysis will be of use in migration studies, and the initial data presented here will be of use to future sulphur isotope studies in this region. As would be expected for central Europe, the low $\delta^{34}S$ values observed in this study do not reflect either a marine dietary

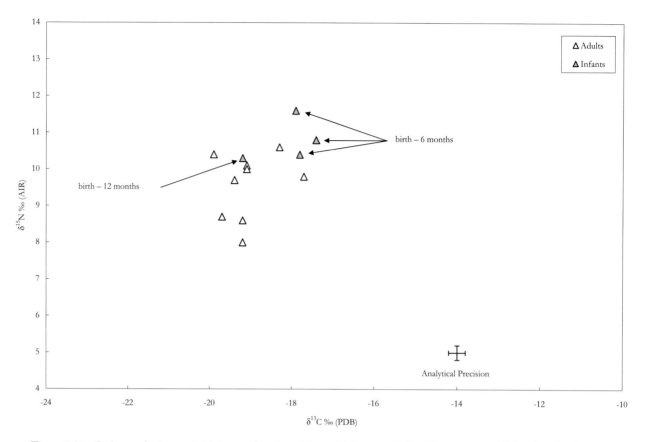

Figure 7.17. Carbon and nitrogen stable isotope data for adults and infants at the La Tène cemetery of Soběsuky, Czech Republic.

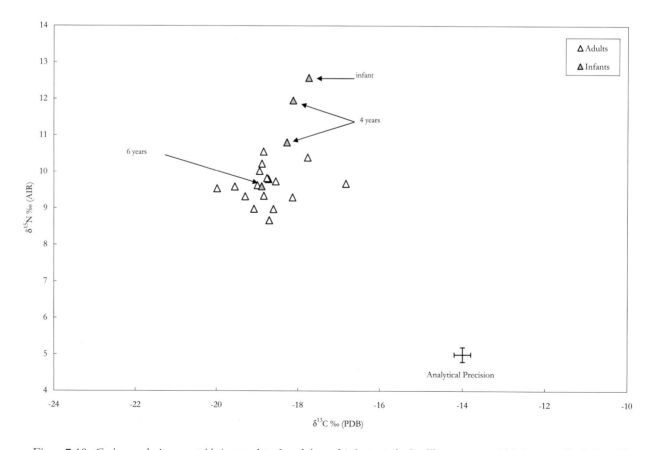

Figure 7.18. Carbon and nitrogen stable isotope data for adults and infants at the La Tène cemetery of Makotrasy, Czech Republic.

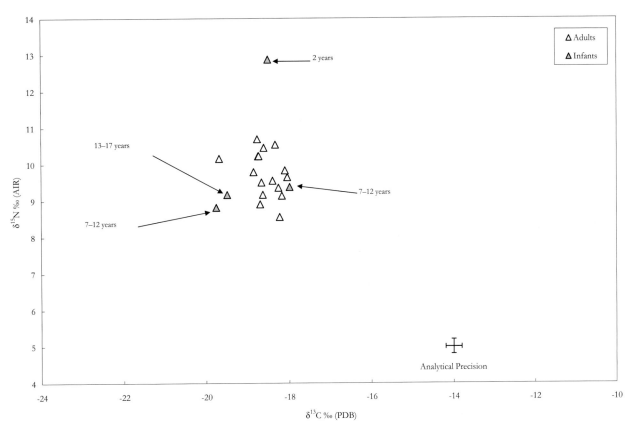

Figure 7.19. Carbon and nitrogen stable isotope data for adults and infants at the La Tène cemetery of Tišice, Czech Republic.

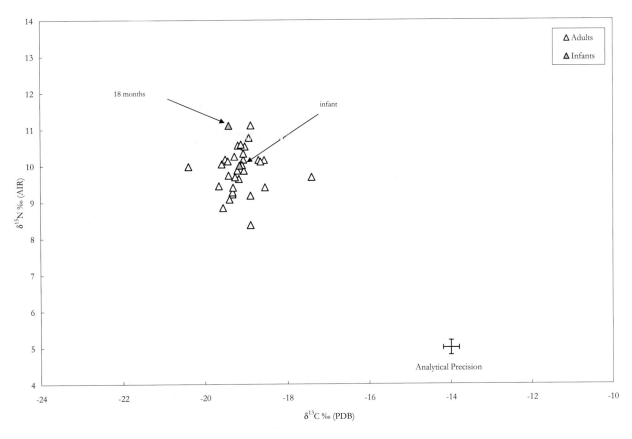

Figure 7.20. Carbon and nitrogen stable isotope data for adults and infants at the La Tène cemetery of Ružyně, Czech Republic.

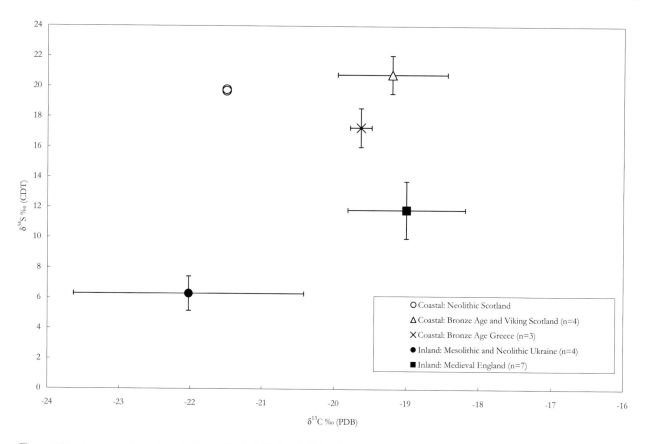

Figure 7.21. Average and standard deviations (1σ) of δ¹³C and δ³⁴S values of human bone collagen taken from five European archaeological sites (adapted from Richards, Fuller and Hedges 2001).

component or a coastal location. There is no doubt that sulphur isotope analysis will be of immense interest to future researchers; however, at present there is a general lack of understanding of the effects of diagenetic alteration on δ³⁴S values and a lack of comparable data from controlled feeding experiments and other archaeological collections that is needed in order to aid interpretation.

Conclusions

This study has attempted to outline the method involved in stable isotope analysis for dietary reconstruction and summarise some of the main findings of an ongoing study that uses these methods to examine diet during the La Tène period in central Europe. This method enables an examination of diet at the level of the individual and can be used to make interpretations regarding some of the more social aspects of prehistoric diet, such as the relationship between diet and social status, the processes of breast-feeding and weaning, as well as some of the practical aspects of diet, such as millet cultivation and consumption. This is the first application of this method to this region, and it is hoped will inspire additional studies of diet in prehistoric central Europe. One interesting finding of this study is the more positive δ¹⁵N values observed in males buried with items of iron weaponry than the remaining male population, a pattern that is

clearly observable in the stable isotope data from Kutná Hora-Karlov and Tišice, but less distinct in the data from Radovesice and Makotrasy. This suggests that a differential dietary system may have existed that was based on 'warrior' status as expressed through the provision of particular grave goods. Access to animal protein in the form of meat and/or dairy produce is the most likely cause of the observed differences in δ¹⁵N values between these social groups. What must be noted is that no information can be gained from stable isotope analysis that will reveal the form of these animal products; which means that the distribution of specific cuts of meat for various social groups would not be detectable using this method. The potential of sulphur isotope analysis has been outlined and initial data has been presented that clearly indicates micro-regional differences in human bone collagen data, suggesting that this method may be of great importance in future migration studies. Additional data from both archaeological and modern bone collagen are needed in order to place the data obtained from this study into context. What is emerging with the increase in use of stable isotope analysis, is the need for co-operation between researchers, and a combined sampling and analysis program that will enable archaeologists to gain the maximum amount of dietary, migration and climatic data possible from a single bone or tooth sample.

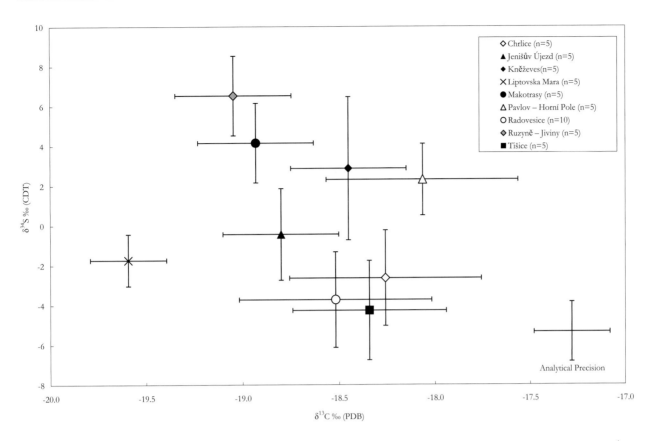

Figure 7.22. Initial δ³⁴S data for human bone collagen from various La Tène period inhumation cemeteries in Bohemia (Jenišův Újezd, Kněževes, Makotrasy, Radovesice, Ruzyně and Tišice), Moravia (Chrlice and Pavlov), and Slovakia (Liptovska Mara).

Acknowledgements

This paper was originally presented on the 10th September 2004 at the 10th Annual Meeting of the European Association of Archaeology in Lyon, for which it received the EAA Annual Student Award. The project was funded by the Natural Environment Research Council as part of a PhD studentship (NER/S/A/2001/06105) at the University of Bradford's Department of Archaeological Sciences. Thanks go to Ken Neal, Andy Gledhill and members of the Palaeodietary Research Group for assistance with the analyses and critical analysis of the isotopic data. Samples were obtained from RNDr. Miloslava Dobisiková and PhDr. Pavel Sankot at the National Museum in Prague, MUDr. Václav Smrčka of the Postgraduate Medical School of Charles University, Prague, PhDr. Petr Holodňak of the Žatec Museum (Czech Republic), PhDr. Petra Stranská of the Archaeological Institute in Prague, and Prof. Maria Teschler-Nicola at the Department of Archaeological Biology and Anthropology at the Natural History Museum in Vienna.

References

Ambrose, S. H., Buikstra, J. and Kreuger, H. W. (2003) Status and gender differences in diet at Mound 72, Cahokia, revealed by isotopic analysis of bone. *Journal of Anthropological Archaeology* 22(3), 217–226.

Ambrose, S. H. (1993) Isotopic analysis of palaeodiets: methodological and interpretive considerations. In M. K. Sandford (ed.) *Investigations of ancient human tissue*, 59–130. Reading, Gordon and Breach Science.

Ambrose, S. H. (1990) Preparation and characterization of bone and tooth collagen for isotopic analysis. *Journal of Archaeological Science* 17, 431–451.

Bender, M. M., Baerreis, D. A. and Steventon, R. L. (1981) Further light on carbon isotopes and Hopewell agriculture. *American Antiquity* 46, 346–353.

Brown, T. A., Nelson, D. E., Vogel, J. S. and Southam, J. R. (1988) Improved collagen extraction by modified Longin method. *Radiocarbon* 30, 171–177.

Buikstra, J. E. and Milner, G. R. (1991) Isotopic and archaeological interpretations of diet in the Central Mississippi Valley. *Journal of Archaeological Science* 18, 319–329.

Chisholm, B. S., Nelson, D. E. and Schwarz, H. P. (1982) Stable carbon isotope ratios as a measure of marine versus terrestrial protein in ancient diets. *Science* 216(4550), 1131–1132.

Čižmář, M. (1978) Keltske pohrebiste v Makotrasich okres Kladnu (Celtic cemetery at Makotrasy in district Kladnu). *Pamatký Archeologické* 69, 117–144.

Čtverák, V. (1986) A fortified settlement of late Hallstatt period at Poříčany (Central Bohemia). In *Archaeology in Bohemia 1981–1985*, 109–114. Prague, Czechoslovak Academy of Sciences.

DeNiro, M. J. and Epstein, S. (1978) Influence of diet on the distribution of carbon isotopes in animals. *Geochimica et Cosmochimica Acta* 42, 495–506.

DeNiro, M. J. and Epstein, S. (1981) Influence of diet on the distribution of nitrogen isotopes in animals. *Geochimica et Cosmochimica Acta* 45, 341–351.

Fuller, B. T., Richards, M. P. and Mays, S. A. (2003) Stable carbon and nitrogen isotope variations in tooth dentine serial sections from Wharram Percy. *Journal of Archaeological Science* 30, 1673–1684.

Grupe, G., Balzer, A. and Turban-Just, S. (2000) Modeling protein diagenesis in ancient bone: towards a validation of stable isotope data. In S. H. Ambrose and M. A. Katzenberg (eds) *Biogeochemical Approaches to Palaeodietary Analysis*, 173–187. New York, Plenum Press.

Hobson, K. A., Alisauskas, R. T. and Clark, R. G. (1993) Stable nitrogen isotope enrichment in avian tissues due to fasting and nutritional stress: implications for isotopic analyses of diet. *Condor* 95, 388–394.

Holodňak, P. (1991) Rescue excavations at Soběsuky in 1985–1990. In *Archaeology in Bohemia 1985–1990*, 210–217. Prague, Institute of Archaeology.

Katzenberg, M. A., Saunders, S. R. and Fitzgerald, W. R. (1993) Age differences in stable carbon and nitrogen isotope ratios in a population of prehistoric maize horticulturalists. *American Journal of Physical Anthropology* 90, 267–281.

Katzenberg, M. A., Herring, D. A. and Saunders, S. R. (1996) Weaning and infant mortality: evaluating the skeletal evidence. *Yearbook of Physical Anthropology* 39, 177–199.

Kuna, M. (1990) Social system of the Iron Age as reflected on the microregional level. *Fonctionnement social de l'âge du fer*, 227–230. Actes de la Table Ronde de Lons-le-Saunier.

Leach, B. F., Quinn, C. J. and Lyon, G. L. (1996) A stochastic approach to the reconstruction of prehistoric human diet in the Pacific region from bone isotope signatures. *Tuhinga: Records of the Museum of New Zealand Te Papa Tongarewa* 8, 1–54.

Le Huray, J. D. and Schutkowski, H. (2005) Diet and social status during the La Tène period in Bohemia: carbon and nitrogen stable isotope analysis of bone collagen from Kutná Hora – Karlov and Radovesice. *Journal of Anthropological Archaeology* 24, 135–147.

Longin, R. (1971) New method of collagen extraction for radiocarbon dating. *Nature* 230, 241–243.

Macko, S. A., Engel, M. H., Andrusevich, V., Lubec, G., O'Connell, T. C. and Hedges, R. E. M. (1999) Documenting the diet in ancient human populations through stable isotope analysis of hair. *Philosophical Transactions of the Royal Society of London, Series B* 354, 65–76.

Mays, S. A., Richards, M. P. and Fuller, B. T. (2002) Bone stable isotope evidence for infant feeding in mediaeval England. *Antiquity* 76, 654–656.

Montgomery, J., Evans, J., Powlesland, D. and Roberts, C. (2005) Continuity or colonization in Anglo-Saxon England? Isotope evidence for mobility, subsistence practice, and status at West Heslerton. *American Journal of Physical Anthropology* 126, 123–138.

Murray, M. L. and Schoeninger, M. J. (1988) Diet, status, and complex social structure in Iron Age Central Europe: Some contributions from bone chemistry. In: D. B. Gibson and M. N. Geselowitz (eds.) *Tribe and Polity in Late Prehistoric Europe: Demography, Production and Exchange in the Evolution of Complex Social Systems*, 155–176. New York, Plenum Press.

Richards, M. P., Fuller, B. T. and Hedges, R. E. M. (2001) Sulphur isotopic variation in ancient bone collagen from Europe: implications for human palaeodiet, residence mobility, and modern pollutant studies. *Earth and Planetary Science Letters* 191, 185–190.

Richards, M. P., Fuller, B. T., Sponheimer, M., Robinson, T. and Ayliffe, L. (2003) Sulphur isotopes in palaeodietary studies: a review and results from a controlled feeding experiment. *International Journal of Osteoarchaeology* 13, 37–45.

Richards, M. P., Hedges, R. E. M., Molleson, T. I. and Vogel, J. C. (1998) Stable isotope analysis reveals variations in human diet at the Poundbury Camp cemetery site. *Journal of Archaeological Science* 25, 1247–1252.

Schoeninger, M. J. and DeNiro, M. J. (1984) Nitrogen and carbon isotopic composition of bone collagen from marine and terrestrial animals. *Geochimica et Cosmochimica Acta* 48, 625–639.

Schoeninger, M. J., DeNiro, M. J. and Tauber, H. (1983) Stable nitrogen isotope ratios of bone collagen reflect marine and terrestrial components of prehistoric human diet. *Science* 220(4604), 1381–1383.

Schurr, M. R. (1997) Stable nitrogen isotopes as evidence for the age of weaning at the Angel site: a comparison of isotopic and demographic measures of weaning age. *Journal of Archaeological Science* 24, 919–927.

Schutkowski, H., Herrmann, B., Wiedemann, F., Bocherens, H. and Grupe, G. (1999) Diet, status and decomposition at Weingarten: trace element and isotopic analyses on Early Medieval skeletal material. *Journal of Archaeological Science* 26, 675–685.

Schweissing, M. and Grupe, G. (2003) Stable strontium isotopes in human teeth and bone: a key to migration events of the late Roman period in Bavaria. *Journal of Archaeological Science* 30, 1373–1383.

Sponheimer, M. and Lee-Thorp, J. (1999) Oxygen isotopes in enamel carbonate and their ecological significance. *Journal of Archaeological Sciences* 26, 723–728.

Turek, J. (1997) Latènskè pohřebiště v Tišicích (okr. Mělník) (La Tène period cemetery at Tišice, district Mělník). *Archeologie ve Středních Čechách* 1, 237–262.

van der Merwe, N. J. and Vogel, J. C. (1978) ^{13}C content of human collagen as a measure of prehistoric diet in woodland North America. *Nature* 276, 815–816.

Van Klinken, G. J. (1999) Bone collagen quality indicators for palaeodietary and radiocarbon measurements. *Journal of Archaeological Science* 26(6), 687–695.

Veleminský, P. and Dobisiková, M. (1998) Demografie a základní antropologická charakteristika pravěkých pohřebišť v Praze 5 – Jinonicích (Demography and basic anthropological characteristics at the prehistoric cemetery at Prague 5 – Jinonice). *Archaeologica Pragensia* 14, 229–271.

Vogel, J. C. and van der Merwe, N. J. (1977) Isotopic evidence for early maize cultivation in New York State. *American Antiquity* 42(2), 238–242.

Waldhauser, J. (2001) *Encyklopedie Keltů v Čechách* (Encyclopaedia of Celts in Bohemia). Prague, Nakladatelství Libri.

White, C., Longstaffe, F. J. and Law, K. R. (2004) Exploring the effects of environment, physiology and diet on oxygen isotope ratios in ancient Nubian bones and teeth. *Journal of Archaeological Science* 31, 233–250.

Wright, L. E. and Schwarcz, H. P. (1999) Correspondence between stable carbon, oxygen and nitrogen isotopes in human tooth enamel and dentine: Infant diets at Kaminaljuyu. *Journal of Archaeological Science* 26, 1159–1170.

Zohary, D. and Hopf, M. (2000) *Domestication of plants in the Old World*. Oxford, University Press.

Appendix

Sample	Context	Bag no.	Species	Element	Collagen Yield	%C	%N	δ13C	δ15N	C/N
SOBA 01	3804	9367	Pig	Mandible	4.3%	43.0	15.4	-20.0	9.8	3.27
SOBA 02	3804	9367	Pig	Mandible	3.7%	43.1	15.1	-20.3	8.9	3.33
SOBA 03	3804	9367	Sheep/goat	Mandible	2.1%	41.8	15.1	-20.8	8.3	3.24
SOBA 04	3804	9367	Cow	Mandible	3.1%	43.4	15.7	-20.7	6.9	3.22
SOBA 05	3804	9367	Sheep/goat	Femur	4.6%	44.2	15.9	-20.7	5.7	3.25
SOBA 06	3804	9367	Horse	Tibia	5.1%	43.8	15.8	-21.2	7.1	3.23
SOBA 07	3804	9367	Cow	Tibia	1.5%	41.4	14.8	-20.2	6.4	3.27
SOBA 08	3804	9362	Sheep/goat	Tibia	3.0%	43.3	15.7	-20.0	7.8	3.22
SOBA 09	3804	9722	Sheep/goat	Mandible	5.2%	42.5	15.2	-20.2	7.0	3.26
SOBA 10	3804	9722	Cow	Mandible	2.8%	43.5	15.5	-20.7	6.4	3.27
SOBA 11	3804	9722	Sheep/goat	Mandible	4.5%	43.5	15.5	-20.6	7.7	3.27
SOBA 12	3804	9722	Pig	Mandible	3.2%	42.5	15.3	-20.7	8.5	3.24
SOBA 13	3714	9079	Cow	Tooth root	3.9%	41.2	14.9	-20.5	6.7	3.24
SOBA 14	3714	9079	Sheep/goat	Femur	4.0%	41.8	14.8	-20.2	7.8	3.29
SOBA 15	3714	9079	Sheep/goat	Tibia	3.2%	43.1	15.5	-18.7	8.4	3.24
SOBA 16	3714	9079	Sheep/goat	Tibia	4.5%	43.4	15.5	-21.0	9.0	3.28
SOBA 17	3714	9091	Cow	Mandible	4.0%	43.4	15.7	-20.3	7.8	3.23
SOBA 18	3714	9091	Sheep/goat	Mandible	4.0%	42.0	15.0	-20.1	7.8	3.26
SOBA 19	3714	9091	Sheep/goat	Tibia	3.8%	40.7	14.7	-20.0	9.2	3.22
SOBA 20	3714	9104	Sheep/goat	Mandible	3.2%	44.0	15.3	-20.5	9.7	3.36
SOBA 21	3658	8942	Sheep/goat	Mandible	3.8%	42.4	15.1	-21.4	6.9	3.27
SOBA 22	3658	8942	Sheep/goat	Mandible	3.6%	44.0	15.7	-20.6	7.6	3.28
SOBA 23	3658	8982	Cow	Mandible	3.9%	43.0	15.4	-20.3	6.4	3.26
SOBA 24	3535	8168	Cow	Mandible	2.3%	41.6	14.9	-21.0	7.3	3.27
SOBA 25	3535	8192	Cow	Tooth root	2.1%	41.5	14.6	-21.1	9.0	3.31
SOBA 26	3532	8004	Sheep/goat	Maxilla	4.0%	43.7	15.7	-20.4	7.1	3.24
SOBA 27	3532	8004	Cow	Femur	4.3%	42.2	15.3	-20.2	4.6	3.22
SOBA 28	3532	4983	Horse	Tooth root	3.8%	42.3	15.3	-21.6	6.3	3.23
SOBA 29	3420	7466	Bird	Humerus	4.0%	43.7	15.2	-20.1	10.3	3.36
SOBA 30	3420	7373	Dog	1st Metacarpal	6.7%	42.0	15.2	-17.5	8.3	3.22
SOBA 31	3419	7248	Cow	Ulna	4.1%	42.5	15.5	-20.7	6.7	3.20
SOBA 32	3419	7408	Cow	Mandible	4.2%	42.0	15.1	-20.9	6.6	3.25
SOBA 33	3419	7408	Sheep/goat	Tibia	4.3%	41.6	15.0	-20.8	6.8	3.23
SOBA 34	3419	7408	Pig	Mandible	3.2%	44.6	15.7	-21.0	8.0	3.32
SOBA 35	3385	7355	Dog	Mandible	4.0%	43.4	15.4	-19.2	9.2	3.28
SOBA 36	3374	7297	Pig	Mandible	2.7%	42.6	15.3	-21.1	8.3	3.25
SOBA 37	3375	7520	Dog	Mandible	0.4%	38.8	13.7	-19.8	10.3	3.31
SOBA 38	3375	7529	Pig	Mandible	3.5%	44.9	15.4	-19.4	9.0	3.40
SOBA 39	3375	7517	Horse	Humerus	4.3%	43.1	15.1	-21.3	6.3	3.32
SOBA 40	3369	7325	Horse	Maxilla	5.3%	45.3	16.1	-21.8	5.8	3.27
SOBA 41	3369	7325	Horse	Tibia	0.5%	41.4	14.5	-22.0	6.7	3.33
SOBA 42	3369	7217	Pig	Mandible	4.0%	43.5	15.4	-20.6	6.0	3.30
SOBA 43	3337	7479	Rodent	Humerus	4.9%	44.1	15.4	-16.7	9.4	3.33
SOBA 44	3337	7185	Dog	Mandible	0.8%	43.2	14.7	-19.1	9.7	3.42
SOBA 45	3337	7185	Pig	Mandible	0.5%	40.1	13.6	-21.3	6.1	3.45
SOBA 46	3337	7204	Rodent	Mandible	3.0%	44.8	15.2	-21.3	12.7	3.44
SOBA 47	3146	6675	Dog	Mandible	2.7%	42.8	15.1	-19.8	7.8	3.31
SOBA 48	3146	6675	Rodent	Humerus	4.4%	44.4	15.7	-20.2	13.3	3.30
SOBA 49	3146	6675	Pig	Mandible	1.9%	69.4	23.4	-20.4	8.6	3.43
SOBA 50	3064	6279	Rodent	Femur	4.1%	43.3	15.2	-21.4	9.7	3.33
SOBA 51	3064	6271	Bird	Femur	4.9%	44.7	15.8	-20.5	5.6	3.30

Table 7.1. Animal bone data from the La Tène period settlement site at Soběsuky.

Sample	Skeleton	Grave/feature	Sex	Age at death	Collagen Yield	%C	%N	δ13C	δ15N	C/N
SOB 01	11343	21/83		14–17	7.1%	45.5	16.0	-18.5	9.7	3.32
SOB 02	12436	288/85		Adult	3.9%	45.1	16.1	-18.3	10.6	3.27
SOB 03	12437	448/85		18–25	2.8%	41.6	14.5	-19.2	8.6	3.36
SOB 03b	12437	448/85		0–1	4.6%	44.1	15.8	-19.2	10.3	3.26
SOB 04	12438	449/85		Adult	6.9%	45.7	16.0	-19.1	10.1	3.32
SOB 05	12439	591/85	Male	46+	3.7%	44.6	15.8	-19.7	8.7	3.29
SOB 06	12440	602/85		Adult	2.9%	44.7	15.9	-19.4	9.7	3.29
SOB 07	12441	612/85		Adult	2.0%	43.5	14.9	-19.1	10.0	3.40
SOB 08	12442	612/85		Adult	1.1%	42.8	14.6	-19.9	10.4	3.42
SOB 09a	12443	613/85		0–0.5	3.0%	44.0	15.8	-17.9	11.6	3.25
SOB 09b	12443	613/85		0–0.5	4.5%	44.2	16.0	-17.4	10.8	3.23
SOB 09c	12443	613/85		0–0.5	4.2%	44.5	16.0	-17.8	10.4	3.24
SOB 10	12444	639a/85		Adult	7.5%	45.3	16.3	-17.7	9.8	3.24
SOB 11	12445	639b/85	Male	26–45	X	X	X	X	X	X
SOB 12	12446	1047/85		Adult	6.4%	44.9	16.1	-19.2	8.0	3.26

Table 7.2. Human bone data from the La Tène period cemetery at Soběsuky (sample SOB 11 lost in transit).

Sample	Skeleton	Grave/feature	Sex	Age at death	Collagen Yield	%C	%N	δ13C	δ15N	C/N
TIS 07	9550	7	Male	46+	2.8%	42.2	14.9	-18.2	9.1	3.30
TIS 08	9551	8	Male	18–25	3.1%	44.1	15.3	-18.7	10.2	3.36
TIS 09	9552	9	Female	26–45	4.1%	43.5	15.3	-18.8	9.8	3.32
TIS 10	9553	10	Male	26–45	4.5%	44.5	15.6	-18.6	10.5	3.32
TIS 11	9554	11		7–12	3.8%	40.4	14.4	-18.0	9.4	3.28
TIS 12	9555	12	Male	26–45	2.7%	43.8	15.2	-18.3	10.5	3.36
TIS 13	9556	13	Male	46+	4.2%	44.6	15.7	-18.2	8.6	3.31
TIS 14	9557	14		13–17	2.9%	42.8	15.0	-19.5	9.2	3.34
TIS 15	9558	15		26–45	4.1%	44.2	15.5	-18.7	10.2	3.33
TIS 16	9559	16	Male	26–45	3.0%	40.3	14.3	-18.7	9.5	3.30
TIS 17	9560	17	Male	18–25	5.0%	44.2	15.6	-18.8	10.7	3.29
TIS 32	9561	32		1.5–2.5	2.8%	40.7	14.1	-18.5	12.9	3.37
TIS 33	9562	33		26–45	4.2%	43.8	15.5	-18.2	9.4	3.30
TIS 50	9563	50	Male	26–45	2.8%	43.7	15.4	-18.1	9.8	3.30
TIS 51	9564	51		26–45	1.3%	31.7	10.8	-19.7	10.2	3.41
TIS 52	9565	52	Female	18–25	1.2%	39.4	13.8	-18.6	9.2	3.32
TIS 53	9566	53		18–25	5.0%	43.8	15.4	-18.0	9.6	3.31
TIS 54	9567	54		18–25	5.0%	44.5	15.6	-18.7	8.9	3.32
TIS 55	9568	55		7–12	1.7%	35.6	12.6	-19.7	8.8	3.30
TIS 56	9569	56	Male	26–45	3.7%	44.8	15.8	-18.4	9.6	3.32

Table 7.3. Human bone data from the La Tène period cemetery at Tišice.

Sample	Species	Element	Collagen Yield	%C	%N	δ13C	δ15N	C/N
JIN 96-1 S/G	Sheep/goat	Radius	1.8%	44.6	16.0	-20.8	5.2	3.26
JIN 96-2 S/G	Sheep/goat	Radius	1.4%	43.7	14.9	-21.1	5.2	3.42
JIN 96-3 S/G	Sheep/goat	Ulna	2.5%	44.5	15.9	-20.8	5.0	3.26
JIN 96-4 S/G	Sheep/goat	Scapula	1.8%	43.2	15.6	-20.7	5.3	3.23
JIN 96-5 S/G	Sheep/goat	Humerus	0.1%	X	X	X	X	X
JIN 96-6 S/G	Sheep/goat	Calcaneous	2.7%	41.7	15.0	-20.0	6.2	3.25

Table 7.4. Animal bone data from grave 96 of the La Tène period cemetery at Jinonice (X=not analysed).

Sample	Skeleton	Grave/feature	Sex	Age at death	Collagen Yield	%C	%N	δ13C	δ15N	C/N
JIN 03F	16097	3		26–45	0.0%	X	X	X	X	X
JIN 04R	16098	4	Male	26–45	5.2%	43.1	15.5	-19.3	9.8	3.25
JIN 05F	16099	5		Adult	5.3%	46.2	16.1	-18.7	9.5	3.35
JIN 06R	16100	6	Female	46+	8.0%	46.5	16.7	-18.9	10.0	3.26
JIN 07R	16101	7	Male	26–45	4.2%	44.8	16.2	-19.6	9.4	3.22
JIN 08F	16102	8		26–45	6.1%	46.1	16.1	-19.1	8.5	3.34
JIN 09F	16103	9		1–6	6.8%	46.5	16.5	-19.7	9.1	3.29
JIN 10F	16104	10		26–45	6.6%	45.6	16.2	-19.1	10.5	3.29
JIN 13aR	16106	13	Male	26–45	2.5%	44.0	15.5	-19.5	12.1	3.31
JIN 13bR	16107	13	Male	18–25	0.9%	31.9	10.7	-19.7	13.2	3.50
JIN 13R	16105	13	Male	Adult	3.9%	44.9	15.6	-19.5	13.1	3.35
JIN 14R	16108	14		1–6	1.9%	34.1	12.1	-19.3	8.7	3.28
JIN 15bF	16110	15		18–25	7.3%	46.7	16.5	-18.2	9.6	3.30
JIN 15F	16109	15		26–45	4.8%	44.4	15.7	-18.8	10.0	3.29
JIN 16F	16111	16		Adult	1.6%	44.4	15.4	-19.9	10.2	3.37
JIN 17aR	16112	17	Female	26–45	3.3%	43.8	15.2	-19.5	13.3	3.37
JIN 17bR	16112	17		Adult	3.9%	40.3	14.3	-19.2	8.8	3.29
JIN 18R	16113	18	Male	46+	5.7%	43.9	15.7	-18.9	9.9	3.26
JIN 19F	16114	19		26–45	4.7%	45.3	15.9	-18.5	9.7	3.32
JIN 21R	16116	21	Female	26–45	3.5%	43.7	15.4	-19.8	10.5	3.31
JIN 22R	16117	22	Female	46+	2.8%	45.2	16.1	-18.3	9.3	3.27
JIN 26R	16118	26	Male	46+	5.8%	47.9	16.8	-18.9	10.3	3.33
JIN 27R	16119	27	Male	46+	3.2%	42.0	15.0	-19.2	9.7	3.26
JIN 33aR	16120	33	Male	26–45	5.8%	46.2	16.5	-18.6	10.0	3.27
JIN 33bF	16120	33		Adult	4.9%	42.9	15.5	-19.2	9.5	3.23
JIN 33cR	16120	33		Adult	8.1%	41.5	15.0	-18.6	9.7	3.23
JIN 34F	16121	34		18–25	2.5%	40.4	14.3	-18.7	9.4	3.30
JIN 35R	16122	35		13–17	6.8%	45.0	16.2	-16.6	10.1	3.25
JIN 36F	16123	36		Adult	6.7%	45.2	16.2	-18.3	9.7	3.25
JIN 37R	16124	37	Female	46+	7.8%	44.2	16.1	-18.6	10.4	3.21
JIN 38F	16126	38	Male	26–45	5.3%	47.2	16.8	-17.6	9.9	3.28
JIN 39F	16127	39	Male	26–45	5.4%	46.1	16.6	-18.4	10.1	3.24
JIN 40aR	16128	40		Adult	6.6%	46.6	16.6	-17.6	9.7	3.28
JIN 40bR	16128	40		Adult	5.9%	44.1	15.7	-17.7	10.6	3.27
JIN 40cF	16128	40	Male	26-45	2.6%	39.5	14.1	-17.8	10.4	3.25
JIN 42R	16130	42	Male	46+	4.3%	44.2	15.8	-17.2	9.0	3.26
JIN 43F	16131	43		26–45	7.8%	43.0	15.6	-17.2	9.6	3.22
JIN 44F	16132	44		Adult	6.1%	39.5	14.1	-18.5	10.2	3.25
JIN 45F	16133	45		Adult	6.0%	45.0	16.0	-18.4	9.9	3.27
JIN 46F	16134	46	Female	Adult	2.0%	45.8	15.7	-19.2	10.3	3.41
JIN 47F	16135	47		Adult	6.2%	43.2	15.5	-18.5	10.0	3.25
JIN 48aF	16136	48		13–17	6.1%	46.4	16.8	-19.1	8.7	3.23
JIN 48bF	16137	48		18–25	3.6%	42.7	15.2	-18.6	9.7	3.28
JIN 49F	16138	49	Male	26–45	3.8%	43.9	15.5	-18.4	9.0	3.30
JIN 50F	16139	50	Female	18–25	4.8%	44.6	16.0	-16.4	9.4	3.25
JIN 53F	16141	53			0.6%	30.6	10.7	-19.5	9.7	3.33
JIN 57F	16142/16143	57			2.3%	44.3	15.5	-18.8	10.7	3.34
JIN 58R	16144	58	Female	18–25	4.1%	45.6	16.2	-18.1	10.0	3.29
JIN 60R	16145	60		1–6	4.1%	45.4	16.0	-20.0	10.8	3.32
JIN 62F	16146	62		13–17	3.0%	44.6	15.9	-18.9	9.1	3.28
JIN 63aF	16147	63		Adult	3.1%	37.2	13.3	-19.0	10.0	3.26
JIN 63bR	16149	63		Adult	2.6%	39.0	13.8	-18.3	9.8	3.31
JIN 64R	16150	64	Male	26–45	5.4%	44.4	15.9	-18.5	10.5	3.26
JIN 71F	16151	71	Female	46+	4.3%	43.7	15.5	-18.0	8.9	3.30
JIN 72F	16152	72	Female	26–45	3.7%	43.6	15.5	-19.4	9.7	3.28
JIN 73R	16153	73	Male	46+	5.4%	43.9	15.7	-18.7	10.3	3.26
JIN 74F	16154	74		Adult	1.4%	37.3	13.2	-18.3	9.7	3.30
JIN 76R	16155	76		Adult	4.6%	43.0	15.4	-19.8	9.2	3.25
JIN 77R	16156	77		18–25	6.4%	45.8	16.2	-20.1	10.0	3.30
JIN 78F	16157	78	Male	26–45	3.3%	36.6	13.1	-19.6	9.2	3.25
JIN 79F	16158	79		Adult	6.8%	44.9	15.9	-18.5	9.1	3.29
JIN 80F	16159	80	Male	26–45	7.3%	44.9	16.1	-19.1	10.1	3.25
JIN 89R	16160	89	Male	26–45	5.9%	42.0	15.1	-18.7	10.1	3.24
JIN 96F	16161	96	Female	26–45	4.7%	41.8	15.0	-19.1	9.0	3.27

Table 7.5. Human bone data from the La Tène period cemetery at Jinonice (X = not analysed).

Sample	Grave	Species	Element	Collagen Yield	%C	%N	δ13C	δ15N	C/N
RUZ COW	7	Cow	Tooth root	2.4%	38.7	13.9	-20.9	8.1	3.24
RUZ PIG 1	15	Pig	Mandible	3.6%	43.2	14.8	-20.2	10.1	3.40
RUZ PIG 2	18	Pig	Tooth root	3.3%	39.1	13.9	-21.1	7.5	3.28
RUZ PIG 3	19	Boar	Femur	3.4%	44.9	15.9	-22.1	6.8	3.29

Table 7.6. Animal bone data from the La Tène period cemetery at Ruzyně.

Sample	Skeleton	Grave/feature	Sex	Age at death	Collagen Yield	%C	%N	δ13C	δ15N	C/N
RUZ 01	8699	1	Male	18–25	2.5%	37.3	13.2	-18.9	9.2	3.30
RUZ 01b	8699	1b	Male	Adult	4.3%	42.0	14.8	-19.1	10.6	3.30
RUZ 03	8701	3		13–17	2.1%	40.1	14.1	-18.9	9.7	3.32
RUZ 04	8702	4	Male	46+	5.3%	44.5	15.8	-18.7	10.2	3.29
RUZ 07	8705	7		13–17	3.2%	41.0	14.6	-18.7	9.9	3.28
RUZ 08	8706	8	Male	46+	4.5%	43.0	15.3	-19.5	10.2	3.28
RUZ 09	8707	9	Male	26–45	2.6%	39.7	14.0	-19.4	9.1	3.30
RUZ 10	8708	10	Male	46+	4.2%	42.4	15.1	-19.4	10.1	3.27
RUZ 11	8709	11		46+	4.7%	43.9	15.6	-18.5	9.4	3.29
RUZ 12	8710	12		26–45	2.9%	42.8	15.0	-19.1	10.2	3.33
RUZ 13	8711	13		18–25	4.1%	41.9	14.9	-19.2	9.6	3.29
RUZ 14	8712	14		13–17	3.7%	44.9	16.0	-17.1	9.4	3.27
RUZ 15	8713	15	Male	46+	3.9%	44.9	16.0	-18.6	10.1	3.27
RUZ 16	8714	16	Male	26–45	3.4%	43.6	15.5	-18.9	11.1	3.28
RUZ 17	8715	17	Male	26–45	3.7%	40.7	14.3	-17.4	9.7	3.32
RUZ 18	8716	18		26–45	7.7%	46.1	16.4	-18.6	10.2	3.29
RUZ 19	8717	19	Male	26–45	0.8%	34.0	11.7	-20.4	10.0	3.40
RUZ 21	8719	21	Male	26–45	7.8%	44.9	15.9	-19.2	10.6	3.30
RUZ 24	8721	24	Male	18–25	7.2%	45.3	16.1	-19.0	9.9	3.28
RUZ 25	8722	25	Male	26–45	5.5%	45.4	16.0	-19.1	10.0	3.31
RUZ 26	8723	26		13–17	4.1%	43.4	15.2	-19.0	11.4	3.32
RUZ 27	8724	27	Male	46+	2.1%	38.6	13.7	-19.3	9.7	3.30
RUZ 28	8725	28		13–17	4.7%	42.3	15.0	-19.6	10.2	3.30
RUZ 29	8726	29		13–17	4.4%	43.1	15.2	-19.2	8.8	3.31
RUZ 30	8727	30		26–45	3.1%	40.9	14.5	-19.3	10.3	3.29
RUZ 31	8728	31		26–45	3.4%	43.3	15.0	-19.4	9.7	3.37
RUZ 32	8729	32		18–25	8.8%	46.8	16.6	-18.9	8.4	3.30
RUZ 34	8731	34		26–45	2.9%	39.4	14.0	-19.3	9.3	3.27
RUZ 35	8732	35		1–6	2.3%	38.5	13.5	-19.1	10.0	3.32
RUZ 36	8733	36		26–45	2.9%	38.2	13.4	-19.6	8.8	3.32
RUZ 37	8734	37			1.7%	38.9	13.7	-18.0	9.8	3.31
RUZ 38	8735	38		1–2	2.5%	41.7	14.5	-19.4	11.1	3.34
RUZ 39	8736	39		18–25	4.3%	42.4	15.1	-19.3	9.2	3.28
RUZ 40	8737	40	Male	26–45	3.0%	44.3	15.6	-19.2	9.9	3.31
RUZ 41	8738	41		13–17	2.6%	37.6	13.4	-19.0	9.2	3.27
RUZ 42	8739	42	Male	18–25	3.6%	43.1	15.2	-19.0	10.5	3.31
RUZ 43	8740	43		13–17	3.6%	42.3	14.9	-18.9	9.6	3.30
RUZ 44	8741	44			2.5%	34.9	12.6	-18.9	8.5	3.24
RUZ 45	8742	45		Adult	2.4%	39.9	13.9	-19.6	9.4	3.34
RUZ 46	8743	46		26–45	8.7%	45.5	16.1	-19.6	10.0	3.30
RUZ 47	8744	47	Male	26–45	3.7%	40.3	14.4	-18.9	10.8	3.26
RUZ 48	8745	48		26–45	3.3%	43.6	15.4	-19.3	9.4	3.31
RUZ 49	8746	49	Female	26–45	1.9%	37.9	13.2	-19.1	10.3	3.35

Table 7.7. Human bone data from the La Tène period cemetery at Ruzyně.

Sample	Skeleton	Grave/feature	Sex	Age at death	Collagen Yield	%C	%N	δ13C	δ15N	C/N
MAK 01	4163	1		5–7	3.6%	44.5	15.7	-18.9	9.6	3.30
MAK 03	4164	3		26–45	1.3%	44.3	15.3	-18.1	9.3	3.38
MAK 05	4166	5	Female	26–45	6.0%	45.0	15.7	-18.6	9.0	3.35
MAK 06-1	4167	6		3–5	6.2%	45.8	16.0	-18.3	10.8	3.34
MAK 06-2	4167	6	Male	26–45	7.4%	45.0	16.1	-18.8	9.8	3.26
MAK 07	4168	7			5.4%	42.7	14.7	-18.4	9.8	3.38
MAK 08	4169	8	Male	Adult	4.9%	44.8	15.9	-17.8	10.4	3.29
MAK 09	4170	9		1–6	4.2%	45.3	15.8	-17.7	12.6	3.34
MAK 10	4171	10		3–5	1.9%	42.2	14.6	-18.1	12.0	3.38
MAK 11	4172	11		26–45	6.2%	44.9	15.8	-19.1	9.0	3.32
MAK 12	4173	12	Female	46+	4.0%	44.4	15.4	-19.6	9.6	3.36
MAK 13	4174	13	Male	26–45	5.6%	45.1	16.0	-18.9	10.0	3.29
MAK 14	4175	14	Female	26–45	5.8%	45.5	16.1	-18.5	9.7	3.29
MAK 15	4176	15	Male	26–45	6.2%	45.6	16.2	-18.8	9.3	3.30
MAK 16	4177	16	Female	26–45	3.9%	45.1	15.5	-18.7	9.8	3.38
MAK 17	4178	17	Male	46+	3.5%	44.0	15.1	-19.0	9.6	3.40
MAK 18	4179	18	Female	26–45	2.3%	43.0	14.9	-16.8	9.7	3.37
MAK 19	4180	19	Female	46+	5.0%	45.3	15.9	-18.7	8.7	3.33
MAK 20	4181	20		Adult	2.4%	43.4	15.2	-18.9	10.2	3.34
MAK 21	4182	21	Male	46+	4.9%	45.8	16.1	-19.3	9.3	3.33
MAK 22	4183	22	Female	18–25	1.0%	43.0	14.5	-20.0	9.5	3.45
MAK 23	7238	23	Male	26–45	3.7%	45.3	16.0	-18.8	10.6	3.30

Table 7.8. Human bone data from the La Tène period cemetery at Makotrasy.

8.   Immigrants on the Isle of Lewis – combining traditional funerary and modern isotope evidence to investigate social differentiation, migration and dietary change in the Outer Hebrides of Scotland

Janet Montgomery and Jane A. Evans

Introduction

Faced with two skeletons in a Viking Period (8th to 9th century AD) cemetery, how can an archaeologist separate the invader from the invaded? Moreover, how can they tell if the migrant came alone or in family groups? Traditionally, archaeologists have employed a variety of methods to identify migrations. These have ranged from historical records, sudden changes in material culture, grave assemblage, burial style and orientation, to more direct studies of skeletal traits such as cranial shape, stature and build. None are wholly objective. Historical records are incomplete and often woefully biased; skeletal traits are difficult to interpret and can vary more within than between populations; and how the burial was arranged may say more about the beliefs and needs of the survivors than those of the deceased. Ancient DNA analysis, should it overcome the difficulties of contamination and damage, cannot easily distinguish the initial invaders from their subsequent descendants. However, isotope analysis of skeletal tissue provides a means of linking people with their geographical, rather than genetic, origins. As the authors of early archaeological applications of the technique pointed out (Ericson 1985; Molleson *et al.* 1986), isotope analysis has the potential to fill this gap. Only the radiogenic isotope systems of strontium and lead will be discussed here; although light stable isotopes such as sulphur and oxygen may also be extremely useful in this regard (Schwarcz *et al.* 1991; Fricke *et al.* 1998; Richards *et al.* 2001, 2003), they either rest on different principles (oxygen) or are obtained by measuring organic tissues (sulphur) which would inevitably necessitate a far lengthier discussion.

Ucko (1969) pointed out over thirty years ago that it

may ultimately prove to be an apparently insignificant difference between burials, for example the placing of the left hand, that identifies the incomer at a particular site. Accordingly, it is vitally important to interpret isotope results within the archaeological context and to keep an open mind. However, we cannot ignore the fact that the heavy metals of strontium and lead have a geological source, and any interpretation must also accord with explanations that conform to geological principles. It is what we do when the archaeological evidence splits the burial population along different lines to the isotopic evidence that presents a conundrum. Is the "hard" geological evidence more reliable than the archaeological, given the fluid nature of human ethnicity, beliefs and culture, or is it also subject to uncertainties and unknowns in how it manifests itself in the human tissues that we analyse, given that people are self-evidently not rocks? This paper attempts to bring these two taskmasters together in a reworking of the nature versus nurture argument, in the hope that it will demonstrate the depth of information that we may potentially retrieve from such work, and how it supports or refutes complementary evidence from funerary and archaeological contexts. We will briefly review archaeological migration theory, the principles, problems and possibilities of applying radiogenic isotope analysis to archaeological tooth enamel, and then attempt to demonstrate in a specific case study from the Outer Hebrides, Scotland, how it may be applied.

Defining migration in archaeology

Migration was all but abandoned in archaeological explanations of cultural change during the 1970s and 1980s when processual theories of diffusion, internal differentiation and co-incident evolution of ideas and artefacts were favoured to explain the sharp discontinuities of the archaeological record (Adams *et al.* 1978). Where once the arrival of immigrants was invoked to explain the sudden change from long to round heads or round to square barrows, processual archaeologists discarded such unfashionable traditionalist explanations in favour of an "immobilist" past where travel was severely curtailed and change was stimulated independently on both sides of the North Sea. In the 1990s, pleas were made to re-instate migration, in all its guises, to its rightful place as a *bona fide* means by which people, artefacts and ideas could move, and to incorporate the long-established and sophisticated migration theories and models from other social sciences (Anthony 1990, 1997; Chapman and Hamerow 1997a; Härke 1998). If, as Anthony (1997, 24) maintains, "cultures don't migrate; people do", then it is, perhaps, to them rather than the remnants of their material culture that we should look for direct evidence of migrations.

However, migration is not necessarily restricted to the exclusive definition of Adams *et al.* (1978, 486), that is, "a simultaneous and permanent movement of substantial numbers of people …which might be expected to leave measurable traces in the cultural, linguistic and skeletal record". It need not mean a simultaneous, permanent migration of many people from one country to another. It does not have to be a single, inexplicable event or even a one-way process. Neither are warfare and military invasion the sole mechanisms (Chapman and Hamerow 1997b), although such events are probably the most visible and best-recorded movements of people. Where, for example, does mobility cease and migration begin? A more inclusive view is expressed by Anthony (1997) using Tilly's (1978) six-fold classification of local, circular, chain, career, colonising and coerced migrations. Here, migration is more akin to mobility in all its forms and includes the more localised social strategies of regular movement within a defined home region, individual migrations and seasonal transhumance. Just as important to archaeology, although perhaps not as prestigious as finding the first Saxon settler to set foot on English soil, is the possibility of identifying mobility between villages, regions or urban and rural environments, and it is Anthony's broader definition of mobility that is used in this paper.

Repeated, cyclical mobility within a restricted area is often very difficult to identify archaeologically and chronologically. However, isotope analysis of several teeth with overlapping mineralization times from a single individual can potentially provide direct, chronologically constrained, evidence for movements of this type (Montgomery *et al.* 2000; Montgomery 2002; Schweissing and Grupe 2003a). The direct analysis of skeletal remains can thus highlight crucial differences between the sexes and age groups resulting from the social processes of marriage, trading, slavery, warfare, in fact, any situation where differentiating between groups is useful. Moreover, the major subsistence and mobility changes predicted at the Mesolithic-Neolithic or the Neolithic-Early Bronze Age transition are ripe for such study. It follows that by extending the study protocols to animals, information can also be obtained about herding practices or the movement, import and export of stock between regions.

Principles, problems and possibilities

In recent years there has been a burgeoning number of studies that have successfully used strontium isotope analysis (Cox and Sealy 1997; Grupe *et al.* 1997; Price *et al.* 2000; Ezzo and Price 2002; Montgomery *et al.* 2003; Schweissing and Grupe 2003a, b; Bentley *et al.* 2004; Price *et al.* 2004), and to a lesser degree lead (Carlson 1996; Montgomery *et al.* 2000; Åberg *et al.* 1998; Montgomery 2002; Chiaradia *et al.* 2003; Muller *et al.* 2003; Budd *et al.* 2004; Montgomery *et al.* 2005), to demonstrate differences between ancient human individuals and populations that we assume arise through eating food sourced from different geological (and hence geographical) regions. Geological strontium and lead enter the biosphere through soil, water and plants and are ingested or inhaled by animals (Fig. 8.1); the majority of the body's burden of both elements is located in the teeth and bones. In archaeological populations, we are more inclined to infer that the people concerned moved from one food source to another. An alternative explanation, of course, and one that happens to a very great extent today, is that the food was transported to them. There are, however, many things that are still not understood about how and when the body incorporates elements such as lead and strontium into bones and teeth and, consequently, precisely what a datum point on a scatterplot or histogram tells us about that individual. Consider, for instance, the simple case of the strontium isotope ratio of a small chip of enamel from a single tooth. Compared to bone, enamel has a very limited period of mineralization followed by negligible post-eruptive turnover. Is it then a snapshot of childhood, when the tooth enamel was forming? The result, perhaps, of a couple of years of dietary inputs? Or just a single summer? Is it an average of the *whole* diet over this time, or can the dietary signature be dominated by a relatively small component of the diet that is calcium deficient or an especially rich or a particularly bioavailable source of strontium? Would the strontium composition of the enamel then be unrepresentative of the diet as a whole? Does the strontium derive mostly from solid food rather than water? How much variation should we realistically expect to see in a fairly self-sufficient farming community? Between siblings? In the dentition of a single indigenous individual? Is the choice of tooth or sampling location on the tooth going to have an effect on this? Is there any incremental isotopic information *within* human enamel that can be obtained, given the complex multi-stage mineralization process and current analytical constraints?

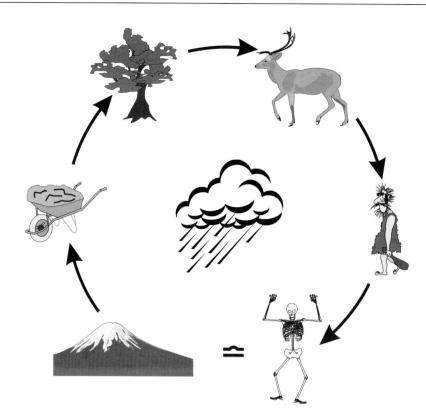

Figure 8.1. Schematic diagram to illustrate the transfer of lead and strontium from the source rock into biological tissues. Water (e.g. rain, groundwater, sea-splash, drinking water) may contribute lead and strontium at all stages.

Surprisingly, very few of these questions currently have answers. Writing this paper presents an opportunity to explore the sources of isotopic variation in humans and what isotope results might be telling us about that individual's behaviour, status, diet and, in particular, geographical origins.

Several excellent, scientifically rigorous explanations of the method and principles of strontium and lead isotope analysis can be found in the literature (*e.g.* Gulson *et al.* 1997; Åberg *et al.* 1998; Capo *et al.* 1998; Beard and Johnson 2000; Price *et al.* 2002). Nevertheless, it is worth reiterating three fundamental points here:

1. Fractionation

Unlike the lighter isotope systems of carbon, nitrogen, oxygen and sulphur, no measurable alteration (*i.e.* fractionation) of strontium or lead isotope ratios occurs in low temperature geological and biological processes (Faure 1986; Graustein 1989; Miller *et al.* 1993; Capo *et al.* 1998; Blum *et al.* 2000). The source of biosphere strontium is rock, and it retains the $^{87}Sr/^{86}Sr$ values characteristic of the source rock when it is weathered into soil, sand, groundwaters and incorporated into plants and animals – predominantly in the skeleton (Fig. 8.1). The same is true of lead. They can be used, therefore, as tracers to link a person to the rocks that are found in the region where they obtained their food, and because different rocks have different ratios due to age, type and history we

can use this to discriminate between individuals with different geographical origins, *providing* the rocks they lived on are sufficiently different (Fig. 8.2) and on the understanding that the elements themselves were not being transported large distances in, for example, food or mineral ores.

2. The sources of strontium and lead

As illustrated in Figure 8.1, although isotopic change is negligible, the resulting skeletal isotope ratios may not be *exactly* the same as the whole source rock because: a) the various components of a heterogeneous rock such as granite may have different isotope ratios and different solubilities, so the strontium released to the food chain may be dominated by the most easily weathered phase rather than representative of the bulk rock; and b) straightforward *mixing* between two or more sources will produce a strontium ratio that is a *weighted average* of the original inputs. The resulting ratio will therefore depend on the *concentration* of strontium in each of the sources. For example, if river water containing very little strontium floods into the sea, it would require an awful lot of this river water in order to produce any measurable change in the strontium *ratio* of the seawater – which is a relatively rich reservoir of strontium. In much the same way, we could imagine the futility of trying to change a tin of deeply pigmented red paint to soft pink by adding white. And hence, why the modern seawater $^{87}Sr/^{86}Sr$ value of

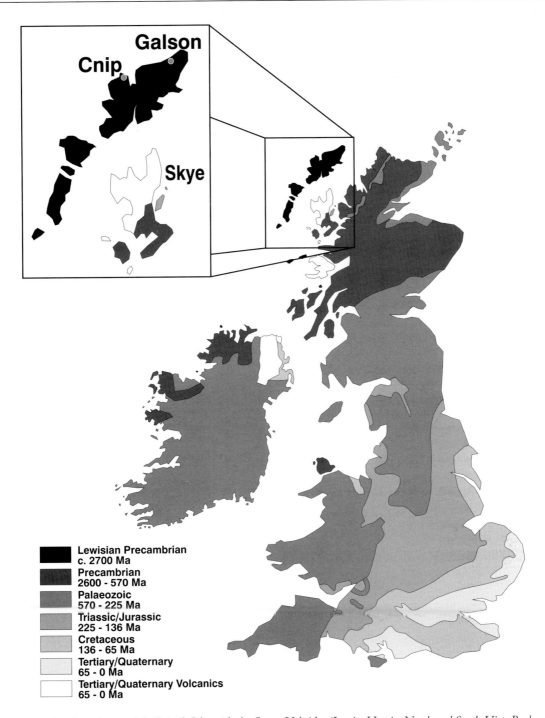

Figure 8.2. Simplified geological map of the British Isles with the Outer Hebrides (Lewis, Harris, North and South Uist, Benbecula etc.) shown in black.

~0.7092 is robustly constant throughout all the world's oceans (Veizer 1989).

Similarly, meat and milk contain little strontium (white paint in our analogy) and are thus likely to have little influence on the skeletal strontium isotope ratio of an individual if the individual is also consuming strontium-rich plants (red paint in our analogy). As an illustration, we could imagine a community who grew their own crops but chose to buy pigs for slaughter at a distant market rather than raising them locally. The strontium isotope ratio of the humans would be controlled by the local plant foods they consumed and their predilection for imported bacon would remain archaeologically invisible unless we also analysed the teeth of the "immigrant" pigs.

The amount of strontium incorporated by animals appears to reflect the amount available from the diet and environment, *i.e.* it is dose-dependent (Comar *et al.* 1956; Boivin *et al.* 1996). Reported values for modern human skeletal and dental tissues are typically 50–300 ppm (Brudevold and Söremark 1967; Underwood 1977; Hancock *et al.* 1989; Elliott and Grime 1993; Montgomery 2002). Animal skeletal tissues exhibit a similar range, although herbivores tend to have higher concentrations than carnivores due to progressive biopurification in the gut and, as already mentioned above, because plants are strontium-rich and animal soft tissues are strontium-poor (Elias 1980; Elias *et al.* 1982; Tuross *et al.* 1989; Bocherens *et al.* 1994; Burton and Wright 1995; Burton *et al.* 2003). Nevertheless, it is extremely rare for any mammalian tissues to exceed 1000 ppm (Radosevich 1993). Strontium concentrations in bone and teeth also vary geographically (Turekian and Kulp 1956; Brudevold and Söremark 1967; Underwood 1977; Burton *et al.* 2003) as a result of regional variations in bedrock geology, water and food, or cultural differences in subsistence strategies and diet. These considerations suggest carnivores can be distinguished from other carnivores inhabiting a different geographic region, and from vegetarians inhabiting the same geographical region on the basis of their strontium concentrations. However, separating vegetarians from plant-eating omnivores will be problematic as even small amounts of plant foods may have a disproportionately large effect on the body's strontium concentration and, hence, isotope ratio. Many studies use elemental Sr/Ca ratios rather than simple strontium concentrations as this enables different components of a foodchain (*e.g.* soil, plants, animals) to be compared. However, if the comparison is between a single tissue type such as enamel, which has a relatively consistent calcium content (~37% by weight), strontium concentrations are a valid discriminator.

Human exposure to natural sources of lead follows a similar pathway. However, it appears that human lead ratios are only linked to the local geology until the advent of widespread metal usage, at which point natural exposure from lead in country rock is swamped by lead of anthropogenic origin and the link is severed (Carlson 1996; Montgomery 2002; Budd *et al.* 2004; Montgomery *et al.* 2005). In Britain, there is a tendency for lead signatures in archaeological populations to move away from a highly variable natural country rock signature and converge on anthropogenic ore-lead, along with a concomitant rise in enamel lead concentration (*i.e.* >0.5 ppm). We have called this phenomenon cultural focussing of human lead signatures (Montgomery *et al.* 2005) and, in England, it appears to have occurred by the Roman period, presumably as a result of intensification of lead mining and use. The timing is, however, clearly geographically and culturally variable and the link may be re-established if lifestyle and status change.

3. Tooth enamel mineralization

All studies that perform chemical or isotopic analysis on samples with a post-mortem history have to address the possibility that the integrity of the ante-mortem information has been compromised. This complex phenomenon is generally given the term diagenesis, and how and whether it occurs is site and sample specific. Given the generally accepted fact that tooth enamel is considerably less prone to diagenetic contamination than dentine or bone, primarily due to its greater density and stability (Glimcher *et al.* 1990; Horn *et al.* 1994; Michel *et al.* 1996; Budd *et al.* 2000; Hoppe *et al.* 2003; Trickett *et al.* 2003; Bentley *et al.* 2004), all the results from humans and animals presented here were obtained from enamel that was very carefully separated from adhering dentine. The data, therefore, give information about the individual's *childhood* diet at some period whilst the tooth crown was mineralizing, irrespective of age at death. For humans especially, the precise timing, progression and duration of enamel *mineralization* as distinct from tooth crown *formation* for each tooth is still poorly understood (Boyde 1989, 1997; Sasaki *et al.* 1997; Fincham *et al.* 1999).

Enamel biomineralisation has been described as "The transformation of what was basically an organic gel to almost pure inorganic mineral (90% mineral by volume) by cellular and biochemical flow processing" (Mann 1997, 264). This process is achieved through the following distinct stages (Robinson *et al.* 1995a, 1995b; Fincham *et al.* 1999):

1. Secretion – of amelogenins and nucleation of crystallites
2. Assembly – of the amelogenins into nanospheres
3. Formation – elongation of thin, ribbon-like crystallites
4. Transition – resorption of the organic matrix and replacement with fluid
5. Maturation – massive increase in mineral ions and lateral growth of crystals.

A tooth's final dimensional parameters of enamel thickness and volume appear to be established during formation of the protein matrix (stages 1–3) when very thin enamel crystallites grow from the enamel-dentine junction to the tooth surface (Robinson *et al.* 1981; Fincham and Simmer 1997; Smith 1998). It is estimated that at this stage the enamel crystallites occupy only ~10% of the immature tissue volume – and hence only about 10% of the final enamel weight (Smith 1998). This protein "scaffold" guides the nucleation and elongation of the enamel crystallites and is eventually resorbed during the transitional phase (*contra* dentine where it mineralizes *in situ*) to permit the enamel crystallites to expand widthways during the maturation phase (stage 5) and occlude the space previously occupied by the organic matrix (Mann 1997; Smith 1998; Fincham *et al.* 1999). In dentine, the protein matrix forms and mineralizes *in situ* within 3–5 days (Hillson 1986, 1996) making the two processes to all intents and purposes simultaneous but, as Hillson (1986, 161) warns, "In enamel, the incremental structures represent matrix formation only – they are seen exactly the same in immature enamel".

It has been demonstrated for some animal species that incremental structures within tooth enamel appear when the primary organic matrix is deposited but that the maturation phase, when the bulk of the mineral ions are deposited, may take a further six months to complete (Robinson *et al.* 1978; Suga 1982; Robinson *et al.* 1987; Balasse 2002; Passey and Cerling 2002; Balasse 2003). Although enamel mineralization is species specific (Boyde 1997), it is clear that in humans also, the timing of enamel formation should not be confused with the timing of mineralization. Most of the lead and strontium in enamel will be incorporated during the massive influx of mineral ions that characterises the maturation phase, and it is not clear how long this process takes in different tooth types (Robinson *et al.* 1981), although some writers estimate maturation may take up to five years in some permanent human teeth (Boyde 1989; Sasaki *et al.* 1997). There is, therefore, no simple relationship between when lead and strontium are incorporated into enamel and such incremental structures. Neither does human enamel mineralize in a simple, single progressive wave of advance from the cusp tip down to the cervix; it appears to progress on several fronts: from the enamel-dentine junction towards the surface; from the outer enamel surface inwards; from the cusp down to the cervix; from the centre of each enamel crystallite – in a similar manner to the growth of tree rings; and thin enamel is likely to mineralize before thicker enamel (Robinson *et al.* 1981, 1987; Boyde 1989; Smith 1998). Robinson *et al.* (1981, 1031) demonstrated that "In the human deciduous incisor... it would appear that the entire labial surface can be at stage 3 at the same time". As stage 3 is the transitional stage that precedes maturation, this suggests that just prior to maturation the cervical enamel has "caught up" with the cuspal enamel, and it is possible that all the enamel on the tooth will go into the maturation phase at the same time. Given that only ~10% of the final mineral content is present when the incremental structures appear, it is highly likely that any chemical information related to the absolute timing of the deposition of the incremental enamel structures of a single tooth will be lost during the maturation phase. Moreover, the length of time human enamel maturation takes (months to years), the timing of its onset, and when during crown formation the maturation phase actually occurs, are not well defined and such parameters may well vary between teeth. For the purposes of lead and strontium analysis, therefore, incremental enamel structures should be regarded simply as relics of formation, fossilized, possibly years later, into the structure of the mature tissue. This study makes no attempt to interpret enamel results on a microscopic scale; results are of bulk enamel values from a single tooth.

A Hebridean case study

To illustrate the application, we will look at burials from the Outer Hebrides, the most northwesterly islands of the British Isles (Fig. 8.2 and Table 8.1). The island chain is geologically homogeneous (Lewisian gneisses and granites) and has a clearly defined geographic boundary (the sea) separating it from places of different geology (and hence isotope ratios) and, we may venture, different subsistence strategies. Whether the sea represented a barrier of any real significance in the periods in question and whether any social or dietary difference existed between Outer Hebrideans and people inhabiting the Inner Hebrides (*e.g.* the Isle of Skye) or the Scottish mainland is debatable, but it clearly presents more of a physical obstacle than, for example, trying to define the area of land utilised by a community and their animals living in central England (Evans and Tatham 2004).

This notwithstanding, in more recent times residents of these islands were regarded as living on the fringes of the European world (Martin 1994; McGowan 1996). This perspective has much to do with viewing the sea as the barrier that it most certainly was to terrestrial wildlife (Serjeantson 1990). Nonetheless, it has been argued that the seas off the west coast of Britain were once an important North Atlantic sea route, that was often quicker and easier to traverse than the equivalent journey overland (Sharples and Parker-Pearson 1999). This would have facilitated contact with Ireland, the western seaboard of Scotland and, particularly well documented in the Norse period, lands to the far north (Armit 1996).

Migration has previously been invoked to explain visible changes in the Hebridean archaeological record such as agriculture, beaker burials, Atlantic roundhouses and the unique long cist burials found at Galson (Armit 1996). Nevertheless, there is little evidence for any substantial population movement to the islands between the initial colonisation during the Mesolithic and the Viking Age (Armit 1996). Moreover, the presence of a seemingly unbroken indigenous pottery tradition from the Early Neolithic through to the 19th century, even during periods when parts of mainland Scotland, and indeed other Viking settlements, were virtually aceramic, would strongly suggest population continuity (Armit 1996; Sharples and Parker-Pearson 1999; Sharples 2001). The cultural affiliation of the inhabitants of Skye and the Western Isles prior to the onset of Viking raiding is, nonetheless, unclear. That they were indigenous Picts or Scots recently arrived from Dalriada (Co. Antrim) in the 5th century AD appears the most likely because both cultures had considerable maritime expertise (Ritchie 1993; Graham-Campbell and Batey 1998). However, the inhabitants of Lewis show no strong cultural affiliations to either group and there is little archaeological and no documentary evidence to support or refute either suggestion (Armit 1996). As Armit (1996, 232) explains, "Even in the Viking Age...the scale of immigration is unclear, as is the question of how far down the social hierarchy significant change occurred." Nonetheless, there is virtually no evidence that any pre-Norse place-names survived on Lewis (Graham-Campbell and Batey 1998) implying Norse settlement was pervasive,

Skeleton code	Sex	Age	Stature estimate	Grave type, alignment and body position	Grave goods	cal. ^{14}C dates (2σ)
Cnip BA	M	M Ad	163 ± 4cm	short cist E-W crouched	plain pottery vessel	1856–1520BC
Gals II	F	Y Ad	165 ± 4cm	long cist W-E extended	None	30–230AD
Gals IV	F	Y Ad	149 ± 4cm	long cist alignment n/k ?extended	None	70–250AD
Gals 74	M	A	169 ± 4cm	not known	None	–
Gals 93	M	A	169 ± 4cm	dug grave W-E flexed	penannular iron brooch, decorated pot, bone pin, textile	110–410AD
Gals 96	M	A	169 ± 4cm	long cist W-E extended	None	60–316AD
Cnip A	F	M Ad	155.5 ± 3.5cm	not recorded – probably simple dug grave	Rich assemblage including pagan Norse jewellery[§]	720–970AD
Cnip B	n/k	~6yrs	–	dug grave S-N flexed	amber bead, stone pendant	778–1006AD
Cnip C	M	M Ad	167 ± 4cm	kerbed E-W extended	None	778–1006AD
Cnip D	M	M Ad	162 ± 4cm	kerbed N-S extended	None	687–974AD
Cnip E	F	M Ad	159.5 ± 3.5cm	kerbed E-W flexed	bone pin, perforated iron plate	717–985AD
Cnip F	n/k	6-9m	–	dug grave NW-SE ?extended	amber beads, decorated bone pin	–
Cnip G	n/k	neonate	–	dug grave E-W crouched	iron rivet, textile	–

Table 8.1. Funerary and skeletal attributes of the individuals from Cnip and Galson, Outer Hebrides, Scotland. Adult ageing follows the standard age ranges recommended by Buikstra and Ubelaker (1994, 9): Young adult (Y Ad) 20–34 years; Middle-aged adult (M Ad) 35–49 years; Old adult (O Ad) 50+ years. For some individuals where preservation was poor, or diagnostic features were absent or ambiguous, the broader classification of Adult (Ad) or not known (n/k) was made by the osteologists concerned.

[§]Assemblage included items considered to be of foreign and indigenous origin: Norse oval gilt bronze brooches; necklace of 44 glass beads; antler comb; bone needle case and two iron needles; 10th century ringed pin; bronze belt-buckle and strap end; sickle; knife; whetstone; and fine linen.

Data sources for Cnip: Dunwell et al. (1996b) fiche 2 G1-G10; Welander et al. (1987); Dunwell et al. (1996a) fiche 4 B9-G14.

Data sources for Galson: Hill (1952); Wells (1953); Neighbour et al. (2002); and M. Bruce personal communication.

and cultural if not physical replacement of the indigenous population occurred. Indeed, the Hebrides were known as Innse Gall or "Islands of the Foreigners" (Ritchie 1993), which suggests migration contributed considerably to their history.

The cemetery at Galson (30–410 AD cal. 2σ) is of Iron Age date, whilst that at Cnip (687–1060 AD cal. 2σ) dates predominantly from the Norse period (Dunwell *et al.* 1996a; Neighbour *et al.* 2002). It should be noted that, in the Hebrides, the Iron Age is not curtailed by the Roman Period and continues uninterrupted until the 9th century AD. All the Iron Age individuals at Galson date from the first millennium AD (Table 8.1). Galson is the only known long cist cemetery in the Hebrides and the recent discovery of a cemetery wall (T. Neighbour, personal communication) strongly suggests that the cemetery was Christian. Although pre-Christian burial in long cists is not unknown and some Scottish and Irish long cists date from the Bronze Age (Proudfoot 1997), it is the size and organisation of the large long cist cemeteries that sets them apart from long cists of earlier date (Proudfoot 1997). If this is so, the dating at Galson makes the arrival of Christianity (and by implication missionaries) to the Hebrides, very early indeed. The majority of individuals excavated to date from Galson were supine burials, aligned E-W with the head to the west, in stone long cists with no extant grave goods (Hill 1952; Wells 1953; Ponting and Bruce 1989; Neighbour *et al.* 2002). However, one individual (Gals 93) had clearly received a very different burial rite; his body was crouched and placed in a simple dug grave with a rare penannular iron brooch, an unused decorated pot, a bone pin at the head and remnants of textile. He was also distinguished from the other occupants by the absence of a skeletal marker – a lateral buttressing of the proximal femur by a flange of bone located just below the third trochanter which is found on most Prehistoric Scottish femora (MacLaughlin and Bruce 1983), including the other Galson individuals and the Bronze Age burial from Cnip (Dunwell *et al.* 1996b; Neighbour *et al.* 2002).

The Norse cemetery at Cnip is the largest and the only known 'family' cemetery dating from the Viking Period in the Hebrides (Table 8.1). Four adults and three juveniles have been excavated to date; one adult female (Cnip A) was buried with an assemblage of pagan Norse grave goods (Welander *et al.* 1987), the richness of the burial contrasting sharply with the graves of the remaining adults (Cnip C, D and E) who were buried in three closely adjacent kerbed graves with few diagnostic grave goods (Dunwell *et al.* 1996a). The Atlantic coast of Lewis is gradually being lost through erosion and both sites have been excavated on a rescue basis. As a consequence, the full extent of neither cemetery is yet known, but they nevertheless pose many interesting questions about the social context of individuals inhabiting the island at two critical times in its history – the coming of Christianity and the Viking Age.

Analytical details

The isotope compositions of strontium and lead were measured using a *Finnigan MAT262* thermal ionisation multi-collector mass spectrometer at the NERC Isotope Geosciences Laboratory, Keyworth, UK, following the procedure given in Montgomery (2002). Isotope dilution was used to obtain lead and strontium concentrations using ^{208}Pb and ^{84}Sr spikes, respectively. The reproducibility of the international strontium standard, NBS 987, during the period of analysis did not exceed ±0.000030 (2σ) or ±0.004% (2σ). All samples were corrected to the value of ^{87}Sr/^{86}Sr = 0.710235 to correct for induced bias through mass spectrometer drift. Strontium isotope data are presented as ^{87}Sr/^{86}Sr ratios. Lead isotope fractionation was monitored with suitable sized (20ng) runs using NBS 981, and data were corrected for fractionation using the associated standards run. The ^{204}Pb ratios are reported in Montgomery (2002), but here we present the ^{208}Pb/^{206}Pb and ^{207}Pb/^{206}Pb ratios, which are used in many archaeological studies and are useful discriminants as they represent the decay products of two different elements: thorium 232, which decays to lead 208; and uranium 235, which decays to lead 207. A further advantage with these ratios is that they avoid the larger errors associated with measuring the low abundance ^{204}Pb isotope in small, low-lead enamel samples. Errors (2σ) on the lead isotope ratios did not exceed ±0.05% for ^{208}Pb/^{206}Pb and ^{207}Pb/^{206}Pb, ±0.16% for ^{208}Pb/^{204}Pb, ±0.13% for ^{207}Pb/^{204}Pb and ±0.01% ^{206}Pb/^{204}Pb. Laboratory contamination, monitored by procedural blanks for both lead and strontium, was negligible.

Lead results

Figure 8.3 displays the lead isotope results (^{208}Pb/^{206}Pb versus ^{207}Pb/^{206}Pb) from humans and animals from the Hebrides. Two Iron Age humans (Gals 93 and IV), and all the Norse humans and cattle cluster in the lower left-hand side of the plot. Such lead signatures are identical to many archaeological individuals from England, and we believe they indicate exposure to anthropogenic sources of lead ore (Montgomery 2002; Budd *et al.* 2004; Montgomery *et al.* 2005). However, they are also indistinguishable from Mediaeval Norwegians (Åberg *et al.* 1998). As there are no sources of lead ore on the Outer Hebrides, this lead must have been imported or accessed elsewhere. English, Welsh and some Irish (but not Scottish) ores can provide such values (Rohl 1996). Figure 4 plots the enamel lead concentration against the ^{208}Pb/^{206}Pb ratio. Two main trends emerge from this plot; high lead concentrations are restricted to ^{208}Pb/^{206}Pb values approximately equal to 2.084, whereas low lead concentrations are coupled with highly variable, non-ore-lead ratios. This inverse correlation between the spread of isotope ratios and lead concentration replicates the cultural focussing of lead burdens observed elsewhere in England (Montgomery *et al.* 2005). In contrast, the Bronze

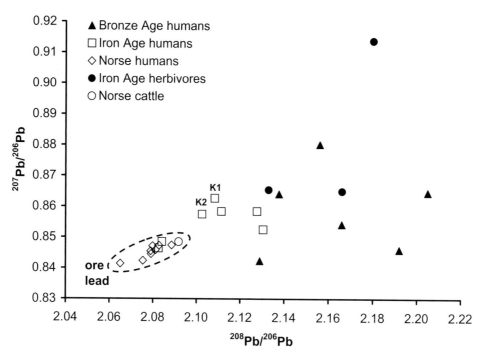

Figure 8.3. Scatterplot of $^{208}Pb/^{206}Pb$ versus $^{207}Pb/^{206}Pb$. Data taken from Montgomery (2002). All the Norse humans and cattle, and two Iron Age humans (Gals 93 and IV) are contained within the dashed oval. Such lead ratios are consistent with ore-lead sources of English, Welsh and eastern Irish (Dublin, Meath, Wicklow and Kildare) origin (Rohl 1996). The remaining Bronze and Iron Age humans and animals have highly variable lead ratios. K1 and K2 are first and second molars from the same individual. 2σ errors are contained within the symbols. Data from Montgomery (2002) and Parker Pearson et al. (2005).

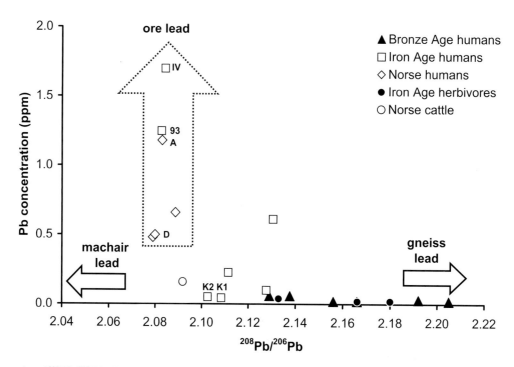

Figure 8.4. Scatterplot of $^{208}Pb/^{206}Pb$ plotted against lead concentration. High lead concentrations are only found in individuals with ore-type lead ~2.084 consistent with English, Welsh and a group of Irish ores from the Dublin region (Rohl 1996). All the Norse humans had anthropogenic ore-lead signatures; concentration samples for Cnip C, E and G failed and cannot be plotted. All the Bronze Age individuals had very low lead concentrations and highly variable lead ratios suggesting natural lead exposure from country rock (gneiss and machair) sources. K1 and K2 are first and second molars from the same individual. 2σ errors are contained within the symbols. Data from Montgomery (2002) and Parker Pearson et al. (2005).

Age humans and animals display the low lead concentrations (<0.06 ppm), coupled with the extremely variable ratios that we would ascribe to natural rock-derived exposure (Montgomery *et al.* 2005).

The Bronze Age humans demonstrate the variability amongst individuals prior to the large-scale lead extraction and exportation that occurred in Britain during the Roman period (Tylecote 1992). They contrast sharply with the increasing homogeneity seen in individuals exposed to lead in later periods, as exposure changes from predominantly geological (Bronze Age) to predominantly anthropogenic (Norse) lead sources severing the link between geology and origins. Lead, therefore, gives us no clear information about the *geographical* origins of the Norse individuals but rather reflects the level of exposure to circulated anthropogenic, rather than natural geological, lead and is thus a cultural, rather than geographical, marker.

In contrast to the consistent isotope ratios amongst the Norse population (humans and cattle) and the consistently low lead burdens of the Bronze Age population, the Iron Age individuals are highly variable: Gals 93 and IV have an entirely ore-dominated ratio which implies a very different childhood exposure to the other Iron Age individuals analysed; the remaining Iron Age individuals appear to have been exposed to little or no anthropogenic lead. The data suggest, therefore, that people could be exposed to highly variable levels (though not sources) of anthropogenic lead in the Hebridean Iron Age, and these results may provide an indication of metal use and circulation, which may change through time, in different locations and with status.

Strontium results

Strontium data from 20 humans, 4 archaeological herbivores (deer, cattle and sheep) and 15 biosphere samples (waters, soils, peat, modern plants and archaeological grains) are displayed, firstly, as a simple histogram (Fig. 8.5), which uses only the ^{87}Sr/^{86}Sr ratios but indicates the number of samples obtained within each group and, secondly, as a scatterplot (Fig. 8.6) which plots two variables: the isotope ratio, and the concentration of strontium in the enamel samples which, as discussed above, can vary both geographically and within a food-chain. Several methods for identifying what magnitude of isotopic difference is meaningful for archaeological interpretations have been suggested (Price *et al.* 2002; Schweissing and Grupe 2003b; Bentley *et al.* 2004; Evans and Tatham 2004). However, the magnitude of a "local" isotopic range is likely to be site, period and context specific. Some sedentary communities will naturally exhibit much larger ranges than others due to both intrinsic and extrinsic factors. The geological and geographical setting (*e.g.* how varied is the geology of the

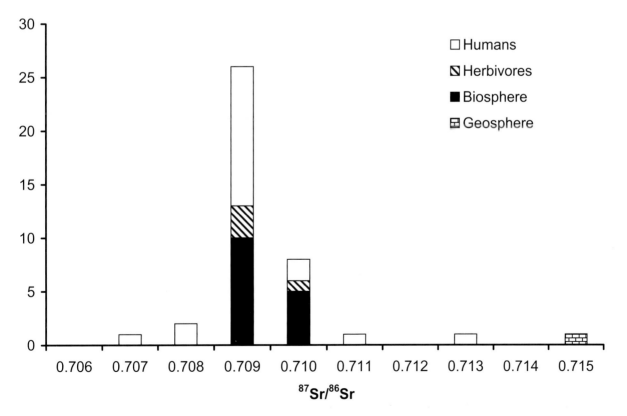

Figure 8.5. Histogram of ^{87}Sr/^{86}Sr values obtained from the Hebrides. Data from Montgomery (2002), Montgomery et al. *(2003; in prep) and Parker Pearson* et al. *(2005).*

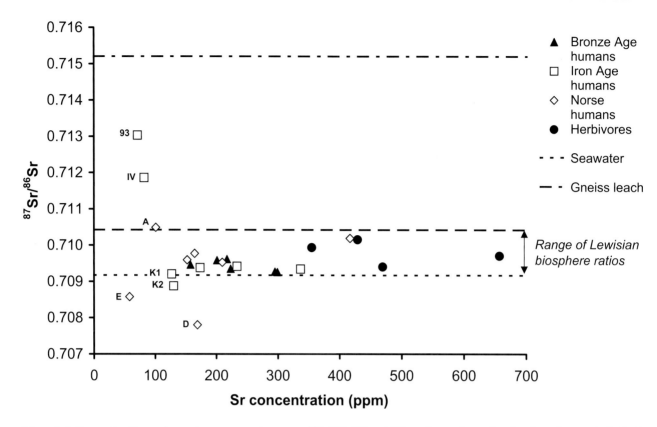

Figure 8.6. Scatterplot of enamel strontium concentrations versus $^{87}Sr/^{86}Sr$ K1 and K2 are first and second molars from the same individual. 2σ errors are contained within the symbols. Data from Montgomery (2002), Montgomery et al. (2003; in prep) and Parker Pearson et al. (2005).

region and how homogeneous is the rock itself? Is the site on a small island? Inland with defined boundaries? Coastal?), and the cultural choices and restrictions on diet and food production strategies that they follow through choice or necessity, will all have a bearing on the observed variability. It is, therefore, a necessary objective to establish what range of strontium isotopes were, and are, available at each site by analysing biosphere samples, whilst acknowledging the difficulties of reconstructing past environmental parameters.

Geological considerations (Faure 1986; Erel *et al.* 1994; Blum and Erel 1997) suggested we might reasonably anticipate that soils, animals and people from Lewis would have strontium isotope ratios that, at least, *reflected* the considerable age of the Lewisian gneiss from which the Outer Hebrides are almost entirely composed; as a broad (but by no means exclusive) rule of thumb, the older the rocks the higher (more radiogenic) their strontium ratio. Figure 8.5 shows the large difference between the gneiss rock leaches (~0.715) and the remaining biosphere samples (>0.709 to <0.711) of burial and cultivation soils, peat, rain, seawater (~0.7092), modern plants and archaeological herbivores. We may deduce from this that the gneiss is contributing very little strontium to the Hebridean biosphere, which poses something of a problem when the premise of identifying immigrants

using strontium is based on linking people to the rocks that crop out in their place of origin. No biosphere samples had $^{87}Sr/^{86}Sr$ values below ~0.7092, which is the value of seawater. Although the humans define a much greater spread, all the Bronze Age humans fall within the biosphere range (Fig. 8.6), as do the three Norse juveniles. This range of $^{87}Sr/^{86}Sr$ values is comparable with values obtained from humans in regions of Triassic and Jurassic sedimentary rocks (Grupe *et al.* 1997; Price *et al.* 2001; Montgomery 2002; Schweissing and Grupe 2003b; Evans and Tatham 2004; Montgomery *et al.* 2005) of considerably younger age than the Precambrian gneiss, from which the Hebrides are predominantly composed.

Strontium is a fairly abundant element in seawater (Libes 1992). Marine-derived strontium can contribute in several ways to a windswept, maritime, island biosphere. In the Hebrides, these would have included rainwater, seawater in the form of sea-splash and spray, marine foods such as fish, and seaweed which can be used both as food and fertilizer. However, perhaps the most significant input is the extensive drift deposits of marine shell-sand (known as machair) that cover large tracts of the west coast and extend up to 2km inland (Owen *et al.* 1996; Gilbertson *et al.* 1999). The Outer Hebrides were a marginal area for agriculture; on Harris less than 1% of the land area is suitable for cultivation, the rest being rock and blanket peat and the 13th century *Chronicles of Man* recorded that "Lewis…(is) but thinly peopled, because it is mountainous and rocky, and almost unfit for cultivation…Olaf took possession …and dwelt there; living, however, very scantily" (Graham-Campbell and Batey 1998). Agriculture and settlement appear to have concentrated progressively on the machair plain throughout prehistory, and by the Iron Age, were largely restricted to machair coastal regions, however, this may simply be a reflection of poor archaeological survival and visibility on the immediately adjacent blacklands and peat covered interior (Sharples *et al.* 2004). The barren island interior supported an impoverished, terrestrial, fauna dominated by deer (Serjeantson 1990; Smith and Mulville 2004) and was mainly exploited for fuel and rough pasture (Armit 1996; Owen *et al.* 1996; Graham-Campbell and Batey 1998). Fieldwork on the machair of South Uist (Sharples and Parker-Pearson 1999) has suggested that the Norse settlement pattern is very similar to that of the preceding Late Iron Age; people farmed the machair and possibly the adjacent, heavier, blackland soils because, faced with the blanket peat, bog and bare rock of the island interior, that was the best option open to them. However, to remain fertile, machair requires constant manuring and fertilising with seaweed and bone (Fenton 1978; Armit 1998; Graham-Campbell and Batey 1998; Sharples and Parker-Pearson 1999), both of which, according to our data (Fig. 8.6), would have had a marine-dominated strontium signature. Marine foods appear to have been an important resource in all periods (Smith and Mulville 2004). So, given the scarcity of foods from non-machair and non-marine sources, the archaeological evidence that people were predominantly living on and cultivating the machair in the first millennium AD, the lack of evidence for any significant food importation or indigenous wildlife other than deer (which have also produced a machair isotope value) and sea-birds to hunt, it is difficult to imagine what significant food sources *were* available to the islanders that could have provided strontium isotope ratios of less than 0.7092 or greater than 0.7105, that is, outside our machair range. Consequently, the archaeological evidence for subsistence strategies coupled with the unique machair environment on the Hebrides lead to the working hypothesis that dietary strontium in all periods is dominated by strontium of marine (*i.e.* ~0.7092) origin with very limited input from the gneiss (Montgomery 2002; Montgomery *et al.* 2003).

Given that high enamel strontium concentrations (~150–400 ppm) were found only in individuals with machair strontium (Fig. 8.6) and that this is also the strontium isotope ratio of the burial soils, an alternative explanation for the distribution of the results would, of course, be that the samples with machair strontium have been subjected to post-mortem contamination and those outside the machair range have not. There are several lines of evidence that indicate this is not the case (Montgomery 2002; Montgomery *et al.* 2003, in prep),

but as this is not within the scope of this paper, and we shall, in any event, concentrate only on the individuals who fall outside this range, this will not be discussed further here.

Only two individuals (Gals 93 & IV) had $^{87}Sr/^{86}Sr$ values that exceeded the biosphere range and approached the values we had expected to characterise indigenous Hebrideans. These were also the only two Iron Age individuals who had ore-lead isotope signatures and high lead concentrations (Figs. 8.3 and 8.4). Admittedly, the total number of skeletons sampled is small, but this is an unavoidable situation because very few prehistoric burials have been excavated from the islands. Nonetheless, these Iron Age individuals *cannot* be dismissed merely as statistical outliers of a population that is normally distributed around a mean centred on machair strontium ratios because, unlike the lighter isotopes of carbon, nitrogen and oxygen, any fractionation of strontium isotope ratios is negligible in low temperature processes. If we recall the example of the red and white paint, one will never obtain a sample of pink paint by simply sub-sampling the pot of red – it has to be mixed with white. Likewise, one will never obtain a strontium ratio of 0.712 by mixing foods with ratios of 0.709 to 0.711, no matter how often it is attempted or how many are introduced to the mix. If the individuals concerned were ingesting any marine-derived strontium at all, they would also have had to ingest a source of strontium equal to or higher than 0.713 that would contribute, through mixing, to the final weighted average. Therefore, for a machair-dweller to have an enamel strontium isotope ratio of 0.713, *sufficient* strontium with a *higher* ratio than 0.713 would have had to have been ingested during childhood in order to balance out the food and drink that has marine/machair strontium ratios to produce the resulting weighted average of 0.713. If we return to our paint analogy and substitute the deeply pigmented red paint with our apparently abundant and strontium-rich machair/marine food resources and the white paint with strontium from the gneiss, it is clear that it would take considerable inputs of gneiss-derived strontium in order to increase an individual's strontium isotope ratio from <0.710 to 0.713 (which, in strontium isotope terms, is a very significant shift) in much the same way that it would be difficult to turn red paint into pink. Moreover, high enamel strontium ratios go hand-in-hand with lower concentrations (Fig. 8.6), suggesting that these individuals obtained their strontium from sources wholly unconnected with the sea or the machair, as it is difficult to envisage how adding the necessary large amounts of high-ratio strontium to a diet already dominated by marine strontium would result in lower enamel strontium concentrations.

Currently, we do not know if there *were* any sources of food or drink available on the island that could provide *sufficient* gneiss-derived strontium >0.713 for humans to subsist on; none have yet been found. It does not seem, therefore, that it would have been possible to survive in this marginal environment without being exposed to marine or machair strontium. If any non-machair sources are found during our current programme of work, it will then be possible to contemplate why these individuals, who also had high exposure to anthropogenic lead, show a much larger contribution from gneiss food sources during their childhood. Is it due to status or cultural differences? Is it because the *bulk* of the strontium is incorporated during a very short period of time rather than being slowly accumulated over a couple of years whilst the crown is mineralizing? This is important because incorporation over a few short months may mean that differences between individuals may result simply from seasonal differences rather than a change of residence or differential status. For example, one child's tooth may have mineralized during the summer months when animals were grazed on the sheilings inland and food was being eked out with wild resources until the harvest came in, whilst his younger sister's enamel mineralized the following winter, when food source, type and quantity may have been quite different. This would lead to considerable variation not only within families but also within the dentition of a single individual. However, if strontium is incorporated slowly over a matter of years rather than months, it is much more likely that any seasonal changes will be averaged out, with the effect of reducing the amount of intra-population variation (Price *et al.* 1985, 2002). Furthermore, the duration, pace and sequence of mineralization varies between teeth, so sample choice will have an impact on how confidently we can identify immigrants.

If we assume that there are no *significant* sources of dietary strontium below 0.7092 or above 0.7110 on the Hebrides, irrespective of seasonal variations, it is possible to propose from this data, therefore, that not only do we have two Norse immigrants to the island in Cnip E (female) and Cnip D (male), but also that Gals 93 (male) and Gals IV (female) could not have grown up on the machair-dominated biosphere that exists on the islands. Such a conclusion would be supported by the high-lead burdens exhibited by these two Iron Age individuals. Two other female burials (Cnip A and burial K) lie just outside the biosphere range but, as explained above, such values cannot arise simply through statistical variation in a normally distributed population unless there are dietary end-member sources in existence that can provide higher strontium ratios than the value obtained for Cnip A and lower strontium ratios than the value obtained for burial K. It is possible that that is indeed the case for Cnip A (*i.e.* the gneiss) but not for burial K. Two teeth (M1 and M2) were sampled from individual K. The value for the earlier mineralising first molar (K1) can be seen directly above that for the second molar (K2), suggesting a move *away* from the machair in later childhood.

Cnip D and E are unlikely to originate from Norway, which is composed of Precambrian gneisses, granites and Palaeozoic sedimentary rocks too old to provide

strontium ratios this low (Åberg 1995; Åberg *et al.* 1998). As a consequence, we can be fairly certain that neither were first generation Vikings from Norway. Norwegian mediaeval teeth have produced $^{87}Sr/^{86}Sr$ ratios ranging from 0.71087 for coastal Bergen, up to 0.73232 from inland sites (Åberg *et al.* 1998). The low $^{87}Sr/^{86}Sr$ values of these two individuals restrict the choice of possible source regions. As already discussed, enamel strontium compositions result from a mixture of the environmental inputs ingested during childhood and are likely to include strontium from local soils *and* rainwater (Fig. 8.1). As rainwater strontium has the seawater composition of ~0.7092 in coastal regions (Capo *et al.* 1998), we would expect their place of origin to provide values *lower* than their resulting enamel value. Thus, we would predict that Cnip D originates from a region yielding a value <0.7078 and Cnip E from a region <0.7086. The two main types of rock that can supply values in this range are basaltic rocks and ancient marine carbonates such as chalk and limestone. Marine carbonates have a minimum value of 0.7071 (Burke *et al.* 1982; McArthur *et al.* 2001) and young basalts can be as low as 0.703 (Dickin 1995). Marine carbonates are a likely substrate for Cnip E but not for Cnip D, as he is close to the minimum chalk composition and, to date, no skeleton excavated from a chalk or limestone burial site in the UK has possessed an enamel $^{87}Sr/^{86}Sr$ value <0.7080 (Montgomery 2002; Evans *et al.* in press). Consequently, the Tertiary Volcanic rocks of the Inner Hebrides, such as the Isle of Skye and Mull, and Antrim in northeastern Ireland provide the nearest potential places of origin for Cnip D (Fig. 8.2), with more distant contenders being Iceland and the Faeroes (Moorbath and Bell 1965; Wallace *et al.* 1994). Archaeological evidence suggests a considerable degree of contact existed between Lewis and all these regions during the Viking Period (Armit 1996), but there is little comparative enamel strontium isotope data available for the Viking Period. The nearest significant Cretaceous chalk outcrops are found in east and southeastern England, and in Denmark, whilst limestones occur in lowland Scotland, southern Wales, northern England and, extensively, in Ireland.

The $^{87}Sr/^{86}Sr$ ratio of the female Cnip A is somewhat inconclusive, falling neither convincingly within the machair field nor high enough to be consistent with the Norwegian origin (Åberg *et al.* 1998) that might be inferred from the accompanying Norse jewellery assemblage. However, there is another way to plot this data which sheds more light on the structure within the Hebridean data set and offers an explanation for the ambiguity inherent in such a result.

A geochemical interpretation

Figure 8.7 shows the same data as Figures 8.5 and 8.6 but it plots the $^{87}Sr/^{86}Sr$ ratios against the *inverse* of the strontium concentration (*i.e.* 1/Sr). An effect of this type

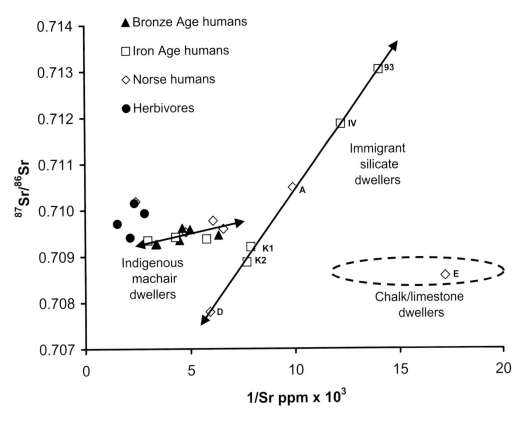

Figure 8.7. Scatterplot of enamel 1/Sr concentration versus $^{87}Sr/^{86}Sr$. Two binary mixing systems are defined by the human data suggesting individuals inhabited two very different biospheres which, particularly in the silicate group ($r^2 = 0.9984$), are tightly constrained by the geological source. K1 and K2 are first and second molars from the same individual. 2σ errors are contained within the symbols.

of plot is to accentuate the differences between people with low strontium concentrations who fall on the right-hand side of the plot whilst minimising differences between individuals with high concentrations. This may seem a little counter-intuitive, but what it does, primarily, is turn a hyperbolic curve into a straight line as illustrated in Figure 8.8. Its usefulness, therefore, becomes apparent when we have people in our population whose diet is composed of two, and only two, discrete sources of strontium. This may sound unrealistic and oversimplified, but it does not require that *types* of foods are restricted, only that they are all grown and grazed on just two types of rock (referred to as end-members) or, alternatively, one type of rock plus rainwater. We could propose, therefore, that people on Lewis, depending on their individual circumstances and food preferences, might all ingest varying amounts of strontium derived from marine and gneiss rock sources. If we imagine that marine strontium is red paint and gneiss strontium white paint, they would emerge in varying shades of pink. They would, on such a plot and with no other significant dietary components, describe a straight "mixing line", with people occupying different positions on the line depending on the relative richness of their diet in the two sources at the time the tooth mineralized. It is quite feasible that the contribution of specific dietary components waxed and

waned both seasonally and over the years, if animal husbandry practices changed, crops failed or marine foods, for whatever reason, became more or less abundant. In other words, the resulting shade of pink depends on the proportions of red to white paint. However, a mixing line relationship requires not only close control over the isotope ratio but also over the concentration and, whilst it may be perfectly reasonable to assume that random mixing of two food types, as illustrated in Figure 8.8, may produce an assortment of *diets* on such a linear array with two identifiable end-members, because there is no opportunity for strontium to be added or taken away, obtaining such a relationship from biological skeletal tissues is not the same thing at all. Although strontium in skeletal tissue may be dose-dependent (Comar *et al.* 1956; Boivin *et al.* 1996), experimental studies have concluded that there is no straightforward, absolute, relationship between the amount of strontium in any given diet and the amount of strontium in the resulting tissue (Elias 1980; Burton and Wright 1995). Biological organisms are not rocks. Physiological processes can act upon the amount of strontium that is finally deposited in tooth enamel at all the stages in its journey from the stomach to its final deposition in enamel. Moreover, strontium is not evenly distributed across all tissues; in mammals, most resides within the skeleton and given bone formation and turnover rates is unlikely to be in constant equilibrium with the diet. Enamel concentrations may be increased or reduced relative to the concentration in any one food type and not all dietary components will contribute equally; indeed some may not contribute at all. Why, then, would we expect to find such a relationship as that illustrated in Figure 8.8 between a human population and its diet?

Figure 8.7 separates the Hebridean individuals into two groups; Cnip E fits into neither group but, as predicted from Figure 8.6, is entirely consistent with individuals excavated from marine carbonates such as chalk and limestone (Montgomery 2002). For ease of reference we have called the two groups machair dwellers and silicate dwellers. Machair dwellers are defined by high strontium concentrations and strontium ratios within the range of biosphere values obtained from the Hebrides. Silicate dwellers are the linear group of individuals whose strontium isotope ratios appear to arise from mixing between two geological end-members with no input from machair, marine or marine carbonate strontium. Such a linear array reflects the compositional range and isotope features seen in silicate rocks of the Inner Hebrides and west coast of Scotland (Fowler et al. 2004). The machair group define a slightly sloping field suggesting that their strontium is predominantly of marine or machair origin with only a very small contribution from the gneiss – consider how far we would have to extend the mixing line before it approached 0.715! Individuals in the machair group appear to be characterised by strontium concentrations in the range of 150–400 ppm. Most archaeological humans analysed to date from England have strontium concentrations in the range 30-100 ppm (Montgomery et al. 2000; Montgomery 2002; Evans and Tatham 2004; Montgomery et al. 2005), including those excavated from inland chalk and limestone sites, which suggests the high concentrations obtained from the

machair group are not simply a result of subsisting on food grown on soils overlying marine carbonate rocks. The herbivores, also, are dominated by marine strontium, although they have much higher enamel concentrations than the humans. This is not unexpected in vegetarians (Tuross et al. 1989; Bocherens et al. 1994). Nor should we be surprised that they do not follow the same trajectory as the humans; they are not consuming the same diet. Furthermore, as already discussed, meat and milk may contribute little to the total strontium budget of omnivores, so it is quite possible that the herbivores are an upper (radiogenic) end-member for the human population, despite falling on the left-hand side of the plot in Figure 8.7. Clearly, the strontium concentration in the herbivore enamel is not directly relevant to human diets, because people do not eat teeth, and meat and milk will contain much less strontium than skeletal tissues.

What is remarkable, given our previous observations on the concentration offset we might expect between the diet of an individual and their enamel, is the extremely good fit ($r^2 = 0.9984$) of the remaining human samples on the silicate mixing line. From a geochemical perspective, this is highly unlikely to arise from co-incidence. As Faure (1986) asserts "The goodness of fit of the data points to a straight line is a test for the validity of the mixing hypothesis and of the assumption that neither the strontium concentrations nor the $^{87}Sr/^{86}Sr$ ratios were modified after mixing had occurred". He is not writing about biological organisms, but the silicate group of individuals do indeed appear to be strongly related in such a simple binary relationship that can be explained through access to food and water that derives from two, non-machair, geological sources: one providing strontium below 0.707 and the other strontium above 0.713. However, in order for these individuals to lie on the mixing line, not only their isotope ratio but also the

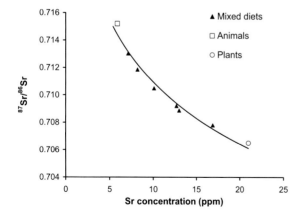 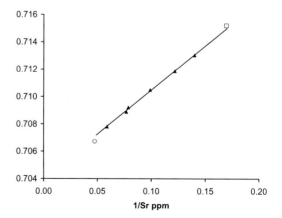

Figure 8.8. Graphs illustrating the transformation of a hyperbolic mixing curve into a straight line in a hypothetical binary system where plants are grown on one type of rock and animals grazed at a different location on a different rock type. The black triangles indicate selected omnivorous diets composed of different proportions of plant and animal foods. The addition of a third source, e.g. drinking water having $^{87}Sr/^{86}Sr = 0.7092$ and a concentration of 0.02 ppm would, if it had any effect at all given the very low concentration, pull the diets away from the mixing line and produce a triangular field of data.

concentration of strontium in their enamel must be very closely controlled by the two geological sources providing the dietary strontium and *not modified subsequently*. Such a finding clearly has implications for studies that use Sr/Ca ratios as an indicator of trophic level and food sources because, as already suggested by Burton *et al.* (2003), it raises the possibility that in some locations geological, rather than biological, processes will control the amount of strontium in skeletal tissue.

Despite the linear relationship between the members of the silicate group, radiocarbon dates from these individuals span nearly 1,000 years and there is little archaeological evidence to link them together. Two are Norse: Cnip A was buried with a characteristically Viking jewellery assemblage and Cnip D with no extant grave goods (Table 8.1). Two are from the high-lead individuals from the Iron Age cemetery at Galson, and whilst Gals 93 (male) is an unusual burial in several ways, Gals IV (female) is not. The two individuals hovering on the edge of the machair field in Figure 8.6 (Cnip A and burial K) fall outside it in Figure 8.7. It is, therefore, unlikely that either were indigenous to the Outer Hebrides. Moreover, what we might have interpreted from Figure 8.6 as a move away from the machair in early childhood for individual K is refuted in Figure 8.7, which suggests the strontium in individual K derives from a non-machair source. One possible region that might provide such mixing oppor-

tunities is the Tertiary Volcanic Province (Fig. 8.2) where young basaltic rocks have extruded through the ancient Lewisian crust, as on the nearby Isle of Skye and Scottish mainland (Fowler *et al.* 2004). This suggests that such a linear relationship may simply be a feature of this unique geological setting and, as illustrated in Figure 8.9, it is certainly the case that linear arrays are not always observed in archaeological studies (*e.g.* Schweissing and Grupe 2003b). Such a large spread in isotope ratios within a single population would be unusual and render it very difficult to apply a blanket cut-off value to identify immigrants in such geological regions. However, the case studies that have been carried out to date have been unavoidably biased towards areas where bone survives, and these are far more likely to be regions of alkaline rock, such as chalk and limestone, than silicate rocks, which frequently produce acidic soils that are not conducive to bone survival.

Alternatively, the factor linking these individuals may be that they originate from quite different places as suggested by the archaeological evidence, but that all these places are regions of silicate rock where there is no input from either marine carbonates or coastal marine strontium, such as the Scottish mainland. This study is still underway but, irrespective of where these individuals originated from, the data appear to provide evidence for an enduring migration stream to the Outer Hebrides.

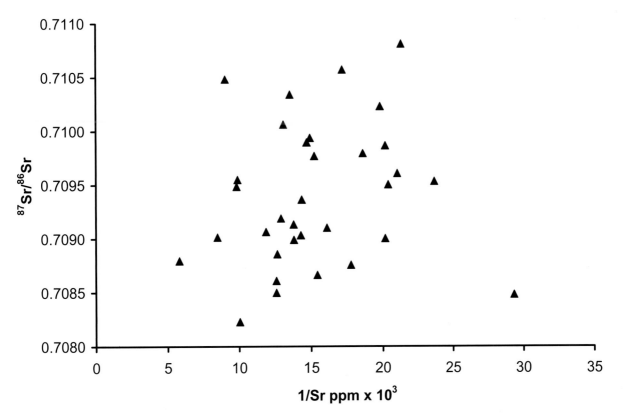

Figure 8.9. Scatterplot of human enamel data for a 5th-7th century AD cemetery in England. The points define a diffuse cloud of data with no clear mixing trends. 2s errors are contained within the symbols. Data from Montgomery et al. (2005).

Discussion

Migration is rarely indiscriminate: "even in distress, people do not move about randomly, but follow kin and co-residents to havens that have an attractive reputation" (Anthony 1997, 27). Chain migration theory predicts that permanent migrants are far more likely to follow family members to known places, or to target places where familiar social systems prevail, than to seek out alternative or new locations. Accordingly, this "brings migrants from a specific home region to a specific destination over a known route, usually to join kin" (Anthony 1990, 903; Anthony 1997, 26). Chain migration between two places can continue for many years, even perhaps generations. Moreover, once established, migration streams are resistant to change and tend to flow in both directions (Anthony 1997). Not only does migration theory thus support what might otherwise be seen as a case of special pleading, that is, that many immigrants to the Outer Hebrides originated from the Isle of Skye, despite archaeological evidence such as Viking grave goods that might suggest otherwise, but it has important implications for studies of aDNA and archaeological skeletal investigations of variation and inherited traits because such kin-focussed migration is recognised as a potential cause of significant variation in allele frequencies between populations (Rogers and Eriksson 1988). It is possible, therefore, that there may be significant differences in the manifestation of metric or non-metric traits between first generation migrants and the indigenous population if they have significantly different genotypes, activity patterns or environment. Unfortunately, in this study, there are too few individuals to draw any valid conclusions from this particular type of evidence.

The strontium and lead data clearly separate the adult male burial Gals 93 and the adult female burial Gals IV from the other Iron Age and Bronze Age burials, not only by geographical origins but also by their environmental exposure to anthropogenic lead, which suggests they inhabited a different cultural environment to that prevailing in the Outer Hebrides during the late Iron Age. The funerary evidence (Table 8.1) would certainly support the conclusion that Gals 93 is culturally different to the other individuals in the Galson cemetery but there is nothing to suggest this for the female burial Gals IV. The non-Norwegian origins of Cnip D and E raise the question of why and how they ended their days on an island purported to have been settled by people of Norwegian origin. One possibility is that they may have arrived as slaves. Archaeological evidence for slavery is rare but it has been argued that this is hardly evidence of absence and archaeologists should "assume access to coerced labour as a priori, in the same way as access to drinking water is assumed" (Taylor 2005, 232). Throughout the Viking period contemporary historical accounts attest to the frequent, often hostile, contact between groups of Vikings led by men of Norse and Danish extraction in the Irish Sea region. Great Britain and Ireland were Christian prior to the arrival of the pagan Norse in the 9th century and the Vikings took large numbers of Christian captives from Great Britain and, notably, northeastern Ireland, often strategically timing their raids to coincide with Christian festivals when many people gathered together (Smyth 1979). Dublin, in particular, was a major Viking slaving colony with small offshore islands being used to hold captives prior to sale (Smyth 1979). The relocation of Cnip D and E to Lewis, which occupied an important position on the main shipping route north, may not, therefore, have been a voluntary one, and they may thus provide evidence for coerced migration, although the kerbstones marking their carefully laid out graves suggest they were finally laid to rest with respect, if scant material wealth. The graves of Cnip C, D and E did not intercut but were so close together and of very similar construction that they are deemed contemporary (Dunwell *et al.* 1996a). The funerary rite is neither definitively Christian nor Norse, but parallels have been drawn with both the typical, Icelandic, Viking Period burial and a Viking Period grave from the Faeroe Islands (Dunwell *et al.* 1996a). The similarity of their burial rite and grave construction provide no obvious hint to archaeologists that they might have originated in three different homelands as suggested by the strontium isotope evidence. Small differences are apparent (Table 8.1): Cnip C and E were aligned E-W in parallel graves with Cnip D N-S at their feet; Cnip C and D were extended burials with no extant grave goods, whilst Cnip E was flexed and recovered with a simple bone pin and perforated metal plate. It may, of course, be argued that slaves being "socially dead" are unlikely to have been accorded burial (Taylor 2005), but archaeological evidence for their disparate origins may be absent because forced displacement ended all connections with their previous life and identity, imposing uniformity in death where none existed in life.

Conclusions

This paper has discussed many of the problems and unknowns involved in the identification of migrants using isotopic data. The influence of drift geology, in particular, have been highlighted as well as how we might interpret human radiogenic isotope data using standard geochemical techniques and explore alternative relationships between individuals, which in turn may allow us to rethink our interpretations and definitions of difference. The range of strontium concentrations, isotopic distribution and degree of variation a population exhibits may change considerably as we move from different geological, geographical and even cultural milieu, but until there are more studies published from a greater variety of such settings, particularly in under-represented regions where archaeological bone survival is poor, we will not see the bigger picture.

No evidence was found for migration to the island in the Bronze Age, but during the first millennium AD the Outer Hebrides appear to have been the destination of both male and female migrants, whether voluntarily or coerced, although we cannot currently determine whether they originated from a multitude of homelands, as suggested by the archaeological evidence, or were principally the result of a migration stream from the Inner Hebrides and Scottish mainland. It would seem that it was only later during the second millennium AD that the Outer Hebrides came to be isolated on the periphery of Europe where we expect "Here be Dragons" to be written on the map. Prior to this, the evidence suggests the islands were home to a cosmopolitan mix of settlers and justly deserved the epithet of the Innse Gall – "Islands of the Foreigners".

References

Åberg, G. (1995) The use of natural strontium isotopes as tracers in environmental studies. *Water, Air and Soil Pollution* 79(1–4), 309–322.

Åberg, G., Fosse, G. and Stray, H. (1998) Man, nutrition and mobility: a comparison of teeth and bone from the medieval era and the present from Pb and Sr isotopes. *The Science of the Total Environment* 224, 109–119.

Adams, W. Y., Van Gerven, D. P. and Levy, R. S. (1978) The retreat from migrationism. *Annual Review of Anthropology* 7, 483–532.

Anthony, D. W. (1990) Migration in archeology: the baby and the bathwater. *American Anthropologist* 92, 895–914.

Anthony, D. W. (1997) Prehistoric migration as a social process. In J. Chapman and H. Hamerow (eds.) *Migrations and invasions in archaeological explanation*, 21–32. British Archaeological Reports International Series 664. Oxford, Archaeopress.

Armit, I. (1996) *The Archaeology of Skye and the Western Isles*. Edinburgh, Edinburgh University Press.

Armit, I. (1998) Human responses to marginality. In C. M. Mills and G. Coles (eds.) *Life on the Edge: Human Settlement and Marginality*, 31–38. Oxford, Oxbow Books.

Balasse, M. (2002) Reconstructing dietary and environmental history from enamel isotopic analysis: Time resolution of intra-tooth sequential sampling. *International Journal of Osteoarchaeology* 12(3), 155–165.

Balasse, M. (2003) Potential biases in sampling design and interpretation of intra-tooth isotope analysis. *International Journal of Osteoarchaeology* 13(1–2), 3–10.

Beard, B. L. and Johnson, C. M. (2000) Strontium isotope composition of skeletal material can determine the birth place and geographic mobility of humans and animals. *Journal of Forensic Sciences* 45(5), 1049–1061.

Bentley, R. A., Price, T. D. and Stephan, E. (2004) Determining the 'local' Sr-87/Sr-86 range for archaeological skeletons: a case study from Neolithic Europe. *Journal of Archaeological Science* 31(4), 365–375.

Blum, J. D. and Erel, Y. (1997) Rb-Sr isotope systematics of a granitic soil chronosequence: The importance of biotite weathering. *Geochimica et Cosmochimica Acta* 61(15), 3193–3204.

Blum, J. D., Taliaferro, E. H., Weisse, M. T. and Holmes, R. T. (2000) Changes in Sr/Ca, Ba/Ca and ^{87}Sr/^{86}Sr ratios between trophic levels in two forest ecosystems in the northeastern U.S.A.

Biogeochemistry 49, 87–101.

Bocherens, H., Brinkman, D. B., Dauphin, Y. and Mariotti, A. (1994) Microstructural and geochemical investigations on Late Cretaceous archosaur teeth from Alberta, Canada. *Canadian Journal of Earth Sciences* 31(5), 783–792.

Boivin, G., Deloffre, P., Perrat, B., Panczer, G., Boudeulle, M., Mauras, Y., Allain, P., Tsouderos, Y. and Meunier, P. J. (1996) Strontium distribution and interactions with bone mineral in monkey iliac bone after strontium salt (S 12911) administration. *Journal of Bone and Mineral Research* 11(9), 1302–1311.

Boyde, A. (1989) Enamel. In B. K. B. Berkovitz (ed.) *Handbook of Microscopic Anatomy: Teeth*, Vol. V/6, 309–473. Berlin, Springer-Verlag.

Boyde, A. (1997) Microstructure of enamel. In D. J. Chadwick and G. Cardew (eds.) *Dental Enamel. Proceedings of the Ciba Foundation Symposium 205*, 18–31. Chichester, John Wiley.

Brudevold, F. and Söremark, R. (1967) Chemistry of the mineral phase of enamel. In A. E. W. Miles (ed.) *Structural and Chemical Organization of Teeth*, 1st ed., Vol. II, 247–277. London, Academic Press.

Budd, P., Montgomery, J., Barreiro, B. and Thomas, R. G. (2000) Differential diagenesis of strontium in archaeological human tissues. *Applied Geochemistry* 15(5), 687–694.

Budd, P., Montgomery, J., Evans, J. A. and Trickett, M. A. (2004) Human lead exposure in England from approximately 5500 BP to the 16th century AD. *The Science of the Total Environment* 318(1–3), 45–58.

Buikstra, J. E. and Ubelaker, D. H. (eds.) (1994) *Standards for Data Collection from Human Skeletal Remains* (Vol. 44). Fayetteville, Arkansas Archaeological Survey.

Burke, W. H., Denison, R. E., Hetherington, E. A., Koepnick, R. B., Nelson, H. F. and Otto, J. B. (1982) Variation of sea-water ^{87}Sr/^{86}Sr throughout Phanerozoic time. *Geology* 10(10), 516–519.

Burton, J., Price, T. D., Cahue, L. and Wright, L. E. (2003) The use of barium and strontium abundances in human skeletal tissues to determine their geographical origins. *International Journal of Osteoarchaeology* 13, 88–95.

Burton, J. H. and Wright, L. E. (1995) Nonlinearity in the relationship between bone Sr/Ca and diet: paleodietary implications. *American Journal of Physical Anthropology* 96, 273–282.

Capo, R. C., Stewart, B. W. and Chadwick, O. A. (1998) Strontium isotopes as tracers of ecosystem processes: theory and methods. *Geoderma* 82(1/3), 197–225.

Carlson, A. K. (1996) Lead isotope analysis of human bone for addressing cultural affinity: a case study from Rocky Mountain House, Alberta. *Journal of Archaeological Science* 23, 557–567.

Chapman, J. and Hamerow, H. (eds.) (1997a) *Migrations and Invasions in Archaeological Explanation*. British Archaeological Reports International Series 664. Oxford, Archaeopress.

Chapman, J. and Hamerow, H. (1997b) On the move again: migrations and invasions in archaeological explanation. In J. Chapman and H. Hamerow (eds.) *Migrations and Invasions in Archaeological Explanation*, 1–10. British Archaeological Reports International Series 664. Oxford, Archaeopress.

Chiaradia, M., Gallay, A. and Todt, W. (2003) Different contamination styles of prehistoric human teeth at a Swiss necropolis (Sion, Valais) inferred from lead and strontium isotopes. *Applied Geochemistry* 18(3), 353–370.

Comar, C. L., Wasserman, R. H. and Nold, M. M. (1956) Strontium-calcium discrimination factors in the rat. *Proceedings of the Society for Experimental Biology* 92, 859–863.

Cox, G. and Sealy, J. C. (1997) Investigating identity and life histories: isotopic analysis and historical documentation of slave skeletons found on the Cape Town Foreshore, South Africa. *International Journal of Historical Archaeology* 1(3), 207–224.

Dickin, A. P. (1995) *Radiogenic Isotopes*. Cambridge, Cambridge University Press.

Dunwell, A. J., Cowie, T. G., Bruce, M. F., Neighbour, T. and Rees, A. R. (1996a) A Viking Age cemetery at Cnip, Uig, Isle of Lewis. *Proceedings of the Society of Antiquaries of Scotland* 125 (1995), 719–752, fiche 714 B719-G714.

Dunwell, A. J., Neighbour, T. and Cowie, T. G. (1996b) A cist burial adjacent to the Bronze Age cairn at Cnip, Uig, Isle of Lewis. *Proceedings of the Society of Antiquaries of Scotland* 125 (1995), 279-288, fiche 272 G271-210.

Elias, M. (1980) The feasibility of dental strontium analysis for diet-assessment of human populations. *American Journal of Physical Anthropology* 53, 1–4.

Elias, R. W., Hirao, Y. and Patterson, C. C. (1982) The circumvention of the natural biopurification of calcium along nutrients pathways by atmospheric inputs of industrial lead. *Geochimica et Cosmochimica Acta* 46, 2561–2580.

Elliott, T. A. and Grime, G. W. (1993) Examining the diagenetic alteration of human bone material from a range of archaeological burial sites using nuclear microscopy. *Nuclear Instruments and Methods in Physics Research Section B: Beam Interactions with Materials and Atoms* 77(1–4), 537–547.

Erel, Y., Harlavan, Y. and Blum, J. D. (1994) Lead isotope systematics of granitoid weathering. *Geochimica et Cosmochimica Acta* 58(23), 5299–5306.

Ericson, J. E. (1985) Strontium isotope characterization in the study of prehistoric human ecology. *Journal of Human Evolution* 14, 503–514.

Evans, J. A., Stoodley, N. and Chenery, C. (in press) A strontium and oxygen isotope assessment of a possible 4th century immigrant population in a Hampshire cemetery, southern England. *Journal of Archaeological Science*.

Evans, J. A. and Tatham, S. (2004) Defining "local signature" in terms of Sr isotope composition using a tenth-twelfth century Anglo-Saxon population living on a Jurassic clay-carbonate terrain, Rutland, UK. In K. Pye and D. J. Croft (eds.) *Forensic Geoscience: Principles, Techniques and Applications, Special Publication Vol. 232*, 237–248. London, Geological Society of London.

Ezzo, J. A. and Price, T. D. (2002) Migration, regional reorganization, and spatial group composition at Grasshopper Pueblo, Arizona. *Journal of Archaeological Science* 29(5), 499–520.

Faure, G. (1986) *Principles of Isotope Geology* (2nd ed.). New York, John Wiley & Sons Inc.

Fenton, A. (1978) *The Northern Isles: Orkney and Shetland*. East Linton, Scotland, Tuckwell Press.

Fincham, A. G., Moradian-Oldak, J. and Simmer, J. P. (1999) The structural biology of the developing dental enamel matrix. *Journal of Structural Biology* 126, 270–299.

Fincham, A. G. and Simmer, J. P. (1997) Amelogenin proteins of developing dental enamel. In D. J. Chadwick and G. Cardew (eds.) *Dental Enamel. Proceedings of the Ciba Foundation Symposium 205*, 118–134. Chichester, John Wiley & Sons Inc.

Fricke, H. C., Clyde, W. C. and O'Neil, J. R. (1998) Intra-tooth variations in $\delta^{18}O$ (PO_4) of mammalian tooth enamel as a record of seasonal variations in continental climate variables. *Geochimica et Cosmochimica Acta* 62(11), 1839–1850.

Fowler, S. J., Bohrson, W. A. and Spera, F. J. (2004) Magmatic evolution of the Skye igneous centre, western Scotland: modelling of assimilation, recharge and fractional crystallization. *Journal of Petrology* 45(12), 2481–2505.

Gilbertson, D. D., Schwenninger, J.-L., Kemp, R. A. and Rhodes, E. J. (1999) Sand-drift and soil formation along an exposed north Atlantic coastline: 14,000 years of diverse geomorphological, climatic and human impacts. *Journal of Archaeological Science* 26, 439–469.

Glimcher, M. J., Cohen-Solal, L., Kossiva, D. and de Ricqles, A. (1990) Biochemical analyses of fossil enamel and dentin. *Paleobiology* 16(2), 219–232.

Graham-Campbell, J. and Batey, C. E. (1998) *Vikings in Scotland: an Archaeological Survey*. Edinburgh, Edinburgh University Press.

Graustein, W. C. (1989) $^{87}Sr/^{86}Sr$ ratios measure the sources and flow of strontium in terrestrial ecosystems. In P. W. Rundel, J. R. Ehleringer and K. A. Nagy (eds.) *Stable Isotopes in Ecological Research*, Vol. 68, 491–512. New York, Springer.

Grupe, G., Price, T. D., Schröter, P., Söllner, F., Johnson, C. M. and Beard, B. L. (1997) Mobility of Bell Beaker people revealed by strontium isotope ratios of tooth and bone: a study of southern Bavarian skeletal remains. *Applied Geochemistry* 12, 517–525.

Gulson, B. L., Jameson, C. W. and Gillings, B. R. (1997) Stable lead isotopes in teeth as indicators of past domicile: a potential new tool in forensic science? *Journal of Forensic Sciences* 42(5), 787–791.

Hancock, R. G. V., Grynpas, M. D. and Pritzker, K. P. H. (1989) The abuse of bone analysis for archaeological dietary studies. *Archaeometry* 31(2), 169–179.

Härke, H. (1998) Archaeologists and migrations: a problem of attitude? *Current Anthropology* 39(1), 19–45.

Hill, W. C. O. (1952) Human skeletal remains from a kitchen midden at Galson, Lewis. *Proceedings of the Royal Physical Society of Edinburgh Sessions 1936–1952* XXIII(1–3).

Hillson, S. (1986) *Teeth*. Cambridge, Cambridge University Press.

Hillson, S. (1996) *Dental Anthropology*. Cambridge, Cambridge University Press.

Hoppe, K. A., Koch, P. L. and Furutani, T. T. (2003) Assessing the preservation of biogenic strontium in fossil bones and tooth enamel. *International Journal of Osteoarchaeology* 13, 20–28.

Horn, P., Hölzl, S. and Storzer, D. (1994) Habitat determination on a fossil stag's mandible from the site of *Homo erectus heidelbergenius* at Mauer by use of $^{87}Sr/^{86}Sr$. *Naturwissenshaften* 81, 360–362.

Libes, S. M. (1992) *An Introduction to Marine Biochemistry*. Chichester, John Wiley & Sons.

MacLaughlin, S. M. and Bruce, M. F. (1983) The shape of the proximal femur in Bronze Age Scots. *Journal of Anatomy* 137, 435–436.

Mann, S. (1997) The biomimetics of enamel: a paradigm for organized biomaterials synthesis. In D. J. Chadwick and G. Cardew (eds.) *Dental Enamel. Proceedings of the Ciba Foundation Symposium 205*, 261–274. Chichester, John Wiley.

Martin, M. (1994) *A Description of the Western Isles of Scotland circa 1695*. Edinburgh, Birlinn (originally published in 1698).

McArthur, J. M., Howarth, R. J. and Bailey, T. R. (2001) Strontium isotope stratigraphy: LOWESS version 3: best fit to the marine Sr-isotope curve for 0-509 Ma and accompanying look- up table for deriving numerical age. *Journal of Geology* 109(2), 155–170.

McGowan, I. (ed.) (1996) *Journey to the Hebrides. Samuel Johnson's A Journey to the Western Isles of Scotland and James Boswell's The Journal of a Tour to the Hebrides with Samuel Johnson*. Edinburgh, Canongate.

Michel, V., Ildefonse, P. and Morin, G. (1996) Assessment of archaeological bone and dentine preservation from Lazaret Cave

(Middle Pleistocene) in France. *Palaeogeography, Palaeoclimatology, Palaeoecology* 126(1/2), 109–119.

Miller, E. K., Blum, J. D. and Friedland, A. J. (1993) Determination of soil exchangeable-cation loss and weathering rates using Sr isotopes. *Nature* 362, 438–441.

Molleson, T., Eldridge, D. and Gale, N. H. (1986) Identification of lead sources by stable isotope ratios in bones and lead from Poundbury Camp, Dorset. *Oxford Journal of Archaeology* 5(2), 249–253.

Montgomery, J. (2002) *Lead and Strontium Isotope Compositions of Human Dental Tissues as an Indicator of Ancient Exposure and Population Dynamics.* Unpublished Ph.D. thesis, University of Bradford.

Montgomery, J., Budd, P. and Evans, J. (2000) Reconstructing the lifetime movements of ancient people: a Neolithic case study from southern England. *European Journal of Archaeology* 3(3), 407–422.

Montgomery, J., Evans, J. A. and Cooper, R. E. (in prep) Resolving archaeological populations with $^{87}Sr/^{86}Sr$ mixing diagrams. *Applied Geochemistry.* Geophysical Research Abstracts EGU 05-A-10020. Paper presented at the EGU General Assembly, Vienna, 2005.

Montgomery, J., Evans, J. A. and Neighbour, T. (2003) Sr isotope evidence for population movement within the Hebridean Norse community of NW Scotland. *Journal of the Geological Society* 160(5), 649–653.

Montgomery, J., Evans, J. A., Powlesland, D. and Roberts, C. A. (2005) Continuity or colonization in Anglo-Saxon England? Isotope evidence for mobility, subsistence practice and status at West Heslerton. *American Journal of Physical Anthropology* 126, 123–138.

Moorbath, S. and Bell, J. D. (1965) Strontium isotope abundance studies and rubidium-strontium age determinations on Tertiary igneous rocks from the Isle of Skye North-West Scotland. *Journal of Petrology* 6, 37–66.

Muller, W., Fricke, H., Halliday, A. N., McCulloch, M. T. and Wartho, J. A. (2003) Origin and migration of the Alpine Iceman. *Science* 302(5646), 862–866.

Neighbour, T., Knott, C., Bruce, M. F. and Kerr, N. W. (2002) Excavation of two burials at Galson, Isle of Lewis, 1993 and 1996. *Proceedings of the Society of Antiquaries of Scotland* 130 (2000), 559–584.

Owen, N., Kent, M. and Dale, P. (1996) The machair vegetation of the Outer Hebrides: a review. In D. Gilbertson, M. Kent and J. Grattan (eds.) *The Outer Hebrides: the last 14,000 years*, Vol. 2, 123–131. Sheffield, Sheffield Academic Press.

Parker Pearson, M., Chamberlain, A., Craig, O., Marshall, P., Mulville, J., Smith, H., Chenery, C., Collins, M., Cook, G., Craig, G., Evans, J. A., Hiller, J., Montgomery, J., Schwenninger, J.-L., Taylor, G. and Wess, T. (2005) Evidence for mummification in prehistoric Britain. *Antiquity* 79, 529–546.

Passey, B. H. and Cerling, T. E. (2002) Tooth enamel mineralization in ungulates: Implications for recovering a primary isotopic time-series. *Geochimica et Cosmochimica Acta* 66(18), 3225–3234.

Ponting, M. R. and Bruce, M. F. (1989) Two Iron-Age cists from Galson, Isle of Lewis. *Proceedings of the Society of Antiquaries of Scotland* 119 (1989), 91-100, fiche 103 F101-G114.

Price, T. D., Bentley, R. A., Lüning, J., Gronenborn, D. and Wahl, J. (2001) Prehistoric human migration in the Linearbandkeramik of Central Europe. *Antiquity* 75(289), 593–603.

Price, T. D., Burton, J. H. and Bentley, R. A. (2002) The characterization of biologically available strontium isotope ratios for the study of prehistoric migration. *Archaeometry* 44(1), 117–135.

Price, T. D., Connor, M. and Parsen, J. D. (1985) Bone chemistry and the reconstruction of diet – strontium discrimination in white-tailed deer. *Journal of Archaeological Science* 12(6), 419–442.

Price, T. D., Knipper, C., Grupe, G. and Smrcka, V. (2004) Strontium isotopes and prehistoric human migration: the Bell Beaker Period in Central Europe. *European Journal of Archaeology* 7(41–60).

Price, T. D., Manzanilla, L. and Middleton, W. D. (2000) Immigration and the ancient city of Teotihuacan in Mexico: a study using strontium isotope ratios in human bone and teeth. *Journal of Archaeological Science* 27, 903–913.

Proudfoot, E. (1997) Excavations at the long cist cemetery on the Hallow Hill, St. Andrews, Fife. *Proceedings of the Society of Antiquaries of Scotland* 126 (1996), 387–454.

Radosevich, S. C. (1993) The six deadly sins of trace element analysis: a case of wishful thinking in science. In M. K. Sandford (ed.) *Investigations of Ancient Human Tissue: Chemical Analyses in Anthropology*, 269–332. Amsterdam, Gordon & Breach.

Richards, M. P., Fuller, B. T. and Hedges, R. E. M. (2001) Sulphur isotopic variation in ancient bone collagen from Europe: implications for human palaeodiet, residence mobility and modern pollutant studies. *Earth and Planetary Science Letters* 191, 185–190.

Richards, M. P., Fuller, B. T., Sponheimer, M., Robinson, T. and Ayliffe, L. (2003) Sulphur isotopes in palaeodietary studies: a review and results from a controlled feeding experiment. *International Journal of Osteoarchaeology* 13(1–2), 37–45.

Ritchie, A. (1993) *Viking Scotland.* London, B.T. Batsford/Historic Scotland.

Robinson, C., Briggs, H. D., Atkinson, P. J. and Weatherell, J. A. (1981) Chemical changes during formation and maturation of human deciduous enamel. *Archives of Oral Biology* 26(12), 1027–1033.

Robinson, C., Fuchs, P., Deutsch, D. and Weatherell, J. A. (1978) Four chemically distinct stages in developing enamel from bovine incisor teeth. *Caries Research* 12, 1–11.

Robinson, C., Kirkham, J., Brookes, S. J., Bonass, W. A. and Shore, R. C. (1995a) The chemistry of enamel development. *International Journal of Developmental Biology* 39, 145–152.

Robinson, C., Kirkham, J., Brookes, S. J. and Shore, R. C. (1995b) Chemistry of mature enamel. In C. Robinson, J. Kirkham and R. C. Shore (eds.) *Dental Enamel: Formation to Destruction*, 167–191. Boca Raton, CRC Press.

Robinson, C., Kirkham, J., Weatherell, J. A., Richards, A., Josephsen, K. and Fejerskov, O. (1987) Developmental stages in permanent porcine enamel. *Acta Anatomica* 128(1), 1–10.

Rogers, A. R. and Eriksson, A. W. (1988) Statistical analysis of the migration component of genetic drift. *American Journal of Physical Anthropology* 77, 451–457.

Rohl, B. (1996) Lead isotope data from the Isotrace Laboratory, Oxford: archaeometry data base 2, galena from Britain and Ireland. *Archaeometry* 38, 165–180.

Sasaki, T., Takagi, M. and Yanagisawa, T. (1997) Structure and function of secretory ameloblasts in enamel formation. In D. J. Chadwick and G. Cardew (eds.) *Dental Enamel. Proceedings of the Ciba Foundation Symposium 205*, 32–50. Chichester, John Wiley.

Schwarcz, H. P., Gibbs, L. and Knyf, M. (1991) Oxygen isotopic analysis as an indicator of place of origin. In S. Pfeiffer and R. F. Williamson (eds.) *Snake Hill: An Investigation of a Military Cemetery from the War of 1812*, 263–268. Toronto, Dundurn Press.

Schweissing, M. M. and Grupe, G. (2003a) Tracing migration events in man and cattle by stable strontium isotope analysis of appositionally grown mineralized tissue. *International Journal of Osteoarchaeology* 13, 96–103.

Schweissing, M. M. and Grupe, G. (2003b) Stable strontium isotopes in human teeth and bone: a key to migration events of the late Roman period in Bavaria. *Journal of Archaeological Science* 30, 1373–1383.

Serjeantson, D. (1990) The introduction of mammals to the Outer Hebrides and the role of boats in stock management. *Anthropozoologica* 13, 7–18.

Sharples, N. (2001) Later prehistory in the Outer Hebrides. *Antiquity* 75, 633–635.

Sharples, N., Parker Pearson, M. and Symonds, J. (2004) The archaeological landscape of South Uist. In R. A. Housley and G. Coles (eds.) *Atlantic Connections and Adaptations. Economies, Environments and Subsistence in Lands Bordering the North Atlantic.* Symposia of the Association for Environmental Archaeology No. 21, 28–47. Oxford, Oxbow Books.

Sharples, N. and Parker-Pearson, M. (1999) Norse settlement in the Outer Hebrides. *Norwegian Archaeological Review* 32(1), 41–62.

Smith, C. E. (1998) Cellular and chemical events during enamel maturation. *Critical Reviews in Oral Biology and Medicine* 9, 128–161.

Smith, H. and Mulville, J. (2004) Resource management in the Outer Hebrides: an assessment of the faunal and floral evidence from archaeological investigations. In R. A. Housley and G. Coles (eds.) *Atlantic Connections and Adaptations. Economies, environments and subsistence in lands bordering the North Atlantic.* Symposia of the Association for Environmental Archaeology No. 21, 48–64. Oxford, Oxbow Books.

Smyth, A. P. (1979) *Scandinavian York and Dublin. The History and Archaeology of Two Related Viking Kingdoms.* (Vol. II). Dublin, Templekieran Press.

Suga, S. (1982) Progressive mineralization pattern of developing enamel during the maturation stage. *Journal of Dental Research* 61, 1532–1542.

Taylor, T. (2005) Ambushed by a grotesque: archaeology, slavery and the third paradigm. In M. Parker Pearson and I. J. N. Thorpe (eds.) *Warfare, Violence and Slavery in Prehistory.* British Archaeological Reports International Series 1374. Oxford, Archaeopress.

Tilly, C. (1978) Migration in modern European history. In W. McNeill and R. Adams (eds.) *Human Migration: Patterns and Policies,* 48–74. Bloomington, Indiana University Press.

Trickett, M. A., Budd, P., Montgomery, J. and Evans, J. (2003) An assessment of solubility profiling as a decontamination procedure for the $^{87}Sr/^{86}Sr$ analysis of archaeological human skeletal tissue. *Applied Geochemistry* 18(5), 653–658.

Turekian, K. K. and Kulp, J. L. (1956) Strontium content of human bones. *Science* 124, 405–407.

Tuross, N., Behrensmeyer, A. K. and Eanes, E. D. (1989) Strontium increases and crystallinity changes in taphonomic and archaeological bone. *Journal of Archaeological Science* 16, 661–672.

Tylecote, R. F. (1992) *A History of Metallurgy.* London, The Institute of Materials.

Ucko, P. J. (1969) Ethnography and archaeological interpretation of funerary remains. *World Archaeology* 1, 262–280.

Underwood, E. J. (1977) *Trace elements in human and animal nutrition* (4th ed.). London, Academic Press.

Veizer, J. (1989) Strontium isotopes in seawater through time. *Annual Review of Earth and Planetary Sciences* 17, 141–167.

Wallace, J. M., Ellam, R. M., Meighan, I. G., Lyle, P. and Rogers, N. W. (1994) Sr isotope data for the Tertiary lavas of Northern-Ireland. Evidence for open system petrogenesis. *Journal of the Geological Society, London* 151, 869–877.

Welander, R. D. E., Batey, C. and Cowie, T. G. (1987) A Viking burial from Kneep, Uig, Isle of Lewis. *Proceedings of the Society of Antiquaries of Scotland* 117 (1987), 149–174.

Wells, L. H. (1953) A note on the human remains from the Gairloch and Galson cist burials. *Proceedings of the Society of Antiquaries of Scotland* 86 (1951–1952), 112–115.

9. Ageing the Past: Examining Age Identity from Funerary Evidence

Rebecca Gowland

Age can be reduced to the simple passage of time, but lots of things are altered in time. Bodies age, societies change and lives are lived (Fry 1996, 117).

Introduction

Age is an important aspect of social identity and organisation and yet for a long time proved to be a blind spot for the social sciences. Archaeologists, until recently, have regarded the cultural experiences of age and ageing to have been uniform across societies and through time (with some exceptions *e.g.*, Sofaer Derevenski 1997a; Gilchrist ed. 2000). While recent studies of gender and ethnicity within archaeology have examined the socially constructed nature of identity and have challenged the imposition of modern Western social models onto past populations, age identity has remained largely under-theorised. As time passes our bodies undergo the biological processes of growth, maturation and, ultimately, degeneration. In this sense, the physical progression of the ageing process is a universal human experience. However, because individuals grow up and grow old within social contexts (Campbell and Alwin 1996, 34) age cannot be reduced to the 'simple passage of time' (Fry 1996, 117). Ethnographic and historical examples reveal that biological, cultural, and chronological concepts of age are intertwined in the formation of age identity in a way that is complicated to unravel. Cultures do not necessarily relate age identity to biological changes (*e.g.* puberty), instead they are more often linked to the fulfilment of social roles such as marriage and parenthood (Schildkrout 1978). As a result there is a great deal of variation in the way in which cultures divide the life course, in the way that they symbolise these divisions, and the extent and manner in which age identity plays a structuring role in society.

It is only recently that the study of age as an aspect of social identity within the field of archaeology has become a pivotal topic for discussion (see Sofaer Derevenski 1997a, 2000; Crawford 1999; Gilchrist ed. 2000). This paper examines the current research on age identity and the potentials and limitations of examining age as an aspect of social identity in the past through the study of archaeological funerary evidence. It draws upon evidence from five early Anglo-Saxon cemeteries and combines skeletal and cultural evidence in order to identify social age groupings and identities, focusing in particular on the 'adult' members of society.

Defining age

Much of the research on age identity to date has been conducted within the fields of social history (*e.g.* Ariès 1963; Pollock 1983; Shahar 1990, 1997; Rosenthal 1996), anthropology (*e.g.* Schildkrout 1978; Fortes 1984; Panter-Brick 1998) and sociology (*e.g.* Prout and James 1990; Arber and Ginn 1991, 1995; Hockey and James 1993). Working within the field of sociology, Ginn and Arber (1995, 2) discussed the relationship between sex and age and argued that: 'a distinction parallel to that between sex and gender needs to be made in relation to age'. Subsequently, several authors have distinguished between different 'types' of age:

1. Physiological/biological age (representing the physical ageing of the body).
2. Chronological age (corresponding to the amount of time that has passed from the moment of birth).
3. Social age (socially constructed norms concerning appropriate behaviour and attitudes for an age group).

It is evident from the majority of cemetery analyses in archaeology that such distinctions remain largely unrecognised within the discipline. For example, the age definitions given for the Anglo-Saxon cemetery of Millgate, Nottinghamshire (Harman 1989, 23) are as follows:

Infant (under 2 years)
Child (2–12 years)
Adolescent (12–18 years)
Adult (over 18 years)
Ageing adult (over 35 years)

These age divisions approximate those reported for many cemetery studies. However, when we deconstruct these categories, it becomes evident that all three definitions of age are being used: the biological age (of the skeleton), which is translated into a chronological age and is then described further by a social age. Because archaeologists tend not to theorise age identity and the way that it operates within society, different definitions of age have been used inter-changeably, as though they mean the same thing. As numerous studies have discussed, terms such as 'child' or 'adolescent' are culturally loaded; they do not simply convey to the reader a chronological age, but a whole schema of appropriate social behaviour and attributes derived from a modern Western context. Imposing these social norms (whether consciously or not) onto the past is a practice that serves not only to perpetuate and validate our current age paradigm, but also to potentially misrepresent the population under study. Crawford (1991, 1999) demonstrated this in her examination of Anglo-Saxon cemetery evidence in conjunction with law codes. She (*ibid.*) found that so-called anomalies in grave good associations (*e.g.* child weapon burials) were actually the result of excavators projecting contemporary age norms onto the past. Clearly, it is necessary for archaeologists to theorise age identity and to consider how it might be accessed in the archaeological record (*cf.* Sofaer-Derevenski 1997a; Gilchrist ed. 2000).

Biology and culture

We cannot deny the biological nature of the ageing process: there is inevitability about this process – interrupted only by fatal illness or accident. However, as Blaikie (1999, 6) states: 'Like every organism the body goes into a state of irreversible decline following maturity. What is contentious is not this physiological fact but how the social frame impinges upon it'. It is well attested, both ethnographically and historically, that age-related social transitions within societies often coincide with physiological parameters (*e.g.* learning to walk or puberty). This biological framework has undoubtedly resulted in a degree of cross-cultural uniformity with respect to particular social age transitions (Schildkrout 1978). There is no absolute universality, however, and a biological milestone viewed as important for age categorisation in one society may be entirely disregarded in another (La Fontaine 1986). For example, menarche is an important stage of physical development for females, often signifying the transition to adulthood. However, this is far from universal; for example, literary evidence relating to the Roman Empire indicates that it had little social significance for females

during this time. The female transition to adulthood was more closely allied with the social event of marriage (Fraschetti 1997, 69; Laurence 2000; Harlow and Laurence 2002).

Archaeologists should also be aware that whether different cultures show synchronicity with respect to their age transitions or not, considerable variation does exist with respect to the *cultural* interpretations of these life stages and the social attributes and responsibilities believed to be held by different age groups within societies (Myerhoff 1984, 307; La Fontaine 1978, 1986). The identity conferred on members of a particular age group is not the naturalised manifestation of their physical development, in the same way that gender roles are not the social expression of biological givens (Moore 1994; Sofaer-Derevenski 1997a).

On a more fundamental level, recent theoretical developments within the social sciences have brought into question the very immutability of the biological transitions that we interpret as important for age grouping. Cultural practices may, in fact, have a profound effect upon the chronological age of attainment of so-called biological goals. For example, walking and talking are viewed as the beginning of personhood in many cultures, both past and present, and yet cultural practices may either significantly delay or advance such abilities (Levine 1998). Biological anthropologists are well aware of the effects that differential cultural practices and the environment may have on factors such as skeletal growth or maturity that are important for age estimation. As the body develops it is, to an extent, taken up and transformed by social factors: biology and culture are largely inter-twined (Shilling 1993; see Sofaer this volume). Through an appreciation of the inter-related nature of biological and cultural aspects of ageing it is hoped that we can examine how the ages that we obtain from skeletal material relate to the social reality of age identity within a particular society and how the changing, ageing body was understood culturally in the past.

Approaches to the study of age identity

Within the sociological literature, the study of age has been broadly divided into two primary approaches: an age differentiated approach that focuses on age grades and cohorts, and the less divisive, life course approach (Marshall 1996). The former perspective has, until recently, dominated much anthropological and sociological research on age. A cohort is defined as a group of people born at approximately the same time that grow up and grow old during a particular period of time. In addition to dividing the lives of individuals into stages, the age cohort approach provides a valuable perspective in that it acknowledges the fact that members of a particular birth cohort will have a unique history and their experience of the ageing process will be correspondingly singular (Uhlenberg and Minor 1996, 208). The experience of being sixty years old in AD 1900, for example, was a very different one from being sixty in the year AD 2000. As Uhlenberg and Minor (1996, 210) state:

> By recognizing that ageing is a dynamic process produced by the collective behaviour of individuals who live within historical and social contexts, this perspective guides attention to the critical factors that change the ageing process over time.

As each cohort ages, considerable continuity in the behaviour of successive age cohorts may exist, however, periods of profound social change can significantly challenge the existing structures and experiences of ageing (Haraven 1995; Uhlenberg and Minor 1996, 208).

Within an archaeological context, while a cemetery may be divided into a series of broad chronological phases, age cohorts are difficult to identify because dating evidence for individual graves is often not specific enough. Although skeletal remains can be grouped according to age categories, it must be recognised that the individuals who comprise them were not all the same age during the same time and this may have impacted upon their experience of ageing. Given that this study draws upon evidence from fifth to sixth centuries AD, a period of rapid social change occurring immediately after the collapse of Roman control, one might expect a certain element of heterogeneity and inconsistency with respect to age-related funerary practice; a factor that may obscure the visibility of age demarcations.

Although the study of age grades and cohorts do provide a useful perspective, there is the tendency in such studies to conceptualise age groupings as homogenous; members of a particular age grade are imbued with particular social norms until their departure into a new age grade. Once categorised, the homogeneity of the age grouping then becomes assumed, without due consideration of the effects of gender, social status and ethnicity (Uhlenberg and Minor 1996, 216; Bradley 1996). It has also been argued within sociology that an emphasis on age grades has tended to focus too much attention on the *differences* between life stages (O'Rand 1996, 189).

One could argue that initial studies concerning age within archaeology were guilty of this also because they focused on specific age categories, most notably childhood (*e.g.* Lillehammer 1989; Sofaer-Derevenski ed. 1994, 1997b, 2000; Crawford 1991, 2000). However, this work was very important for redressing the balance of academic neglect of archaeologically excluded age groups and for beginning a discourse on age in archaeology.

When discussing age, many authors now find it useful to refer to the life course; the period of time from conception to death (*e.g.* Harlow and Laurence 2002). An important principle of life course analysis is that one life phase can only be understood in relation to the way that identities are played out over the entire life course. This approach, rather than focusing on a series of demarcated age groups, concentrates instead on 'life pathways' and the entry/exit transitions that occur throughout the trajectory of life in a more holistic manner (Moen 1996, 180).

Marshall (1996, 22) described the life course perspective as an: 'explicit attempt to view the individual biography within the context of society, and to take a historical perspective on both the individual and society'. A life course approach would seem preferable for archaeological studies of age, in part because it allows for a greater sensitivity towards the fluidity of age related shifts in identity, particularly with respect to gender and status over time (O'Rand 1996, 192–3). When using archaeological funerary evidence we do need to employ age groupings because skeletal ageing techniques are not specific enough, but it is still possible to view these in a more fluid way in accordance with life course analysis. When looking at rites of passage, the crossing of transitions between age boundaries, archaeologists can use this approach to examine the interaction and tensions between age and other aspects of the social persona. Such a study has been undertaken by Sofaer Derevenski (1997a) who examined the relationship between age, sex and gender in relation to burial practices in Copper Age Hungary, noting that these aspects of identity are almost inextricably intertwined.

In sum, it can be said that the questions that we need to explore with respect to the past include:

– How did past populations conceptualise and structure their life course?
– What particular characteristics were each of these stages imbued with and how were they symbolised?
– How did age interact with other aspects of the social persona such as gender and status?
– How are these age transitions managed?

Funerary evidence

The present study draws upon the analysis of a sample of skeletons from five cemeteries of early Anglo-Saxon date (fifth to sixth centuries AD) located in Oxfordshire and Hampshire (Table 9.1). While this study focuses in more detail on the 'adult' members of the burial societies, it was necessary to analyse the burials of all ages in order to contextualise the treatment of these individuals within that of the entire life course.

Recent studies have made it apparent that archaeology has treated 'adulthood' as the unspoken hegemony, and the past has been viewed in overtly adult terms. It is the paradoxical nature of such dominant discourses, however, that their assumed normality leaves them under-theorised. This was apparent in initial studies of gender, where as part of the feminist reaction against the androcentrism of archaeological narratives, the concept of femininity was explored in depth, while masculinity received little theoretical attention (*cf.* Hadley ed. 1999). A similar reaction, this time against adult-centric views of the past, contributed to the focus on childhood in archaeological

Region	Site	Period	No. Ind.
Upper Thames	Berinsfield (Boyle *et al.* 1995)	Early Anglo Saxon	119
Upper Thames	Abingdon (Leeds and Harden 1936)	Early Anglo Saxon	129
Hampshire	Worthy Park (Hawkes and Grainger 2003)	Early Anglo Saxon	109
Hampshire	Portway (Cook and Dacre 1985)	Early Anglo Saxon	71
Hampshire	Alton (Evison 1988)	Early Anglo Saxon	50

Table 9.1. The cemetery sample (NB information on grave goods were obtained from the cited reports).

studies of age. As a result, the social criteria necessary for the attainment of adulthood in the past and the multitude of ways in which societies may perceive adulthood (if at all) are relatively unexplored territory in archaeology. The experience of being an adult within a particular society has tended to be perceived as homogenous, however, sociological studies have demonstrated that it is in fact enormously variable and dependent upon gender, status, ethnicity and age.

Ageing the skeleton

The skeletal remains from all of the cemeteries in the study sample were analysed by the present author in order to estimate age and determine sex. Within the field of biological anthropology, maturational/degenerative information from the skeleton is always related to chronological age by comparing skeletal age indicators to models derived from skeletons of known age (Beall 1984). However, this process of skeletal ageing may be seen to be problematic on a number of levels. Firstly, because skeletal age has a limited ability to act as an indicator of chronological age, particularly once skeletal maturity has been achieved. Secondly, because age in chronological terms may have little relevance for the population being studied, instead age may have been understood in relative terms (*e.g.* age sets) (Fortes 1984). The first problem has dominated research on age within biological anthropology, particularly over the last two decades. It is primarily a result of individual and population level variation in the timing and manifestation of age-related skeletal changes. However, the problem is further compounded by statistical biases associated with current ageing methods and a lack of standardisation in the skeletal age estimation methods used (*e.g.* Bocquet-Appel and Masset 1982, 1985; Aykroyd *et al.* 1997, 1999; Hoppa and Vaupel ed. 2002).

Bocquet-Appel and Masset (1982) demonstrated that the age distributions obtained for archaeological populations were, to some extent, dependent on the age structure of the known age reference sample from which a particular ageing technique was devised. In effect, they argued that the age distributions produced for a given cemetery could depend as much on the ageing method(s) chosen as on the actual age structure of the archaeological sample. This brings into question the validity of comparing age profiles of cemeteries that have used

different age estimation techniques. This is one important reason for the re-analysis of the skeletal remains for the purposes of this study – though in not all instances had a skeletal report been undertaken at all (*e.g.* Abingdon).

This statistical bias has also been shown to be responsible for the under-ageing of older individuals within past populations (Aykroyd *et al.* 1997, 1999). This is partly because many of the current ageing methods are based on known age samples derived from forensic contexts that have age distributions very unlike those that we would expect to find in attritional cemeteries (where individuals died more 'naturally' from factors such as infections, old age, *etc.*). The problems associated with statistical bias are currently being addressed by a number of authors, primarily using methods based on Bayes' Theorum (*e.g.* Hoppa and Vaupel ed. 2002).

For the purposes of this study the ages-at-death of the immature skeletons were derived from observations of dental development and eruption (Moorrees *et al.* 1963a, b), long bone length and skeletal maturity indicators. Different cultural practices and the environment may significantly affect long bone growth and skeletal maturity. In order to account for this, Millard and Gowland (in prep) developed growth profiles specific to the cemetery populations analysed in the present sample and skeletal maturity indicators were studied in relation to dental development.

The 'adults' were aged using the pubic symphyses (Brooks and Suchey 1990), auricular surfaces (Lovejoy *et al.* 1985), late fusing epiphyses (Webb and Suchey 1985) and dental attrition. The molar wear of all dentitions present were scored according to a numerical system adapted from Brothwell's (1981) charts and seriated in a database so that individual dentitions could thus be aged relative to one another.

Sex, gender and the skeleton

Sexing skeletons is considered to be much more straight-forward and reliable than estimating age at death. On a basic level, there are a number of morphological and metrical differences between male and female skeletons, particularly in the regions of the pelvis and skull, which form the basis of sex determination techniques. The sex estimation of the adult skeletal material analysed in this study was conducted using methods described in Krogman and Iêcan (1986) and Buikstra and Ubelaker (1994).

Generally, in cemetery studies, biological sex is viewed as static and fixed; we have male and female categories. Gender on the other hand is perceived as distinct from biological sex; it represents the cultural interpretation of these bodily differences (Gilchrist 1999; Sørensen 2000). In funerary archaeology information concerning gender is usually derived from the cultural variables while skeletal information is seen as relevant only in providing a biological basis. While this distinction between sex and gender has been enormously useful and influential in archaeology, numerous authors have suggested that it does not stand up to scrutiny and have challenged this divide (see Sørensen 2000; Soafer this volume for a discussion).

On a basic level, the biology of 'sex' in terms of skeletal morphology is far from 'fixed'. A number of sexing categories are used by biological anthropologists because the extent and nature of sexual dimorphism exhibited by skeletons varies considerably both within and between populations. This was observed in the analysis of the skeletons in this study in terms of both the degree of overlap and characteristics of some of the sexually dimorphic features expressed. As a result, it was often necessary to slightly adjust skeletal sexing criteria accordingly.

In addition to these problems of variability and overlap in sexual dimorphism, studies have demonstrated that the criteria employed when assigning sex to a skeleton are not totally objective. For example, sex assessment based on the skull (which survives much more frequently than the pelvis, albeit often in a fragmentary state) is reliant on features of robusticity. Walrath *et al.* (2004) demonstrated that the lack of clear description/definition concerning the levels of robusticty which constitute a male as oppose to a female skull leads to a considerable amount of inter-observer variability based on individual traits. Previous studies demonstrated that researchers are more likely to sex intermediate specimens as male, presumably because they are less able to accept a robust female (Weiss 1972). Thus, one could argue that current gender paradigms and norms concerning physical sexual aesthetics infiltrate supposedly objective scientific methodologies (see also Stone and Walrath, this volume). Other studies have, however, contradicted these findings (*e.g.* Meindl *et al.* 1985) or have found no such bias (*e.g.* Molleson and Cox 1993), and it would seem that the variability is largely down to the differing degrees of sexual dimorphism.

It is also important to note that sexually dimorphic features do not remain static throughout the life course. It is not possible, for example, to determine the sex of skeletons prior to the completion of skeletal maturity. Even in live infants and young children, material culture plays a big part in allowing us to distinguish boys from girls, when clothed. Ethnographically and historically, children are often seen to have an ambiguous gendered identity, which then alters as they develop and their identity becomes more strongly aligned with adult gender/sexuality.

During adulthood morphological sexual characteristics do not remain static either. For example, it has been shown that adult males on reaching skeletal maturity tend to have less well-defined supraorbital ridges and generally less robust facial features than those of mid-adult males. It has been argued by Walker (1995) that this may be a factor leading to the identification of fewer young males within skeletal populations (instead they are categorised as females, or of indeterminate sex). In very advanced years, some facial characteristics of males again become altered. For example, age-related edentulism leads to resorption of the bone of the mandible giving it a more gracile, or feminine appearance. Conversely, the cranio-facial characteristics of females may become more masculine with advancing age (Meindl *et al.* 1985). Post-menopausal alterations in hormones often lead to a thickened cranial vault (Ortner and Putschar 1985) that may also result in incorrect determinations of sex, particularly when the skull is fragmentary. As well as having palaeodemographic repercussions, these changing characteristics may have more profound implications concerning social identity; the fluidity of physical features with age both contributing to and reinforcing changing perceptions of masculinity and femininity throughout the life course.

Age-related grave good patterns

The above discussion has emphasised the changing nature of the human skeleton throughout the life course. The following analysis will link this evidence to the material components of the burial record with the aim of high-lighting any age-related grave good patterning, in particular amongst the older individuals buried in the cemeteries studied. Burials in early Anglo-Saxon England are particularly rich in grave goods and therefore lend themselves to this type of analysis. Grave goods are the focus of most funerary analyses because material objects are key to the communication and expression of social identity (Sørensen 2000). Grave goods can be viewed as a way in which past societies symbolically constructed, reinforced, or subverted social norms (Lucy 1998). Subsequently, when examined in conjunction with skeletal evidence, they provide a unique, though by no means straightforward, way of accessing past social identities.

Numerous studies have examined the gender symbolism of grave artefacts from the early Anglo-Saxon period (*e.g.* Pader 1982; Brush 1993; Lucy 1997, 1998; Stoodley 1999; Knüsel and Ripley 2000). Items of material culture are traditionally perceived by archaeologists to be gendered because of their repeated and exclusive association with individuals of a particular biological sex. Grave goods, therefore, become 'masculine', feminine' or, if found with both sexes, 'gender neutral'. While it has been recognised that there are shortcomings with this terminology (Knüsel and Ripley 2000; Scull 2000), the terms do fulfil a useful discursive function and, with some caveats, will be retained here. Comparatively few studies looking at gender symbolism from this time period have also examined the way that objects may also reflect age identity – beyond the Western adult/child dichotomy (for exceptions see Stoodley 1999; Crawford 1999).

Previous studies of the early Anglo-Saxon period have demonstrated that burials exhibiting a feminine gender are far more common than masculine burials and that more artefact types participate in the construction of a feminine identity (*e.g.* Pader 1982; Brush 1993; Stoodley 1999, 78). This was also noted at the cemeteries in this study, with the exception of Worthy Park, Hampshire, where masculine burials (*i.e.* burials with weapons) slightly outnumber feminine burials. Overall, at the sites examined here, general fluctuations were observed in both the proportion of individuals accorded 'gendered' grave goods and the composition of burial assemblages throughout the life course (Fig. 9.1). Some regional differences were also noted between the Oxfordshire and Hampshire sites and a brief discussion of these will be presented below.

This study does not focus too much on the burials of 'children' as these have been discussed at length elsewhere (*e.g.* Crawford 1991, 1999). However, a brief examination of the burials of the young from these cemeteries is required in order to contextualise the grave good patterns of the older individuals within the life course as a whole. One of the most striking patterns amongst the immature individuals is the apparent increase in the quantity and variety of grave goods from the age of 4–7 years. A similar pattern has been observed in previous studies by Stoodley (1999, 110) and Lucy (1998, 45). Focusing, first of all, on 'feminine' assemblages, it is notable that these increase markedly from 8–12 years, particularly at the sites of Abingdon and Berinsfield. At the other sites (all in Hampshire) gendered grave good assemblages were only

consistently buried with individuals at the slightly older age of 13–17 years. While gendered items such as brooches were buried with individuals from the age of one year they tend to be present only singly and were not worn in the 'adult' female style (one on each shoulder) until 8–12 years of age. All individuals in the 13–17 year age group with feminine assemblages were buried with brooches in the 'adult' manner.

This evidence may suggest that a shift in social status is occurring (for presumably female children) at around this age threshold, and that this transition coincides with the expression of a more strongly signified gender identity. There are, however, some subtle differences in the composition of the grave good assemblages between these young individuals and those of older females. For example, although saucer brooches are one of the most common brooch types overall, these were never buried with individuals below 18 years of age (Stoodley (1999, 115–116) has also noted at other sites that saucer brooches were not buried with young individuals). The brooches buried with individuals between 4–7 years are exclusively disc brooches, as are the majority of brooches in the 8–12 year age group. Overall, these brooch types are fairly uniform and smaller in size than those buried with 'adult' females. These younger individuals also tend to be buried with far fewer beads, particularly compared to the age category of 18–24 years (Fig 9.2). Could it be that females underwent an age transition beginning about the age of 8–12 years that saw a shift in gender status, and then a further transition around the age of 18 years, the latter possibly signifying marital status?

Finally, another interesting distinguishing feature of the assemblages of these younger individuals (between 8–17 years) is that they had a strikingly higher proportion of items of personal adornment that may be considered 'Roman' in style or origin (Fig. 9.3). It is interesting that

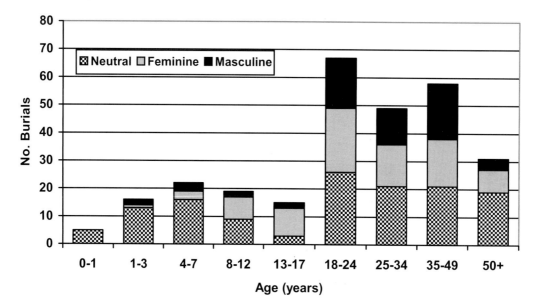

Figure 9.1. Number of individuals in each age group with 'gendered' burials.

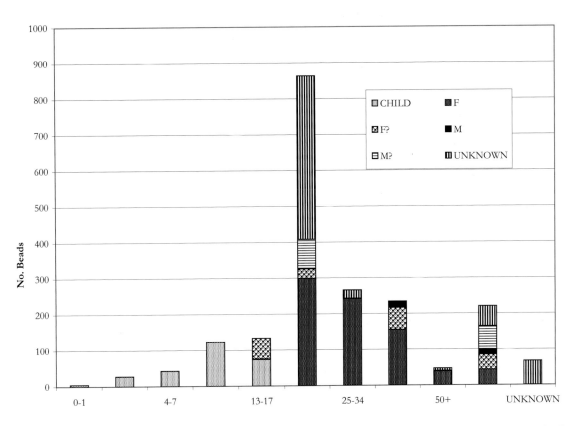

Figure 9.2. Quantity of beads buried with each age and sex at the early Anglo-Saxon cemeteries. There are a large number of individuals of 'unknown sex' in the 18–24 year age category. These were primarily the result of poor preservation, but also a result of ambiguity in the sexually dimorphic features.

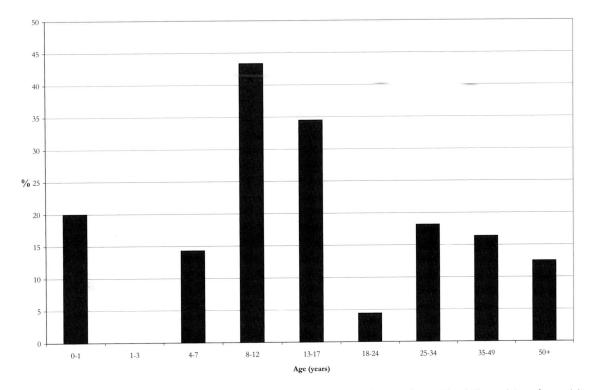

Figure 9.3. The proportion of items of personal adornment in each age group that may be considered 'Roman' in style or origin.

there is an age-related component to the presence of 'Roman' objects in Anglo-Saxon graves as these had often been attributed in the past to the expression of a 'native' Romano-British identity or aspiration (Gowland, in press).

When examining those females usually classed as 'adults' some age-related differences between the young and older ends of the spectrum were also noted amongst the cemetery sample. It has been noted elsewhere that there is a decrease in grave goods buried with older 'adult' females compared to younger ones (Stoodley 1999). If one examines the quantity of goods buried with each female age group, one does see what at first appears to be a significant drop in goods buried with older females, particularly over the age of 50 years. However, this relates primarily to the fact that there are fewer older females represented in the sample. At the cemeteries in this study it was observed that, in fact, approximately equal proportions of females in all age groups were provided with grave goods and that the average quantity of grave goods also remained approximately the same (with the exception of Abingdon where there is a decrease from the age of 35 years).

There are, though, some age-related differences in terms of the types of grave goods that constitute the burial assemblages. Older females were generally buried with slightly fewer items of personal adornment than younger females, although the difference was not very marked (Fig. 9.4). One of the most notable age-related features of burial amongst the females in this sample was the large deposits of beads found with the 18–24 year group (Fig. 9.2). While beads were also buried with the older female age groups, these tend not to be in the same quantities. Other differences relate to brooch types, with younger 'adult' female burials exhibiting much more uniformity in brooch types – predominantly saucer and disc brooches. This was particularly apparent at the sites of Worthy Park and Abingdon. By contrast, older females were buried with a wide variety of brooch types and comparatively few were buried with saucer brooches. This may reflect age-related symbolism in everyday dress, if one assumes that this did not differ profoundly from burial costume.

Overall, a smaller proportion of older females were buried with 'feminine' assemblages when compared to younger females. The grave assemblages of older females more often contained 'gender neutral' items, such as buckles and buckets. Stoodley (1999, 108) also found a decline in 'feminine' items of grave goods with age (although the extent of this was overstated). Recent studies of the early Anglo-Saxon period have begun to stress the significance of these 'gender neutral' burials, both in terms of their frequency and implications for the binary gender system that has been envisaged for this period (*e.g.* Lucy 1998; Knüsel and Ripley 2000, 178).

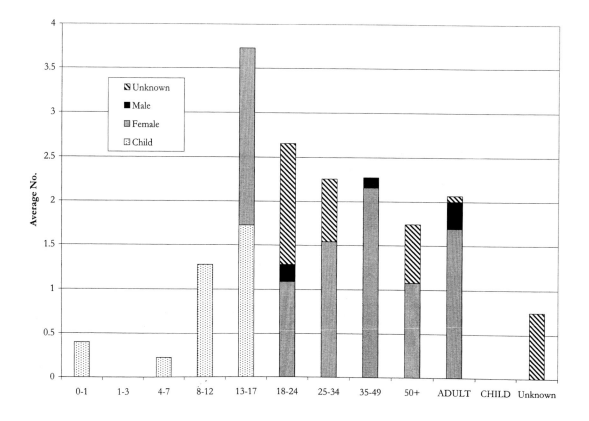

Figure 9.4. The average number of items of personal adornment buried with individuals in each age and sex group from the entire Anglo-Saxon cemetery sample (calculated from those buried with grave goods only).

Overall, individuals at each extreme of the life course spectrum, the very young and very old, tend to exhibit fewer grave goods and a greater proportion of gender neutral burial assemblages (Fig. 9.1). Often these are also interpreted as representing 'low status' graves (*e.g.* Halsall 1996), however, an alternative interpretation could be that gender was simply not an over-riding characteristic at these stages of the life course. For older females, items of jewellery may well have been passed on to daughters at marriage or left as heirlooms.

Stoodley (1999, 80, 106) refers to 'grades of femininity' and discusses the gender neutral grave assemblages of some older females as demarcating a change in identity associated with the menopause. Ethnographic literature has demonstrated that a shift in female identity is often observed in old age and only occasionally coincides with the menopause. More often it is only indirectly associated with physiological age. For example, the marriage of a child, or widowhood may precipitate a transition to a new gender/age identity with the accompanying material and social norms (Rasmussen 1987, 1991). Often this age transition, far from resulting in reduced status, involves empowerment and freedom from the social constraints that govern the behaviour of younger females.

Amongst males at early Anglo-Saxon cemeteries, burial with weapons is a common practice. Härke (1990, 1992) importantly suggested that these may not simply represent

'warrior' graves, but may be symbolic of other aspects of social identity. The cemeteries examined for the present study, along with the findings of others (*e.g.* Härke 1995; Stoodley 1998, 1999; Crawford 1999), demonstrate that there is also an age-related element to this rite, albeit not one that is straightforward to interpret. In this analysis it was found that while individuals below the age of 13 years were occasionally buried with a spearhead, the youngest to be buried with a shield was 16 years old and only those over 18 years were buried with a sword. It has previously been stated that a sword was buried with a juvenile at Abingdon (*e.g.* Brush 1993, 166; Stoodley 1999) based upon the report by Leeds and Harden (1936) which stated that Skeleton 42 was that of an 'adolescent'. However, personal examination of the skeletal remains indicated that this individual was in fact aged between 18–24 years. From the age of 18–24 years there was a dramatic increase in the number of males buried with weapons (Fig. 9.5), which quite possibly indicates an important shift in social identity/status at this stage in the life course.

Several authors (*e.g.* Härke 1995; Stoodley 1998, 1999) have argued that the majority of individuals accorded the weapon burial rite were young adult males. This ties in with images of warriors in 'prime' physical condition, rather than older males. In the present analysis, it was observed that at two of the early Anglo-Saxon cemeteries (Berinsfield and Abingdon) a smaller proportion of males

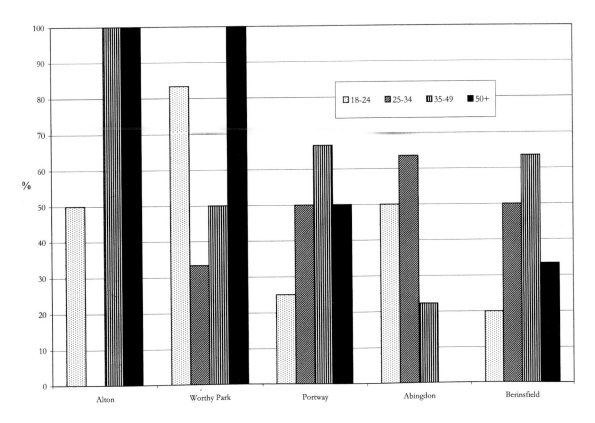

Figure 9.5. Percentage of each age group buried with weapons at the early Anglo-Saxon cemeteries.

over the age of 50 years were indeed buried with weapons compared to other 'adult' age groups, although the difference was not as marked as has previously been suggested (*e.g.* Stoodley 1998, 1999). At Berinsfield and Abingdon, while males over the age of 50 years were more frequently buried with 'gender neutral' burial assemblages, those with weapons tended to have a higher average number of weapons than younger males. Brush (1993, 203) also found that those burials containing the most elaborate weapon sets were of older males. Furthermore, at the early Anglo-Saxon cemeteries of Alton, Worthy Park and Portway (all in Hampshire) there was no drop in the proportion of individuals buried with weapons in the older age categories (Fig. 9.5). As observed in the examination of grave goods buried with 'children' and females, subtle regional differences are also apparent in male assemblage patterns between the Oxfordshire and Hampshire sites. It would seem from the present analysis that the notion of weapon burials being predominantly those of young adult males has been overstated. If these weapon burials also represent a social status, then there is no clear diminution of this amongst older males at early Anglo-Saxon cemeteries, contra the suggestions of previous studies. It is possible that this was because older males were survived by adult children asserting their own social position through the funeral rites they accorded their father (Knüsel pers. comm.) (NB a practice not evident in the burial of mothers).

This leads to the point that when interpreting burial assemblages in terms of social identity, it should be remembered that as people get older, not only does their identity alter, but so too does that of the principal mourners. Archaeologically, this can be most clearly observed from the epigraphic evidence throughout the Roman Empire. For example, a female was commemorated by her parents in youth, after marriage by her spouse, and in old age by her children (Parkin 1992). Age and gender identity are lived relationally; therefore, the variation in funerary practice accorded to females throughout various life course stages could be reflecting and reproducing the changing relationships of the dead person with age. The increase in burial wealth associated with females buried in their early twenties, for example, may not necessarily reflect an increase in social status, or gendered identity, but a shift in the identity of the primary mourner and their relationship to the deceased.

Conclusion

This paper has attempted to place the age and sex data retrieved from the skeleton within a theoretical context. There are clearly a number of problems when attempting to explore age as an aspect of social identity in the past that relate to our inability to reliably estimate chronological age. Furthermore, while it is easy to be over-simplistic in our interpretations of material culture associations, it is important to note that the social meaning imbued by

material culture may be far from straightforward. Material culture is just as likely to subvert and transform, as to reflect and conform to social norms, and this may be particularly so when associated with the dead, whose relationship to the living may be one that necessitates a subversive use of material culture items.

Despite these caveats, archaeology is uniquely placed to provide important insights into how age identity changes over time and the material symbols though which age is expressed. The majority of archaeological cemetery analyses have not considered the fluid nature of age and gender identity and instead have adopted a very rigid modern Western view of the adult/child, male/female distinction (though there are some exceptions *e.g.* Sofaer Derevenski 1997a; Stoodley 1999). As a result, the symbolism of funerary practice has often been obscured or misinterpreted because it falls outside modern social parameters. However, we need not simply reproduce our own social paradigms from past material culture, but through the cemetery data, seek to identify those age/gender thresholds that have symbolic and social significance within the populations under study. By taking a more reflexive approach to the archaeological data, we are able to suggest not only that certain goods are associated with either a masculine, or feminine gender, but also observe the fluidity and plurality of gender and status, as expressed in burial, with age.

Finally, archaeologists have overlooked the relationship between the changing physical nature of the body as it ages and the way in which this may influence and in, turn, be affected by social factors. The influence of cultural beliefs and practices on the physical body in terms of the timing of age-related 'biological' changes is potentially profound. In turn, the physical condition of the body has an important part to play in social identity. We cannot, therefore, reduce the idea of age to a binary opposition of biological versus cultural age: the two are largely irreducible. This requires further consideration and future studies of past age identity must be sensitive to this complex inter-dependence.

Acknowledgements

I would like to thank Chris Knüsel, Dawn Hadley, Sam Lucy, John Pearce and Tim Thompson for their valuable comments on an earlier draft of this paper. This research was undertaken as part of my PhD (funded by the AHRB) and I'm grateful for the supervision of Sam Lucy and Andrew Millard and their useful comments throughout. Any errors, of course, remain my own.

References

Arber, S. and Ginn, J. (1991) *Gender and Later Life*. London, Sage.
Arber, S. and Ginn, J. (1995) Choice and constraint in the retirement of older married women. In S. Arber and J. Ginn (eds.) *Connecting Gender and Ageing: A Sociological Approach*, 69–86. Milton Keynes, Open University Press.

Ariès, P. (1962) *Centuries of Childhood*. (Translated from the French by R. Baldock). London, Jonathan Cape.

Aykroyd, R. G., Lucy, D., Pollard, A. M., and Solheim, T. (1997) Technical note: Regression analysis in adult age estimation. *American Journal of Physical Anthropology* 104, 259–265.

Aykroyd, R. G., Lucy, D., Pollard, A. M., and Roberts, C. A. (1999) Nasty, brutish, but not necessarily short: a reconsideration of the statistical methods used to calculate age at death from adult human skeletal and dental age indicators. *American Antiquity*, 64, 55–70.

Beall, C. M. (1984) Theoretical dimensions of a focus on age in physical anthropology. In D. I. Kertzer and J. Keith (eds.) *Age and Anthropological Theory*, 82–95. Ithaca, New York, Cornell University Press.

Blaikie, A. (1999) *Age and Popular Culture*. Cambridge, Cambridge University Press.

Bocquet-Appel, J.-P. and Masset, C. (1982) Farewell to palaeodemography. *Journal of Human Evolution* 11, 321–333.

Bocquet-Appel, J.-P. and Masset, C. (1985) Palaeodemography: resurrection or ghost? *Journal of Human Evolution* 14, 107–111.

Boyle, A., Dodd, A., Miles, D. and Mudd, A. (eds.) (1995) *Two Oxfordshire Anglo-Saxon Cemeteries: Berinsfield and Didcot*. Thames Valley Landscapes Monograph No 8. Oxford, Oxford University Committee for Archaeology.

Bradley, H. (1996) *Fractured Identities*. Cambridge, Polity Press.

Brooks, S. T. and Suchey, J. M. (1990). Skeletal age determination based on the os pubis: a comparison of the Ascadi-Nemeskeri and Suchey-Brooks methods. *Human Evolution* 5, 227–238.

Brothwell, D. R. (1981) *Digging Up Bones*. Second Edition. Ithaca, Cornell University Press.

Brush (1993) *Adorning the Dead: The Social Significance of Early Anglo-Saxon Funerary Dress in England*. Unpublished Ph.D. thesis, University of Cambridge.

Buikstra, J. and Ubelaker, D. H. (1994). *Standards For data Collection From Human Skeletal Remains*. Fayetteville, Arkansas, Ankara Archaeological Survey Research series no. 44.

Campbell, R. T. and Alwin, D. F. (1996) Quantitative approaches; toward an integrated science of aging and human development. In R. H. Binstock. and L. K. George (eds.) *Handbook of Aging and the Social Sciences*, 31–51. Fourth Edition. New York: Academic Press.

Cook, A. M. and Dacre, M. W. (1985) *Excavations at Portway, Andover 1973–1975*. Oxford, Oxford University Committee for Archaeology.

Crawford, S. (1991) When do Anglo-Saxon children count? *Journal of Theoretical Archaeology* 2, 17–24.

Crawford, S. (1999). *Childhood in Anglo-Saxon England*. Sutton, Stroud.

Evison V. I. (1988) *An Anglo-Saxon Cemetery at Alton, Hampshire*. Hampshire, Hampshire Field Club Monograph 4.

Fortes, M. (1984) Age, generation, and social structure. In D. I. Kertzer and J. Keith (eds.) *Age and Anthropological Theory*. 99–122. Ithaca, New York: Cornell University Press

Fraschetti, A. (1997) Roman youth. In G. Levi and J.-C. Schmitt (eds.) *A History of Young People in the West*. Vol. 1, 51–82. Cambridge, Massachusetts, Harvard University Press.

Fry, C. (1996) Age, aging and culture. In R. H. Binstock and L. K. George (eds.) *Handbook of Aging and the Social Sciences*. 118–135. Fourth Edition. New York: Academic Press.

Gilchrist, R. (1999). *Gender and Archaeology: Contesting the Past*. London: Routledge.

Gilchrist, R. (2000) Archaeological biographies: realizing human lifecycles, -courses and -histories. *World Archaeology* 31, 325–328.

Ginn, J. and Arber, S. (1995) 'Only connect': gender relations and ageing. In S. Arber, and J. Ginn (eds.) *Connecting Gender and Ageing: A Sociological Approach*, 1–14. Buckingham: Open University Press, 1–14.

Gowland, R. L. (in press) Beyond ethnicity: symbols of social identity in fourth to sixth centuries England. *Anglo-Saxon Studies in Archaeology and History*

Hadley, D. M. ed. (1999) *Masculinity in Medieval Europe*. London, Longman

Halsall, G. (1996) Female status and power in early Merovingian Central Austrasia: the burial evidence. *Early Medieval Europe* 5, 1–24.

Haraven, T. K. (1995) Changing images of ageing and the social construction of the life course. In M. Featherstone and A. Wernick (eds.) *Images of Ageing*, 119–134. London, Routledge.

Härke, H. (1990) "Warrior graves". The background of the Anglo-Saxon weapon burial rite. *Past and Present* 126, 22–43.

Härke, H. (1992) Changing symbols in a changing society: the Anglo-Saxon weapon burial rite in the seventh century. In M. Carver (ed.) *The Age of Sutton Hoo*, 149–166. Suffolk, The Boydell Press.

Härke, H. (1995) Discussion of the finds. In Boyle, A., Dodd, A. and Miles, D. (eds.), 1996. *Two Oxfordshire Anglo-Saxon Cemeteries: Berinsfield and Didcot*, 67–74. Oxford, Thames Valley Landscapes Monograph 8.

Harman, M. (1989) Discussion of the finds: Cremations. In A. G. Kinsley (ed.) *The Anglo-Saxon Cemetery at Millgate, Newark-on-Trent, Nottinghamshire*, 23–25. Nottingham, Department of Classical and Archaeological Studies, University of Nottingham.

Harlow, M. and Laurence, R. (2002) *Growing up and Growing Old in Ancient Rome*. London, Routledge.

Hawkes, C. S. and Grainger, G. (2003) *The Anglo-Saxon Cemetery in Worthy Park, Kingsworthy, near Winchester*. Oxford, Oxford University School of Archaeology Monograph No. 59.

Hockey, J. and James, A. (1993) *Growing Up and Growing Old*. London, Sage.

Hoppa, R. D. and Vaupel, J. W. eds. (2002) *Paleodemography: Age Distributions from Skeletal Samples*. Cambridge, Cambridge University Press

Knüsel, C. and Ripley, K. (2000) The Berdache or man-woman in Anglo-Saxon England and Early Medieval Europe. In W.O. Frazer and A. Tyrrell (eds.) *Social Identity in Early Medieval Europe*, 157–191. London and New York, Leicester University Press.

Krogman, W. M. and Iscan, M. Y. (1986) *The Human Skeleton in Forensic Medicine*. Springfield, Illinois, Charles Thomas.

La Fontaine, J. S. (ed.) (1978) *Sex and Age as Principles of Social Differentiation*. London, Academic Press.

La Fontaine, J. (1986) An anthropological perspective on children in social worlds. In M. Richards and P. Light (eds.) *Children of Social Worlds*, 10–30. Cambridge, Polity Press.

Laurence, R. (2000) Metaphors, monuments and texts: the life course in Roman culture. *World Archaeology* 31, 442–455.

Leeds, E. T. and Harden D. B. (1936) *The Anglo-Saxon Cemetery at Abingdon, Berkshire*. Oxford, University of Oxford, Ashmolean Museum.

Levine, R. A. (1998) Child Psychology and anthropology: an environmental view. In C. Panter-Brick (ed.) *Biosocial Perspectives on Children*, 102–130. Cambridge, Cambridge University Press.

Lillehammer, G. (1989) A child is born. The child's world in an archaeological perspective. *Norwegian Archaeological Review* 22, 89–105.

Lovejoy, C. O., Meindl, R. S., Pryzbeck. T. R. and Mensforth, R. P. (1985) Chronological metamorphosis of the auricular surface of the ilium: A new method for the determination of adult skeletal age at death. *American Journal of Physical Anthropology* 68, 15–28.

Lucy, S. J. (1997) Housewives, warriors and slaves? Sex and gender in Anglo-Saxon burials. In J. Moore and E. Scott (eds.) *Invisible People and Processes*, 150–168 London and New York: Leicester University Press.

Lucy, S. J. (1998) *The Early Anglo-Saxon Cemeteries of East Yorkshire: An Analysis and Re-Interpretation.* Oxford: B.A.R Brit. Ser. 272.

Marshall, V. W. (1996) The state of theory in aging and the social sciences. In R. H. Binstock and L. K. George (eds.) *Handbook of Aging and the Social Sciences*, 12–30. Fourth Edition. New York, Academic Press.

Meindl, R. S., Lovejoy, C. O., Mensforth, R. P. and Don Carlos, L. (1985) Accuracy and direction of error in sexing of the skeleton: implications for paleodemography. *American Journal of Physical Anthropology* 68, 79–85.

Millard, A. and Gowland, R. L. (in prep) Long bone growth in late Roman and early Anglo-Saxon populations.

Moen, P. (1996) Gender, age and the life course. In R. H. Binstock and L. K. George (eds.) *Handbook of Aging and the Social Sciences*, 181–187. Fourth Edition. New York, Academic Press.

Molleson, T. and Cox, M. (1993) *The Spitalfields Project Volume 2. The Anthropology. The Middling Sort.* York, C.B.A. Research Report 86.

Moore, H. (1994) *A Passion for Difference.* Cambridge, Polity Press.

Moorrees, C. F. A., Fanning, E. A., and Hunt, E. E. (1963a) Formation and resorption of three deciduous teeth in children. *American Journal of Physical Anthropology* 21, 205–213.

Moorrees, C. F. A., Fanning, E. A., and Hunt, E. E. (1963b) Age variation of formation stages for ten permanent teeth. *Journal of Dental Research* 42, 1490–1502.

Myerhoff, B. (1984) Rites and signs of ripening: the intertwining of ritual, time, and growing older. In D. I. Kertzer and J. Keith (eds.) *Age and Anthropological Theory*, 305–330. Ithaca, New York, Cornell University Press.

O'Rand, M. A. (1996) The cumulative stratification of the life course. In R. H. Binstock and L. K. George (eds.) *Handbook of Aging and the Social Sciences.* Fourth Edition, 188–207. New York, Academic Press.

Ortner, D. J. and Putschar, W. G. J. (1985) *Identification of Pathological Conditions in Human Skeletal Remains.* Washington, Smithsonian Institution Press.

Pader, E.-J. (1982) *Symbolism, Social Relations and the Interpretation of Mortuary remains.* Oxford, B.A.R. Brit. Ser. 130.

Panter-Brick, C. (ed.) (1998) *Biosocial Perspectives on Children.* Cambridge, Cambridge University Press.

Parkin, T. G. (1992) *Demography and Roman Society.* Baltimore, John Hopkins University Press.

Pollock, L. A. (1983) *Forgotten Children.* Cambridge, Cambridge University Press.

Prout, A. and James, A. (1990) A new paradigm for the sociology of childhood? Provenance, promise and problems. In A. James and A. Prout (eds.) *Constructing and Reconstructing Childhood*, 7–33. Basingstoke, Falmer Press.

Rasmussen, S. J. (1987) Interpreting Androgynous woman: female aging and personhood among the Kel Ewey Tuareg. *Ethnology* 26, 17–30.

Rasmussen, S. J. (2000) From childbearers to culture bearers: transition to post-childbearing among Taureg women. *Medical Anthropology* 19, 91–116.

Rosenthal, J. T. (1996) *Old Age in Late Medieval England.* Philadelphia, University of Pennsylvania Press.

Schildkrout, E. (1978) Age and gender in Hausa society: socio-economic roles of children in urban Kano. In L. La Fontaine (ed.) *Sex and Age as Principles of Social Differentiation*, 109–138. London, Academic Press

Scull, C. (2000) How the dead live: some current approaches to the mortuary archaeology of England in the fifth to eighth centuries A.D. *Archaeology Journal* 157, 399–406.

Shahar, S. (1990) *Childhood in the Middle Ages.* London, Routledge.

Shahar, S. (1997) *Growing Old in the Middle Ages: 'Winter Clothes us in Shadow and Pain'.* (Translated from the Hebrew by Yoel Latan). London, Routledge.

Shilling, C. 1993. *The Body and Social Theory.* London, Sage Publications.

Sofaer Deverenski, J. (1994) Where are the children? Accessing children in the past. *Archaeological Review from Cambridge* 13 (2), 7–33.

Sofaer Deverenski, J. (1997a) Age and gender at the site of Tiszapolgár-Basatanya, Hungary. *Antiquity* 71, 875–889.

Sofaer Deverenski, J. (1997b) Engendering children, engendering archaeology. In J. Moore and E. Scott (eds.) *Invisible People and Processes*, 192–202. London, Leicester University Press.

Sofaer Derevenski, J. ed. (2000) *Children and Material Culture.* London, Routledge

Sørensen, Stig, M. L. (2000) *Gender Archaeology.* London, Polity Press.

Stoodley, N. (1998) Post-migration age structure and age-related grave goods in Anglo-Saxon cemeteries in England. *Studien zur Sachsenforschung* 11, 187–197.

Stoodley, N. (1999) *The Spindle and the Spear: A Critical Enquiry into the Construction and Meaning of Gender in the Early Anglo-Saxon Burial Rite.* Oxford: B.A.R. Brit. Ser. 288.

Uhlenberg, P. and Minor, S. (1996) Life course and aging: a cohort perspective. In R. H. Binstock and L. K. George (eds.) *Handbook of Aging and the Social Sciences*, 208–228. Fourth Edition. New York, Academic Press.

Walker, P. L. (1995) Problems of preservation and sexism in sexing: some lessons from historical collections for palaeo-demographers. In S. R. Saunders and A. Herring (eds), *Grave Reflections: Portraying the Past through Cemetery Studies*, 31–48. Toronto: Canadian Scholars Press.

Walrath, D. E., Turner, P., Bruzek, J. (2004) Reliability test for the visual assessment of cranial traits for sex determination. American Journal of Physical Anthropology 125, 132–137.

Webb, P. A. O. and Suchey, J. M. (1985) Epiphyseal union of the iliac crest and medial clavicle. *American Journal of Physical Anthropology* 68, 457–466.

Weiss, K. M. (1972) On the systematic bias in skeletal sexing. *American Journal of Physical Anthropology* 37, 239–250.

10.   Gender, Bioarchaeology and Human Ontogeny

Joanna R. Sofaer

Introduction

Osteoarchaeologists have only relatively recently engaged with the concept of gender as a cultural construction, more often being explicit regarding an awareness of data in terms of sex distributions in a field where determination of biological sex is seen as a fundamental parameter. While there remain many more references to sex rather than gender in osteological papers (Walker and Cook 1998), there is nonetheless a trend towards increasing awareness and insistence on the distinction between sex and gender within osteoarchaeology with specific discrimination between the terms (Pearson 1996; Armelagos 1998; Grauer and Stuart-Macadam 1998; Walker and Cook 1998; Mays and Cox 2000; Sofaer Derevenski 2000).

The development of gender as a concept arose in the social sciences from an awareness of the complexity of relationships and behaviours surrounding the lives of men and women, suggesting that it is not contingent solely upon biology (*e.g.* Ortner and Whitehead 1981; Collier and Yanagisako 1987; Hess and Ferree 1987; Shaver and Hendrick 1987; Moore 1988, 1994; del Valle 1993; Cornwall and Lindisfarne 1994; Lorber 1994). It was therefore considered necessary to maintain a distinction between sex and gender as observation of biological difference alone cannot describe or explain social behaviour. As Moore (1994, 71) points out, 'the obvious fact of biological differences between women and men tells us nothing about the general social significance of those differences; and although human societies the world over recognise biological differences between men and women, what they make of those differences is extraordinarily variable. We cannot deal, therefore, with the observable variability in the cultural construction of gender across the world or through historical time simply by appealing to the indisputable fact of sexual difference'.

The meaning and application of the term 'gender' is not, however, universal. Within the discipline of archaeology as a whole, the relationship between sex and gender has been increasingly debated and called into question (see Gilchrist 1999; Sørensen 2000). Following Butler (1990, 1993), the concepts of sex and gender have been deliberately collapsed with both being identified as cultural constructions (Meskell 1998, 2001; Gilchrist 1999; Gosden 1999; Joyce 2000a and b; Bachand *et al.* 2003). As part of this trend there has been a move towards seeing gender as a redundant category and giving sex primacy. Advocates of the cultural construction of sex and gender have tried to claim ground from the so-called 'natural' sciences by using biology, in particular genetics and the osteological analysis of the human skeleton, to undermine its own tenets. Such arguments have obvious relevance for archaeologists working with human remains.

This chapter explores the uses to which the human skeleton has been put for contrasting understandings of the relationship between sex and gender in archaeology. The first of these relates to the methodological use of osteologically determined sexed skeletons in a perspective where sex and gender are considered conceptually distinct. Here biological sex is considered an important hook upon which to hang interpretations by making associations between sexed individuals and gendered artefacts. The second relates to the ways in which the role of biological sex is brought into question through an insistence on the culturally constructed character of sex in a perspective where sex and gender are considered conceptually inseparable. Despite different ways of configuring the sex-gender relationship, both approaches result in a series of tensions between theory and method. These originate from common assumptions regarding the immutability and stability of the biological body, which is frequently contrasted with the fluidity of cultural phenomena. Bioarchaeological understandings of the human skeleton, however, identify it as dynamic. Not only do people grow, mature and senesce, but the ways that they lead their lives materially shape their bodies. In this perspective, sexed bodies are subject to biological change throughout the life course. I want to suggest that we move towards an understanding of gender that takes biological processes into account and that is situated in terms of human development, where human development is understood to embrace both biology and culture. Gender is an ontogenetic process that can be explored through the human skeleton.

Uses of the human skeleton where sex and gender are considered distinct

In archaeologies where sex and gender are considered distinct, sex is understood in terms of biology and is determined from the skeleton. Sex is thus defined by differences between males and females that are determined at conception and enhanced in subsequent physiological development (Armelagos 1998, 1). Sex differences include chromosomal differences, genitalia, and morphological differences in the skeletal anatomy of men and women that are related to hormonal differences between them (Mays 1998; Mays and Cox 2000). In archaeological contexts, determination of sex in adults normally takes the form of the visual assessment of morphological characteristics of the skeleton. The pelvis and skull are generally considered the single most reliable areas for sex determination, the former reflecting functional differences between men and women related to childbirth (Mays 1998; Mays and Cox 2000). The skeleton is understood as a proxy for what is observed in the living because the skeleton is the frame for the flesh. Despite the advent of DNA analysis which is seen by some as the way forward, particularly as a solution to problems of sexing immature skeletons (Brown 1998, 2000; Stone 2000), this currently plays a limited role in archaeology. The establishment of sex through the classification of individual bodies as male and female is seen as the province of osteoarchaeology.

Archaeological method commonly infers gender by way of associations between 'sexed' skeletons and 'gendered' objects in mortuary contexts (Whitehouse 2002) as patterns of grave goods are identified in relation to male or female bodies. Reaction against the prioritisation of grave goods has seen the emergence of a commonly expressed concern with accuracy that identifies the use of osteological sex determinations as being more secure than a potentially ethnocentric identification of objects as male or female without reference to the skeletal body (*cf.* Tarlow 1999, 12). Thus osteological sex determinations act as the foundation for archaeological analysis. As sexed and therefore 'known' the skeletal body is accorded a privileged status in the archaeological study of gender.

Using the skeletal body as the methodological key to archaeologies of gender, however, results in a series of tensions between the apparent inferential simplicity of method and the complexity of theory. The practice of mapping gender (a social construction) onto sex (the biological sexed skeleton) seems to indicate methodological uncertainty in how to approach gender as a cultural construction. While the concept of gender appears to set out a cultural agenda, the practice of associating objects with sexed bodies would logically seem only to conflate sex and gender by using the same variable to examine both (Sofaer Derevenski 1998; Sørensen 2000). The distinction between sex and gender becomes one of material (human bones vs. artefacts) rather than of concept. Furthermore, an *a priori* division of grave goods into two categories corresponding to male and female that links the duality of the sexes with a universal assumption of the bimodal distribution of grave goods, assumes a high degree of congruence between the identity and activities of the deceased in life. But given that gender is a social construction, equating such a complex aspect of social life with the single variable of sex seems somewhat reductive. Archaeological practice is problematic because while it sets out a theoretical distinction between sex and gender, it simply ends up categorising people through sex and so returns to biology. This results in methodological and epistemological confusion regarding the character of gender. Lacking the direct ethnographic observation of person-object interaction, archaeologists can neither disassociate objects from the biology of the individual without losing a point of reference, nor associate objects with the body without falling into the trap of biological determinism.

The body acts not as the focus of interpretation, but as a reference point around which interpretations of surrounding artefacts are made. In other words, interpretations focus on the patterning and distribution of grave goods in relation to bodies rather than on the bodies themselves. In cases where there are no objects with bodies, this approach implies either that it is not possible to access gender in the past, or that gender was not important, thereby potentially conflating burial traditions with social structures. Despite some recent attempts to examine gender through osteoarchaeology (*e.g.* Grauer and Stuart-Macadam 1998; Hollimon 1992, 2000a; Sofaer Derevenski 1998, 2000; Peterson 2002), gender often seems to be located outside the body, constructed external to the person who was gendered in life. Archaeological method sets up a dichotomy between person and object, although the material world is crucial to the construction of gender through practice since gendered individuals made and used those artefacts (Sørensen in press). This leads to tension, for without gendered individuals there can be no gendered meaning. Archaeological method leaves the impression that identity resides in objects rather than in the people themselves. The body is used as a stepping stone to interpretation, rather than central to the project of an engendered archaeology.

Uses of the human skeleton where sex and gender are considered inseparable

Where sex and gender are considered inseparable, sex is understood as a cultural construction rather than a natural given. It is seen as a product of discourse brought into being over time through reiterative performances as people behave in particular ways (Butler 1990, 1993). Those in favour of collapsing sex and gender argue against sex being fixed at birth and instead focus on the ways that people are able to manipulate and change the perception of their bodies by others. This perspective is based on awareness of historical changes in perceptions of sex in the history of medicine on one hand (*e.g.* Laqueur 1990) and on the complexity of sex identity identified by reference to transsexuals, transvestites, and historical and ethnographic accounts (*e.g.* Blackwood 1984; Herdt 1994; Roscoe 1998) on the other. Concern with sexuality as an aspect of individual sexed experience has been emphasised alongside the idea that what people make of sex is not just reproductive (*e.g.* Nordbladh and Yates 1990; Gilchrist 1999; Voss 2000; Hollimon 2000b; Meskell 2002). Arguments for sex as a cultural construction thus suggest that pigeon-holing people as male or female from birth on the basis of sex characteristics does not allow for potential fluidity and choice in the expression and experience of sex.

A key element of this position in archaeology is the questioning of biological understandings of sex in terms of the binary categories male or female (*e.g.* Nordbladh and Yates 1990; Knapp and Meskell 1997; Gilchrist 1999; Hodder 1999; Arnold 2002). It is argued that sex cannot be comprehended through two categories alone as there is a range of variation in the expression of sex characteristics at both genotypic and phenotypic levels. Advocates point to the existence of individuals with chromosomal, gonodal, endocrine and phenotypic abnormalities including Klinefelter syndrome (47XXY), Turner syndrome (45XO) and Testicular Feminization syndrome (46XY) as suggesting a wider non-binary range of sex variation. Hence the binary division of sex is a socio-historical product and sex should instead be seen as a fluid spectrum (Nordbladh and Yates 1990; Knapp and Meskell 1997; Gilchrist 1999; Hodder 1999). The relevance of such insights to archaeology is, however, doubtful in as much as the skeletal implications of such configurations are unclear. People do not see each other as genes but as bodies in the world, and it is difficult to know how they could be recognised in past populations (Mays and Cox 2000), especially given their relative rarity in living groups. The total frequency of intersex babies with a range of abnormalities relating to genotype (non-XX or non-XY combinations, including Klinefelter syndrome and Turner syndrome), is estimated to average 0.193% of total live births (Blackless *et al.* 2000, 159). Intersex conditions linked to hormonal causes are estimated to average 1.516% of live births (Blackless *et al.* 2000, 159), although figures vary between populations.

Critiques of the binary division of sex also point to the way that osteoarchaeologists score skeletal material. Both British and US guidelines to the standards for recording human remains advise the use of five categories from which to choose when recording morphological features of the skull and pelvis in the adult skeleton on a scale of typical male – probable male – sex unknown – probable female – typical female (Brickley and McKinley 2004; Buikstra and Ubelaker 1994). In determining sex, osteoarchaeologists score observations in terms of this range of options and, on the basis of the category in which the majority of observable characteristics lie, determine the sex of the individual. Again, advocates for the cultural construction of sex, argue that this reflects a continuum of variation and so sex is a spectrum (Nordbladh and Yates 1990; Yates 1993). While there is a wide range of phenotypic variation in the skeletal expression of sexually dimorphic traits even within normal XX or XY chromosomal combinations, such an argument misconstrues the principles that lie behind osteological assessments which are rather to do with degrees of certainty in determination rather than absolute correspondence with a range of sexes. Using a method based on rank scoring explicitly recognises potential variation in the expression of sex, while a multifactorial approach takes into account a range of different characteristics in order to acknowledge the complexity of the process of classification. Overall, however, males and females fall into distinct groups because they are dimorphic. Scoring methods thus represent a potential range of permutations, but in reality variation in expression of sex is not evenly distributed along a spectrum, but rather exists within two categories. What is of importance for sex determination is the strength of dimorphism at a population level since some populations display a greater degree of dimorphism than others. In addition, the relevance of biological variation in terms of a cultural reality is unclear (Sørensen 2000, 46–47). Arguments based on the skeletal expression of sex verge on biological determinism. As Sørensen (2000, 47) points out, what is at stake here is not whether sex exists but our ability to classify it. On one hand arguments for the cultural construction of sex dismiss the relevance of osteological sexing to the social understanding of biological sex, yet on the other hand they use highly categorical concepts of sex at the chromosomal level that are very much modern conceptions.

Where the binary division of sex into male and female is considered to be a produced representation that is the product of discourse, biological notions of sex are said to be specific cultural statements created through particular cultural practices (Nordbladh and Yates 1990; Meskell 1996, 1998, 2001; Gosden 1999, 146–150; Conkey 2001, 344; Joyce 2000b; for a discussion see Sørensen 2000, 47; Houston and McAnany 2003, 34). In archaeology, the practices in question are those involved in the osteological determination of sex (Claassen 1992). Following Foucault (1978), the process of sexing bodies is understood to produce sex, which does not exist prior to its description. Consequently, sex is a cultural construct. Bias in sexing towards males is used as evidence of this construction

(Arnold 2002), although the extent of such bias has not been systematically demonstrated. The logical extension of the constructionist argument is that osteological sexing of the human body and the use of osteological determinations are inappropriate to archaeological practice since they are based on universalist principles that are incompatible with arguments concerning the discursiveness of sex. Significantly, most of those workers who emphasise the construction of sex do not deal with skeletal material or mortuary contexts, but with studies of the body using textual records or traditional material culture, thereby avoiding the skeletal body.

The idea that sex is a construction because the method that leads to it is a construction would seem to conflate two quite different arguments. It is possible to acknowledge that the particular notion of sex as it is understood in osteoarchaeology is the product of a particular contextual and historical perspective on the basis that the act of creating scientific knowledge is a social act (Harding 1986; Jones 2002) without suggesting that osteological determinations do not form a useful axis of analysis. Furthermore, the aim of osteoarchaeology is to find ways of analysing the variation that is *already* observed in the skeleton; despite scepticism regarding osteological sexing in parts of the archaeological community (Hodder 1999, 114–115), osteoarchaeology is not a form of alchemy that is able to create something from nothing. For example, at the site of Spitalfields where coffin plates gave the name (and hence sex) of individuals, Molleson and Cox (1993) tested the reliability of osteological sexing methods and reported that 98% of adult skeletons were successfully identified. Sex differences also have implications for other aspects of skeletal biology (Armelagos 1998). For example, a range of factors, including diet and exercise, may contribute to low bone density (osteopenia) and osteoporosis, but these are more commonly found in women due to pregnancy, lactation and menopause (Weaver 1998). Osteoarchaeological sexing is a practice concerned with understanding categories and variability within categories, where what is at stake is not the existence of differences between bodies because this is taken for granted, but the assessment that understanding bodies in this particular way is of importance. There may then be many different ways of understanding what sex is under different historical conditions, but this potential plurality does not undermine the relevance of osteological notions of sex for archaeology since osteological assessments allow the potential importance of biological sex for past human groups to be explored. 'Sex as an analytical concept is not *per se* a prescriptive term establishing either how societies should be or necessarily revealing the variation which social concepts of sex suppress, rather it is a term aiming at understanding social categorisation and practices that are prescriptive in terms of how bodies are understood' (Sørensen 2000, 48).

Sex has a material reality. It is not simply a represen-tation. Rejection of biological sex as an axis of analysis removes people and their participation in social relations from the real world in which people live, situating it instead in a notional world of symbolic constructs (*cf.* Ingold 1991). To account for the regulation of sex in archaeological contexts we must take cognizance of differences between bodies and we do this by reference to the skeleton. An osteological approach to sex may be a form of cultural construction, but as an effective way of dealing with the material reality of sex by providing categories that can be investigated in terms of their social relevance and means of regulation in the past it has a clear contribution to make. Osteological categorisations of the physical body do not prohibit or remove the need to examine how sex is socially understood and regulated. The production of osteoarcheological knowledge does not preclude its interpretation in terms of social relations or what people may, or may not, have made of differences between bodies.

It is thus precisely because osteoarchaeological methods for the determination of sex are culturally specific ways of identifying sex, that we need to consider gender, otherwise we run the risk in archaeology either of falling back into biological determinism or of cutting ourselves off completely from the possibility of accessing the potential ways that differences between bodies can be socially regulated and understood. Such an approach does not deny that people have to come to grips with their sexed bodies and that they have sexual experiences, but by allowing for the possibility of gender a potentially greater complexity of human life can be explored. Arguing that both sex and gender are culturally constructed does not logically require that gender becomes an invalid concept, or indeed that sex and gender can be used interchangeably (Sørensen 2000). Sex and gender need not be equivalent and maintaining the possibility of both sex and gender allows for a range of possibilities in analysis that collapsing sex with gender as a single form of construction seems to preclude (Sørensen 2000). The problem is how to 'forge an understanding of gender that neither underestimates nor neutralizes its relationship to sex, while at the same time, neither reducing nor negating its social dimension' (Sørensen 2000, 57).

The rejection of biology is also problematic since advocates of collapsing sex and gender still work with some universal notion of human nature, even if any such conception is overtly treated with suspicion. Thus while they do generally tend to mean that 'difference' comes first, despite the rhetoric of rejecting biology they retain clear ties to biologism (Morton 1995, 103–4) as they are still tied to a notion of the human being or of humanity that unifies the discipline of archaeology. As Morton (1995, 104) points out, it seems intuitively paradoxical to speak of the 'cultural construction of human beings' because human beings tend to be globally defined at the level of the species *Homo sapiens*, a strictly biologically defined entity.

Common tensions between method and theory in the archaeology of gender

Despite contrasting views of the role of biological sex in relation to gender, both perspectives suffer from a lack of clarity and consistency in terms of the relevance of the physical body to archaeological understandings of gender. Their different tensions emerge, however, from the same common origin in as much as the biological body is treated as synonymous with sex, where the expression of sex throughout the life course is regarded as static. For those who consider sex and gender to be distinct, this has meant that because of the difficulties involved in accurately determining the sex of sub-adult remains, the study of gender has tended to focus on adults. Young individuals who cannot be easily sexed osteologically are excluded, although there is no *a priori* reason why they too may not be gendered. Objects are divided into two mutually exclusive categories relating to male and female. Artefacts which cannot be associated in this manner are frequently dropped from the analysis and are implicitly regarded as non-gendered. The mapping of gender onto sex is thus unable to take into account the ways that the physical expression of sex changes over the life course in relation to skeletal maturation and how this may, or may not, be related to the construction of gender (Sofaer Derevenski 1997a and b, 2000; Gowland 2001, 2004). This results in gender becoming a means of classification rather than of exploration (Sørensen 2000) that in practice often tends to assume that gender is stable throughout the life course, thereby precluding the fluidity that is a particularly useful element of the concept and that is inherent in understanding it as culturally dependent and learnt. Where sex and gender are considered inseparable, biological sex is rejected as an analytical axis on the basis that it is fixed and static in contrast to the fluidity of cultural construction. This position tends to conflate genetics with biology and fails to distinguish between developmental differences and genetic ones (Morton 1995; Ingold 1998). The effect of identifying the biological body as synonymous with sex as static has been a disengagement with mortuary contexts and work with human remains. It has been replaced by a focus on living embodiment, particularly through work on iconographic representations that somewhat paradoxically seems to lack 'real' bodies. While such work has constructively explored temporal dimensions to the construction of identity over the life course through the iteration of social acts (*e.g.* Joyce 2000a and b, 2003), it has placed relatively little emphasis on physical changes to the body. A perception of the biological body as fixed underlies even feminist thinking, although this is ostensibly denied by statements that we cannot understand our biological selves except through culture, thus perpetuating an 'additive model' of culture superimposed onto nature (Birke 1999, 44).

The identification of the biological body as synonymous with sex results from a common division between "natural" and "cultural" bodies that forms one of the most 'tenacious mental habits' (Duden 1991, vii). Thus the biological osteological body is perceived as an immutable, unchanging and stable substrate in contrast to the culturally constructed body, which is temporally variable and flexible. In this scheme, the biological body, while seen as a vehicle of social and cultural activities, is differentiated and divorced from other realms of culture and society, implying the existence of some kind of biological entity that is separate from the cultural life of the body (Duden 1991, vii; Ingold 1998). For advocates of sex and gender as distinct this perception of stability of the biological body lends it a reality or authenticity that the changeable, and perhaps more fickle, cultural body is seen to lack. By contrast, for advocates of sex and gender as inseparable this stability means that the physical body becomes irrelevant to discussions of culture as fluid. Furthermore, this notion of stability is taken to mean universality in the human body such that bodies are everywhere regarded as similar. This is further extended to an association with the impersonality of the biological body, which, separated from culture, is not only seen as common to all, but hence cannot be regarded as in any way individual or personal in the way that the fluid culturally constructed body is.

The stability of the biological body can be questioned on two main counts. First, while genetic sex may be fixed at conception, the expression of sex inevitably changes over the course of people's lives as they grow, mature and senesce. For example, bodies develop sex characteristics in puberty. Interest in the ways that the expression of sex changes over the life course has long been a focus of osteoarchaeology arising from methodological concerns over the accuracy of sex determination and appreciation of its limitations. Indeed, a significant corpus of the osteoarchaeological literature deals with the possibilities and difficulties provided by changes to the body over the life course as well as their use, misuse and calibration. This emphasis on the body as dynamic is radically different to external perceptions of osteoarchaeology as simply pigeon-holing people as male or female. Second, sex is identified as synonymous with biology by virtue of the skeletal body being understood as a kind of substrate. Outside archaeological discussions of gender, however, biology refers to process rather than substrate (Birke 1999), where biology relates to development rather than genetics, and the social is part of the domain of lived experience rather than its categorical representation (Ingold 1998, 25). These distinctions are crucial because they shift the emphasis towards a developmental perspective that investigates the relationship between people and the world rather than seeing the body as a static given. It is worth exploring these notions further as they lead to the use of biology of the body in a way that may help to resolve some of the tensions in existing archaeological approaches.

Plasticity and human development

Biological processes follow particular patterns or stages defined by the limited range of responses of human tissue and regulatory mechanisms (Lovejoy _et al._ 2003). Nonetheless, the development of the body is not simply related to inevitable processes of growth and degeneration or the product of a genetic inheritance. The human body is plastic and the _specific way_ in which a body develops is related to the totality of the environment in which a person is situated, where environment is understood as comprising both so-called natural and cultural phenomena (Roberts 1995), including the actions of self and of others in the world.

The principle of plasticity underlies the bioarchaeological approach to the study of the human skeleton. It is a key concept in contemporary human biology (Roberts 1995; Hulse 1981) and is defined as 'systematic changes within the person in his or her structure and/or function' (Lerner 1984, xi) or 'the capability of being moulded' (Roberts 1995, 1) that refers to a process of functional adaptation to the environment affecting both the soft tissues and bony structures of the body (Roberts 1995). It differs from acclimatization (a short term reversible adaptive process) and evolution (genetic adaptation over generations) (Schell 1995), being defined in terms of dynamic irreversible modifications that are not heritable (Lasker 1969), where the phenotype is defined as an expression of the genotype in a particular environment (Knüsel 2000). It begins in utero. Thus it is increasingly understood that effects of the mother's environment in relation to the class and health status of pregnant women influence the child's intrauterine experience and the body of the foetus. Mothers who eat poor diets, use drugs and consume excessive alcohol during pregnancy are more likely to have intellectually impaired children (Dickens 2001) while smoking, poor maternal fat stores and heavy weight-bearing activity in late pregnancy lead to a lower neonatal bone mass and increased risk of osteoporosis later in life (Godfrey _et al._ 2001; Cooper _et al._ 2002). The potential for plasticity exists throughout the life course (Roberts 1995), although there are periods when it may exhibit more or less plasticity. Thus for example, intentional cranial deformation or cranial deformation by cradleboarding takes advantage of the heightened plasticity of the infant body (Ortner and Putschar 1985; Aufderheide and Rodriguez-Martin 1998; Torres-Rouff 2002).

The plasticity of the human skeleton provides a framework for understanding synchronic and diachronic contrasts between otherwise similar human groups. It can be seen in, for example, the effect of nutrition on human growth. Numerous studies have shown that improved nutrition leads to greater body size (Boldsen 1995; Bogin 2001, 1999) as exemplified in studies of migrants and their children (see Roberts 1995; Coleman 1995). The skeleton also responds to damage, disease or mechanical stress. Following traumatic injury, over time bones may heal, sometimes with considerable deformity (Roberts 2000). Disease processes have a synergistic relationship to the environment in which people live and work (Kelley 1989; Roberts and Manchester 1995; Roberts and Cox 2003). Thus the prevalence of types of infectious diseases and the health risks people run have changed as human lifeways have changed, a classic example of this being the domination and spread of pathogens such as those causing smallpox and cholera in urban communities with a high population density (Kelley 1989; Roberts and Cox 2003). Bone responds to disease and palaeopathological bone changes represent an adaptation by forming bone (proliferative changes) and/or destroying bone (destructive changes), or a mixture of the two (Roberts and Manchester 1995). Conditions of prolonged and continued stress imposed by habitual, or occupational activity can also cause bone to deform with the development of irregularities of osseous and dental tissues (Kennedy 1989; Rubin _et al._ 1990). The mechanical load applied to living bone through, for example, weight-bearing or muscular tension influences the morphology and density of bone (Lanyon _et al._ 1982; Lanyon 1987; Cowin 2001), although the complexities of the relationship between stress trajectories and trabecular architecture have been increasingly recognised and form a focus of investigation (Cowin 2001). Bone remodelling is greatest under cyclical loading, as in movement (Martin and Burr 1989). Bone may also respond to stress with accelerated degenerative changes to joints (osteophytosis and osteoarthritis) which result not only from the inevitable process of ageing, but for which, in general terms, the primary contributing factor is mechanical stress on the skeleton (Radin _et al._ 1972; Radin 1982; Peyron 1986; Larsen 1997).

There is a growing body of literature which has examined activity-related change in skeletal samples with varying degrees of success using musculoskeletal stress makers, nonpathological articular modifications, directional asymmetry, cross-sectional geometry of bone, and pathological lesions, the latter including degenerative changes to joints and trauma (_e.g._ Jones _et al._ 1977; Merbs 1983; Ruff _et al._ 1984; Kelley and Angel 1987; Robb 1994; Baud 1996; Pálfi and Dutour 1996; Sperduti 1997; Stirland 1993, 1998; Steen and Lane 1998; Mays 1999; Peterson 2002; Ciranni and Fornaciari 2003; Weiss 2003; Eshed _et al._ 2004; Stock and Pfeiffer 2004). Capasso _et al._ (1998) published an _Atlas of Occupational Markers on Human Remains_ while Kennedy (1989) describes 140 markers of occupational stress reported in published medical and anthropological sources. At one end of the spectrum researchers have identified skeletal changes related to specific activities such as horseriding (_e.g._ Pálfi 1992), canoeing and kayaking (Lai and Lovell 1992; Lovell and Lai 1994; Hawkey and Street 1992), or postural and upper limb modifications associated with grinding foodstuffs (Ubelaker 1979; Bridges 1989; Molleson 1989, 1994; Miles 1996). At the other, observed skeletal modifications have been regarded as more general and non-specific indications of life-style (*e.g.* Cohen and Armelagos 1984; Kennedy 1998). Controversy exists regarding the extent to which it is possible to specifically identify such changes in terms of particular activities (Jurmain 1990; Stirland 1991; Rogers and Waldron 1995; Knüsel *et al*. 1997). Many workers emphasise that the precise aetiology of many traits are currently poorly understood and that a specific modification 'may not be attributable to a single activity pattern, but rather a wide range of habitual behaviours' (Capasso *et al*. 1998, 5 cited in Knüsel 2000, 382). The effects of stress on the skeleton are often described anecdotally and there is a need to accumulate more base-line data on the impact of known activities on the skeleton by examining historically and ethnographically documented populations where possible (Sofaer Derevenski 2000). Where musculoskeletal stress makers are used, preferential consideration of groups of muscles that function together is desirable (Stirland 1998).

While teeth do not remodel in the same way as bones, they too respond to stress and mechanical forces. Stress during tooth formation can result in disturbance to the growing tooth enamel resulting in pits or a band of thinner enamel known as dental enamel hypoplasia (Goodman and Rose 1990). Dental enamel hypoplasia has been related to a wide range of conditions including fever, low birth weight, starvation, congenital infections and weaning (see Goodman and Rose 1991; Hillson 1996; Larsen 1997), although in some cases the significance of weaning for their formation may be coincidental (Blakey *et al*. 1994; Larsen 1997). The rate of tooth wear is related to diet and patterns of dental macrowear and microwear reflect the relative consumption of foodstuffs (*e.g.* Smith 1984; Schmidt 2001; see Larsen 1997) as well as the use of teeth for grip in daily tasks (*e.g.* Turner and Anderson 2003).

Despite caveats regarding the extent to which it is possible to make direct links between particular activities or lifeways and osseous modifications, the plasticity of the body means that the body is never pre-social and is contextually dependent. Plasticity is a developmental phenomenon that exists from birth to death (Lerner 1984, 3) and lends the body its historicity. The body is a dynamic developmental system, not an unchanging entity simply waiting to be manipulated and socially constructed. It exists within an environment with which it has a recursive relationship (Ingold 1998). This means that the body cannot exist in some kind of natural pristine state as it affects, and is affected by its surroundings, both intentionally and unintentionally. The body as it is found at death is brought into being over the life course through repeated socially defined actions. Such a contextual view of development means that the body is constantly reworked and is never finished. As Ingold puts it, '....throughout life the body undergoes processes of growth and decay, and that as it does so particular skills, habits, capabilities and strengths, as well as debilities and weaknesses, are enfolded into its very constitution' (Ingold 1998, 26–27).

Plasticity is not, however, limitless. Because processes of modification of the human skeleton are governed by its physical properties, types of modification are not infinite, although individual skeletons may manifest it to different degrees. The degree to which the human body may be influenced is complex and multifactorial, being affected by a large number of factors including age, sex and predispositions (Bridges 1991; Larsen 1997). Furthermore, as well as lending potential, the environment also places limits on the body. It is just as wrong to depict human beings as infinitely malleable by saying that 'any' human organism can participate in 'any' social or cultural environment (Morton 1995, 118) as to suggest that bodies are fixed entities. While the plasticity of the body means that it can be identified as expressive of social values, the body is not a pre-existing passive biological container to be filled with culture (Ingold 1998, 26–27). Humans grow in an environment provided by the presence and activities of others and are active in their own development through engaging in social relations (Ingold 1998; Toren 1999, 2001). There is a growing corpus of literature showing that social relations affect how a child develops in later life (Dickens 2001), suggesting that those early experiences become 'biologically embedded' (Keating and Miller 1999, 232). These experiences drive future actions and create constraints as well as possibilities. Our experiences are thus related to those of our parents and carers. We literally embody our history and because our history is created through our relations with others, we also embody the history of our relations with them, thereby tapping into their histories too (Toren 1999, 2).

Resolving common problems: skeletons, gender and ontogeny

This emphasis on plasticity and process shifts the study of gender away from the use of the skeletal body as a means of classification, towards an appreciation of biology in terms of human ontogeny through the engendering of people, and the use of the skeleton as a site for the investigation of gender in its own right. In other words, since gender is key to social relations, gendered behaviour is learnt, and gendered actions have the potential to be expressed by the body since skeletal remains can be regarded as the product of human action, one fruitful avenue may be to use gender as an heuristic concept to explore the processes leading to the development of contextually specific bodies. Configured in this way, the issue is not whether bodies are natural or cultural because they are both, but the trajectories that different bodies follow over their lives, the variables that cause bodies to develop in particular ways, and the ways that that the expression of gender changes over time. A first step in addressing the tensions between method and theory in the archaeology of gender can be taken through a bioarchaeological approach that recognises the potential of the body for the material expression of gender, where gender is the outcome of human agency and related to social practice.

Bioarchaeological studies of gender have looked primarily at the gendered division of labour. For instance, food preparation may involve strenuous, repetitive work such as pounding or grinding which is carried out on a regular basis from a young age and places repeated physical stress on particular locations on the body. Molleson (1989, 1994) found that female skeletons from the Mesolithic and Neolithic site of Tell Abu Hureyra, Syria, showed metatarsal-phalangeal modifications in the first metatarsals with degenerative changes to the margins of the joint facets in older individuals. She suggested that alterations to the joint were probably the result of prolonged hyperdorsiflexion of the toes while kneeling. Such a posture while grinding cereal is depicted in Assyrian and Egyptian dynastic tomb art (Molleson 1989). Bridges (1989) suggested that pounding corn with long wooden pestles held with both hands may have led to an increase in diaphyseal bone thickness and strength, along with a reduction in bilateral asymmetry of the humerus in Mississippian females compared to Archaic females. The major motions involved in this activity were flexion and extension at the elbow as the forearms were first drawn up together and then forcibly straightened to drive the pestle into the mortar (Bridges 1989, 1985). Thus although most people preferentially use one hand over another in skilled tasks contributing to a tendency towards asymmetry in bone morphology and mineral density in paired skeletal elements in the arms and shoulder girdle (Steele 2000), as both arms were used in pounding, the forces on both arms would have been equivalent, resulting in reduced asymmetry.

Other gendered activities have also been inferred from skeletal remains on the basis of their socio-cultural and archaeological context. Merbs (1983) identified osteoarthritis of the ulnarcarpal and radioulnar joints, especially on the left hand of Inuit women, as a result of holding skins in the right hand and cutting them with the left. Lovell and Dublenko (1999) suggested that lesions on some of the skeletons of men from the cemetery at the 19th century trading post at Fort Edmonton, Canada, were consistent with 'mushing' (driving a dog sled), while those on the single preserved female from the site may have been related to the arduous domestic chores documented at the fort. At the ethnographically and historically documented 16th-19th site of Ensay in the Outer Hebrides, differences between the sexes in the prevalence and distributions of osseous changes along the spine could be related to highly structured differences in activities. In particular, load-bearing by women using baskets known as 'creels' to carry peats for fuel and wet seaweed for fertiliser resulted in a characteristic posture which disrupted 'normal' patterns of osseous change down the spine (Sofaer Derevenski 2000). By contrast, in the Medieval English countryside, though labour was divided between the sexes with men responsible for the

majority of heavy lifting and women carrying out tasks in the domestic arena, outside the home the division of labour was rather fluid (Bennett 1987). Distinctions in skeletal modifications of the spine between males and females from the site of Wharram Percy were less marked suggesting broadly similar lifestyles (Sofaer Derevenski 2000). In a recent study of the transition to agriculture in the Levant using musculoskeletal stress markers of the upper limb, Eshed *et al.* (2004) found that changes in activity patterns between the Natufian hunter-gatherers and Neolithic farmers led to an overall increase in stress in the farming population with women taking on a greater proportion of subsistence activities compared to Natufian females. Differences in diet between men and women have also been a focus of investigation. In an early study exploring the links between food and gender relations Hastorf (1991) used botanical and isotopic data to suggest differential access to foodstuffs that she related to changes in Andean women's political position during Inka rule. More recent studies have explored the relationship between gender, group membership, and status through diet (*e.g.* White *et al.* 1993; Schulting and Richards 2001; Privat *et al.* 2002; Cucina and Tiesler 2003; Ambrose *et al.* 2003) indicating the potentially complex ways in which gender was played out.

The bioarchaeological perspective generates a specific understanding of gender where gender is identified in terms of modifications to the body distinct from morphological or genetic aspects of the body that can be understood as sex. The skeletal body is culturally constructed – gendered actions produce gendered bodies – but this is in the most fundamental *material* way. Gender is not just a mental construction situated in the realms of discourse, but the material and the ideal are aspects of each other (*cf.* Toren 1999). As Moore (1994, 85) puts it, 'It is not that the material world, as a form of cultural discourse, reflects the natural division of the world into women and men, but rather that cultural discourses, including the organisation of the material world, actually produce gender difference in and through their workings. It is not that our bodies naturally evince gender differences, or any other form of difference, it is rather that these differences are produced as an effect upon them'. Gender is thus defined as 'that which is materially expressed in the human body'. While this may be narrow and in some ways exclusive, it lends itself to the construction of hypotheses while retaining the potential to reveal new layers of non-artefactually based information. The material expression of gender explored in individual skeletons lends insights into the wider social regulation of gender, while allowing for an appreciation of similarity and difference between individuals in the manner in which they express gender; modifications identified in a single individual are difficult to identify as gender but need to be situated within patterns explored in terms of the expression of gender on a group level.

Clearly, not all gendered activities carried out by an individual or in relation to that individual by others during his or her lifetime will have an effect on the skeleton. Traces of those that do may only refer to particularly stressful and sustained actions or episodes. Osseous changes take time to develop and the corporeal expression of gender may vary at different points in the life course. Skeletal modifications may become exaggerated with age as a result of the cumulative effects of gender and its interaction with inevitable age-related processes of growth and degeneration. Such older individuals, or those who have a propensity to form bone, should not be seen as more gendered than others; it is the pattern rather than the severity of modifications which are of interest. We also need to be aware of the dangers of making direct links between osseous modifications and specific activities given the variability and complexities involved in the development and assessment of osseous modifications. A fine enough level of discrimination must be applied to the collection of data through the separate recording of morphologically and aetiologically distinct osseous changes.

Conclusion

By studying the people themselves, bioarchaeology offers the potential for a people-centred approach that resolves existing tensions between method and theory in archaeological approaches to the study of gender. Such an approach does not mean, however, that we need forget about objects. Rather, they are vital to social practice and complement investigations of gender that appreciate the problems and potentials of osteological data.

A bioarchaeological approach to the investigation of gender, with all its variation and potential ambiguity in expression, means that gender becomes an exploratory concept and a way of investigating patterns, rather than a way of allocating people to genders in a categorical fashion. A variety of archaeologically accessible skeletal attributes become linked aspects of a single, multi-faceted construction in as much as the material expression of gender in the skeletal body can also be related to a range of other variables that may potentially affect it. In particular, since this understanding of gender *as material* identifies it as being produced over the lifetime of individuals in terms of the gradual construction of the body, development of gender becomes closely linked to age. Gender is an ontogenetic process that emerges over time.

Bioarchaeology is about how bodies come into being. Sexed bodies are subject to biological change throughout the life course and biological processes provide an axis through which to explore gender as the body is formed in particular ways through engagement in the world. Accessing gender through the skeleton does not mean that gender is understood as biological or as biologically determined. Rather, it is a question of how the skeleton is interpreted in terms of it being the product of social action and of biology together.

References

Ambrose, S., Buikstra, J. and Harold, W. (2003) Status and gender differences in diet at Mound 72, Cahokia, revealed by isotopic analysis of bone. *Journal of Archaeological Science* 22 (3), 217–226.

Armelagos, G. J. (1998) Introduction: sex, gender and health status in prehistoric and contemporary populations. In A.L. Grauer and P. Stuart-Macadam (eds.) *Sex and Gender in Paleopathological Perspective*, 1–10. Cambridge, Cambridge University Press.

Arnold, B. (2002) "Sein und Werden": Gender as process in mortuary ritual. In S. Milledge Nelson and M. Rosen-Ayalon (eds.) *In Pursuit of Gender. Worldwide Archaeological Approaches*, 239–256. Walnut Creek, AltaMira Press.

Aufderheide, A. C. and Rodriguez-Martin, C. (1998) *The Cambridge Encyclopaedia of Human Paleopathology*. Cambridge University Press, Cambridge.

Bachand, H., Joyce, R. A. and Hendon, J. A. (2003) Bodies moving in space: ancient Mesoamerican sculpture and embodiment. *Cambridge Archaeological Journal* 13 (2), 238–247.

Baud, C. (1996) Paléopathologie du travail. In *L'identité des populations archéologiques. XVIe Rencontres international d'archéologie et d'histoire d'Antibes*, 207–210. Sophia Antipolis: Éditions APDCA.

Bennett, J. M. (1987) *Women in the Medieval English Countryside: Gender and Houshold in Brigstock Before the Plague*. Oxford, Oxford University Press.

Birke, L. (1999) Bodies and Biology. In J. Price and M. Shildrick (eds.) *Feminist Theory and the Body*. Edinburgh, Edinburgh University Press.

Blackless, M., Charuvastra, A., Derryck, A., Fausto-Sterling, A., Lauzanne, K. and Lee, E. (2000) How sexually dimorphic are we? Review and synthesis. *American Journal of Human Biology* 12, 151–166.

Blackwood, E. (1984) Sexuality and gender in certain Native American tribes: The case of cross-gender females. *Signs* 10, 27–42.

Blakey, M., Leslie, T. E. and Reidy, J. P. (1994) Frequency and chronological distribution of dental enamel hypoplasia in enslaved African Americans: a test of the weaning hypothesis. *American Journal of Physical Anthropology* 95, 371–383.

Bogin, B. (1999) *Patterns of Human Growth*, 2nd edition. Cambridge, Cambridge University Press.

Bogin, B. (2001) *The Growth of Humanity*. New York, Wiley-Liss.

Boldsen, J. L. (1995) The place of plasticity in the study of the secular trend for male stature: an analysis of Danish biological population history. In C. G. N. Mascie-Taylor and B. Bogin (eds.) *Human variability and plasticity*, 75–90. Cambridge, Cambridge University Press.

Brickley, M. and McKinley, J. (eds) (2004) *Guidelines to the Standards for Recording Human Remains*. Southampton and Reading, BABAO and Institute of Field Archaeologists.

Bridges, P. S. (1985) Structural changes of the arms associated with the habitual grinding of corn. *American Journal of Physical Anthropology* 66, 149–150.

Bridges, P.S. (1989) Changes in activities with the shift to agriculture in the southeastern United States. *Current Anthropology* 30, 385–394.

Bridges, P.S. (1991) Degenerative joint disease in hunter-gatherers and agriculturalists from the southeastern United States. *American Journal of Physical Anthropology* 85, 379–391.

Brown, K.A. (1998) Gender and sex – what can ancient DNA tell us? *Ancient Biomolecules* 2, 3–15.

Brown, K.A. (2000) Ancient DNA applications in human

osteoarchaeology: achievements, problems and potential. In M. Cox and S. Mays (eds.) *Human Osteology in Archaeology and Forensic Science*, 455–473. London, Greenwich Medical Media.

Buikstra, J. E. and Ubelaker, D. H. (eds) (1994) *Standards for Data Collection from Human Skeletal Remains*. Fayetteville, Arkansas Archeological Survey.

Butler, J. (1990) *Gender Trouble. Feminism and the Subversion of Identity*. New York, Routledge.

Butler, J. (1993) *Bodies that Matter. On the Discursive Limits of "Sex"*. New York, Routledge.

Capasso, L., Kennedy, K. A. R. and Wilczak, C. (1998) *Atlas of Occupational Markers on Human Remains*. Teramo, Edigrafital SPA.

Ciranni, R. and Fornaciari, G. (2003) Luigi Boccherini and the Barocco cello: an 18th century striking case of occupational disease. *International Journal of Osteoarchaeology* 13 (5), 294–302.

Claassen, C. (1992) Questioning gender: An introduction. In Claassen, C. (ed.) *Exploring gender through archaeology. Selected papers from the 1991 Boone conference*, 1–9. Madison, Prehistory Press.

Cohen, M. N. and Armelagos, G. J. (eds) (1984) *Paleopathology at the Origins of Agriculture*. Orlando, Academic Press.

Colemen, D. (1995) Human migration: effects on people, effects on populations. In C. G. N. Mascie-Taylor, and B. Bogin (eds.) *Human Varaiability and Plasticity*, 115–145. Cambridge, Cambridge University Press.

Collier, J. F. and Yanagisako, S (eds) (1987) *Gender and kinship: Essays Toward a Unified Analysis*. Stanford, Stanford University Press.

Conkey, M. (2001) Epilogue: thinking about gender with theory and methods. In C. F. Klein (ed.) *Gender in Pre-hispanic America: A Symposium at Dumbarton Oaks 12 and 13 October 1996*, 341–362. Dumbarton Oaks, Washington, DC.

Cooper, C., Javaid, M. K., Taylor, P., Walker-Bone, K., Dennison, E. and Arden, N. (2002) The fetal origins of osteoporotic fracture. *Calcified Tissue International* 70, 391–394.

Cornwall, A. and Lindisfarne, N. (eds) (1994) *Dislocating masculinity: Comparative ethnographies*. London, Routledge.

Cowin, S. C. (2001) The false premise in Wolff's Law. In S. C. Cowin (ed.) *Bone Mechanics Handbook*, 2nd edition, 30–1–30–15. Boca Raton, CRC Press.

Cucina, A. and Tiesler, V. (2003) Dental caries and antemortem tooth loss in the Northern Peten area, Mexico: A biocultural perspective on social status differences among the Classic Maya. *American Journal of Physical Anthropology* 122 (1), 1–10.

del Valle, T. (ed) (1993) *Gendered Anthropology*. London, Routledge.

Dickens, P. (2001) Linking the social and natural sciences: is capital modifying human biology in its own image? *Sociology* 35 (1), 93–110.

Duden, B. (1991) *The Woman Beneath the Skin: A Doctor's Patients in Eighteenth-Century Germany*. Cambridge, Mass, Harvard University Press.

Eshed, V., Gopher, A., Galili, E. and Hershkovitz, I. (2004) Musculoskeletal stress markers in Natufian hunter-gatherers and Neolithic farmers in the Levant: The upper limb. *American Journal of Physical Anthropology* 123 (4), 303–315.

Foucault, M. (1978) *The History of Sexuality. Volume 1. An Introduction*. London, Penguin.

Gilchrist, R. (1999) *Gender and Archaeology. Contesting the Past*. London, Routledge.

Godfrey, K., Walker-Bone, K., Robinson, S., Taylor, P., Shore, S., Wheeler, T. and Cooper, C. (2001) Neonatal bone mass: influence of parental birthweight, maternal smoking, body composition and activity during pregnancy. *Journal of Bone and*

Mineral Research 16, 1694–1703.

Goodman, A. H. and Rose, J. C. (1990) Assessment of systemic physiological perturbations from dental enamel hypoplasias and associated histological structures. *Yearbook of Physical Anthropology* 33, 59–110.

Goodman, A. H. and Rose, J. C. (1991) Dental enamel hypoplasias as indicators of nutritional status. In M. A. Kelley and C. S. Larsen (eds.) *Advances in Dental Anthropology*, 279–293. New York, Wiley-Liss.

Gosden, C. (1999) *Anthropology and Archaeology: A Changing Relationship*. London, Routledge.

Gowland, R. (2001) Playing dead: implications of mortuary evidence for the social construction of childhood in Roman Britain. In G. Davies, A. Gardner, and K. Lockyear (eds.) *TRAC 2000: Proceedings of the Tenth Annual Theoretical Roman Archaeology Conference*, 152–168. Oxford, Oxbow.

Gowland, R. (2004). Ageing the past: examining age identity from funerary evidence. Paper presented at the European Association of Archaeologists Xth annual meeting. Lyon.

Grauer, A. L. and Stuart-Macadam, P. (eds) (1998) *Sex and Gender in Paleopathological Perspective*. Cambridge, Cambridge University Press.

Harding, S. (1986) *The Science Question in Feminism*. Ithaca, N.Y., Cornell University Press.

Hastorf, C. (1991) Gender, space and food in prehistory. In J. M. Gero and M. W. Conkey (eds.) *Engendering Archaeology: Women and Prehistory*, 132–159. Oxford, Blackwell.

Hawkey, D. E. and Street, S. R. (1992) Activity-induced stress markers in prehistoric remains from the eastern Aleutian Islands. *American Journal of Physical Anthropology (Supplement)* 14: 89

Herdt, G. (ed) (1994) *Third Sex, Third Gender: Beyond Sexual Dimorphism in Culture and History*. Cambridge, Mass, MIT Press.

Hess, B. B. and Ferree, M. M. (eds) (1987) *Analysing Gender: A Handbook of Social Science Research*. Newbury Park, Sage.

Hillson, S. (1996) *Dental Anthropology*. Cambridge, Cambridge University Press.

Hodder, I. (1999) *The Archaeological Process: An Introduction*. Oxford, Blackwell.

Hollimon, S. E. (1992) Health consequences of sexual division of labour among prehistoric Native Americans: The Chumash of California and the Arikara of the North Plains. In C. Claassen, (ed.) *Exploring Gender Through Archaeology. Selected Papers from the 1991 Boone Conference*, 81–88. Madison, Prehistory Press.

Hollimon, S. E. (2000a) Sex, health, and gender roles among the Arikara of the northern plains. In A. E. Rautman (ed.) *Reading the Body. Representations and Remains in the Archaeological Record*, 25–37. Philadelphia, University of Pennsylvania Press.

Hollimon, S. E. (2000b) Archaeology of the 'Aqi: Gender and sexuality in prehistoric Chumash society. In R. Schmidt and B. Voss (eds.) *Archaeologies of Sexuality*, 179–196. London, Routledge.

Houston, S. D. and McAnany, P. A. (2003) Bodies and blood: critiquing social construction in Maya archaeology. *Journal of Anthropological Archaeology* 22 (1), 26–41.

Hulse, F. S. (1981) Habits, habitats and heredity: a brief history of studies in human plasticity. *American Journal of Physical Anthropology* 56, 495–501.

Ingold, T. (1991) Becoming persons: consciousness and sociality in human evolution. *Cultural Dynamics* 4 (3), 355–378.

Ingold, T. (1998) From complementarity to obviation: on dissolving the boundaries between social and biological anthropology, archaeology and psychology. *Zeitschrift für Ethnologie* 123, 21–52.

Jones, A. (2002) *Archaeological Theory and Scientific Practice*, Cambridge,

Cambridge University Press.

Jones, H. H., Priest, J. D., Hayes, W. C., Tichenor, C. C. and Nagel, D. A. (1977) Humeral hypertrophy in response to exercise. *Journal of Bone and Joint Surgery* 59A, 204–208.

Joyce, R. A. (2000a) Girling the girl and boying the boy; the production of adulthood in ancient Mesoamerica. *World Archaeology* 31 (3), 473–483.

Joyce, R. A. (2000b) *Gender and Power in Prehispanic Mesoamerica.* Austin, University of Texas Press.

Jurmain, R. (1990) Paleoepidemiology of a central California prehistoric population from CA-ALA-329: II. Degenerative disease. *American Journal of Physical Anthropology* 83, 83–94.

Keating, D. and Miller, F. (1999) Individual pathways in competence and coping. In Keating, D. and Hertzman, C. (eds.) *Developmental Health and the Wealth of Nations.* New York, Guilford.

Kelley, M. A. (1989) Infectious disease. In M. Y. Iscan and K. A. R. Kennedy (eds.) *Reconstruction of Life from the Skeleton,* 191–199. New York, Alan R. Liss.

Kelley, J. O. and Angel, J. L. (1987) Life stresses of slavery. *American Journal of Physical Anthropology* 74, 199–211.

Kennedy, K. A. R. (1989) Skeletal markers of occupational stress. In M.Y. Iscan and K. A. R. Kennedy (eds.) *Reconstruction of life from the skeleton,* 129–160. New York, Alan R. Liss.

Kennedy, K. A. R. (1998) Markers of occupational stress: conspectus and prognosis of research. *International Journal of Osteoarchaeology* 8 (5), 305–310.

Knapp, B. and Meskell, L. (1997) Bodies of evidence on Prehistoric Cyprus. *Cambridge Archaeological Journal* 7 (2), 183–204.

Knüsel, C. J. (2000) Bone adaptation and its relationship to physical activity in the past. In M. Cox and S. Mays (eds.) *Human Osteology in Archaeology and Forensic Science,* 381–401. London, Greenwich Medical Media.

Knüsel, C. J., Göggel, S. and Lucy, D. (1997) Comparative degenerative joint disease of the vertebral column in the medieval monastic cemetery of the Gilbertine priory of St. Andrew, Fishergate, York, England. *American Journal of Physical Anthropology* 103, 481–495.

Lai, P. and Lovell, N. C. (1992) Skeletal markers of occupational stress in the fur trade: a case study from a Hudson's Bay Company fur trade post. *International Journal of Osteoarchaeology* 2, 221–234.

Lanyon, L. E. (1987) Functional strain in bone tissue as an objective, and controlling stimulus for adaptive bone remodelling. *Journal of Biomechanics* 20, 1083–1093.

Lanyon, L. E., Goodship, A. E., Pye, C. J. and MacFie, J. H. (1982) Mechanically adaptive bone remodelling. *Journal of Biomechanics* 15, 141–152.

Laqueur, T. (1990) *Making Sex. Body and Gender from the Greeks to Freud.* Cambridge, Massachusetts, Harvard University Press.

Larsen, C. S. (1997) *Bioarchaeology. Interpreting Behaviour from the Human Skeleton.* Cambridge, Cambridge University Press.

Lasker, G. (1969) Human biological adaptability. *Science* 166, 1480–1486.

Lerner, R. M. (1984) *On the Nature of Human Plasticity.* Cambridge, Cambridge University Press.

Lorber, J. (1994) *Paradoxes of Gender.* New Haven, Yale University Press.

Lovejoy, C. O., McCollum, M. A., Reno, P. L. and Rosenman, B. A. (2003) Developmental biology and human evolution. *Annual Review of Anthropology* 32, 85–109.

Lovell, N. and Dublenko, A. (1999) Further aspects of fur trade life depicted in the skeleton. *International Journal of Osteoarchaeology* 9,

248–259.

Lovell, N. C. and Lai, P. (1994) Lifestyle and health of voyageurs in the Canadian fur trade. In A. Herring and L. Chan (eds.) *Strength and Diversity: A Reader in Physical Anthropology,* 327–343. Toronto, Canadian Scholars Press.

Martin, R. B. and Burr, D. B. (1989) *Structure, Function and Adaptation of Compact Bone.* New York, Raven.

Mays, S. (1998) *The Archaeology of Human Bones.* London, Routledge.

Mays, S. (1999) A biomechanical study of activity patterns in a medieval human skeletal assemblage. *International Journal of Osteoarchaeology* 9, 68–73.

Mays, S. and Cox, M. (2000) Sex determination in skeletal remains. In M. Cox and S. Mays (eds.) *Human Osteology in Archaeology and Forensic Science,* 117–130. London, Greenwich Medical Media.

Merbs, C. F. (1983) *Patterns of Activity-Induced Pathology in a Canadian Inuit Population.* Ottawa, Archaeological Survey of Canada. National Museum of Man Mercury series 119.

Meskell, L. (1996) The somatisation of archaeology: institutions, discourses, corporeality. *Norwegian Archaeological Review* 29, 1–16.

Meskell, L. (1998) The irresistible body and the seduction of archaeology. In D. Monsterrat (ed.) *Changing Bodies, Changing Meanings: Studies of the Body in Antiquity,* 139–161. London, Routledge.

Meskell, L. (2001) Archaeologies of Identity. In I. Hodder (ed.) *Archaeological Theory Today,* 187–213. Cambridge, Polity Press.

Meskell, L. (2002) *Private Life in New Kingdom Egypt.* Princeton, New Jersey, Princeton University Press.

Miles, A. E. W. (1996) Humeral impingement on the acromion in a Scottish island population of c.1600 A.D. *International Journal of Osteoarchaeology* 6 (3), 259–288.

Molleson, T. (1989) Seed preparation in the Mesolithic: the osteological evidence. *Antiquity* 63 (239), 356–362.

Molleson, T. (1994) The eloquent bones of Abu Hureyra. *Scientific American* 271, 70–75.

Molleson, T. and Cox, M. (1993) *The Spitalfields Project. Volume 2 – The Anthropology. The Middling Sort.* York, Council for British Archaeology, Research Report 86.

Moore, H. (1988) *Feminism and Anthropology.* Cambridge, Polity Press.

Moore, H. (1994) *A Passion for Difference: Essays in Anthropology and Gender.* Cambridge, Polity Press.

Morton, J. (1995) The organic remains: remarks on the constitution and development of people. *Social Analysis* 37, 101–118.

Nordbladh, J. and Yates, T. (1990) This perfect body, this virgin text: between sex and gender in archaeology. In I. Bapty and T. Yates (eds.) *Archaeology After Structuralism,* 222–237. London, Routledge.

Ortner, D. and Putschar, W. (1985) *Identification of Pathological Conditions in Human Skeletal Remains.* Washington, Smithsonian University Press.

Ortner, S. and Whitehead, H. (1981) *Sexual Meanings: The Cultural Construction of Gender and Sexuality.* Cambridge, Cambridge University Press.

Pálfi, G. (1992) Traces des activités sur les squelettes des anciens Hongrois. *Bulletin et Mémoires de la Société d'Anthropologie de Paris* 4 (3–4), 209–231.

Pálfi, G. and Dutour, O. (1996) Les marqueurs d'activité sur le squelette humain. Aspects théoriques et application à des séries ostéoarchéologiques européennes. In *L'identité des populations archéologiques. XVIe Rencontres international d'archéologie et d'histoire d'Antibes,* 245–269. Sophia Antipolis: Éditions APDCA.

Pearson, G.A. (1996) Of sex and gender. *Science* 274 (5285), 328–329.

Peterson, J. (2002) *Sexual Revolutions. Gender and Labor at the Dawn of Agriculture*. Walnut Creek, AltaMira Press.

Peyron, J.G. (1986) Osteoarthritis. The epidemiologic viewpoint. *Clinical Orthopaedics* 213, 13–19.

Privat, K. L., O'Connell, T. C. and Richards, M. (2002) Stable isotope analysis of human and faunal remains from the Anglo-Saxon cemetery at Berinsfield, Oxfordshire: dietary and social implications. *Journal of Archaeological Science* 29 (7), 779–790.

Radin, E. L. (1982) Mechanical factors in the causation of osteoarthritis. *Rheumatology* 7, 46–52.

Radin, E. L., Paul, I. L. and Rose, R. M. (1972) Mechanical factors in osteoarthritis. *Lancet* 1, 519–522.

Robb, J. (1994) Skeletal signs of activity in the Italian Metal Ages: methodological and interpretative notes. *Human Evolution* 9, 215–229.

Roberts, C. (2000) Trauma in biocultural perspective: past, present and future work in Britain. In M. Cox and S. Mays (eds.) *Human Osteology in Archaeology and Forensic Science*, 337–356. London, Greenwich Medical Media.

Roberts, C. and Cox, M. (2003) *Health and Disease in Britain. From Prehistory to the Present Day*. Thrupp, Stroud, Sutton Publishing Limited.

Roberts, C. and Manchester, K. (1995) *The Archaeology of Disease*. Stroud, Sutton.

Roberts, D. F. (1995) The pervasiveness of plasticity. In N. Mascie-Taylor, and B. Bogin, (eds.) *Human Variability and Plasticity*, 1–17. Cambridge, Cambridge University Press.

Rogers, J. and Waldron, T. (1995) *A Field Guide to Joint Disease in Archaeology*. Chichester, Wiley.

Roscoe, W. (1998) *Changing Ones: Third and Fourth Genders in Native North America*. New York, St Martin's Press.

Rubin, C. T., McLeod, K. J. and Bain, S. D. (1990) Functional strains and cortical bone adaptation: Epigenetic assurance of skeletal integrity. *Journal of Biomechanics* 23, 43–54.

Ruff, C. B., Larsen, C. S. and Hayes, W. C. (1984) Structural changes in the femur with the transition to agriculture on the Georgia coast. *American Journal of Physical Anthropology* 64, 125–136.

Schell, L. M. (1995) Human biological adaptability with special emphasis on plasticity: history, development and problems for future research. In N. Mascie-Taylor and B. Bogin (eds.) *Human Variability and Plasticity*, 212–237. Cambridge, Cambridge University Press.

Schmidt, C. W. (2001) Dental microwear evidence for a dietary shift between two nonmaize-reliant prehistoric human populations from Indiana. *American Journal of Physical Anthropology* 114 (2), 139–145.

Schulting, R. and Richards, M. (2001) Dating women and becoming farmers: new palaeodietary and AMS evidence from the Breton Mesolithic cemeteries of Téviec and Hoëdic. *Journal of Archaeological Science* 20 (3), 314–344.

Shaver, P. and Hendrick, C. (eds) (1987) *Sex and Gender*. Newbury Park, Sage.

Smith, B. H. (1984) Patterns of molar wear in hunter-gatherers and agriculturalists. *American Journal of Physical Anthropology* 63, 39–56.

Sofaer Derevenski, J. (1997a) Engendering children, engendering archaeology. In J. Moore and E. Scott (eds.) *Invisible People and Processes*, 192–202. London, Leicester University Press.

Sofaer Derevenski, J. (1997b) Linking Gender and Age as Social Variables. *Ethnographisch-Archäologischen Zeitschrift* 38 (3 & 4), 485–493.

Sofaer Derevenski, J. (1998) Gender Archaeology as Contextual Archaeology. A Critical Examination of the Tensions between Method and Theory in the Archaeology of Gender. Unpublished PhD thesis. University of Cambridge.

Sofaer Derevenski, J. (2000) Sex differences in activity-related osseous change in the spine and the gendered division of labor at Ensay and Wharram Percy, UK. *American Journal of Physical Anthropology* 111 (3), 333–354.

Sørensen, M.L.S. (in press) On gender negotiation and materiality. In S. Hamilton (ed.) *Women's Work*. Sussex Archaeological Society.

Sørensen, M.L.S. (2000) *Gender Archaeology*. Cambridge, Polity Press.

Sperduti, A. (1997) Life condition of a Roman Imperial Age population: occupational stress markers and working activities in Lucus Feroniae. *Human Evolution* 12, 253–267.

Steele, J. (2000) Skeletal indicators of handedness. In M. Cox and S. Mays (eds.) *Human Osteology in Archaeology and Forensic Science*, 307–323. London, Greenwich Medical Media.

Steen, S. L. and Lane. R, W. (1998) Evaluation of habitual activities among two Alaskan Eskimo poulations based on musculoskeletal stress markers. *International Journal of Osteoarchaeology* 8, 341–353.

Stirland, A. (1991) Diagnosis of occupationally related palaeopathology: can it be done? In D. Ortner and A.C. Aufderheide (eds.) *Human Paleopathology: Current Syntheses and Future Options*, 40–47. Washington DC, Smithsonian Institution Press.

Stirland, A. (1993) Asymmetry and activity-related change in the male humerus. *International Journal of Osteoarchaeology* 3, 105–113.

Stirland, A.J. (1998) Musculoskeletal evidence for activity: problems of evaluation. *International Journal of Osteoarchaeology* 8 (5), 354–362.

Stock, J. T. and Pfeiffer, S. K. (2004) Lone bone robusticity and subsistence behaviour among Later Stone Age foragers of the forest and fynbos biomes of South Africa. *Journal of Archaeological Science* 31 (7), 999–1013.

Stone, A. C. (2000) Ancient DNA from skeletal remains. In M. A. Katzenberg and S. Saunders R. (eds.) *Biological Anthropology of the Human Skeleton*, 351–371. New York, Wiley-Liss.

Tarlow, S. (1999) *Bereavement and Commemoration. An Archaeology of Mortality*. Oxford, Blackwell.

Toren, C. (1999) *Mind, Materiality and History. Explorations in Fijian Ethnography*. London, Routledge.

Toren, C. (2001) The child in mind. In H.Whitehouse (ed.) *The Debated Mind. Evolutionary Psychology versus Ethnography*, 155–179. Oxford, Berg.

Torres-Rouff, C. (2002) Cranial vault modification and ethnicity in Middle Horizon San Pedro de Atacama, Chile. *Current Anthropology* 43 (1), 163–171.

Turner, G. and Anderson, T. (2003) Marked occupational dental abraison from Medieval Kent. *International Journal of Osteoarchaeology* 13 (3), 168–172.

Ubelaker, D. H. (1979) Skeletal evidence for kneeing in prehistoric Ecuador. *American Journal of Physical Anthropology* 51, 679–686.

Voss, B. L. (2000) Feminisms, queer theories, and the archaeological study of past sexualities. *World Archaeology* 32 (2), 180–192.

Walker, P. L. and Cook, D. C. (1998) Gender and sex: Vive la difference. *American Journal of Physical Anthropology* 106 (2), 255–259.

Weaver, D. S. (1998) Osteoporosis in the bioarchaeology of women. In A.L. Grauer and P. Stuart-Macadam (eds.) *Sex and Gender in Paleopathological Perspective*, 27–44. Cambridge, Cambridge University Press.

Weiss, E. (2003) Effects of rowing on humeral strength. *American*

Journal of Physical Anthropology 121 (4), 293–302.

White, C. D., Healy, P. F. and Schwarcz, H. P. (1993) Intensive agriculture, social status, and Maya diet at Pacbitun, Belize. *Journal of Anthropological Research* 49, 347–375.

Whitehouse, R. (2002) Gender in the South Italian Neolithic: a combinatory approach. In S. Milledge Nelson and M. Rosen-Ayalon (eds.) *In Pursuit of Gender. Worldwide Archaeological Approaches*, 15–42. Walnut Creek, AltaMira Press.

Yates, T. (1993) Frameworks for an archaeology of the body. In C. Tilley (ed.) *Interpretative Archaeology*, 31–72. Oxford, Berg.

11.   The Gendered Skeleton: Anthropological Interpretations of the Bony Pelvis

Pamela K. Stone and Dana Walrath

Introduction

Demographic analyses of archaeological populations report higher rates of mortality for women of childbearing ages compared to men of the same ages. This differential death rate is often used to suggest that isolated biological aspects of pregnancy and birth place females at risk, rather than as a reflection of the inferior social status of women in past societies (Ashworth *et al.*1976; Blakely 1977; Clarke 1977; Lovejoy *et al.* 1977; Lallo *et al.* 1978; Owsley and Bradtmiller 1983; Martin *et al.* 1991). These studies echo the early days of archaeological inquiry that reconstructed the social roles of women to fit the androcentric gender norms of the practicing archaeologists of the time (Fratt 1991; Gero and Conkey 1991; Nelson 1997). Women of the past were rendered as passive agents; tied to the kitchen (or food preparation area), immobilized as they gave birth, raised the children, and taught their daughters how to be good wives. These "housewives" were depicted as less essential than men, the hunters and traders, to the maintenance of community and society.

Similarly, the image of the passive social female also pervades interpretations of the female physical body, particularly in Euro-American discourse on childbirth. With the medicalization of childbirth in the 1920s to the 1950s, interpretation of female pelvic morphology as inadequate for childbirth began not only within obstetrical practice, but within anthropology as well. In obstetric practice, "delicate" early 20th century women requested anesthesia for relief from the unbearable pain of labour (Rooks 1997). Expert physicians delivered neonates from the pelvic bones surrounding and impinging upon the birth canal while mothers remained in a state of "twilight sleep." During this time period, anthropologists, grounded in the same gender norms as medical doctors, formulated a model of species-wide obstetrical difficulty (Walrath 2003). Paleoanthropologists began to focus on sex differences in pelvic morphology, using these analyses in studies aimed at reconstructing the evolution of bipedalism, increased brain size, and the human birth process. This evolutionary discourse depicts the female pelvis as passive and ill-equipped for childbirth without cultural assistance.

We argue here that the gendered discourse on the evolution of childbirth and contemporary Euroamerican birth practices perpetuate preconceptions concerning the mortality of young females in archaeological profiles. We critically examine the 'obstetrical hazard' model common to evolutionary and bioarchaeological studies as well as biomedicine. This model relies upon static interpretations of the pelvic girdle to promote a notion of species-wide difficulty during childbirth. We suggest that this model, has limited bioarchaeological interpretations of women's lives by invariably attributing deaths of young females to childbirth.

Childbirth, a dynamic process involving the biology and behaviour of the birthing mother and child in a particular biocultural context, can be only partially inferred from isolated pelvic measurements. Contextualization of these bioarchaeological data can situate static metric features in the dynamic biocultural frameworks of the past and present. By removing gendered interpretations of female pelvic anatomy and childbirth, bioarchaeologists can begin to link metric features to the biocultural contexts of the past. We present a bioarchaeological analysis of Pueblo pelvic remains as an example of interpretations revealed through biocultural contextualization.

Further, because contemporary biocultural contexts can also provide evidence for the interpretation of bioarchaeological data, we offer a brief review of factors contributing to female morbidity and mortality related to the complications of pregnancy and childbirth. We suggest that the high rates of reproductive morbidity and mortality experienced by women in the developing world and disenfranchised sub-populations in industrialized nations (WHO 2001; Maine and Chavkin 2002) provide evidence of structural violence against women rather than of species-wide obstetrical problems. By joining skeletal data with a systematic evaluation of ecological and biocultural factors affecting women's morbidity and mortality, new perspectives on the intersection of women's health and culture through time can emerge.

The pelvis and birth in human evolution

Reconstruction of the birth process in human evolutionary studies is a tale of compromise told within the evolutionary paradigm of paleoanthropology. In this tale, the birth of large-brained young and the advent of bipedalism place competing demands on the pelvis of the human female. Physical anthropologists traditionally cite male pelvic morphology as illustrating the pure, unfettered adaptation to bipedal locomotion while the functional morphology of the female pelvis is interpreted as a compromise between the structural requirements of bipedal locomotion and those of childbirth (Krogman 1951; Napier 1967; Lovejoy 1981; Tague 1986, 1992; Trevathan 1987; Berge 1993; Rosenberg and Trevathan 1996). This compromise is not considered entirely successful. Instead, the competing demands of bipedalism and childbirth are said to leave humans with what Washburn (1960) termed an "obstetrical dilemma." Underscoring this and using the language of his time, Krogman (1951, 56) stated "there can be no doubt that many of the obstetrical problems of Mrs. H. Sapiens are due to the combination of a narrower pelvis and a bigger head in the species." The notion of an inherent obstetric dilemma persists today in anthropological introductory texts and standard references (for examples see: Jones *et al.* 1994; Jurmain *et al.* 2002).

The 'obstetrical hazard' model of paleoanthropology supports biomedical birth practices (Walrath 2003) while conforming to gender norms emphasizing female dependence (Jordan 1978; Martin 1987, 1996; Davis-Floyd 1992). At the same time, because the birth process is not preserved in either the fossil or archaeological records, this model relies heavily upon Euro-American birth practices to support its claims. Hospital-based birth is used as evidence for the danger of birth rather than as a set of medical beliefs and practices embedded in the gender norms of Euro-American cultures (Kitzinger 1972; Shaw 1974; Jordan 1978; Scully 1980; MacCormack 1982; Martin 1987, 1996; Ginsburg and Rapp 1991, 1995; Davis-Floyd 1992).

The analysis of pelvic morphology has the potential to provide insight into the health of women in the past. However, in order to effectively incorporate this osteo-logical information, the gender roles of women in the past and present need to be taken into account. Gendered approaches to childbirth in the present interfere with the interpretation of pelvic remains from the past, resulting in an incomplete perspective on female health. Through an awareness of these gendered interpretations, bio-archaeologists can return to a contextualized analysis of

the bones, thus contributing to a comprehensive understanding of the effects of gender on health in the past.

Measuring pelves

Many studies that assess the pelvis in an evolutionary context focus on variation in pelvic size and shape to understand the evolution of sex differences in humans (Segebarth-Orban 1980; Hager 1989; Tague 1991, 1992, 1995; Sibley *et al.* 1992; Berge 1993). In addition, sexual dimorphism has been used to examine differences in the growth process for males and females (Williams 1922; Greulich and Thoms 1944; Coleman 1969; Crelin 1969; Tague 1992; La Velle 1995). Though Tague (1992, 88) notes that "there remains disagreement in the iden-tification and obstetric significance of [most] pelvic dimorphisms," childbirth is generally used to account for sex differences in metric pelvic features (Sibley *et al.* 1992; MacDonald *et al.* 1997). The gendered notion of inherent 'obstetrical hazard' interferes with interpreting these sex differences in pelvic morphology as an indication of successful adaptation to childbirth.

The anthropological focus on sexual dimorphism of the pelvis is a relatively recent phenomenon. Before the medicalization of childbirth, anthropological interest in the pelvis was limited to the study of differences among so called "racial types" rather than sexual dimorphism (Hoyme 1957; Walrath 2003). With the switch to a focus on sex differences, anthropologists drew heavily on existing interpretations of pelvic morphology developed in Euro-American obstetrics. These biomedical models in turn retained the emphasis on pelvic types derived from earlier anthropological models in which male and female pelves were defined as gynecoid, android, anthropoid, or platypelloid depending upon their shape (Fig. 11.1). During this period, normal pelvic measurements, now used as standards to which skeletal populations are compared, were defined within biomedical practice based on average values observed in gynecoid pelves. These seemingly neutral metric features of the pelvis incorporate the social meanings of the times. Measurement was part of the gendered model of childbirth emphasizing 'obstetrical hazards' and the inability of females to bear young without assistance (Kitzinger 1972; Shaw 1974; Jordan 1978; Scully 1980; Martin 1987; Davis-Floyd 1992). Expert physicians measured pelves to determine their adequacy for childbirth.

Metric analyses of the pelvic girdle paint a static picture of pelvic morphology. These static anthropometric measurements focus on the true obstetric pelvis, which is that portion of the pelvis lying below and including the pelvic inlet (Fig. 11.2), representing the area of obstetric significance since it includes the bony canal through which the foetus must pass (Sibley *et al.* 1992). To describe a "normal" pelvis obstetricians divide the bony canal into three functional planes which include: the pelvic inlet, midpelvis, and outlet (Caldwell and Moloy 1933; Greulich and Thoms 1938; Thoms 1956; Davis 1997; MacDonald *et al.* 1997). "Normal" pelvic dimensions were defined according to average fetal cranial dimensions (Oxorn 1986; Sibley *et al.* 1992; MacDonald *et al.* 1997). A "flattened" or platypelloid pelvis, one that is attenuated in an antero-posterior dimension was clinically seen as a problem. It is defined metrically as a pelvis with a transverse diameter exceeding the anteroposterior diameter by 3 cm or more (MacDonald *et al.* 1997).

These measurements were assessed through X-ray Pelvimetry, a standard part of hospital-based obstetric practice before the hazards of radiation were known. As these hazards came to light, obstetricians began to assess "pelvic adequacy" through the rate at which labour progressed. Today, radiographic measurement of the "fit" between an individual maternal pelvis and foetal head occurs only in very limited clinical circumstances (Morgan *et al.* 1986) and labour duration is generally used to assess pelvic adequacy (Davis-Floyd 1992). Nevertheless, whether the standards of normal labour are reckoned in units of distance or time, the biomedical approach begins with the assumption that the female pelvis is frequently inadequate for childbirth and that medical intervention corrects these natural flaws.

While standards and "norms" offer a means to quantify differences in pelvic shape and size among populations, they are of limited use for predicting individual birth outcomes. Individual life-history, as well as foetal and maternal health over the course of a pregnancy, is far more important for successful birth. Though these qualitative data are absent from osteological analyses, some of these features may be inferred from bio-archaeological analyses aiming to reconstruct a comprehensive picture of life in the past. By contrast, discussions of pelvic morphology in past populations tend to focus only on metric features derived from biomedical practice. Osteological analyses tend to ignore cultural buffers and influences. As a result, the beliefs and practices of biomedicine are reinforced through the 'obstetrical hazards' model, while other cultural practices more likely to have influenced the birth process for pre-colonial women are neglected.

The pelvis in bioarchaeological interpretations

Bioarchaeological investigation has much to contribute to hypotheses accounting for early death of some women in precontact times. The contextualization of pelvic remains without the overbearing influence of the 'obstetrical hazards' model will allow for better reconstruction of the reproductive lives of women in the past. This is a contested area of study, as some researchers claim that the majority of deaths of young women are

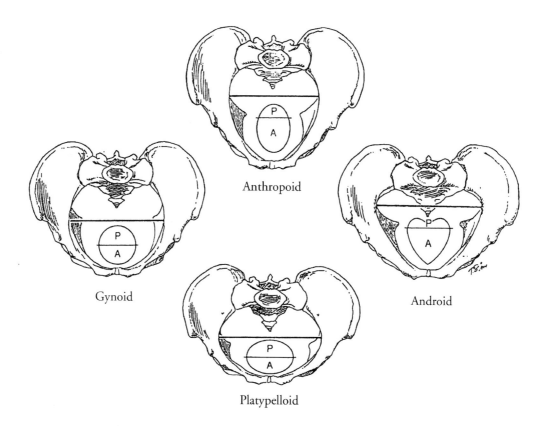

Figure 11.1. Pelvic "types" from Williams Obstetrics. *These types were incorporated into biomedical obstetrics from physical anthropology in the 1930s. The flattened of "platypelloid" pelvis can pose birthing difficulties.*

related to reproduction (Blakely 1977; Lovejoy *et al.* 1977; Lallo *et al.* 1978; Martin *et al.* 1991), while others suggest that these deaths are likely *not* due to reproduction (Wells 1967; Ives 1994). We will argue that the multi-faceted approach of bioarchaeology allows for the complex interplay between biology and culture, thus providing a deeper understanding of the myriad of factors surrounding the early death of young women in the past.

Archaeological populations

Several anthropological studies utilize obstetric standards to examine the role of compromised birth canal dimensions in females dying young (Angel 1978; Cook 1984; Tague 1986; Arriaza *et al.* 1988; Sibley *et al.* 1992). While others (Owsley and Bradtmiller 1983) report the prevalence of foetal remains *in utero* they never discuss the use of pelvic metrics to assess their findings. Instead, this study assumes these deaths are related to pregnancy and birth complications.

The best evidence for ascertaining the degree of perinatal mortality in archeological contexts comes from Arriaza and colleagues (1988) and Sibley and coworkers (1992). These researchers examine direct evidence of possible childbirth death of the mother and neonate through analyses of female pelvic remains (both mummified and skeletal) some of which still retained the neonate *in utero*.

Arriaza and coworkers examined 128 pre-Columbian female mummies of childbearing ages (range 12–45 years) from Chile. Their study revealed that 14% of women (average age 30.3) died as a result of childbirth complicated deaths (CCD) with early death of non-pregnant females (average age 28.6), representing 30.9% of their sample. In addition, even the CCD deaths were not necessarily due to pelvic morphology. Metric analyses indicate that the females who died as a result of CCD presented "normal" pelvic measurements.

These authors also examined some early Chilean cultural practices related to birth, such as stomach binding and squatting position, in conjunction with metric analyses. Some cultural practices, such as squatting during childbirth, are known to enhance pelvic size and allow for easier passage of the neonate (King 1909; Drosin 1923; Gardosi *et al.* 1989; Golay *et al.* 1993; Hanson 1998). Historically, Chilean women practiced squatting as well as wrapping a belt around their abdomen just before the birth of the child to place external pressure on the uterus to facilitate pushing the baby through the birth canal (Arriaza *et al.* 1988). Some of the Chilean mummies examined were found buried in a squatting position with birthing belts tied around their abdomens. While this suggests death during childbirth, it is also possible that these mummies represent women symbolically placed in the culturally established birthing positions due to their dying from a variety of other causes while in a pregnant state.

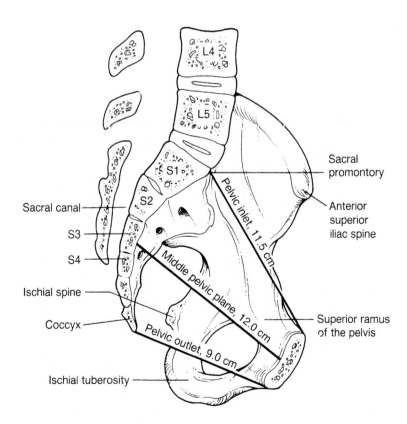

Figure 11.2. Sagittal Diameters of the pelvis and the three planes of the true pelvis (Danforth's Obstetrics and Gynecology).

In their conclusions, Arriaza and colleagues (1988, 40) note that "when age is related to childbirth, it becomes apparent that problems occur in both young and old …[but] more deaths were found in mature females". This study finds no link between pelvic dimensions and birth outcome suggesting instead that other variables, such as multiple pregnancies and births, alongside of ill health and increasing age, most likely played large roles in the mortality of women of childbearing ages. Finally, it is also worth noting that the 21 CCD deaths in their sample span a 2700 year time period. This also suggests that while CCD may contribute to early death for some women, other factors account for the early mortality of most women.

Using both mummified and skeletal human remains, Sibley and coworkers (1992) examined 36 individuals, with ages estimated to range between 19–44 years, from Sudanese Nubia. These authors focused their attention on the standard pelvic planes (inlet, midpelvis, and outlet), and classification system as set forth by Thoms (1934). These data revealed that 3% of Nubian females present with flat pelvic dimensions. Due to the generally smaller stature of the Nubian women their pelves were also generally smaller than American pelvic standards in use in a clinical setting resulting in "at least 1/3 to 1/2 of the sample being diagnosed as contracted" (Sibley *et al.* 1992, 427). Such "clinically normal" parameters derived from larger, well nourished (American) populations are problematic in archaeological contexts. Smaller size in the past may be a reflection of normal human variation or it may reflect restricted growth due to nutritional stress (Angel 1978; Goodman *et al.* 1988). Thus, both these studies reveal that while childbirth and associated complications place added stress on reproductive-aged women, a larger complex picture of health and lifestyle needs to be examined before we can relegate reproductive-aged death to the biology of human birth.

A few studies present compelling ethno-archaeological data to suggest factors beyond the birth process as the causal agents for early death in some women. For example, Ives (1994) combines an exhaustive reconstruction of herbal medicinals and traditional midwifery practices to show the potential for relatively good reproductive outcomes. She (1994, 80) suggests that the reasons for women's early deaths are related to factors such as "subsistence strategy, socio-political development, disease environment, ecology, and historical context," rather than 'obstetrical hazards.' This work is compelling, yet like many other studies on reproduction in the past (Blakely 1977; Clarke 1977; Owsley and Bass 1979; Owsley and Bradtmiller 1983) Ives has limited empirical data to support her contentions. Nevertheless, we agree with Ives that subsistence strategy, socio-political factors, disease environment, ecology, and historical context all factor into patterns of poor health and differential treatment of women. Each of these factors is intricately linked with women's lives and plays a role in quality of life

and ability to reproduce with or without complications.

Rather than begin with a gendered notion of 'obstetrical hazard' the bioarchaeological approach focuses on teasing apart the components affecting the morbidity and mortality of women of childbearing ages. Occupation, subsistence strategy and other social, political, and historical processes affect both the culture and biology of birth. For example, contemporary studies on women's health have shown that strenuous physical effort and calorie intake together have a synergistic effect on pregnancy, parturition and maternal health (Prichard 1970; Thomas *et al.* 1970; Naeye 1981; Moerman 1982; Russo and Cramoy 1984; Harris and Ross 1987; Brown *et al.* 1991; Doyle 1995; Leavitt 1999). In addition, globally, contemporary statistics reveal the highest incidence of compromised health and maternal infant mortality occurs in regions economically marginalized by controlling world forces (Crosette 1996; Dierks 1996; Duke and Conly 1997; WHO 2001; Maine and Chavkin 2002). Clearly a relationship exists between Ives' (1994) primary factors *and* early reproductive mortality for women. Empirical physical data are needed to clarify how these interacting variables work with regard to reproduction, lifestyle/workloads, and longevity in archaeological contexts.

A bioarchaeological picture of the gendered pelvis

Combined archaeological, biological, and ethnographic analyses can link women's health to changes in habitation and food production. In turn, these models can be used in bioarchaeological research to expand our understanding of how cultural activities can be deduced from skeletal remains and correlated with biological consequences. A working knowledge of the traditional cultural values and practices can indicate a complex bio-cultural relationship between the physiological stressors of reproduction and lifestyle.

Classic notions of early precontact populations assumed that all women are biologically prepared to bear children at full fecundity levels, and that these females die early as a result of high fecundity rates and associated birth complications. The pre-contact reproductive woman is defined through the examination of differential mortality at early ages between women and men. Demographic data from a number of archaeological sites demonstrate high mortality at early ages for precontact women (Blakely 1977; Lovejoy *et al.* 1977; Lallo *et al.* 1978; Martin *et al.* 1991). However, studies such as these rely only on age-at-death as the indicator of 'obstetrical hazard' without considering other factors that may have contributed to the early death of many women.

The resident Pueblo populations of the American Southwest have long been the subjects of extensive anthropological study and have recently been used to assess gender differences in all aspects of life. Ethnographic accounts document ceremonial practices, kinship, and traditional behaviors surrounding subsistence, building, and craft production (Waters 1963; Hungry Wolf 1980; Meltzer 1981; Dutton 1983; Cordell 1984; Hegmon and Trevathan 1996; Crown 2000). In addition, early accounts of Pueblo life from missionary and explorer diaries suggest a wide range of occupations for men and women (Judd 1925; Simpson 1964; Black 1984; Niederman 1988; Babcock 1991; Fratt 1991; Lowell 1991; Underhill 1991; Gabriel 1992). Syntheses of these early ethnographic works along with archaeological and physical data indicate that activities and use of space within Pueblo communities were divided along gender lines. These studies place women in a variety of labour intensive activities over the course of their lifetime (Lowell 1991; Martin and Frayer 1997; Hays-Gilpin 1998; Kamp 1998, 2002; Crown 2000). In addition, a number of studies published focus on the relationship between diet and health status for Ancestral Pueblo peoples (Palkovich, 1984; Stodder, 1984; Goodman *et al.* 1988; Martin *et al.* 1991). These studies report high rates of ill health and early death for women (18–30) when compared to males in the same age cohorts and mirror the demographics of other archaeological studies (Ashworth *et al.* 1976; Blakely 1977; Lovejoy *et al.* 1977; Lallo *et al.* 1978; Owsley and Bradtmiller 1983). Despite the evidence of poor health among reproductive-aged Pueblo women in the past, higher morbidity and earlier mortality is attributed primarily to 'obstetrical hazards' rather than other causes. None of these researchers focus on the pelvis in these interpretations to support their contentions of obstetrical complications, nor do they suggest other potential reasons for early death of young females.

A bioarchaeological examination of pelvic morphology within the context of a well-studied population, such as the Pueblo of the American Southwest, provides insight into the early death of reproductive aged women. When pelvic measurements are assessed it becomes clear that the osteological evidence does not necessarily indicate the hazards of childbirth that gendered interpretations of the past suggested. In fact, skeletal data combined with ethnographic information about the Puebloan peoples make a convincing case for the absence of physical (pelvic) obstetric hazards.

As with Arriaza *et al.* (1988), Stone (2000) examined patterns of early death for women in Ancestral Pueblo populations focusing on pelvic morphology. This sample represents geographically related but often temporarily separated skeletal remains from Ancestral Pueblo groups found within Chaco Canyon, Canyon de Chelly and Canyon del Muerto, spanning AD 400–1200 (Basket Maker II-III, Early (I &II) and Late (III) Pueblo periods). Employing pelvic measurements as the only quantifiable tool available the sample included 44 females with ages estimated to range between 17 and 55 years (30.2 average) in which pelvic shape and size in relation to birth process and rates of flattened pelvic dimensions were assessed. Pelvic measurements taken included the standard

obstetric planes and classifications as outlined by Sibley and coworkers (1992) and supported by Davis (1997) and MacDonald *et al.* (1997). Stone's results indicate that Ancestral Puebloan women presented pelvic dimensions similar to American "norms" (Table 11.1). These data were then compared to similar analyses conducted by Tague (1986) from other Amerindian osteological samples (Indian Knoll; Pecos Pueblo; Libben; Haida) and the Nubian pelves assessed by Sibley *et al.* (1992). The data on Ancestral Pueblo pelvic remains suggest pelvic adequacy and successful childbirth rather than 'obstetrical hazard.'

These metric analyses also provide information about the average pelvic shape and size of Amerindian and Nubian pelves. In a general sense, these data indicate similarity across a variety of populations as all the average measurements are within two standard deviations of the American norms. In a few instances, these static measurements indicate some difference in pelvic shape. For example, as described above, relatively small transverse dimensions of the pelvic inlet and midplane are seen in the Nubian sample (Sibley *et al.* 1992). Similarly, in the Pecos Pueblos sample, antero-posterior dimensions are relatively small when compared to the other populations, but transverse dimensions are nearly identical to the American normal. While this population variation is interesting, it provides limited information about individual birth outcomes. The labour process and the emerging neonate are not preserved to provide a direct link between maternal death and childbirth. Interestingly, the pelvic morphology in isolation strongly suggests the absence of obstructed birth canals, the proverbial 'obstetrical hazard' among Pueblo women. We suggest that the notion of birthing difficulty is imposed upon women of the past even when their bones appear 'normal' according to American biomedical criteria due to gendered beliefs about human birthing difficulty. The use of static pelvic measurements to suggest that death at a reproductive age is due to 'obstetrical hazards,' regardless of whether these measurements indicate pelvic adequacy or constraint, indicates that female morbidity and mortality is likely due to other causes.

Rather than using contemporary beliefs about inherent birthing difficulty to contextualize skeletal remains from the past we propose instead analysis of the complex history of heredity, environmental stresses, and cultural activities that may have contributed to the quality and length of a woman's life. As described above, archaeological and ethnographic investigation of Pueblo societies indicates a gendered division of labour as well as a gendered relationship between diet and ill health. Together with the osteological evidence for pelvic adequacy, a different picture emerges regarding the morbidity and mortality of women of child-bearing age. Their deaths appear related to more generalized aspects of social status encompassing heavy work loads, dietary stress, and poor health rather than species-wide 'obstetrical hazards.' More recent

Dimensions	US Normal		Ancestral Pueblo[1]	Indian Knoll[2]	Pecos Pueblo[2]	Libben[2]	Haida[2]	Kulubnarti[3]
Pelvic Inlet Anteroposterior	10.5	X	10.3	10.8	9.1	9.8	11.2	10.3
		S.D.	0.9	0.7	0.8	0.8	1.0	0.8
		N	43	28	42	11	15	36
Transverse	13.5	X	12.6	13.4	13.4	13.4	13.5	11.6
		S.D.	0.7	0.7	0.6	0.7	0.8	0.7
		N	44	33	54	12	19	36
Pelvic Midplane Anteroposterior	11.5	X	11.8	12.0	11.8	12.6	13.8	11.5
		S.D.	1.1	1.0	0.9	0.7	1.0	0.7
		N	38	4	6	-	8	36
Transverse	10.5	X	10.3	11.2	9.9	-	11.0	9.1
		S.D.	0.8	1.0	1.0	-	0.5	0.7
		N	10	4	6	-	8	36
Pelvic Outlet Anteroposterior	11.5	X	11.4	11.4	11.4	12.1	13.5	11.0
		S.D.	1.1	0.9	0.9	0.6	1.0	0.7
		N	36	30	43	8	15	36

[1] Data from Stone (2000)
[2] Data from Tague (1986)
[3] Data from Sibley *et al.* (1992)
-, data not available

Table 11.1. *Ancestral Pueblo[1] pelves compared to other North American Groups[2] and Kulubnarti, Nubian's[3] (measurements in cm).*

populations provide additional data to support this bioarchaeological approach.

Historical populations

In eighteenth-century populations of Europe, evidence of environmental and cultural stressors is preserved in pelvic morphology and related medical concerns. For example, physicians of this period focused on the sagittal diameter of the pelvis (Fig. 11.2) reflecting the clinical concern with pelvic flattening due to the pathology of osteomalacia and rickets (Loudon 2001). These bone disorders are the direct result of Vitamin D deficiency leading to rickets in growing girls and osteomalacia in adult women. Vitamin D deficiency derives primarily from limited exposure to sunshine through mechanisms such as forced indoor labour, industrial pollution, or behavioural restrictions (Stuart-Macadam 1989). These disorders were common, particularly among the poor, in northern European cities at that time (Caldwell and Moloy 1933; Moir 1946; Angel 1978; Stuart-Macadam 1989; Loudon 2001). Furthermore, it is reported that the high incidence of these disorders coincides directly with very high rates of maternal death in Europe for this time period, and were seen as the causal factor in obstructed labours (Loudon 2001). Today, osteomalacia, rickets and other childhood growth disorders still account for obstetrical complications in some populations (Akiel *et al.* 1982; Serenius *et al.* 1984; Martorell 1989). Of course, such birthing difficulties evident in the

bones of the pelvis stem from specific pathology rooted in biological and cultural interaction rather than from species-wide 'obstetrical hazards.'

Similarly, in a comprehensive historical analysis of perinatal mortality in Utrecht, Netherlands between 1880 and 1940 Ward (2003) did not link perinatal deaths to obstructed birth canals. Instead a powerful association is found between perinatal mortality and low birth weight. Ward's finding, consistent over a sixty year period, indicates that other factors such as overall maternal health and age play an important role in reproductive morbidity and mortality.

Contemporary women's health and links to the past

Recent scholarly work on women's health in cross-cultural contexts demonstrates that patterns of ill health derive from gender-based political and economic structures rather than female biology (*e.g.* Brettell and Sargent 1993; McElmurry *et al.* 1993; Finkler 1994; Doyle 1995; WHO 2001; Maine and Chavkin 2002). Women in marginal and agricultural settings today are vulnerable to higher rates of morbidity and early mortality due to preventable pregnancy-related health problems, and it is likely that these reproductive-related deaths are exacerbated by labour demands (WHO 2001). World-wide studies on pregnancy-related deaths in developing nations demonstrate that prolonged and obstructed labour, combined with hemorrhage and infections, account for the deaths of at least 600,000 women yearly (Crosette 1996; Duke and Conly 1997; WHO 2001). It has been shown that these "at-risk" women work long hours at both subsistence activities and child rearing (Harris and Ross 1987). The disproportionate distribution of these deaths in the developing world and disenfranchised sub-populations in industrialized states reflects the biological consequences of social structures as opposed to species-wide 'obstetrical hazards.'

Other likely contributors to maternal morbidity and mortality are sex bias in the allocation of food and medicine to female infants and children (Waldron 1987; Manderson 1999; Rousham 1999). Reproductive sequelae have been documented in adults who were malnourished as children (Martorell 1989; Rush 2000). Furthermore, health data on the effects of gender inequality presented at the 1995 "World Conference on Women" in Beijing revealed that, even though women live longer than men, they experience more chronic illness and disability over their lifetime (Martin 1997). The gendered division of labour, vulnerability to reproductive tract infections, feminization of poverty, and prostitution all levy a strong effect on the reproductive health of women in the present (Doyle 1995; Maine and Chavkin 2002). The clear relationship between women's lower social position and poor health status in the present supports an association between gender asymmetries and increased health risks for women into the pre-colonial past (Bentley *et al.* 1993; Goodman *et al.* 1995; Martin 1997). Contemporary studies provide important models for the relationship between reproduction, workloads and mortality in past populations, and may inform the focus on 'obstetrical hazards' as the sole cause of early death for young females in archaeological populations.

Reproductive morbidity and mortality provide a window onto the complex inter-relationships and health hazards affecting the quality of women's lives (Nelson *et al.* 1994). The bioarchaeological tool kit used to study these questions needs to be balanced between the traditional osteological approaches (such as osteometry, analysis of diet through stable isotopes, and paleo-pathology) and theories and methods from cultural anthropology. This unified approach will allow bio-archaeologists to improve their underlying theories, to broaden the questions they choose to ask, and to maximize the information garnered from available skeletal remains. Bioarchaeological studies exploring the relationships between the physical body and gender identity can thus frame new questions examining women's roles in society (Gero and Conkey 1991; Walde and Willows 1991; Goodman *et al.* 1995; Spielmann 1995; Martin 1997; Crown 2000).

Conclusions

In the past, biological anthropologists and bio-archaeologists have tended to employ biomedical accounts of reproduction as though they were strictly scientific accounts not shaped by culture. Ginsburg and Rapp (1991, 330) emphasize that "no aspect of women's reproduction is a universal or unified experience nor can such phenomena be understood apart from the larger social context that frames them." Because the scientific disciplines of biomedicine and paleoanthropology established a doctrine of inevitable 'obstetrical hazard', cause of death for reproductive aged females in archaeological populations was overwhelmingly attributed to childbirth. Movement away from this single inter-pretation to reconstruct a more complete picture of women in the past involves incorporation of cultural perspectives on several levels.

First, in order to fully explore the relationship between the reproductive body and the construction of social and self identity in the past, the effects of contemporary Euro-American gender roles on scientific discourse on repro-duction must be taken into account. Exposing these influences will allow bioarchaeologists to reconstruct more complete versions of the experienced body and identity of people as members of societies from the past. Thus the inherently incomplete archaeological evidence will not be filled in with biases and beliefs, such as the notion of 'obstetrical hazard' that appears 'natural' and 'correct' solely because it fits with established gender norms.

Without a pseudo-scientific story about the natural basis for birthing difficulties, the social, political, and economic origins of reproductive morbidity and mortality can be discovered for women in the past as they have been documented in the present. This encompasses the second level at which the incorporation of gender in the present can contribute to the reconstructions of repro-duction in the past. The contemporary and historical documentation of gender based food distribution, labour patterns, and poverty provides data to substantiate a link between gender and reproductive morbidity and mortality. These data indicate that simple attribution of death of a woman of reproductive age to childbirth, obscures the social dimensions of poor reproductive health outcomes of women. Such biocultural analyses reveal the mechanisms by which social processes impact human biology. We advocate for the incorporation of this integrated biocultural perspective linking gender and health in bioarchaeological analyses.

Third, equipped with an understanding of the social and biological mechanisms through which gender roles affect reproductive morbidity and mortality, bio-archaeological analyses can include more complete versions of the experienced body and identity of people as members of societies from the past. The high death rates of young women in some archaeological populations thus become an indication of the inferior social status of women and will aid in the reconstruction of the roles of women in past societies. This framework might lead to new interpretations of archaeological data as investigators strive to determine biosocial mechanisms for female mortality in the societies they study.

To embody identity in the past for women requires a reevaluation of the models that underlie anthropological reconstructions of women's biology and behaviour. By expanding the study of reproduction to include ways contemporary gender roles influence scientific models, and the effects of gender on women's health in the past and present, anthropology can move beyond assumptions of 'obstetrical hazard' to suggest specific ways of assessing women's identity in the past. This methodology crosscuts and integrates several sub-disciplines (biology, archaeology, biocultural adaptation, medicine, public health, and ethnography). It offers an innovative approach that begins to link skeletal, archaeological, and ethnographic data, thereby placing women's health in the past in a broader context. This task is analytically challenging because much of the information and documentation has been rooted in androcentric analyses and remains compartmentalized within the boundaries of anthropological subfields.

As we progress through the twenty-first century, more studies need to be carried out that are inclusive and combine many disciplines and perspectives. The discussion of gender, ideology, and power within anthropological frameworks requires that skeletal data be integrated with other archaeological and ethnographic studies to fully understand the (pre)historical and long-term dynamics that include men, women, and children. It also requires a healthy reflexivity about our own scientific theories with an awareness of how gender norms and other socio-cultural values become interpolated into seemingly neutral scientific work. With an integrated bioarchaeological approach, contextualized osteological remains add considerably to the database of information that examines the history of women's health.

References

Akiel, A. S. H., Raber, H., Al Meshari, A. A. A. and Kidess, E. A. I. (1988) Low dose CT Pelvimetry in Saudi Females. *Saudi Medical Journal* 9(2): 173–81.

Angel, J. L. (1978) Pelvic inlet form: a neglected index of nutritional stress. *American Journal of Physical Anthropology* 48, 378.

Arriaza, B., Allison, M. and Gerszten, E. (1988) Maternal mortality in pre-columbian Indians of Arica, Chile. *American Journal of Physical Anthropology* 77, 35–41.

Ashworth, J. T., Allison, M., Gerszten, E. and Pezzia, A. (1976) The pubic scars of gestation and parturition in a group of pre-columbian and colonial Peruvian mummies. *American Journal of Physical Anthropology* 45, 85–90.

Babcock, B. A. (1991) *Pueblo Mothers and Children*. Santa Fe, New Mezico, Ancient City Press.

Bentley, G. R., Goldberg, T. and Jasienska, G. (1993) The fertility of agricultural and non-agricultural traditional societies. *Population Studies* 47, 269–281

Berge C. (1993) *L'Evolution de la Hanche et du Pelvis des Hominidés: bipédie, parturition, croissance, allométrie*. Paris, CRNS Editions.

Black, M. (1984) Maidens and mothers: an analysis of Hopi corn metaphors. *Ethnology* 23, 279–288.

Blakely, R. L. (1977) Sociocultural implications of demographic data from Etowah, Georgia. In R. L. Blakely (ed.), *Biocultural Adaptation in Prehistoric America*, 45–66. Athens, University of Georgia Press.

Brettell, C. B., and Sargent, C. F. (1993) *Gender in a Cross Cultural Perspective*. Upper Saddle River, New Jersey, Prentice Hall.

Brown, H. L., Fan, Y. and Gonsoulin, W. H. (1991) Obstetric complications in young teenagers. *Southern Medical Journal* 84, 46–48.

Caldwell, W. E. and Moloy, H. C. (1933) Anatomical variations in the female pelvis and their effects in labor with a suggested classification. *American Journal of Obstetrics and Gynecology* 26, 824–41.

Clarke, S. (1977) Mortality trends in prehistoric populations. *Human Biology* 49(2), 181–186.

Coleman, W. H. (1969) Sex differences in the growth of the human bony pelvis. *American Journal of Physical Anthropology* 31, 125–152.

Cordell, L. S. (1984) *Prehistory of the Southwest*. New York, Academic Press.

Cook, D. C. (1984) Subsistence and health in the lower Illinois valley: osteological evidence. In M. N. Cohen and G. J. Armelagos (eds.), *Paleopathology at the Origins of Agriculture*, 237–270. Orlando, Academic Press.

Crelin, E. S. (1969) The development of the bony pelvis and its changes during pregnancy and parturition. *Transactions of the New York Academy of Sciences (2)* 31, 1049–1058.

Crosette, B. (1996) New tally of world tragedy: women who die giving life. *New York Times*, June 11, A12.

Crown, P. (2000) *Women and Men in the Prehispanic Southwest: Labor, power and prestige*. Santa Fe, School of American Research Press.

Davis, E. (1997) *Heart and Hands: A Midwife's Guide to Pregnancy and Childbirth. Third Edition*. Berkeley, Celestial Arts.

Davis-Floyd, R. E. (1992) *Birth as an American Rite of Passage*. Berkeley, University of California Press.

Dierks, B. W. (1996) The UN Fourth World Conference on Women. *National Women's Studies Association Journal* 8(2) 82–90.

Doyle, L. (1995) *What Makes Women Sick: Gender and the Political Economy of Health*. New Brunswick, New Jersey, Rutgers University Press.

Drosin, L. (1923) The dorso-squatting position in obstetrics. *International Journal of Medicine and Surgery*, 423–427.

Duke, R. C., and Conly, S. (1997) The population explosion is over. *The New York Times Magazine*, Sunday, December 14. Letters.

Dutton, B. P. (1983) *American Indians of the Southwest*. Albuquerque, University of New Mexico Press.

Finkler, K. (1994) *Women in Pain: Gender and Morbidity in Mexico*. Philadelphia, University of Pennsylvania Press.

Fratt, L. (1991) A preliminary analysis of gender bias in the sixteenth and seventeenth century Spanish colonial documents of the American Southwest. In D. Walde and N. D. Willows (eds.) *The Archaeology of Gender Proceedings of the 22nd Annual Chacomool Conference*, 245–251. Calgary, The Archaeological Association of the University of Calgary.

Gabriel, K. (1992) *Marietta Wetherill: Reflections on Life with the Navajos in Chaco Canyon*. Boulder, Colorado, Johnson Books.

Gardosi, J., Hutson, N. and Lynch, C. (1989) Randomised controlled trial of squatting in the second stage of labour. *The Lancet* 74–77.

Gero, J. and Conkey, M. (1991) *Engendering Archaeology: Women and Prehistory*. Cambridge, Massachusetts, Blackwell Press.

Ginsburg F. and Rapp, R. (1991) The politics of reproduction. *Annual Review of Anthropology*. 20, 311–343.

Ginsburg F. and Rapp, R. (1995) *Conceiving the New World Order: The*

Global Politics of Reproduction. Berkeley, University of California Press.

Goodman, A. H., Thomas, R. B., Swedlund, A. C. and Armelagos, G. J. (1988) Biocultural perspectives on stress in prehistory, historical, and contemporarypopulation. *Yearbook of Physical Anthropology* 31, 169–202.

Goodman, A. H., Martin, D. L. and Armelagos, G. J. (1995) The biological consequences of inequality in prehistory. *Rivista di Antropologia* 73, 1–9.

Golay, J. Vedem, S. and Sorger, L. (1993) The squatting position for the second stage of labor: effects on labor and on maternal and fetal well-being. *Birth* 20, 73–78.

Greulich, W. W. and Thoms, H. (1938) The dimensions of the pelvic inlet of 789 White females. *Anatomical Record* 72, 45–51.

Greulich, W. W. and Thoms, H. (1944) The growth and development of the pelvis of individual girls before, during and after puberty. *Yale Journal of Biology and Medicine* 17, 91–97.

Hager, L. (1989) *The Evolution of Sex Differences in the Hominid Bony Pelvis*. Ph.D. Dissertation, University of California at Berkeley.

Hanson, L. (1998) Second-stage positioning in Nurse-Midwifery practices: Part 1: position use and preference. *Journal of Nurse-Midwifery* 43(5), 320–325.

Harris, M. and Ross, E. B. (1987) *Death, Sex and Fertility: Population Regulation in Preindustrial and Developing Societies*. New York, Columbia University Press.

Hays-Gilpin, K. and Whitley, D. S. (eds.) (1998) *Reader in Gender Archaeology*. New York, Routledge.

Hegmon, M. and Trevathan, W. R. (1996) Gender, anatomical knowledge, and pottery production: Implications of an anatomically unusual birth depicted on Mimbres pottery from southwestern New Mexico. *American Antiquity* 61(4), 747–754.

Hoyme, L. H. (1957) The earliest use of indices for sexing pelves. *American Journal of Physical Anthropology* 15, 537–46.

Hungry Wolf, B. (1980) *The Ways of My Grandmothers*. New York, William Morrow.

Ives, V. S. (1994) *Reassessing Childbirth-Related Mortality in Prehistoric Populations*. Unpublished MA. thesis, Arizona State University.

Jones, S., Martin, R.D. and Pilbeam, D.R., (1994) *The Cambridge Encyclopedia of Human Evolution (Cambridge Reference Book), Reprint edition*. Cambridge, Cambridge University Press.

Jordan, B. (1978) *Birth in Four Cultures: A Crosscultural Investigation of Childbirth in Yucatan, Holland, Sweden, and the United States*. Montreal, Eden Press Women's Publications.

Judd, N. M. (1925) Everyday life in Pueblo Bonito. *National Geographic* 48(3), 227–262.

Jurmain, R., Nelson, H., Kilgore, L. and Trevathan, W. (2002) *Introduction to Physical Anthropology, Ninth edition*, Belmont, California, Wadsworth.

Kamp, K. A. (ed.) (2002) *Children in the Prehistoric Puebloan Southwest*. Salt Lake City, University of Utah Press

Kamp, K. A. (1998) *Life in the Pueblo: Understanding the Past through Archaeology*. Prospect Heights, Illinois, Waveland Press.

King, A. M. (1909) The significance of posture in obstetrics. *New York Medical Journal*, November 27, 1054–1058.

Kitzinger, S. (1972) *The Experience of Childbirth*. Baltimore, Penguin Books.

Krogman, W. (1951) The scars of human evolution. *Scientific American* 185, 54–57.

Lallo, J., Armelagos, G. J. and Rose, J. C. (1978) Paleoepidemiology of infectious disease in the Dickinson Mounds population. *Medical College of Virginia Quarterly* 14, 17–23.

La Velle, M. (1995) Natural selection and development of sexual

variation in the human pelvis. *American Journal of Physical Anthropology* 98, 59–72.

Leavitt, J. W. (1999) *Women and Health in America: Historical Readings, Second Edition*. Madison, University of Wisconsin Press.

Loudon, I. (2001) *Death in Childbirth: An International Study of Maternal Care and Maternal Mortality 1800–1950*. Oxford, Claredon Press.

Lowell, J. C. (1991) Reflections of Sex Roles in the Archaeological Record: Insights from Hopi and Zuni Ethnographic Data. In D. Walde and N. D. Willows (eds.) *The Archaeology of Gender Proceedings of the 22nd Annual Chacomool Conference*, 452–461. Calgary, The Archaeological Association of the University of Calgary.

Lovejoy, C. O. (1981) The origin of man. *Science* 211, 341–350.

Lovejoy C. O., Meindl, R. S., Pryzbeck, T. R., Barton, T. S., Heiple, K. and Knotting, D. (1977) Paleodemography of the Libben site, Ottawa County, Ohio. *Science* 198, 291–293.

MacDonald, P. C., Grant, N. F., Levene, K. J., Gilstrap, L. C., Hawkins, G. D. V. and Clark, S. L., editors, (1997) *Williams Obstetrics, Twentieth Edition*. New York, Appleton & Lange.

MacCormack, C. P. (1982) *Ethnography of Fertility and Birth*. London, Academic Press.

Maine D. and Chavkin W. (2002) Maternal mortality: global similarities and differences. *Journal of the American Western Medical Association,* 57(3),127–130.

Manderson, L. (1999) Social meanings and sexual bodies: gender sexuality and barriers to women's health care. In T. M. Pollard and S. B. Hyatt (eds.) *Sex, Gender, and Health*, 75–93. Cambridge, Cambridge University Press.

Martin, D. L. and Frayer, D. W. (1997) *Troubled Times: Violence and Warfare in the Past*. Amsterdam, Overseas Publishers Association, Gordon and Breach Publishers.

Martin, D. L., Goodman, A. H., Armelagos, G. J. and Magennis. A. L. (1991) *Black Mesa Anasazi Health: Reconstructing Life from Patterns of Death and Disease*. Southern Illinois University at Carbondale, Center for Archaeological Investigations, Occasional Paper No.14.

Martin, D. L. (1997) Women's bodies, women's lives: biological indicators of gender differentiation and inequality in the southwest. Paper presented at for "Sex Roles and Gender Hierarchies in Middle Range Societies: Engendering Southwestern Prehistory" School of American Research Advanced Seminar, Santa Fe, New Mexico. March 2–6.

Martin, E. (1987) *The Woman in the Body*. Boston, Beacon Press Books.

Martin, E. (1996) The egg and the sperm: how science has constructed a romance based on stereotypical male-female roles. In C. F. Sargent and C. B. Brettel (eds.) *Gender and Health: an International Perspective*, 29–43. Upper Saddle River, New Jersey, Prentice Hall.

Martorell, R. (1989) Body size, adaptation, and function. *Human Organization* 48(1), 284–290.

McElmurry, B. J., Norr, K. F. and Parker, R. S. (1993) *Women's Health and Development*. Boston, Jones and Bartlett.

Meltzer, D. (1981) *Birth: An Anthology of Ancient Texts, Songs, Prayers, and Stories*. San Francisco, North Point Press.

Moerman, M. L. (1982) Growth of the birth canal in adolescent girls. *American Journal of Obstetrics and Gynecology* 151, 528–532.

Moir, J. C. (1946) The use of radiology in predicting difficult labour. *Journal of Obstetrics and Gynaecology* 53, 487.

Morgan, M., Thurnau, G. and Fishburne, J. (1986) The fetal-pelvic index as an indicator of fetal-pelvic disproportion: a preliminary report. *American Journal of Obstetrics Gynecology* 155, 608–613.

Naeye, R. L. (1981) Teenaged and pre-teenaged pregnancies: consequences of the fetal-maternal competition for nutrients. *Pediatrics* 67, 146–150.

Napier, J. (1967) The antiquity of human walking. *Scientific American* 216, 56–66.

Nelson, S. M. (1997) *Gender in Archaeology*. Walnut Creek, California, Alta Mira Press.

Nelson, B. A., Martin, D. L., Swedlund, A. C., Fish, P. R. and Armelagos, G. J. (1994) Studies in disruption: demography and health in the prehistoric American Southwest. In G. J. Gumerman and M. Gell-Man (eds.) *Understanding Complexity in the Prehistoric Southwest*, 222–235. Santa Fe Institute Studies in the Sciences of Complexity.

Niederman, S. (1988) *A Quilt of Words: Women's Diaries, Letters and Original Accounts of Life in the Southwest (1860 –1960)*. Boulder, Johnson Books.

Owsley, D. W. and Bass, W. T. (1979) A demographic analysis of skeletons from the Larson Site (39WWZ), Walworth County, South Dakota: vital statistics. *American Journal of Physical Anthropology,* 51, 145–154.

Owsley, D. W. and Bradtmiller, B. (1983) Mortality of pregnant females in Arikara Villages: osteological evidence. *American Journal of Physical Anthropology* 61, 331–336.

Oxorn, H (1986) *Oxorn-Foote Human Labor and Birth, Fifth Edition*. Norwalk, CT, Appleton-Century-Crofts.

Palkovich, A. M. (1984) Agriculture, marginal environments, and nutritional stress in the prehistoric Southwest. In M. N. Cohen and G. J. Armelagos (eds.) *Paleopathology at the Origins of Agriculture*, 425–461. New York, Academic Press.

Prichard, J. A. (1970) *Anemia's complicating Pregnancy and the Puerperium*. National Research Council, Food and Nutrition Board. Maternal Nutrition and the Course of Pregnancy. Washington D.C.: National Academy of Sciences, 74–109.

Rooks, J. P. (1997) *Midwifery and Childbirth in America*. Philadelphia, Temple University Press.

Rosenberg, K.R. and Trevathan, W. (1996) Bipedalism and human birth: the obstetrical dilemma revisited. *Evolutionary Anthropology* 4, 161–168.

Rousham E.R. (1999) Gender bias in South Asia: effects on child growth and nutritional status. In T. M. Pollard and S.B. Hyatt (eds.) *Sex, Gender, and Health,* 37–52. Cambridge, Cambridge University Press.

Rush D. (2000) Nutrition and maternal mortality in the developing world. *American Journal of Clinical Nutrition* (suppl.) 72, 212S–40S.

Russo, P. and Cramoy, C. (1984) Nutrition and pregnancy. In M. Winick (ed.), *Nutrition in the Twentieth Century*, 49–90. New York, John Wiley.

Scott, J. R., Di Saia, P. J., Hammond, C. B. and Spellacy, W. N. (1999) *Obstetrics and Gynecology*. Philadelphia, Lippincott, Williams and Wilkins.

Scully, D. (1980) *Men Who Control Women's Health: the Miseducation of Obstetrician-Gynecologists*. Boston, Houghton Mifflin.

Segebarth-Orban, R. (1980) An evaluation of the sexual dimorphism of the human innominate bone. *Journal of Human Evolution* 9, 601–607.

Serenius, F., Elidrissy, A. T. and Dandona, P. (1984) Vitamin D nutrition in pregnant women at term and in newly born babies in Saudi Arabia. *Journal of Clinical Pathology* 37(4), 444–7.

Shaw, N. Y. S. (1974) *Forced Labor: Maternity Care in the United States*, New York, Pergamon Press.

Sibley, L. M., Armelagos, G. A. and Van Gerven, D. P. (1992) Obstetric dimensions of the true pelvis in a medieval population

from Sudanese Nubia. *American Journal of Physical Anthropology* 89, 421–430.

Simpson, J. L. (1964) *Journal of Military Reconnaissance from Santa Fe, New Mexico to the Navajo Country*. Reports of the Secretary of War, Sen. Exec. Doc. 64, 31st Congress, 1st Session, Washington D.C., 1850. Oklahoma City, Reprinted by the University of Oklahoma Press.

Speilmann, K. A. (1995) Glimpses of gender in the prehistoric Southwest. *Journal of Anthropological Research* 51(2), 91–102.

Staurt-Macadam, P. (1989) Nutritional deficiency diseases: a survey of scurvy, rickets, and iron deficiency anemia. In M. Iscan and K. A. R. Kennedy (eds.) *Reconstructions of Life from the Skeleton*, 210–222. New York, Alan R. Liss, Inc.

Stodder, A. W. (1984) Bioarchaeological investigations of protohistoric Pueblo health and demography. In C. Larsen (ed.) *In the wake of Contact: Biological Responses to Conquest,* 97–107. New York, Wiley-Liss.

Stone, P. K. (2000) *Paleoobstetrics: Reproduction Workload and Mortality for Ancestral Pueblo Women*, Unpublished Ph.D. Thesis, University of Massachusetts, Amherst Massachusetts

Tague, R. G. (1986) *Obstetric Adaptations of the Human Bony Pelvis*. Unpublished Ph.D. Thesis, Kent State University, Ohio.

Tague, R. G. (1991) Commonalties in dimorphism and variability in the anthropoid pelvis, with implications for the fossil record. *Journal of Human Evolution* 21, 153–176.

Tague, R. G. (1992) Sexual dimorphism in the human bony pelvis, with a consideration of the Neanderthal pelvis from Kebara Cave, Israel. *American Journal of Physical Anthropology* 88, 1–21.

Tague, R. G. (1995) Variation in pelvic size between males and females in nonhuman anthropoids. *American Journal of Physical Anthropology* 97, 213–233.

Thomas, A. M., Hytten, F. E., and Billewicz, W. Z. (1970) The energy costs of human lactation. *British Journal of Nutrition* 24, 565–72.

Thoms, H. (1934) What is a normal pelvis? *Journal of the American Medical Association* 102(25), 2075–2076.

Thoms, H. (1956) *Pelvimetry*. New York, Paul B. Hoeber Inc. Medical Books Department of Harper Brothers.

Trevathan, W. R. (1987) *Human Birth: An Evolutionary Perspective*. Hawthorne, New York, Aldine de Gruyter.

Underhill, R. (1991) *Life in the Pueblos*. Santa Fe, New Mexico, Ancient City Press.

Walde, D. and Willows, N. (1991) *The Archaeology of Gen*der. Proceedings of the 22nd Annual Chacmool Conference. Calgary: Archaeology Association of the University of Calgary.

Waldron, I. (1987) Pattern and causes of excess female mortality among children in developing countries. *World Health Statistics Quarterly* 40, 194–210.

Walrath, D. (2003) Rethinking pelvic typologues and the human birth mechanism. *Current Anthropology*, 44(1), 5–31.

Ward, W.P. (2003) Perinatal mortality in Utrecht, The Netherlands, 1880–1940. *Economics and Human Biology*, 1(3), 379–398.

Waters, F. (1963) *The Book of the Hopi*. New York, Penguin Books.

Washburn, S (1960) Tools and human evolution. *Scientific American* 203, 3–15.

Wells, C. (1967) Weaver, Tailor or Shoemaker? An osteological detective story. *Medical Biological Illustrations* 17, 39–47.

Williams, J. T. (1922) Normal variation in type of the female pelvis and their obstetrical significance. *American Journal of Obstetrics and Gynecology III*, 345–351.

World Health Organization (2001) Maternal Mortality in 1995, Geneva: Estimates Developed by WHO, UNICEF, UNFPA.

12.   The Osteology of Monasticism in Medieval England

Simon Mays

Introduction

Monasticism began as a movement in the deserts of the Middle East in the third century AD. The first monastic communities in England appear to date to the 7th century. The Viking raiding of the ninth century virtually destroyed English monasticism, but it revived in the 10th century with the defeat of the Viking threat (Aston 2000). There were over 1000 monastic communities in late Medieval England (Coppack 1990, 12); most of these were founded before the end of the 13th century and continued to function until the Dissolution (1536–1540), when monastic life was abruptly extinguished and the property of the religious orders seized by the Crown.

Because of the integral role played by religious orders in Medieval society, and because of the richness of the record, both in terms of upstanding ruins and below ground archaeology, the study of monasticism has long been an important focus in British Medieval archaeology. Initially, the emphasis was on the study of the structure and layout of the buildings which made up the monastic complex (Coppack 1990). The last two decades, however, have seen a shift toward greater study of the economic role of monasteries and their management of the environment (Gilchrist 1995, 4–5).

Within the traditional, buildings-orientated framework there was little role for human osteology. The potential for human osteological work to contribute to the newer approaches emphasising economy and environment would appear somewhat greater. For example, dietary studies enable a focus on an aspect of the 'consumer' side of the monastic economy, and since disease experience may be profoundly influenced by living conditions, palaeopathology has a potentially important role in the study of the interactions between monastic communities and their environment.

Although attempting to reconcile historical and archaeological evidence has long been a part of monastic archaeology, recent approaches have attempted a more ambitious integration, treating the two strands of evidence on an equal basis rather than archaeology playing a subservient role (*e.g.* Gilchrist 1995). The ability of human osteology to shed light directly on aspects of monastic lifestyle means that it has an important role in complementing the evidence from written sources, which are rather sparse and imperfect in this regard. Most written evidence on monastic daily life consists of strictures ('Rules') concerning how life should be lived rather than the way it actually was. Some sources, such as monastic accounts (Harvey 1993) or contemporary social comment (Lawrence 1984), are exceptions. However, it is often difficult to relate monastic accounts to actual lifestyle, even for aspects such as diet upon which they have fairly direct bearing, and many contemporary descriptions of monastic life, particularly those critical of the religious orders, have to be viewed largely as propaganda, a product of the social and political context in which they were written.

Despite its potential, the influence of human osteology on monastic archaeology has to date been small. To some extent, this reflects the lack of suitable material; there are relatively few skeletal assemblages from monastic sites which can confidently be identified as of monastic brethren rather than of lay benefactors or patrons. It is also a symptom of the wider problem of the marginalisation of human osteology within archaeology, due largely to differing academic traditions (Mays 1998a). Recent years have, however, seen movement toward reintegration of human osteology into mainstream archaeology. A consequence of this has been the beginnings of problem-orientated work on monastic skeletal remains. It is timely, therefore, to review the role of skeletal remains in shedding light on monastic life in medieval England.

In the sections which follow, aspects of the Rules which governed monastic life of monks, canons and friars in the Middle Ages are discussed. Passing on to the skeletal evidence, the problems in distinguishing burials of religious from those of layfolk at monastic sites will be examined, and some archaeological sites where it has proved possible to identify significant groups of monastic burials will be itemised. A critical discussion of what has so far been learnt of monastic life from osteological evidence will be presented, and possible future directions suggested.

The nature of monastic life

A monastic community is one whose members have withdrawn from the distractions and temptations of the secular world in order to devote themselves to serving God, principally through devotion and prayer. Members of a monastic order lived a communal life in a single-sex community, were celibate, renounced private property, observed a strictly regulated life, and owed obedience to a common superior. On death, members of the community were generally buried within the monastic precinct. Monastic life, as well as involving rigid routines of prayer and devotion to God, also meant a distinct lifestyle in terms of basic physical aspects, such as the degree and type of physical labour undertaken, and the type of diet consumed.

The basis for most monastic life in the Middle Ages was the Rule of St Benedict, a 6th-century Italian monk. His Rule was widely adopted by monastic communities from the 9th century onwards, and although by the 11th century modifications had taken place in observances, it continued to provide the foundation for monastic life right up until the Dissolution. The Rule provided an ordered routine for the monastic day. The aim was the conquest of sensuality and self-will through strict discipline, so that the individual was totally receptive to the will of God. The prime purpose of those who professed a monastic life was prayer, in the belief that their intercession would help save mankind. The day therefore consisted of a liturgical framework around which other activities were structured. Outside the hours of common prayer, the waking day was divided into periods of work and study. Benedict emphasised the value of manual labour: it had an ascetic and an economic function – it kept men humble and helped provide for the material needs of the community (Lawrence 1984, 30). As well as manual labour in fields and gardens, tasks might include domestic chores and, if monks had the skills, craft activities (Lawrence 1984, 30; Burton 1994, 164).

The Benedictine Rule's prescriptions with regard to food were designed to create a diet which was adequate but not lavish. The emphasis was on bread and vegetables, and on moderate quantities. Meat was forbidden, except for the sick, although fish could be substituted (Dickinson 1961; White 1993).

In the late 10th century, the *Regularis Concordia*, a code compiled for English Benedictine houses, altered the monastic regime, so that the liturgy became the overwhelming element, relegating manual work to a token (Burton 1994, 160). There were also relaxations con-cerning the amount of food permitted, although meat was still proscribed (*op cit.* 166–167).

During the Middle Ages, periodic attempts were made by some orders to return to a more literal interpretation of the Benedictine Rule, thereby restoring a more rigorous monastic regime. For example, the Cistercians, present in England from the 12th century, instituted a return to what they considered a more pristine observance of the Rule of St Benedict, reinstating manual labour and a more austere diet (Lawrence 1984, 151; Burton 1994, 167). However, in general, there was a trend toward dilution of self-denying ordinances as the Medieval period wore on (Dickinson 1961). For example, until the 13th century abstinence from meat seems to have been usual among Benedictine orders, but this appears to have broken down somewhat after about 1200 when abstinence seems only to have been partial (Bond 1988). The Cistercians held out somewhat longer against consumption of meat; only in the 14th century did dispensations start to appear, but thereafter meat-eating gradually increased (Greene 1992, 147; White 1993).

With the growth of monastic estates during later medieval times, an increasing number of monks were occupied with managerial tasks rather than manual labour (Lawrence 1984, 31). Domestic tasks also began to be undertaken by hired servants, rather than by the brethren themselves (Burton 1994, 164).

In the later Middle Ages, two new types of monastic order sprang up, the canons regular and the friars. Canons regular were groups of clergy living under a monastic regime. In most instances they did little in the way of pastoral work, this being delegated to secular clergy; the emphasis was on an enclosed monastic existence, separated from the world (Dickinson 1961, 78). Some houses, such as those for clergy serving cathedrals and major churches, were situated in towns; others were located in more isolated rural areas (Aston 2000, 94). From the 12th century, various orders of the canons regular established houses in England, including the Premonstratensians, Augustinians and the Gilbertines. Some Gilbertine establishments were double houses of men and women.

Canons regular observed the Augustinian Rule, which is based upon a letter written to a group of nuns by St Augustine of Hippo in the early 5th century AD. This was not a detailed and systematic prescription for the monastic day but a brief document giving general spiritual advice. Individual houses were, subject to official approval, left to reinforce this with various rules and observances of their own, generally borrowed from Benedictine monastic practice. This meant that there was significant variation in observance between houses of canons (Dickinson 1961, 77). In general, the regime was less severe than that of the early Benedictine houses. Diet was more generous and the attitude to meat-eating more relaxed. Partial abstinence from meat was a popular compromise (Dickinson 1950, 182), and it seems probable that the proportion of meat in the diet increased over time (White 1993). Study and intellectual persuits were commended in place of physical labour (Lawrence 1984, 140). With the general relaxation of monastic ordinances in the later part of the Medieval period there became little important difference between the regime of many Benedictine and Augustinian houses (Dickinson 1961, 77).

The friars differed from the Benedictine monks and the canons regular in that they rejected the ownership of property and were mendicant. They had an active pastoral mission, preaching and ministering to layfolk. Because of their dependence on charity and their evangelical role, their houses were situated in urban areas. The friars came to England in the 13th century. There were four major orders, the Dominicans (Friars Preachers or Blackfriars), the Carmelites (Whitefriars), the Franciscans (Friars Minor or Greyfriars) and the Austin Friars. The friars were the great success story of the 13th century, and by 1300 most towns had at least one friary and some had houses of all four major orders.

Dominican, Carmelite and Austin friars organised their monastic regime according to the Augustinian Rule. Because of their mendicancy and their active evangelising, physical labour played little part (Lawrence 1984, 205). The Franciscans based their regime on the teachings of St Francis of Assisi. There was an emphasis on poverty and, at least initially, they refused to own their own buildings or to handle money. St Francis had envisaged that at least some brethren would be engaged in manual work, but, in practice, physical labour only played a minor role (Dickinson 1961, 89). As with other monastic orders, ordinances governing the regime of friars were relaxed during the centuries leading up to the Dissolution, although the friars never possessed the great wealth and estates of the monasteries (Lawrence 1994, 218–228).

Burials at religious houses

Donations from lay families were an important source of income for all the monastic orders and, for the friars, were virtually the sole source of support. By providing financial aid to a religious house, a lay family reaped a variety of benefits, chiefly of a spiritual and social nature. This is illustrated by the role played by religious houses as places of burial for patrons or benefactors. For a lay family, burial of the dead within a monastic precinct was a means of asserting social identity and religious piety, and of helping to ensure intervention of the prayers of brethren for the souls of the departed (Harding 1992). Indeed, for many, the main aim of providing financial support was to secure a burial place within the monastic precinct, especially within the church (Astill and Wright 1993). From the point of view of the religious order, providing a place of burial supplied a service to the lay family, and was of direct financial benefit, both through a gift, often associated with a request for burial, and with the expectation of continuity of support from the family

(Burton 1994, 219). The friars were particularly successful at attracting burials of the richer members of society, but for all religious orders burials of layfolk came to be an important element in cementing relationships with families who provided financial support, even among those such as the Cistercians whose ordinances initially forbade it (Burton 1994, 218).

Given the presence within monastic precincts of burials of both layfolk and of members of the resident religious community, the challenge is to try and distinguish the two. There is generally little in the way in which the corpse was laid out, or in the manner of burial, to distinguish interments of the monastic community from those of layfolk, but the two were generally segregated spatially. For wealthier layfolk, the church was a popular choice of burial place (Coppack 1990, 59), but lay burial might also occur within a designated cemetery area within the precinct. The cemetery area reserved for burial of members of the resident religious community was conventionally situated to the east of the church (Coppack 1990, 60). Few archaeological investigations of religious houses have investigated the eastern cemetery area in detail, but those which have generally found that burials were almost entirely male. Given that the sites investigated were male houses, this supports the interpretation of burial grounds for brethren. Some published sites in England which have yielded large collections of remains of resident religious communities are detailed in Table 12.1.

Although interpreted as specifically for brethren, it is notable that all the burial areas identified in Table 12.1 contain some interments of women or children. In some instances (St Mary, Stratford Langthorne and St Andrew, Fishergate, York) these were noted as being at the margins of the part of the cemetery excavated, suggesting that the excavated area simply extended into areas used for lay burial.

A consideration when interpreting child burials in apparent monastic cemeteries is that most medieval religious houses accepted oblates; offspring given up in childhood to a monastery by their parents to be brought up as monks or nuns, so that children aged seven years upwards lived within monastic communities (Lawrence 1984, 32; Burton 1994, 174). Child burials in areas thought reserved for brethren may thus represent oblates. Child oblates were a major source of recruitment to medieval monasteries (although Cistercian houses refused to accept them). The practice was formally proscribed in 1215. Although it was still permissable after this date to accept children for education they were not committed to a monastic life, and from this time the number of children in monastic houses dwindled rapidly (Lawrence 1984, 33). After this date, burials of immature individuals in cemetery areas seemingly for brethren are more likely to be offspring of lay benefactors or, if adolescent, servants or novices in the monastic house.

There is historical evidence that segregation of lay and

Site	Order	Date	Location of monastic burials	Date of monastic burials	N	M	F	U	J	Sex ratio	Source
St Saviour, Bermondsey	Cluniac monks	1089–1538	East of church	1089–1430	193	137	8	47	1	17:1	Connell and White (forthcoming)
St Andrew, Fishergate, York	Gilbertine canons	1195–1538	East of church	1195–early 14th cent.	51	47	3	0	1	16:1	Stroud and Kemp (1993)
St Mary, Stratford Langthorne, London	Cistercian monks	1135–1538	North and east of church	1135–1538	647[†]	536	28	55	28	19:1	White (2004)
Merton Priory	Augustinian canons	1140–1540	Chapter house, cemetery to east of church	1140–1540	35	34	1	0	0	34:1	Waldron (1985a)
Bordesley Abbey	Cistercian monks	1138–1538	East of church	1138–1538	128	49	7	67	5	7:1	Hirst and Wright (1989)

Table 12.1. Some large collections of monastic burials excavated from sites in England.

Key: N= total number of burials in area interpreted as burial ground of monastic brethren, [†]=includes a few burials from within the conventual church; M= males; F=females; U=unsexed adults; J=juveniles.

religious burials may not always have been absolute. For example, Cistercian monks could bury two lay friends in the cemetery (Astill and Wright 1993). In his survey of burials at Blackfriars friaries, Palmer (1891) notes instances of lay benefactors requesting burial next to a particular friar. Lay patrons might request rights of confraternity, an association with a religious house which might entitle them to receive prayers on the anniversary of their deaths and other spiritual privileges. Some might go further and, on their deathbeds, take the habit to die as a monk, canon or nun. There are even records of lay women being clothed as Cistercian monks on their deathbeds (Lawrence 1984, 217). This might potentially result in lay individuals being buried in the monastic cemetery. At Monk Bretton Priory (South Yorkshire) and Bardney Abbey (Lincolnshire), both Benedictine houses, grave-slabs commemorating monks were found in the church nave along with those of benefactors. This may indicate that some monks were buried alongside layfolk (although it is also possible that the grave-markers had been moved (Coppack 1990, 60)).

In addition to the eastern cemetery, another place traditionally used for the burial of religious brethren, particularly high-ranking individuals, is the chapter house (Coldstream 1986, 157; Coppack 1990, 72). However, laity, if they were considered sufficiently important, might also be buried there (Daniell 1997, 96). There is archaeological evidence for both practices. At some sites, chapter house burials are solely of adults and all those which could be sexed are male (*e.g.* Ipswich Blackfriars (Mays 1991a), Ipswich Whitefriars (Mays 1991b), Gilbertine Priory of St Andrew, Fishergate, York (Stroud and Kemp 1993) and St Gregory's Priory of Augustinian

canons, Canterbury (Anderson 2001)), supporting the idea that they were burials of brethren. On the other hand, the chapter houses at Merton Priory (Waldron 1985a) and Linlithgow Whitefriars (Stones 1989) included burials of females and at the Oxford Blackfriars the burials of children (Edwards 1976), findings which indicate lay burial.

It is notable that there is a paucity of burials from pre-Conquest monastic communities or from nunneries. One of the few excavations at female monastic houses to produce significant quantities of skeletal remains is that at the late medieval Nunnery of St Clement, York. Of 132 burials which could be sexed, 89 were female and 43 male (Dawes, nd), suggesting that part of the nuns' cemetery may have been excavated. Whether burials of religious women can be distinguished from lay burials is unclear, as the site has yet to be published. A possible female monastic site of pre-Conquest date was identified at Nazeingbury, Essex (Huggins 1978). Here 153 burials were excavated. There were few juveniles, and the sex ratio among the adults was 2.6:1 in favour of females (Putnam 1978). An interpretation offered by the excavator was that this was an unsuspected early nunnery. The burials showed no spatial segregation by sex so identifying those of nuns (if nunnery this was) would be difficult.

Osteological evidence for monastic life

Diet

Bone stable isotope studies

Traditionally, diet in earlier populations has been investigated in skeletal material by examination of the frequency of pathological lesions, particularly dental diseases such as caries (*e.g.* Moore and Corbett 1978). However, in the last two decades, chemical techniques, particularly bone stable isotope analyses, have greatly increased the palaeodietary information potentially obtainable from human remains (Larsen 1997, 270–301; Mays 2000a). The most widely used stable isotopes for the purposes of dietary reconstruction are those of carbon and nitrogen. Marine foods generally show higher levels of carbon-13 and nitrogen-15 than do terrestrial foods. This difference is passed on to the bones of the consumer. Carbon and nitrogen stable isotope ratios (measured as $\delta^{13}C$ and $\delta^{15}N$) in bone collagen potentially yield information concerning the proportion of dietary protein derived from marine foods. A few isotope studies have investigated medieval monastic diet.

Carbon stable isotope work on skeletons from the Gilbertine Priory of St Andrew, Fishergate, York revealed that monastic brethren consumed a greater proportion of seafood in their diets than did layfolk, with marine resources providing up to one-third of dietary protein among the former (Mays 1997). The monastic burials were also observed to show a lower rate of dental caries. This too might be connected with a heavy marine diet. The flesh of marine animals is non-cariogenic, and the high fluoride content of many seafoods may inhibit the development of caries. Given that monastic dietary ordinances proscribed meat (albeit only partially in the case of the Augustinian Rule followed by the Gilbertine order) but permitted fish to be substituted, the results were interpreted as consistent with the idea that monastic ordinances were exerting an influence over eating habits, at least during the first two centuries of the priory's existence, from which the sampled burials derived.

The only other stable isotope work on monastic burials from England of which I am aware is the analysis of a single burial, dating from the 11th-13th century, from the monk's cemetery at Malmesbury Abbey, Wiltshire, a Benedictine monastery. Mirroring the York results, this individual also showed a substantial seafood component in his diet, despite the inland location of the site (Mays 1998b).

Recently, Polet and Katzenberg (2003) have reported carbon and nitrogen isotopic results from some monastic burials from Dunes Abbey, Koksijde, Belgium. This was a Cistercian house, and the burials sampled date from the 12th-15th century. Results showed greater seafood consumption at this site compared with lay inland sites. As with the York Fishergate material, this group also showed a low caries rate.

At St Mary, Stratford Langthorne, 4% of teeth were carious, a rather low rate compared with other Medieval collections (White 2004), suggesting a distinct monastic diet. High seafood consumption, as observed at the sites discussed above, would be one possible explanation, but isotopic study would be required to confirm this. The caries rates at Merton Priory and the Abbey of St Saviour,

Bermondsey were not exceptional (Waldron 1985a; Connell and White, forthcoming). There is no published osteological report on Bordesley Abbey.

DISH and monastic life
In an attempt to look at the quantity of food eaten rather than dietary composition, various workers have investigated the prevalence of DISH (diffuse idiopathic skeletal hyperostosis) in medieval remains. DISH is a progressive ossification of the spinal ligaments, particularly in the thoracic segment, leading to ankylosis (bony fusion) of vertebrae (Fig. 12.1). There is also extra-spinal ossification at ligamentous and tendinous insertions. Clinical studies

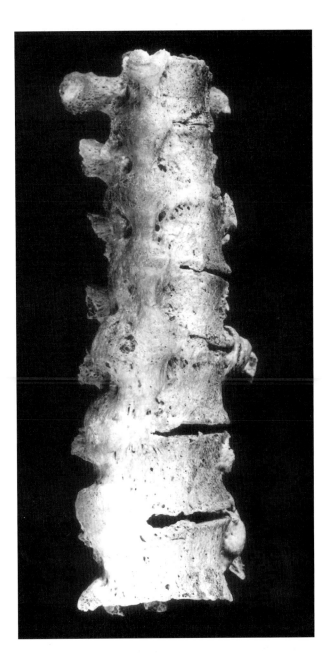

Figure 12.1. Seven thoracic vertebrae from Wharram Percy. They are united by a thick, flowing, right-sided osteophyte. These changes are characteristic of DISH.

have shown a link between DISH and high body weight and late onset diabetes (Julkunen *et al.* 1971; Vezyroglou *et al.* 1996; Lenchik *et al.* 1996; McAlindon *et al.* 1996; Mata *et al.* 1997).

Various workers have claimed a high prevalence of DISH among skeletons from monastic cemeteries and have cited this as evidence of over-eating and consequent obesity among the monks. The first to suggest an association between DISH and monastic lifestyle was Waldron (1985b). Among 35 burials from Merton Priory, three showed the condition, a prevalence of 8.6%. He compared this with a well-known study of modern Europeans by Julkunen *et al.* (1971). Julkunen *et al.* (1971) took radiographs of the thoracic spine of living subjects and scored DISH as present if at least two complete bony bridges between vertebrae were visible; no cases were found in individuals under 40, the prevalence among those over 40 was 2.8%. Waldron (ibid.) suggested that the higher prevalence at Merton Priory suggested that obesity was a problem among the Augustinian canons.

Based on only three cases of disease, Waldron's (1985b) finding of a higher DISH prevalence in the medieval canons than among modern Europeans is clearly not statistically valid, but since this publication, other studies have appeared purporting to show an association between DISH and monastic burials. Some of these (*e.g.* Rogers and Waldron 2001) are problematic in that they deal with burials which appear to be a mixture of brethren and layfolk and it is impossible to determine to which category the skeletons showing DISH belong. Others deal with a single or a few burials so that no statistically valid patterns can be established (*e.g.* de la Rua and Ortue 1992). Because DISH is a progressive disease, authors should state clearly the degree of ossification necessary to elicit a positive diagnosis for the condition, but the diagnostic criteria cited in many palaeopathological publications are frustratingly vague. For example, Janssen and Maat (1999) reported signs of DISH among all 27 skeletons of canons from St Servaas Basilica, Maastricht. The extent of ossification in individual skeletons is unclear, but it appears that some of their cases show spinal changes insufficient to qualify as diagnostic of DISH according to the Julkunen *et al.* (1971) criteria.

Other studies (Stroud and Kemp 1993; White 2004; Connell and White, forthcoming) deal with numbers large enough potentially to produce statistically valid results, and although they use different diagnostic criteria, and differing methods to calculate prevalence rates, the reports contain sufficient information to enable some comparisons to be drawn. The nature of the data from these sites makes comparison with modern studies, such as Julkunen *et al.*'s (1971), problematic, but in any event a better strategy for evaluating the hypothesis of increased DISH in monastic burials would seem to be to compare with medieval non-monastic material. In the paragraphs which follow, I attempt to draw comparisons between the results of the above studies and the non-monastic group

from the deserted medieval village of Wharram Percy.

The skeletons excavated from the churchyard at Wharram Percy represent primarily ordinary peasants. All the skeletons (N=687) have been examined by the present writer. Medieval peasants were among the poorest members of what was a very hierarchical society, and documentary sources indicate that their diet was often inadequate (Gies and Gies 1990). Osteological study of the Wharram Percy skeletons (Mays 1995, 1999a) confirms that nutritional stress was marked in this group. If the prevalence of DISH is elevated in monastic brethren on account of over-eating and obesity, then the frequency in the monastic burials ought to be greater than at Wharram Percy where we know nutrition was poor.

At St Saviour, Bermondsey, Connell and White (forthcoming) indicate that 15 of the 193 burials showed DISH. All cases were male, giving a frequency of 15 of a total of 137 male burials excavated, or 10.9%. The 15 cases identified include those showing spinal disease and those with extra-spinal manifestations.

At Wharram Percy, eight individuals showed at least one complete bony bridge between thoracic or lumbar vertebral bodies as a result of ossification of the anterior longitudinal ligament, 21 showed spinal ligamentous ossification to a degree insufficient to result in bony union of any thoracic or lumbar vertebrae, and two showed extra-spinal manifestation only (*i.e.* widespread ossification at ligamentous and tendinous insertions). Of this total of 31 individuals, 28 were male. At Wharram Percy a total of 360 adult burials were excavated of which 211 were male. Taking the presence of spinal or extra spinal ossification as indicative of a positive score for DISH (in order to match the method published for St Saviour), the prevalence with regard to total adult burials recovered is 31/360 (8.6%), or 28/211 (13.3%) for males. These figures resemble those from St Saviour.

Turning to St Mary, Stratford Langthorne, White (2004) indicates the presence of 22 cases of DISH among 253 male vertebral columns examined, a frequency of 8.7%. In addition to the fully developed condition, vertebral columns where at least four vertebrae showed right-sided exuberant osteophytic growth were included in the total. Applying these diagnostic criteria to the Wharram Percy remains gives a total of 12 cases of which 11 are male. If one uses as the denominator male vertebral columns for which the combined total of thoracic and lumbar vertebrae preserved is at least four, then the frequency at Wharram Percy is 11/157 or 7%. There is no statistically valid difference between this prevalence figure and that from St Mary, Stratford Langthorne.

At St Andrew, Fishergate, York, there were six cases of DISH among the 51 burials from the eastern cemetery (Stroud and Kemp 1993). DISH was diagnosed as present if there was some ankylosis of vertebral bodies or if there were interlocking osteophytes. Applying similar criteria to the Wharram Percy burials gives a total of 17 cases of which 16 are male. The prevalence with respect to all male adults excavated is therefore 7.6%. This is statistically indistinguishable from the frequency in the Fishergate eastern cemetery.

One should be cautious in interpreting the above results, given the difficulties in precise matching of methods for diagnosing and determining the prevalence of DISH, and because of the impossibility of age-matching of samples (which, given the age progressive nature of DISH would have been the ideal) due to important differences in the methods for determining age at death. However, the three assemblages from St Saviour, Bermondsey, St Mary, Stratford Langthorne and St Andrew, Fishergate, York are the largest and best reported collections of monastic burials currently available from England, and hence are the collections of choice for a meta-analysis of the frequency of DISH. The low nutritional status of the Wharram Percy population would be expected to provide a good contrast if the monastic groups had a high caloric intake. There is nevertheless no evidence of a higher rate of DISH in the monastic collections.

Comparing the frequency of DISH at Wharram Percy and in modern Europeans is also instructive. At Wharram Percy, five individuals satisfied the criteria of Julkunen *et al.* (1971) for the diagnosis of DISH of at least two complete bony bridges between thoracic vertebral bodies. This gives a frequency, expressed with respect to adults aged 40 years or more with at least three thoracic vertebrae

surviving, of 5/149 = 3.4% (Mays 2000b). This resembles the prevalence of 2.8% found for Europeans today by Julkunen *et al.* (1971). It is probable that obesity is more frequent among modern Europeans than in the medieval peasants from Wharram Percy, for whom being over-weight was hardly likely. Given the above, it may be (as I have argued elsewhere (Mays 2000b)) that, although an association between DISH and obesity has been found in some well-controlled clinical studies, it is likely that this association is insufficiently strong for the frequency of obesity to be an important determinant of the prevalence of DISH at a population level. Observations on living populations are consistent with this. Julkunen *et al.* (1971) found that, despite their observation that weight: height index was greater in DISH cases than in controls, regional differences in DISH frequency which they observed could not be ascribed to population differences in obesity.

Activity patterns

Within limits, living bone adapts structurally to the loads imposed upon it, bone being added where it is needed and resorbed where it is not. In the shaft of a tubular bone, an increase in mechanical forces (from, for example, vigourous physical activity) may result both in an increase in the amount of cortical bone and in an alteration to its distribution in cross-section so that more is disposed further from the neutral axis (Fig. 12.2). These changes have the effect of increasing the strength of the shaft so

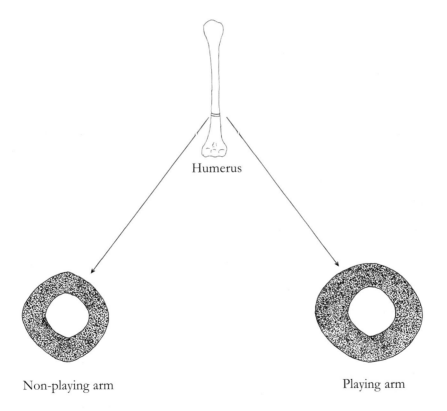

Figure 12.2. Cross-sections of the humeri of a professional tennis player. The response of bone to increased mechanical forces is illustrated in the heavily thickened bone in the racket arm. Based on Jones et al. *(1977).*

that it is better able to resist the forces placed upon it. Analysis of cross-sectional morphology of long-bones is increasingly being used as a complementary technique to those based upon studying pathological changes, such as degenerative joint disease, for investigating activity regimes in past populations.

To my knowledge only two published osteological studies have focussed specifically on activity patterns among medieval religious brethren. Both used the remains from the Gilbertine priory of St Andrew, Fishergate, York. Analysis of cross-sectional properties of humeri (Mays 1999b) indicated reduced diaphysial strength among the canons at St Andrew, Fishergate than among layfolk buried in the priory. This was interpreted as indicating a reduction in heavy physical activity among the brethren, at least in tasks which loaded the upper limbs. This was thought consistent with the Rule of St Augustine which commended study and intellectual pursuits in place of manual labour.

An earlier study of the York material (Knüsel *et al.* 1997) attempted to investigate activity patterns using degenerative joint disease of the vertebral column. Although degenerative joint disease is thought to be related to mechanical factors (Jurmain 1999), these workers failed to find any differences in the pattern of disease between monastic and lay burials. The results of these two studies seem to suggest that differences in activity patterns were preserved in humeral diaphysial morphology but not in the degenerative joint disease data. It may be that the frequency of degenerative joint disease is not a very good indicator of habitual activity, even at a population level, and the vertebral column may not be the best focus for study (Knüsel *et al.* 1997). It is also worth bearing in mind that bone diaphysial morphology and the occurrence of degenerative joint disease may be conveying different information. The biomechanical factor most closely associated with the development of degenerative joint disease is repetitive impact loading across a joint (*e.g.* Radin and Paul 1971; Simon *et al.* 1972). On the other hand, diaphysial remodelling appears to be a response to general mechanical forces acting on a bone shaft (Ruff 1992; Larsen 1997, 195–199).

Infectious disease

The distinctive nature of monastic communities and their separation, to a greater or lesser degree, from lay society may potentially influence the burden of infectious disease compared with secular society. Although all monastic orders interacted with the secular world, the relative isolation of many of the contemplative orders may have helped them avoid outbreaks of infectious disease which were commonplace in Medieval towns. The standards of sanitation in medieval monastic houses were exceptional for the time, and the nutrition and shelter enjoyed by the inmates may also have been better than the norm in the medieval period (Hatcher 1986). These factors would be expected to help to reduce morbidity. On the other hand,

even rural monasteries received a constant stream of visitors (many of whom may have travelled considerable distances) and urban houses, especially of friars, had regular contact with townsfolk (Lawrence 1984, 192f; Hatcher 1986; Burton 1994, 221). These factors would have aided the transmission of disease into monastic communities, and the close-knit, communal lifestyle of a monastic house would have aided the spread of disease between inmates. The balance between the effects of these positive and negative factors would, of course, have depended upon the specific nature of the monastic house in question.

To my knowledge, no problem-orientated research has been carried out looking at infectious disease in monastic skeletal material. However, a little data has been published in bone reports. The prevalence of specific infections, such as tuberculosis, is too low (as it generally is in skeletal samples) to permit meaningful comparative analysis of prevalences. However, non-specific signs of infectious disease (i.e. those where the cause of the infection cannot be determined) are more frequent and hence lend themselves rather better to quantitative analysis. An important way in which infectious disease manifests in the skeleton is via periostitis, the sub-periosteal deposition of new bone upon existing bone surfaces. At St Andrew, Fishergate, York, periostitis appears to be less frequent among the burials from the monastic cemetery than in burials from other areas (Stroud and Kemp 1993). By contrast, at St Mary, Stratford Langthorne, periostitis seems to be rather frequent – one third of all lower legs were said to show the condition (the lower leg bones are the usually most common sites of periostitis) (White 2004). This frequency is greater than at Wharram Percy (where 9% of individuals showed periostitis – counting not only lower leg lesions but those on other bones as well – Mays 1998a), or at the medieval London churchyard of St Nicholas Shambles, where periostitis was 'rare' (White 1988). Although the possibility of significant inter-observer error in the scoring of periostitis should not be completely ruled out, it seems more likely that the above results represent real patterns in the skeletal data. Interpretation of these patterns is, however, difficult because a complex array of factors, in addition to the prevalence of infection experienced by the community, affect the rate of bone lesions seen in a skeletal population. For example, it takes time for infectious disease to produce skeletal changes, so collections which show little in the way of skeletal lesions may do so simply because few had enough resistance to infectious disease to survive long enough for it to affect the skeleton.

Conclusions

The relatively few assemblages of monastic burials currently available limits our knowledge of the skeletal biology of earlier monastic communities. Particular lacunae include a paucity of material from pre-Conquest houses or from nunneries. Although the investigation of some research themes, such as comparison of life in male and female monastic communities, must await the acquisition of suitable skeletal assemblages, there is much that remains to be done with the material we do have. Aspects which could be explored include questions of the distinctiveness of monastic communities compared with secular ones and the extent of differences in lifestyle between different monastic houses. As was discussed above, some work has already been done on the former, particularly in terms of diet and activity patterns. However it would be useful to extend this to other aspects. Problem orientated work on infectious disease is sorely needed. Careful study of infectious lesions in skeletal material may help us to understand patterning in lesion prevalence. For example, recording, in individual cases, whether lesions were remodelled (which would suggest that the individual recovered from the episode of infection which produced them) or were active at time of death (implying that the individual succumbed) would help address the role of the resistance to disease in influencing prevalences of skeletal lesions. It would also be useful to re-assess age at death in monastic and coeval lay skeletal collections using consistent methodology. (Meta-analysis of age at death using published osteological reports is unrewarding due to major differences in techniques for estimating adult age.) This may augment the very limited documentary evidence on age at death in monastic communities (Russell 1948, 189–192; Hatcher 1986), and may help determine whether the distinctiveness of monastic life is reflected in different mortality patterns.

Differences in lifestyles between the various monastic orders might be expected if the different ordinances had a real effect on the daily life of brethren. Using skeletal remains, it should be possible to investigate whether there is evidence of differences in diet, physical activity patterns or other aspects between some of the orders, although further assemblages would be required to explore this more fully. It would also be of value to investigate change over time in these respects, given the documentary evidence for a relaxation in regime among most monastic orders during the later Middle Ages, but for this we will need more precisely dated material.

In addition to exploring new research directions, we also need critically to re-assess what we think we already know about the skeletal biology of early monastic communities. A case in point is the notion that monastic burials show high levels of DISH and that this shows habitual gluttony and consequent obesity among brethren. Firstly, it is debatable whether the link between high body mass and DISH is strong enough for the frequency of DISH to be used as an indicator of obesity in past populations. Secondly, although the link between DISH and monastic burials seems widely accepted, it is not one which bears rigorous scrutiny: there is no published, statistically valid evidence for a higher rate of DISH among medieval monastic burials than among non-monastic medieval material. A proper, systematic re-evaluation of

the prevalence of the disease in medieval monastic and non-monastic assemblages would have to be carried out to provide a definitive solution to the question of whether DISH is more frequent in monastic groups. The meta-analysis conducted above suggests that the answer produced by such an exercise is likely to be negative.

Simply applying established scientific techniques to skeletal material is likely to yield significant new insights into monastic life in the Middle Ages, but methodological innovations are likely to increase the information potentially available from the study of human remains. For example, analysis of carbon and nitrogen stable isotopes and of bone biomechanics has already yielded useful insights and simply carrying out similar analyses on assemblages where this has not already been done would be useful. However, recent developments in these fields hold the promise that new dietary information and more fine-grained distinctions in activity patterns may be obtainable. As well as being greater in marine foods, $\delta^{15}N$ increases as one ascends a food chain, may be markedly elevated in freshwater fish and mammals, and varies in different classes of plants according to the way in which they obtain nitrogen (Katzenberg 2000). With careful analysis of the results, and the use of animal bone controls, information on these aspects of monastic diets may potentially be obtained. It is possible that analysis of carbon stable isotopes in bone mineral and in cholesterol extracted from bone may provide new dietary data; these components appear to provide information on whole diet rather than just the protein part (references in Mays 2000a). More advanced methods of measuring bone cross-sectional morphology, including high resolution CT scans (*e.g.* Bridges *et al.* 2000), are becoming more widely available, and allow more accurate estimation of bone strength and hence, potentially, the teasing out of more subtle differences in activity patterns.

Recent work indicates that stable isotopes of oxygen, strontium and lead in tooth enamel from ancient human remains may provide information on residential mobility (references in Mays 2000a). Studies of monastic burials might help shed light on whether particular monasteries recruited predominantly from the local population or whether intake came from further afield.

In summary, the amount of problem-orientated work on human remains from monastic cemeteries is rather small. Nevertheless, sufficient has been carried out to show the potential of human osteology for shedding light on medieval monasticism, and methodological developments continue to increase the information obtainable from human skeletal remains. There are few skeletal assemblages available which can be identified with certainty as of religious rather than layfolk, and if this continues to be the case our knowledge of the skeletal biology of monastic communities will necessarily remain rather patchy. In order to harness fully the potential of osteoarchaeology to shed light on monastic life, further assemblages are needed.

Acknowledgements

Thanks are due to Bill White and Brian Connell for permitting access to their unpublished data on the human bones from St Saviour, Bermondsey, and to York Archaeological Trust for supplying a copy of Jean Dawes' unpublished osteological report on the Nunnery of St Clement.

References

Anderson, T. (2001) The human remains. In M. Hicks and A. Hicks (eds) *St Gregory's Priory, Northgate, Canterbury Excavations 1988–1991*, 338–370. Canterbury, Canterbury Archaeological Trust.

Astill, G. G. and Wright, S. M. (1993) Perceiving patronage in the archaeological record: Bordesley Abbey. In M. Carver (ed.) *In Search of Cult: Archaeological Investigations in Honour of Philip Rahtz*, 125–137. Woodbridge, Boydell.

Aston, M. (2000) *Monasteries in the Landscape*. Stroud, Tempus.

Bond, C. J. (1988) Monastic fisheries. In M. Aston (ed.) *Medieval Fish, Fisheries and Fishponds in England*, 69–112. British Archaeological Reports (British Series) No. 182(i). Oxford, British Archaeological Reports.

Bridges, P. S., Blitz, J. H. and Salano M. C. (2000) Changes in long bone diaphysial strength with horticultural intensification in west-central Illinois. *American Journal of Physical Anthropology* 112, 217–238.

Burton, J. (1994) *Monastic and Religious Orders in Britain*. Cambridge, Cambridge University Press.

Coldstream, N. (1986) Cistercian architecture from Beaulieu to the dissolution. In C. Norton and D. Park (eds) *Cistercian Art and Architecture in the British Isles*, 139–159. Cambridge, Cambridge University Press.

Connell, B. and White, W. (forthcoming) The Human Bone. In A. Steele *Excavations at the Monastery of St Saviour, Bermondsey – Southwark*. London, Museum of London.

Coppack, G. (1990) *Abbeys and Priories*. London, Batsford / English Heritage.

Daniell, C. (1997) *Death and Burial in Medieval England*. London, Routledge.

Dawes, J. (nd) The Human Bones. In D. A. Brinklow, J. D. Dawes and S. Donaghey (eds), *Structural and Burial Evidence for the Nunnery of St Clement, Clementhorpe*, 4–24. Manuscript on file at York Archaeological Trust, York.

Dickinson, J. C. (1950) *The Origin of the Austin Canons*. London, SPCK.

Dickinson, J. C. (1961) *Monastic Life in Medieval England*. London, A and C Black.

Edwards, E. (1976) The human remains. In G. Lambrick and H. Woods, Excavations at the Second Site of the Dominican Priory, Oxford. *Oxoniensia* 41, 168–231.

Gies, F. and Gies J. (1990) *Life in a Medieval Village*. New York, Harper and Row.

Gilchrist, R. (1995) *Contemplation and Action: The Other Monasticism*. Leicester, Leicester University Press.

Greene, J. P. (1992) *Medieval Monasteries*. Leicester, Leicester University Press.

Harding, V. (1992) Burial choice and burial location in medieval London. In S. Bassett (ed.) *Death in Towns*, 119–135. Leicester, Leicester University Press.

Harvey, B. (1993) *Living and Dying in England 1100–1540. The Monastic Experience*. Oxford, Clarendon.

Hatcher, J. (1986). Mortality in the fifteenth century: some new evidence. *Economic History Review* 34, 19–38.

Hirst, S. M. and Wright, S. M. (1989) Bordesley Abbey church: a long-term research excavation. In R. Gilchrist and H. Mytum (eds) *The Archaeology of Rural Monasteries*, 295–311. British Archaeological Report (British Series) No. 203. Oxford, British Archaeological Reports.

Huggins, P. J. (1978) Excavation of a Belgic and Romano-British farm with middle Saxon cemetery and churches at Nazeingbury, Essex, 1975–6. *Essex Archaeology and History* 10, 29–116.

Janssen, H. A. M. and Maat, G. J. R. (1999) *Canons Buried in the "Stiftskapel" of the Saint Servaas Basilica at Maastricht AD 1070–1521*. Barge's Anthropologica No. 5. Leiden, Barge's Anthropologica.

Jones, H. H., Priest, J. D., Hayes, W. C., Tichenor, C. C. and Nagel, D. A. (1977) Humeral hypertrophy in response to exercise. *Journal of Bone and Joint Surgery* 59A, 204–208.

Julkunen, H., Heinonen, O. P. and Pyorala, K. (1971) Hyperostosis of the spine in an adult population. *Annals of the Rheumatic Diseases* 30, 605–612.

Jurmain, R. (1999) *Stories From the Skeleton: Behavioral Reconstruction in Human Osteology*. London, Gordon and Breach.

Katzenberg, M. A. (2000) Stable isotope analysis: a tool for studying past diet, demography, and life history. In M. A. Katzenberg and S. R. Saunders (eds) *Biological Anthropology of the Human Skeleton*, 305–327. New York, Wiley-Liss.

Knüsel, C. J., Göggel, S. and Lucy, D. (1997) Comparative degenerative joint disease of the vertebral column in the medieval monastic cemetery of the Gilbertine priory of St Andrew, Fishergate, York. *American Journal of Physical Anthropology* 103, 481–495.

Larsen, C. (1997) *Bioarchaeology: Interpreting Behavior From the Human Skeleton*. Cambridge, Cambridge University Press.

Lawrence, C. H. (1984) *Medieval Monasticism*. London, Longman.

Lawrence, C. H. (1994) *The Friars*. London, Longman.

Lenchik, L., Andresen, R., Sartoris, D.J., Sledge, P.A., Morton, D.J. and Barrett-Connor, E.L. (1996). Risk Factors for Diffuse Idiopathic Skeletal Hyperostosis. *Journal of Bone and Mineral Research* 11 Supplement 1, S578.

Mata, S., Fortin P.R., Fitzcharles, M., Starr, M.R., Joseph, L., Watts, C.S., Gore, B., Rosenberg, B., Chhem, R.K. and Esdaile, J.M. (1997) A Controlled Study of Diffuse Idiopathic Skeletal Hyperostosis. *Medicine* 76, 104–117.

Mays, S. (1991a) *The Medieval Burials from the Blackfriars Friary, School Street, Ipswich Suffolk*. Ancient Monuments Laboratory Report 16/91. London, English Heritage.

Mays, S. (1991b) *The Burials from the Whitefriars Friary Site, Buttermarket, Ipswich, Suffolk*. Ancient Monuments Laboratory Report 17/91. London, English Heritage.

Mays, S. (1995) The relationship between Harris lines and other aspects of skeletal development in adults and juveniles. *Journal of Archaeological Science* 22, 511–520.

Mays, S. (1997) Carbon stable isotope ratios in medieval and later human skeletons from northern England. *Journal of Archaeological Science* 24, 561–567.

Mays, S. (1998a) The Archaeological Study of Medieval English Human Populations. In J. Bayley (ed) *Science in Archaeology, An Agenda for the Future*, 195–210. London, English Heritage.

Mays, S. (1998b) *Notes on the 'Malmesbury Monk'*. Manuscript on file at the Ancient Monuments Laboratory, English Heritage, Portsmouth.

Mays, S. (1999a) Linear and appositional long bone growth in earlier human populations: a case study from medieval England. In R. D. Hoppa and C. M. Fitzgerald (eds) *Human Growth in the Past: Studies From Bones and Teeth*, 290–312. Cambridge, Cambridge University Press.

Mays, S. (1999b) A biomechanical study of activity patterns in a medieval human skeletal assemblage. *International Journal of Osteoarchaeology* 9, 68–73.

Mays, S. (2000a) New directions in the analysis of stable isotopes in excavated bones and teeth. In M. Cox and S. Mays (eds) *Human Osteology in Archaeology and Forensic Science*, 425–438. London, Greenwich Medical Media.

Mays, S. (2000b) Diffuse idiopathic skeletal hyperostosis (DISH) in skeletons from two medieval English cemeteries. *Journal of Palaeopathology* 12, 25–36.

McAlindon, T.E., Chaisson, C., LaValley, M., Zhang, Y., Kauppila, L. and Felson, D.T. (1996). Are individuals with diffuse idiopathic skeletal hyperostosis (DISH) at increased risk of diabetes mellitus (DM)? *Arthritis and Rheumatism* 39 Supplement, S113.

Moore, W. J. and Corbett, M. E. (1978) Dental caries experience in man. In N. H. Rowe, ed. *Diet, Nutrition and Dental Caries*, 3–19. Ann Arbor, University of Michigan School of Dentistry and the Dental Research Institute.

Palmer, C. F. R. (1891) Burials at the priories of the Black Friars. *The Antiquary* 23, 122–126; 24, 28–30, 76–79, 117–120, 265–269.

Polet, C. and Katzenberg, M. A. (2003) Reconstruction of the diet in a medieval monastic community from the coast of Belgium. *Journal of Archaeological Science* 30, 525–533.

Putnam, G. (1978) Analysis of the skeletal material. In P. J. Huggins, Excavation of a Belgic and Romano-British farm with middle Saxon cemetery and churches at Nazeingbury, Essex, 1975–6. *Essex Archaeology and History* 10, 29–116.

Radin, E. L. and Paul, I. L. (1971) Response of joints to impact loading. *Arthritis and Rheumatism* 14, 356–362.

Rogers, J. and Waldron, T. (2001) DISH and the monastic way of life. *International Journal of Osteoarchaeology* 11, 357–365.

de la Rua, C. and Ortue, J. M. (1992) Health conditions in a monastic community of the Basque Country (16th and 17th centuries). *Journal of Palaeopathology* 4, 193–200.

Ruff, C. (1992) Biomechanical analysis of archaeological human skeletal samples. In S. R. Saunders and M. A. Katzenberg (eds) *Skeletal Biology of Past Peoples: Research Methods*, 37–58. New York, Wiley-Liss.

Russell, J.C. (1948). *British Medieval Population*. Albuquerque, University of New Mexico Press.

Simon, S. R., Radin, E. L., Paul, I. L. and Rose, R. M. (1972) The response of joints to impact loading – II: in vivo behavior of subchondral bone. *Journal of Biomechanics* 5, 267–272.

Stones, J. A. (1989) *Three Scottish Carmelite Friaries. Excavations at Aberdeen, Linlithgow and Perth 1980–1986*. Society of Antiquaries of Scotland Monograph No. 6. Edinburgh, Society of Antiquaries of Scotland.

Stroud, G. and Kemp, R. L. (1993) *Cemeteries of St Andrew, Fishergate*. The Archaeology of York, Volume 12/2. York, York Archaeological Trust.

Vezyroglou, G., Mitropoulos, A., Kyriazis, N. and Antoniadis, C. (1996). A metabolic syndrome in diffuse idiopathic skeletal hyperostosis. A controlled study. *Journal of Rheumatology* 23, 672–676.

Waldron, T. (1985a) *A Report on the Human Bone From Merton Priory*. Ancient Monuments Laboratory Report 4483. London, English Heritage.

Waldron, T. (1985b) DISH at Merton Priory: evidence for a "new" occupational disease. *British Medical Journal* 291, 1762–1763.

White, E. (1993) The measure of the meat: monastic diet in medieval England. In, C. A. Wilson (ed) *Food for the Community. Special Diets for Special Groups*. Sixth Symposium on Food and Society. Edinburgh, Edinburgh University Press.

White, W. (1988). *The Cemetery of St Nicholas Sambles, London*. London, London and Middlesex Archaeology Society.

White, W. (2004) The Human Bone. In B. Barber, S. Chew, T. Dyson and B. White *The Cistercian Abbey of St Mary Stratford Langthorne, Essex*. MoLAS Monograph Series 18. London, Museum of London.

13. Text, Space and the Evidence of Human Remains in English Late Medieval and Tudor Disease Culture: Some Problems and Possibilities

Isla Fay

Illness is the night-side of life, a more onerous citizenship. Everyone who is born holds dual citizenship, in the kingdom of the well and in the kingdom of the sick. Although we all prefer to use only the good passport, sooner or later, each of us is obliged, at least for a spell, to identify ourselves as citizens of that other place (Sontag 1991, 3).

Lesions, language, and the social importance of disease

Diseases have two forms. The first is uniquely personal, the occurrence of physiological failure. This is the *fact* of disease itself, recognised, in the burial record, by characteristic lesions in human tissues. Charting the past profile of this phenomenon is the work (as traditionally perceived) of the palaeopathologist.

The second form is *conceptual*, made up of language and discourse. As such, it leaves no corporeal residue, and is thought to be invisible to the palaeopathologist or funerary archaeologist. And yet, it is the conceptual type that determines what it is like to take up that 'more onerous citizenship' in 'the kingdom of the sick' (Sontag 1991, 3). It is *disease culture*, and it consists of all kinds of thinking attached to the very notion of disease itself.

The definition of these abstractions is not pre-determined by the nature of the physical, *factual* form; rather, it is influenced by human expectations – expectations of the functional capacity of the diseased individual, his or her economic productivity, personal culpability and social usefulness (Finlay 1999). Other explanatory frameworks that are generally employed to account for events in the physical world – be they theological, ecological or cosmographical – also influence ideas about health and sickness. Consequently, the processes of naming, grouping and explaining diseases are culturally contingent and do not transcend time and space. In the words of M. D. Grmek:

Notions of disease and even of particular diseases...are explanatory models of reality, not its constitutive elements...They interpret a complex empirical reality and presuppose a certain medical philosophy or pathological system of reference. So, for example, one can say that there exists a person who is sickly, coughs, spits blood and grows thin, and one can say that the bacillus that pervades his organism and produces characteristic lesions on his lungs...also exists in the strict sense of the word, but one cannot say the same for tuberculosis. Its existence is bound up with a well-articulated conceptual structure and a particular medical ideology (1989, 1).

The 'conceptual structures' of disease culture develop out of the relationship between, and the circumstances surrounding, both the diagnostician and the sick individual. For example, when certain sixteenth-century civic activists in Flanders and England congratulated themselves that:

the dysfygured syghtes of...uysured pore men ar not now sene, all roughe and scouruy and ronnynge with matter both vgely to loke on and euyll smellynge to the nose, and ouer that, to some tender stomakes lothsome... (Salter 1926, 69).

(the disfigured sights of the faces of poor men are no longer seen, all rough and scurvy and running with matter, which is both ugly to look on and evil smelling to the nose, and moreover, loathsome to some stomachs...)

they were not, as a twenty-first century mind might suppose, making an empirical survey of the realities of contemporary urban standards of living – or at least, not in the modern sense of the phrase. The tract was that of the 1525 Ypres Poor Relief scheme, whose dual purpose was to rid society of 'counterfeit' (or fraudulent) beggars who chose not to work, and to identify the genuinely sick and incapacitated members of the poor who should be transferred to the seclusion of a hospice (Salter 1926; Rawcliffe 2004b). Informed by our own concepts of public health, we read this passage in terms of germ theory and deprivation. These were not, however, the conceptual structures that governed how its 'contagious' subjects were originally seen.

The gravity of the tract's proposals reflected social anxiety about a new and virulent epidemic known to English contemporaries as the *pox*. As with many other diseases, contemporaries considered the *pox* (infamously associated with illicit or promiscuous sexual activity) to be linked to personal transgressions. Medical theory, expressed in the increasingly popular *regimen sanitatis*, counselled against overindulgence in the 'agents necessary to life'; which included the consumption of food and drink, the evacuation of sexual or other bodily excretions, and physical rest, a scheme that tessellated neatly with Christian condemnations of excess, immorality and sloth (Rawcliffe 1995a; Arrizabalaga *et al.* 1997; Wear 2000). The poor of Ypres – who (according to the tract's authors) appeared lazy, gluttonous and drunk, and revelled in 'other vyces not to be named' – were accountable for their own physical suffering because they paid no heed to the golden rule of 'temperance' (Salter 1926, *passim*). These were *standards of living* in a pre-modern sense. The physical condition of beggars had ramifications for society as a whole. In the same way that a man's body required a moderate lifestyle, so did the 'the hole corps' (or *body politic*) of the civic community. Contagious and immoral paupers seemingly assaulted the well-being of society on every level, spreading decay and disorder in the urban environment (Salter 1926, *passim*). Evidently, the symptomatology of their encrusted, scaly heads was framed not only by the empirical realities of disease lesions, but also by *social symbolism*.

Diseases, as they are constructed in language, therefore, cease to be wholly personal and become interpersonal (Horden 2000, 21; Hsu 2002, 9). Sometimes, the notions attached to particular diseases translate into the 'punitive or sentimental fantasies' of the sort Sontag sought to expose: "not the real geography [of the kingdom of the sick], but stereotypes of national character" (1991, 3). Social expectations also determine the content of medical praxis and systems of support. They inform what kind of healing personnel should be consulted – whether secular or clerical, mortal or divine – and at what point in a disease process. Similarly, they determine which therapies or prophylactic measures might be employed in order to maintain or regain health. Until very recently, investigations in the plane of disease culture were the preserve of medical historians and anthropologists (Rawcliffe 1995a; Getz 1998; Pelling 1998; Wear 2000; Hsu 2002).

This kind of interpretation is thought to be fundamentally different to that practised by other scholars (including palaeopathologists) who analyse the *material* manifestations of illness. From the perspective of disease culture, we need to ask if the expectations and explanations surrounding pathological events vary across time and place, and if there is any merit in seeking (as a focus upon the primary phenomenon of disease lesions seemingly encourages) an essential or *common* disease experience.

Disciplinary distinctions

Scholarship has become both polarised and dogmatic over the issue of disease as a material entity. According to Harley (1999, 418) 'the view of disease from within the history of medicine is...very different from that deployed by palaeopathologists or historical epidemiologists'. It appears that the first, exclusively hermeneutic perspective interprets the nuances of past disease experiences by restructuring them in their own cultural terms. The second, materialist approach inevitably misrepresents and obscures the original event with anachronistic and facile conflations of distinct medical paradigms. How did the work of 'disease-materialists' come to be seen as so myopic? Are Harley's claims justified?

For their part, palaeopathologists and osteo-archaeologists have traditionally been quite catholic in their methods, engaging with the evidential bases of anthropology, history and sociology (Wells 1965a; Roberts 1986, 1991; Grauer 1991, *passim*; Bassett 1992). More recently they have turned to these allied disciplines not only for corroborative evidence, but for theoretical positions as well (Roberts and Cox 2003, 1, 221 ff., 383–4; Lewis 2002a). This development has opened up new possibilities for research into disease culture. However, methodological, taxonomic and specimen-based research (which provided the analytical and diagnostic tools of the discipline from its early, post-war development) also continues today.

The (so-called) 'case study' – which describes the appearance of lesions in specific disease processes – traditionally represents the largest proportion of palaeo-pathological output (Larsen 1997; Mays 1997; Roberts and Cox 2003, 22–23). These studies were originally undertaken with a cumulative academic project in mind: to chart out the historical prevalence of the full range of osteologically visible diseases, thereby demonstrating how the *modern* disease burden developed. Calvin Wells, a medical doctor who wrote many articles on palaeo-pathological subjects in the 1960s and 1970s, captured this forward-looking spirit in his paper 'Two mediaeval cases of malignant disease':

> Today [carcinomata]...in bone are extremely common. In early burial grounds, they are remarkably rare...In view of th[is] rarity...it is important to record all specimens which are discovered. Eventually, a pattern of types and distributions may emerge (Wells 1964, 1611).

The heirs of the 'case study' – the palaeopathological sections of archaeological cemetery studies – pursue the same aim, endeavouring to capsulize the raw material for future palaeoepidemiological study. However, the nature of bone itself has forced a reappraisal of the original project (Wood *et al.* 1992; Waldron 1994). Similarly, it has proved very difficult to generate meaningful prevalence rates for diseases in the past owing to the variable ways in which the relevant data was collected, archived and published (Roberts and Cox 2003, 384). Because of this, case studies and bone reports have attracted criticism for focusing exclusively on the morphology and prevalence of skeletal lesions, at the expense of analyzing the human context of disease. Due to the constraints of time and funding, it is not always possible (particularly in a commercial context) to produce a report upon a skeletal assemblage which not only records its pathological and biological parameters, but also situates it within a social and spatial context. Rebecca Gowland has recently observed that palaeopathological findings thus risk becoming *objectified*, rendered 'immutable' and 'universal'; that is independent from the 'historically ...*specific* condition of human identity' and irrelevant to the (subjective) interpretation of the cultural context of the funerary environment (Gowland 2004, 136).

Methodological improvements continue to develop, and faith is again placed in the possibility of reconstructing patterns of diseases in the past (Boldsen 2001; Brickley and McKinley 2004). But scholarly anxiety over the situation has generated a trenchant position, namely that palaeopathologists should seek out avenues of research in which the evidence of skeletal material is more widely, and immediately, useful (Roberts and Cox 2003, 383). As we shall see, the original project's perceived sterility is perhaps the most visible aspect of palaeopathology to scholars outside the discipline. Yet, palaeopathologists have, for a long time, endeavoured to augment case studies and bone reports with wider research imperatives. Wells himself, in concert with contemporary colleagues, played a major role in establishing this tradition, when he sought out evidence for the 'ways of life', living conditions and even the medical culture of past peoples (Wells 1964, 1611; Wells 1965a and b; Weiss and Møller-Christensen 1971). Particularly over the last twenty years, a model of palaeopathological study has developed which challenges the view of lesions as singular, isolated events. Researchers are now expected to demonstrate *why* and *how* they develop with reference to wider physiological processes and the total sum of disease experiences suffered by an individual. This encourages a broader, ecologically and culturally relevant view of disease (Larsen 1997, 6–63; Gowland 2004, 137). These *biocultural* principles have placed issues such as status, social organisation and human behaviour at the forefront of palaeopathological enquiry.

In tandem with the long term drive to evaluate individual lesions in the context of the body as a social entity, is a dialogue with archaeologists (further stimulated by the continental influence of *anthropologie de terrain*), which encourages scrutiny of exactly how diseased bodies were deposited within graves, and their relationships to the wider funerary environment (Duday, this volume; Duday *et al.* 1990). This theme has been explored most fully in *osteobiographies*, that is analyses of the health status of individuals with reference to the spatial and cultural aspects of their burial context. Funerary behaviour is here understood to be a reflection of attitudes towards a diseased individual, and, by extension, towards the

concepts of disease and functional impairment themselves (Knüsel 1999; Gowland 2004). Multidisciplinary approaches to disease in the burial record have also occasionally uncovered direct evidence of healing practice in the form of remedial or prophylactic artefacts, which can be linked to contemporary medical ideologies and theories (Janssens 1987; Knüsel *et al.* 1995; Knüsel 2002).

However, palaeopathologists *en masse* have not addressed how disease as a conceptual structure was understood in the past, seemingly preferring a narrative grounded in present, biomedical paradigms. Indeed, they are proud of the extent to which their subject informs medical science. The usefulness to clinical leprology of Vilhelm Møller-Christensen's analysis of medieval human remains is, for example, justly celebrated (Andersen and Manchester 1992, 121–122; Roberts and Manchester 1995, 3; Bennike 2002, 137). No one would doubt the value of palaeopathology in this respect. But for those whose primary concern focuses upon the 'historically specific' and 'culturally contingent', the biocultural agenda is seemingly eclipsed by a large body of work which highlights the particularity and consistency of disease lesions over time. In a characteristically witty and painterly article, published in 2000, the historian, Peregrine Horden, contended that:

> in the history of pre-modern – let us say, pre-nineteenth-century – public health measures, sewers and skeletons are not quite enough. A materialist-biological account will clearly capture some of the story...But it will do that only in the narrow terms of biomedicine and demography, ignoring other aspects...such as purification, or the sense of community (18).

Horden challenges that it is through examination of the *actions* ('ritual'), *symbolism* and *metaphor* generated by disease experiences, that the notion of disease is itself understood. Scrutiny of contemporary documents is, he suggests, the best way to reconstruct the disease cultures of the past – the means that 'avoids anachronistic 'biologism'' (2000, 28). Despite the rhetoric, Horden's article demonstrates an underlying sympathy towards analysis of the spatial and material aspects of disease culture. In other quarters, a greater sense of frustration is displayed towards the perceived aims of palaeopathologists. Witness Harley's response to Dutour's edited volume, *L'Origine de la syphilis en Europe: avant ou après 1493?*:

> The old argument about whether medieval European society experienced syphilis, as currently defined, has little relevance for historians of medicine. *New diseases have to be defined in order to be experienced, so it is their invention and the social response [to them] that is of interest to historians*...Instead of biomedical specificity, perhaps we should be thinking in terms of sociocultural specificity (1999, 418, 434, my emphasis).

The issue of *specificity* (by which historians mean the specificity of pathogens) is an important one, although palaeopathologists and funerary archaeologists have yet to address it in detail. Syphilis, the argument goes, only exists in medical culture after 1905, when the treponeme was isolated for the first time. Other terms with which it has been associated – including the *pox* – were more inclusive than this purely bacterial identity (Arrizabalaga *et al.* 1997). To put it another way, both syphilis and the *pox* are constituent parts of the *second form* of disease. (In Grmek's terminology, they are 'explanatory models' of an 'empirical reality'). Both may, in a given time and place, share features on the *primary* physiological level. But this relationship is neither essential nor universal (Arrizabalaga *et al.* 1997). To contemporaries, the *pox* shared aetiological and semiotic associations with both scurvy (as we have seen in the Ypres poor relief scheme) and leprosy – each disease was a more or less external expression of a fundamental internal corruption (Boorde 1552, fos 10v–11r; Pelling 1998, 95). The resonances and inter-connectedness of disease in the medieval past are obscured, therefore, by unreflective deployment of modern diagnostic criteria.

Yet, specificity does not pose insuperable problems; there is still life (as it were) in the funerary record. In the absence of medical intervention, some chronic diseases (*including* treponemal diseases, but also leprosy, tuberculosis, crippling osteopathies and, potentially, some congenital mental disorders) have serious and obvious consequences for their sufferers: consequences that would have been recognised by their immediate community and which can still be inferred, osteologically, by us (Roberts and Manchester 1995; Ward 1996). Modern palaeo-pathological explorations of disease culture re-evaluate the consequences of physiological changes *for each individual body* in which they are displayed. The diagnosis of 'specific, biomedical' conditions (like syphilis) is thus useful only in so far as it facilitates communication between scholars, or is *demonstrably* consonant with historical nosology in a particular time and place.

With leprosy at any rate, we can be additionally assured of some measure of semiotic consistency. Excavation of the cemetery of the leprosarium of St James and St Mary Magdalene, Chichester, and other, similar institutions, confirms that the radical changes of physiology that are today called *leprous*, were also considered *leprous* in the medieval past. The same lesions in the bones of the face, hands, feet and legs are present in each case (Lewis *et al.* 1995; Fay 2002; Lewis 2002b). This remains true even if we accept that, at points in the past, 'leprosy' was a term that embraced an eclectic mixture of symptoms and spiritual or social connotations that are no longer associated with the disease as it is understood in the West. This is a departure from the general thrust of historical scholarship over the last twenty years which has relegated medieval leprosy to the position of a diagnostic or social catchall, an approach perhaps best represented by the evocative words of R. I. Moore, first published in 1987:

the diagnosis of leprosy [in the medieval period] was capable of providing...a flexible principle upon which almost anybody might be excluded from the community on the basis of a minimal consensus that they ought to be (79).

The fingers of historiography penetrate deeply into the cognitive plane of disease. But disease culture is not just about the sum of intellectual achievements, epistemic campaigns, or the diffusion of medical doctrine. It is also about praxis, manners, customs and *attitudes* at the level of individual interaction. Funerary archaeology has the potential to contribute significantly to our understanding of the 'definition' and 'experience' of bodily illness, as well as the 'social response' to it: features that historians consider to be the quintessence of disease culture. Concomitantly, the palaeopathological and historical projects are not as distinctive as they at first appear. One enlists documentary sources to reconstruct how disease culture informs human behaviour and the use of space (Jenner 1997a; Horden 2000). The other employs *material* evidence of the same phenomenon. An examination of both archives and archaeological reports from Norwich – 'the most healthful city in England' according to a long tradition of civic propaganda – serves to highlight how human remains can reveal aspects of disease culture 'at work' in the most layered, structured and particular way (Rawcliffe 2004a and b; Fay *in prep.*).

The evidence from Norwich: a healthful and pleasant citye

Burial was the last word in an ongoing discourse about the body, articulated at some length during the medieval and Tudor period. To understand this fully it is necessary to consider briefly the concepts of *symbolism*, *social cohesion*, *purity* and *pollution* which historians have identified as the indigenous categories of 'public health' in the past (Horden 2000).

In the late medieval and Tudor mentality, there existed a close association between order (or 'health') in the social hierarchy and order (or 'cleanliness') in the urban environment. These concepts sustained a dynamic relationship with one another and were expressed through analogies with Christ's mystical body, the revivified ancient concept of the *body politic* and current medical theory (Salter 1926, 9; James 1983; Mayer 1989; Rubin 1991; Pelling 1998, 64; Logan and Adams, 2000, *passim*; Maddern 2004). By the late sixteenth century, Norwich had developed a unique reputation for successful management on both fronts.

Medieval and early modern citizens thought that the environment played a crucial role in spreading disease. Many of the waste products which naturally accumulated in the nooks and crannies of urban space – such as stagnant water, hay, muck, blood, offal and, not least, the 'ded and stynkyng' corpses of humans and animals – were considered sources of pestilential vapours (Horrox 1994). This idea was familiar to contemporaries through vernacular manuscripts, printed tracts and oral culture from at least the late fourteenth century onwards, when an 'information revolution' met and stimulated the desire for human control over the natural world (MacCraken

1961, 702; Henderson 1992; Horrox 1994, 95–110, 158–206; Murray Jones 1994, 100; Rawcliffe 1995b, 75–81; Jones 2004; Rutledge 2004). Accordingly, Norwich's urban oligarchy waged regular campaigns to clean up the urban environment in order to preserve the health of the populace (Rawcliffe 2004b; Fay *in prep.*). In 1558, the Norwich born physician and polymath, William Cuningham, celebrated these principles in a 'prospect' or plan of the city (Fig. 13.1). This, in combination with the accompanying text, constituted a self-conscious emulation of the Hippocratic chorographic text *Airs, Waters, Places* – the basis of the medieval idea that local topography directly influenced health status. Norwich's lush, green open spaces and fast-flowing river featured prominently in Cuningham's (somewhat idealised) plan, arguing for its status as a naturally 'healthful and pleasant citye' (Cuningham 1968, f. 174; Lloyd 1978, 148–169; Pelling 2004; Fay *in prep.*).

The idea that a locality could be more or less salubrious would have been self-evident to Norwich's residents, who could observe the phenomenon in practice. In 1570, the civic authorities conducted a city-wide census of the poor, which demonstrated that some neighbourhoods contained higher concentrations of chronically crippled or bedridden residents than others (Pound 1971). One northern district, the ward of Fyebridge, housed a number of paupers who could no longer work owing to physical incapacity (Fig. 13.2). The head count of chronic sick – as

a proportion of the total number of recorded paupers – was higher in Fyebridge than in either of the neighbouring (but otherwise similar) wards of Coslany and Colgate (6.4%, 3.2% and 4.5%, respectively, Pound 1971, 68–93). A different state of affairs prevailed in the central districts situated south of the river, closer to the economic hub. The rich and populous ward of Mid Wymer, for example, housed the smallest proportion of poor compared to every other district in Norwich. Additionally, those paupers who were resident in the ward seem to have enjoyed relatively good health (Pound 1971, 11, 60–63). Widowhood, old age and low-income employment accounted for impoverishment in Mid Wymer; a very different picture to that presented by the 'lame', 'deaf', 'blind', 'lunatick' and 'veri sick' residents in the north, where the burden of social dependency must have been correspondingly heavier (Pound 1971, *passim*).

Ordinary men and women contributed to the elite's sanitizing agenda with alacrity, often presenting each other in the local neighbourhood ('leet') courts for environmental infractions (Hudson 1892; Rees Jones 2000, 134–140). For example, in 1390/1 (whilst national epidemics ravaged the country, reportedly carrying off many children and adolescents), one local resident, William Gerard, was accused of depositing the decomposing corpse of a horse in the high street, thereby encouraging infection (*habuit unum equum per longum tempus iacentem in Regia via iuxta ecclesiam Sancti Michaelis de Colgate in magnum abhominacionem*

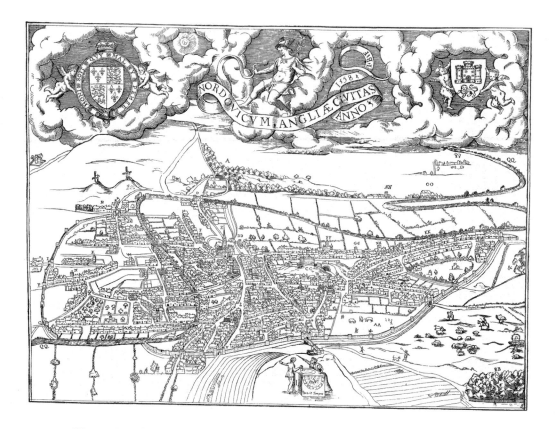

Figure 13.1. Cuningham's Map of Norwich. Courtesy of the Norfolk Heritage Centre.

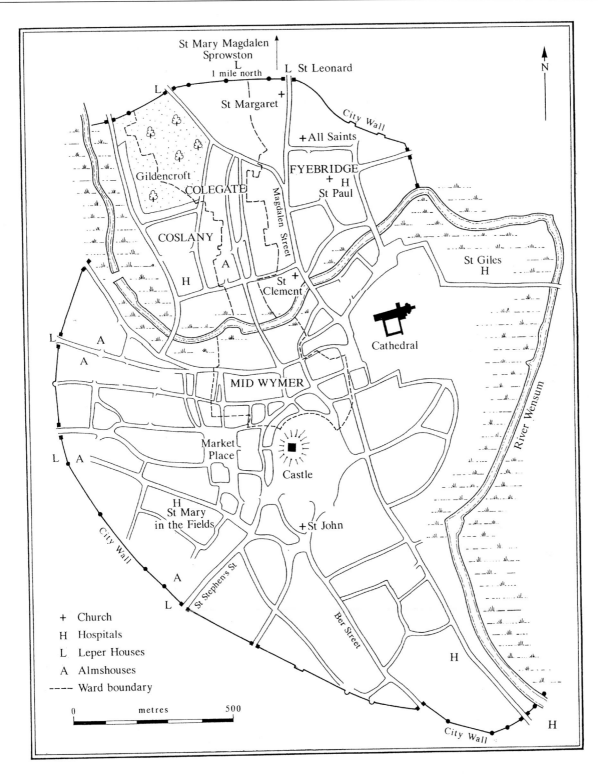

Figure 13.2. Places mentioned in the text. Map by Philip Judge, School of Environmental Sciences, University of East Anglia.

et corrupcionem: Hudson 1892, 75). Like their counterparts in London, the jurors serving in Norwich leet courts probably had a fixed series of routine inquisitions or questions to put to witnesses concerning stagnant waste, the control of animals and the presence of lepers in the neighbourhood, all of which might imperil the health of others (Carpenter 1861, 287–292; Hudson 1892, *passim*; Rawcliffe 2004b, 304–7). Taking the metaphor of the body politic to its logical conclusions, the civic elite had to preserve harmony in the smallest social units, including marriages, households and neighbourhoods. At the same time as reporting potential sources of miasma (which themselves promoted neighbourly discord) the citizens were encouraged to inform on the activities of prostitutes, night-walkers, illegal traders and strangers, whose behaviour also seemed to threaten urban order and purity (Maddern 2004). This prolonged campaign to eliminate all potential sources of urban 'pollution' (which, in the sixteenth century saw the implementation of a scheme not unlike that adopted in Ypres) led one contemporary commentator, with a dose of sarcasm, to label Norwich "another Utopia" because the people lived 'in such good order', the streets were 'kept so cleanly', and there was hardly a beggar to be seen (Park 1804, 170; Rawcliffe 2004b, 306, 322–324).

Norwich citizens were, therefore, acutely aware of the relationship between the health of each individual component of the body politic, and that of society as a whole. This picture can be amplified from the archives of other civic governments of the period (Sabine 1933, 1934 and 1937; Carr 1997; Goldberg 1999 and 2001). Historians have long recognised the wider implications of campaigns against 'pigs and prostitutes', demonstrating that anxiety about transience, difficult interpersonal relationships and the economy were expressed in terms of assaults upon the urban body (Sennett 1994; Jenner 1997b; Goldberg 1999, 2001). The role played by the fabric of medieval and early modern towns in generating and communicating disease culture has also been readily recognised (Jenner 1997a ; Horden 2000). But the importance of the actual, physical body and of diseases as real, *material* entities has been overlooked in recent scholarship. This is surprising because the register of ideas that incorporated the axis of putrefaction, disease, community and environment in contemporary mentalities existed within a larger, cosmological and teleological framework, in which the physical body was central.

The cosmos, the body and the burial record in concept and practice

During the many epidemics which occurred periodically from 1348 to the seventeenth century, the putrefaction of substances within the environment was thought to derive not only from immediate causes – privies, muck heaps, stagnant water and the like – but also from an 'ultimate' cause, the admonitory will of God. This principle centred on the idea that man was a *microcosm* of the universe: a Christianised version of an Ancient Grecian theory, which itself informed the influential Hippocratic treatise *Airs, Waters, Places*. Changes within the physical world were thought to impact directly upon the physiological functions of the body. Over all these things, God of course had control; fundamentally, therefore, physical corruption had *spiritual* significance (Lloyd 1978; Horrox 1994, 173–4; Rawcliffe 1995a; Horden 2000).

In conjunction with these external, cosmological influences upon the body, an individual's predispositions or behaviour were considered of prime importance in disease formation. In a fourteenth-century plague tract (known as the *Treatise of John of Burgundy* to historians, itself the most famous and widely circulated of all the advice literature produced in response to successive epidemics) one author postulated that the effects of corrupt air were contingent upon a *primary* putrefaction, located within the body (Keiser 2003). Men and women "stuffed full of evil humours" would be most at risk "for as Galen says in the book of fevers, the body suffers no corruption unless the material of the body has a tendency towards it" (Horrox 1994, 185). Putrefaction in the environment, then, had to encounter putrefaction within the body for it to have a harmful effect. By the same token, putrefaction of the body contributed to the miasmic burden of the environment; as we have seen, unburied corpses (whether human or animal) were often cited as a contributory factor in generating epidemic disease (Henderson 1992; Pickett 1994; Rawcliffe 1995b, 78; Harding 2000, 175).

The putrefactive process (as precipitated in the living body) was part of God's plan for each human soul. Advice manuals, in counselling their readership to prepare for death, encouraged sufferers with the exhortation that "infirmity before death is like a purgatory...it cometh by divine dispensation". A temporary test was necessary for each man, "to the end that he go not to *eternal* pain" (Comper 1977, 63). "The longest vice and sin" naturally resulted in the most deforming and debilitating diseases. But the rewards in such cases (including leprosy) were also proportionally greater. The corruption and putrefaction which took place in the body – in disease and after death – were, therefore, part of "the career of the Christian"; a staging post in the journey to resurrection and final judgement when the body (bound in life to an inevitable process of decay) would be purified; its deformities rectified in the final triumph over decomposition (Bynum 1995, *passim*; Wear 2000, 138). The second mental register of contemporary medico-spiritual culture therefore comprised an intricate but stable relationship between the cosmos, man, death, decay and resurrection (Fig. 13.3). The final, earthly platform for the expression of these ideas was, of course, the burial ground, where spatial organisation signified an assumed hierarchy of worthiness to mortal and divine onlookers (Bymun 1995, 204; Harding 2000, 139). Did those marked out by disease receive differentiated treatment in this context?

Normally, every member of the Christian community aspired to a familiar model of funerary observances and protocols, whose structure, length and content depended upon their status, the resources available and the payment of a mortuary fee (Harding 1989, 113, 123; Wieck 1999; Harding 2000, 176–184). Sometimes, however, circumstances contrived to produce a situation in which people could not be given the kind of burial they and their family might have hoped for. For example, a succession of epidemics in England and on the continent in the fourteenth century necessitated the excavation of grave pits in order that large numbers of corpses could be quickly disposed of (Hawkins 1990; Harding, 2000, 185). Anxiety amongst the middle and upper classes (who feared a similarly ignoble fate) and a pre-existing association between pit burials and heresy apparently led to a new scrutiny of burial practices in some European countries following the first waves of plague (Wakefield and Evans 1969, 274; Cohn 2000, 29). Other members of the community, whether during times of epidemics or not, never exercised much agency over the form and manner of their eventual interment. These, the very poor, were forced to rely on the chance and circumstance of a charitable burial, a feature of medieval life compelled not only by practical necessity, but also by a doctrinal commission. Burying the dead was one of the seven 'Comfortable Works' – a series of spiritually sanctioned, practical obligations which medieval men and women seem to have taken seriously if the building of hospitals (the institutional manifestation of the Comfortable Works) is a guide (Rawcliffe 2003). We might anticipate, therefore, that exigency and poverty were the features that impacted with most force upon traditional burial mores, and were responsible for the truncation or abandonment of normal funerary observances. The infamous, distinctive practices adopted in the burial of suicides and criminals suggests, however, that we must take seriously the idea that spiritual and personal status also influenced the exact form of an individual's final interment (Gordon and Marshall 2000, *passim*). As we have seen, the perceived role of personal agency in bringing about disease encouraged an ambivalent

response to the chronic sick, who simultaneously might be held responsible for their own suffering, and viewed as receptacles of divine grace (Rawcliffe 1995a, 8). Was this also reflected in funerary provisions?

Certain, post-medieval commentators made clear that they expected the most alarming and wretched members of the chronic sick to be given a distinctive status by their burial. The eighteenth-century antiquarian, Francis Blomefield, related a local tradition in his *Essay Towards a Topographical History of Norfolk*, which united the themes of disease with religious and material 'pollution'. He described a tomb in the churchyard of St Clement that was orientated on a north-south alignment – an obvious inversion of the Christian norm. Under this, the legend went, lay the body of a leper (Blomefield 1806, 459–46; Fig. 13.2). According to Blomefield, the parish agreed to accept this individual only after several others had refused to do so. Yet those responsible for carrying out the interment clearly intended that the grave and its occupant should be visibly distinguished from the mass of the Christian faithful. North-south graves of the Reformation period have been interpreted as "an easily recognisable piece of symbolism indicating that the [buried individual] was considered a heretic and an outcast from the Christian church" (Duffy 2001, 131).

Blomefield suspected that some of the story's details were false (he conjectured, for example, that lepers in fact had a parochial right to be interred at St Clement's), although he did not challenge the appropriateness of this mode of inhumation. The story – whatever its provenance or veracity – is allusive for eighteenth-century attitudes towards disease and status, but cannot be read as a straightforward reflection of medieval practice. Leprosy itself seems to have diminished and perhaps disappeared entirely in England by the time Blomefield was writing (Roberts and Cox 2003, 330); the picture he painted was, therefore, inevitably based upon retrospective and received opinions. Despite both Victorian glosses of the subject and contemporary associations between disease and sin in sermon literature, lepers had unique role in the medieval Christian community (Peyroux 2000, 185). Whilst attitudes certainly hardened from the fourteenth century (when an increased emphasis was placed upon the risks of contagion) there is no doubt that in the high Middle Ages the leper was seen as a recipient of divine favour. The opportunity to regain spiritual health was a situation "worthy of honour as well as pity": leprosy chastised sinners whilst "simultaneously providing the occasion for their redemption" (Rawcliffe 1995a, 1; Satchel 1998, 26; Rawcliffe 2004b, 305; Rawcliffe *forthcoming*). Lepers (and the non-leprous, but spiritually distinguished members of the healthy community who associated with them) also enjoyed special importance owing to the perceived efficacy of their prayers and their renunciation of worldly attachments (Peyroux 2000).

Fortunately, Blomefield's legend can be counterpoised with osteoarchaeological findings to develop a more

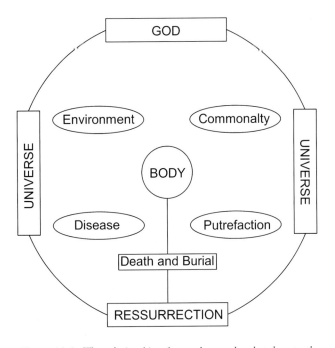

Figure 13.3. The relationship of cosmology and eschatology to the human body.

nuanced picture. Material evidence for the burial treatment of 'lepers' – along with other chronically sick citizens and the very poor – is plentiful in Norwich's medieval archaeological record, providing a unique insight into the final stages of their 'Christian careers'. Specifically, the study of human remains provides an opportunity to challenge the caricature of the outcast leper, and provides a context from which to understand medieval attitudes towards chronic disease in general.

Burial Locations for the Chronic Sick in Medieval and Tudor Norwich

In Norwich, several institutions made specific provisions for the burial of the chronic sick. The hospitals of St Giles (the Great Hospital), Norman's Spital (also known as St Paul's) and the *leprosarium* of St Mary Magdalen, Sprowston, all had their own burial grounds, into which were deposited the bodies of the more or less decrepit residents. There is no evidence that Norwich's (several) other hospitals, alms houses and *leprosaria* provided any similar service; like the one mentioned by Blomefield, they probably buried their dead in the cemetery of the parish in which they stood. No archaeological excavations have taken place in these areas to date, although a sewer trench outside the hospital of St Mary Magdalen did reveal a small number of remains apparently indicating the presence of *lepromatous leprosy* (the low resistance form of Hansen's Disease/leprosy that leads to facial disfigurement) within the buried population (Fig. 13.2; Norfolk Historic Environment Record 670-NF67). Excavation *has*, however, uncovered comprehensive evidence for the manner of burial of similarly affected individuals prior to the advent of this house and of Norwich's six other, suburban *leprosaria*. During the tenth and eleventh centuries, at least nineteen and possibly as many as thirty-five individuals suffering from *lepromatous leprosy* were buried in the parish cemetery of St John Ber Street, situated to the south of the old Saxon defences at an important entry point of the city (Fig. 13.2; Anderson 1996; Shepherd Popescu, *forthcoming*).

The burial context of one of these individuals helps to demonstrate attitudes towards disfiguring disease at this time. Skeleton 13055, a male of about 16–19 years of age, was buried in a chalk and clay-lined grave, suggesting that he enjoyed distinguished personal status in life (Anderson 1996, 54; Shepherd Popescu, *forthcoming*). Additionally, this individual suffered from chronic infection in the lower limbs and rhinomaxillary area of the face, indicating soft tissue damage almost certainly caused by *Mycobacterium leprae*. Whether his community would have called him a *leper*, however, is currently unclear. The religious and cultural movements which brought about the foundation of the first English leper houses – themselves an important indicator of early twelfth-century attitudes towards the disease – began after the Norman Conquest, as the result of a stimulus that St John's itself will, in future, help to explain (Shepherd Popescu, *forthcoming*).

Nonetheless, this young individual would have suffered observable physiological changes, loss of sensation and, probably, painful 'reaction' episodes which caused tissue injury and illness (Jopling, 1984; Stanford and Stanford 2002). Resources and personal reputation were, in this case, seemingly more important contributors to social standing than sickness.

Between *c*.1100 and 1468, one of Norwich's most northerly parishes, St Margaret's (part of the impoverished Fyebridge ward, mentioned above), seems to have catered especially for the burial of individuals with a range of debilitating chronic diseases, including leprosy (Fig. 13.2). The cemetery is already known to palaeopathologists through the work of Ann Stirland who identified in the population cases of tuberculosis; treponemal disease; non-specific, chronic infections; nutritional deficiencies; trauma and a possible instance of a neuromuscular dystrophy (Stirland 1994; Stirland 1996; Stirland 1997; Stirland, *forthcoming*). All of these conditions imply personal histories characterised, to a greater or lesser extent, by impoverished environmental circumstances, periods of pain and illness and compromised physical ability (Jopling 1984; Roberts and Manchester 1995, 151; Stirland 1997). It might have been difficult for several of these individuals to find remunerative employment within the city's economy; as we shall see, many were seemingly forced to rely on the Christian charitable obligation to bury the dead.

The cemetery is remarkable not only for the startling catalogue of human suffering evident in its human remains, but also for the range of burial customs found there. Altogether, it provides a rather different picture to the Ber Street site. Here, economy and disease seemed to have produced a cocktail of social responses to the deceased. St Margaret's was partially excavated in 1987, yielding a total of 436 articulated skeletons. Of these, over 40 per cent were buried in graves containing more than one individual. Forty-nine graves were excavated which housed between two and seven corpses each, and, in one case, twelve individuals were placed in a single grave. Many corpses within these group interments were also deposited in a prone (face down) position, or otherwise aligned on an axis deviating from the east-west norm (Stirland, *forthcoming*). Figure 13.4 (Grave 480) illustrates the kind of practice employed. The grave was constructed in order to hold four bodies, one of which was deposited in a prone position. Like the 'leper grave' observed by Blomefield (1806), it was aligned on a north-south axis. To contemporary eyes, the situation would have seemed abject.

Across the site as a whole, however, no simple relationship existed between disease status and the inversions of normative funerary practice; most of the conditions seen (with the exception of the possible case of neuromuscular dystrophy) were represented in both the (normative) individual and (non-normative) group burials from the site. In what remains of this paper, the

Figure 13.4. Grave 480, St Margaret's Fyebridgate. Courtesy of Jayne Bown, Norfolk Archaeological Unit.

context of these burials is explored using documentary, archaeological and palaeopathological evidence, in an attempt to better understand how disease might have influenced personal status during the period.

The cemetery of St Margaret, Fyebridgegate, in comparative context

It is necessary to place the group burials of St Margaret's into a local and national context in order wholly to appreciate the range of practices recorded. Group burials are not a phenomenon unique to this site, and generally signify periods of heightened mortality. Moreover (although they necessitate an initial outlay of money and man power) such burials require relatively little space or investment compared to an equivalent number of individual graves (Harding 1993). They are a means, therefore, of conserving the expenditure of both cash and labour. Analogous practice elsewhere suggests they were employed in a number of different circumstances, and that they carried a range of cognitive meanings. The late Saxon parish cemetery of St John Ber Street, mentioned earlier, also contained a group interment (Shepherd-Popescu *forthcoming*). The individuals there were deposited in supine positions and aligned on an east-west axis; they were, therefore, buried within the bounds of normal depositional custom. A similar concern for the preservation of order can be seen in a group burial at the hospital of St Mary Spital, London (Thomas *et al.* 1997, 122), and, most significantly, at two mass burial trenches at the Royal Mint site in East Smithfield – a Black Death cemetery which catered for 292 individuals (Hawkins 1990, 638–641). At the latter site, only two individuals were buried in non-normative modes – one was in a prone and one in a 'crouched' position. Even at a time of mass mortality, therefore, the *mores* of Christian practice were still considered important. Further afield, but still of comparative value, is another plague cemetery, that of the rue Jean-François Leca, Marseilles, dating to 1720–22. Here again, individuals were deposited with "un soin particulier" (Dutour *et al.* 1994). Inversions of the norms of practice in the excavated area were minimal, but included the prone ('procubitus') burial of a mature female, and a group of four, misaligned corpses, which were thought to represent simultaneous depositions into the trench. The excavators considered these uncharacteristic interments to be a result of the urgency and difficulty surrounding burial logistics during an epidemic, and not a conscious attempt to diminish the personal status of the dead (Dutour *et al.* 1994, 193).

Some concern to preserve order at St Margaret's – in contrast to other burials at the site and despite apparent exigency – is demonstrated by Grave 324, which contained four closely-packed skeletons, laid out in the 'proper' fashion (Fig. 13.5). Two of these individuals were

probably infected by bacteria of the *treponema* genus. Skeletons 227 and 305 both displayed lytic cranial changes, which in life would have been associated with infected soft tissue lesions (Stirland 1994; Stirland, *forthcoming*). A further four individuals from the site displayed other lesions also suggestive of one of the *treponematoses*. These included skeleton 68, a mature adult female. Again, this corpse was buried in a group interment, but one in which practice appeared to be normative (site 780N Norfolk Archaeological Unit Archive). The remaining three were buried in single graves. Whether or not they were thought to be suffering from a discrete disease entity is not known. The similarity of the lesions present in the corpses of Sk. 227 and 305 may have been recognised by contemporary observers, as they were simultaneous interments. At any rate, they could not have been considered victims of the *pox*. This is despite both the modern association between *treponemal* disease and the historical *pox*, and the place that 'ulcers' and 'pustules' (redolent of soft tissue changes associated with the observed skeletal lesions) were later to occupy in that disease's perceived symptoms. This was because the *pox* only made its impact on medicine, literature and the civic mentality from the 1490s onwards, when the cemetery

Figure 13.5. Grave 324, St Margaret's Fyebridgegate. Courtesy of Jayne Bown, Norfolk Archaeological Unit.

had already fallen out of use (Arrizabalaga *et al.* 1997, 25 and *passim*).

Even though the corpses of skeletons 68, 227 and 305 were apparently deposited with care, some circumvention of the processes of a desirable burial occurred here. Copper alloy lace tags were associated with three of the skeletons in Grave 324 (including Sk. 227 and 305), suggesting that they were buried in their clothes (Stirland *forthcoming*). Normally, a body would be stripped and washed, sewn into a shroud and placed into a coffin – actions depicted in fifteenth-century continental Books of Hours and widely practised in contemporary hospitals (Binski 1996; Rawcliffe 2003). Indeed, even the plague victims of Marseilles were stripped and bound in bed sheets (Dutour *et al.* 1994). Expediency and a lack of interested personnel to undertake these activities would account for their apparent neglect at St Margaret's. Perhaps surprisingly, these 'shortcuts' seem to have been less likely to occur in times of very high mortality (like the plague), when many eyes were turned towards mortuary provision, than in the gradual accretion of group burials in this peripheral suburb of Norwich.

In fact, the parish is known to have been economically, socially and topographically marginal, suggesting that it was lowly or disreputable personal standing, rather than disease status alone, which resulted in the apparently substandard mortuary situation of the group burials of St Margaret's. The cemetery was positioned at the most northerly entrance point to the city, just within the fortifications (Fig. 13.2). For the first century of its use (that is, from about 1100) the area between the cemetery and the city defences was used for large open cast iron-pan or gravel quarries. Subsequently, metal working industries were accommodated in the same location, creating a particularly insalubrious environment according to contemporary medical sensibilities (Rawcliffe 1995a, 39; Atkin and Evans 2002, 159, 182). A further look at the patterns of land use in the north of the city confirms the impression that this parish was a backwater. The intramural lands to the west of the church were taken up by private crofts, the precincts of St Augustine's church and a twelve-acre expanse of farmland called the Gildencroft (Atkin and Evans 2002, 177; Ayers 2003, 101). To the southeast of the cemetery was the suburb around St Paul's hospital, itself 'an island of urban development situated in open fields' (Rawcliffe 1995c, 62). Low density settlement seems to have remained the norm into the sixteenth century, when space was available for barns, gardens and orchards to be laid out in the immediate vicinity of what had been the parish church of St Margaret (Atkin and Evans 2002, 183). This semi-agrarian topography, however, did not preclude the possibility of areas of localised population density within the domestic accommodation that *did* exist in the parish during the years of the church's use. A combination of corporate land-holdings, a strong rental market and (until the mid-fourteenth century) rapid population growth contrived to produce enclaves across Norwich where rows of densely packed housing overlooked the same streets as tracts of undeveloped or open land (Rutledge 1995; Atkin and Evans 2002, 78). In such circumstances the sub-division and multiple occupation of properties was common with a correspondingly deleterious effect on standards of living (Rutledge 1995, 11–13). Today, low socio-economic status and population density are associated with the development of leprosy and tuber-culosis, so it is unsurprising that these conditions surface in the burial record of northern Norwich (Jopling 1984).

A little more is known about the personal standing of some of the people interred at the cemetery. In common with most parish cemeteries, this seems to have been variable. Cyst burials excavated along the street frontage suggest that some members of the parish population desired, and could be provided with, a measure of distinction in the manner of their burial (site 780N, NAU archive). The goods that others left behind were apparently not sufficient to provide for such privileges – or else they were considered not to merit them. A reference to the parish made after 1245 gave it the suffix *ubi supeliunter suspensi*, 'where the hanged are buried' (Hudson 1910, 12; Ayers 2003, 98). The city gallows were in fact situated nearby, outside the defences. Executed bodies would have fallen within the ambit of charitable burials and some of the excavated groups may plausibly contain the bodies of criminals who – though committed to Christian ground – had placed themselves outside the bounds of acceptable behaviour (Harding 2000, 174; Whyte 2003).

It is very likely that the cemetery was also used by the leper house of St Leonard, a humble institution situated directly outside Magdalen gate, which consisted of a collection of wooden buildings and (probably) a chapel (Fig. 13.2). The first, extant record of the house derives from 1335. In all probability, however, it existed for much longer – several of the city's other leper houses were similarly first mentioned in the early fourteenth century, reflecting a period of 'documentary florescence' rather than a rash of new foundations. St Leonard's is thought to have been a particularly early foundation, and it is likely that most of the other *leprosaria* were also built at some point during the twelfth century (Rawcliffe 1995c; Satchel 1998).

St Leonard's stood on land which was part of the parish of St Margaret's until the church was dissolved in the later fifteenth century. The population then transferred worship to the nearby church of All Saints (Fig. 13.2). Burial rights were also conveyed to the latter parish: two wills of 1448 and 1466, made by residents of the leper house, requested burial there, and give a clear picture of the social position of the inmates. The testaments of Henry Wellys and his relation, Richard, document the lives of apparently literate and devout individuals, who (in every respect other than their disease status) were not unlike their fellow citizens. Richard was in fact quite well off and enjoyed a network of friends and family. Henry bequeathed a missal to All Saints, suggesting that he was interested in the details of funerary masses, having perhaps taken a prayerful role in the funerals of others. Similarly, Richard requested a commemorative trental mass after his death, for the sake of his soul's health. The brethren of St Leonard's were particularly well suited to comply with his commission; the prayers of lepers were widely believed to have a heightened efficacy, and, in Norwich, were enlisted by a succession of Bishops and citizens (Rawcliffe 1995c, 51–2; Norfolk Record Office NCC Reg. Jenkkys, f. 43 and Aleyn, f.9).

A closer look at the interment patterns of individuals who displayed osseous evidence of *M. leprae* (apparently consonant with the medieval concept of 'leprosy') bears out the interpretation of historians that no single leprous identity or monolithic response to the disease existed in the period. Six individuals who fall into this category were excavated from St Margaret's. The burial of one of these, Sk. 618, inverted typical Christian practice and is discussed further below. Four others, however, were buried in individual graves according to the norm. The remaining 'leprous' individual, Sk. 252, was interred in a grave which had the proportions of an ordinary, single interment. The corpse was placed in a supine position, with its head to the west, and would have been unremarkable, therefore, were it not for a second skeleton (253) which was deposited above it. Sk. 253 displayed lesions suggesting neuromuscular dystrophy, which have already been the subject of publication (Stirland 1997). The excavators recorded that the manifest pathologies of this individual prevented the corpse from being manipulated into a normative position. Instead, it was deposited prone and 'crouched', with its head proximate to the pelvis of Sk. 272 – a pattern which, if intentional, would constitute a highly unusual funerary practice (site 780N, NAU archive). It is not, however, clear whether these were really simultaneous interments, or if the grave was accidentally reopened when Sk. 273 was buried (Jayne Bown, *pers comm.*). In any event – and despite the legend penned by Blomefield – the majority of 'leper' burials at the site seem to have been normative. It is difficult to infer a specific intention to degrade the bodies of such individuals on the part of those in charge of interments.

The Wellys' relative wealth and the apparently uncompromised modes of 'leper' burial are, moreover, a salutary reminder that life in the area was perhaps not always as bleak as hindsight seems to suggest. When St Margaret's church was first built it augured for a programme of urban reform and population expansion, a counterpoise to that taking place south of the river where the castle, cathedral, market and nearby French borough were under construction (Fig. 13.2). The foundation of St Margaret's drew settlement northwards from the old, fortified Saxon town, reviving what had been a major axial route through the borough prior to the Conquest (Atkins and Evans 2002, 155–156; Ayers 2004, 13). Soon after the cemetery

came into use, the suburb of St Paul's – with its monastic hospital and church – was also constructed nearby (Ayers 2004, 18). If we include the hospital of St Mary Magdalen at Sprowston (St Paul's institutional counterpart to the north, also constructed in the early twelfth century) the area could boast a wealth of spiritual services for its anticipated population (Atkins and Evans 2002, 156). Yet the aspirations for this northern area of the Fyebridge ward seem never to have come to fruition. As early as 1254, the benefice of St Margaret's was considered too meagre to qualify for ecclesiastical taxation, and fast declining population levels precipitated its final closure in 1468, by which point the cemetery had probably been out of use for some time (Hudson 1910, 12; Tanner 1984, 164; Atkins and Evans 2002, 163).

There is little evidence to suggest that individuals with leprous and treponemal lesions were in any way vilified after death. Other forms of group interment at the site, however, show far less concern for the particulars of burial custom, and present a rather different picture. Two graves were orientated on a north-south axis, in distinction from those surrounding them, without any apparent reason (such as the presence of a building) which might necessitate such an arrangement (site 780N, NAU archive). Grave 480 has already been mentioned. None of the skeletons removed from it displayed any evidence of chronic disease. In Grave 624, on the other hand, the dead included Sk. 694, an adult suffering from chronic osteomyelitis following a fracture to the mandible or lower jaw (a suppurative infection of the bone cavity, which, in this case, probably resulted from a severe and chronic lesion in associated soft tissue structures). A mature adult (Sk. 695), who displayed osseous malformation of the lower limbs suggestive of childhood rickets, was also excavated from this group (Stirland *forthcoming*). In the case of the first individual, a history of pain and temporary incapacity can be assumed. The long-term functional implications for the second individual were probably minor. Nonetheless, they may well have suffered an inauspicious start in life; urban overcrowding, dietary deficiency and a chronically underfed mother can contribute to rickets (Roberts and Manchester 1995, 174). Mediolateral bowing of the tibiae would have also given Sk. 695 a characteristic gait. Three of the five individuals deposited in Grave 624 were buried in a prone position, including the two just mentioned. Because there is no apparent practical reason for this treatment, it seems reasonable to interpret the structure of the grave and the configuration of the corpses within it as a deliberate means of differentiating and degrading the occupants.

Another grave at St Margaret's which seems to reinforce, at least superficially, the idea that the point of interment was used to make spiritual or social statements about the dead is Grave 276. This grave contained twelve individuals, of whom nine were buried face down. It was not wide enough to accommodate a single layer of corpses, though it was deep, with steep vertical sides (Fig. 13.6).

According to the excavators, three of the individuals had their hands behind their backs in a position which suggests they had been bound. The positions of some skeletons in this group suggest that they were unshrouded though no evidence associated textiles or other clothing remains was found. Two corpses were also interred with their heads to the east (site 780N, NAU archive). At least one met a violent death. Skeleton 374 displayed a perimortem sharp-force fracture to the skull (Stirland 1996, 96). Another (skeleton 618) displayed gross bilateral lytic lesions of the feet (comprising the destruction of both fifth metatarsals) and periostitis (or chronic inflammation of the membrane enveloping bone) of the fibulae and tibiae (Stirland, *forthcoming*). These changes are strongly suggestive of infection by *Mycobacterium leprae*, and are similar to the lesions seen in the graveyards of medieval leper houses.

The closest analogy on British soil to this multiple interment may be found in the mass grave dug after the Battle of Towton (1461), where excavations revealed thirty-six articulated skeletons. The order in which the corpses were deposited within the Towton grave has been reconstructed. Just under half the corpses (n = 16) were buried in prone positions, although not according to any obvious pattern (Sutherland 2000, 40). This probably resulted from a desire on behalf of those filling the grave to minimise the energy they expended on the procedure – energy which would have been more quickly consumed if care was taken to ensure that all corpses were placed 'the right way up'. There was more consistency in the alignment of individuals within the grave. The first and largest cohort of corpses was aligned west-east, with the head to the west, a situation which was reversed for the next ten burials (of which only one was prone). Only the final four interments were obviously erratic, with one aligned north-south, and the others variably placed with their heads to either the west or east. It was not possible to determine whether the manner of interment signified "the scale of the number of dead to be buried, and the problems of their interment" or de-Christianising and humiliating intentions on behalf of the grave's overseers (*ibid.* 43). Similar caveats apply at St Margaret's. In the case of Grave 276 (unlike that at Towton) no single event can be evoked to account for the presence of many corpses requiring burial at the same time. Indeed, the approximate time of their deaths may be the only thing that these individuals had in common, particularly if this grave also represents a charitable burial. The presence of a putative 'leper' in this group should not, therefore, be understood as an act of denigration motivated simply by that individual's disease status.

Figure 13.6. Grave 276, St Margaret's Fyebridgegate. Courtesy of Jayne Bown, Norfolk Archaeological Unit.

Depositional praxis and disease status

How do we account for variation in the deposition of the chronic sick at St Margaret's? Diseases commonly associated with low socio-economic status, population density and compromised individual immunity are all present in the site's profile. Given the historical context of the area, we can be fairly certain that the majority of individuals interred at the site belonged to the ranks of the urban poor. I suggest, therefore, that expediency and a low level of personal agency over burial form accounts for the kind of practice seen. The internal evidence of the site's osteoarchaeological record does not suggest a simple picture of medieval antipathy towards the sick dead; in fact, the contrasting pictures provided by graves 324 and 480 implies that other aspects of personal status determined the form of an individual's funerary treatment.

Two features – evident at the mass grave at Towton – remain illuminating for the customs seen at St Margaret's churchyard, namely the desire to minimise the energy expended in funerary arrangements, and an apparently erratic depositional pattern which governed the placement of the final interments. At St Margaret's, there is a relationship between the number of individuals awaiting burial at any one time, and the number of 'inverted' or non-normative practices seen within the grave. Less than thirty per cent of graves containing between two and four corpses demonstrate non-normative practices (Table 13.1). The proportion was much higher when five or more individuals awaited burial. Prone, or misaligned depositions seem to occur, therefore, when the task of burial was difficult and exacting. Often group interments would begin in a normative fashion. This was the case in Grave 153, which contained one individual apparently suffering from Paget's Disease – a painful metabolic, possibly viral,

condition (Fig. 13.7). The first three skeletons were laid out with their heads to the west, and in a supine position. As at Towton, the orientation of the next layer of corpses was reversed, probably reflecting a desire to 'level' the burial group in preparation for back filling. The final individual in this interment seems to have been cast into the grave. It has already been demonstrated at Towton that those responsible for the multiple interment grew increasingly careless as their task neared its end. Seemingly, as the group graves at both sites were filled (regardless of their relative size) it became more difficult to manipulate the bodies into the correct position without entering the grave itself.

Altogether, the evidence seems to suggest that the highly unusual burial practices at St Margaret's resulted from the urgency and logistical difficulties of disposing of a relatively large number of burials at any one time – a fact that those in charge were repeatedly required to look squarely in the face. The marginal status of the parish suggests that many of the burials would have served individuals for whom a full mortuary fee was not forthcoming, for one reason or another. In such circumstances, it seemed expedient to conduct group interments. In the cases of only two graves – those aligned on a north-south axis – does this model fail satisfactorily to explain the pattern of deposition. The north-south graves would have left a permanent mark on the cemetery landscape, because the mound covering them would remain at odds with the rest. It is possible that the alignment of Grave 624 resulted from the manifest disease status of two of the occupants, yet this does not tally with the general picture. Others exhibiting gross, pathological changes (including the 'lepers' and *treponemal* cases deposited in single graves) were processed in the ordinary way.

No. of individuals in grave	No. of graves	No. of individuals with chronic disease/infection of bones	No. of graves including pathological individuals	Percentage of graves including non-normative practices*	Percentage of individuals with chronic disease/infection of bones
2	15	4	3	20.0	13.3
3	18	4	3	27.8	7.4
4	5	7	4	20.0	35.0
5	4	3	2	100.0	15.0
6	3	4	3	67.7	22.2
7	3	3	2	100.0	14.3
12	1	2	1	100.0	16.7

Table 13.1. Showing the extent of non-normative burial practices and chronic pathologies in the multiple burials of St Margaret, Fyebridgegate. * *Individuals deposited prone, on their side, or with head to north, south or east.*

Figure 13.7. Grave 153, St Margaret's Fyebridgegate. Courtesy of Jayne Bown, Norfolk Archaeological Unit.

Conclusion

This site demonstrates that the old maxims concerning leper burials (which presuppose absolute segregation, without giving full attention to the precise context of funerary space) are too crude. Medieval attitudes towards the chronic sick were ambivalent and variable, reflecting not simply their disease burden, but also their wider economic, social and familial status (Rawcliffe, *forthcoming*). The degree of spiritual kudos accorded to the inmates of St Leonard's would have distinguished them from the morally disreputable figure of the felon whose cemetery, at St Margaret's, they happened to share (Whyte 2003). Such 'lepers' should be considered with reference to provisions made at St Mary Magdalen, Sprowston, located not more than a mile to the north (Fig. 13.2). That house, in comparison to St Leonard's, could boast not only a flint coursed infirmary and a burial ground for the dead but also a role in the ecclesiastical and – owing to its annual fair – communal life of the city (Rawcliffe 1995c). Hierarchies and differences clearly existed, therefore, even within disease groups.

By combining osteoarchaeological evidence with documentary and topographical analysis, we can view Norwich's diseased dead in their proper context. Medieval and Tudor citizens were acutely aware of the relationship between poverty and disease (Pelling 1998). The individuals buried at St Margaret's seem to represent a section of the urban poor that – unlike the sick inmates of the city's hospitals – remained active and visible in the urban landscape. A nexus of theories about the environment, city space and putrefaction eventually led the authorities (already concerned to curtail the influence of apparently disruptive citizens) to wage campaigns against urban pollution in all its forms – issues that also exercised humanist scholars and found expression in Cuningham's eulogy of Norwich's salubrious virtues. The social archaeology of funerary remains has, therefore, much to offer the disciplines of medical history and palaeopathology through its careful scrutiny of the *precise* context of burial practice. But it is not without difficulty. Of the hermeneutic approach to disease culture, three leading historians made the following statement:

> In dealing historically with words we are in effect making a kind of translation, from the past to the present. Everybody familiar with a second language recognises the dangers of facile translation. Some words simply do not have an adequate partner in other languages. It is easy to see that there are cultural reasons for this. The same difficulty of translation is evident in translating from the culture of the past (Arrizabalaga *et al.* 1997, 17).

Words are not the only form of evidence which requires translation. Interpretations of material phenomenon are also elusive, but equally beset by pitfalls. When palaeopathologists describe osseous lesions in terms of wider consequences for the body (placing them the context of an individual's life history) they should be facilitating that translation and not obscuring it. Ultimately, our desire to demonstrate an adequate appreciation of the language deployed in the disease culture of the past should not tempt us to forget that physical experiences prompted the invention or cognitive framing of diseases in the first place.

Acknowledgements

I would like to thank Chris Knüsel and Becky Gowland for inviting me to submit this paper, and also for their patience, support and feedback; Carole Rawcliffe for her advice and encouragement, her time generously given, her specific comments about this paper, and innumerable references that have made it possible; Ann Stirland and an anonymous reviewer for their responses on an earlier version; Jayne Bown for permission to consult the archives of the Norfolk Archaeological Unit, including a pre-publication copy of the text *Criminals and Paupers,* and to reproduce photographs of St Margaret's; Clive Wilkins-Jones and the Norfolk Heritage Centre for permission to reproduce Cuningham's plan; Elizabeth Shepherd Popescu, Cambridge Archaeological Unit (formerly of NAU), for allowing me to see sections of her forthcoming work on excavations at Norwich Castle; Mike Evans for, Philip Judge and Rik Hoggett for help with images; and finally, Silvia Bello, of the Natural History Museum, to whom I owe references to the plague pits of Marseille. For my parents.

References

Andersen, J. G., and Manchester, K. (1992) The rhinomaxillary syndrome in leprosy: a clinical, radiological and palaeo-pathological study. *International Journal of Osteoarchaeology* 2, 121–129.

Anderson, S. (1996) *Human Skeletal Remains from Timberhill, Castle Mall, Norwich (Excavated 1989–91)*. Ancient Monuments Laboratory Report 73/96. Portsmouth, English Heritage.

Arrizabalaga, J., Henderson, J. and French, R. (1997) *The Great Pox: The French Disease in Renaissance Europe*. New Haven and London, Yale University Press.

Atkin, M., and Evans, D.H. (2002) *Excavations in Norwich 1971–1978, Part III*. East Anglian Archaeology 100. Norwich, The Norwich Survey/ Norfolk Museums and Archaeology Service.

Ayers, B. (2003) *Norwich: A Fine City*. Stroud, Tempus.

Ayers, B. (2004) The urban landscape. In C. Rawcliffe and R. Wilson (eds.) *Medieval Norwich*, 1–28. London and New York, London and Hambledon.

Bassett, S. (ed.) (1992) *Death in Towns: Urban Responses to the Dying and the Dead 100–1600*. Leicester, London and New York, Leicester University Press.

Bennike, P. (2002) Vilhelm Møller-Christensen: his work and legacy. In C. Roberts, M. Lewis and K. Manchester (eds.) *The Past and Present of Leprosy: Archaeological, Historical, Palaeopathological and Clinical Approaches*, 135–148. Oxford, Archaeopress.

Binski, P. (1996) *Medieval Death: Ritual and Representation*. London, The British Museum Press.

Blomefield, F. (1806) *An Essay Towards a Topographical History of the County of Norfolk, Volume IV*. London, Miller.

Boldsen, J.L. (2001) Epidemiological approach to the palaeo-pathological diagnosis of leprosy. *American Journal of Physical Anthropology* 115, 380–387.

Boorde, A. (1552) *The Breuiary of Healthe*. London, Witham Powell.

Brickley, M. and McKinley, J. (2004) *Guidelines to the Standards for Recording Human Remains*. Institute of Field Archaeologists Paper No. 7. Southampton and Reading, BABAO and IFA.

Bynum, C.W. (1995) *The Resurrection of the Body in Western Christianity, 200–1336*. Lectures in the History of Religion, n.s. 15. New York, Columbia University Press.

Carpenter, J. (1861) *Liber Albus: The White Book of the City of London*. Ed. H. T. Riley. London, Richard Griffin.

Carr, D. R. (1997) From pollution to prostitution: supervising the citizens of fifteenth-century Salisbury. *Southern History* 19, 24–41.

Cohn, S. K. (2000) The place of the dead in Flanders and Tuscany: towards a comparative history of the Black Death. In B. Gordon and P. Marshall (eds.) *The Place of the Dead: Death, Ritual and Remembrance in Late Medieval and Early Modern* Europe, 17–43. Cambridge, Cambridge University Press.

Comper, M. M. (ed.) (1977) *The Book of the Craft of Dying and Other Early English Tracts Concerning Death*. New York, Arno Press.

Cuningham, W. (1968) *The Cosmographical Glasse*. Amsterdam and New York, Da Capo Press.

Duday, H., Courtaud, P., Crubézy, E., Sellier, P. and Tillier, A-M. (1990) L'anthropologie 'de terrain': reconnaissance et interprétation des gestes funéraires. *Bulletin et Mémoires de la Société d'Anthropologie de Paris* (n.s.) 2, 29–50.

Duffy, E. (2001) *The Voices of Morebath: Reformation and Rebellion in an English Village*. New Haven and London, Yale University Press.

Dutour, O., Signoli, M., Georgeon, E. and Da Silva, J. (1994) Le charnier de la grande peste de Marseille (Rue Leca). *Préhistoire Anthropolgie Méditerranéennes* 3, 191–203.

Fay, I. H. H. (2002) *The experience of leprosy in the middle ages: the cemetery of SS. James and Mary Magdalene, Chichester*. Unpublished M.Sc. dissertation, University of Bradford.

Fay, I. H. H. (in prep.) *Health and sickness in medieval and Tudor Norwich*. PhD thesis, University of East Anglia.

Finlay, N. (ed.) (1999) *Disability and Archaeology. Archaeological Review from Cambridge* 15.

Getz, F. (1998) *Medicine in the English Middle Ages*. Princeton and Chichester, Princeton University Press.

Goldberg, P. J. P. (1999) Pigs and prostitutes: streetwalking in comparative perspective. In K. J. Lewis, N. J. Menuge and K. Phillips (eds.) *Young Medieval Women*, 173–193. Stroud, Sutton.

Goldberg, P. J. P. (2001) Coventry's 'Lollard' programme of 1492 and the making of *Utopia*. In R. Horrox and S. Rees-Jones (eds.) *Pragmatic Utopias: Ideas and Communities 1200–1630*, 97–116. Cambridge, Cambridge University Press.

Gordon, B., and Marshall, P. (2000) *The Place of the Dead: Death and Remembrance in Early Modern Europe*. Cambridge, Cambridge University Press.

Gowland, R. (2004) The social identity of health in late Roman Britain. In B. Croxford, H. Eckharat, J. Mead and J. Weekes (eds.) *TRAC 2003: The Proceedings of the Thirteenth Annual Theoretical Archaeology Conference, Leicester, 2003*, 135–147. Oxford, Oxbow Books.

Grauer, A.L. (1991). Patterns of life and death: The palaeo-demography of medieval York. In H. Bush and M. Zevelebil (eds.) *Health in Past Societies: Biocultural Interpretations of Human Skeletal Remains in Archaeological Contexts*, 67–80. Oxford, Tempus.

Grmek, M.D. (1989) *Diseases in the Ancient Greek World*. Trans. M.

and L. Muellner. Baltimore and London, John Hopkins University Press.

Harding, V. (1989) 'And one more may be laid there': the location of burials in early modern London. *London Journal* 14, 112–129.

Harding, V. (1993) Burial of the plague dead in early modern London. In J. A. I. Champion (ed.) *Epidemic Disease in London*, 53–64. Centre for Metropolitan History Working Papers 1, 53–64. London, Centre for Metropolitan History.

Harding, V. (2000) Whose body? A study of attitudes towards the dead body in early modern Paris. In B. Gordon and P. Marshall (eds.) *The Place of the Dead: Death and Remembrance in Late Medieval and Early Modern Europe*, 170–187. Cambridge, Cambridge University Press.

Harley, D. (1999) Rhetoric and the social construction of sickness and healing. *Social History of Medicine* 12, 407–435.

Hawkins, D. (1990) The Black Death cemeteries and the new London cemeteries of 1348. *Antiquity* 64, 637–642.

Henderson, J. (1992) The Black Death in Florence: medical and communal responses. In S. Bassett (ed.) *Death in Towns: Urban Responses to the Dying and the Dead, 100–1600*, 136–150. Leicester, London and New York, Leicester University Press.

Horden, P. (2000) Ritual and public health in the early medieval city. In S. Sheard and H. Power (eds.) *Body and City: Histories of Public Health*, 17–40. Aldershot, Ashgate Publishing Limited.

Horrox, R. (1994) *The Black Death*. Manchester and New York, Manchester University Press.

Hudson, W. (eds.) (1892) *Leet Jurisdiction in the City of Norwich During the XIIIth and XIV Centuries*. Seldon Society 5. London, Quaritch.

Hudson, W. (1910) The Norwich taxation of 1254 so far as it relates to the diocese of Norwich. *Norfolk Archaeology* 17, 46–155.

Hsu, E. (2002) Medical anthropology, material culture and new directions in medical archaeology. In P. A. Baker and G. Carr (eds.) *Practitioners, Practices and Patients: New Approaches to Medical Archaeology and Anthropology*, 1–15. Oxford, Oxbow Books.

James, M. (1983) Ritual drama and the social body in the late medieval English town, *Past and Present* 98, 3–29.

Janssens, P.A. (1987) A copper plate on the upper arm in a burial at the church in Vrasene (Belgium). *Journal of Paleopathology* 1, 15–18.

Jenner, M. (1997a) Underground, overground: pollution and place in urban history, *Journal of Urban History* 24, 97–110.

Jenner, M. (1997b) The great dog massacre. In W. Naphy and P. Roberts (eds.) *Fear in Early Modern Society*. Manchester, Manchester University Press.

Jones, C. (2004) Discourse communities and medical texts. In I. Taavitsainen and P. Pahta (eds.) *Medical and Scientific Writing in Late Medieval English*, 23–36. Cambridge, Cambridge University Press.

Jopling, W. H. (1984) *Handbook for Leprosy*. Third edition. London, William Heineman.

Keiser, G. (2003) Two medieval plague treatises and their afterlife in early modern England. *Journal of the History of Medicine and Allied Sciences* 58, 292–324.

Knüsel, C. J. (1999). Orthopaedic disability: some hard evidence. In N. Finlay (ed.) *Disability and Archaeology. Archaeological Review from Cambridge* 15, 31–53

Knüsel, C. J. (2002) Of crystal balls, political power and changing contexts: what the clever women of Salerno inherited. In P. A. Baker and G. Carr (eds.) *Practitioners, Practices and Patients: New Approaches to Medical Archaeology and Anthropology*, 172–194. Oxford, Oxbow Books.

Knüsel, C. J., Kemp, R. L., and Budd, P. (1995) Evidence for remedial medical treatment of a severe knee injury from Fishergate Gilbertine monastery in the city of York. *Journal of Archaeological Science* 22, 369–384.

Larsen, C. S. (1997) *Bioarchaeology: Interpreting Behaviour from the Human Skeleton*. Cambridge, Cambridge University Press.

Lewis, M. E., Roberts, C. A., and Manchester, K. (1995) Inflammatory bone changes in leprous skeletons from the medieval hospital of St James and Mary Magdalene, Chichester, England. *International Journal of Leprosy* 63, 77–85.

Lewis, M. E. (2002a) *Urbanization and Child Health in Medieval and Post-Medieval England*. British Archaeological Reports, British Series 339. Oxford, Archaeopress.

Lewis, M. E. (2002b) Infant and childhood leprosy: past and present. In C. Roberts, M. Lewis and K. Manchester (eds.) *The Past and Present of Leprosy: Archaeological, Historical, Palaeopathological and Clinical Approaches*, 135–148. Oxford, Archaeopress.

Lloyd, G. E. R. (ed.) (1978) *Hippocratic Writings*. London, Penguin.

Logan, G.M. and Adams R. M. (eds.) (2000) *Thomas More's Utopia*. Cambridge, Cambridge University Press.

MacCraken, H. N. (ed.) (1961) *The Minor Poems of John Lydgate*. Early English Text Society 192. 2 vols. London and New York, Oxford University Press.

Maddern, P. (2004) Order and disorder. In C. Rawcliffe and R. Wilson (eds.) *Medieval Norwich*, 189–212. London and New York, Hambledon and London.

Mayer, T. F. (eds.) (1989) *A Dialogue Between Pole and Lupset*. Camden fourth series, 37. London, Royal Historical Society.

Mays, S. (1997) A perspective on human osteoarchaeology in Britain. *International Journal of Osteoarchaeology* 7, 600–604.

Moore, R. I. (1987) *The Formation of a Persecuting Society: Power and Deviation in Western Europe 950–1250*. Oxford, Oxford University Press.

Murray Jones, P. (1994) Information and science. In R. Horrox (ed.) *Fifteenth-Century Attitudes: Perceptions of Society in Late Medieval England*, 97–111. Cambridge, Cambridge University Press.

Park, T. (ed.) (1804) *Nugae Antiquae II*. London, Vernor and Hood.

Pelling, M. (1998) *The Common Lot: Sickness, Medical Occupations and Urban Poor in Early Modern England*. London, Longman.

Pelling, M. (2004) Health and sanitation to 1750. In C. Rawcliffe and R. Wilson (eds.) *Norwich Since 1550*, 117–137. London and New York, Hambledon and London.

Peyroux, C. (2000) The leper's kiss. In S. Farmer and B. H. Rosenwein (eds.) *Monks and Nuns, Saints and Outcasts: Religion in Medieval Society*, 172–188. *Essays in Honor of Lester K. Little*. Ithaca and London, Cornell University Press.

Pickett, J.P. (1994) A translation of the "Canutus" plague treatise. In L. M. Matheson (ed.) *Popular and Practical Science of Medieval England*. Medieval Texts and Studies, 11. East Lansing, Colleagues Press.

Pound, J. (ed.) (1971) *The Norwich Census of the Poor, 1570*. Norfolk Record Society 40. Norwich, Norfolk Record Society.

Rawcliffe, C. (1995a) *Medicine and Society in Later Medieval England*. Stroud, Sutton Publishing.

Rawcliffe, C. (ed.) (1995b) *Sources for the History of Medicine in Late Medieval England*. Kalamazoo, Western Michigan University.

Rawcliffe, C. (1995c). *The Hospitals of Medieval Norwich*. Studies in East Anglian History 2. Norwich, Centre for East Anglian Studies.

Rawcliffe, C. (2003) The seventh comfortable work: charity and mortality in the medieval hospital. *Medicina & Storia* 3, 11–35.

Rawcliffe, C. (2004a) Introduction. In C. Rawcliffe and R. Wilson (eds.) *Medieval Norwich*, xix–xxxvii. London and New York, Hambledon and London.

Rawcliffe, C. (2004b) Sickness and health. In C. Rawcliffe and R. Wilson (eds.) *Medieval Norwich*, 301–324. London and New York, Hambledon and London.

Rawcliffe, C. (*forthcoming*) Isolating the medieval leper: ideas – and misconceptions – about segregation in the middle ages. In P. Horden (ed.) *Freedom of Movement in the Middle Ages: People, Ideas, Goods.* Proceedings of the Twentieth Harlaxton Symposium.

Rees Jones, S. (2000) Household, work and the problem of mobile labour: the regulation of labour in medieval English towns. In J. Bothwell, P. J. P. Goldberg and W. M. Ormrod (eds.) *The Problem of Labour in Fourteenth-Century England*, 133–153. York Medieval Press. Woodbridge, Boydell and Brewer.

Roberts, C. (1986) Leprosy and leprosaria in medieval Britain. *MASCA Research Papers in Science and Archaeology* 4, 15–21.

Roberts, C. (1991) Trauma and its treatment in the British historic period: a design for multidisciplinary research. In D. J. Ortner and A. C. Aufderheide (eds.) *Human Palaeopathology: Current Synthesis and Future Options*, 225–40. Washington DC, Smithsonian Institution Press.

Roberts, C., and Cox, M. (2003) *Health and Disease in Britain from Prehistory to the Present Day.* Stroud, Sutton Publishing.

Roberts, C., and Manchester, K. (1995) *The Archaeology of Disease.* Stroud, Sutton Publishing.

Rubin, M. (1991) *Corpus Christi: The Eucharist in Late Medieval Culture* Cambridge, Cambridge University Press.

Rutledge, E. (1995) Landlords and tenants: housing and the rented property market in early fourteenth-century Norwich. *Urban History* 22, 7–24.

Rutledge, E. (2004) Economic life. In C. Rawcliffe and R. Wilson (eds.) *Medieval Norwich*, 158–188. London and New York, Hambledon and London.

Sabine, E. (1933) Butchering in medieval London. *Speculum* 8, 335–53.

Sabine, E. (1934) Latrines and cesspools of medieval London. *Speculum* 9, 306–320.

Sabine, E. (1937) City cleaning in medieval London. *Speculum* 12, 19–43.

Salter, F. R. (1926) *Some Early Tracts on Poor Relief.* London, Methuen.

Satchel, A. (1998) The emergence of leper houses in medieval England, 1100–1250. Unpublished PhD thesis, University of Oxford.

Sennett, R. (1994) *Flesh and Stone: The Body and the City in Western Civilisation.* London and Boston, Faber and Faber.

Shepherd Popescu, E. (*forthcoming*) *Norwich Castle Excavations and Historical Survey, 1987–98, Part I: Anglo-Saxon – c. 1345.* Norwich, East Anglian Archaeology.

Sontag, S. (1991) *Illness as Metaphor and AIDS and its Metaphors.* London, Penguin.

Stanford, J. L. and Stanford, C. A. (2002) Leprosy: a correctable model of immunological perturbation. In C. Roberts, M. Lewis and K. Manchester (eds.) *The Past and Present of Leprosy:*

Archaeological, Historical, Palaeopathological and Clinical Approaches, 25–38. Oxford, Archaeopress.

Stirland, A. (1994) Evidence for pre-Columbian treponematosis in medieval Europe. In O. Dutour, G. Pálfi, J. Bérato and J-P Brun (eds.) *L'Origine de la Syphilis en Europe: Avant ou Après 1493?*, 109–115 and 300. Paris, Éditions Errance.

Stirland, A. (1996) Patterns of trauma in a unique medieval parish cemetery. *International Journal of Osteoarchaeology* 6, 92–100.

Stirland, A. (1997) Care in the medieval community. *International Journal of Osteoarchaeology* 7, 587–590.

Stirland, A. with contributions by B. Ayers and J. Bown (*forthcoming*) *Criminals and Paupers: The Graveyard of St Margaret in Combusto, Norwich.*

Sutherland, T. (2000) Recording the Grave. In V. Fiorato, A. Boylston and C. Knüsel (eds.) *Blood Red Roses: The Archaeology of a Mass Grave from the Battle of Towton AD 1461*, 36–44. Oxbow, Oxford.

Tanner, N. P. (1984) *The Church in Late Medieval Norwich, 1370–1532.* Studies and Texts 66. Toronto, Ponitifical Institute of Medieval Studies.

Thomas, C., Sloane, B. and Philpotts, C. (1997) *Excavations at the Priory and Hospital of St Mary Spital, London.* London, Museum of London Archaeology Service.

Wakefield, W. L. and Evans, P. (1969) *Heresies of the High Middle Ages: Selected Sources Translated and Annotated.* New York, Columbia University Press.

Waldron, T. (1994) *Counting the Dead: The Epidemiology of Skeletal Populations.* Chichester, J. Wiley.

Ward, S. (1996) A consideration of mental retardation in pre-modern England: historical and anthropological perspectives with a case study. Unpublished M.Sc. Dissertation, University of Bradford.

Wear, A. (2000) *Knowledge and Practice in English Medicine, 1550–1680.* Cambridge, Cambridge University Press.

Weiss, D. L., and Møller-Christensen, V. (1971) Leprosy, echinococcosis and amulets: a study of a medieval Danish inhumation. *Medical History* 15, 260–267.

Wells, C. (1964) Two medieval cases of malignant disease. *British Medical Journal* 20, 1611–1612.

Wells, C. (1965a) Fifteenth-century wood-carvings in St. Mary's Church, Bury St. Edmunds. *Medical History* 9, 286–288.

Wells, C. (1965b) *Osteogenesis imperfecta* from an Anglo-Saxon burial ground at Burgh Castle, Suffolk. *Medical History* 9, 88–89.

Whyte, N. (2003) The deviant dead in the Norfolk landscape. *Landscapes* 4, 24–39.

Wieck, R.S. (1999) The death desired: Books of Hours and the medieval funeral. In E. E. DuBruck and B. J. Gusick (eds) *Death and Dying in the Middle Ages*, 431–476. New York, Peter Lang.

Wood, J. W., Milner, G. R., Harpending, H. C. and Weiss, K. M. (1992) The osteological paradox: problems of inferring prehistoric health from skeletal samples. *Current Anthropology* 33, 343–367.

14. 'Of No More Use to Men Than in Ages Before?':[1] The Investiture Contest as a Model for Funerary Interpretation

Christopher J. Knüsel

Preamble

The act of burial can be as much about succession as it is about commemoration. The *Investiture Contest* or *Controversy* developed from the contentions surrounding the investiture of clerics that came to a head in the late 11th-century A.D. At the heart of this controversy was the desire to control the naming of successors to vacated ecclesiastical sees, usually at the death of the incumbent, a right claimed by both temporal (*i.e.* the crowned heads of Europe) and spiritual rulers (the Pope). At stake was the governance of society made physical in the conferment of the episcopal ring and crosier at the investiture. The social and political contentions arising from succession may better explain the repeated occurrence of elaborate and liminal burials encountered in prehistory and proto-history, as well as history.

The Investiture Contest

In the winter of 1077, the Emperor Henry IV knelt in the snow at Canossa in the northern Italian Alps. Barefoot, the penitent Emperor spent three days in the snow before he was permitted to confess himself and receive absolution from the reform-minded Pope Gregory VII (the formidable, one-time Cardinal Hildebrand). In this self-effacing, yet politically astute manoeuvre, the Emperor found himself released from excommunication, a situation with both severe spiritual and temporal ramifications. As an excommunicate, the Emperor was denied the support of his bishops and noble barons (who were prohibited from communicating with an excommunicate), Church services, and a Christian burial should he die. He lost rights to taxes garnered from the granting of charters and other official documents, and the funds necessary to support the imperial army. He also found himself fleeing his realm, which had been thrown into chaos as his noble liegemen, barons, and bishops exercised much desired autonomy from the Imperial Curia which, as King and Emperor-apparent, Henry headed and, as an excommunicated temporal ruler, over which he could no longer claim suzerainty.

The relationship between the spiritual and temporal realms has long been an uneasy one in a number of historical and ethnographic societies (see, for example, Winkelman 1990; Atkinson 1992; Vitebsky 1995; Humphrey 1996; Hamayon 1996), and that which came to a head in medieval Europe had a long, contentious and confusing history that frequently inspired political intrigue, civil strife, and blood-letting. Without a formal relationship established between the Bishop of Rome (the Pope) and the Roman Emperor, the succession to these titles had relied on a mix of Germanic Law and Roman Law Codes, as well as extensive political manoeuvring due to the inherent tensions between these juridical documents and the variable practices which they spawned. Still, practices gave rise to precedent and precedent was supported by symbols and ceremony that, at times, appeared to clarify the issue.

In A.D. 751, perhaps after receiving papal approval, the Frankish bishops or, possibly even Pope Stephen II, himself, anointed Pippin or Pepin (a descendant of Pepin I of Landen), the Mayor of the Palace, with chrism (holy oil) to mark his inauguration as Pippin III, King of the Franks, and the first of the Carolingian dynasts. The ceremony seems to have arisen as an innovation, perhaps to legitimate what, in essence, was usurpation at the expense of the last Merovingians, who were removed from power by taking holy vows and entering monastic life. Whatever the specifics of these events were, it is clear that later sources presented a much more orderly and elaborated view of Pippin's emergence than was in actuality the case (Collins 1998; McKitterick 1997, 2000).

At any rate, later Frankish annals presented these ceremonies as contributing to the transition, and they came to represent the succession of power among the Carolingians (McKitterick 2000). Crowning, however, appears to have been added to the ceremony later in the course of the 8th century and may have been in imitation of Byzantine practice (Nelson 1987). In the year 800 A.D. Charlemagne was crowned Holy Roman Emperor by Leo III in Rome, an action that set forth a precedent in the relationship between Pope and Emperor. In this act, Charlemagne acceded to the *Imperium* once held by the Roman emperors, but his title and his symbols had been conferred *upon* him by the Pope whom he pledged to protect and support. It is likely that Charlemagne accepted the title in order to be seen as an equal to the Byzantine Emperor in Constantinople (Tierney and Painter 1970), but this act of fealty to the Pope was of far greater import to Charlemagne's and Leo's successors.

By the 11th century, due to political happenings since 800 A.D., the Holy Roman Emperors had claimed the right to consecrate the Pope after an oath of allegiance had been sworn by the incumbent to the Emperor. In performing this rite at the highest level, the Holy Roman Emperor donned the symbols of the Patriciate, a green mantle, ring, and gold crown (MacDonald 1932). In a similar vein, secular rulers and aristocrats had invested candidates in a ceremony that involved conferment of the symbolic episcopal crosier and ring. The crowned heads of Europe had grown accustomed to and dependent upon appointing bishops to the sees founded within their kingdoms; as secular clergy, bishops ruled secular lands and acted as royal and imperial servants in return for the wealth of the land granted them, the so-called benefice. These positions conferred substantial social, economic (in land, tithes, and taxes), and political power on the holder. Tradition had made the proprietary church- one founded by a lay aristocrat- a normal part of the diocesan landscape of the Early Middle Ages such that the system of lay investiture (*i.e.* by secular aristocrats) penetrated from the highest to the lowest of ecclesiastical offices, from the Pope down to the parish priest.

Originally, in both Roman and Canon (Church) Law and in the practices of the early Church, the clergy and community of the faithful nominated and elected individuals to vacant sees. From the fifth century onwards, through the system of feudal obligation, the temporal and spiritual aristocrats developed a system in which they agreed to confirm each other's candidates. Because of the vast wealth in land, people and their products, buildings, and goods accruing to holders, the purchase of titles (simony) very early on became a part of feudal practice, payments being made by a family on behalf of a male relation to ensure investiture. Once invested, these feudal bishop-barons could be relied upon to provide men and goods in support of the undertakings of their temporal lords. By the 12th-century, the extent to which this practice had become ingrained comes with the now

seemingly ironic offer of 1,000 pounds made by Tedald, the Bishop of Arrezzo, in order to secure his bid for the Papacy, a position from which he pledged to rid the Church of simoniacs (MacDonald 1932).

The Church had been complicit in maintaining the purchase of benefices through clerical marriage, a practice that was long permitted among the secular clergy (but not among cloistered monks) – from Pope to priests – by the ancient Church and which was common in the 11th century. Such marriages supported those who wished to maintain Church property within the family by inheritance from father to son, sometimes even permitting the alienation of Church lands when the son did not wish to take up his father's spiritual vocation (MacDonald 1932).

In the latter half of the 11th century, through a reform movement fuelled by monastic ideal (which included interdicts against marriage and vows of celibacy), successive Popes tried to reverse this practice and release the Papacy from what they saw as lay interference in ecclesiastical affairs. This struggle involved legists, high imperial and church officials, and armed men that enforced decisions made by rival factions. In 1075, Gregory VII attempted to carry to conclusion a series of reforms intended to strengthen the Church's hand in naming successors and, in this desire, he clashed with the Holy Roman Emperor Henry IV, who saw these moves as a threat to his political, social, and economic rights that had become bound up with and visible in the act of investiture. As Henry saw them, these were sacral duties, rights and privileges inherited from imperial forebears and ordained by God. On the other hand, Pope Gregory believed not only in his spiritual link to the divine, but also in his temporal ability to wield the sword to enforce his wishes.

The clash between Henry and Gregory ended with the sacking and partial burning of Rome by a mixed South Italian Norman and Saracen army, slavery for many of the city's inhabitants, and Gregory's eventual death a year later in 1085, as an exile in Salerno. Henry was eventually crowned Emperor on Easter Sunday 1084, in a ceremony performed by Pope Clement III, who Henry had invested as Pope on the previous Palm Sunday. Even with numerous subsequent attempts to harmonise temporal and spiritual powers, the overlap between them continued to cause contention and contest with the death of each temporal and spiritual office-holder, as well as those of their noble supporters and retainers, throughout the Middle Ages.

The theoretical link

There is a generalised tension between particularism and unity in socio-political structures. Within societies, this tension produces internal contradictions towards one or the other that not only accommodates but also facilitates group and individual endeavour, producing in the process what Crumley (1995) has termed 'heterarchy'. Heterarchy emerges when contemporary material remains from a past time indicate different kinds of social structures and power relations (see Crumley 1995, Levy 1995). Crumley argues that the study of power shifts can indicate how these occur and under what circumstances power structures constitute both stable and unstable governance. A hierarchy of values may appear to be enshrined at one social, spatial, and temporal scale, while at another or different scale, this hierarchy is not so straight-forward (Crumley 1995, Ashmore 2002). Thus societies and parts of societies can move between hierarchy and more shared and dispersed power structures, as well as encompassing both at once. Ianone (2002) has recently suggested that the tensions between these opposed social forces are part and parcel of societies, and they are responsible for the social changes that created the Maya state. The tension between kin-based social structures and the establishment of non-kin elites that cross-cut such kin-based relationships and that characterise state-level societies is at the heart of this apparent unevenness in the archaeological record. He suggests that because these forces produce fluctuations in the landscape of power they are most amenable to historical approaches designed specifically to deal with change, such as the historical *Annales* approach that looks at long-term change with reference to short-term events.

With regard to more recent politics, Verdery (1999, 24) comments along similar lines: "Political actors pursue their activities in arenas both large and small, public and private; the overlap and interference of the arenas shape what goes on in any one of them. Because human activity nearly always has affective and meaningful dimensions and takes place through complex symbolic processes… politics… [is] a realm of continual struggles over meanings, or signification." Like Verdery, Parker-Pearson (1993, 226) highlights the political nature of burial when he concludes: "These [processes that can be identified from the funerary record] are the use of the dead for political legitimation, the identification of the dead with a distant past, the naturalization of the social order by reference to a supernatural or ancestral hierarchy, the inversion of traditional funerary practices, the appropriation of components from other rituals, and the emulation of restricted practices by inferior social groups." Individuals responsible for the burying of the dead express not only their status, but also their socio-political aspirations as pretenders to unoccupied social positions, and this influences the manner and form of burial. Therefore, the body of the deceased and its context can be seen as a symbolic vessel for the claimant's desires as much as a commemoration of the dead individual.

This use of the dead would be expected to become more frequent and more obtrusive at rapid social transitions. In her analysis of the momentous transition to a post-socialist, global political system in Eastern Europe, Verdery (1999) demonstrates the way in which the preserved remains of dead leaders and physical rep-

resentations of the politically famous (or infamous) dead, such as statues, are used to support and shape socio-political concerns of the living. The dead are used to recreate and draw links to the past in order to legitimate and add credence to claims to rights and privileges made by the living. Although she notes that these political events occur at many social levels simultaneously, those that occur among the leadership are most prominent. There are both historical and ethnohistorical examples of the burials of leaders that reflect astute consideration for their political symbolism.

Brown (1985) notes that, although individual burial in propitious places has a long legacy in medieval Europe, the first tomb effigies – elaborate above-ground markers – of individual rulers date to the late 12th century (*cf.* Steane 1993, Duffy 2003, for the English monarchy). She links this phenomenon to spiritual concerns for the soul on the part of the deceased monarch, the financial rewards that establishments hosting such remains and their effigies could expect, but also, importantly, that the arrangement and re-arrangements of these tombs and, in the case of St. Denis, traditional burial church of the French monarchy, that these edifices and the corporeal remains they contained reflected the 'spiritual status of the king of France' (Brown 1985, 241) that was on a par with the earthly remains of saints. These saintly or sacred kings formed a key asset in anti-papal politics (Hallam 1982). These changing perspectives and the circumstance in which they were embedded can be seen as an extension of the political aspirations of individual monarchs since the time of Charles the Bald and the last Carolingians in the 9th century through to the desecrations of the French Revolution (1789) and subsequent restoration of the monarchy in the 19th century. Brown (*ibid.*, 243) writes, "For descendants and successors, imposing tombs dedicated to their ancestors and predecessors served as testimony to dynastic greatness and redounded to their own temporal welfare. Further, the cult of the ancestral dead served to shore up feelings of insecurity harboured by those whose claims to the authority they had inherited were questionable. As to the religious establishments where the rulers' bodies were interred, striking memorials testified to the continuing presence of the distinguished dead within their walls and thus won the houses both the renown and also the prospect of donations from those drawn to view and venerate the monuments."

In short, those who controlled the destiny of the dead also had a better grip on political power and the machinery of the state. In 1306, Philip IV 'Le Bel' (the 'Fair') succeeded in first canonising and then translating the body of his grandfather, Louis IX, hence St. Louis, from his foundation church, St. Chapelle, on the Ile de la Cité in Paris to St. Denis, the burial church of the French monarchy. The body of the saint and his tomb were placed next to those of his predecessors, Philip II Augustus and Louis VIII, leaving enough room for the insertion of Philip's own burial between that of the Saint and his parents' graves. In this way Philip emphasised the legitimacy of the earlier and contested Capetian dynasty, whose earliest members, Hugh Capet (died 996 A.D.) and Robert the Pious (died 1031 A.D.), had adopted St. Denis, the burial church of their Carolingian predecessors, as their own (Hallam 1982, Wyss 1997). Philip also inserted the tomb of his mother, Isabelle of Aragon, and his father, Philip III, and their associated earthly remains in the areas formerly reserved for Merovingian and Carolingian graves. There was thus no longer a spatial division within the church between the earlier Merovingian and Carolingian lineages and his own (Brown 1985). Philip's political message was made physical in this re-ordering; he had a long and distinguished dynastic lineage that included the Merovingian kings, descendants of Clovis, the first Christian king of the Franks (see below), and the Carolingian kings, descendants of Charlemagne, that would live beyond him. No doubt, too, a monarch associated with the abduction, if not the death, of the aged Pope Boniface VIII (an event that precipitated the so-called Babylonian Captivity that saw the French-backed Papacy installed in Avignon), also saw the opportunity to benefit from the proximity of his saintly grandfather for spiritual reasons.

Kirch (1980) provides another example of the modulating influence of longer-term political events on social ranking among historically known Tongan chiefdoms of 19th century Polynesia. In his analysis of protohistoric tombs, Kirch notes that the tomb of the Tu'i Tonga ('The Lord of Tonga') Paulaho, a descendent of a lineage of sacred chiefs, was of less elaborate construction – as measured by the height of the facing of tomb walls and tomb volume – than that of a certain Finau, the ranking chief of Vava'u. If social ranking had been the only criteria upon which his study had been based, this relationship would have been counter-intuitive. By the early 19th century, though, when Captain James Cook visited the islands, the line from which Finau was descended had achieved a dominant political and economic position through military conquest, eclipsing the traditionally more socially powerful, yet politically less effectual Tu'i Tonga. The less elaborate burial, then, reflects the shifting historical and political relationship between the two lineages and its leaders.

These examples demonstrate the potential socio-political importance of burial, as well as the aspirations of individuals responsible for the changes noted in the funerary record. Given such evidence, it seems odd that similar arguments have not been used to interpret changes in the funerary record for other places and other times. What follows considers why this has come to be the case.

The individual in prehistory

A number of researchers argue that due to the incompleteness and differential preservation of past material remains in the archaeological record, long and medium-term change can more easily be addressed than that involving short-term events which are the result of individual action or agency (*cf.* Bintliff 1991, Pauketat (2001) refers to these as macroscale and microscale events). Carver (2002, 135) summarises the current epistemological climate by noting that "… nothing could be more unfashionable than to credit historical events, change, or invention to an individual", but he also cautions that it is also "… not sufficient to say that the actions of individuals were only ephemeral within a broader *longue durée*." Through 'ancestralisation' of the past and as an apparent outgrowth of the notion of a collective mentality that has come to dominate prehistory (see also Whitley 2002), the individual has been lost to archaeological discourse. Last (1995, 148–149) notes the effect of an archaeological narrative predicated on long-term change that 'reduces agents to epiphenomena of structures'. Individual motivations, whether singular or in groups, have been removed from discourse as a result. Individuals become mere epiphenomena of social change, perhaps reflective of change in some poorly perceived way but in no way acting a part in such change. Curiously, this mirrors the situation in the integration of human remains in archaeological discourse, which often (although not always) come as individual burials that differ in their positioning, placement, demarcation, grave types, inclusions of objects, all of which might be summed up in their degree of 'monumentalisation' or 'memorialisation', qualities that to some are reducible, for comparative purposes, to 'energy expenditure' (Tainter 1978), the social *persona* (Binford 1972), or social rank (Pebbles and Kus 1977). The deceased also possesses, to use a term borrowed from forensic anthropology, 'individuating' features. These consist of identifying personal details such as age-at-death, sex (gender being a social construct that might be indicated by the sex of the deceased and the types of objects, burial positioning, or grave and its marker), kinship (through non-metric trait analysis, craniofacial dimensions and, possibly and more problematically, aDNA analysis), signs of life experiences such as healed (ante-mortem) and unhealed (peri-mortem) injuries or treatments (such as trepanation or amputation, for example), bony reactions to infection, disease, and disorder that relate to the health of the individual, stature and body proportions related to nutrition and socio-economic factors under which the individual grew and developed, and physiognomy (robusticity, asymmetrical development) that relate to physical activity, in addition to diet and geographical origin (from isotopic analyses).

Due to individual human life-spans, individuals have a short shelf-life. By the very nature of the human life-span, then, individual actions are relatively short-term events in the *Annaliste* sense, but a string of like-minded leaders can become part of conjunctures through motivating medium-term change that can form a *longue durée*, long-term change, if practices are continued by even longer-term successors. Therefore, the transmission of power is a potential social *tour-de-force* and a powerful metaphor for prolonged stability or, when such transmission is broken, disruptive change. Social change moderated in this way depends not only on there being leaders, but also on the type of person that occupies a particular position of authority at any particular time. Although the actions of the 'the common person' may be of a scale too small to be perceived, the same may not hold for leaders in the past whose burial often requires unusual and unique social and ritual sanctions (*cf.* Ucko 1969).

Agency in archaeology

In the introduction to Dobres and Robb's (2000) volume, *Agency and Archaeology*, the editors stress that 'eclectic tendencies' (p.10) have gripped the application of agency in archaeological discourse and interpretation. Although they feel that the ambiguity and contradictions thrown up by these differing uses are often compelling, ambiguity and contradiction is of greater interest if it is seen to play a part in the past, rather than acting to obscure understanding and communication in the present. The term 'agency' has been used to represent everything from the quality of agency itself, to conscious action, its unintended consequences, as well as a descriptive category that explains material patterning in the archaeological record. Agency, then, might refer to an individual; a group, such as a lineage, clan, caste or class; institutions, such as a ruling council; a workshop or craft specialist; a council of elders; or a sodality, such as a warrior society; or a dominant individual, such as a paramount leader or a ritualist.

Gillespie (2001) characterises problems with agency as an inability to reconcile how individuals are connected to society, its social structure, and social organisation. She argues that in the past the tendency was to see individuals as autonomous, self-interested actors, what she sees as an anachronistic (and Western) notion of the 'individual' as an historically contingent construct. She recommends using the notion of 'personhood' or 'selfhood' to bridge the gap between the individual and society. Personhood is derived from the enactment of relationships as part of everyday lived experience between people, groups, people and objects (as in a gift that cements a relationship) and between the living and the dead. Pauketat (2001) has also independently emphasised the problematic relationship between individual actors and the society that structures their actions. In his view (*ibid.*, 79) the failings of some recent approaches to agency (individual action) may be described as "...a trend toward methodological individualism, often overlooking the central importance of the process of 'structuration', the continuous creation of the conditions that govern practice, as opposed to particular agents."

Much of the hesitancy to ascribe individual motivation to archaeological patterns concerns an underestimation of the symbolic content of depositions. In describing the various theoretical uses of symbols in archaeological discourse, from those who posit that symbolic meaning is either beyond our comprehension or of no import to understanding how societies were structured in the past, to those who argue that symbols and their manipulation are fundamental to power and prestige, Robb (1998) notes that a conflictual view of the interplay of symbols may have more to do with perceptions of modern politics than it does with what he sees as essentially conservative ancient societies that tended to preserve fixed meanings for symbols. He also argues (Robb 1998, 339) that such a view encourages "all of symbolic life [to] become superficial, without historical or psychological roots – a transitory juxtaposition of images on a screen." As with the apparent ubiquity of the ancestors in dictating the form and content of funerary rites in the past (see Whitley 2002), this approach, in Robb's (1998, 339) view, seems to end with "generic portraits applicable to virtually any society." Although it seems wise to recommend caution in attributing individuality in the past based on symbolic relations, it may be that certain social transformations – such as a shift from one type of burial rite to another – arise from very similar social circumstances and indeed are part and parcel of the need to break with a largely conservative past.

Because individuals partake in long traditions that determine the form and appearance of their social roles to separate individual motivation from them is difficult. In the archaeological past, this may be due to the rarity of individuals pre-eminent enough to both influence social change and whose funerary treatment is visible to the archaeologist in a manner sufficient enough to be seen as individuals in the past. It is also a facet of an incomplete understanding of sequential change in the funerary context (dating) and burials being treated as cultural indicators of ethnicity based on group membership over considerable time-spans. Individual motivation in the past may be shielded from us, at present, not because it is an under-theorised concept, but because what we are seeking is rare and requires a synthetic and diachronic approach to, and knowledge of, the remains of burials and the context in which they occur. The origins of this rarity are due to vagaries introduced by archaeological preservation, coverage, and visibility, but also because too little has been made of the physical remains of the deceased in archaeological discourse to date. The problem with agency has been that researchers have concentrated on objects, landscapes and spatial relationships, but have not sufficiently linked these developments to the human beings who were the agents in the past (see contributions to Hill and Gunn 1977). Human remains are the corporeal remains of these agents. The further synthesis of these remains with other archaeological data would advance the cause of agency in the past.

Repetitive patterns are considered to relate to social memory, a process that has been linked to the creation of the ancestors, a social collectivity, with whom the living identify. Verdery (1999) contends that these social memories can be manipulated to both celebrate, remember, and 'ancestralise' the deceased. They may, however, also be used to erase individuals and groups from memory or re-invent them by emphasising different qualities of the person or group that serve emergent socio-political purposes; individuals' may be figuratively revived and their burials and re-burials commemorated but with their motivations and intentions re-ascribed. "History is remade, rewritten" (Rév 1995, 32). Although there are many individual sets of human remains from the past, it may be that individualism is limited in the past. In some cases, individuals may follow socio-politically embedded precepts under which their individuality may be disguised and unacknowledged in burial, or equally, they may be one among many people who aspire to positions of social prestige, to which only a few or even only one may attain (*cf.* Fried 1967). Funerary rites can, indeed, re-enforce community and social hierarchy and norms for the grand majority, yet this would act to set off unusual rites for individuals in even more stark contrast. Uniqueness- non-repetitive patterning- seems to be one, perhaps enduring, expression of individuality in the past (*cf.* Johnson 2000 for unique features of castle design of powerful individuals).

It is likely the political message of one or some that will make the greatest impact on the funerary record because these individuals provide the context, if not the motivation, for such changes in funerary rites. The more individualised the burial – its unique, propitious location and form, appearance, dress, and accoutrements – the more tumultuous and radical the shift in power. The uniqueness of burials ascribes to the act of deposition an even more portentous and a powerful social statement. Especially in pre-state societies the transfer of goods from one individual to another may be more about obtaining status and allies than about becoming materially wealthy (*cf.* Mauss 1990). The funerary domain, perhaps above all else, reflects this pre-occupation of the living.

Childéric and Clovis in the borderlands between prehistory and history

Sometime in the year 481 or 482 A.D. the Merovingian paramount, Childéric, died (James 1982) and his eldest son, Clovis, acceded to his father's position (*Liber Historiae Francorum* II.25), although what that entailed remains very much a matter of historical speculation. Identified variously as a Roman provincial ruler (Wood 1994), 'a Roman general' (Steuer 1989), one of the 'frankischer kleinkönig' (Anon. 1980), an administrator of *Belgica Secunda* (Kazanski 1997), or as 'King of the Salian Franks' (Kazanski 1997), Gregory of Tours in his *Liber Historiae Francorum* refers to Childéric as simply 'King of the Franks', a grand sobriquet for a leader that may have been little more than a chieftain with limited regional authority (especially compared with the position his son,

Clovis, attained) among many whose names Gregory mentions in connection with northern Gaul (*contra* Werner 1991). He seems to have acted in concert with the Romans, having aided the Roman general Aegidius in a war waged against the Visigoths in 463 A.D., one of a number of territorial conflicts that dominated northern Gaul in the late fifth century.

Although known from historiography, who Childéric was relies heavily on the discovery and excavation of a tomb replete with grave inclusions in modern Tournai, Belgium, on 27 May 1653, which "…put [Childéric] on the scholarly map…" (James 1988, 59) and which Wood (1994, 40) describes as "…perhaps the richest royal burial from the medieval period." This grave is perhaps the earliest ever recorded that contains an object identifying the occupant: a signet ring bearing the inscription CHILDERICI REGIS, and a portrait of an individual with long braided hair (a symbol of power among Germanic peoples), holding a shield and spear and wearing the *paludamentum*, the mantel of a Roman officer, and a neck chain (Fig. 14.1). Childéric's status as an ally of the Romans and, perhaps, leader of mixed Roman and Frankish warriors, rather than coming from chroniclers' accounts, is linked to the inclusion in the grave of a gold cruciform fibula or brooch that would have fastened the *Paludamentum*. Both the brooch and mantel are seen as insignia of a Roman officeholder (Kazanski 1997), objects presented to worthies at their investiture by the Emperor (James 1982). Werner (1991) argues that the presence of the signet ring, which he believes would have been used to confirm juridical acts, and the brooch and mantel, suggest that Childéric had become integrated into the late Roman state machinery. It seems as likely, though, that these objects may have been conferred as gifts to seal an alliance. Whether or not they confirmed juridical rights

Figure 14.1. The signet ring, found in Tournai, Belgium, near the church dedicated to St. Brice, which identified the grave as Childéric's (Reproduced with permission of the Ashmolean Museum, Oxford).

beyond those accorded a regional tribal leader seems less obvious, especially in the absence of an established bureaucracy, a system that does not seem implicated in an increasingly fragmented empire with unstable borders and waning political control.

Whatever Childéric's relationship was with the Romans, the full significance of this link was not realised until Clovis consolidated and extended the Merovingian dynasty's control of, first, northern Gaul and then beyond. Among Clovis' many recorded actions the most emphasised by later writers centres on his conversion to Christianity in about the year 500 A.D. Although we cannot know for certain what his personal motives were, this conversion appears to have resulted in Clovis' gaining the support of the Gallo-Roman populace (Moorhead 1985). Moorhead (1985, 339) characterises conversion by once pagan, yet Romanised Germanic leaders as "...a *rite de passage* for barbarians on the way to becoming civilized..." He emphasises that the goal in imitating the Gallo-Roman populace was not to woo this group but rather was a "culturally motivated desire to be like the Gallo-Romans." Roman Catholicism, then, could be seen as part of a package that propelled the Merovingian dynasty from being mere allies of the Romans under Childéric's suzerainty to being seen as the equal of them.

Recent insights into religious conversion reveal the political value of adopting what was, already in Clovis' time, a world religion. From anthropological studies of more recent conversions, Hefner (1993, 28) notes that the "hallmark of the world religions... is their subordination of local spirits, dialects, customs, and territory to a higher spiritual cosmology. They declare the superiority of God or gods over low spirits, scriptural Word over local babble, transregional clerics over local curers, and a Holy Land or lands over local territory." Thus Childéric's burial and Clovis's conversion mark a transition from a belief system focused on the community and its relationship to its own exclusive gods to a doctrinally-based, transcendental one attained through initiation into a large community of the faithful and adherence to strict moral codes (*cf.* Russell 1994: 48). Christian conversion, then, suited a leader who desired the breakdown of the old social order established on local influence and control with one that focused on a larger and more pan-regional society with non-local control. In his analysis of Germanic kinship structure, Murray (1983, 64–65) writes, "Kinship was a crucial factor in all... activity, but its uses and groupings were fluid, and probably on the whole not long lasting.... If kinship groupings or kinship-based groups lay behind many political, military and social institutions, these were groups leavened not merely by blood relationship and lordship but by a strong dose of personal preference and allegiance, and economic and personal interest. It was a situation that offered mobility and choice, and which at times would result in the conflicting claims and obligations which are

the stuff of epic." This fluid social structure also made it unstable and resistant to supra-regional authority.

Clovis's actions see him intimating links with the Eastern Empire, perhaps like Charlemagne two centuries later (see Moreland and van de Noort 1992), striving to be the equivalent of the Eastern Emperor. This is peer polity interaction (see Renfrew 1986) that suggests a similar approach to power and power relations within Europe for at least a millennium. In this policy Clovis achieved success, having received recognition in the form of a consular office from the Eastern Emperor Anastasius. He adopted the titles of 'consul' and 'augustus' says Gregory (II.38). The symbolism of Clovis' dress leaves little doubt as to his political aspirations. Gregory tells us that: "In St. Martin's church he stood clad in a purple tunic and the military mantle, and he crowned himself with a diadem" (*Liber Historiae Francorum* II.38). As well as his choice of the imperial purple, Clovis' imitation of the 4th-century Emperor Constantine comes to the fore in much else. Like Constantine, he converts to Christianity after receiving a sign of divine support in the form of victory (in battle against the Alamans) (*Liber Historiae Francorum* II.30). He, like Constantine in his foundation of a new capital, Constantinople, founds a new capital in Paris (*Liber Historiae Francorum* II.38). Clovis is interred in his new capital in the Church of the Holy Apostles, thus sharing the same dedication as the Church in which Constantine was interred 200 years previously in Constantinople (Périn 1992). Here, though, we may be seeing what Gregory of Tours wished us to see – that the obvious similarities supported Gregory's contention that Clovis was indeed 'like some new Constantine' (*Liber Historiae Francorum* II.31). Perhaps Gregory's comments should be seen as panegyric or as a justification for what had become established norm in his own day. The symbolism of Clovis' actions suggests that he may not only have been imitating the material form of Constantine's imperial style but also its symbolic meaning. When the Roman Emperor Constantine was inhumed in the Church of the Holy Apostles in Constantinople, the tombs of the Apostles were placed on either side of his own. Constantine was the first emperor to be inhumed and also the first whose passing was not marked by a funeral pyre; this new funerary procedure ensured Christian immortality such that the Emperor's biographer, Eusebius, noted that Constantine continued to rule the Empire in death as he had in life (Price 1987). The implications of these innovations may not have been lost on Clovis, who desired the same long-lasting rule. Important, too, in the adoption of a new religion is a rejection of what came before and the social order that drew support from it. Comparing the burials of the father, Childéric, and the son, Clovis, can disentangle potentially misleading metaphors and aspirations.

Although Tournai was the capital of *Belgica Secunda*, its selection as the burial place of Childéric remains obscure. In an area that later became the location of a church dedicated to St. Brice, the immediate area of the burial appears to have been distinguished by little more than a Roman road running to the northeast, some 25 metres away. No previously existing church has been found on the site that pre-dates the 9th century (Brulet 1990). An area around the burial that is devoid of features suggests the presence of a tumulus (see Fig. 14.2 for an example), measuring some 20 to 40 metres in diameter (Brulet 1991), perhaps once containing a chamber that was 2.2 metres deep (Anon., 1980). This tumulus became the central focus for later burials dating from the 5th and 7th centuries. Three large ditch features containing the articulated remains of 21 horses surround and border the area of the tumulus at a distance of about 20 metres. All of these ditch deposits may not be of the same date, but they do date from the first half of the Merovingian period and could be contemporaneous with Childéric's burial (Gilot 1991). Based on their size and proportions, these horses were, for the most part, geldings (seven) and stallions (seven), with one possible mare and three foals less than a year and a half old at death represented, all of which had been placed in the ditches without any standard orientation (Ghenne-Dubois 1991). This spatial patterning suggests that Childéric's burial was a founder's burial, of a type that is known from a variety of other near-contemporary locations (Brulet 1991). The mix of Roman

influences with those that are much more akin to un-romanised Germanic practices lend an ambiguity to the burial. The church of St. Brice, founded within 10 metres of Childéric's burial, and later burials do not respect the earlier features. This apparent phase change indicates that, despite the presence of a mound, the location and significance of the burial was, in a relatively short time, forgotten.

Although the Roman trappings of the burial reflect links to the Late Roman Empire, many of the inclusions are unique, including a gold bull's head; 300 gold cicadas, symbols of eternal life (Werner 1964), that may once have decorated garments Werner 1964) or, alternatively, a horse harness (James 1988); the extensive range of garnet encrusted gold cloisonné jewellery and large gold bracelet belie a connection with the sumptuary and symbols that promoted and maintained leadership among northern and central European peoples in the fifth century. A purse containing 100 gold coins minted in Constantinople between AD 476 and 491 attests to connections, at once perhaps political and certainly symbolic of external links, with the Eastern Empire (Werner 1964, Kazanski 1997). A further 200 silver coins dating from Republican Rome to the reign of Constantius II (340–361) (Anon 1980), provide links with an even deeper Roman past (see Table 14.1).

Figure 14.2. A reconstructed tumulus at L'Archéodrome du Bourgogne (Source: author).

Inclusion	Prestige	Sumptuary (worn on the body)	Exotica (symbolic of external links)	Ceremonial	Martial	Spiritual
Shield	√?	√?		√?	√?	
Long Sword (*spatha*)		√?		√?	√?	
Scramasaxe		√?		√?	√?	
Hatchet (*francisca*)					√?	
Lance					√?	
Cruciform fibula	√	√?		√	√	
100 gold coins, dated from Emperor Theodosius (450 A.D. to Emperor Zeno (476–491 A.D.)	√		√			
200 silver coins, Republican Roman to Constantius II (340–361 A.D.)	√		√			
300 gold cicadas	√	√?		√		√
Gold bracelet	√	√?				√
Signet ring depicting *Paludamentum*	√	√?		√		
Cloisonné jewellery (purse)	√	√?	√			
Bull's head	√	√?		√		√
Horses	√			√	√	√
Chamber/mound	√			√		√

Table 14.1. Summary of Childéric's Persona *based on occurrences in other male burials of the period.*

The multiple horse burials, perhaps with one included in full harness in the tumulus itself, is a pre-Christian practice (Ghenne-Dubois 1991). This practice became a focus for suppression of monastic missionaries in later years, not only due to its ritualistic opposition to Christian practices, but, perhaps more importantly, because horses were used to display social pre-eminence and their sacrifice may have formed part of the ceremonies that accompanied changes in leadership (*cf.* Knüsel and Ripley 2000), but simultaneously also had symbolic funerary associations for individuals and groups in the Early Medieval period (see Bond and Worley, this volume and Williams 2001). Horses and their sacrifice were bound up with offerings to both Freyr, a fertility deity, and perhaps most strongly with Odin/Wodan, a sky god associated with warfare, the dead, magic, and poetry among Nordic peoples (Simek 1993, see also discussion in Brulet 1991, 21). Writing in the first century A.D., Tacitus ascribed a sacral quality to horses; horses played a role in rituals involving divination and the consultations of 'kings and priests' (*Germania* 10). The horses, then, could, in addition to being signs of conspicuous destruction of wealth, also symbolise a sacral link between Germanic rulers and the gods with whom rulers acted as intermediaries and who provided good luck. Frankish paramounts seem to have associated themselves closely with Odin/Wodan and have been described as "Wotanic kings", the bull with a solar disk between its horns found among the grave inclusions symbolising the link between Childéric's interment and the sky god, Odin/Wodan (Russell 1994, 175). Given the presence of numerous weapons in the burial, including a long sword or *spatha,* decorated with gold; a *scramasaxe* or short, thrusting sword; a lance; a hatchet or *franzisca,* and a shield, the martial component of Childéric is emphasised and represented, further strengthening the link with the war-faring aspect of Odin/Wodan's constitution.

James (1988, 61) proffers that a crystal ball came to be associated with Childéric's grave due to the disturbance of a neighbouring grave during the excavation in 1653. If part of the interred material associated with Childéric, however, it may symbolise an association with healing powers (see Knüsel 2002). Childéric's burial, then, is a syncretic mix of powerful and splendid symbols of the warrior, the ceremonialist, the sacred leader, a person of far-flung relations with the powerful- all of those items linked to the fifth century social and political climate, gathered together, deposited in one place, and subsequently forgotten.

It is unclear who arranged the burial of Childéric in Tournai, although it seems likely that Clovis did (Steuer 1989). Although Gregory of Tours provides considerable detail of Clovis' place of burial, with regard to Childéric's he reports nothing. This silence is matched only by the silence of more recent sources about the physical remains of the body interred in the tumulus at Tournai. Of these, nothing is said in more recent treatments, although the human remains are described as being "gut erhaltenen Gebeinen" ("well-preserved bones"), which were also found with an additional cranium deemed to be that of a female (Anon. 1980). Childéric is, indeed, the epitome of the body being used as a clotheshorse (see the Introduction to this volume). We do not know what Childéric looked like- the nature of his physique (robusticity), how tall he was, how old he was at death (a figure which is not recorded in historical documents either), what his health status was at death, in what manner he died, and whether or not he bore the physical signs of active participation in warfare in the form of weapon injuries (see Knüsel 2005) or biomechanical alterations (see Knüsel 2000, Rhodes and Knüsel, 2005) that would help us to separate the symbolic from the martial component of the weapons included in the burial, perhaps in conjunction with metallurgical analysis of the weapons themselves for evidence of use. Due to this absence and the lack of recorded placement of the objects with respect to the human remains, we really do not know what sort of leader Childéric was (see question marks in Table 14.1).

On the other hand, Gregory tells us that Clovis was 45 years of age at death (in 511 A.D.) and by calculation he must have been only 15 years of age when his father died in 481–482 A.D. Clovis' own church burial (at the Church of the Holy Apostles, hence known as St. Geneviève, in Paris) (see Périn 1992) harkened to the saintly defender of the city (Geneviève, over whose grave the church was built) against Attila's Huns, the power of a supreme deity,

an indomitable Emperor who converted to Roman Catholicism, and the venerable Church with its antecedents in the Roman world. Whether or not the 15-year-old anticipated the course of events that would transform him into 'some new Constantine' in the 480s, the intervening 30 years allowed him the time to usher in a new order that inspired his successors and, moreover, their supporters. Clovis' burial and likely the obsequies leading to it inspired Charlemagne's own burial within an annex Charlemagne himself had added to the cathedral at Aachen, three hundred years later (Fig. 14.3). Einhard tells us in his *Vita Caroli (Life of Charlemagne)* that the burial of Charlemagne was arranged by others in the absence of knowing the wishes of the dead Emperor (although see Dierkens (1991) and Collins (1998, 136-137), who emphasise the geographical and political centrality, respectively, of Aachen within the Carolingian Empire). Later, still, Clovis's interment would inspire the French monarchy to establish a burial church at St. Denis, which contained an effigy of Clovis, if not his actual remains (Brown 1985, Périn 1992) (Fig. 14.4). The link between Clovis and the later monarchs seems well-established from material remains and in historiography. This stands in contrast to Childéric's tomb from which the body was, apparently, never removed in antiquity.

Clovis' actions may have instilled a sense of solidarity during a social change that would see the creation of

Figure 14.3. The octagonal basilica and cupola at Aachen Cathedral built by Charlemagne that became his burial location. Clovis' burial location, in an annex, would have been a similar, although less grand, structure (Source: author).

hereditary rule for himself and his descendants, the creation of written laws, the *Lex Salica*, from oral tradition, and an institutionalised inequality in power and power relations embodied in the first episcopal council in 511 A.D., in which Clovis met with the bishops of Gaul (Becker 2003). Clovis's violent policy towards his own kin, recounted by Gregory of Tours, marks a forceful shift from kin-based rule that characterises pre-state chiefly societies (see Earle 1987, 1997, Kristiansen 1991) to that of sole ruler with the power of life and death over all those with whom he came into contact. Gregory reports that Clovis made the following comment: "How sad it is that I live among strangers like some solitary pilgrim, and that I have none of my own relations left to help me when disaster threatens" of which Gregory comments obliquely, "He said this not because he grieved for their deaths, but because in his cunning way he hoped to find some relatives still in the land of the living whom he could kill" (*Liber Historiae Francorum* II, 42). Gregory, though, was in no doubt about the result of these actions: "By doing this he spread his dominion over the whole of Gaul." By attacking his own kin, Clovis was removing those who, in the old chiefly tribal order, could act to undermine his desire for personal power and pave the way for dynastic aggrandisement beyond his own death.

The transition to Clovis' rule was made in the traditional manner. Childeric's finery was interred in hoard-like splendour, within a chamber, beneath a mound. It seems that such a large burial was intended to be conspicuous; it did attract interments around it after its creation for a period afterwards. The burial, though, can also be seen as the first act in a political play that anticipates Clovis acting 'like some new Constantine' (*Liber Historiae Francorum* II.31). Given the advanced age of some of the objects interred, such as the coins, the burial might be seen as an anachronistic appeal to the past that was intended to unify potential followers behind the new leader. Clovis' accession would likely have been aided by a display of conspicuous largesse to the dead 'king', his father, and that likely extended to the pretender's would-be supporters (Bullough 1983). As Steuer (1989, 107) observes, "The objective of the activities surrounding burial was to determine the rank not merely of the deceased, but also of the group to which she/he belonged, especially its head." In this act that one might see as commemorative, Clovis marked his ascendancy by removing the symbols of his father's leadership, burying him (or allowing him to be buried by others) in the old chiefly style beneath a mound (more reminiscent of earlier Iron Age practice than his own church burial that was to come). Where Childéric's power resided in links to old divinities, objects, kin, and alliances with the regional potentates of the waning Empire, Clovis' would reside in a supreme deity with links to Constantine, the Imperial

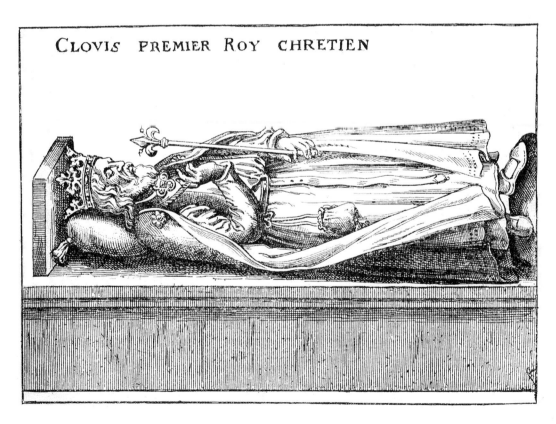

Figure 14.4. A 17th-century reconstruction of Clovis's tomb. Here his appearance has been up-dated to correspond with the regalia of later medieval kingship (Reproduced with permission of the Boydell Press).

Roman state, its unifying authority and, ultimately, to Clovis himself as an inheritor of this legacy. Clovis' tomb was a church made in stone that evinced permanence, while Childéric's was of earth and wood, perishable, impermanent, located in an area that was to lose its significance.

Childéric's remains, the weapons and symbolic sumptuary that would have been seen to characterise his authority in death, as they appear to have done in life, were locked away and forgotten in the act of burial. Their removal left the political space necessary for Clovis to forge a more centralised leadership, one more fit to his desire to exert his authority over a much larger and more highly integrated, yet nascent Merovingian state. The interment of the signet ring bearing the potentate's likeness and name- the object linked perhaps to what would later become juridical, stately control- marked a juridical death as well as a physical one. No-one henceforth could claim to be or act on behalf of the dead potentate. Part of the physical reality of the dead leader's identity had been removed, leaving a memory that could be manipulated or, as seems the case for later commentators, left unelaborated.

As much as the manner and form of Childéric's burial attests to much that one could call individual- unique- and unsurpassed in splendour, size, and grandeur for its time and place- it represents a continuation with the past. Clovis' own burial, though, represents a rupture with tradition. His burial marks the final part of his vision for what would become the Merovingian state. Given that Clovis' contemporaries carried out this act of burial, it seems to have been in harmony with their aspirations as well. Both burials look to the past for inspiration, but they are different pasts. Childéric's is older and traditional in that it looks to the pre-Roman past for inspiration, suffused as it is with pre-Christian symbols of belief and leadership, while Clovis' recreates that of a more prox- imate past, one that recalled that of a divine and Christian Emperor who lived nearly 200 years previously. Childéric's burial owed its creation to practices recorded in oral tradition (orthopraxy), while Clovis' drew on those recorded in historical documents (orthodoxy). Childéric's relied on the conspicuous largesse of chiefly prerogative, while Clovis' looked forward to the apparent permanence of dynastic succession. The success of Clovis' political intentions can be measured in the way in which the written record of his father is so adumbrated, and his father's burial so completely expunged from memory, its politically powerful symbolic content dimmed and locked away.

Conclusion

In his study of the Ndembu of Central Africa, Victor Turner (1995, 10) noted that: "As we became increasingly part of the village scene, we discovered that very often decisions to perform ritual were connected with crises in the social life of villages." Death marks one of these periods of crisis in that each death changes the social structure of the living community. The impact of death has a scalar quality in that some deaths touch the lives of many more people, directly or indirectly, than do others due to their position in the social structure (cf. Binford 1972). Although all deaths create a period of uncertainty and social disruption, the death of an incumbent leader is socially and politically portentous because, as Fried (1967) noted, there are often more individuals who are capable- or at least feel themselves capable- of assuming the dead incumbent's position than can actually accede to that position. Others, too, may wish to and do influence the ceremonial rite of passage to better accommodate their personal agenda. These competing desires create an atmosphere of uncertainty that leads to contest and, often, controversy as those who wish to occupy the social position of the deceased vie with one another through re- aligning themselves and others within the social structure. Much is at stake. Investiture entitles and enables one. It permits access to sumptuary clothing and objects denied to others. It carries with it the rights to land and resources. It acknowledges the right to perform ceremonies and warrants community support in undertakings.

In societies with a well-developed bureaucracy, pre- cedent has been enshrined in legal codes, a type of historical record, that fosters an atmosphere of stately, organised, and premeditated transition underlined by ceremonies, the significance of which draws on the orthodoxy of the written word. In Imperial Rome, the apotheosis of the dead emperor through the funeral pyre was organised by his successor and the senate because "...of the need to create and define roles, both for the emperor and the Roman elite" (Price 1987, 83). Not until the High Middle Ages in both France and England did the dying king become synonymous with the heir- apparent; successor and predecessor appeared as the same person with regard to the office, the *dignitas*, which continued despite the demise of the incumbent (Kantorowicz 1957). The successor, usually the eldest son, took the throne immediately upon the death of his father and predecessor, eventually without even the previously requisite formal investiture, which sometimes came a considerable time afterwards and in which the Church played a increasingly vanishing role in the course of the Middle Ages. In later medieval society the *dignitas* or office was thus conceived of as separate from the office- holder. Kantorowicz (1957) argued that this dualism developed from medieval Christian political theology and had no antecedents in antiquity. This system removed some of the uncertainty from political transitions and ordained inheritance of political control. Eventually, it would create divine right monarchs.

In many pre-state societies, the office and title and the individual are not discrete and the ruler is also seen to be intimate with or to personify a deity (see Mauss 1990, Rowlands 1994). In such societies, there is a less formal succession because leadership is personalised. The successor to such a leader must be seen to be the equivalent or the better of the deceased leader, and this requires elaborate ritual display that involves neutralising or assuaging the claims of would-be pretenders, usually through transfer of commodities or rights and privileges (gift exchange). In societies without legal codes or where such codes are unclear, out-moded, or contradictory, precedent is guided by unwritten orthopraxy embedded in oral histories, remembered and embellished stories of past circumstances, events and group (lineage, clan, or caste) or individual action. The ceremonies that surround the death of incumbents and that accompany the investiture of new leaders to replace them represent a social affirmation of the right to succeed and, for some, to rule. Although both orthodoxy and orthopraxy contribute to the creation of social memory (the how and why of action), of the two, orthopraxy is the more labile, less concrete, likely because its precepts and accompanying ceremonies and their significance are only completely and intimately remembered and understood by the few- or, even, the one. The dead leader is an active participant in the creation of social memory as pretenders manipulate the physical demise and the social disruption that follows to both ease and provide justification for their own accession. The dead and the manner in which they are treated thus act as signposts to and symbols for past political circumstance. Their handling thus reveals aspects of the intentions and actions of those to whom succession is made. The dead may be eulogised and memorialised by some after death or, alternatively, their physical demise may be used to provide the context for re-interpretation and affirmation of social change.

With the more recent excavations in Tournai in the vicinity of what was once Childéric's tumulus, as Brulet (1991, 11) notes, burials dating from the later fifth to the seventh centuries – that is from little time before Childéric's burial to a little time after his burial – have been excavated. In other words, some people, even in the time of Clovis, continued to be buried with his deceased predecessor father. In what may be a sign of disaffection, regional loyalty, or the maintenance of old practices, in the continued burials, one may perceive the seeds of what transpired after Clovis' reign. After Clovis' death the territory he controlled was divided among his four sons, and until the 8th century, the Frankish political terrain was inhabited by many kings- being a king's son did not guarantee succession (Nelson 1987). The unity that Clovis fought to create was not maintained for long after his death. After his death, Gregory of Tours' *History* records civil strife, internecine warfare, assassination, and political murder after political murder. Gregory, himself, was aware of the effects of these changes. In the introduction to Book V of his *Liber Historiae Francorum,* he writes: "It gives me no pleasure to write of all the different civil wars which afflicted the Frankish people and their rulers… The Franks ought, indeed, to have been warned by the sad fate of their earlier kings, who, through, their inability ever to agree with each other, were killed by their enemies. If only you kings had occupied yourselves with wars like those in which your ancestors larded the ground with their sweat, then the other races of the earth, filled with awe at the peace which you imposed, might have been subjected to your power! Just think of all that Clovis achieved, Clovis, the founder of your victorious country…" Gregory laments the particularism and disunity to which he credits the potential demise of the Franks. Due to the cultural syncretism that was conversion to Christianity in the fifth century, rather than the precepts of Christian philosophy superseding those of the warrior-leaders who converted, it was the warrior-leaders who transformed Christianity, injecting it with a warrior ethic that would last beyond the Middle Ages (*cf.* Russell 1994). The interplay between Christianity and older forms of belief fostered Clovis' political aims. He substituted the worship of the old gods for that of the one all powerful god and, in the process, aligned himself with the spiritual leaders in their Roman diocesan enclaves within his realm.

In the quotation that inspires the title to this contribution, the *Beowulf* poet is anachronistic. The buried wealth was not a meaningless gesture, as he seems to intimate, but one through which succession to the rights and privileges of the deceased was mediated and ultimately decided. Clovis' ascendancy was marked by removing the symbols of his father's reign, burial of him and them in the old chiefly style beneath a mound. In this case, the material value of such objects was far less than their symbolic value, predicated on their association with pre-Christian beliefs and practices. Therefore, their inclusion in the grave removed them from the world of the living. They were lost and forgotten among the dead, which contributes to our lack of full comprehension of their meaning today. Perhaps unexpectedly, the individual in prehistory and protohistory may be glimpsed not only in their own burial but also- perhaps more clearly- in that of their predecessor.

Note

1 *Beowulf* (Ll. 3168).

Acknowledgements

Carol Palmer, on more than one occasion, listened to the ideas that eventually became this paper and then read the result and made comments upon and improved them. Becky Gowland, John Moreland, and John Robb also made extensive, helpful and thought-provoking comments on this paper, for which I am most appreciative. I thank the Research Seminar Series, Department of Archaeology, University of Sheffield, and *The Connectors and Catalysts* conference at the Institute for Medieval Studies, University of Leeds, for the opportunity to air versions of and receive comments on the views expressed in this paper, as well as successive years of Master's students in funerary archaeology at Bradford, whose enthusiasm, interest, and thoughtful criticism have been so beneficial in helping me to hone these ideas. These people and organisations are, of course, blameless for any remaining deficiencies in this piece.

References

Anon. (1980) *Gallien in der Spätantike. Von Kaiser Constantin zu Frankenkönig Childerich. Katalog zur Ausstellung,* Mainz am Rhein, Romisch-Germanishe Zentralmuseum, Forschungsinstitüt für Vor und Frühgeschichte.

Anon. (1999) *Beowulf.* Translated by Seamus Heaney. London, Faber and Faber.

Ashmore, W. (2002) 'Decisions and dispositions': socializing spatial archaeology. *American Anthropologist* 104 (4), 1171–1183.

Atkinson, J. M. (1992) Shamanisms today. *Annual Review of Anthropology* 21, 307–330.

Becker, M. (2003) *Charlemagne.* New Haven and London, Yale University Press.

Binford, L.R. (1972) Mortuary practices: Their study and potential. In L.R. Binford (ed.) *An Archaeological Perspective,* 108–243. New York, Seminar Press.

Bintliff, J. (1991) The Contribution of an *Annaliste*/Structural History Approach to Archaeology. In J. Bintliff (ed.) *The Annales School and Archaeology,* 1–33. Leicester, Leicester University Press.

Brown, E. A. R. (1985) Burying and unburying the Kings of France. In R.C. Trexler (ed.) *Persons in Groups,* 241–266. Binghamton (NY), Medieval and Renaissance Texts and Studies 36.

Brulet, R. (1990) *Les Fouilles du Quartier Saint-Brice à Tournai 1*: L'Environnement Funéraire de la Sépulture de Childéric. Louvain-la- Neuve, Département d' Archéologie et d'Histoire de l'Art.

Brulet, R. (1991) *Les Fouilles du Quartier Saint-Brice à Tournai 2*: L'Environnement Funéraire de la Sépulture de Childéric. Louvain-la- Neuve, Département d' Archéologie et d'Histoire de l'Art.

Bullough, D. (1983) Burial, community and belief in the early medieval west. In P. Wormald, D. Bullough, and R. Collins (eds.) *Ideal and Reality in Frankish and Anglo-Saxon Society,* 177–201. Oxford, Blackwell.

Carver, M. (2002) Reflections on the meanings of monumental barrows in Anglo-Saxon England. In Sam Lucy and Andrew Reynolds (eds.) *Burial in Early Medieval England and Wales,* 132–143. London, The Society for Medieval Archaeology.

Collins, R. (1998) *Charlemagne.* Basingstoke and London, MacMillan Press.

Crumley, C. L. (1995) Heterarchy and the analysis of complex societies. In R. M. Erhenreich, C. L. Crumley, and J. E. Levy (eds.) *Heterarchy and the Analysis of Complex Societies,* 1–5. Arlington (VA.), Archaeological Papers of the American Anthropological Association Number 6.

Dierkens, A. (1991) Autour de la tombe de Charlemagne: considerations sur les sépultures et les funérailles des souverains carolingiens et des membres de leur famille. *Byzantion* 61: 156–180.

Dobres, M. -A. and Robb, J. E. (2000) Agency in archaeology: paradigm or platitude. In Dobres, M. -A. and J. E. Robb (eds.) *Agency in Archaeology,* 3–17. London and New York, Routledge.

Duffy, M. 2003. *Royal Tombs of Medieval England.* Stroud, Gloucestershire, Tempus.

Earle, T. (1987) Chiefdoms in archaeological and ethnohistorical perspective. *Annual Review of Anthropology* 16, 297–308.

Earle, T. (1997) *How Chiefs Come to Power: The Political Economy in Prehistory.* Stanford, Stanford University Press.

Einhard the Stammerer (1969) *Life of Charlemagne.* Translated by Lewis Thorpe. Harmondsworth, Penguin Books.

Fried, M.H. (1967) *The Evolution of Political Society.* New York, Random House.

Ghenne-Dubois, M.- J. (1991) Les sépultures de chevaux. In R. Brulet (ed.) *Les Fouilles du Quartier Saint-Brice à Tournai,* 23–34. Louvain-La-Neuve, Département d'Archéologie et d'Histoire de l'Art.

Gillespie, S. D. (2001) Personhood, agency, and mortuary ritual: a case study from the ancient Maya. *Journal of Anthropological Archaeology* 20, 73–112.

Gilot, É. (1991) Datation au ^{14}C. In R. Brulet (ed.) *Les Fouilles du Quartier Saint-Brice à Tournai,* 47–49. Louvain-La-Neuve, Département d'Archéologie et d'Histoire de l'Art.

Gregory of Tours (1974) *The History of the Franks.* Translated by Lewis Thorpe. Harmondsworth, Penguin Books.

Hallam, E.M. (1982) Royal burial and the cult of kingship in France and England, 1060–1330. *Journal of Medieval History* 8, 359–380.

Hamayon, R. (1996) Shamanism in Siberia: from partnership in supernature to counter-power in society. In N. Thomas and C. Humphrey (ed.) *Shamanism, History, and the State,* 76–89. Ann Arbor, University of Michigan Press.

Hefner, R. W. (1993) World building and the rationality of conversion. In R.W. Hefner (ed.) *Conversion to Christianity: Historical and Anthropological Perspectives on a Great Transformation,* 3–44. University of California Press, Berkeley.

Hill, J. N. and Gunn, J. (1977) *The Individual in Prehistory: Studies of Variability in Style in Prehistoric Technologies.* New York, Academic Press.

Humphrey, C. (1996) Shamanic practices and the state in northern Asia. In N. Thomas and C. Humphrey (ed.) *Shamanism, History, and the State,* 191–228. Ann Arbor, University of Michigan Press.

Ianone, G. (2002) *Annales* history and the ancient Maya state: Some observations on the "dynamic model". *American Anthropologist* 104(1), 68–78.

James, E. (1982) *The Origins of France: From Clovis to the Capetians, 500–1000.* London and Basingstoke, Macmillan Press.

James, E. (1988) *The Franks.* Oxford, Basil Blackwell,

Johnson, M. (2000) Self-made men and the staging of agency. In M. -A. Dobres and J. E. Robb (eds.) *Agency in Archaeology,* 213–231. London and New York, Routledge.

Kantorowicz, E. H. (1957) *The King's Two Bodies: A Study in Medieval Political Theology.* Princeton, Princeton University Press.

Kazanski, M. (1997) *Les Francs: Précurseurs de l'Europe.* Les Musées de la Ville de Paris, Paris.

Kirch, P.V. (1980) Burial structures and societal ranking in Vava'u, Tonga. *Journal of the Polynesian Society* 89(3), 291–308.

Knüsel, C.J. (2000) Activity-related changes in casualties from the medieval battle of Towton, A.D. 1461, In V. Fiorato, A. Boylston, and C.J. Knüsel, (eds.) *Blood Red Roses: The Archaeology of a Mass Grave from Towton, A.D 1461,* 103–118. Oxford, Oxbow Books.

Knüsel, C.J. (2002) Of crystal balls, political power, and changing contexts: what the clever women of Salerno inherited. In P. A. Baker and G. C. Carr (eds.) *Practitioners, Practices, and Patients: New Approaches to Medical Archaeology and Anthropology,* 172–194. Oxford, Oxbow Books.

Knüsel, C.J. (2005) The evidence of warfare – subtle stigmata. In M. Parker Pearson and I. J. N. Thorpe (eds.) *Violence, Warfare, and Slavery*, 49–65. British Archaeological Reports International Series 1374. Oxford, Archaeopress.

Knüsel, C. J. and Ripley, K. M. (2000) The Man-Woman or 'Berdache' in Anglo-Saxon England and Post-Roman Europe. In W. Frazer and A. Tyrrell (eds.) *Social Identity in Early Medieval Britain*, 157–191. Leicester, Leicester University Press.

Kristiansen, K. (1991) Chiefdoms, states, and systems of social evolution. In T. Earle (ed.) *Chiefdoms: Power, Economy, and Ideology*, 16–43. Cambridge, Cambridge University Press.

Last, J. (1995) The nature of history. In I. Hodder, M. Shanks, A. Alexandri, V. Buchli, J. Carman, J. Last, and G. Lucas, (eds.) *Interpreting Archaeology: Finding Meaning in the Past*, 141–158. London, Routledge.

Levy, J. E. (1995) Heterarchy in Bronze Age Denmark: Settlement Pattern, Gender, and Ritual. In R. M. Ehrenreich, C. L. Crumley, and J. E. Levy (eds.) *Heterarchy and the Analysis of Complex Societies*, 41–53. Arlington (VA.): Archeological Papers of the American Anthropological Association Number 6.

MacDonald, A. J. (1932) *Hildebrand (Gregory VII)*. London, Methuen and Co. Ltd.

Mauss, M. (1990) *The Gift: The Form and Reason for Exchange in Archaic Societies*. Translated by W.D. Halls. London, Routledge.

McKitterick, R. (1997) Constructing the past in the early middle ages: the case of the Royal Frankish annals. *Transactions of the Royal Historical Society* 7, 101–29.

McKitterick, R. (2000) The illusion of royal power in the Carolingian annals. *English Historical Review* 115, 1–20.

Moreland, J. and van de Noort, R. (1992) Integration and social reproduction in the Carolingian Empire. *World Archaeology* 23(3), 320–334.

Moorhead, J. (1985) Clovis' motives for becoming a Catholic Christian. *Journal of Religious History* 13(4), 329–339.

Murray, A. C. (1983) *Germanic Kinship Structure: Studies in Law and Society in Antiquity and the Early Middle Ages*. Toronto, Pontifical Institute of Mediaeval Studies.

Nelson, J. L. (1987) The Lord's anointed and the people's choice: Carolingian Royal Ritual. In D. Cannadine and S. Price (eds.) *Rituals of Royalty: Power and Ceremonial in Traditional Societies*, 137–180. Cambridge, Cambridge University Press.

Parker Pearson, M. (1993) The powerful dead: archaeological relationships between the living and the dead. *Cambridge Archaeological Journal* 3(2), 203–229.

Pauketat, T. R. (2001) Practice and history in archaeology: an emerging paradigm. *Anthropological Theory* 1(1), 73–98.

Périn, P. (1992) The undiscovered grave of King Clovis I (died 511). In M.O.H. Carver (ed.) *The Age of Sutton Hoo: The Seventh Century in North-western Europe*, 255–264. Woodbridge, Suffolk, The Boydell Press.

Peebles, C. and Kus, S. (1977) Some archaeological correlates of ranked societies. *American Antiquity* 42, 421–448.

Price, S. (1987) From noble funerals to divine cult: the consecration of Roman Emperors. In D. Cannadine and S. Price (eds.) *Rituals of Royalty: Power and Ceremonial in Traditional Societies*, 56–105. Cambridge, Cambridge University Press.

Renfrew, C. (1986) Introduction: peer polity interaction and socio-political change. In C. Renfrew and J. Cherry (eds.) *Peer Polity Interaction and Socio-political Change*, 1–18. Cambridge, Cambridge University Press.

Rév, I. (1995) Parallel autopsies. *Representations* 49, 15–39.

Robb, J. E. (1998) The archaeology of symbols. *Annual Review of Anthropology* 27, 329–346.

Rhodes, J.A. and Knüsel, C.J. (2005) Activity-related skeletal change in medieval humeri: cross-sectional and architectural alterations *American Journal of Physical Anthropology* 128(3), 536–546.

Rowlands, M. J. (1994) The cultural economy of sacral power. In P. Ruby, (ed.) *Les Princes de la Protohistoire et l'Émergence de l'État*, pp. 165–172. École française de Rome, Naples and Rome.

Russell, J. C. (1994) *The Germanization of Christianity: A Sociohistorical Approach to Religious Transformation*. New York, Oxford University Press.

Simek, R. (1993) *Dictionary of Northern Mythology*. Woodbridge, Suffolk, D.S. Brewer.

Steane, J. (1993) *The Archaeology of the Medieval English Monarchy*. London, Batsford.

Steuer, H. (1989) Archaeology and history: proposal on the social structure of the Merovingian kingdom. In K. Randsborg, (ed.) *The Birth of Europe: Archaeology and Social Development in the First millennium A.D.*, 100–123. Rome, L'Ermadi Bretschneider.

Tainter, J. A. (1978) Mortuary practices and the study of prehistoric social systems. In M.B. Schiffer (ed.) *Advances in Archaeological Method and Theory* 1, 105–141.

Tierney, B. and Painter, S. (1970) *Western Europe in the Middle Ages, 300–1475*. New York, Knopf.

Turner, V. (1995) *The Ritual Process: Structure and Anti-Structure*. Aldine de Gruyter, New York.

Ucko, P. J. (1969) Ethnography and archaeological interpretation of funerary remains. *World Archaeology* 1(2), 262–280.

Verdery, K. (1999) *The Political Lives of Dead Bodies: Reburial and Postsocialist Change*. New York, Columbia University Press.

Vitebsky, P. (1995) *The Shams: Voyages of the Soul Trance, Ecstasy and Healing from Siberia to the Amazon*. London, Macmillan.

Werner, J. (1964) Frankish royal tombs in the Cathedrals of Cologne and Saint-Denis. *Antiquity* XXXVIII, 201–216.

Werner, J. (1991) Données nouvelles sur la sépulture royale de Childéric. In R. Brulet (ed.) *Les Fouilles du Quartier Saint-Brice à Tournai*, 14–22. Louvain-La-Neuve, Département d'Archéologie et d'Histoire de l'Art.

Whitley, J. (2002) Too many ancestors. *Antiquity* 76, 119–26.

Williams, H. (2001) An ideology of transformation: cremation rites and animal sacrifice in early Anglo-Saxon England, in N. Price (ed.) *The Archaeology of Shamanism*, 193–212. London and New York, Routledge.

Winkelman, M. J. (1990) Shamans and other magico-religious healers: a cross-cultural study of their origins, nature, and social transformations. *Ethos* 18(3), 308–352.

Wood, I. (1994) *The Merovingian Kingdoms, 450–751*. London and New York, Longman.

Wyss, M. (1997) Saint-Denis (France): du mausolé hypothétique du Bas-Empire à l'ensemble basilical carolingien. In G. De Boe and F. Verhaeghe (eds.) *Death and Burial in Medieval Europe – Papers of the 'Medieval Europe Brugge 1997' Conference*. Vol. 2, 111–114.

15. Skeletal Evidence and Contexts of Violence in the European Mesolithic and Neolithic

Rick Schulting

Introduction

Violence is a powerful way of interacting, in the past no less so than in the present (Riches 1986; Schröder and Schmidt 2001). Even the threat of violence can have major consequences for human behaviour, both that of the aggressor and that of the (intended) recipient, and both at the individual and the group level. Views of prehistoric societies that fail to take full account of how violence can be strategically employed at various levels, from the individual to the largest sociopolitical grouping, and of how it can structure social relations, run the risk of presenting very sanitised and incomplete accounts. Larry Keeley's (1996) concept of the 'pacified past' at least in part describes the situation with regard to views of earlier prehistoric Europe where Mesolithic and Neolithic society has often been portrayed as peaceful and co-operative, in outlook if not always in practice (Whittle 1996, 4, 277). Examples of interpersonal violence are known, but, with some notable exceptions, little account has been taken of the wider implications of this evidence, and they have tended to be dismissed as isolated incidents. Within the last few years, a number of papers have appeared that are beginning to document and discuss the extent of skeletal evidence for prehistoric violence, although putting these examples into a population perspective, and under-standing the causes and consequences of violence within prehistoric communities, are areas that still require investigation.

The European Mesolithic and Neolithic are fruitful areas for an exploration of violence, as they can be tied in with a series of questions relating to environmental change, population movement and density, levels of social complexity, the introduction of farming, and a variety of new cultural practices, including different approaches to the land, and to the dead. In order to realise this longer-term goal, however, it is first necessary to achieve a better understanding and integration of the different lines of evidence for violence – graphic representations, artefacts, architectural and settlement remains, as well as skeletal remains. What the skeletal evidence can, uniquely, contribute to this discussion is a direct measure of the actual prevalence of interpersonal violence (as opposed to a symbolism and ideology of violence), and the forms it takes. A complete survey of the relevant skeletal evidence – let alone the other lines of evidence – is beyond the scope of this paper; a number of such summaries of varying compass are available (*e.g.*, Vencl 1984; 1999; Wahl and König 1987; Makkay 2000; Guilaine and Zammit 2001; Peter-Röcher 2002; Thorpe 2003; Orschiedt 2005). Instead, a series of themes will be explored using selected examples (Fig. 15.1), in an attempt to illustrate the extant range of skeletal evidence for interpersonal violence and how it might be interpreted. Specifically, discussion touches upon: embedded projectile points, both direct and 'inferred'; healed and unhealed cranial trauma; post-cranial trauma; cut-marks; mass graves; and special contexts. Concurrently, the examples presented under each heading are discussed in light of the context(s) for violence that might be implicated. It is recognised that overlap exists in these categories, but they may still be usefully discussed separately, particularly as to some extent they seem to reflect different behaviours.

Skeletal evidence and contexts for violence

Embedded projectiles

Projectiles directly embedded in bone are fairly straight-forward and uncontroversial as evidence of interpersonal violence. While it is possible that on occasion such injuries represent accidents, this must be considered as a very rare event. The earliest European examples of embedded projectiles derive from two Italian Epipalaeolithic sites: San Teodoro and Grotte des Enfants (ca. 13,000 BP) (Bachechi *et al.* 1997; Dastague and de Lumley 1976). From then to the end of the Neolithic (and later of course), there are examples in both stone and bone known from across most of Europe, though, unsurprisingly, our knowledge of their distribution through space and time is intermittent (Bégouën *et al.* 1922; Péquart and Péquart 1937; Becker 1952; Corcoran 1967; Selkirk 1971; Ebbesen 1985; Wahl and König 1987; Léotard *et al.* 1988; Larsson 1989; Lubell *et al.* 1989; Cordier 1990; Campillo *et al.* 1993; Armendariz *et al.* 1994; Lynch and O'Donnabhain 1994; Balakin and Nuzhnyi 1995; Polet *et al.* 1996; Chapman 1999; Makkay 2000; Wysocki and Whittle 2000; Lillie 2004; Roksandic 2004).

Far more problematic are cases in which penetration is inferred from the location of the projectile in relation to the skeleton (*e.g.*, Pitt-Rivers 1898; Piggott 1962; Atkinson 1965; Albrethsen and Brinch Petersen 1976; Pryor 1976; Whittle 1991; Guilaine and Zammit 2001). This comprises a large number of examples, which are, with some exceptions, often interpreted as grave offerings rather than evidence of violence. The idea that these represent

grave offerings needs to be approached with caution, as the goal in bow and arrow or spear conflict is not to hit bone, but to penetrate vital organs. Thus the presence of cases in which a point is found embedded in bone, and survives in this position to be found by the excavator, and is subsequently recognised, must be a small subset of all those individuals struck by projectiles (see Milner 2005; Wendorf 1968). Equally, we must be cautious in assuming that these cases *do* represent violence, unless patterning can be demonstrated (*e.g.*, in the unusual position of projectile points *vis à vis* the skeleton compared to the more usual pattern within a culture), or close inspection of the skeleton reveals small nicks or cuts on bone consistent with the passing of a projectile. Nevertheless, it is certain that projectile injuries are under-represented, in part through poor preservation and inadequate examination of the surviving material itself, and in part because bone would not always be struck in the first place. This whole area needs further research, in which the study

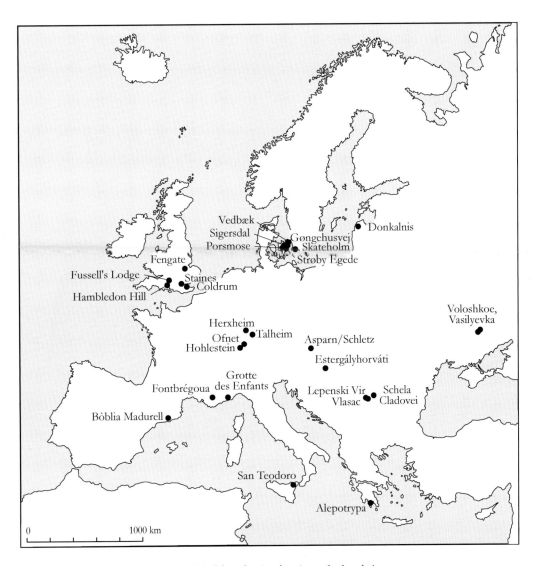

Figure 15.1. Map showing locations of selected sites.

of impact fractures on the projectile points themselves should also feature. In addition, the analysis of blood residues on projectiles and other cutting implements offers enormous possibilities that have been little explored. Although the technique remains controversial, some of this potential is suggested through recent analysis of the famous Tyrolean 'Man in the Ice', where, in conjunction with DNA analysis of the blood residues on his associated clothing and weapons, it has been possible to posit the involvement of four other individuals in the events leading up to this individual's violent death high in the Alps (Ives 2003). Mirroring some investigations on skeletal remains, it is also worth noting that a decade passed before the projectile embedded in the body's back was discovered, despite extensive study and radiography.

A little investigated aspect of known projectile point injuries involves a detailed synthesis, analysis and discussion of the angle of entry, and hence the position of the victim relative to the assailant. In terms of understanding the context of the event, this is potentially of great importance; at the simplest level, a projectile entering from the back has different implications from one entering the front of the body, and could indicate ambush, or a rout. Guilaine and Zammit's (2001, Figure 39) very useful diagrammatic summary of Neolithic and Chalcolithic projectile injuries in France shows that, as with the Ice Man, a number of points did penetrate from behind. Other noteworthy points emerge from a consideration of the overall distribution of injuries (Fig. 15.2). Firstly, it is clear that hits to the torso are artificially under-represented: the ribs comprise a larger proportion of the torso than the vertebral column, and yet register no embedded points (although at least one point embedded in a rib is noted in Guilaine and Zammit's Appendix 1). This is probably due to a combination of poor preservation and often cursory examination of this material (*cf.* Wysocki and Whittle 2000). Secondly, the spread of injuries around the body is relatively random, including seven examples that struck the lower

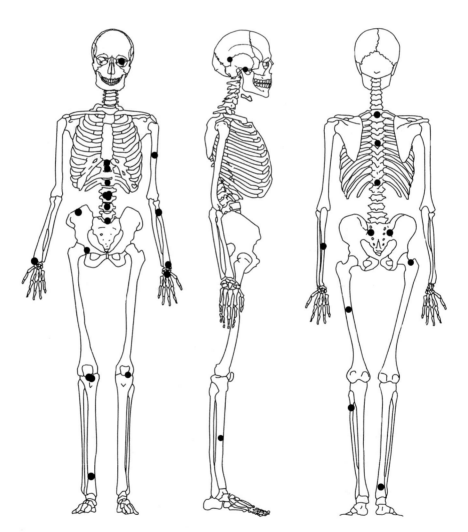

Figure 15.2. Composite figure of 33 embedded projectile points from 32 individuals from Neolithic and Chalcolithic France (and one Mesolithic individual). Compiled from Guilaine and Zammit (2001, Figure 39). Where sex is reported, all are male. This is a subset of the actual number of embedded projectile points, as only those points with a very specific location on the skeleton are included. In total Guilaine and Zammit (2001, 196 and Appendix 1) report more than 60 embedded points, mainly from Chalcolithic contexts.

half of the leg. The leg may have been an intentional target, such as seen in New Guinea, where the use of defensive shields covering the torso left the legs exposed. A demobilising injury to the leg would be followed by a killing thrust with a hand-held spear (Milner 2005). Alternatively, it could imply the flight of an arrow near the end of its trajectory, suggesting an exchange occurring at some distance, reminiscent of more formal 'arranged' battles seen among a number of small-scale societies ethnographically (Gardner and Heider 1974; McKnight 1986; Keeley 1996).

A number of cases do provide more detail concerning the actual angle of penetration. One of the most interesting of these is a Neolithic adult male from Bòblia Madurell in Spain. The angle of an embedded flint point in a lower thoracic vertebra indicates that the arrow must have penetrated from below, thus: 'it would seem obvious that individual MF-18 was situated high up...' (Campillo *et al.* 1993, 150). This could imply the positioning of this individual on top of a natural or built fortification, with the assailant firing from below. The opposite situation may be indicated by a Neolithic adult male skeleton from Porsmose, Denmark, with a long bone point embedded in its nasal cavity, and another in its chest (Becker 1952, Figures 1 and 2). The point in the nasal cavity is at an extreme upwards angle, indicating either that the arrow was at the end of a long, high trajectory, or, in light of the above example, that the assailant was firing downwards from high above the victim. If the victim were already lying on the ground, then a shot to the face may have been given at close range as a *coup de grâce*, particularly given the point in the chest, which was fired from the same direction but does not appear to be at such an extreme angle. But it might also be suggested that the assailant was positioned in a tree (a difficult position from which to fire a bow), or on an artificial raised platform. This interpretation, though speculative, begins to suggest some possible scenarios, including those of shooting from ambush (offensive) or from a sentry post (defensive). The watchtowers erected by the Dani of Papua New Guinea provide an example of the latter (Gardner and Heider 1974, Figure 1).

Where sex is known, the great majority of acceptable examples of embedded projectile points cited in the literature appear to be male. This applies in Britain (Schulting and Wysocki forthcoming) and Denmark (Bennike 1985), and is seen very clearly in Guilaine and Zammit's (2001, 340–344) summary of the French Neolithic/Chalcolithic, where all examples of sexed individuals (11) with embedded points are male. There are exceptions, such as the Epipalaeolithic adult female and child noted above. Nevertheless, this robust trend is noteworthy, especially as there appears to be less sex-related patterning in other forms of injury (particularly cranial fractures) (Bennike 1985; Wahl and König 1987; Papathanasiou *et al.* 2000; Schulting and Wysocki forthcoming). This may indicate a different context for the 'violence at a distance' seen with bow and arrow, as opposed to the face-to-face confrontations often

implicated by cranial injuries (though some may reflect sling or thrown stone injuries).

Cranial trauma

The identification of healed cranial trauma is relatively straightforward, though its origin may not be. Unhealed, peri-mortem (at or near the time of death) injuries can be more difficult to recognise. Based on the author's own research on earlier Neolithic skeletal collections in Britain, it can be suggested that in general the prevalence of both forms of cranial trauma are under-represented in the *recent* literature (the literature of the nineteenth century, by contrast, abounds with claims of 'cleft' skulls and violent death (Thurnam 1865, 1869), many of which cannot be supported by modern criteria (Schulting and Wysocki 2002; forthcoming). While some cases may represent accidents, the most common cause of both healed and unhealed cranial trauma is widely accepted to be interpersonal violence (Ortner and Putschar 1985; Ubelaker and Adams 1995; Lovell 1997).

There is abundant and widespread evidence for healed and unhealed cranial trauma across Europe (though overall prevalence remains poorly documented except in a few cases). A series of Mesolithic sites in the Iron Gates area show considerable evidence of cranial trauma, as well as embedded projectile points and post-cranial trauma, specifically parry-type fractures (Roksandic 2004). Once again emphasising the need for re-examination of skeletal assemblages, two sites – Vlasac and Lepenski Vir – were originally reported as not showing any signs of violent trauma (see Chapman 1999, Table 1), yet Roksandic (2004) documents convincing examples of both healed and perimortem cranial trauma and an embedded bone projectile point. Interestingly, there seems to be considerable variability in the prevalence of interpersonal violence between sites on the two sides of the Danube. Denmark also has a surprisingly high proportion of trauma in the Mesolithic, mainly healed blunt force cranial trauma (Bennike 1985; 1987; 1997; Grøn and Skaarup 1991). At one point, Bennike (1985, Table 14) was able to report an prevalence of cranial trauma of over 40% for the Danish Mesolithic; this figure becomes substantially lower with the inclusion of subsequent finds, but it still remains high within the context of prehistoric Europe. Though the overall prevalence appears to be considerably lower (less than 10%), there are still at least some 20–30 individuals with cranial injuries spanning the Danish Neolithic (Bröste *et al.* 1956; Bennike 1985, Table 15; 2003; Ebbesen 1985). For both periods, the majority of cases involve males and are healed, so that these figures cannot be taken as the prevalence of violent death. There is also a high proportion of healed injuries from the Neolithic site of Alepotrypa Cave in Greece (Papathanasiou *et al.* 2000), and both healed and unhealed injuries from the Neolithic of the eastern Baltic (Butrimas and Jankauskas 1998).

A recent re-examination of earlier Neolithic crania, predominantly from southern Britain, has reported 31 probable injuries, mainly blunt force trauma (Schulting and Wysocki 2002; forthcoming). Both males and females appear equally affected. In Britain, as in Denmark, there is usually only one injury per individual, but there are a number of examples with multiple injuries. Among the latter is an adult male from Fussell's Lodge with three small, well-healed depressed fractures along the top of the cranium; whether this is evidence of repeated bouts of violence, or whether they all occurred at the same time, is not possible to determine. For both Denmark and Britain, the majority of Neolithic examples derive from chambered tombs and earthen long barrows – *i.e.*, the normative mortuary contexts for the period – raising questions over the context of violence, such as whether the injured individuals originated from within the community, or outside of it.

In addition, a number of trepanations have been reported for the period under consideration (Gaillard 1883; Bennike 1985; Brenot and Riquet 1977; Alt *et al.* 1997a; Lillie 2003; Roberts and McKinley 2003; Silva 2003). These warrant mention here for two reasons. Firstly, it may be that one of the main reasons for performing the operation was to treat cranial trauma suffered as a result of violence (Bennike 1985, 98; Ortner and Putschar 1985, 96; Alt *et al.* 1997a). This is suggested very strongly in the Danish Neolithic, where most trepanations are to the anterior part of the left parietal and frontal of male crania (Bennike 1985, Figure 45). Secondly, it can be difficult to distinguish – particularly with the partial and fragmentary material that is often all that survives – between healed trepanations and healed depressed fractures (Brothwell and Blake 1966; Bennike 2003; Schulting and Wysocki forthcoming).

Though there is some regional variability, in general the cranial injuries noted above appear to involve a wider segment of the population than the projectile injuries, at least in terms of adolescent and adult men and women. Children are less frequently represented, although this may be, in part, a survival and recovery bias (the exceptions provided by mass graves such as Ofnet, Talheim and Asparn-Schletz are addressed below). Cranial trauma invokes different contexts for violence from projectiles, including face-to-face conflict between individuals. The fact that – apart from mass grave contexts – a large proportion of cranial injuries are healed could suggest a more controlled form of violence in which the death of the participants was not seen as appropriate (though there are issues with the difficulty of identification of peri-mortem fractures that require consideration). Possible contexts for the violence represented by healed cranial injuries vary widely, from 'domestic' conflict, self-inflicted injury, ritualised combat, martial training, to survival of injuries that were actually of lethal intent. Differentiating between these is a difficult task, although on occasion other contextual evidence can be brought to bear. Among the most intriguing examples of healed cranial injury is an adult female from the Danish

Mesolithic site of Gøngehusvej (Brinch Petersen *et al.* 1993) (Fig. 15.3). The position of a bone pin and red ochre beside a deep depressed fracture suggests that the woman pinned her hair here, or wore a cap of some kind, as though to cover up the injury, which was likely to have been visible in life. This is very unlike the situation seen in some societies with formal bouts of ostensibly non-lethal combat, in which scars from interpersonal conflict are emphasised as badges of honor (Chagnon 1997).

Non-lethal, 'ritualised' (the degree of formality is highly variable) conflict is not uncommon cross-culturally, both within and between communities (McKnight 1986; Chagnon 1988; 1997; Halbmeyer 2001). At the same time, many cultures make a strong distinction between in-group and out-group violence, with the former condemned and the latter tolerated or, more often, extolled (Bohannon and Bohannon 1953; Paige and Paige 1981; McKnight 1986; Halbmayer 2001; Schwandner-Sievers 2001; Stewart and Strathern 2002). Although violence may certainly occur within the group, its severity, and the lethality of the weapons that may be used, are very often different from violence directed at the out-group. This is not a simple dichotomy (although in some cases it can be made so), but rather one of nested kin and social relationships, as summed up very well in an Arab proverb: 'I against my brother; I and my brother against my cousin; I, my brother and my cousin against the next village; all of us against the foreigner' (quoted in Paige and Paige 1981, 129). But the presence of non-lethal forms of interpersonal violence does not necessarily negate the presence of more deadly violence, particularly when undertaken between communities. Such encounters can escalate, leading to deaths, which in turn need to be avenged; events can rapidly spiral out of control. It is equally important to remember that individuals often *do* survive injuries of lethal intent, and so we should not jump to the conclusion that all healed injuries result from ritualised combat. Rather, a variety of contexts should be envisaged and explored on a case-by-case basis.

Peri-mortem cranial injuries present some of the same interpretative possibilities taken to a more extreme form, but also include new contexts, such as the massacre of captives and non-combatants, punishment killing for social transgression, and sacrifice. Killing for social transgression or for sacrifice are difficult to distinguish archaeologically, though there are possibilties in this regard (see Taylor 2002). Some probable cases of sacrifice are considered below under 'special contexts'.

Post-cranial trauma

Post-cranial trauma is more difficult to deal with on a number of accounts: 1) although most healed fractures are easily recognisable, criteria for the recognition of peri-mortem injuries lag behind those for the cranium (though this situation is changing – see Knüsel 2005); 2) the often poor state of preservation and high degree of frag-mentation of the post-cranial skeleton make this material

Figure 15.3. Adult female with healed depressed fracture from Mesolithic site of Gøngehusvej, Vedbæk, Zealand. The position of the bone pin by the head is atypical for the Mesolithic; such pins are usually found in the region of the torso. (Photo courtesy of Erik Brinch Petersen.)

much more difficult to work with than crania when investigating evidence for trauma; and 3) even where healed or unhealed fractures can be demonstrated, the more likely cause is often accident rather than interpersonal violence. There are exceptions to the last-mentioned point, most notably the hands, ribs and the facial region, which are often affected in modern studies of interpersonal violence (Lovell 1997). Unfortunately, the state of preservation comes into play here, as these bones are small or fragile and thus far less likely to survive and be recovered.

While fractures of the ulna – so-called 'parry fractures' – do survive better, their relationship to interpersonal violence has been questioned (Lovell 1997). Nevertheless, they may be investigated as part of a suite of injuries to see whether any patterning exists. For example, if fractures of the ulna were more common in skeletal assemblages also showing higher frequencies of cranial injuries to the left side of the head, it would strongly suggest an association between the two, and the existence of face-to-face conflict. Parry fractures do not seem common in Mesolithic and Neolithic Europe, though a number of examples have been noted (Brothwell 1961; Brothwell and Blake 1966; Lubell *et al.* 1989; Whittle 1991; Robb 1997; Butrimas and Jankauskas 1998; Roksandic 2004; Schulting and Wysocki forthcoming). The fact that only healed examples are mentioned is likely a bias caused by the difficulties noted above.

There are cases in which more extreme post-cranial trauma has been claimed. When this is part of a set of other injuries, a context of violence can be strongly indicated, as is the case with an adult male burial from the Mesolithic site of Skateholm I in southern Sweden, found with a transverse stone projectile point embedded in the pelvis (Larsson 1989). Not only was the skeleton partially disarticulated, but Persson and Persson (1984, 20) note that '... the cranium, pelvis and the majority of long extremity bones seem to have been split asunder, in all probability prior to interment'.

Cut-marks and intentional modification

Another aspect of both cranial and post-cranial remains involves cut-marked bone. The identification of these is usually fairly straightforward, given the development of criteria for distinguishing stone and metal cut-marks, animal gnawing, post-depositional erosion, and what might be called excavation or curation trauma (Potts and Shipman 1981; Shipman 1981; Cook 1991). Recent examinations of material from both new excavations and older museum collections are identifying an increasing number of examples of cut-marked human bone from Mesolithic and Neolithic sites across northwestern Europe (Villa *et al.* 1986; Leitão *et al.* 1987; Andersen 1988; Evans and Simpson 1991; Mordant and Mordant 1992; Boulestin and Gomez de Soto 1995; Baxter 1999; Boulestin 1999; Cauwe 2001; Schulting and Davis n.d.; Schulting and Wysocki 2002; forthcoming; Murphy 2003; Smith and Brickley 2004; Wysocki and Fernández-Jalvo forthcoming). Some cut-marks are quite subtle, and a number have no doubt been missed on material that has not been closely examined. Thus the prevalence of cut-marked human bone is very likely under-represented. But its interpretation is another matter. The majority of examples have been seen in a context of post-mortem processing of the dead for ritual purposes. Certainly the location of most of the cut-marks suggests dismemberment or defleshing. But the possibility of cannibalism has also been raised, and debated (Villa *et al.* 1986; Kneipp and Büttner 1988; Villa 1992; Boulestin and Gomez de Soto 1995; Lescot 1996; Boulestin 1999; Cauwe 2001; Taylor 2002).

Even if accepted in some cases, and this seems likely (Villa 1992), cannibalism need not bear any relationship to interpersonal violence (see Knüsel and Outram, this volume). The practice may instead pay tribute to a revered person after death, or may be undertaken for other ritual reasons, or as a last recourse during times of starvation. Other forms of cannibalism, however, are more likely to occur in a context of violence, such as the eating of a dispatched enemy, either as an insult (being treated like an animal), or as an attempt to absorb certain of their qualities. The best line of evidence for violent cannibalism would be to find peri-mortem injuries not related to butchery, together with evidence of butchery and consumption. This is hard to demonstrate on the basis of the available evidence, though the similar treatment of animal and human remains as food debris, such as seen at the Neolithic site of Fontbrégoua (Villa *et al.* 1986; Villa 1992), does not immediately suggest a strongly ritualised or respectful context.

Another context for cut-marks involves the taking of body parts either as mementos, or as trophies. The former is interpreted in an in-group context of keeping a 'relic'

from a loved one, or a revered ancestor, while the latter term is here employed in relation to an act intended to constitute an insult to the dead, and/or a boast to the living (of one's own community as well as of those further afield). The widespread practice of taking scalps, particularly well-documented in North America (Larsen 1997), provides one of the best examples of this. Butrimas and Jankauskas (1998) report a case of scalping from the Lithuanian Neolithic site of Donkalnis, though more detail would be needed on the exact location of the cuts for this to be accepted without reservation. Scalping has also been tentatively suggested for some of the crania at the Bavarian Mesolithic site of Ofnet, discussed further below (Frayer 1997, 201). A cranium from the Neolithic site of Coldrum in southeast England exhibits peri-mortem fractures and cut-marks found on the left temporal just above the external auditory meatus (Fig. 15.4). This has been interpreted as possible evidence for the removal of the ear as a trophy (Schulting and Wysocki forthcoming), a practice documented in a Euroamerican tradition up to at least the Vietnam War (Abler 1992, 16).

The skeletal assemblage at the recently excavated Linearbandkeramik (LBK) enclosure of Herxheim included the remains, often highly fragmentary, of some 450 individuals found mainly in the two ditches surrounding the site. Only a small fraction of this number was represented by the more usual LBK pattern of a single articulated burial in a pit. Crania were by far the most frequent element, and many had been intentionally shaped into skull caps (calottes) by the removal of the facial area and the base of the cranium (Orschiedt *et al.* 2003). They may have been intended as containers, though for what is not yet known. The initial view of the site was one in

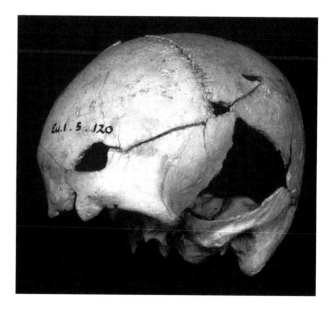

Figure 15.4. Adult female showing peri-mortem cranial fractures, from Neolithic site of Coldrum, Kent, England. (Photo by author.)

which violence played a major role in accounting for the state and context of the human remains (Häusser 1998). More recent analysis, however, has called this into question; a number of healed cranial injuries are present, but few if any peri-mortem injuries, leading to the suggestion that this may be part of a normative mortuary rite (Orschiedt *et al.* 2003). However, as this practice is rarely, if ever, seen elsewhere in the LBK, it is at present only 'normative' in the context of Herxheim, which raises questions over why it was being done there. The interpretation of this site will need to await fuller analysis, which is still in its preliminary stages.

Mass graves

In light of recent events in the Balkans, Iraq, Rwanda and elsewhere, the term 'mass grave' is an emotive and highly charged one, immediately calling to mind images of extreme violence and repression. There are prehistoric precedents in Neolithic Europe that are in some ways comparable, in that they often seem to present an image of one-sided conflict – a better term might be massacre – rather than an even-sided fight. Whether this image is true or not is another matter, but in some situations a strong case can be made. One of the most important sites of this type is the late LBK site of Talheim in southern Germany, where 34 men, women and children were found thrown unceremoniously into a large pit (Wahl and König 1987). This treatment is clearly anomalous when contrasted with normative LBK burial practice, the body lying carefully flexed on its side, with grave offerings often present (Jeunesse 1996). Moreover, the signs of violent death are clear at Talheim: 18 individuals had each received up to three massive blows to the head, including adult males and females as well as children. At least one adult had been shot in the head with a flint-tipped projectile, and an additional four examples of projectile trauma were found in the postcrania (Wahl and König 1987). The location of some injuries to the back of the head suggests an execution style killing, or at least the killing of helpless prisoners or non-combatants. At an even larger scale, the remains of some 67 individuals, many of which exhibit peri-mortem injuries, have been recently found at the late LBK enclosure of Asparn-Schletz in Austria (Teschler-Nicola *et al.* 1996; Windl 1996; 1999; 2001). Although discussed here as a 'mass grave', it appears that, unlike Talheim, the human remains at Asparn/Schletz were not buried at all, but were thrown into the enclosure ditch and left accessible to scavengers. This is supported by the presence of typical carnivore (canid) scavenging marks on the human bone assemblage (Teschler-Nicola *et al.* 1996, 9–10). A recent dating programme has confirmed that both Talheim and Asparn-Schletz are consistent with an interpretation as single events (Wild *et al.* 2004).

Another mass grave is seen in the recently discovered Late Neolithic Lengyel site of Estergályhorváti in southwest Hungary (Makkay 2000), where some 25–30 individuals were packed haphazardly into a pit with no

grave goods. The material was highly fragmentary and recovered under less than ideal conditions, yet it is noteworthy that the single relatively complete cranium shows a peri-mortem injury caused by a sharp instrument. Another cranial fragment also exhibited evidence of a peri-mortem injury. This suggests, however tentatively, the possibility that the whole group may have met with violent death; if this is accepted, then the fact that the individuals are all older adolescent and adult males strongly suggests a context of raiding or warfare (Makkay 2000). However, given the highly fragmented state of the remains and problematic recovery, such an interpretation must remain tentative.

Talheim could represent the entire population of a small late LBK hamlet, and indeed a degree of genetic relationship is suggested by the distribution of non-metric skeletal traits (Alt *et al.* 1997b). Thus the goal at Talheim may have been the extermination of a local group, rather than raiding for women, livestock or goods. This is a fairly common pattern in warfare in small-scale societies and is often associated with the kind of excessive brutality seen on some of the Talheim remains (Keeley 1996; Larsen 1997). A cranium from the Early Neolithic causewayed enclosure of Staines in southern England is similar in this respect, with probable multiple blows and decapitation (confirmation of the peri-mortem injuries is made problematic by excessive plaster reconstruction) (Robertson-Mackay 1987; Schulting and Wysocki forthcoming). Another common goal of warfare is the capture of women (Donald 1997; Otterbein 2000), and, in fact, the presence of three times as many adult males as females at Asparn/Schletz has led to the suggestion that the 'missing' young women were being taken as captives (Teschler-Nicola *et al.* 1996; see also Gronenborn 2001). While intriguing, this interpretation should be treated with some caution, as it makes certain assumptions about the nature of the event(s), such as that women were originally present in equal numbers to men. It does receive support, however, from the presence of ca. 30% children and young adolescents. If the dead represented a raiding or war party, as proposed for Estergályhorváti, then it should be composed predominantly of older adolescent and adult males (though it should be noted that there is ethnographic evidence for the occasional participation at some level of women in war parties (Ewers 1994)).

The most important aspect for present purposes is that mass graves provide the strongest skeletal evidence for large-scale interpersonal violence; thus, they imply a greater degree of organisation both in defence and in attack, and so justify speaking of inter-group, rather than intra-group, violence. Events on this scale can resonate across space and time, through the telling and re-telling of incidents of violence so that they become part of cultural memory, creating a climate of fear and mistrust, and instigating cycles of revenge, what Schröder and Schmidt (2001) have termed the 'violent imaginary' (see also Ember and Ember's (1992) 'socialization for mistrust'). This violent imaginary is a crucial resource to be drawn upon in further acts of violence. Specialised war leaders are likely to emerge under such situations, although the degree to which their authority during conflicts is transferable to other times and other socio-political contexts is likely to be highly variable.

Other cases of simultaneous multiple burials (where this is not the normal burial mode for the society) present an interpretive challenge that, to date, appears to have received relatively little attention. At the extreme, this can take the form of mass graves with tens of individuals, but this need not always be the case. The point here is that, in small communities, simultaneous multiple deaths would be expected to be a relatively rare event (Frayer 1997, 183). There are exceptions, of course, such as when the death of a mother is followed by the death of her young infant, if no other nursing women are present, or willing to care for the child (this may be more often a social matter than a physiological one). This is often the explanation given for the double burial of an adult and a child, though it is worth commenting that in a fair number of cases the adult is male (*e.g.*, Péquart and Péquart 1937; Larsson 1989). Other exceptions would include accidents affecting a number of people at one time, disease, or starvation. But when one or more individuals in a multiple burial show evidence of violent death, then the question must arise as to the nature of the deaths of all the others. Thus, at Talheim, it is not necessary to demonstrate that each and every individual exhibits peri-mortem injuries in order to infer that all were victims of violence. The interpretation is less secure in a case like the multiple Neolithic burial at Fengate in eastern England. Here, an adult male was found with a projectile point between two ribs – though not embedded – in a grave together with an adult female and two children (Pryor 1976). A similar example is provided by Mesolithic grave 19 at Vedbæk, where a bone point was found lodged – again, not embedded – between two cervical vertebrae of an adult, found in a triple grave with another adult and a child (Albrethsen and Brinch Petersen 1976). (While the individual with the lodged point is often presented as male, the sex of this individual is actually quite ambiguous (Bennike 1985, 104; C. Meiklejohn pers. com.)). Unlike Talheim and Asparn/Scheltz, however, the bodies at these two sites had been laid out in their graves with some care, in a position more usual for their region and time period. The difference in burial treatment may be explained by the scale of the event, by who was doing the burying, and under what conditions (*e.g.*, in haste?). But, assuming that the projectile points are indeed the cause of death in the above two examples, how are the other individuals in the grave to be interpreted?

Then there are the even more problematic cases of mass graves in which there is no evidence of injury. A good example of this is the Mesolithic site of Strøby Egede, Denmark, with eight individuals of both sexes and ranging in age from neonate to elderly adult, all carefully laid out in a single large pit with grave goods (Brinch Petersen 1990). An important consideration with multiple graves is the ability to satisfactorily demonstrate contemporaneity of the individuals interred. The kind of very detailed analysis of the skeleton's position advocated by the French *anthropologie de terrain* approach can be usefully brought to bear here (Duday *et al.* 1990; Nilsson Stutz 2003). But in this case, at least, the burial seems to represent a single event, and this raises the question of the cause of death of so many individuals at, or very near, one time. The apparent absence of skeletal evidence of violent injury (though it should be noted that it has not been possible to fully examine the skeletons – C. Meiklejohn pers. com.) dictates that this is not the first explanation to be considered, but nevertheless the possibility must arise. Accident, such as drowning, infectious disease or starvation are other possibilities, though the prevalence of such a virulent infectious disease in a relatively scattered and small population (even if argued to be dense by the standards of hunter-gatherers) would not be expected to have been high. The demography of the group, including all age groups, would also be unusual for all but the most virulent diseases, as indeed it would be for starvation.

Special contexts

Lastly, there is the case of human remains from what might be referred to as special contexts. A good example of this would be the two adult males found under the burnt palisade and rubble collapse of the bank of an Early Neolithic causewayed enclosure at Hambledon Hill, in southwest England (Mercer 1988; 1999, 154). Both males had leaf-shaped projectile points in close association, and, though not directly embedded, these may be inferred to have been shot into the body. But even without this corroborative evidence, the circumstances of the burnt and collapsed palisade would be highly suggestive of a large-scale violent event responsible for the deaths of at least the two male adults, and presumably others that were not so fortuitously preserved. Indeed, the remains of four other individuals may have been involved in the same or another similar event (Mercer 1988, 104). A very different kind of special context is seen at two Danish Neolithic bog body sites, Bolkilde and Sigersdal. There are no skeletal injuries here, but one of the two individuals from each of these sites was found with a rope around its neck, strongly implying a sacrificial context (Bennike and Ebbesen 1986; Bennike *et al.* 1986; Ebbesen 1993). A sacrificial context may also be invoked in cases of so-called 'foundation burials' from the Late Neolithic Lengyel culture of Central Europe (Makkay 2000).

Special contexts need not involve the complete skeleton. There is abundant, though regionally and chronologically variable, evidence for the removal of the head from the fully fleshed body in both the Mesolithic and Neolithic in Europe. This is distinct from the widespread Neolithic practice of moving elements of the skeleton, particularly the cranium, once in a dry, defleshed state (Piggott 1962; Smith 1965; Cauwe 1996; 2001). Evidence for the removal of the fleshed head consists of the articulated cranium, mandible, and a number of upper cervical vertebrae. The frequent presence of cut-marks on the cervical vertebrae provides further confirmation, but the mere finding of these elements together is quite convincing on its own. More problematic are river finds of isolated crania (Bradley and Gordon 1988; Knüsel and Carr 1995), though these potentially offer another kind of special context, particularly when there can be higher than average traumatic injuries represented (Turner *et al.* 2002). These aside, there are a number of cases from Neolithic Britain with skulls and vertebrae in pits or ditches, such as the enclosure at Staines (Schulting and Wysocki forthcoming). The practice could be seen either in the context of ancestor veneration, or of trophy-taking; where peri-mortem injuries are present, as claimed for Staines (Robertson-Mackay 1987), the latter is clearly implicated. But it is not necessary to regard ancestor veneration and trophy-taking as mutually exclusive, since the idea that the head is the core of personhood and of spiritual power can easily lead to both behaviours. That is, if using the head of one's ancestor in rituals brings prosperity and protection to the individual and to the community, then taking the head of a member of a rival group not only removes that potentiality from that group, but may transfer it to one's own (Hoskins 1996).

Perhaps the best known examples of head removal and deposition in special contexts are the Mesolithic 'skull nests' of southwest Germany, most notably Ofnet, but also Kaufertsberg and Hohlestein-Stadel (Birkner 1926; Gieseler 1951; Frayer 1997; Orschiedt 1998; 2005). Two shallow pits were found within Ofnet cave, one containing from 27 to 31 skulls and the other six; thus, the site could have been equally considered under the previous 'mass graves' section. The skulls, including four or five males, seven to ten females and 16 children, were carefully arranged facing the cave's entrance, and sprinkled with red ochre, and a number were associated with abundant shell and animal tooth ornamentation. The presence of cervical vertebrae, many showing cut-marks, indicates that the heads were removed from fleshed bodies, and do not represent the secondary burial of defleshed skulls. More tellingly for the interpretation of these finds, a number of the skulls display peri-mortem fractures, consistently of an elliptical shape suggesting an axe-like implement (Frayer 1997; Gieseler 1951; Orscheidt 1998; 2005). The number reported varies in the different accounts, but in all cases represents a significant proportion of the total, from as 'low' as ca. 25% (Orscheidt 2005) to as high as 50% (Frayer 1997, 192). The males exhibit the greatest frequency of injuries, with over half being to the back of the head (Orscheidt 2005). A number of crania also exhibit cut-marks. The Hohlestein pit held the skulls of an adult man, a woman, and a young child, again with red ochre. Recent re-analysis confirms earlier interpretations

that all three exhibit peri-mortem injuries, as well as cut-marks indicating decapitation (Orschiedt 1998).

Without the abundant evidence for violent trauma at Ofnet and Hohlestein, it would be tempting to treat the skull nests as a local normative mortuary practice, as very few other forms of human burial are known from the region at this time (Jochim 1998). But the evidence for violence clearly puts these finds into another context altogether. This is not to say that all need refer to the same behaviour. Indeed, there is some debate over whether each 'nest' at Ofnet represents a single depositional event (Orschiedt 2005). However, the connections between the crania and the cervical vertebrae, if these can be sustained, would be improbable if the pit was opened on a number of occasions for new additions, as would the integrity of the pierced tooth and shell ornamentation with specific individuals. And the cervical vertebrae would be unlikely to be present at all if the heads were curated elsewhere over a period of time before being deposited in the pits, unless, as Armit (in press) has recently suggested, the curation of dried heads is considered as a possibility. The context in which such practice might take place then becomes of interest, particularly in light of the observed peri-mortem injuries (e.g., the heads of enemies?). Although further work on dating is certainly warranted, six of the seven currently available radiocarbon estimates are consistent with a single depositional event, or, at most, a brief period of use (Hedges *et al.* 1989; though see Orschiedt 2005 for an opposing view). Assuming contemporaneity, the number of individuals in the larger pit could represent a sizeable proportion of any local community; indeed, this could easily be the entire membership of a small foraging band. This could, then, represent a very violent, and, for the Mesolithic, large-scale event. That the heads were subsequently treated in a very formal and ritualistic way provides a contrast with Talheim, where the victims of a massacre were thrown haphazardly into a mass grave. Those responsible for the deposition of the heads at Ofnet, Kaufertsberg and Hohlestein may have been either the perpetrators, or members of the group from which the victims derive (assuming these are not one and the same, although it is difficult to envisage a scenario in which killing as many as 31 members of one's own group was seen as legitimate). In either case, one could devise a scenario in which this treatment of the dead was seen as necessary, such as to appease otherwise vengeful ghosts.

Despite the similar end result, Hohlestein seems to present a very different context for violence than Ofnet. The child's skull here appears to be hydrocephalic (Czarnetzki 1983 cited in Orschiedt 1998, 156); this is a condition caused by the accumulation of cerebrospinal fluid in the brain, hence its common name 'water on the brain'. The condition may be related to the child's death, and perhaps to all three deaths, in a context of sacrifice (Gronenborn 1999). Hydrocephaly can develop very quickly in infants, causing abnormally rapid growth of the head and bulging fontanelles (Bannister and Tew 1991). This would be very noticeable in itself; moreover, the condition can be accompanied by a whole suite of symptoms – including vomiting, poor coordination, and seizures – that may have provoked fear in the community, leading to the killing of the child and its parents. Future analysis of ancient DNA of the Hohlestein group would be useful in corroborating this idea.

The marking out of people with disabilities for violent death has also been noted for the Danish Neolithic and Bronze Age, where it seems that a disproportionate number of bog skeletons show skeletal abnormalities (Bennike 1985; 1999; Bennike *et al.* 1986; Ebbesen 1993). Two bog skeletons from the Early Neolithic site of Døjringe both exhibit marked abnormalities of the humerus, and in one case also spina bifida (Bennike 1985, 219–222). In addition, both individuals show cranial trauma, two healing trepanations in the case of Døjringe I (perhaps intended as a treatment for spina bifida), and a probable healed depressed fracture for Døjringe II.

Conclusions

The above discussion has touched upon the various lines of skeletal evidence for interpersonal violence in the Mesolithic and Neolithic of Europe. Interpretation is often far from straightforward, but then violence itself is equally not a simple phenomenon. Nevertheless, it has been possible in this brief review to suggest various contexts for violence, including encounters between mainly adult males using projectile weaponry, both at some distance and possibly in ambush; some form of non-lethal conflict, whether domestic or ritualised; large-scale raiding or warfare; capture of women; violent cannibalism; head-taking; and sacrifice. A discussion of the actual prevalence of violent trauma at different times and in different places across Europe has been beyond the scope of this paper, but is clearly an area that requires attention. Even then, the skeletal evidence, of course, only provides one aspect of the picture, in some ways a very limited one, and it is essential to see how the actual prevalence and contexts for violent injury and death correlate with other lines of evidence. Only then will it be possible to explore the causes and consequences of violence in the context of Mesolithic and Neolithic society and the great changes that were happening at this juncture in European prehistory.

Acknowledgements

I would like to thank the editors of this volume for their patience, Joanna Ostapkowicz and Ian Armit for a host of useful comments, and Chris Meiklejohn for discussions concerning the Vedbæk and Strøby Egede material. Thanks also to the reviewers for their comments, criticisms and suggestions, which have greatly improved the clarity of the paper. Any remaining faults are, of course, the sole responsibility of the author.

References

Abler, T. (1992) Scalping, torture, cannibalism and rape: an ethnohistorical analysis of conflicting cultural values in war. *Anthropologica* 34, 3–20.

Albrethsen, S. E. and Brinch Petersen, E. (1976) Excavation of a Mesolithic cemetery at Vedbæk, Denmark. *Acta Archaeologica* 47, 1–28.

Alt, K. W., Jeunesse, C., Buitrago-Télley, C. H., Wächter, R., Boës, E. and Pilcher, S. L. (1997a) Evidence for stone age cranial surgery. *Nature* 387, 360.

Alt, K. W., Vach, W. and Wahl, J. (1997b) La reconstitution "genetique" de la population de la fosse commune Rubanée de Talheim (Allemange). In C. Jeunesse (ed.), *Le Néolithique Danubien et ses Marges entre Rhin et Seine*, 1–8. Strasbourg, Cahiers de l'Association pour la Promotion de la Recherche Archéologique en Alsace.

Andersen, N. H. (1988) Hygind. *Journal of Danish Archaeology* 7, 248.

Armendariz, J., Irigaray, S. and Etxeberria, E. (1994) New evidence of prehistoric arrow wounds in the Iberian Peninsula. *International Journal of Osteoarchaeology* 4, 215–222.

Armit, I. (in press) Inside Kurtz's compound: headhunting and the human body in prehistoric Europe. In M. Bonogofsky (ed.), *Skull Collection, Modification and Decoration*. Oxford, British Archaeological Reports, International Series.

Atkinson, R. J. C. (1965) Wayland's Smithy. *Antiquity* 39, 126–133.

Bachechi, L., Fabbri, P.-F. and Mallegni, F. (1997) An arrow-caused lesion in a Late Upper Paleolithic human pelvis. *Current Anthropology* 38, 135–140.

Balakin, S. and Nuzhnyi, D. (1995) The origin of graveyards: the influence of landscape elements on social and ideological changes in prehistoric communities. *European Prehistory* 7, 191–202.

Bannister, C. M. and Tew, B. (eds) (1991) *Current Concepts in Spina Bifida and Hydrocephalus*. Cambridge, Cambridge University Press.

Baxter, M. (1999) Dancing with the dead in a mass grave. *British Archaeology* 50, 6–7.

Becker, C. J. (1952) Skeletfundet fra Porsmose ved Næstved. *Fra Nationalmuseets Arbejdsmark* 1952, 23–30.

Bennike, P. (1985) *Palaeopathology of Danish Skeletons*. Copenhagen, Akademisk Forlag.

Bennike, P., Ebbesen, K. and Jørgensen, L. B. (1986) Two Early Neolithic skeletons from Bolkilde Bog, Denmark. *Antiquity* 60, 199–209.

Bennike, P. and Ebbesen, K. (1986) The bog find from Sigersdal: human sacrifice in the Early Neolithic. *Journal of Danish Archaeology* 5, 85–115.

Bennike, P. (1987) Menneskeknogler fra Stenalderbopladsen på Argusgrunden – Beboernes Udseensde og Helbredstilstand. *Fortidsminder og Kulturhistorie* 8, 94–106.

Bennike, P. (1997) Death in the Mesolithic. Two old men from Korsør Nor. In L. Pedersen, A. Fischer and B. Aaby (eds), *The Danish Storebælt Since the Ice Age*, 99–105. Copenhagen, A/S Storebælt Fixed Link.

Bennike, P. (1999) The Early Neolithic Danish bog finds: a strange group of people! In B. J. Coles, J. M. Coles and M. Schou Jørgensen (eds), *Bog Bodies, Sacred Sites and Wetland Archaeology*, 27–32. Exeter, WARP 12.

Bennike, P. (2003) Ancient trepanations and differential diagnoses: a re-evaluation of skeletal remains from Denmark. In R. Arnott, S. Finger and C. U. M. Smith (eds), *Trepanation: History, Discovery, Theory*, 95–115. Lisse, Swets & Zeitlinger.

Bégouën, H., Cugulières, H. and Miquel, H. (1922) Vertèbre humaine traversée par une lame en quartzite. *Revue Anthropologique* 32, 230–232.

Birkner, F. (1926) Das Jungpaläolithikum in Bayern. *Der Bayersiche Vorgeschichtsfreund* 6, 13–16.

Bohannon, P. and Bohannon, L. (1953) *The Tiv of Central Nigeria.* London, International African Institute.

Boulestin, B. and Gomez de Soto, J. (1995) Le cannibalisme au Néolithique: réalité et sens. *"La Mort". Passé, Présent, Conditionel,* 59–68. La Roche-sur-Yon, Groupe Vendéen d'Etdues Préhistoriques.

Boulestin, B. (1999) *Approche Taphonomique des Restes Humaines. Le Cas des Mésolithiques de la Grotte des Perrats et le Problème du Cannibalisme en Préhistoire Récente Européenne.* Oxford, BAR International Series 776.

Bradley, R. and Gordon, K. (1988) Human skulls from the River Thames, their dating and significance. *Antiquity* 62, 503–509.

Brenot, P. and Riquet, R. (1977) La trépanation Néolithique. *Archéologia* 104, 8–17.

Brinch Petersen, E. (1990) Nye grave fra Jægerstenalderen, Strøby Egede og Vedbæk. *Nationalmuseets Arbejdsmark* 1990, 19–33.

Brinch Petersen, E., Alexandersen, V. and Meiklejohn, C. (1993) Vedbæk, graven midt i byen. *Nationalmuseets Arbejdsmark* 1993, 61–69.

Brothwell, D. (1961) The palaeopathology of early British man: an essay on the problems of diagnosis and analysis. *Journal of the Royal Anthropological Institute* 91, 318–344.

Brothwell, D. R. and Blake, M. L. (1966) The human remains from Fussell's Lodge long barrow: their morphology, discontinuous traits and pathology. *Archaeologia* 100, 48–63.

Bröste, K., Jørgensen, J. B., Becker, C. J. and Brøndsted, J. (1956) *Prehistoric Man in Denmark. A Study in Physical Anthropology.* Copenhagen, Einar Munksgaard.

Butrimas, A. and Jankauskas, R. (1998) Mesolithic and Neolithic graves in Lithuania: data on the transition from foraging to food production. In M. Zvelebil, R. Dennell and L. Domanska (eds), *Harvesting the Sea, Farming the Forest: The Emergence of Neolithic Societies in the Baltic Region,* 219–223. Sheffield, Sheffield Academic Press.

Campillo, D., Mercadal, O. and Blanch, R.-M. (1993) A mortal wound caused by a flint arrowhead in individual MF-18 of the Neolithic period exhumed at Sant Quirze del Valles. *International Journal of Osteoarchaeology* 3, 145–150.

Cauwe, N. (1996) Les sépultures collectives dans le temps et l'espace. *Bulletin de la Société Préhistorique Française* 93, 342–352.

Cauwe, N. (2001) Skeletons in motion, ancestors in action: Early Mesolithic collective tombs in southern Belgium. *Cambridge Archaeological Journal* 11, 147–163.

Chagnon, N. A. (1988) Life histories, blood revenge, and warfare in a tribal population. *Science* 239, 985–992.

Chagnon, N. A. (1997) *Yanomamö* (5th edition). Orlando, Harcourt Brace.

Chapman, J. (1999) The origins of warfare in the prehistory of central and eastern Europe. In J. Carman and A. Harding (eds), *Ancient Warfare,* 101–142. Stroud, Sutton.

Cook, J. (1991) Preliminary report on marked human bones from the 1986–1987 excavations at Gough's Cave, Somerset, England. In N. Barton, A. J. Roberts and D. A. Roe (eds), *The Late Glacial in North-West Europe: Human Adaptation and Environmental Change at the End of the Pleistocene,* 160–168. London, Council for British Archaeology, Research Report 77.

Corcoran, J. X. W. P. (1967) Excavation of three chambered cairns at Loch Calder, Caithness. *Proceedings of the Society of Antiquaries of Scotland* 98, 1–75.

Cordier, G. (1990) Blessures préhistoriques animales et humaines avec armes ou projectiles conservés. *Bulletin de la Société Préhistorique Française* 87, 462–481.

Dastague, J. and de Lumley, M. A. (1976) Las maladies des hommes préhistoriques du Paléolithique et du Mésolithique. In M. A. de Lumley (ed.), *La Préhistoire Français, vol. I,* 621–622. Paris, Éditions du Centre National de la Recherche Scientifique.

Donald, L. (1997) *Aboriginal Slavery on the Northwest Coast of North America.* Berkeley and Los Angeles, University of California Press.

Duday, H., Courtaud, P., Crubézy, E., Sellier, P. and Tiller, A.-M. (1990) L'Anthropologie 'de terrain': reconnaissance et interprétation des gestes funéraires. In E. Crubézy, H. Duday, P. Sellier and A.-M. Tiller (eds), *Anthropologie et Archéologie: Dialogue sur les Ensembles Funéraires,* 29–50. Paris, Bulletin et Mémoirs de la Société d'Anthropologie de Paris n.s. 2.

Ebbesen, K. (1985) Nordjyske gravkister med indgang: Bøstrup-Kisterne. *Aarbørger for Nordisk Oldkyndighed og Historie* 1983, 5–65.

Ebbesen, K. (1993) Sacrifices to the powers of nature. In S. Hvass and B. Storgaard (eds), *Digging into the Past. 25 Years of Archaeology in Denmark,* 122–125. Aarhus, Aarhus University Press.

Ember, C. R. and Ember, M. (1992) Resource unpredictability, mistrust, and war: a cross-cultural study. *Journal of Conflict Resolution* 36, 242–262.

Evans, J. G. and Simpson, D. D. A. (1991) Giants' Hill 2 long barrow, Skendleby, Lincolnshire. *Archaeologia* 109, 1–46.

Ewers, J. C. (1994) Women's roles in Plains Indian warfare. In D. W. Owsley and R. Jantz (eds), *The Skeletal Biology of the Plains,* 325–332. Washington, D.C., Smithsonian Institution Press.

Frayer, D. W. (1997) Ofnet: evidence for a Mesolithic massacre. In D. L. Martin and D. W. Frayer (eds), *Troubled Times: Violence and Warfare in the Past,* 181–216. Amsterdam, Gordon and Breach.

Gaillard, M. (1883) Fouilles des dolmens de Port-Blanc (St-Pierre-Quiberon). *Bulletin de la Société d'Anthopologie de Paris* 6, 292–316.

Gardner, R. and Heider, K. G. (1974) *Gardens of War.* Harmondsworth, Penguin.

Gieseler, W. (1951) Die Süddeutschen Kopfbestattungen (Ofnet, Kaufertsberg, Hohlestein) und ihre Zeitliche Einreihung. *Aus der Heimat* 59, 291–298.

Gronenborn, D. (1999) A variation on a basic theme: the transition to farming in southern central Europe. *Journal of World Prehistory* 13, 123–210.

Gronenborn, D. 2001. Zum (möglichen) Nachweis von Sklaven/Unfreien in prähistorischen Gesellschaften Mitteleuropas. *Ethnographische-Archäologische Zeitschrift* 42, 1–42.

Grøn, O. and Skaarup, J. (1991) Møllegabet II – A submerged Mesolithic site and a "boat burial" from Æro. *Journal of Danish Archaeology* 10, 38–50.

Guilaine, J. and Zammit, J. (2001) *Le Sentiér de la Guerre: Visages de la Violence Préhistorique.* Paris, Éditions du Seuil.

Halbmayer, E. (2001) Socio-cosmological contexts and forms of violence: war, vendetta and suicide among the Yukpa of north-western Venezuela. In B. E. Schmidt and I. W. Schröder (eds), *Anthropology of Violence and Conflict,* 50–75. London, Routledge.

Häusser, A. (ed.) (1998) *Krieg oder Frieden? Herxheim vor 7000 Jarhen.* Herxheim, Landesamt für Denkmalplfege.

Hedges, R. E. M., Housley, R. A., Law, I. A. and Bronk Ramsey, C. (1989) Radiocarbon dates from the Oxford AMS system: *Archaeometry* datelist 9. *Archaeometry* 31, 207–234.

Ives, S. (2003) Was ancient Alpine 'iceman' killed in battle? *National*

Geographic News http://news.nationalgeographic.com/news/ 2003/10/1030_031030_icemandeath.html

Jeunesse, C. (1996) Variabilité des pratiques funéraires et différenciation sociale dans le Néolithique Ancien Danubien. *Gallia Préhistoire* 38, 249–286.

Jochim, M. A. (1998) *A Hunter-Gatherer Landscape: Southwest Germany in the Late Paleolithic and Mesolithic.* New York, Plenum Press.

Keeley, L. H. (1996) *War Before Civilization: The Myth of the Peaceful Savage.* Oxford, Oxford University Press.

Kneipp, J. and Büttner, H. (1988) Anthropophagie in der Jüngsten Bandkermik der Wetterau. *Germania* 66, 490–497.

Knüsel, C. and Carr, G. D. (1995) On the significance of the crania from the River Thames. *Antiquity* 63, 162–169.

Knüsel, C. J. (2005) The physical evidence of warfare – subtle stigmata? In M. Parker Pearson and I. J. N. Thorpe (eds), *Warfare, Violence and Slavery in Prehistory,* 49–65. Oxford, British Archaeological Reports, International Series 1374.

Larsen, C. S. (1997) *Bioarchaeology: Interpreting Behavior from the Human Skeleton.* Cambridge, Cambridge University Press.

Larsson, L. (1989) Late Mesolithic settlements and cemeteries at Skateholm, southern Sweden. In C. Bonsall (ed.), *The Mesolithic in Europe,* 367–378. Edinburgh, John Donald.

Leitão, M., North, C. T., Norton, J., da Veiga Ferreira, O. and Zbyszewski, G. (1987) A Gruta Pré-Histórica do Lugar do Canto, Valverde (Alcanede). *O Arqueólogo Português* 5, 37–65.

Lescot, F. (1996) La Grotte des Perrats à Agris. *L'Archéologue, Archéologie Nouvelle* 22, 9–15.

Léotard, J.-M., Cauwe, N., Bastin, B. and Gilot, E. (1988) Un ossuaire Néolithique aux Roches de Freyr à Dinant. *Activités 86 à 87 du S.O.S. Fouilles* 5, 73–88.

Lillie, M. C. (2004) Fighting for your life? Violence at the Late-Glacial to Holocene transition in Ukraine. In M. Roksandic (ed.), *Violent Interactions in the Mesolithic,* 89–96. Oxford, British Archaeological Reports, International Series 1237.

Lillie, M. C. (2003) Cranial surgery: the Epipalaeolithic to Neolithic populations of Ukraine. In R. Arnott, S. Finger and C. U. M. Smith (eds), *Trepanation: History, Discovery, Theory,* 175–188. Lisse, Swets & Zeitlinger.

Lovell, N. C. (1997) Trauma analysis in paleopathology. *Yearbook of Physical Anthropology* 40, 139–170.

Lubell, D., Jackes, M. and Meiklejohn, C. (1989) Archaeology and human biology of the Mesolithic-Neolithic transition in southern Portugal: a preliminary report. In C. Bonsall (ed.), *The Mesolithic in Europe,* 632–640. Edinburgh, John Donald.

Lynch, A. and Ó Donnabháin, B. (1994) Poulnabrone portal tomb. *The Other Clare* 18, 5–7.

Makkay, J. (2000) *An Early War: The Late Neolithic Mass Grave from Esztergályhorváti.* Budapest, J. Makkay.

McKnight, D. (1986) Fighting in an Australian Aborigine supercamp. In D. Riches (ed.), *The Anthropology of Violence,* 136–163. Oxford, Basil Blackwell.

Mercer, R. J. (1988) Hambledon Hill, Dorest, England. In C. Burgess, P. Topping, C. Mordant and M. Maddison (eds), *Enclosures and Defences in the Neolithic of Western Europe,* 89–106. Oxford, Bar International Series 403(i).

Mercer, R. J. (1999) The origins of warfare in the British Isles. In J. Carman and A. Harding (eds), *Ancient Warfare,* 143–156. Stroud, Sutton.

Milner, G. R. (2005) Nineteenth-century arrow wounds and perceptions of prehistoric warfare. *American Antiquity* 70, 144–156.

Mordant, D. and Mordant, C. (1992) Noyen-sur-Seine: a Mesolithic waterside settlement. In B. Coles (ed.), *The Wetland Revolution in Prehistory,* 55–64. Exeter, The Prehistoric Society and WARP.

Murphy, E. (2003) Funerary processing of the dead in prehistoric Ireland. *Archaeology Ireland* 17, 13–15.

Nilsson Stutz, L. (2003) *Embodied Rituals and Ritualized Bodies.* Lund, Acta Archaeologica Lundensia.

Orschiedt, J. (2005) The head burials from Ofnet cave: An example of warlike conflict in the Mesolithic. In M. Parker Pearson and I. J. N. Thorpe (eds), *Warfare, Violence and Slavery in Prehistory,* 67–73. Oxford, British Archaeological Reports, International Series 1374.

Orschiedt, J. (1998) Ergebnisse einer neuen Untersuchung der Spätmesolithischen Kopfbestattungen aus Süddeutschland. *Urgeschichtliche Materialhefte* 12, 147–160.

Orschiedt, J., Häußer, A., Haidle, M. N., Alt, K. W. and Buitrago-Téllez, C. H. (2003) Survival of a multiple skull trauma: the case of an early Neolithic individual from the LBK enclosure at Herxheim (Southwest Germany). *International Journal of Osteoarchaeology* 13, 375–383.

Ortner, D. J. and Putschar, W. G. J. (1985) *Identification of Pathological Conditions in Human Skeletal Remains.* Washington, D.C., Smithsonian Institution.

Otterbein, K. F. (2000) Killing of captured enemies: a cross-cultural study. *Current Anthropology* 41, 439–443.

Paige, K. E. and Paige, J. M. (1981) *The Politics of Reproductive Ritual.* Berkeley, University of California Press.

Papathanasiou, A., Larsen, C. S. and Norr, L. (2000) Bioarchaeological inferences from a Neolithic ossuary from Alepotrypa Cave, Diros, Greece. *International Journal of Osteoarchaeology* 10, 210–228.

Persson, O. and Persson, E. (1984) *Anthropological Report on the Mesolithic Graves from Skateholm, Southern Sweden. I. Excavation Seasons 1980–1982.* Lund, Institute of Archaeology, Report Series no. 21.

Peter-Röcher, H. (2002) Krieg und Gewalt: zu den Kopfdepositionen in der Großen Ofnet und der Diskussion um kriegerische Konflikte in prähistorischer Zeit. *Praehistorische Zeitschrifte* 77, 1–28.

Péquart, M., Péquart, S.-J., Boule, M. and Vallois, H. (1937) *Téviec, Station-Nécropole du Mésolithique du Morbihan.* Paris, Archives de L'Institut de Paléontologie Humaine XVIII.

Piggott, S. (1962) *The West Kennet Long Barrow.* London, HMSO.

Pitt-Rivers, L.-G. (1898) *Excavations at Cranborne Chase, Vol. IV.* Privately Printed

Polet, C., Dutour, O., R., O., Jadin, I. and Louryan, S. (1996) A healed wound caused by a flint arrowhead in a Neolithic human innominate from the Trou Rosette (Furfooz, Belgium). *International Journal of Osteoarchaeology* 6, 414–420.

Potts, R. B. and Shipman, P. (1981) Cutmarks made by stone tools on bones from Olduvai Gorge, Tanzania. *Nature* 291, 577–580.

Pryor, F. (1976) A Neolithic multiple burial from Fengate. *Antiquity* 50, 232–233.

Riches, D. (1986) The phenomenon of violence. In D. Riches (ed.), *The Anthropology of Violence,* 1–27. Oxford, Basil Blackwell.

Robb, J. (1997) Violence and gender in Italy. In D. L. Martin and D. W. Frayer (eds), *Troubled Times: Violence and Warfare in the Past,* 111–144. Amsterdam, Gordon and Breach.

Roberts, C. and McKinley, J. (2003) Review of trepanations in British antiquity focusing on funerary context to explain their occurrence. In R. Arnott, S. Finger and C. U. M. Smith (eds), *Trepanation: History, Discovery, Theory,* 55–78. Lisse, Swets & Zeitlinger.

Robertson-Mackay, R. (1987) The Neolithic causewayed enclosure at Staines, Surrey: excavations 1961–63. *Proceedings of the Prehistoric Society* 53, 23–128.

Roksandic, M. (2004) Contextualising the evidence of violent death in the Mesolithic: burials associated with victims of violence in the Iron Gates Gorge. In M. Roksandic (ed.), *Violent Interactions in the Mesolithic*, 53–74. Oxford, British Archaeological Reports, International Series 1237.

Schröder, I. W. and Schmidt, B. E. (2001) Introduction: violent imaginaries and violent practices. In B. E. Schmidt and I. W. Schröder (eds), *Anthropology of Violence and Conflict*, 1–24. London, Routledge.

Schulting, R. and Davis, M. (n.d.) Report on cut-marks identified on Neolithic human remains from Bryn-yr-Hen-Bobl. Unpublished report on file with the author.

Schulting, R. and Wysocki, M. (Forthcoming) "In this chambered tumulus were found cleft skulls...": an assessment of the evidence for cranial trauma in the British Neolithic. An assessment of evidence for cranial trauma in the British Neolithic. *Proceedings of the Prehistoric Society*.

Schulting, R. and Wysocki, M. (2002) Cranial trauma in the British earlier Neolithic. *Past* 41, 4–6.

Schwandner-Sievers, S. (2001) The enactment of 'tradition': Albanian constructions of identity, violence and power in times of crisis. In B. E. Schmidt and I. W. Schröder (eds), *Anthropology of Violence and Conflict*, 97–120. London, Routledge.

Selkirk, A. (1971) Ascott-under-Wychwood. *Current Archaeology* 24, 7–10.

Shipman, P. (1981) Applications of scanning electron microscopy to taphonomic problems. *Annals of the New York Academy of Sciences* 276, 357–385.

Silva, A. M. (2003) Trepanation in the Portuguese Late Neolithic, Chalcolithic and Early Bronze Age periods. In R. Arnott, S. Finger and C. U. M. Smith (eds), *Trepanation: History, Discovery, Theory*, 117–130. Lisse, Swets & Zeitlinger.

Smith, I. F. (1965) *Windmill Hill and Avebury: Excavations by Alexander Keiller 1925–1939*. Oxford, Clarendon Press.

Smith, M. and Brickley, M. (2004) Analysis and interpretation of flint toolmarks found on bones from West Tump long barrow, Gloucestershire. *International Journal of Osteoarchaeology* 14, 18–33.

Stewart, P. J. and Strathern, A. (2002) *Violence: Theory and Ethnography*. London, Continuum.

Taylor, T. (2002) *The Buried Soul*. London, Fourth Estate.

Teschler-Nicola, M., Gerold, F., Kanz, F., Lindenbauer, K. and Spannagl, M. (1996) Anthropologische Spurensicherung: Die Traumatischen und Postmortalen Veränderungen an den Linearbandkeramischen Skelettresten von Asparn/Schletz. *Archäologie* 7, 4–12.

Thorpe, I. J. N. (2003) Anthropology, archaeology, and the origin of war. *World Archaeology* 35, 145–165.

Thurnam, J. (1865) On the two principal forms of ancient British and Gaulish skulls. Part II. *Memoirs of the Anthropological Society* 1865, 459–519.

Thurnam, J. (1869) On ancient British barrows (Part I. Long barrows). *Archaeologia* 42, 161–244.

Turner, A., Gonzalez, S. and Ohman, J. C. (2002) Prehistoric human and ungulate remains from Preston Docks, Lancashire, UK: problems of river finds. *Journal of Archaeological Science* 29, 423–433.

Ubelaker, D. H. and Adams, B. J. (1995) Differentiation of perimortem and postmortem trauma using taphonomic indicators. *Journal of Forensic Sciences* 40, 509–512.

Vencl, H. (1984) War and warfare in archaeology. *Journal of Anthropological Archaeology* 3, 116–132.

Vencl, S. (1999) Stone Age warfare. In J. Carman and A. Harding (eds), *Ancient Warfare*, 57–72. Stroud, Sutton.

Villa, P., Courtin, J., Helmer, D., Shipman, P., Bouville, C. and Mahieu, E. (1986) Un cas de cannibalisme au Néolithique. Boucherie et rejet des restes humaines et animaux dans la grotte de Fontbrégoua (Salernes, Var). *Gallia-Préhistoire* 29, 143–171.

Villa, P. (1992) Cannibalism in prehistoric Europe. *Evolutionary Anthropology* 1, 93–104.

Wahl, J. and König, H. (1987) Anthropologisch-Traumologische Untersuchung der Menschlichen Skelettreste aus dem Bandkeramischen Massengrab bei Talheim, Kreis Heilbronn. *Fundberichte aus Baden-Wurtemberg* 12, 65–193.

Wendorf, F. (1968) Site 117: A Nubian Final Paleolithic graveyard near Jebel Sahaba, Sudan. In F. Wendorf (ed.), *The Prehistory of Nubia*, 954–995. Dallas, Southern Methodist University Press.

Whittle, A. (1991) Wayland's Smithy, Oxfordshire: excavations at the Neolithic tomb in 1962–63 by R.J.C. Atkinson and S. Piggott. *Proceedings of the Prehistoric Society* 57, 61–101.

Wild, E. M., Stadler, P., Häusser, A., Kutschera, W., Steier, P., Teschler-Nicola, M., Wahl, J. and Windl, H. J. (2004) Neolithic massacres: local skirmishes or general warfare in Europe? *Radiocarbon* 46, 377–385.

Windl, H. (1996) Archäologie einer katastrophe und deren Vorgeschichte. *Rätsel um Gewalt und Tod vor 7,000 Jarhen: Eine Spurensicherung*, 7–29. Asparn a.d. Zaya, Museum für Urgeschichte.

Windl, H. (1999) Makabres ende einer kultur? *Archäologie im Deutschland* 1999, 54–57.

Windl, H. (2001) Erdwerke der Linearbandkeramik in Asparn an der Zaya/Schletz, Niederösterreich. *Preistoria Alpina* 37, 137–144.

Wysocki, M. and Whittle, A. (2000) Diversity, lifestyles and rites: new biological and archaeological evidence from British earlier Neolithic mortuary assemblages. *Antiquity* 74, 591–601.

Wysocki, M. and Fernández-Jalvo, J. (forthcoming) Cut-marked human postcranial bones from two British Neolithic chambered tombs: evidence for post-mortem dismemberment?

16. Beneath the Façade: A Skeletal Model of Domestic Violence

Shannon A. Novak

Introduction

Every year, between one and two million women in the United States are injured by their male partners (Melnick *et al.* 2002). In many countries around the world, 20% to 70% of women report having been physically abused by a partner (Heise 1994). Quite consistently, a woman is more likely to be the victim of assault by a known male than by a stranger (Crowell and Burgess 1996). When strangers are assailants, the attacks result in fewer and less severe injuries than those seen in domestic assaults (Spedding *et al.* 1999).

Domestic assaults result in more injuries to women than do rape, mugging, and car accident combined (Bachman and Carmody 1994). The immediate physical effects include contusions, fractures, miscarriages, hearing loss, gastrointestinal disorders, depression, anxiety, and suicide (Campbell 2002; Heise 1995). Over the long term, there are dramatic consequences for the health and mortality of women and their children (Asling-Monemi *et al.* 2003).

Given the prevalence of domestic violence in modern societies, physical anthropologists must consider whether this behavior was present in prehistory and, if so, what the biological consequences might have been for individuals and populations. The tenets of evolutionary theory and data from nonhuman primates suggest that males are motivated to use physical force to coerce females (*e.g.* Smuts 1992; Daly and Wilson 1994; Handwerker 1998). Such coercion may be mitigated, however, by social and ecological constraints (Rodseth and Novak 2000), giving rise to wide variability in levels of gender violence.

Through the assessment of skeletal trauma, bioarchaeologists have attempted to identify domestic violence in the archaeological record. In some cases, healed traumatic lesions in female skeletons have been compared with assault patterns in contemporary clinical studies (*e.g.* Shermis 1982; Alvrus 1996; Walker 1997). Although these studies provide useful heuristics, their application to prehistoric skeletons remains problematic.

The aim of the present research was to identify a trauma pattern that could be used statistically to test hypotheses about domestic violence in prehistory. A clinical study documented injury patterns in known cases of accident and domestic assault. The distribution of soft- and hard-tissue lesions across the patients' bodies were assessed using multivariate statistics for those locations on the body that best discriminated between accident and assault. From these anatomical locations, a general linear model was developed to test the aetiology of skeletal wounds in unknown cases. A small skeletal sample from the Great Basin was used to illustrate the utility of the model in a prehistoric context.

It is worth pausing here to clarify the underlying assumptions of this study. In keeping with recent evolutionary theory (Ridley 2003; West-Eberhard 2003), I assume that the environment – both physical and social – *always* mediates between genes and phenotypes. Despite the lingering perception that an evolutionary analysis implies genetic determinism, such analysis has actually provided "massive documentation of a heretofore widely underestimated capacity for adaptive condition-sensitive behavior and development" (West-Eberhard 2003, 5). In this light, it is fallacious to assume that "genetic" traits are invariant while "learned" or "acquired" ones are plastic. In fact, the aim of the present research is to analyse *variation* in the physical coercion of women, not to universalise one particular pattern. As a result, I do not assume that domestic assaults have a common, cross-cultural signature. In any case, if there were such a signature, it would not indicate genetic, as opposed to environmental, control over the behaviour.

Background

Ethnography and primatology

To understand domestic violence, it should be viewed in

a broad comparative context. Ethnographic evidence can tell us about the cross-cultural patterning of abuse, while behavioural primatology can shed light on the analogs of such abuse in species closely related to humans. For present purposes, three issues are of special interest: which females are most at risk, what factors motivate males to inflict abuse, and what strategies females can use to defend themselves against abuse.

Ethnographic accounts are vital to an anthropological understanding of the prevalence, frequency, and motivations of wife beating (*e.g.* Romanucci-Ross 1973; Burbank 1994; Counts *et al.* 1999; Abraham 2000; McClusky 2001). These studies consistently report that the primary victims of assault by intimate males are parous females, and that jealousy, as a result of real or imagined sexual infidelity, motivates most of the attacks. High levels of gender violence are associated with economic inequality between the sexes, masculine ideals of male dominance, economic and decision-making authority by males, and violent interpersonal conflict resolution. Conversely, low levels of gender violence are correlated with female power outside the home, community intervention in violent episodes, presence of all-female work groups, and sanctuary from violence by friends and family (Levinson 1989; Heise 1994; Counts *et al.* 1999).

One limitation of the existing ethnographic literature is a lack of quantitative data on injury patterns. A recent study in a foraging-horticultural society has helped to fill this gap. Sugiyama (2004) interviewed 40 Shiwiar men and women in the Ecuadorian Amazon about the types of injuries and illnesses they had experienced over their lives. The aim of the study, it should be noted, was not to investigate violence but to shed light on the evolution of low mortality rates as a result of healthcare provisioning. The focus, in other words, was on the *consequences* rather than the causes of injuries. As a result, however, Sugiyama's data are of limited use in the present context. For example, of the 20 females included in the study sample, only five were between the ages of 21 and 40 (seven were young girls below the age of 10, while another six were between 11 and 20). As a result, little is known about the patterning of injuries in parous women, precisely those at greatest risk for domestic violence. In any case, some form of "violence" (including both "assaults" and "fights") accounted for eight soft-tissue injuries and one fracture in the females (Sugiyama 2004, Tables 3 and 6). The circumstances surrounding this violence are unknown.

Nonhuman primate studies suggest that social organization and gender relations are affected by environmental constraints, especially the quality and distribution of resources (Wrangham 1979, 1980, 2000). In apes, female dispersal and a lack of stable coalitions among females results in their susceptibility to male coercion. For example, male chimpanzees use physical force to guard and intimidate females, and to "encourage" the formation of consortships (Smuts and Smuts 1993).

Evolutionary psychology suggests that jealously guarding or sequestering a mate enhances male fitness, since it serves to prevent cuckoldry (*e.g.* Daly *et al.* 1982; Daly and Wilson 1994; Buss and Malamuth 1996; Wilson and Daly 1998). In some species, by associating with a particular male, a female can reduce the level of assault (Smuts 1985; Smuts and Smuts 1993; Wrangham and Peterson 1996; Mesnick 1997). As a result, a coalition with a male is often preferred over alliances with other females (*cf.* Wrangham 2000). Violent attacks on females can cause serious injury (Lovell 1990; Jurmain and Kilgore 1998) and thus carry potential fitness costs.

In summary, then, three patterns emerge from behavioural observation of humans and other primates: parous females are most at risk of violence, males are motivated by cues of sexual infidelity, and females face a trade-off between forming coalitions with particular males or with a group of females to defend themselves against assault.

Skeletal studies

Informed by observations of nonhuman primates and ethnographic accounts, skeletal studies of past populations have been used to investigate the temporal depth and patterning of violent behavior (see review in Walker 2001). Because interpersonal violence can leave traces in the skeleton, it may be possible to identify such violence without directly observing it. Fracture morphology, location, and state of healing have been used by bioarchaeologists to identify interpersonal violence in the past. While many of these studies have focused on injuries related to warfare (*e.g.* Walker 1989; Willey 1990; Milner *et al.* 1991; Owsley and Jantz 1994; Lambert 1997), a number have considered domestic assault as the cause of healed skeletal lesions in females.

As early as 1910, Elliot-Smith and Wood-Jones attributed healed cranial and forearm fractures in Nubian female skeletons to wife beating. Similar conclusions have been drawn for skeletal populations from the Sudan (Alvrus 1999) and Australia (Webb 1995). In North America, skeletal evidence of female-directed violence is reported for precontact sites in Michigan (Wilkenson and Van Wagenen 1993; Wilkenson 1997), Tennessee (Smith 1996), Colorado (Martin 1997), California (Lambert 1997). These more recent studies incorporate the skeletal findings within a cultural and historical framework, considering factors that may exacerbate female-directed violence, such as resource stress, status relations, abduction, and warfare.

With this said, however, the overriding criterion used to identify domestic violence is trauma to the head, face, and forearm in female skeletons. These locations are based on injury patterns identified in contemporary clinical research on assault. Shermis (1982) first compared prehistoric skeletal trauma to the locations of soft-tissue domestic assault injuries reported by women in a shelter. While not statistically validated, his observations of facial, thoracic, and limb injuries to female skeletons from California and South Dakota closely corresponded to the areas in which domestic assault victims said they were struck by a "hard or painful blow" (Shermis 1982, 148). Subsequent to these findings, numerous clinical studies have refined a set of trauma patterns that aid in the identification of domestic assault victims.

Contemporary clinical studies

In medical settings, severe injuries from domestic violence include trauma to the teeth (Gutmann and Gutmann 1995), orbital fractures (Hartzell *et al.* 1996), and fractures of the mandible, zygomaxillary complex, and nasal bones (Shepherd *et al.* 1990; Zachariades *et al.* 1990; Ochs *et al.* 1996; Greene *et al.* 1997; Huang *et al.* 1998). Victims are most likely to receive injuries to the face, and it has been suggested by some clinicians that, in the absence of evidence for a car accident, trauma to the face should be considered a result of domestic violence (Hartzell *et al.* 1996; Ochs *et al.* 1996; Gilthorpe *et al.* 1999; Perciaccante *et al.* 1999).

While these studies provide useful patterns to compare to prehistoric skeletal lesions, the juxtaposition of the trauma sets remains problematic. Data are often pooled in the clinical studies in such a way that it is impossible to tease apart patterns by sex, skeletal element, or type of assault. For example, although Hussain *et al.* (1994), Kjaerulff *et al.* (1989), and Ström (1992) provide detailed soft- and hard-tissue injury findings for known cases of assault, in the final analysis, the sexes are pooled and only Ström (1992) considered postcranial lesions.

In fact, the vast majority of the clinical literature fails to consider the distribution of trauma *across* the body and focuses instead on the craniofacial region. This is a result, in part, of who does the research, with most of it conducted by dentists (*e.g.* McDowell *et al.* 1992; Gutmann and Gutmann 1995), oral and maxillary surgeons (*e.g.* Shepherd *et al.* 1990; Greene *et al.* 1997; Perciaccante *et al.* 1999), and plastic surgeons (*e.g.* Hartzell *et al.* 1996; Huang *et al.* 1998). Even with such detailed craniofacial focus, many of these studies lack control samples and focus solely on trauma from domestic assault (*e.g.* DeMoss and DeMoss 1994).

As emphasized by Jurmain and Kilgore (1998), an epidemiological approach to skeletal trauma is needed and, in particular, the combined distribution of cranial and postcranial injuries should be evaluated to infer causality. With these considerations in mind, I designed a clinical study to facilitate a more direct comparison between modern and prehistoric skeletal lesions.

Clinical study

Bradford Royal Infirmary

The clinical portion of the research was conducted in the casualty unit of the Bradford Royal Infirmary (BRI) in northern England. This large emergency center serves the City of Bradford and the surrounding region of West Yorkshire, an area with a population of 484,500 in 1997. Bradford District comprises a densely populated urban center, smaller satellite towns and villages, and a large rural region. The area is also ethnically diverse, with a native British population and large immigrant communities, primarily from rural north Pakistan.

For this clinical study, a trauma center in Britain was preferable to an American facility. One advantage is that the stringent gun control laws in Britain ensure that firearms are kept in very few private homes. This reduces the likelihood of gun-related accidents or assaults. In fact, none of the cases surveyed for this study involved gunshot trauma. Because many domestic assaults in the U.S. involve firearms, these cases are problematic for drawing comparisons with historic or prehistoric evidence.

Another advantage to the British context is that there is no legal mandate in the U.K. requiring medical providers to report domestic assaults to the police. When victims of such assaults are admitted to the casualty unit, treatment is provided on a confidential basis and attending nurses and physicians generally do not report the incident to the police. In contrast, many states in the U.S. have laws that require healthcare providers to notify the police of an assault (Houry *et al.* 2002). This requirement may lead female patients to misrepresent the cause of their injuries to protect an intimate partner or family member from prosecution (Feldhaus *et al.* 2003). For the same reason, many victims in the U.S. avoid medical treatment altogether.

Finally, the British National Health Service guarantees medical treatment to all individuals presenting at an emergency center. As a result, women from many backgrounds use such facilities, regardless of their social or economic status. While patients in the U.K. are encouraged to visit their primary physician for routine care or to receive a referral to the emergency center, this is not a perquisite for treatment. As a result, the BRI casualty unit often treats minor aches, pains, and abrasions, as well as more serious life-threatening injuries. This clinical study recorded a broad range of injuries from both accidents and domestic assaults.

Sample and data collection

To select the domestic violence sample, a hospital database provided a list of patients who were female, 15 to 65 years in age, and admitted during a one-year period for assault. Because the ICD (International Classification of Diseases) computer codes did not distinguish between domestic and other types of assault, domestic assault victims had to be identified by reading the original patient files.

The control sample consisted of females, 15 to 65 years in age, who had been admitted to the casualty unit during the same year as the assault patients, but in this case for non-vehicular, accidental injuries. Because the number of accident cases was so large for this one-year period, the sample was reduced to the months of December and July. One winter month and one summer month were selected to account for seasonal differences in accidental injuries. As with the domestic assault sample, a list of patients was generated and the original files consulted. In both samples, patients were excluded from the study if the cause of the injury was misclassified when coded in the computer, if the handwriting by the physician was illegible, or if the injury had been produced by a modern mechanical device. If patients presented multiple times during the year, only the first hospital visit was retained for the study.

Using reports from physicians and radiographers, each patient's wounds were illustrated and coded on body schematics (Table 16.1). Individual wounds were coded for the force and weapon used, the resulting wound manifestation, and the level of tissue damage (Table 16.2). Medical files were consulted for basic demographic information about each patient and to recover the patient's original remarks about the causes and context of the accident or assault.

Methods of analysis

From the trauma schematics, a computer database was used to document each subject's lesions in 54 zones of the body. Ideally, the analysis would compare trauma patterns by skeletal element, but the variable size and anatomical position of these elements can result in some regions being over-enumerated. For example, Zones 1 through 9 include all facial bones, but because of the small size of such elements, a single blow can affect multiple bones. As a result, an analysis by element can inflate the number of blows. Conversely, a single blow to Zone 31, the anterior superior right arm, would affect only a single zone. To facilitate statistical analysis and avoid confounding zones, the original 54 regions were compressed into 10 loci (Table 16.1). The reduced loci include gross target areas (*e.g.* the face) whose underlying bones (*e.g.* frontal, lacrimal, nasal, maxilla, zygomatic, mandible, or dentition) might be affected by a single blow.

The distribution of trauma by subject was coded for the 10 loci as either present (1) or absent (0). When a lesion from a single blow affected multiple zones, each affected zone would be coded for the presence of trauma. If multiple wounds were present in a single locus, the presence of lesions would be recorded but not their number. As a result, the total number of wounds does not equal the number of loci affected.

Although the primary interest of this study was to differentiate assault from accident trauma in skeletal remains, the distribution of soft-tissue injuries were also evaluated to determine areas of the body at risk for skeletal trauma. Therefore, each subject had to be coded for wound distribution in two data sets. Because soft-tissue damage is also present in cases of skeletal trauma, all lesions were included in the first data set. A second data set was created for each subject that exhibited hard-tissue injuries.

Locus	Zone	Anatomical Area
1	1	nasal
	2	L. maxilla
	3	R. maxilla
	4	L. zygomatic
	5	R. zygomatic
	6	L. mandible
	7	R. mandible
	8	L. frontal
	9	R. frontal
2	10	L. parietal
	11	R. parietal
	12	L. temporal
	13	R. temporal
	14	L. occipital
	15	R. occipital
3	16	L. ant. neck
	17	R. ant. neck
4	18	L. clavicle
	19	R. clavicle
	20	L. chest
	21	R. chest
	22	L. abdomen
	23	R. abdomen
5	24	L. ant. femur
	25	R. ant. femur
	26	L. ant. tib/fib
	27	R. ant. tib/fib
	28	L. sup. foot
	29	R. sup. foot
6	30	L. ant. humerus
	31	R. ant. humerus
	32	L. ant. ulna/rad
	33	R. ant. ulna/rad
	34	L. palmar hand
	35	R. palmar hand
7	36	L. post. neck
	37	R. post. neck
8	38	vertebrae
	39	R. back
	40	L. back
	41	R. buttocks
	42	L. buttocks
9	43	R. post. femur
	44	L. post. femur
	45	R. post. tib/fib
	46	L. post. tib/fib
	47	R. planar foot
	48	L. planar foot
10	49	R. post. humerus
	50	L. post. humerus
	51	R. post. ulna/rad
	52	L. post. ulna/rad
	53	R. post. hand
	54	L. post. hand

Table 16.1. Wound location by locus, zone, and anatomical area.

Force	Manifestation		Weapon	Tissue Damage
1 Blunt	1	Contusion	1 Substrate	1 Affects bone
	2	Abrasion	2 Unknown	2 No effect on bone
	3	Laceration	3 Mouth	
	4	Bite	4 Hand/fist	
	8	Tooth loss	5 Foot	
	9	Puncture	6 Knife	
2 Sharp	5	Cut	7 Other object	
	6	Stab	8 Multiple body	
3 Thermal	7	Burn	9 Body and object	
4 Other				

Table 16.2. Injury codes for body map documentation.

Age Interval	Age-Group Midpoint
15 – 24	19.5
25 – 34	29.5
35 – 44	39.5
45 – 54	49.5
55 – 64	59.5
65 – 74	69.5

Table 16.3. Ten-year age categories and age-group midpoints.

Descriptive statistics were produced and tests of proportion were conducted to evaluate the soft- and hard-tissue injuries by location for accident and assault subjects. A stepwise discriminant function analysis (DFA) was used to test whether or not the accident and domestic assault patients could be separated, based on the injury location variables measured for each group (SAS 1989). A DFA was conducted using principal component analysis on matrix indices calculated from between- and within-group variance. Using the variables identified in the DFA, a general linear model (GLM) was produced to develop a prediction equation.

The dependent variables in this study were the categories of domestic assault and accident, and the independent variables included 10 injury loci and age of the patient. Age was included as an independent variable because of the considerable difference in the age distributions of assault victims as opposed to accident victims. To tailor this study for use with prehistoric skeletons, ages were compressed into 10-year categories and the midpoint of this category was used for the analysis (Table 16.3). Such conservative categories were used because of the known difficulties involved in determining the biological age of an adult skeleton (*e.g.* Nawrocki 1998; Suchey and Katz 1998).

Results

Descriptive statistics

This study drew on trauma histories of 673 women. The domestic assault sample included 194 women, aged 16 to 63 years. The ages of these women clustered between 16 and 41 years (Fig. 16.1), with a mean of 30 years (s.d. 7.98). A total of 544 domestic assault wounds were documented, with an average of 2.8 wounds per woman. Nearly all of these injuries were produced by blunt force

trauma (99%) and a large majority resulted in damage to soft tissue only (93%). A fraction of the lesions (7%), however, did affect bone.

The accident sample contained 479 women, aged 16 to 65 years. The mean age of accident patients was 36 years (s.d. 13.2), and in contrast to the domestic assault subjects, this sample has a flatter distribution. While 94% of the domestic assault victims were under age 42, the age of accident patients must be extended to 60 to account for the same proportion of cases. Accidental injuries were the result of falls (54%) and other miscellaneous mishaps (46%). A total of 557 accidental wounds were documented, with an average of 1.2 wounds per woman. Damage to soft tissue only occurred in 79% of the lesions, while 21% of the injuries affected bone.

Accident and assault patients had a nearly equal number of soft-tissue wounds, but accidents were responsible for a greater proportion of hard-tissue lesions. When the distributions on the body of accident and assault lesions are compared, however, different patterns emerge. Because the primary focus of this study is the patterning of hard-tissue injuries, the soft-tissue findings are only briefly discussed here, to give some indication of the regions of the body at risk of fracture (see Novak 1999 for more detail).

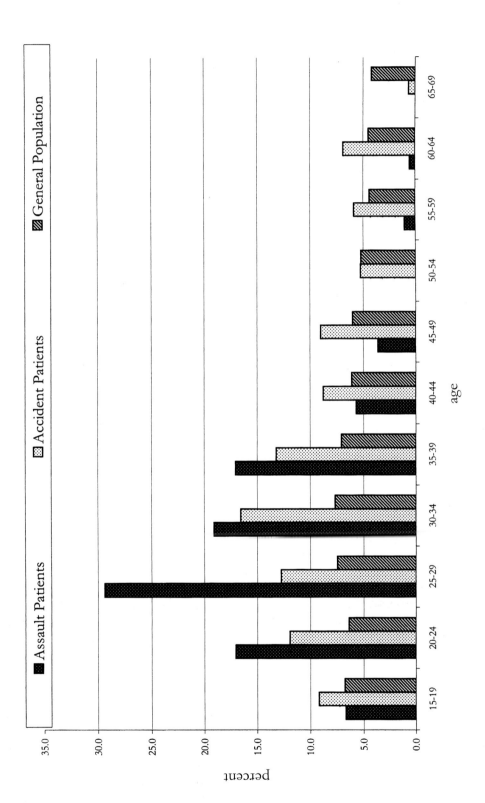

Figure 16.1. Age distribution for BRI assault and accident patients, and age distribution of the female population in Bradford, 1997 (City of Bradford, 1996).

Locus	Assault		Accident		Standard		
	Frequ.	%	Frequ.	%	Error	z-value	p-value
Face	134	35.5	44	7.2	0.0268	10.5562	0.0000
Head	48	12.7	44	7.2	0.0201	2.7231	0.0031
Ant. neck	18	4.8	1	0.2	0.0111	4.1513	0.0000
Chest	30	8.0	11	1.8	0.0150	4.1098	0.0000
Ant. lower limbs	28	7.4	191	31.5	0.0232	-10.3675	0.0000
Ant. upper limbs	27	7.2	89	14.7	0.0196	-3.8367	0.0002
Post. neck	12	3.2	1	0.2	0.0092	3.2844	0.0000
Back	20	5.3	15	2.5	0.0132	2.1548	0.0116
Post. lower limbs	12	3.2	75	12.4	0.0161	-5.6871	0.0000
Post. upper limbs	48	12.7	136	22.4	0.0241	-4.0126	0.0001
Total	377	100.0	607	100.0			

Table 16.4. BRI soft-tissue injury location difference.

Soft-tissue findings

For each patient, 10 locations on the body were coded for presence or absence of soft-tissue wounds. Across all patients, injuries were coded as present in a total of 984 loci, 377 from domestic assaults and 607 from accidents (Table 16.4). Assault injuries to the face are predominant, followed distantly by those to the head and posterior upper limb. Accidental soft-tissue injuries affect primarily the anterior lower limb, followed by the posterior and anterior arms. A two-population proportions test and z-test show that the percentages differ at eight loci at the $\alpha = .001$ level, and at two loci at the $\alpha = .05$ level (Table 16.4). While these findings strongly suggest a difference by locus in domestic assault and accidental wounds, the pattern of lesions across each subject's body is of primary interest. For this assessment, multivariate analysis is required.

A stepwise DFA (discriminant function analysis) was conducted to determine what combination of variables might distinguish domestic assault from accident as the cause of a patient's wounds. A total of 671 domestic assault and accident patients were considered for analysis (two subjects were eliminated due to missing data). Eleven variables were entered in the analysis, including the 10 body loci and age by 10-year age midpoint. The significance level to enter and to keep a variable in the equation was set at $\alpha = .05$. Originally, at this significance level, all loci and ages were determined to be useful in discriminating between the two groups. The possibility of a significant finding by chance alone is likely when all variables remain in a discriminant function model (Manly 1994). As a result, the analysis was run again at the more stringent level of $\alpha = .01$.

Six variables proved to be useful in discriminating between the two groups, including the face, head, anterior neck, posterior neck, chest, and age of the victim (Table 16.5). The partial R^2 values indicate that the face provides

Locus	Partial R^2	F Statistic	Prob. F
Face	0.3777	406.049	0.0001
Head	0.0438	30.601	0.0001
Ant. neck	0.0467	32.666	0.0001
Post. neck	0.0357	24.630	0.0001
Age	0.0361	24.923	0.0001
Chest	0.0243	16.439	0.0001

Table 16.5. Summary statistics from soft-tissue discriminant function analysis.

the most explanatory value in differentiating an assault victim from an accident victim. Locations on the body that did not enter the equation as good discriminators at the soft-tissue level were the anterior and posterior upper limbs, anterior and posterior lower limbs, and the back.

Hard-tissue findings

Domestic assaults result in hard-tissue injuries that affect five loci, for a total of 35 observations (Table 16.6). The posterior head, neck, and lower limbs do not exhibit fractures from domestic assault. Fractures to the face are predominant, followed distantly by those to the upper limbs and anterior torso. Accidental injuries affect the bone at seven loci, for a total of 140 observations. The posterior head and neck do not display hard-tissue accidental injuries and the torso is only minimally affected. A two-population proportions test and z-test indicate that the percentages differ significantly at three loci.

A total of 150 subjects who displayed hard-tissue trauma in one or more loci were entered into the stepwise DFA. Eleven variables were entered in the analysis,

Locus	Assault Frequ.	%	Accident Frequ.	%	Standard Error	z-value	p-value
Face	23	65.7	4	2.9	0.0815	7.7164	0.0000
Head	0	0.0	0	0.0	0.0000	no test	no test
Ant. neck	0	0.0	0	0.0	0.0000	no test	no test
Chest	2	5.7	1	0.7	0.0399	1.2539	0.0217
Ant. lower limbs	0	0.0	50	35.7	0.0405	-8.8192	0.0000
Ant. upper limbs	3	8.6	16	11.4	0.0544	-0.5250	0.3150
Post. neck	0	0.0	0	0.0	0.0000	no test	no test
Back	1	2.9	3	2.1	0.0307	0.2326	0.4012
Post. lower limbs	0	0.0	17	12.1	0.0276	-4.3988	0.0158
Post. upper limbs	6	17.1	49	35.0	0.0754	-2.3687	0.0000
Total	35	100.0	140	100.0			

Table 16.6. BRI hard-tissue injury location difference.

including the 10 body loci and the subject's age-group midpoint. The face, chest, anterior lower limb, and victim's age were determined to be the best variables to discriminate between accident and domestic assault. All variables remained in the analysis at the $\alpha = .05$ level (Table 16.7). Again, as in the soft-tissue model, the face provides the most explanatory value.

A GLM (general linear model) was run to develop a predictive model using the three body loci and age variables identified in the discriminate function analysis. All four variables remain significant at the $\alpha = .05$ level and the overall general linear model is highly significant (p=.0001). The R^2 value of the GLM indicates that nearly 59% of the variation is explained. The following predictive equation was produced to determine group inclusion as domestic assault or accidental injury based on hard-tissue lesions:

$$\hat{y} = - 0.442371 + 1.420588 \text{ (face)} + 1.13328257 \text{ (chest)} - 0.214 \text{ (a. lower limb)} - 0.008361 \text{ (age group)}$$

The calculation requires a 1 or 0 to be entered for each subject as a multiplier for each variable according to whether a fracture does (1) or does not (0) affect a bone in the corresponding locus. The midpoint of a victim's age in a 10-year age category is entered as a multiplier for this variable (see Table 16.3). If the predicted y is greater than zero, the injury is due to a domestic assault; if less than zero, an accident is predicted to have caused the injury. It is obvious from the equation that fractures of the face and chest positively weight the prediction toward domestic assault and, conversely, fractures of the lower limb and an older age increase the negative multiplier toward a prediction of accident. When all possible combinations of fracture location and age are calculated using the GLM, the majority of combinations result in a prediction of assault (Table 16.8). Only the combination of chest and lower limb loci changes group classification

Locus	Partial R^2	F Statistic	Prob. F
Face	0.5107	154.477	0.0001
Chest	0.0837	13.421	0.0003
Age	0.0448	6.849	0.0098
Ant. lower limbs	0.0302	4.514	0.0353

Table 16.7. Summary statistics from hard-tissue discriminant function analysis.

from assault to accident with increasing age.

To assess the model's accuracy in discriminating between domestic assault and accident, the subjects were reassessed using the GLM (Table 16.9). Overall, the model does well, predicting 91% of the cases correctly. The accident victims were identified correctly in the majority of cases (96%). The domestic assault victims, however, were less successfully classified using the model. Though nearly 76% of the domestic assault cases were correctly predicted, 24% were misclassified as accidents.

While this seems a bit discouraging, a close examination of the misclassified subjects shows that all have fractures to the upper limbs (*i.e.* arms, wrists, or hands). If the model equation is examined, only fractures of the face, chest, and lower limb should be evaluated, since these are the only variables that discriminate between the two groups. The cause of fractures in the upper limb loci cannot be differentiated by location using this model.

Assessing the model

To assess the validity of the BRI model, it was applied to an independent data set. Using police reports and photographs from Salt Lake City, Utah, 188 cases of domestic assault were documented and coded by age and wound

AFFECTED LOCI			EVENT BY AGE-GROUP MIDPOINT					
Face	Chest	A. lower limbs	19.5	29.5	39.5	49.5	59.5	69.5
		1	*accident*	*accident*	*accident*	*accident*	*accident*	*accident*
	1		assault	assault	assault	assault	assault	assault
	1	1	assault	assault	assault	assault	*accident*	*accident*
1			assault	assault	assault	assault	assault	assault
1		1	assault	assault	assault	assault	assault	assault
1	1		assault	assault	assault	assault	assault	assault
1	1	1	assault	assault	assault	assault	assault	assault

Table 16.8. All possible wound combinations by age and predicted event.

Actual Group	No. of Cases	Predicted Group Membership	
		Accident (%)	Domestic Assault (%)
Accident	117	112 (95.73)	5 (4.27)
Domestic Assault	33	8 (24.24)	25 (75.76)
Percentage of cases correctly classified: 91.33			

Table 16.9. Results of BRI hard-tissue classification (N=150).

loci. Because the hard- and soft-tissue models can differentiate between accident and assault only for the loci present in the equation, the assessment was limited to 157 soft-tissue cases (83%) and 37 hard-tissue cases (53%). The BRI soft-tissue equation correctly predicts 96.2% of the cases (see Novak 1999). The hard-tissue model classifies 94.6% of the domestic assault cases correctly (Table 16.10). Having tested the model in a second known context, it was now possible to apply it to a case in which the aetiology of the wounds was unknown.

Application to the prehistoric Great Basin

From approximately AD 400 to 1300, while the Anasazi were flourishing to the south, a Formative group known as the Fremont occupied the eastern Great Basin and parts of the western Colorado Plateau. Approximately 2000 years ago, these foragers sporadically cultivated maize to supplement wild food resources in their diet. Some groups remained nomadic, relying solely on wild foods, while others practiced periodic farming (Simms 1986; Madsen and Simms 1998). Approximately 1700 years ago, larger, more sedentary hamlets appeared in areas where intensive horticulture could be practiced. Maize appears to have been a major food source at these locations (Coltrain 1993; Coltrain and Leavitt 2002), and its production was facilitated by pottery and new tools. Above-ground storage facilities are found in association with larger, semi-subterranean living areas.

Caldwell Village (42UN95), a large site by Fremont standards, is located in northeastern Utah at the base of the Uinta Mountains. Excavation identified 22 pithouses, storage units, and an irrigation canal (Ambler 1966). Based on superposition of the excavated pithouses, no more than 18 of these structures would have been occupied at any one time, although many additional houses may have been present at the site. Dating of the site is problematic. A single radiocarbon estimate of AD 520 has been dismissed as too early and ceramic analysis suggests that the site dates from approximately AD 1050 (Ambler 1966).

The human skeletal remains recovered from Caldwell Village include a total of nine burials: three adult males, five adult females, and one juvenile (Table 16.11). Their interment was unsystematic and mortuary offerings were limited to the occasional grinding stone.

All of the female skeletons from the site are small and gracile, and sexual dimorphism is pronounced. Pathology in the younger women includes premature thinning of the cortical bone and two are afflicted by congenital spinal abnormalities. Two other females have infectious skeletal lesions. A middle-aged female has disseminated periostitis from a non-specific infectious disorder, while a young adult female has lesions indicative of spinal tuberculosis (Pott's disease).

In addition to these pathological conditions, all of the female skeletons have well-healed antemortem cranial or facial trauma. Healed nasal-maxillary fractures (Fig. 16.2)

Actual Group	No. of Cases	Predicted Group Membership	
		Accident (%)	Domestic Assault (%)
Soft-Tissue Domestic Assault	157	6 (3.8%)	151 (96.2)
Hard-Tissue Domestic Assault	37	2 (5.4%)	35 (94.6)

Table 16.10. Results of SLC hard-tissue test case.

Burial #	Sex	Age	Antemortem Trauma	Pathological & Anomalous Conditions
UMNH 39	Male	30-34	None	None
UMNH 89	Female	23-29	R. nasal and maxilla fracture	Pott's disease Ankylosis of r. humerus, ulna & radius
UMNH 91	Female	20-24	Depression fracture on frontal	Congenital ankylosis of cervical vertebrae 2/3 Congenital ankylosis of thoracic vertebrae 6/7 Congenital pseudarthrosis of cervical vertebra 1
UMNH 92	Female	20-24	Two depression fractures on posterior l. parietal	Ankylosis of cervical vertebra 1 to occipital condyles Accessory thoracic vertebra
UMNH 94	Male	60+	None	Congenital ankylosis of cervical vertebrae 5/6 Ankylosis of sacroiliac joints Spondylolysis of lumbar vertebra 5 Generalized osteoporosis
UMNH 95	Female	60+	Depression fracture on frontal Fracture of l. clavicle	Generalized osteoporosis
UMNH 96	Male	55-59	Fracture of nasal bones Fracture of r. third rib	Ankylosis of sacroiliac joints Contact facets on r. ribs 1 and 2 Cribra orbitalia
UMNH 193	Female	35-39	Fracture of l. nasal and maxilla	Periostitis on radii, tibiae, and fibulae
UMNH 194	Ind.	.5-1.5	None	None

Table 16.11. Human remains from Caldwell Village, including trauma and pathological conditions.

are present in two individuals, and healed cranial fractures of the frontal and occipital bones are evident in the other three females. A single postcranial fracture was identified in the left clavicle of the oldest female.

The skeletal trauma model developed at the Bradford Royal Infirmary was used to reanalyse the lesions in the Fremont skeletons from Caldwell Village. Four of the five adult females' antemortem wounds could be assessed using the regression formula from the clinical study (Table 16.12). The model classifies all four of the cases of facial fracture as the result of domestic assault. In the fifth case (UMNH 92), the model could not assess the aetiology because the depression fractures occurred in the posterior parietal. In this region of the head, the DFA could not distinguish trauma caused by domestic assault from trauma caused by accident.

Discussion

Material evidence

The BRI soft-tissue findings were consistent with those reported in previous clinical studies (*e.g.* Zachariades *et al.* 1990; Hussain *et al.* 1994, Gutmann and Gutmann 1995; Hartzell *et al.* 1996; Muellemann *et al.* 1996; Ochs *et al.* 1996; Abbott 1997; Greene *et al.* 1997). Six variables proved to be useful in discriminating between accidents and assaults. The face, head, anterior neck, posterior neck, chest, and age of the victim were retained in the DFA, while the anterior and posterior upper limbs, anterior and posterior lower limbs, and the back were not useful discriminators. The face provided the most explanatory value in differentiating an assault trauma from an accidental trauma in soft tissue.

While relatively few of the BRI domestic assaults affected bone, when they did, the fractures were distributed in a distinct pattern. Skeletal trauma was focused in the face, with the highest frequency of fractures found in the nasal bones. For example, the risk of a nasal fracture in the BRI domestic assault sample is one fracture for every three blows to this facial region alone. Hard-tissue injuries to the face and chest provide the most explanatory value for domestic assault, while the lower limb and older age weight the GLM toward accidents.

When the GLM was applied to BRI subjects exhibiting hard-tissue injuries, 91% of the cases were correctly classified. Ninety-six percent of the accident victims were correctly classified by fracture pattern, as were 76% of domestic assault victims. All misclassifications of domestic assault trauma as accidental were the result of fractures in the upper limb locus – a location that should not be assessed with this model. Because the GLM formula has a large negative constant and a negative age weighting, subjects assessed for injuries that were not incorporated into the model will be classified by default as victims of accidents. When the same GLM was tested with the Salt Lake City sample, using only assault victims with fractures in the face, chest, or lower limbs, 95% of the domestic assault cases were correctly classified.

It is important to reiterate that the upper limb locus (arms, wrists, and hands) were not retained in either the soft- or hard-tissue DFA. In fact, not a single domestic assault produced a fracture that might be interpreted as the result of parrying a blow. Assault victims, however, have upper limb fractures that affected the humerus (n=1), ulnae/radii (n=3), and metacarpal/phalanges (n=4). Trauma to the ulnae and radii is located in or near the joints and these fractures are indistinguishable from those resulting from a fall. In fact, none of these fractures resulted from parrying a blow, but rather occurred when the assault victim fell or was thrown to the ground. As a result, based solely on location, these fractures cannot be differentiated from accidental falls. This is an interesting finding, since forearm "parry" trauma has been offered as evidence for assault in prehistoric skeletons (Elliot-Smith and Wood-Jones 1910; Wells 1964; Angel 1974; Shermis 1982; Smith 1996). Given the results of this study (see also Kilgore *et al.* 1997; Lovell 1997; Walker 2001), the cause of forearm fractures should be inferred with great caution.

While the upper limbs remain a problematic variable, age repeatedly entered both the hard- and soft-tissue DFA. Consistent with behavioral observations of humans and other primates, the age distribution of the BRI domestic assault patients mirrored a fertility curve (Fig. 16.1). The age of these women clustered between 16 and 41 years, while the average age (36 years) and range (s.d. 13.2) of accident patients was much higher. The difference in age distribution is reflected in the GLM model, in which a negative multiplier for this variable accounts for the increasing risk of accident-related trauma in older women. For example, in the hard-tissue GLM (Table 16.8), a woman with a combined chest and lower limb fracture would be classified as an assault victim until the age of 55. After this age, the fracture combination would be attributed to an accident.

In a clinical setting, a woman's age might well be a useful variable for determining the aetiology of her wounds. In a prehistoric skeleton, however, determining the biological age at which an individual experienced traumatic injuries remains problematic. For example, the older female (UMNH 95) from Caldwell Village had a

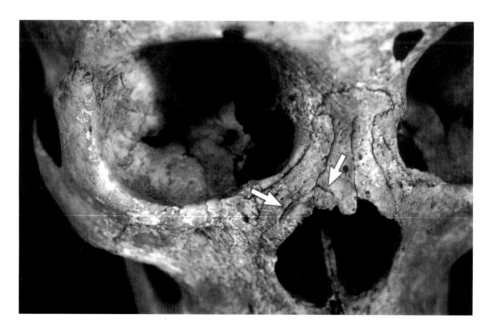

Figure 16.2. Healed fracture in right nasal and maxilla of UMNH 89.

healed depression fracture on the frontal and a second healed fracture in the left clavicle (Table 16.12). Both fractures were well-healed, indicating that these traumatic events could have occurred at any point during her 60+ years. Furthermore, applying the GLM to this female assumes that the fractures in the frontal and clavicle occurred during a single event.

Both of these problems could be overcome by assessing only perimortem (unhealed) trauma, because the age of the victim and timing of the traumatic event should correspond to each other. However, because the women in the BRI clinical setting survived their assaults and accidents, the model is valid only for assessing skeletal lesions that are healing or already healed. Cases of lethal trauma were not evaluated in this study but remain a topic for future investigation.

Inferring social context

We are left with the question of how skeletal indicators of interpersonal violence can be interpreted behaviourally (Jurmain and Bellifemine 1997). Three issues in particular complicate the application of the model developed here, especially in cases from prehistory.

(1) *Who meets the definition of an "intimate" male?* While contemporary data indicate that women are most at risk of being assaulted by an intimate male, can intimate relationships be identified in prehistory? There are no clear criteria for identifying husbands or other male partners in the past. For example, if a woman receives wounds long after being captured by raiders (Jorgensen 1980), should

this be considered "domestic" assault? Especially given that these women often enter the households of their captors, should such behavior be considered, as in the case of chimpanzees, sexual coercion to "encourage" consortships? Answers to such questions are beyond the scope of this paper, but must be considered in future research.

(2) *What if the assailant is not a male?* The BRI study was limited to cases of domestic violence in which the assailant was male. It is also worth considering the effects of female-inflicted trauma. Only a small fraction of the BRI and Salt Lake City cases of domestic assault were female-on-female. These assaults were characterised by numerous abrasions but rarely by serious injuries. This pattern is consistent with anecdotal reports in the cross-cultural literature (*e.g.* Burbank 1988; Cook 1992; Campbell 2002). In some cases, however, female assailants do cause serious injuries, especially when a weapon is used (*e.g.* Schuster 1983; Bolger 1991; Burbank 1994; Webb 1995). Future research must examine the socioecological contexts of female-female conflict (*e.g.* Lamphere 1974).

(3) *What if the trauma is not the result of assault?* A number of bioarchaeological studies have identified injury patterns that mimic the effects of interpersonal violence (*e.g.* Smith 1996; Wakely 1996). Alternative causes of craniofacial fracture include self-induced trauma during mourning rituals (Tyson 1977; Webb 1995), and accidental injuries suffered while herding large domesticates (Busch *et al.* 1986) or participating in recreational sports (Walker 1997). Other confounding variables may be introduced

Burial Number	Age	Antemortem Trauma	AFFECTED LOCI			AGE GROUP MIDPOINT	y PREDICTED	PREDICTED EVENT
			Face	Chest	A. lower limb			
UMNH 89	23–29	Fx r. nasal and maxilla	1	0	0	29.5	0.731568	assault
UMNH 91	20–24	Depression fx on frontal	1	0	0	19.5	0.815178	assault
UMNH 92	20–24	Two depression fx on l. parietal	0	0	0	19.5	*	*
UMNH 95	60+	Depression fx on frontal; fx l. clavicle	1	1	0	59.5	1.614563	assault
UMNH 193	35–39	Fx l. nasal and maxilla	1	0	0	39.5	0.647958	assault

* affected locus not in model and cannot be predicted

Table 16.12. Application of hard-tissue model to Caldwell Village skeletal remains.

by the physical environment itself. Terrain and climate may have predisposed some women to a high risk of accidental injury (*e.g.* Grauer and Roberts 1996; Kilgore *et al.* 1997; Alvrus 1999). Seasonality was considered for the contemporary BRI accident sample, but there were no statistical differences in winter and summer trauma patterns.

Conclusion

The BRI model was developed in a Western industrial context and has yet to be tested in other ethnographic settings. In particular, field studies of wound patterning in small-scale societies would probably lead to refinements or revisions of the model. At the same time, we must not idealise so-called traditional societies as a privileged site of inquiry into human behaviour. All contemporary humans, including hunter-gatherers, have been affected directly or indirectly by Western commodities, politics, and pathogens. As Sugiyama (2004, 385) notes, "no single extant or prehistoric group could provide a comprehensive snapshot of the pathogenic, foraging, social, and demographic conditions that form the parameters of our evolutionary history." Yet the corollary is that no human group, including a Western industrial society, should be considered irrelevant to an evolutionary analysis. The approach taken here aims to develop and refine evolutionary principles of human behavior by studying such behavior in as many different contexts as possible.

In extending the present research to other societies, it must be recognised that domestic violence is a specific form of conflict, quite distinct from what is usually called "political" conflict, in both its causes and its consequences. Domestic assault tends to involve a continuing, intimate, and socially sanctioned relationship between perpetrator and victim, who are usually of opposite sex. For all these reasons, it stands apart from the various forms of public violence, including war, spectacle, and "street crime." Acknowledging the distinct nature of domestic violence is the first step to understanding its historical effects on women's health, fitness, and mortality.

Acknowledgements

Because of the sensitive nature of this study, collection of the data would have been impossible without the support of Drs. Keith Manchester, Michael Smith, and Tony Shenton of the Bradford Royal Infirmary, and, at the Salt Lake City Police Department, Sgt. Dana Orgill and George Throckmorton. Todd Grey, John McCullough, Dennis O'Rourke, Douglas Owsley, and Lars Rodseth provided valuable comments, critiques, and encouragement, and Terry Allen's statistical expertise is evident throughout this study. The research was funded by the Department of Archaeological Sciences at the University of Bradford and a Marriner Eccles graduate fellowship at the University of Utah. This study was reviewed and approved by the General University Institution Review Board for human subject study at the University of Utah (G020196-01), subsequent to approval by the review boards of the Salt Lake City Police Department and the Bradford Royal Infirmary. And finally, a special thanks to Rebecca Gowland and Christopher Knüsel for the invitation to participate in this edited volume. Theirs and the anonymous reviewer's comments were especially insightful.

References

Abbott, J. (1997) Injuries and illness of domestic violence. *Annals of Emergency Medicine* 29, 781–785.

Abraham, M. (2000) *Speaking the Unspeakable: Marital Violence Among South Asian Immigrants in the United States.* New Brunswick, Rutgers University Press.

Alvrus, A. (1996) *Fracture Patterns among the Nubians of Semna South, Sudan.* Unpublished Master's thesis. Department of Anthropology, Arizona State University, Tucson.

Alvrus, A. (1999) Fracture patterns among the Nubian of Semna South, Sudanese Nubia. *International Journal of Osteoarchaeology* 9, 417–429.

Ambler, J. R. (1966) Caldwell Village. *University of Utah Anthropological Papers* No. 84. Salt Lake City.

Angel, J. L. (1974) Patterns of fracture from Neolithic to modern times. *Anthropologiai Közlemények* 18, 9–18.

Asling-Monemi, K., Rodolfo, P., Ellsberg, M. C. and others (2003) Violence against women increases the risk of infant and child mortality: A case-referent study in Nicaragua. *Bulletin of the World Health Organization* 81, 10–16.

Bachman, R. and Carmody, D. C. (1994) Fighting fire with fire: The effects of victim resistance in intimate versus stranger perpetrated assaults against females. *Journal of Family Violence* 9, 317–331.

Bolger, A. (1991) *Aboriginal Women and Violence.* Darwin, Australian National University, North Australia Research Unit.

Burbank, V. K. (1988) Female aggression in cross-cultural perspective. *Behavioral Science Research* 21, 70–100.

Burbank, V. K. (1994) *Fighting Women.* Berkley, University of California Press.

Busch, H., Jr., Cogbill, T., Landercasper, J. and Landercasper, B. (1986) Blunt bovine and equine trauma. *Journal of Trauma* 26, 559–560.

Buss, D. M. and Malamuth, N. M. (eds.) (1996) *Sex, Power, Conflict: Evolutionary and Feminist Perspectives.* New York, Oxford University Press.

Campbell, J. C. (2002) Health consequences of intimate partner violence. *Lancet* 359, 1331–1336.

City of Bradford (1996) Population forecast for Bradford District. CBMDC Corporate Services, City Hall Research Section. Bradford.

Coltrain, J. B. (1993) Fremont corn agriculture: A pilot stable carbon isotope study. *Utah Archaeology* 1993, 49–56.

Coltrain, J. B. and Leavitt, S. W. (2002) Climate and diet in Fremont prehistory: Economic variability and abandonment of maize agriculture in the Great Salt Lake Basin. *American Antiquity* 67, 453–485.

Cook, H. B. K. (1992) Matrifocality and female aggression in Margariteno society. In K. Bjorkqvist and P. Niemela (eds.) *Of Mice and Women: Aspects of Female Aggression*, 149–162. San Diego, Academic Press.

Counts, D.A., Brown, J. K. and Campbell, J. C. (eds.) (1999) *To Have and to Hit: Cultural Perspectives on Wife Beating*. Chicago, University of Illinois Press.

Crowell, N. A. and Burgess, A. W. (eds.) (1996) *Understanding Violence Against Women*. Washington DC, National Academy Press.

Daly, M. and Wilson, M. (1994) Evolutionary psychology of male violence. In J. Archer (ed.) *Male Violence*, 253–288. London, Routledge.

Daly, M., Wilson, M. and Weghorst, S. (1982) Male sexual jealousy. *Ethology and Sociobiology* 3, 11–27.

DeMoss, B. C. and DeMoss, C. J. (1994) Dental detection of domestic violence victims. *Texas Dental Journal* March, 25–26.

Elliott-Smith, G. and Wood-Jones, F. (1910) Fractured bones and dislocations. In *The Archaeological Survey of Nubia Report for 1907–1908*, Volume II, Report on the Human Remains. Cairo, National Printing Department.

Feldhaus, K. M., Houry, D., Utz, A. and Dewitt, C. (2003) Physicians' knowledge of and attitudes toward a domestic violence mandatory reporting law. *Annals of Emergency Medicine* 41, 159.

Gilthorpe, M. S., Wilson, R. C., Miles D. R. and Bedi, R. (1999) Variations in admissions to hospital for head injury and assault to the head. Part 1: age and gender. *British Journal of Oral and Maxillofacial Surgery* 37, 294–300.

Grauer, A. L. and Roberts, C. A. (1996) Paleoepidemiology, healing, and possible treatment of trauma in Medieval cemetery population of St. Helen-on-the-Walls, York, England. *American Journal of Physical Anthropology* 100, 531–544.

Greene, D., Raven, R., Carvalho, G. and Maas, C. S. (1997) Epidemiology of facial injury in blunt assault: Determinants of incidence and outcome in 802 patients. *Arch Otolaryngol Head Neck Surgery* 123, 923–928.

Gutmann, J. L. and Gutmann, M. S. E. (1995) Cause, incidence, and prevention of trauma to teeth. *Dental Clinics of North America* 39, 1–13.

Handwerker, W. P. (1998) Why violence? A test of hypotheses representing three discourses on the roots of domestic violence. *Human Organization* 57, 200–208.

Hartzell, K. N., Botek, A. A. and Goldberg, S. H. (1996) Orbital fractures in women due to sexual assault and domestic violence. *Ophthalmology* 103, 953–957.

Heise, L. L. (1994) Violence against women: The hidden health burden. *World Bank Discussion Papers*, No. 255. Washington DC, The World Bank.

Heise, L. L. (1995) Violence, sexuality, and women's lives. In R. G. Parker and J. H. Gagnon (eds.) *Conceiving Sexuality*, 109–134. New York, Routledge.

Houry, D., Sachs, C. J., Feldhaus, K. M. and Linden, J. (2002) Violence-inflicted injuries: Reporting laws in the fifty states. *Annals of Emergency Medicine* 39, 56–60.

Huang, V., Moore, C., Bohrer, P. and Thaller, S. R. (1998) Maxillofacial injuries in women. *Annals of Plastic Surgery* 41, 482–484.

Hussain, K., Wijetunge, D. B., Grubnic, S. and Jackson, I. T. (1994) A comprehensive analysis of craniofacial trauma. *Journal of Trauma* 36, 34–47.

Jorgensen, J. (1980) *Western Indians*. San Francisco, Freeman.

Jurmain, R. and Bellifemine, V. I. (1997) Patterns of cranial trauma in a prehistoric population from central California. *International Journal of Osteoarchaeology* 7, 43–50.

Jurmain, R. and Kilgore, L. (1998) Sex-related patterns of trauma in humans and African apes. In A. L. Grauer and P. Stuart-Macadam (eds.) *Sex and Gender in Paleopathological Perspective*, 11–26. Cambridge, Cambridge University Press.

Kilgore, L., Jurmain, R. and Van Gerven, D. (1997) Palaeoepidemiological patterns of trauma in a medieval Nubian skeletal population. *International Journal of Osteoarchaeology* 7, 103–114.

Kjaerulff, H., Jacobsen, J., Aalund, O., Albrektsen, S. B., Breiting, V. B., Danielsen, L., Helweg-Larsen, K., Staugaard, H. and Thomsen, J. L. (1989) Injuries due to deliberate violence in areas of Denmark. III. Lesions. *Forensic Science International* 41, 169–180.

Lambert, P. M. (1997) Patterns of violence in prehistoric hunter-gatherer societies of coastal southern California. In D. L. Martin and D. W. Frayer (eds.) *Troubled Times: Violence and Warfare in the Past*, 77–109. Toronto, Gordon and Breach.

Lamphere, L. (1974) Strategies, cooperation, and conflict among women in domestic groups. In M. Z. Rosaldo and L. Lamphere (eds.) *Woman, Culture, and Society*, 97–112. Stanford, Stanford University Press.

Levinson, D. (1989) *Family Violence in Cross-Cultural Perspective*. Newbury Park, CA, Sage Publications.

Lovell, N. C. (1990) *Patterns of Injury and Illness in Great Apes*. Washington DC, Smithsonian Institution Press.

Lovell, N. C. (1997) Trauma analysis in paleopathology. *Yearbook of Physical Anthropology* 40, 139–170.

Madsen, D. B. and Simms, S. R. (1998) The Fremont complex: A behavioral perspective. *Journal of World Prehistory* 12, 255–336.

Manly, B. F. J. (1994) *Multivariate Statistical Methods*. London, Chapman and Hall.

Martin, D. L. (1997) Violence against women in the La Plata River valley (AD 100–1300). In D. L. Martin and D. W. Frayer (eds.) *Violent Times: Violence and Warfare in the Past*, 45–75. Toronto, Gordon and Breach.

McDowell, J. D., Kassebaum, D. K. and Stromboe, S. E. (1992) Recognizing and reporting victims of domestic violence. *Journal of the American Dental Association* 123, 44–50.

McClusky, L. J. (2001) *"Here, Our Culture is Hard": Stories of Domestic Violence from a Mayan Community in Belize*. Austin, University of Texas Press.

Melnick, D. M., Maio, R. F., Blow, F. C., Hill, E. M., Want, S. C., Pomerantz, R., Kane, M. L., Graham-Bermann, S., Weber, J. and Farber, M. (2002) Prevalence of domestic violence and associated factors among women on a trauma service. *Journal of Trauma* 53, 33–37.

Mesnick, S. L. (1997) Sexual alliances: evidence and evolutionary implications. In P. A. Gowaty (ed.) *Feminism and Evolutionary Biology: Boundaries, Intersections, and Frontiers*, 207–260. New York, Chapman and Hall.

Milner, G. R., Anderson, E. and Smith, V. G. (1991) Warfare in late prehistoric west-central Illinois. *American Antiquity* 56, 581–603.

Muellemann, R. L., Lenaghan, P. A. and Pakieser, R. A. (1996) Battered women: injury locations and types. *Annals of Emergency Medicine* 28, 486–492.

Nawrocki, S. P. (1998) Regression formulae for estimating age at death from cranial suture closure. In K. J. Reichs (ed.) *Forensic Osteology: Advances in the Identification of Human Remains*, 276–292. Springfield, Charles C. Thomas.

Novak, S. A. (1999) Skeletal manifestations of domestic assault: a predictive model for investigating gender violence in prehistory. Unpublished Ph.D. dissertation, Department of Anthropology, University of Utah, Salt Lake City.

Ochs, H. A., Neuenschwander, M. C. and Dodson, T. B. (1996) Are head, neck and facial injuries markers of domestic violence? *Journal of the American Dental Association* 127, 757–761.

Owsley, D. W. and Jantz, R. L. (eds.) (1994) *Skeletal Biology in the Great Plains: Migration, Warfare, Health, and Subsistence.* Washington DC, Smithsonian Institution Press.

Perciaccante, V. J., Ochs, H. A. and Dodson, T. B. (1999) Head, neck, and facial injuries as markers of domestic violence in women. *Journal of Oral and Maxillofacial Surgery* 57, 760–762.

Ridley, M. (2003) *Nature via Nurture: Genes, Experience, and What Makes Us Human.* New York, HarperCollins.

Rodseth, L. and Novak, S. A. (2000) The social modes of men: Toward an ecological model of human male relationships. *Human Nature* 11, 335–366.

Romanucci-Ross, L. (1973) *Conflict, Violence, and Morality in a Mexican Village.* Palo Alto, National Press Books.

SAS, Inc. (1989) *STAT User's Guide*, version 6, 4th ed. Cary NC, SAS Institute, Inc.

Schuster, I. (1983) Women's aggression: An African case study. *Aggressive Behavior* 9, 319–331.

Shepherd, J. P., Shapland, M., Pearce, N. X. and Scully, C. (1990) Pattern, severity, and aetiology of injuries in victims of assault. *Journal of the Royal Society of Medicine* 83, 161–162.

Shermis, S. (1982) Domestic violence in two skeletal populations. *Ossa* 9–11:143–151.

Simms, S. (1986) New evidence of Fremont adaptive diversity. *Journal of California and Great Basin Archaeology* 8, 204–216.

Smith, M. O. (1996) "Parry" fractures and female-directed interpersonal violence: implications from the late archaic period of west Tennessee. *International Journal of Osteoarchaeology* 6, 84–91.

Smuts, B. B. (1985) Sisterhood is powerful: aggression, competition and cooperation in nonhuman primate societies. In M. Haug, D. Benton, B. F. Brain and B. J. Olivier (eds.). *The Aggressive Female*, 115–135. Weesp, Duphar Publications.

Smuts, B. B. (1992) Male aggression against women: An evolutionary perspective. *Human Nature* 3, 1–44.

Smuts, B. B. and Smuts, R. W. (1993) Male aggression and sexual coercion of females in nonhuman primates and other animals: Evidence and theoretical implications. *Advances in the Study of Behavior* 22, 1–63.

Spedding, R. L., McWilliams, M., McNichol, B. P. and Dearden, C. H. (1999) Markers for domestic violence in women. *Journal of Accidental and Emergency Medicine* 16, 400–402.

Ström, C. (1992) Injuries due to violent crimes. *Medicine Science Law* 32, 123–132.

Suchey, J. M. and Katz, D. (1998) Applications of pubic age determination in a forensic setting. In K. Reichs (ed.) *Forensic Osteology: Advances in the Identification of Human Remains*, 204–236. Springfield, Charles C Thomas.

Sugiyama, S. (2004) Illness, injury, and disability among Shiwiar forager-horticulturalists: Implications of health-risk buffering for the evolution of human life history. *American Journal of Physical Anthropology* 123, 371–389.

Tyson, R. A. (1977) Historical accounts as aids to physical anthropology: Examples of head injury in Baja California. *Pacific Coast Archaeological Society Quarterly* 132, 52–58.

Wakely, J. (1996) Limits to interpretation of skeletal trauma: Two case studies from Medieval Abingdon, England. *International Journal of Osteoarchaeology* 6, 76–83.

Walker, P. L. (1989) Cranial injuries as evidence of violence in prehistoric southern California. *American Journal of Physical Anthropology* 80, 313–323.

Walker, P. L. (1997) Wife beating, boxing, and broken noses: skeletal evidence for the cultural patterning of violence. In D. Martin and D. W. Frayer (eds.) *Violent Times: Violence and Warfare in the Past*, 145–179. Toronto, Gordon and Breach.

Walker, P. L. (2001) A bioarchaeological perspective on the history of violence. *Annual Review of Anthropology* 30, 573–596.

Webb, S. (1995) *Palaeopathology of Aboriginal Australians.* Cambridge, Cambridge University Press.

Wells, C. (1964) *Bones, Bodies and Disease.* New York, Praeger Publishing.

West-Eberhard, M. J. (2003) *Developmental Plasticity and Evolution.* New York, Oxford University Press.

Wilkenson R. G. (1997) Violence against women: Raiding and abduction in prehistoric Michigan. In D. Martin and D. W. Frayer (eds.) *Violent times: Violence and Warfare in the Past*, 21–43. Toronto, Gordon and Breach.

Wilkenson R. G. and Van Wagenen, K. M. (1993) Violence against women: prehistoric skeletal evidence from Michigan. *Midcontinental Journal of Archaeology* 18, 190–216.

Willey, P. (1990) *Prehistoric Warfare on the Great Plains: Skeletal Analysis of the Crow Creek Massacre Victims.* New York, Garland Publishing.

Wilson, M. and Daly, M. (1998) Lethal and nonlethal violence against wives and the evolutionary psychology of male sexual proprietariness. In R. E. Dobash and R. P. Dobash (eds.) *Rethinking Violence Against Women*, 199–230. Newbury Park, CA, Sage Publications.

Wrangham, R. W. (1979) On the evolution of ape social systems. *Social Science Information* 18, 335–368.

Wrangham, R. W. (1980) An ecological model of female-bonded primate groups. *Behaviour* 75, 262–300.

Wrangham, R. W. (2000) Why are male chimpanzees more gregarious than mothers? A scramble competition hypothesis. In P. Kappeler (ed.) *Primate Males: Causes and Consequences of Variation in Group Composition*, 248–258. Cambridge, Cambridge University Press.

Wrangham, R. W. and Peterson, D. (1996) *Demonic Males.* New York, Houghton Mifflin Company.

Zachariades, N., Koumoura, F. and Konsolaki-Agouridaki, E. (1990) Facial trauma in women resulting from violence by men. *Journal of Oral and Maxillofacial Surgery* 48, 1250–1253.

17.   Fragmentation of the Body: Comestibles, Compost, or Customary Rite?

Christopher J. Knüsel and Alan K. Outram

Introduction

One of the most inimical ways to debase a people is to declare them cannibals – eaters of their own kind. The association between cannibalism and immorality, depravity, and base iniquity has contributed to the long-term interest in the behaviour. It has become a common-place pejorative applied to exotic peoples, enemies, and strangers – sometimes and, more innocuously perhaps, to titillate fascination and, more sinisterly and more often, to dehumanise another group. Tuzin (1983, 62) characterises the Ilahita Arapesh's (of northeastern New Guinea) attitude towards the cannibalism of the down-stream Sepik, "… as an amused, faintly condescending interest that is morally neutral in tone…' and that those who engage in such consumption are described as an 'another kind of man'. The apparent relativism of this statement, although lacking in obvious contempt or fear, provides the basis upon which difference could be accentuated to justify actions at another time or under different circumstances. The use of the term 'cannibalism' among both Europeans and non-Europeans (see Strathern 1982, Rumsey 1999) to make a people less than human – with real social and political consequences for those so-labelled – prompted Arens (1979) to deny that the behaviour had ever been practised. Others have argued that it did occur upon occasion in a number of circumstances and for a variety of reasons. About the same time that Arens was writing, for example, Marvin Harris (1977, 126) remarked that:

> As recently as fifty or a hundred years ago, small-scale sacrifice of prisoners of war and the redistribution of their flesh were common practices in hundreds of pre-state societies scattered across Africa south of the Sahara, South-East Asia, Malaysia, Indonesia, and Oceania. I have reason to believe, however, that eating human flesh was never an important aspect of the redistributive feasts in the culture which immediately preceded the rise of states in Mesopotamia, Egypt, India, China, or Europe.

In this passage, Harris not only supports the wides-pread occurrence of cannibalism, he also provides a social context for the behaviour.

Since literary accounts of purported cannibalism appear to defy even the most probing textual and inter-textual analyses, an obvious complement to this literature is the study of the physical evidence for the behaviour as recovered from archaeological remains. Since archaeo-logical studies also produce texts, they are not immune from the same literary polemic of other written accounts, however. Many of the early accounts based on archaeological remains interpreted bone breakage as resulting from cannibalism before the full range of archaeological signatures of the behaviour could be distinguished from others. Early on, an apparent absence or rarity of formal burials and scattered and broken human bones found on sites was enough to suggest that corpses had either been exposed or cannibalised (Clark 1962, Ucko 1969).

In an otherwise very descriptive and matter-of-fact account of the strata and features excavated at the Charlbury Camp hillfort in Dorset, England, when Whitley (1943, 103) addresses herself to the human remains encountered, she writes:

> The floor [of what was interpreted to be the remnants of a wooden hut] was made up of a layer of fine trampled mud, but over everything a mass of human and animal bones, pottery, and charcoal lay scattered about in great confusion… They [the human remains] were not in articulation, so could not have been *in situ*, but may be the remains of early defenders of the rampart subsequently disturbed by the builders of the hut; human bones were actually found in the packing of one of the post-holes, so they must have been lying about when the hut was built. Cannibalism is another possible explanation; in any case, the phenomenon provides a striking instance of the casual treatment of human remains after death…

From the frequent occurrence of such assessments, it seems many of them were simply suppositions that were in vogue at a particular time to throw into stark contrast the lives of ancestors and peoples who were at a far remove in both space and time and thus, by implication, culturally and socially very different from ourselves. Alternatively, they could be interpreted as untested hypotheses. In support of the former interpretation, it seems that exposure and excarnation have superseded cannibalism to explain the occurrence of scattered human bones on sites (see, for example, Cunliffe 1992, Hill 1995, Carr and Knüsel 1997). These shifting interpretations have less to do with the appearance and patterning of the remains, but seem to draw their inspiration more from general perceptions of past societies and a desire to make sense of apparently unburied and thus 'non-normative' depositions of human remains – in many instances from sites where the context is no longer clear.

Several of these early assessments of supposed cannibalism have been more recently denied. Early on, cannibalism was invoked to explain the occurrence of fragmented crania of the Zhoukoudian *Homo erectus* specimens. The occurrence of neurocrania with broken off viscero-cranial elements, found in conjunction with burnt remains, longitudinally fractured hominid long bones, and consistently broken mandibulae were offered as defining characteristics to support such an interpretation. It is now clear that the evidence for fire at Zhoukoudian, one of the often-stated co-requisites for cannibalism, has recently been demonstrated to be the result of fluviale processes (Goldberg *et al.* 2001). The fragile nature of the viscero-cranial skeleton and the absence of *bona fide* cutmarks on these remains seem to deny an association with cannibalism and, instead, suggest a taphonomic process and carnivore feeding as responsible for their fragmented state (Binford and Ho 1985, Binford and Stone 1986).

Similarly, in a more recent 7th century AD setting, Brothwell (1971) argued that an individual known as Q1, recovered from the Neolithic long mound at Maiden Castle in Dorset, England (Wheeler 1943, plate XLII), had sustained multiple injuries from an edged metal weapon and that circular traumatic cranial lesions had resulted from a mutilating attack. Brothwell (*ibid.*) surmised that they were unlikely to have been the result of an attempt to remove the brain, as had previously been suggested. This assessment relied as much on the presumed context and antiquity of such occurrences as they did on evidence that could be uniquely associated with the consumption of human flesh and the systematic refutation of alternatives (see Brothwell 1961 for similar sentiments).

Although refutation of such pronouncements has also occasioned the re-analysis of some early-excavated assemblages (see, for example, White and Toth 1991), some early investigators were aware of the importance of what, today, are considered archaeological indicators of cannibalism. In the 1870s, after examining human remains from shell middens in the southern U.S. state of Florida, Jefferies Wyman, Curator of the Peabody Museum, Harvard University, suggested cannibalism as being

responsible for disarticulated human remains found in unusual burial circumstances that had been broken in a manner similar to that identified in animal remains found in the same sites. Using ethnographic and ethnohistoric accounts, he also suggested that signs of dismemberment present in human remains, similar to those employed by more recent Amerindians in animal carcass butchery, were also an identifiable feature of cannibalism (cited in Buikstra, forthcoming, White 1992, 10). What is compelling about these earlier treatments is not only the easy alacrity with which cannibalism was interpreted in many of them, but the wide variation in the archaeological signatures used in supporting arguments. Although the former is less obviously the case in more recent years, the variation in the latter has been retained to the present day. This contribution addresses the nature of the physical evidence for cannibalism, examines the protocols to support its study, and considers a social context for the behaviour.

Archaeological arguments and equifinality

In the last few years, cannibalistic behaviour has once again been posited to have existed among the Neanderthals of the Middle (Fernàndez-Jalvo *et al.* 1999, Defleur *et al.* 1999) and Upper Palaeolithic (Andrews and Fernández-Jalvo 2003), in the Neolithic of France (Villa and Mathieu 1991), and among the Anasazi of the American Southwest (White 1992, Turner and Turner 1995, 1999), as well as to have been present among pre and protohistoric Fijians, where the behaviour is recorded by early European visitors to the area (DeGusta 1999). Given the wide geographic and temporal span covered, it would seem that a practice once considered nothing more than a means of dehumanising indigenous populations during colonial expansion (see Arens 1979) was widespread long before European colonisers took to the seas. Moreover, cannibalism appears to have an established legacy within Europe itself that stretches back to Middle Palaeolithic populations, some of which have been posited to represent pre-*sapiens* species on phylogenetic grounds.

There are other explanations for fragmented assemblages (see also Hurlbut 2000). These include the disturbance of primary burials (compost), customary mortuary rites involving defleshing of the dead and/or secondary burial, and peri-mortem torture and mutilation of individuals or of the corpse. Some instances of cannibalistic behaviour have been questioned and denied on the grounds of physical examination of the remains (DeGusta 2000) and on suspected misinterpretation of the ethnographic record (Murphy and Mallory 2000). Trinkaus (1985) examined the Archaic *Homo sapiens* (Neandertal) Krapina material and argued that the incised marks on these remains were the result of defleshing (*cf.* Russell 1987a and b) as part of a mortuary rite, an interpretation also levelled to explain similar occurrences on the Archaic *Homo sapiens* Bodo cranium (White 1986) and, most recently, on the Stw 53 cranium, a late

Australopithecine or early member of the genus *Homo* specimen from Sterkfontein, South Africa (Pickering *et al.* 2000).

A number of researchers have argued that cutmarks located in the vicinity of joints represent evidence of immediate post-mortem dismemberment. Ethnographic accounts of this behaviour abound (see Huntingdon and Metcalf 1991, 85, for a discussion of cleaning bones among the Berawan of northern Borneo). In Europe, medieval people retrieved the bones of saints for inclusion in reliquaries or for separate interment elsewhere (Mafart *et al.* 2004). The bodies of saints were not only defleshed and dismembered in these instances, but they were also often boiled to aid this process (Brown 1981). Dismemberment of the dead may also be practiced as a form of denigration of a defeated foe; Liston and Baker (1996), Olsen and Shipman (1994), and Scott *et al.* (2002) provide examples. Verano (1986, 2001) presents an excellent example of dismemberment related to trophy collection at the Moche Period site at Pacatnamu, Peru, *c.* 1100 AD, where the left radius was removed from three ritually murdered individuals buried in a haphazard fashion. A similar intent may be responsible for the 75 weapon-injured, decapitated males from the pre-Roman Iron Age site at Ribemont-sur-Ancre, département de la Somme, France (Brunaux 1998, Duday 1998). Injuries in these instances are indicative of peri-mortem trauma (breakages of bone that occur around the time of death) from stone (Walker and Long 1977, Shipman and Rose 1983, Wahl and König 1987, Frayer 1997) and metal (see Berryman and Symes 1998, Novak 2000, Boylston *et al.* 2000, Boylston 2000, Knüsel 2005) weapons (Fig. 17.1). If these individuals had survived – even for a week or two's duration – there would be signs of healing in the form of woven, porous bone around the site of injury, some of which may be visible only through microscopic analysis

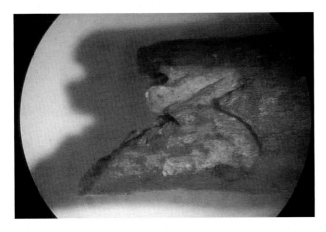

Figure 17.1. Close-up of peri-mortem trauma in the right ulna of Towton 30 from the late medieval Battle of Towton (AD 1461). This fracture possesses spalling (chips removed from the cortical bone surface) associated with a parry fracture (Photograph: A. R. Ogden and the first author).

(Barber 1929, 1930). These are then instances of peri-mortem trauma that do not appear to involve consumption of human flesh. Fragmentation and dismemberment of human corpses due to weapon or tool trauma, however, might be expected to accompany cases of denigration of the deceased, of which cannibalism may also play a part.

Cannibalism as metaphor

Cannibalism may be invoked in a metaphorical sense and whether or not these references refer to the actual practice in the past remains a question in many parts of the world (see Pickering (1999) for a discussion of Australian Aboriginal metaphors involving 'cooked flesh' and Sahlins (1985) on 'cooked men' in Fijian society). In Papua New Guinea, there is a popular tradition of cannibals having lived in a distant time, and common speech draws on the presumed existence of such individuals (see Goldman 1999). Strathern (1982) discusses the use of terms such as 'to eat' to describe marriage, sexual intercourse, and exchange among the Melpa of the Western Highlands of New Guinea. In the context of a reprisal killing in the same area, the Big Man, Ongka (cited in Strathern 1979, 76), reports the following event:

> They [the men involved] prepared various stuffs which were tough and prickly as adjuncts to their ritual… These things they scraped on to the pig's blood, cut the livers into small pieces over this, and made long sausages. The other meat they seasoned thoroughly too and prepared to dance out with fine decorations the next day. They added shreds of parsley and suet to the spices they had made. Finally, they took out the special red ochre powder and rubbed it all over the livers. A big-man got up, made small piles of all of this for each person and distributed them to each man of the group. Then each man said he was eating a particular part of the man they had killed- his head, tongue, liver, kidneys, leg, stomach, lower intestine, penis, testicles. They name each part of his body, including the bones, down to the last bit. Of course, they were actually only eating the pigs' livers.

Sahlins (1985, 112–113) remarks on the same theme in Polynesia. He writes, "…Polynesian social life is a universal project of *cannibalisme généralisé,* or even of endo-cannibalism, since the people are genealogically related to their own 'natural' means of subsistence." In these societies major staple foods, like taro or the sweet potato, are related to all else, including people, through common descent. Thus by cooking these tubers in an oven, people are in essence removing what is considered divine in them, and by consuming them, cannibalise a human relation. Similarly, the *kava* root that provides an infusion that is consumed in the installation ceremony of Fijian rulers is understood to be the 'child of the land' that is ritually killed by spear thrusts (*i.e.* harvested), prepared and served by young warriors to the ruler (Sahlins 1985, 95ff). As Sahlins (1983, 88) notes: "The problem, of course, is that cannibalism is always 'symbolic', even when it is 'real'."

Cannibalism is thus bound up with notions of ritual, magic, warfare and ceremony, as well as the practices subsumed within these (Tuzin and Brown 1983). These close links, though, do not necessarily mean that all instances relate to mythic practices, but they may provide a context and cosmology for the act for those who engage in it.

Archaeological indicators of cannibalism

Suitably rigorous methods for the study of complex and unusual peri-mortem treatment of human remains, at sites where cannibalism is a possible interpretation, have only surfaced – gradually and in an accretional manner – within the last ten to fifteen years. The field has developed to a large extent in response to the discovery of human remains in unusual (*i.e.* non-normative) circumstances among Anasazi sites in the American Southwest (*e.g.* White 1992; Turner 1993; Turner and Turner 1992, 1993, 1995, 1999). Individuals at these sites number between one and thirty plus, and they are found scattered within domestic settings, such as on the floors of rooms within pueblo complexes or semi-subterranean pithouses. These are considered unusual because they occur as multiple burials in the same stratum, lack grave good inclusions, and possess no standard body position or spatial location, a pattern that is different from the contemporary burial norm in the region – what the Turners refer to as 'considerate burial' (Turner and Turner 1999, 39ff.). In their 1999 volume, *Mancorn: Cannibalism and Violence in the Prehistoric American Southwest*, the Turners provide a synthesis and gazetteer of the Anasazi sites that contain these non-normative burials. They support the interpretation of cannibalism in some, while denying it in others based on the presence or absence of a series of assemblage characteristics, including most fundamentally and most commonly, the presence of intentional, peri-mortem bone breakage, in addition to cutmarks, evidence

for burning, anvil or hammerstone abrasions (Fig. 17.2), and the absence or crushing of vertebrae to facilitate the recovery of fat from these highly cancellous-filled elements. They also address the context for the behaviour using analogies drawn from sites in contemporary pre-historic Mexico, where institutionalised cannibalism was practised, and from ethnographic accounts of animal butchery.

The Turners' longer-term research efforts have been supplemented by White's (1992) book, *Prehistoric Cannibalism at Mancos 5MTUR-2346*, which is based on a detailed analysis of a single site assemblage from Mancos Wash in southwestern Colorado, USA. Since the over-arching theme of these studies is that people, like animals, are used for food, White (1992, 100) stressed the need to integrate the physical anthropologist's detailed knowledge of human anatomy with the zooarchaeologist's under-standing of human-induced taphonomic factors. He (1992, 108) outlined the important data categories that support this type of study: preservation, fracture, tool-marks, percussion, gnawing, burning and fragment dimensions. Like the Turners, White has also developed criteria by which to identify cannibalism in the archaeo-logical record. Because these authors worked in parallel, the names of these features are similar but not identical, although all are complementary and none are contra-dictory.

White (1992, 425) identifies two main groupings of features: those related to processing of human remains and another set that relates to the extent of animal access to the remains after processing. The first of these is heavily reliant on the mechanical properties of fresh bone to characterise the nature and timing (*i.e.* peri-mortem or post-mortem) of bone fragmentation. These include peri-mortem fractures (fractures produced around the time of death), including cranial remains exhibiting internal vault release (bevelling of the endocranial surface of the cranium) (see Fig. 17.3), inner conchoidal scars (in the

Figure 17.2. A sheep metapodial (an endo-cortical view of which appears in Fig. 17.4) bearing an impact scar (towards the left and bottom of the bone) and anvil abrasions (Photograph: the authors).

medullary canal of long bones from being broken with a hammerstone) (see Fig. 17.4), crushing, percussion pits (again from hammerstones) (Fig. 17.2), adhering flakes (from impacts with tools), peeling ('twig' peel or longitudinal spalls or bone splinters from impacts) (Fig. 17.1), cutmarks, chopmarks, polishing (or 'pot polish') of fractured ends of bones, intentional scraping (as in drawing a blade over bone), percussion striae (multiple curvilinear depressions from the use of a stone anvil) (Fig. 17.1), and burning. The most important feature added by White (1992) is the impact or conchoidal scars that are formed as part of the marrow extraction processing of bones and could thus be included with anvil abrasion marks, which are also called striae and consist of multiple

Figure 17.3. The bevel formed by internal vault release in a cranium from an unstratified individual 1 from the battle of Towton (Photograph: Eric Houlder)

parallel scratches (see Turner and Turner 1995, Fig. 4). In a more recent study, Fernández-Jalvo *et al.* (1999) separate percussion marks from chopmarks – the former relate to marks left on a defleshed bone impacted to obtain access to the medullary canal, while the latter is a mark related to the process of dismemberment.

Pot polish, a novel feature identified by White (1992, 120–128) and synonymous with the Turners' end-polishing, has since been incorporated in the trait list by Turner and Turner (1999, 20–21 and Figs. 2.7 and 2.8). White (1992, 347, Fig.13.3) also noted human tooth puncture marks on human hand remains. These are considered as complementary but not defining features of cannibalised remains. Pot polish results from using a bone fragment to scrape fat deposits from the inside of ceramic vessels. This is a feature found in some, but not all, site assemblages in the American Southwest (see Turner and Turner 1999, Billman *et al.* 2000). White (1992, 124) performed an experimental study using cervid remains and ceramic vessels, but he noted that the extent of the polishing seen was not observed in the archaeological material. Moreover, Kantner (1999, 84) draws attention to the lack of experiments under which such polish might be produced under other circumstances, including post-depositional ones. Curiously, human tooth punctures have not played a substantial role, even given their apparently obvious importance (see below). White (1992) also highlighted the importance of distinguishing features related to animal activity from those associated with human processing, such as the multiple grooves produced by rodent incisors when they gnaw bones and the pits in the cortical surface and underlying cancellous bone produced by the teeth of carnivores ('carnivore damage').

Figure 17.4. An inner conchoidal scar in the medullary canal of sheep metapodial (the same element as that in Fig. 7.2). This is similar to the bevel seen in cranial trauma (Photograph: C. Palmer and the authors).

Many of these features were anticipated and identified by Villa and colleagues (1986a and b, 1988) in their earlier analysis of Fontbrégoua Cave, a habitation site dating to the Early and Middle Neolithic and located in Provence, France, where three adults, one adolescent, two children and one child of indeterminate age were found (Villa and Mahieu 1991). As in the American Southwest, the remains from Fontbrégoua differed in their placement and treatment from contemporary normative burials. These researchers compared human and non-human animal remains found at the site and established the near contemporaneity of features through a combination of conjoining exercises and non-calibrated C14 dates. They used scanning electron miscroscopy to distinguish cutmarks on human and animal remains to distinguish them from abrasions made by trampling, which are shallow and more dispersed than are those made with stone implements. In addition, these authors characterised and compared element frequency, peri-mortem bone breakage, fracture, cutmark, impact scar, and discard pattern frequencies between animal and human remains from the site. They also recorded evidence for non-human gnawing of remains in order to gauge the potential effect of non-human animal activity in the creation of the assemblage.

Although they considered evidence for both boiling and roasting of remains, they were not able to identify either type of preparation through chromatographic analysis of collagen or through amino acid analysis directed at determining if the bone had been heated to temperatures greater than 150°C. In addition to these biochemical considerations, another unique feature of these authors' research is that they provided matched comparisons between cutmarks on human skeletal elements and those found on the remains of various animal species represented at the site based on their anatomical position. In this way, they noted differing treatment of the scapula and cranial remains based on anatomical differences between humans and animals, but similarities in the treatment of all other elements between different animal species. Human patterns were not identical to any particular species, but had similarities to animals of diverse size, ranging from martens, foxes, badgers, and dogs to wolves and domesticated sheep, pigs, and cattle. The authors noted the absence in some groups of remains of certain elements, such as crania, limb extremities or portions of the axial skeleton. Compared to the vertebrae from non-human species, human vertebrae were less well-represented at the site, which the authors attribute to the selection of parts for differing uses, such as immediate consumption at the site, as opposed to transport of some parts for consumption elsewhere.

In summary, then, potential archaeological indicators of cannibalism are:

1. Human and animal remains found in the same context and in the same spatial relationships (through recording and conjoining) meaning that the discard history is similar.

2. Element representation is similar between humans and animals.

3. Patterns of bone modification are similar – cut and chop marks, percussion striae, anvil abrasions, internal vault release (bevelling), adhering flakes, inner conchoidal scars, crushing of cancellous bone, and peeling of cortical bone. The remains have these features in the same frequency and anatomical location.

4. Peri-mortem fractures are similar in both human and faunal remains. These are indicative of processing to retrieve marrow and brains for consumption.

5. Evidence for burning and/or cooking of both whole elements and of previously fractured elements. These features relate to similar preparation of human and non-human animal remains.

6. The presence of human tooth impressions.

Additional observations act as covering arguments to discount certain influences on the formation and appearance of the assemblage. These include:

7. Little evidence of carnivore or rodent gnawing. As a covering signature, the absence of such tends to exclude other animal activities in the processes observed.

8. No age or sex dependent aspect of the assemblage – both males and females, infants, children, adolescents, and adults may be included in the palaeodemographic profile (i.e. unlike battle-related sites, where males predominate). In other words, in most cases the age-at-death profile is most like a catastrophic palaeodemographic assemblage, one that includes individuals of both sexes and all ages.

9. No evidence for mortuary ritual, such as care in the placement and positioning of the deceased, grave cuts, or burial treatment, or artefact inclusions that respect the body.

Applications

Table 17.1 provides an over-view of assemblages of human remains that researchers have analysed for cannibalistic intent. They represent robust and holistic treatments of human remains in their archaeological context. The majority of these come from published journal articles, and some have been the subject of publication on more than a single occasion by different researchers (*e.g.* Cowboy Wash, Krapina).

As can be seen from the table there are not only a number of differences in the recording methods used, but also in the types of information recorded and how this information is presented in the text. Perhaps one of most obvious shortcomings of these studies is the lack of combined human and animal remains analysis that would permit direct comparisons between assemblages from the same site. This is despite the implicit understanding that

Study, Author And Date	Zone	Frag. Level	Fracture Types	Impact	Indet. Inc.	Preservation	Gnaw	Burn	Cook	Conjoin	Min No.	Trauma/ Butchery	Animal Integ.
Mancos 5MTUMR, Colorado, USA White 1992	NO	YES IND	YES COD	YES COD	YES	YES SEM	YES SEM	YES LEV COD	YES POL	YES EXT	YES	YES COD SEM	YES D*
Fontbrégoua, Provence, France Villa et al. 1986/1991	NO	YES DAT IND	YES COD	YES COD	YES	YES	YES	YES	YES ALT	YES EXT	YES	YES COD SEM	YES LD
Gran Dolina, Atapuerca, Burgos, Spain Fernándo-Jalvo et al. 1999	NO	YES DAT	?**	YES COD	NO	YES	NO	NO	NO	YES EXT	YES	YES COD SEM	YES LD
Canyon Butte, Arizona, USA Turner et al 1992	NO	YES IND	YES COD	YES COD	NO	NO	YES	YES LEV COD	NO	NO	YES	YES COD	NO
Largo-Gallina, New Mexico, USA Turner et al. 1993	NO	YES IND	YES COD	YES COD	NO	NO	YES	YES COD	NO	NO	YES	YES COD	NO
Chaco-Canyon, New Mexico, USA Turner 1993	NO	YES IND	YES COD	YES COD	NO	YES	YES	YES LEV COD	YES POL	YES LIM	YES	YES COD	NO
Krapina, Croatia Trinkaus 1985, Russell 1987a and b	NO	NO	YES COD	YES COD	NO	YES	YES SEM	NO	NO	NO	NO	YES COD PIC SEM	YES LD
Moula-Guercy, Ardéche, France Defleur et al. 1999	NO	YES IND	YES PIC	YES	NO	YES	YES	NO	NO	YES EXT	YES	YES	YES FI
Franklin Expedition, King William Island, Canadian Arctic Keenleyside et al. 1997	NO	NO	YES***	NO	NO	YES	YES	YES	NO	NO	YES	YES COD	NO
Kodiak Island, Alaska, USA Simon 1992; Simon and Steffian 1994	NO	NO	NO PIC	NO	NO	NO	YES	YES	NO	NO	YES	YES COD PIC	NO

Table 17.1. Comparison of the Methods Employed in the Identification of Cannibalism. (For key, see page 261.)

Study, Author And Date	Zone	Frag. Level	Fracture Types	Impact	Indet. Inc.	Preservation	Gnaw	Burn	Cook	Conjoin	Min No.	Trauma/Butchery	Animal Integ.
St. Lawrence Iroquoian Roebuck Site, Ontario, Canada Jamieson 1983	NO	NO	NO	NO	NO	NO	YES	YES LEV	YES	NO	YES	YES COD PIC	NO
Cowboy Wash, Colorado, USA Lambert et al. 2000a, and b, Billman et al. 2000	NO	YES IND	NO	YES	NO	NO	YES	YES LEV	YES	YES EXT	YES	YES COD	NO
Navatu, Fiji DeGusta 1999	NO	YES IND PIC	YES IND COD	YES COD	YES	YES	YES	YES P/A	YES	YES EXT	YES	YES COD	YES FI
Vunda, Fiji DeGusta 2000	NO	YES IND PIC	YES IND COD	YES COD	YES	YES	YES	YES P/A	YES	YES EXT	YES	YES COD	YES FI
Saunaktuk, Northwest Territories, Canada Melbye and Fairgrieve 1994	NO	NO	NO	NO	NO	NO	NO	NO	NO	NO	NO	YES COD PIC	NO
Grinell Site Graver et al. 2002	NO	YES IND	YES IND PIC	YES COD	NO	NO	YES	YES	YES POL ALT	YES LIM	YES	YES COD PIC	NO
Backhoe Village, Utah Novak and Kollman 2000	NO	YES IND	YES	YES IND	YES	YES	NO	YES	YES POL ALT	YES LIM	YES	YES COD PIC	NO
Ram Mesa, New Mexico Ogilvie and Hilton 2000	NO	YES IND	YES	YES IND	NO	YES	YES	YES COD	YES	YES EXT	YES	YES COD PIC	NO
Alferd (sic) Packer Case Rautman and Fenton 2005	NO	YES	YES COD	YES	NO	YES	YES	YES	YES	NO	YES	YES COD PIC	NO
Gough's Cave, Somerset, England Andrews & Fernández-Jalvo 2003	NO	YES IND PIC	YES****	YES	NO	YES	YES	YES	YES	YES	YES	YES COD PIC	YES

Table 17.1. Continued. (For key, see opposite.)

* Method would have been fully integrated if faunal material were available in the actual sample studied.
** Only identification of peeling which can be related to green bone fracture, but no systemic description of fracture types.
*** Indeterminate due to weathering.
**** Hindered by gluing of fragments.

Note: Impact includes consideration of anvil marks.

Abbreviations:
D = Discussion of animal remains but no direct comparison of data given (not given or material not available or methods differ)
C = Comparison with similar data derived from other analyses
LD = Limited direct comparison – comparison of a selection of criteria using same methods
FI = Full direct comparison – animal and human material recorded with fully integrated methodology
SEM = Scanning Electron Microscopy employed to confirm difficult interpretation of surface features
LIM = Limited Conjoining carried out
EXT = Extensive conjoining carried out
IND = Use of a index method to represent fragmentation level (e.g. a ratio or % complete figures)
DAT = Full data on degree of fragmentation based on size classification of fragments
P/A = Presence absence of particular butchery/trauma marks and burning
COD = Coded approximate position of identified butchery/trauma marks, fracture scars and burning
PIC = Pictorial record of exact position of identified butchery/trauma marks, fracture scars and burning
LEV = Level of burning recorded
POL = Microscopic analysis for "pot polish"
ALT = Signs of physical and chemical alteration from cooking

Key to Table 17.1.

in cases of cannibalism, people are treated like animals. Sometimes, the lack of a combined analysis is due to the lack of animal remains, as is the case for White's (1992) study of Mancos 5MTUMR-2346 and the Krapina assemblage. This scarcity of animal assemblages also influences the work of the Turners. In these instances, researchers attempt to draw on contemporary remains from other sites, a practice that has been questioned by Villa and Mahieu (1991) on the grounds that the excavated material may have been collected using different protocols and is thus not comparable. For example, the faunal remains recovered from Combe Grenal, used for comparison with the remains from Krapina, were limited to articulations, and the excavators did not retain fragments from long bone diaphyses. Moreover, due to the selective nature of the Krapina remains, no attempt was made to characterise relative frequencies of fragmentation, a feature that is fundamental to analysis.

The frequency and intensity of fragmentation permits comparison of the peri-mortem and taphonomic history of human and animal bone assemblages. Interpretation of these frequencies has produced the greatest controversy and difference of opinion (see Villa *et al.* 1986a and b; Villa and Mahieu 1991; White 1992; Turner 1993; Turner and Turner 1995, 1999; Billman *et al.* 2000). Turner (1995, see also Turner and Turner 1999) has suggested threshold percentages to support an interpretation of cannibalism, but these have not been maintained in any categorical way in more recent treatments,

with studies tending to rely on direct comparisons of frequencies between human and animal remains from the same or other near-contemporary site.

Archaezoologists often use the degree of fragmentation of animal remains to indicate intensity of processing that may reflect the economic and environmental context of their exploitation (see Outram 1999, 2003). DeGusta (1999) uses the same reasoning when he notes that the difference between the Navatu cannibalised remains and those from the American Southwest is largely due to the apparent less intensive marrow exploitation of the Fijian inhabitants, as represented in the frequency of percussion pits and crushing. Presumably, the same would apply to cannibalised humans where the intensity of processing could relate to the circumstances under which human flesh was consumed, but would also be affected by cultural practices that dictated the amount and portions of, and manner in which, humans could be consumed.

The studies in Table 17.1 rely on NISP (number of identifiable specimens) and MNI (minimum numbers of individuals) as a means to record human remains, while none rely on MNEs (minimum number of elements), which is a standard treatment employed more recently by faunal analysts due to the fragmentary and disarticulated nature of faunal assemblages. This method of analysis has recently been adopted by the authors in conjunction with a zonation method of recording (Dobney and Reilly 1988, Knüsel and Outram 2004). The zonation method produces an MNE that is a better reflection of representativeness than the maximum number produced by NISP and the minimum number produced by MNI.

Very few studies quantify the number of indeterminate fragments. This results in an inability to determine the intensity of fragmentation, as well how this differs between axial, mainly cancellous and thus fat-bearing bones, and those from the appendicular skeleton with their considerable cortical bone coverage and endo-cortical fat stores. Without these, absent vertebrae could be interpreted as a taphonomic signature due to lack of preservation and/or animal activity or as the result of a processing behaviour (see Outram 2001, Outram *et al.* 2005). A tally of fragment size and whether fragments come from the axial or appendicular skeleton permit inferences to be made about the apparently unrepresented skeletal elements, as well as to quantify the intensity of fragmentation and better compare human and animal remains directly (Outram 2001, Outram *et al.* 2005).

It is also important to consider the presence of dry fractures, which are rarely explicitly considered in the studies found in Table 17.1. Dry fractures occur when the amount of collagen in the bone has been reduced and the mechanics of bone fracture altered as a consequence (Fig. 17.5). Micro-cracks caused by loss of both water and collagen result in features that distinguish dry from peri-mortem fractures. Peri-mortem fractures are identified on the basis of their smooth, sharp and helical appearance in fresh bones (Knüsel 2005). Dry fracture morphology may resemble that found in fresh bones in part, but deviations from this appearance result in roughened, corrugated fracture surfaces and steps in the fracture outline. The dryer the bone, the rougher and straighter (diagonal, longitudinal, transverse, stepped or columnar, rather than spiral) the fracture outlines become. Straight diagonal breaks are most easily confused with true helical (*i.e.* peri-mortem) fractures. The presence of dry fractures would indicate the remains had been moved from a primary context in the past and have been employed as an indicator for secondary burial (see Valentin and Le Goff 1998, Outram 2002). Although Ogilvie and Hilton (2000) mention dry fractures in their treatment, there is no indication of their frequency or where they occurred in their sample. Their presence, though, in this assemblage would suggest disturbance or manipulation of the remains in the past.

The significance of dry bone fracture frequencies is revealed in Dongoske *et al.*'s (2000, 183) cautionary example relating to three disarticulated bone assemblages recovered during the construction of the La Plata Highway in New Mexico, citing an unpublished report presented at the 1993 annual meeting of the Society for American Archaeology. A detailed taphonomic analysis of these remains revealed that: "…one of the assemblages was due to carnivore damage and recent (trenching) damage, one

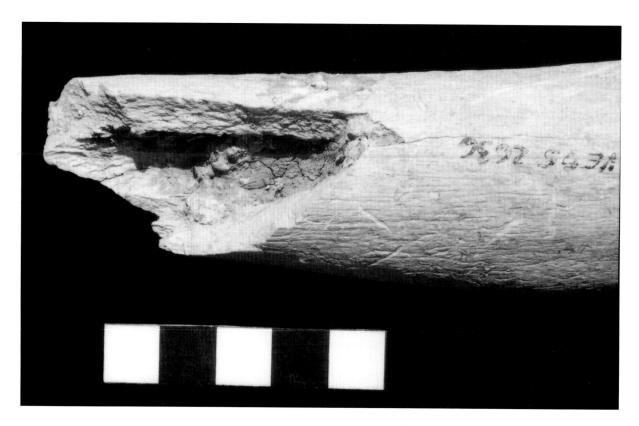

Figure 17.5. A dry fracture of a left femoral diaphysis from the Bronze Age site of Velim Skalka, Czech Republic (Photograph: C. Palmer and the authors).

was due to ancient movement of remains and secondary burial, and one was likely due to some human activity involving dismemberment and intentional arrangement." This assessment is no different from that offered by the Turners, who analysed the same material, but they sustained the argument for cannibalism for the last assemblage, but not for the other two. They (1999, 316) write: "The considerable post-mortem damage we found in the human bone assemblage was due to excavation... We can easily distinguish between peri-mortem damage and that caused by recent excavation and archaeological techniques. However, the other criteria for proposing cannibalism are unquestionably present, although in low frequencies." What is implicated here is not only a difference in interpretation based on the frequency of characteristics, but also one that invokes a problem with distinguishing features on the trait list to support cannibalism as opposed to other possibilities. Presumably, without explicitly saying so, the Turners used the presence of dry fractures to reject an interpretation of cannibalism for the second of these assemblages characterised by the 'ancient movement of remains and secondary burial'.

Lastly, few treatments present drawings of the placement and position of cutmarks and other features on human and animal skeletons. There is often no similar record of the pattern of burning, although sometimes this information can be extracted from the text. This absence makes comparison between sites difficult, if not impossible. Information on the patterning of burning is essential if, for example, immolation is to be separated from the roasting or oven-cooking of remains and whether exposure to flame occurred before or after fragmentation. This may be due to the lack of obvious individuals among these remains, but a simple sample-wide line-drawing like those in Keenleyside's (1997), Villa *et al.*'s (1986b), and Rautman and Fenton's (2005) treatments is a good complement to tabular information, as are line-drawings of affected skeletal elements, as in the articles by Simon (1992) and Simon and Steffian (1994). Both the Turner's volume and White's are replete with high quality photographs that are essential to documenting the alterations to bone, but there are far fewer – or none at all – in many cases.

The earliest instances of cannibalism – in the absence of burning

The earliest evidence of cannibalism comes from Middle Palaeolithic sites that have produced remains ascribed to Archaic *Homo*, Neanderthals and their precursors in Europe (pre-Neanderthals or *Homo antecessor*) (Arsuaga *et al.* 1999). Defleur *et al.* (1999) report on remains from Baume Moula-Guercy, Ardèche, southern France, deriving from six Neandertals (two adults; two adolescents, aged 15 and 16 years of age at death; and two children, aged six and seven years of age at death), dating to isotope stage 5 (80,000–120,000 years ago). They were found commingled with faunal remains, mainly of red deer, *Cervus elaphus*, along with stone tools (with little lithic débitage). The similar finds context, element representation (taking anatomical differences between species into consideration), fragmentation, and processing information (as represented by cutmarks, percussion pits, anvil striae, adhering flakes, inner conchoidal scars, crushing of cancellous bone, and cortical bone peeling) suggests that the discard pattern and treatment of these remains were similar. Conjoined human elements, found three metres apart, and evidence for splitting of long bone shafts suggest retrieval of marrow from the medullary canal after diaphyses had been broken open. There is no mention of evidence for burnt remains and, given the evidence for on-site processing, these remains may have been consumed in a raw state or prepared elsewhere.

Absence of evidence for burning appears to be a feature of European prehistoric sites. No evidence for cooking or heating was noted in either human or animal remains at Fontbrégoua Cave (discussed above). Villa *et al.* (1986b) note that animals and humans were treated in a similar manner, however. They identify cutmarks in similar locations made by the same type of implement – one was found in association with the human remains. Interestingly, the human and animal remains were segregated in different features, for which conjoining exercises demonstrated single short-term periods of accumulation. Both human and animal bones showed evidence not only for dismemberment in the form of jointed remains, but also that the muscle tissue had been filleted from the bones prior to consumption. Humans, like wild animals at the site, appear to have been butchered in groups, while domestic species were butchered singly. Villa and colleagues (1986b) note that the splintering of both human and animal bone is similar with similar frequencies of impact scars noted. Furthermore, this evidence for marrow extraction and the discard of these remains differs from the contemporary inhumation rite practised in the area during the Neolithic and that these patterns also contrast with those associated with secondary burial practices (see Villa and Mahieu 1991). Based on the absence of neuro-crania from the assemblage and cutmarks to the viscero-crania that are present these researchers argue for ritual retrieval of crania and exo-cannibalism (*cf.* Turner and Turner 1992). There does not appear, however, to be evidence for violent trauma that one might anticipate if cannibalism occurred as a result of hunting (and killing) humans. Therefore, this site presents substantial evidence for the consumption of human flesh but without evidence for exposure to fire.

Instances of survival cannibalism

There is no doubt that cannibalism has taken place under conditions of extreme distress and deprivation, both physical and mental (Tuzin 1983). One of the best-studied historical cases is that of the Donner Party, a wagon train that was trapped by winter weather in 1846–1847. Numbering some 87 persons, this group experienced not only cannibalism but also violence among the males, over half of whom perished (Grayson 1990). In another example, Keenleyside *et al.* (1997) note that among the ice-locked crew of the Franklin Expedition, lost in the search for a Northwest Passage in 1848, the position of cutmarks near articular surfaces and possible peri-mortem breakage (although levelled tentatively by these authors due to weathering of the fractured surfaces) on approximately one-third of the fragmented and scattered human remains is consistent not only with cannibalism but also with defleshing or removal of soft tissue. The assessment of cannibalism is sustained, in this instance, by contextual and circumstantial evidence that supports historical accounts of the loss of the crew. This support includes the morphology of the cutmarks being consistent with the use of metal implements (not stone as used by the indigenous Inuit), other material culture (personal items and items of clothing), and oxygen isotope signatures that attest to a European, rather than an Arctic origin for these human remains. Above all, it is the eye-witness accounts collected from Inuit after the event that attest to cannibalism. Multiple cutmarks on the remains of the hands, for which the authors cannot attach significance, may perhaps attest to defence injuries. The drawing of the placement of them suggests that they were made to the palmar surface, a position that is consistent with individuals grabbing a cutting weapon while defending themselves from attack (see Novak 2000 for examples).

Although White (1992) refrained from interpreting the heavily fragmented assemblage from Mancos Wash, Colorado, using factor analysis of the indicators of cannibalism, Kantner (1999) has more recently demonstrated that this assemblage is unique among American Southwest sites previously analysed and identified as containing non-normative burials. This site, then, may be best associated with climatic deterioration and survival cannibalism.

In a case of historically documented murder/cannibalism, Rautman and Fenton (2005) record a combination of peri-mortem cranial trauma with a minority of post-cranial defence injuries affecting the upper limbs and evidence for defleshing in a group of late nineteenth-century males killed and subsequently cannibalised by Alferd (*sic*) Packer. In this example, the authors note the lack of cutmarks associated with disarticulation, e.g. without cutmarks found on the articular surfaces, with 95% of these marks occurring near the proximal or distal ends of the long bones and the remaining 5% (only nine cutmarks), found in the mid-diaphysial region. The authors suggest the patterning of these cutmarks relates to filleting of muscle tissue from the bone. They contrast this with defleshing marks that tend to be more randomly distributed on the bone. The lack of disarticulation and bone breakage associated with marrow extraction sets this instance off from those

associated with the Anasazi of the prehistoric American Southwest. The authors, like DeGusta (1999, see below) in his treatment of Fijian cannibalism, note that cultural and culinary differences play a substantial role in the form cannibalism may take.

The earliest, best-developed case for cannibalism comes from the karstic cave site of Gran Dolina, Atapuerca, Burgos, northwest Spain. Here, 80 fossil remains of a minimum of six individuals, dating to before 750,000 years ago, were found commingled with 200 lithic artefacts and faunal remains that included animals such as mammoths, cave bears, canids, foxes, lions, cats, weasels, horses, boars, as well as fallow, roe, and red deer, bison, and 'Irish Elk' (*Megaloceros* sp.). The part representation of this assemblage demonstrates that the most commonly occurring elements are metapodials, phalanges, ribs, isolated teeth, and vertebrae. Unlike the situation at American Southwest sites, vertebrae are found in a higher proportion than are metapodials and phalanges. The authors attribute this discrepancy to the absence of boiling of vertebrae. Conversely, the scapula, humerus, ulna, sacrum, pelvis, fibula, tibia, calcaneum and astragalus are entirely absent from the assemblage. Limb bone fragments overall were rare (one femoral and two radial fragments), so the assemblage was predominately made up of axial elements. The palaedemographic profile of the hominids and fauna (MNI=22) are similarly dominated by infants and juveniles, with the hominids represented by two infants, 3–4 years old; two adolescents, one 14 years old, a second 11 years old; and two sub-adults, 16–18 years of age at death. Roughly 25% of the hominid specimens possess cutmarks and the hand elements also possess these, which the authors believe relates to cuts made when these elements were held in the mouth. In addition, there are conchoidal scars, percussion marks, peeling, and adhering flakes represented in the assemblage, damage induced by fracturing bones to reveal the medullary canal.

In comparison to Anasazi assemblages, including that from Mancos Wash, there is greater evidence for conchoidal scars, peeling and adhering flakes, features of the Atapuerca assemblage that the authors relate to differences in treatment of the remains, perhaps due to the absence of fire and greater difficulty in the dismemberment process without it. The hominid remains share these features with the medium-sized mammals at the site, presumably due to the ease with which elements from these species can be broken by bending with the hands, as opposed to the greater force needed to break large mammal bones. Limb bones of all species were heavily fragmented to reveal the medullary canal. This difference may also explain the greater number of cranial cutmarks among the Atapuerca hominid remains as compared to those of animals. This lack of preparation may also be responsible for the relative abundance of vertebral and rib fragments in this assemblage since these are usually under-represented in other assemblages previously investigated for cannibalism due to rendering them for grease. Due to what seems to be a temperate climate and abundant species diversity, the authors suggest that the Atapuerca remains relate to dietary or gastronomic cannibalism, rather than to survival cannibalism. They see no evidence for any ritual behaviour evident in this assemblage, as for example, may have characterised the Krapina assemblage and that from Neolithic Fontbrégoua. Based on the demographic profile of hominids found in the Simo de los Huesos, of which Gran Dolina is a part, these individuals represent a catastrophic assemblage, rather than an attritional one (i.e. one that characterises a slow accumulation of deaths), as indeed does the assemblage from Krapina (Bocquet-Appel and Arsuaga 1999). Although this assumes that these individuals died over a relatively short time, the profile reveals an age-at-death expected of a group of individuals living at the same time (i.e. a living population), an observation that is consistent with mortality independent of age or sex, as has been noted in other suspected cases of cannibalism from the American Southwest.

Compost

Disturbance of primary burials shortly after interment, but when the bone contains substantial amounts of collagen, may mimic the peri-mortem breakage patterns of remains said to be cannibalised. Based on observations of peri-mortem breakage, Simon (1992) and Simon and Steffian (1994) argue that scattered, disarticulated multiple human bones from the excavation of a Pacific Eskimo site (Kachemak Tradition, 733 to 2701 B.P.) on Crag Point, Kodiak Island, south-central Alaska, represent a complex mortuary rite rather cannibalism, as had been argued previously. This complex mortuary rite involved processing of the bodies of the dead and of human bone, in addition to retention of skeletal elements removed from desiccated or skeletonised bodies for ceremonial purposes.

These researchers identify three types of interment: primary inhumation, multiple disarticulated inhumation that was at least partially fleshed when consigned to the ground, and scattered human remains. The last of these appear to result from the disturbance of primary inhumations, perhaps in the performance of retrieving human skeletal remains, and would thus be better described as a form of secondary mortuary rite. Only the scattered remains possess evidence of animal scavenging and were also, unlike the inhumations, the only remains to bear evidence of cultural modifications consisting of cutmarks, defleshing (*i.e.* incised marks), burning, drilled holes and two types of peri-mortem breakage, single fractures on single elements and multiple fractures of bones indicative of a reduction sequence. These features were found on sub-adult and adult female remains only, although the authors point out that this may simply reflect the fact that the elements involved were those for which sex and age-at-death could be determined.

At this site, cannibalism is denied on the grounds that the interred elements lack features of those found scattered- cultural modification and animal gnawing – and that these interred remains are found in contexts that seem to have been disturbed as part of secondary funerary rites when elements had been removed for ceremonial purposes, or when burials, perhaps in a desiccated state, had been added to cairn-like structures and disturbed earlier burials. Simon (*ibid.*, 146) indicates that cannibalism might be implicated when cutmarks, peri-mortem breakage, and burning are found on skeletal material from the same feature and when "independent data", such as historical accounts or oral tradition, suggest that human cannibalism occurred among a particular group of people at a particular place, and at a particular time. Simon and Steffian (1994, 86) conclude that the currently available data do not support, or discount, the possibility that traumatic death occurred or that human bones were processed for consumption at Crag Point.

It seems unwarranted to demand "historical accounts" to support interpretations of prehistoric events. Such a statement seems to fundamentally question the notion that archaeological remains can reflect cultural and social change. Melbye and Fairgrieve (1994, 57–58) elaborate upon this point in their analysis of the remains from the Inuit Saunaktuk site in Canada's Northwest Territories. They write: "… we know of no corroborating independent data (such as historical accounts or oral tradition) at a particular time and place in south-central Alaska (or for the entire Arctic for that matter), which supports a mortuary custom of slashing or chopping the deceased, defleshing and dismembering the body, splitting the long bones, and scattering the remains in a random fashion about the site." These authors rely on evidence for substantial peri-mortem trauma in scattered and disarticulated human bone found in association with two dwellings dated to AD 1370 ± 57 to support an interpretation of massacre. Although the authors entertain and, indeed, support the interpretation of the remains as cannibalised, they do not attempt to demonstrate this possibility by comparison with other assemblages. The human remains demonstrate cutmarks especially affecting the viscero-cranial skeletal that the authors argue were intended to remove tissue and disfigure the deceased. They further identify evidence of torture in the form of medio-laterally gouged holes in the epicondylar region of three femora and one humerus in at least two different adults. Ethnographic sources attest to a practice whereby the knees were pierced with an object, by which the transfixed person was dragged. They also note substantial evidence for cranial trauma, as well as slash (*i.e.* chop) marks that suggest further cranial and infra-cranial injuries as well as numerous cutmarks that appear to relate to dismemberment. They argue that longitudinally split long bones represent cannibalism of mainly children and adolescents (24 of 35 individuals). These remains were then discarded and denied normative burial rites and left to decompose on the surface of the site.

Customary rites and endo-cannibalism

Cannibalistic behaviour may be part of a mortuary rite associated with consumption of the intimate dead (see Keesing 1975, 164–165). Diamond (2000) relates the story of how he became a second-hand 'witness' to cannibalism during fieldwork in Papua New Guinea, when he was informed that the departure of one of his team had been precipitated by the death of his son-in-law and that he had to return to his village to partake in eating his body. This form of cannibalism, known as endo-cannibalism, relates to a proscribed mortuary rite that is found in various parts of the world. Goldman (1999, 14) defines this practice as "the consumption of flesh from a member of one's 'insider' group… and seems most usually associated with ideologies about the recycling and regeneration of life-force substances." Exo-cannibalism he relates to the consumption of flesh from outsiders, such as defeated war enemies, that often includes some form of peri-mortem mutilation and head-hunting to retrieve trophies.

One of the enduring problems with records of cannibalism is that the mortuary type of cannibalism, endo-cannibalism, is confused with exo-cannibalism, single acts of denigration such as eating a vanquished foe(s) or, even, institutionalised cannibalism, represented by repeated highly ritualised acts of cannibalism of many individuals (also referred to as "gustatory cannibalism"). This confusion also extends to mortuary rites that involve defleshing the dead, sometimes involving boiling or burning. Pickering (1999, 66) recounts the following practice from the Mary River area of Queensland, Australia: "The body was reportedly skinned and decapitated, the legs were cut off at the knees and thighs and the arms removed. The anatomical portions were then defleshed through scraping and cutting. The bones were broken to get out the marrow, not for eating, but as part of the flesh disposal process. The flesh was then buried, while the scraped bones were distributed amongst relatives." In this instance no flesh is consumed, as has been noted in other cases of ritual defleshing of human remains.

Using ethnographic examples, Kantner (1999) posits that in instances where mortuary rites produce peri-mortem fragmentation, the resulting burials would not be intermingled with animal remains, and there would be evidence of formalised and standardised burial treatment. These aspects, therefore, could be used to dissociate mortuary rites, even those involving endo-cannibalism, from exo-cannibalism, although Villa *et al.* (1986a and b) noted that at Fontbrégoua human remains were in separate contexts from those that contained animal remains, yet still sustained their argument that the remains had been exo-cannibalised based on the under-representation of human cranial remains that may have been collected for ritual reasons.

At the Iron Age (*c.* third-second century BC) Tuvan burial ground at Aymyrlyg, Siberia, Murphy and Mallory (2000) note evidence for both dismemberment, with cutmarks found in the vicinity of articular joint surfaces and, more infrequently, for defleshing, which was especially evident on the scapulae, pelvic girdle, and femora. Even though the occasional burial was found in a disarticulated state lacking proper anatomical alignment, remains treated in this manner were interred separately from those of others and were not fragmented. None of the bones had been broken open to reveal the medullary canal, and none were burnt or demonstrated evidence of having been boiled (*i.e.* there was no pot polish, see below). On this evidence the authors argue for mortuary preparation and the secondary interment of those who died away from the winter settlement. Taylor (2002, 82) questions this assessment; he argues that the lack of bone breakage does not necessarily mean that the flesh removed was not eaten. He notes that in Herodotus' account of the Issedones, predecessors of those people living in the region in the 3rd-2nd century BC, were said to cut off the flesh alone for consumption, after cooking it. This appears to be a form of endo-cannibalism. Herodotus (4.26) says that sons of a dead man chop up the corpse, mix it with the flesh of goats and sheep, and serve the mixture as part of a feast, while retaining the gilded head of the man as a sacred image. Because the individuals described by Murphy and Mallory (*ibid.*) are found singly and are not commingled, this example seems to bear out Kantner's hypothesis, except that these remains are not heavily fragmented. It may be, then, that the Fontbrégoua remains are also better interpreted as deriving from endo-cannibalism – especially in the absence of trauma that would suggest a violent encounter (see above).

Trinkaus (1985) previously argued on the basis of circumstantial evidence that the fragmentation of the Krapina remains was due to rock falls and excavation trauma and that striations found on the bones were due to post-depositional processes. He supported this assessment by comparing the skeletal part representation of the Krapina remains with unburied and buried Neanderthal and anatomically modern human remains. This comparison showed that the Krapina remains more closely resembled the skeletal part representation of the buried samples than they did the unburied ones. The element representation included, for example, many of the more delicately constructed bones, such as scapulae and juvenile claviculae. Furthermore, it is unusual to find so many hand and foot phalanges as represented in Trinkaus' (1985) diagrams. The absence of these remains is often one of the indicators of secondary interment (*cf.* Orschiedt 1997, Valentin and Le Goff 1998) and thus their presence at Krapina would suggest another accumulation mechanism.

In a subsequent analysis, Russell (1987a and b) studied the fragmented remains and the cutmark evidence from Krapina. She assessed all cutmarks and determined whether they were ancient or recent. In the absence of impact scars, Russell interpreted the longitudinally split long bones as having derived from carnivore activity. She then compared the cutmark distribution of the Krapina hominid remains with butchered animals from the Middle Palaeolithic Dordogne site of Combe Grenal and a Late Woodland (AD 1320 ± 75 years) Amerindian ossuary sample from Juntunen, Bois Blanc Island, Michigan, USA, where ethnographic records from the following historic period documented a secondary burial rite involving defleshing and reburying of human remains. The placement of cutmarks on the Krapina remains more closely resembles those of the Juntunen material than they did the butchery marks of the Combe Grenal material. Based on this analysis, she argued that the Krapina material derived from a mortuary rite involving defleshing of skeletal elements to obtain 'clean' bones. This cleaning of bones produced multiple and repeated, short incised marks in a 'ladder-series' arrangement that Russell (1987b) associated with scraping dried tissue from bones prior to interment (*cf.* Olsen and Shipman 1994).

One of the most intriguing studies of the physical evidence of cannibalism is DeGusta's study of Fijian remains from two sites, Navatu (1999) and Vunda (2000), both found on the island of Viti Levu, Fiji. Fiji has long been associated with cannibalism, the concept being used metaphorically (see above), in addition to instances of the behaviour being recorded ethnohistorically (Sahlins 1983). These treatments are unique in that, using the same methods, DeGusta (1999) sustains the argument for cannibalism at Navatu, while denying that the behaviour existed at Vunda.

Disarticulated shell midden material at Navatu, dating to between 100 BC to AD 1900, contains the commingled remains of humans with other non-human taxa, mainly fish, but also including pig, dog, bat (*Pteropus* sp.), rat (*Rattus exulans* and *norvegicus*) and, from more recent periods, goat and cattle, as well as turtles and a variety of bird species. DeGusta (1999) compares the fragmentary commingled human and non-human remains, found in middens, with Late Period burials dating from roughly AD 1800 to 1900. He notes greater similarity between the midden human material and the medium-sized mammal remains than he does with the remains from human burials. Breakage (fracture type) pattern and fragmentation are statistically significantly similar between the medium mammals and humans and different from contemporary human burials. Burning, cutmarks with peeling, percussion pits, and crushing are also characteristics of the medium mammal and human material in the midden, albeit these features are represented in relatively small numbers and are variable among taxa. All of these features are absent in the human burials. Perhaps indicative of differences in cooking methods, the evidence for the pattern of burning associates humans with fish and reptiles, while small and medium-sized mammals and birds form a separate group.

The majority of the human remains that exhibit burning are cranial and mandibular elements, 67 of 165 fragments. Post-cranial burnt bones included hand elements (N=9), a fragment of a foot phalanx, femoral fragments, one rib fragment, and a thoracic vertebral fragment. Essentially, then, burning affects the extremities more often than it does the thorax. This is in keeping with individuals who have been exposed to fire in a complete state (*cf.* Owsley *et al.* 1995, Ubelaker *et al.* 1995). From the appearance of the burnt elements in DeGusta's Figure 4, it is clear that burning occurred after fragmentation in that all surfaces are affected, including those from within articulations and those that exhibit peri-mortem fractures (*cf.* Novak and Kollman 2000).

DeGusta (1999) compares the assemblage from Navatu with that from Juntunen, previously analysed by Russell (1987a and b, see above), and notes that the Fijian assemblage is more fragmentary and has a lower percentage of cutmarks than does this defleshed and secondarily buried assemblage from Michigan. These observations are consistent with Russell's hypothesised differences between mortuary treatment and other behaviours. Moreover, samples derived from violent encounters and secondary burial from the Crow Creek, South Dakota, massacre site (AD 1325) are less fragmented, have a different pattern of element representation- far fewer hand and foot bones and far more *ossa coxae*, mandibulae, and sacra- and no cutmarks or evidence of burning. The midden remains are also distinctively different from Fijian normative burials, but also differ from suspected instances of cannibalism from the American Southwest Anasazi sites of Mancos and Chaco Canyon, where differences in breakage, burning, crushing, and percussion pit frequencies exist. These differences DeGusta attributes to cultural or sample composition differences. Like Villa and colleagues (1986a and b), DeGusta argues that the similarity between the human and non-human remains indicates that either both were processed for consumption or they were processed similarly but were not consumed.

At Vunda, DeGusta (2000) made a similar comparison between medium mammal remains and those of humans, and with human burials. Here, however, he found that breakage (fracture type) and fragmentation to be more common in the midden remains than they are in the human burials. Cutmarks and burning, although found to be less common than breakage and fragmentation in the midden, are virtually absent in the burials. Similarly, peeling, percussion pits, and crushing are rare in both the midden material and in the burials. There are no statistically significant differences between human remains found in the middens and the human burials. The medium mammals possess higher frequencies of cutmarks and burning, percussion pits, and peeling than do the human remains. Because the modifications between the midden human material is not different from that in burials and the medium mammals are somewhat distinct, DeGusta (2000) rejects the hypothesis that the appearance and distribution of the Vunda human remains were the result of cannibalism. He also notes that the Vunda material is different from that from Navatu in post-cranial part representation and in its evidence for burning, cutmarks, and peeling. Based on these differences, he ascribes the distribution of midden human remains to having derived from disturbed burials. Again, the presence of dry fractures would have helped to support this argument.

Exo-cannibalism: cannibalism as denigration

In order to distinguish amongst the types of situations in which cannibalism occurs the context is all-important. The key between differentiating mortuary rites involving dismemberment and endo-cannibalism is the evidence for denigration of the deceased. Gardner (1999) records cannibalism in the context of raids carried out by men from the Mianmin of central New Guinea in 1960. These raids were undertaken to obtain wives from neighbouring peoples. The men encountered in these raids were killed, their bodies decapitated and entrails removed, and the dismembered remains carried away to be eaten. In addition, a captured, crippled woman who, due to her disability, had trouble keeping up with the raiding party was also killed and parts of her body were also consumed.

Kantner (1999) noted some features of assemblages from the American Southwest that would be expected to occur in instances of cannibalism, in addition to cutmarks, signs of dismemberment, and burning. These are the removal of body parts – hands, feet, or heads – as trophies, evidence of scalping, and most importantly evidence for violent trauma to long bones and crania but in a manner that would not be consistent with marrow or brain extraction. Evidence for denigration might include evidence for a non-normative burial, although this, alone, would not distinguish the patterning of human remains from those of other non-normative rites. The best evidence for denigration would be to find unusual burials with evidence of butchery, like that that characterises animal processing, along with evidence for substantial violence in the form of overkill injuries. Overkill injuries are multiple injuries that are in excess of those necessary to cause death. They would be similar to those meted to war captives who were beaten and wounded and, eventually, butchered and consumed.

One of the most revealing discussions of this type of evidence comes, again, from the American Southwest, where the question is not only about the status of the human remains, but is also coloured by perspectives of the modern descendants of indigenous peoples living in the area today. Dongoske *et al.* (2000, 188) make the following remark: "We also are concerned with how allegations of cannibalism in the popular press affect contemporary Native Americans, especially descendants of the Ancestral Puebloans." There is no doubt that this type of study produces highly eye-catching leaders in the popular press, but this polemical situation has also precipitated one of the fullest and most frank discussions of the evidence that has appeared in print to date.

The discussion centres on the fragmented remains of four adults, two adult males and one probable adult male, and an adult female, found inside the largest pithouse, Feature 3, and a child of roughly 11 years of age at death found in the ventilator shaft of the same pithouse at the Cowboy Wash site (5MT10010) in southwestern Colorado, USA. Another two individuals, a child aged about 7.5 years and an adolescent aged about 14 years at death, were found in pithouse Feature 13, the smallest pithouse, at the same site. These burials differed in their appearance and context from primary midden interments from the site. Unlike the latter remains, these were found scattered on the floors of the pithouses, with parts of the same individuals (identified by conjoined elements, skeletal part representation, and developmental age criteria) found in different locations within these structures. Fifty percent of the long bone diaphyses of these individuals had been shattered, producing 1150 pieces in total. These fragments possess numerous peri-mortem breaks in the form of spiral, hinge and conchoidal fractures, as well as evidence of crushing of elements and peeling of cortical bone surfaces, cutmarks, chopmarks, percussion pits and striae. A small minority of elements also demonstrate evidence of burning, both before and after breakage (Lambert *et al.* 2000b), which the authors interpret as evidence for roasting. There was no evidence for pot polish, although the authors concede that the pale colouration of the remains may indicate boiling. The vertebrae were under-represented, as were hand elements. All of the vertebrae recovered bore peri-mortem fractures, which supports the interpretation that they had been crushed. The context in which these remains were found suggest rapid abandonment of the pithouses, which were left to decay into dereliction as standing structures afterwards. The collapse of these structures did not, apparently, play a role in the peri-mortem breakage of the remains (Lambert *et al.* 2000b). The presence of utilitarian and items of personal adornment support the rapid abandonment of the site under what may have been circumstances of distress.

The analysis of this site is unique due to the bio-chemical analyses applied to potsherds and to a human coprolite found in another pithouse nearby, pithouse Feature 15. Analysis of a number, but not all, of the potsherds showed traces of human myoglobin (which are distinct from those of other animals), a protein found in human muscle tissue, but not in the skin, mucosal lining, or blood of humans. The only potsherds that did produce a positive result came from the remnants of a cooking pot found in association with the viscero-cranial remains of the adolescent found in pithouse Feature 3. The coprolite produced evidence for human myoglobin – and only humanly-derived myoglobin – to the exclusion of that of other animals. It was found in the hearth of pithouse

Feature 15 in an unburnt state, suggesting that it had been deposited after the hearth's last use (Marlar *et al.* 2000). Lastly, using blood residue analysis, two but not all stone tools, and these from pithouse Feature 13 (that associated with the child and adolescent remains), showed signs of human blood (Marlar *et al.* 2000).

This evidence benefited from further clarification offered by the authors after Dongoske *et al.* (2000) questioned the context and interpretation of the human remains, as well as the reliability of the analytical methods used to obtain the results. Dongoske *et al.* (2000, 186) also provide a competing scenario that sees the patterning of these remains resulting from an attack in which individuals were hacked to death (as in modern-day Kosovo and Rwanda), some of whom fell into or over fires and were burned, after which the survivors returned to perform perfunctory burials and, shortly thereafter, abandoned the site. These authors' critique clarified a number of issues. Lambert *et al.* (2000b) did not find evidence of carnivore and other animal activity, such as gnawing and tooth punctures, which indicates that animal activity did not appear to contribute to the patterning of the assemblage. In addition, it is possible that missing elements may have been removed and deposited elsewhere on the surface and lost from the archaeological record as a result (Lambert *et al.* 2000b). Dongoske *et al.* (2000) also question the residue analyses on the stone tools, drawing on the rather unsubstantiated history of such analyses in archaeology. Lambert *et al.* (2000b) reply that previous analyses relied on under-developed laboratory protocols and that such residues relate to the last use of the tool only. The blood could not have come from an abrasion of the skin of those using the tool because blood from such an event would have been removed with subsequent use. With regard to the coprolite, it did not contain any floral material and can be differentiated from other animal dung, including that of dogs, who ingest bone when eating (none was found and neither was dog fur incorporated as a result of self-grooming). The deposit of this coprolite, although in another pithouse, was coeval with the deposition of the human remains and abandonment of other structures at the site.

Other critiques of the cannibalism hypothesis have concentrated on mutilation of the dead to explain the patterning observed. Although the evidence from the American Southwest seems clear evidence for the butchery and subsequent burning of human remains after dismemberment, based on ethnographic evidence of more recent southwestern groups, Darling (1998) and Ogilvie and Hilton (2000) posit that similar fracturing, dismemberment, and defleshing could be the result of the treatment meted to suspected witches, who were not, apparently, the subject of cannibalism. The bodies of such individuals were dismembered or struck with stones in order to disable the corpse so that it would no longer trouble the living. Although neither Darling nor Ogilvie

and Hilton present osteological comparative evidence for the peri-mortem treatment of witches, to demand this of researchers would involve the same constraints as does demonstrating cannibalism itself, the use of human corpses in experimental studies. However, that these assemblages may relate to the presence of notions of witchcraft is not incompatible with other interpretations, including cannibalism, especially if the treatment of witches changed form more recently. In the distant past perhaps suspected witches were consumed. Darling (1998) notes, for example, that witchcraft and cannibalism are linked concepts among the peoples of the American Southwest in the recent past, and this may suggest that the two had some physical relationship in the past. It may not be coincidence that Hough's earliest record of what he interpreted as cannibalised human remains discovered in 1901 recorded the burial of a 'medicine man', an individual interred with ritual paraphernalia similar to that of more recent Zuni priests, near to these assemblages (Turner and Turner 1992). Whatever the case, it may be that both witch execution and cannibalism were relatively rare events that were quite variable in their expression when they did occur. This seems to pose, at present, an insurmountable problem for distinguishing the two behaviours from one another (although see below).

From the same region, Graver *et al.* (2002) argue for extreme violence after their analysis of human remains found at the Grinnell site, Colorado, in what they interpret as a small ceremonial centre dating the late Pueblo II/early Pueblo III periods. The human remains, dated by dendrochronology to 1244 AD were found in a cist adjoining a kiva in a 'mass burial', a position that is reminiscent of the deposition at Cowboy Wash, Colorado, although the latter is found in a pithouse, rather than in a kiva. The remains of eight individuals: three pre-teen children; two subadults 16 to 21 years of age at death; and three adults, two young adult females and a young adult male, were found scattered and disarticulated (i.e. not in proper anatomical alignment) on the floor of a cist and on the floor of the kiva outside the cist, while some were found within a corrugated pot that sat on top of the cist and was surrounded by human bones. The bones were heavily fragmented (only 24, mainly crania, were whole) with spiral fractures occurring on most of the long bone fragments and cutmarks concentrating mainly in the cranial remains (N=126) with another 45 found on post-cranial elements, and with seven chopmarks on a single tibia fragment with these marks predominately found on the proximal and distal ends. Most of the cutmarks on the crania occurred in the nasal, orbital, frontal, maxilla and mandible. Some 5.6% had either been burnt (N=10) or charred (N=11). On the basis of this evidence, the authors interpret that these remains had sustained both sharp and blunt force traumatic injuries, the crania having been flayed (*i.e.* skinned or defleshed), and the body disarticulated, as if butchered. On the basis of what they describe as a low prevalence of burning, however, and in the absence of anvil abrasions and pot polish, these authors reject an interpretation of cannibalism. Due to the presence of blunt force cranial trauma that occurs on 20% of the cranial remains and crushing of the viscero-cranial skeleton they argue that, instead, these individuals had been beaten to death, after which their bodies were defleshed and the bones further fragmented. In this instance the authors emphasise the traumatic injuries over the evidence for fragmentation to argue in support of an assessment of endemic violence in the American Southwest.

For the ninth-century Backhoe Village site in south-central Utah, USA, Novak and Kollman (2000) make a similar assessment of the remains of nine individuals (five adult males; two adult females, broadly aged from young to older adults; and two juveniles, one roughly nine years and the other about six years of age at death). In this group, evidence for blunt force trauma to the viscero- and neuro-cranial areas and scalping is accompanied by cutmarks, the location of which, near joint surfaces, suggests disarticulation, with anvil abrasions, percussion scars, crushing and peeling evident on long bones, and a relative absence of vertebrae indicating peri-mortem fragmentation. Some of the peri-mortem fragments had also been exposed to fire after they had been fragmented, as indicated by their fracture surfaces being blackened. Based on the sequence of these events, these authors support an interpretation of cannibalism. This level of burning is higher (57%) than that noted by Graver *et al.* (2002) but, like these authors, Novak and Kollman (2000) did not find evidence for pot polish. Uniquely, Novak and Kollman suggest that the thoracic cavity had been flayed and spread based on the pattern of peeling noted in the vicinity of the angle of the ribs. The level of burning, then, separates these two interpretations.

In another interpretation of remains as evidence for violence, Ogilvie and Hilton (2000) present arguments surrounding the remains of 13 individuals, including males, females, children, and infants, ranging in age from one year to over 40 years of age at death, recovered from a Basketmaker III pithouse and kiva, located about 800 m apart. The remnants of the kiva, or ceremonial structure, contained the remains of 12 of these individuals, while the pithouse contained only those of a 30–40 year old female. The kiva remains were found scattered and commingled in the bench and floor areas, with a smaller concentration on an ash lens in the hearth area. These remains were found in association with an artefactual assemblage that included hammerstones, stone flakes, and bone awls; residue analysis of the hammerstones produced signatures of primate blood (presumably, likely to be human since North America has not had natural populations of that Order, other than humans, since the Eocene). These remains were so fragmented that only 23% (651 from 2823 specimens) could be identified to element and thus the authors concentrated primarily on the cranial material in their analyses. In addition to fragmentation, these authors also found evidence of peri-mortem

fractures on 19.6%, burning on 10.9%, cutmarks (1.2%), and impact marks (9.6%), as well as evidence for rodent gnawing and scratching. The cutmarks predominate on the cranial remains (including avulsion of the crowns of anterior teeth) of both adults and children. The authors contend that the fragmentation is in excess of that required for processing of remains for consumption and that the extent of blunt force trauma is responsible for an under-representation of mainly cranio-facial and vertebral elements in both mature and immature individuals, although to a lesser extent in mature individuals. They support an interpretation that these remains represent ritualised violence directed at witches in that entire families were executed in the recent ethnohistoric period by stoning, cutting up, and burning. This assemblage stretches the occurrence of such assemblages further back into prehistory, before 750 AD, and predates the apparent efflorescence of these assemblages in the later Puebloan period in the American Southwest.

In a later American Northeast example, dating to 1390 ± 100 AD, Jamieson (1983) argued for prisoner sacrifice and, possibly, cannibalism based on cutmarked, burnt, and scattered human bones from the Roebuck Site, in eastern Ontario. There is good evidence from this site for defleshing in the form of horizontal cutmarks along the diaphyses of long bones and the manufacture of beads from human bone, gorgets from portions of human crania drilled with holes, and possibly awls or daggers made from human ulnae. Jamieson (*ibid.*) notes, however, that the butchery marks might relate to mortuary rites and, without information on fracture type- whether dry or peri-mortem- it remains a possibility that, as the author avers, ploughing had disturbed the site, and this more recent phenomenon is responsible for the appearance of the remains. Based on the demographic profile of the humanly modified cranial bones, including a minority of children and females, Jamieson suggests that prisoner-sacrifice was practiced. This association, though, is made with scant reference to the presence of peri-mortem injuries that might indicate such an activity; the only mention of this type of evidence comes with Jamieson's observation of cuts along the suprameatal crest of two temporal bones that he surmises may relate to removal of the ear. Cutmarks are distributed in a pattern suggestive of dismemberment, after which some bones and their flesh were exposed to fire, evidence that could relate to cannibalism. Curiously, Jamieson argues for the certainty of prisoner-sacrifice, but remains much less supportive of cannibalism to explain the patterning and appearance of the remains from the site. Ultimately, the interpretation of the assemblage hinges on practices recorded in the ethnohistoric record of the region.

Here, we see the predominating influence of the context in which researchers pose their questions, analyse, and interpret their data. This observation is at odds with the published sentiments of Turner and Turner (1999, 24), who contend that: "... it is our theoretical position that bone alone can generate a reliable reconstruction of the death history of a burial or charnel deposit." White (1992, 364), too, although not explicitly supporting this position, argues for further analysis of museum collections, rather than focusing on on-going excavation material. These sentiments are difficult to sustain after reviewing the published literature. It seems that the context is the starting point for such studies because the non-normative nature of them is the first aspect to draw attention in excavation. It is also fundamental to the interpretation of the remains. One of the more recent examples of disarticulated and burnt remains of 41 adults and subadults, mixed with the remains of rats, birds, and fish, comes from the island of Mangaia, southern Cook Islands, in a rock shelter used by humans between 1390 and 1470 AD (Steadman *et al.* 2000). The authors describe this rock shelter as a ritualistic site where "…human body parts, as well as some fish, rats and a few birds were cooked in earth ovens…". These remains are more like the fragmented human remains, possibly from sacrifices, found at temples (*Marae*) on the island than they are like cave burials. This disparity leads the authors to suggest that the rock shelter remains do not appear to be in a mortuary context (Antón and Steadman 2003).

White (1992, 422ff.) lays out the sequence of procedures that are required in the analysis of heavily fragmented and scattered human remains. These are: discovery, exposure, recording, labelling, lifting, transport, washing, sorting by element, attribute recording, refitting, anatomical analysis, photography, and curation. The first six parts of this sequence occur *before* the assemblage reaches the laboratory, while the remaining seven occur once the material reaches the laboratory. Much of this sequence occurs prior to material leaving the field. This emphasises the importance of the context and relationships among parts of the assemblage that can only be recovered in the field. It is the absence of these early parts of the procedure that make interpretations of mortuary treatment difficult to distinguish from one another. The possibility exists, as well, that remains may have gone through more than a single process and the unique signatures are inter-mixed.

Kantner (1999) relies heavily on the archaeological context to aid the interpretation of his factor analyses of sites in the American Southwest exhibiting non-normative burials. One of the three groupings comes from sites with taphonomic indicators associated with heavily fragmented human remains of, in the main, males. These appear to have been rarely intentionally inhumed but were found scattered indiscriminately on the floors of pueblo complex rooms. These individuals possess evidence of inter-personal violence in the form of embedded projectile points and peri-mortem breakage that did not involve heavy fragmentation of the remains, although there are peri-mortem fractures due to what has been interpreted as resulting from rocks being thrown down from above on the individuals. They lack pot polish, anvil abrasions, cutmarks, and evidence of burning. There is no apparent absence of vertebrae and a reduced frequency of fragmented remains. Nearly all of these sites date to Pueblo III times (AD 1100–1300).

In Kantner's second grouping, which dates to the preceding Pueblo II period (*c.* AD 900 to 1100), are sites that have produced fragmented remains, but include some intentional burials and also those that display pot polish and evidence for scalping. These remains, though, are not found in association with non-human animal remains and consist of groups of all ages and both sexes buried together or in close proximity. A benign climate at this time seems to mitigate against an explanation of survival cannibalism, but evidence for extreme violence- scalping and multiple peri-mortem cranio-facial fractures- and the presence of pot polish in the context leads Kantner (1999, 93) to characterise these as indicative of possible cannibalism. Given the evidence for extreme violence, the cannibalism appears to have been performed to denigrate the deceased and, perhaps, as a means of intimidation and humiliation.

In summary, then, Kantner (1999) argues that these sites represent two different behaviours. Those from Pueblo II times are brutalised casualties of warfare with perhaps some cannibalism, while those from the succeeding Pueblo III period are more likely to represent war casualties who had sustained peri-mortem injuries as a result of violent conflict. The palaeodemographic profiles seem also to support this difference with the latter being mainly males, while the former includes groups of both sexes and more variable ages at death. These profiles, then, are much like the mass graves found at Early Neolithic sites, as at Schletz in Austria (Teschler-Nicola *et al.* 1999) and Talheim in Germany (Wahl and König 1987), as opposed to that from Towton, England (Fiorato *et al.* 2000), which contained the remains of males, solely, and are thus more like the Pueblo III sites described by Kantner (1999).

The context of cannibalism and commensal politics in world later prehistory

The question of cannibalism has been posed within the framework of more recent fascination with the behaviour and its dehumanising features. This framework has contributed to a polemical atmosphere that has as much to do with recent history and ethnic tensions as it does with past history and events. As a result considerations of the social context of cannibalism have been overshadowed by modern reactions to the behaviour. For example, instances have been ascribed to social pathology (Turner 1993, Turner and Turner 1999), a very modern concept. Today, cannibalism is treated as a criminal activity (the raiders discussed by Gardner (1999), above, were tried in court and incarcerated for their actions). Under what social circumstances might such a practice have been given significance in the past, though? In instances of survival cannibalism, one could posit that the behaviour occurred under stressful environmental circumstances, whether among stranded seafarers (see above) or among protein-starved Aztecs (Harner 1977), although the latter has manifest socio- political overtones, while the former may be attributed to the vicissitudes of climate (*cf.* Fagan 2000).

Many recent studies of food have considered it as more than a means of sustenance and have attempted to delve into the symbolic and social aspects of food and its consumption (Dietler 1990, 2001; Hamilakis 1998; Hamilakis and Konsolaki 2004). These studies indicate that certain foods – meats and various beverages especially – are consumed rather infrequently and only for certain special occasions, such as during festivals or rites of passage. In the absence of evidence for widespread and sustained cannibalism, it would seem that if human flesh was consumed, then this consumption may have been sporadic and, like survival cannibalism, occurred only under very particular circumstances.

Food, its acquisition, preparation, and consumption are intimately linked to obtaining pre-eminent social status, as well as maintenance of the social structure and social organisation of society. A number of researchers have linked the mass consumption of food to feasting (Hayden 1996, Parker Pearson 1999), a social behaviour that takes on a greater role under conditions of emergent or developed social inequality. The social significance of feasting intensifies with the adoption of and dependence on agricultural products that can be stored to support mass consumption (Hayden 1990). Dietler (1996) identifies three patterns of feasting within the political economy: the entrepreneurial, the patron-client, and the diacritic. Although he did not discuss these in the context of cannibalism, all of these could be seen to operate in instances of cannibalism.

The first of these, entrepreneurial feasting, is associated with the work-party feast, in which an individual provides food and refreshment in order to bring together a sufficient work-force to complete an undertaking that brings increased social prestige to the host. Williams (cited in Carneiro 1990, 206) noted that: "Human bodies are sometimes eaten in connection with the building of a temple or canoe; or on launching a large canoe; or on taking down the mast of one which has brought some chief on a visit; or for feasting of such as take tribute to a principal place." The second of these, the patron-client feast, is a formalised use of the feast to symbolically legitimise unequal social power and is associated with the lavish feasts of chiefs in pre-state societies. As Carneiro (1990, 205) remarks, "Although commoners were allowed to partake of human flesh, it was chiefs who were by far the most accomplished cannibals. Many of the Fijian chiefs were famous for the quantity of human flesh they had consumed." The third of these types of feast, the diacritic, involves the use of special foods and special means of preparation and/or service that symbolically reifies rank differences in social groups. This type involves elaborate service vessels from which exotic or difficult to produce foods or drinks are served. These may be similar to those found in ancient Mesoamerica, where powerful individuals engaged in sacrifice and consumption on special feast days associated with a deity when the "…sacrificed person is quartered and the meat is prepared as a meal with squash flowers for the gentlemen and principals, who eat it in a ritual manner" (Fernández, quoted in Turner and Turner 1999, 417).

Hayden (1996, 137ff) argues that these socially competitive feasts can be identified in the archaeological record by the following:

1. Abundant resource bases capable of providing surpluses
2. Special foods used for feasting
3. Special vessels used for serving feasting food
4. The use of prestige items that food surpluses could be converted into
5. The occurrence of special grounds or structures where feasting events could be held
6. The occurrence of 'Triple A' (ambitious, aggressive, accumulative) individuals having more wealth and influence than others in the community. They are also called aggrandizers, accumulators, and acquisators.

The question is, then, does cannibalistic behaviour fit within this scheme. Given that there seems to be no evidence that any human society subsists for any extended period of time solely on eating members of their own kind (save, perhaps among the Aztecs), the act of cannibalism should be seen, perhaps, as an extension of feasting. From the published literature, the vessels that would have served this purpose would help us to understand how such actions were perceived. Were such vessels, like the corrugated pots found with human remains in them in the American Southwest or the 'great red and yellow bowl', similarly associated with the remains of humans found at Azcapotzalco, Mexico, dating from the Teotihuacán period (Harner 1977), considered part of feasting paraphernalia? If so, one would expect to find evidence of cannibalistic behaviour associated with certain kinds of vessels and special implements, such as the 'cannibal forks' of Fiji (Carneiro 1990, 204) reserved for consumption of feasting foods, including human flesh. Turner and Turner (1999) note the ceremonial and ritual context of sacrificial and cannibalistic rites in Mesoamerican feasts centred on the consumption of special foods, including those derived from humans. This may involve bouts of consumption where a number of individuals are consumed, or indeed, only one, perhaps to symbolise the triumph of the consumer and his or her group over the consumed. This is often done to capture the essence or the personal strength of the individual consumed, but can also be viewed, simultaneously, as an act of supreme denigration and disempowerment by those contributing individuals who are eaten (see Carneiro 1990).

Kantner (1999) places what appear to be the relatively rare instances of cannibalism in the American Southwest in this context, where Pueblo II times are characterised by social inequality on a much grander scale than in preceding Basketmaker and Pueblo I (prior to AD 900) times (see also Haas 1990). Turner and Turner's (1999) survey supports the view that the period between 900 and 1300 AD in the area occupied by the Anasazi experienced violence on a previously unprecedented scale. In their review of 76 sites with evidence of fragmented remains found in non-normative burial contexts, Turner and Turner (1999) accept 38 of 76 sites to be valid; 286 individuals of all ages and both sexes come from these sites and fit the criteria for cannibalism.

Importantly, another 445 individuals from their survey had sustained injuries due to violent trauma, again with all ages and both sexes being affected. These include five sites associated with towers interpreted as defensive structures that occur in the Largo Gallina area of New Mexico (Turner and Turner 1993). They do not meet the criteria for cannibalised remains but appear to have resulted from violent raids initiated in the area in the same period, 1100–1300 AD, in which suspected cannibalism also occurred. Although they possess some of the same features of cannibalised remains, such as a lack of formal burial of multiple individuals, evidence for peri-mortem burning in one case (from what has been interpreted as a result of a burning roof collapse), and fragmentation of remains, they lack the level of fragmentation, anvil abrasions, and cutmarks associated with cannibalised remains. In addition, these bodies are mostly complete, with vertebrae well-represented. When they do possess anvil abrasions, these are associated with signs of peri-mortem trauma in the form of embedded projectile points, mutilation, scalping, and body part removal (hands and feet) as trophies. Viscero-cranial trauma in these remains occurs without the anvil abrasions that would indicate butchery directed at removal of the brain. Importantly, the sex profile of these remains is skewed with the remains of males outnumbering those of females in a 5:1 (26 to 5) ratio and with the majority (51 out of 55) over the age of 12 years at death. Thus the association of these remains with defensive structures, the evidence for peri-mortem trauma, and the nearly entirely adult male make-up of these sites serves to differentiate them from those with evidence for cannibalised remains. Turner and Turner (1993) note that two of these sites could have resulted from cannibalism had they demonstrated evidence for burning or heating of remains. It is thus highly possible that the two forms of behaviour, violence and cannibalism, could co-occur at the same site, just as they seem to co-occur in time.

On the basis of previously identified material culture connections with Mesoamerican state-level societies (including the burial of an individual exhibiting dental modification like that practiced in Mesoamerica, see Geller, this volume), where there is ample evidence of institutionalised sacrifice and cannibalism recorded ethnographically, ethnohistorically, and through the study of human remains – Turner and Turner (1999, 484) argue that "…the majority of Chaco Anasazi cannibal episodes resulted from acts of violent terrorism, possibly combined with ritual, incited by a few zealous cultists from Mexico and their descendant followers who possessed the deadly knowledge of certain Mexican socio-religious and warfare practices." Cannibalism in this context may have been used as a means of social control and intimidation. It would have served to cement the loyalty of the group by distinguishing the prestige and power of leaders who could dehumanise others by transmuting them into comestibles, while acting as a warning to dissenters, as well as outsiders. In this context, it is perhaps illustrative to note that at Cowboy Wash 5MT10010 the only meat consumed by those leaving behind their droppings was apparently human (Billman *et al.* 2000, Lambert *et al.* 2000b, 404). This uniquely human signature suggests that the consumption of human flesh may have occurred over a very short time, more like that associated with consumption of a special food in a feast.

Conclusion and further research

From the appearance of Table 17.1, the procedures for studying assemblages of peri-mortally fragmented remains are not uniform, nor is their reporting. It is also clear that the level and standard of recording requires more sustained attention. There are many examples reviewed here (those for which there is only a "YES" indicated) where a particular feature is only mentioned but without identifying the level or intensity of the feature noted. The depiction of features, too, needs to be improved with further use of photographs, line drawings of the location of traits for comparison across sites, and greater use and publication of SEM images in order to bolster interpretations. It comes as no surprise, then, that in summarising the osteological features associated with an interpretation of cannibalism, Kantner (1999, 84) writes: "The conclusion, therefore, is that none of the taphonomic criteria constitutes definitively convincing evidence for the occurrence of cannibalism." He (*ibid.*) envisions the application of biochemical evidence as a means of refining the arguments to support the interpretation of cannibalism. The Cowboy Wash site in southwestern Colorado has since seen the application of such evidence, where biochemical analysis of faeces in association with human skeletal remains with cutmarks consistent with those resulting from butchery appears to have confirmed that the bodies of individuals were consumed in the prehistoric American Southwest during Pueblo times (*c.* 1150 AD) (Marlar *et al.* 2000). Due to the unusual contextual features of this site, the protocol is unique, combining osteological, archaeological, and biochemical evidence of excreted faeces, and not applicable in the others reviewed here.

In the absence of such evidence, it is particularly clear that there is no single trait or traits of an assemblage that can be easily and uniquely associated with cannibalism. In their consideration of the influence of cultural values on the form that cannibalism takes, Rautman and Fenton (2005, 338) note that "…'cannibalism per se has no necessary correlation with any particular postmortem treatment of the human body." The easy alacrity with which scattered human remains were linked with cannibalism in the past can certainly no longer be sustained. What, though, of cannibalism itself from the study of bone assemblages? It seems that, although there are well-founded means to demonstrate that human remains have been processed, there is no clear way to distinguish a mortuary treatment involving defleshing and dismemberment from cannibalism. The longitudinal splitting and fragmentation of some assemblages do not fit easily with this mortuary rite, however, but this combination of features is recorded ethnographically, such as with the treatment of suspected witches in the American Southwest. The separation of bone fragments over an area, though, seems inconsistent with this peri-mortem treatment, where – in the absence of subsequent disturbance – helically broken bone fragments would be expected to be found in close approximation to one another– like the victims of suspected rock falls.

Distinguishing endo-cannibalism from exo-cannibalism may depend on finding evidence for cannibalistic behaviour in conjunction with evidence for peri-mortem injuries, although as in Graver *et al.*'s (2002) and Novak and Kollman's (2000) examples, this is often seen as evidence for death in violent circumstances without invoking cannibalism. At the present time, it is clear that there is no agreed upon means by which to distinguish endo-cannibalism from exo-cannibalism, although as noted above some of the associated part representations and spatial patterns may be suggestive of each of these (see Villa *et al.* 1986b, Kantner 1999). Due to similarities between carnivore damage to human remains and those modified by humans, a fundamental covering argument must be to exclude carnivore involvement in the creation of such assemblages. Part of torture or ceremony, though, might also include feeding animals on human flesh, the fate of the torsos of sacrificed individuals that were fed to animals in the ruler's zoo in the Aztec Empire (Harner 1977).

Whether researchers interpret heavily fragmented human remains as evidence for prisoner-sacrifice (Jamieson 1983), witch torture and killing (Darling 1998), genocidal attack (Dongoske *et al.* 2000), being beaten to death (Graver *et al.* 2002), survival cannibalism (Keenleyside *et al.* 1997), gastronomic cannibalism (Fernández-Jalvo *et al.* 1999), civil war (Novak and Kollman 2000), massacre (Melbye and Fairgrieve 1994), ritualised violence (Ogilvie and Hilton 2000), institutionalised cannibalism (Turner and Turner 1999), raiding and cannibalism (Lambert *et al.* 2000a and b), or social pathology (Turner 1993), all seem to agree

that these human remains indicate periods of local environmental and/or social instability that produced interpersonal violence and, in some cases, what may have been endemic warfare (see also LeBlanc 1999). Novak and Kollman (2000) document similar bone pattern assemblages at the ninth-century Backhoe Village site in south-central Utah, USA, among Fremont horticulturalists that predate the Anasazi sites further to the south, so the same types of human remains deposits may also be found in the Great Basin, outside the Anasazi Culture area. In essence, then, this may be part and parcel of the development of more highly socially integrated (*i.e.* complex) societies in this area. As Earle (1987, 293) notes: "Intense warfare characterizing stateless societies may favor [the development of] regional chiefdoms." In others, similar patterning may be minimally interpreted as an elaboration of funerary rites, whether cannibalism can be sustained or not.

Essentially, no-one disagrees with the evidence for peri-mortem fracturing and most of the physical features (save, perhaps, pot polish – see Kantner 1999) and unusual burial contexts of these assemblages. What is more revealing about these various arguments is that researchers are more accepting of the occurrence of what must have been endemic violence for decades, if not centuries, perpetrated on men, women, children, and infants – even seeing such an interpretation as 'more conservative' (Graver *et al.* 2002) than one of cannibalism. This perhaps has more to say about how violence is viewed (and accepted) today. Apparently, modern dispositions are better able to cope with interpretations of what must have been considerable brutality and cruelty to the living or, potentially, desecration of the deceased if fragmentation occurred immediately after death, as long as it was perpetrated without then eating the flesh of the deceased.

In the absence of faecal material (*i.e.* coprolites) upon which to perform biochemical assays, it seems that one of the most direct forms of evidence for cannibalised human remains may be tooth punctures like those noted by White (1992) on the Mancos remains, and which DeGusta (1999, 225) notes as an untested possibility in the Navatu remains from Fiji. If this type of evidence could be clearly distinguished from similar punctures produced by animals, then this would seem to be an immensely important indicator of cannibalism. At least, it would suggest mastication of human bones by humans. Tooth puncture marks from some carnivore species have been differentiated from measurements made on moulds of the pits produced by animal teeth (Pickering *et al.* 2004 and references therein). These could be supplemented by SEM analysis to aid further differentiation of human and non-human tooth marks (see also Blumenshine *et al.* 1996). Perhaps due to the lack of comparative studies, this feature of the Mancos remains has not received much attention in literature published since. Kantner (1999) in his synthesis of the taphonomic features of apparently cannibalised remains does not mention it.

As in other instances when arguments are based on the physical evidence of human remains, the recovery and recording of the burial context and knowledge of the general pattern of the mortuary variability of a given region over contiguous periods of time is essential. If cannibalism is an adjunct to, or an extension of, feasting and power politics, then the potential of environmental upheaval to produce or exacerbate these processes needs to be addressed as well, if for no other reason than to rule out cases of cannibalism related to short-term environmental disturbances. As White (1992) has previously noted, there is a need for further experimental work on taphonomic aspects of animal and human remains assemblages. These are required to be specific to different environmental circumstances (*cf.* Andrews and Cook 1985).

In the absence of analogous controlled instances of human cannibalism (cases of modern human cannibalism being rare and the physical features of such remains being unpublished as far as the authors are aware), interpretive models based on analogies drawn from the behaviours of non-human primate hunting and consumption of kills might provide some additional insights. As White, the Turners, and other researchers have noted, the assemblages associated with suspected cannibalism possess a relative absence of vertebrae, a feature usually attributed to the preparation and consumption of these cancellous-filled bones, but which could also be associated with variable preservation and heavily disturbed deposits (see Outram 2004), some of which may represent post-mortem manipulation of the dead, as in secondary burial. In a study of chimpanzee carnivory at Gombe National Park, Tanzania, Plummer and Standford (2000) noted the relative paucity of these elements in hunted red colobus monkey (*Colobus badius*) remains, which make up only a little over 2.0 % of the surviving remains. Cranial elements (60.0%) and hemi-mandibulae (40.0%) contributed the greatest number of surviving elements, with those of the appendicular skeleton and pectoral and pelvic girdles falling in between, forming between 11.1 and 22.2 % of remains. These authors also note the occurrence of chimpanzee canine puncture marks in the crania of these monkeys. As in the earliest instances of cannibalism (see above), these remains were not cooked or roasted before consumption. This type of non-human primate data, although drawn from a study of a small number of individuals (N=5) appears to provide some support for the association of some of the indicators of cannibalism with archaeologically retrieved assemblages thought to have been cannibalised by humans. This type of research is a good complement to investigations of human remains with a recent history or reports of cannibalism (*cf.* Rautman and Fenton 2005). Without these further controls and concerted efforts, it may not be possible to dissociate closely related mortuary behaviours and our interpretations will continue to be held hostage to equifinality.

Acknowledgements

The authors thank Carol Palmer (University of Sheffield), Alan R. Ogden (University of Bradford), and Eric Houlder for their photographs that appear in this contribution. We also thank Shannon Novak (Idaho State University), Tim Taylor (University of Bradford), Carol Palmer and Becky Gowland for their reviewers' comments on an earlier draft of this piece.

References

Andrews, P. and Cook, J. (1985) Natural modifications to bones in a temperate setting. *Man* (N.S.) 20, 675–691.

Andrews, P. and Fernández-Jalvo, Y. (2003). Cannibalism in Britain: taphonomy of the Creswellian (Pleistocene) faunal and human remains from Gough's Cave (Somerset, England). *Bulletin of the Natural History Museum (Geol.)* 58 (supp.) 59–81.

Antón, S. C. and Steadman, D. W. (2003) Mortuary patterns in burial caves on Mangaia, Cook Islands. *International Journal of Osteoarchaeology* 13, 132–146.

Arens, W. (1979) *The Man-eating Myth: Anthropology and Anthropophagy*. New York, Oxford University Press.

Arsuaga, J.-L., Martínez, I., Lorenzo, C., Garcia, A., Muñoz, A., Alonso, O. and Gallego, J. (1999). The human cranial remains from Gran Dolina Lower Pleistocene site (Sierra de Atapuerca, Spain). *Journal of Human Evolution* 37, 431–457.

Barber, C. G. (1929) Immediate and eventual features of healing in amputated bones. *Annals of Surgery* XC, 985–992.

Barber, C. G. (1930) The detailed changes of healing bone in amputated stumps. *Journal of Bone and Joint Surgery* 12, 353–359.

Berryman, H. E. and Symes, S. A. (1998) Recognizing gunshot and blunt cranial trauma through fracture interpretation. In K. J. Reichs, and W. M. Bass (eds.) *Forensic Osteology: Advances in the Identification of Human Remains* (second edition), 333–352. Springfield (IL), Charles C. Thomas.

Billman, B. R., Lambert, P. M. and Leonard, B. L. (2000) Cannibalism, warfare, and drought in the Mesa Verde region during the 12th century AD *American Antiquity* 65(1), 145–178.

Binford, L. R. and Ho, C. K. (1985) Taphonomy at a distance: Zhoukoudian, "The cave home of Beijing Man"? *Current Anthropology* 26(4), 413–442.

Binford, L. R. and Stone, N. M. (1986) Zhoukoudian: a closer look. *Current Anthropology* 27(5), 453–475.

Blumenshine, R. J., Marean, C. W. and Capaldo, S. D. (1996) Blind tests of inter-analyst correspondence and accuracy in the identification of cut marks, percussion marks, and carnivore tooth marks. *Journal of Archaeological Science* 23, 493–507.

Bocquet-Appel, J.-P. and Arsuaga, J.-L. (1999) Age differences of hominid samples at Atapuerca (SH) and Krapina could indicate accumulation by catastrophe. *Journal of Archaeological Science* 26, 327–338.

Boylston, A. E. (2000) Cranial trauma in past British populations. In M. Cox and S. Mays (eds.) *Human Osteology in Archaeology and Forensic Science*, 357–380. London, Greenwich Medical Media.

Boylston, A., Knüsel, C. J., Roberts, C. A. and Dawson, M. (2000). Investigation of a Romano-British Rural Ritual in Bedford, England. *Journal of Archaeological Science* 27, 241–254.

Brothwell, D. R. (1961) Cannibalism in early Britain. *Antiquity* XXXV, 304–307.

Brothwell, D. R. (1971) Forensic aspects of the so-called Neolithic skeleton Q1 from Maiden Castle, Dorset. *World Archaeology* 3(2), 233–241.

Brown, E. A. R. (1981) Death and the human body in the later Middle Ages: the legislation of Boniface VIII on the division of the corpse. *Viator: Medieval and Renaissance Studies* 12, 221–270.

Brunaux, J.-L. (1998) Un monumental trophée celtique à Ribemont-sur-Ancre (Somme). *Etudes et Documents Fouilles 4, Les Celtes: Rites Funéraires en Gaule du Nord entre le VIᵉ et le 1ᵉʳ Siècle avant Jesus-Christ*, 107–113. Namur, Ministère de la Région Wallone.

Buikstra, J. (forthcoming) An historical introduction. In J. Buikstra and L.A. Beck (eds) *Bioarchaeology: Peopling of the Past.* London, Elsevier.

Carneiro, R. L. (1990) Chiefdom-level warfare as exemplified in Fiji and the Cauca Valley. In J. Haas (ed.) *The Archaeology of War*, 190–211. Cambridge University Press, Cambridge.

Carr, G. C. and Knüsel, C. J. (1997) An assessment of the evidence for exposure burial in the Iron Age of southern England, In A. Gwilt and C. Haselgrove, (eds.) *Reconstructing Iron Age Societies: New Approaches to the British Iron Age.* 167–173. Oxbow Monograph 71.

Clark, G. (1962) *Prehistoric England.* London, Batsford.

Cunliffe, B. (1992) Pits, preconceptions, and propitiation in the British Iron Age. *Oxford Journal of Archaeology* 11, 69–83.

Darling, J. A. (1998) Mass inhumation and the execution of witches in the American Southwest. *American Anthropologist* 100, 732–752.

Defleur, A., White, T. D., Valensi, P., Slimak, L. and Créget-Bonnoure, É. (1999) Neanderthal cannibalism at Moula-Guercy, Ardèche, France. *Science* 286, 128–131.

DeGusta, D. (1999) Fijian cannibalism: osteological evidence from Navatu. *American Journal of Physical Anthropology* 110, 215–241.

DeGusta, D. (2000) Fijian cannibalism and mortuary ritual: bioarchaeological evidence from Vunda. *International Journal of Osteoarchaeology* 10, 76–92.

Diamond, J. M. (2000) Talk of cannibalism. *Nature* 407, 25–26.

Dietler, M. (1990) Driven by drink: The role of drinking in the political economy and the case of early Iron Age France. *Journal of Anthropological Archaeology* 9, 352–406.

Dietler, M. (1996) Feasts and commensal politics in the political economy: food, power, and status in prehistoric Europe. In P. Wiessner and W. Shieffenhövel (eds.) *Food and the Status Quest*, 87–125. Providence and Oxford, Berghahn Books.

Dietler, M. (2001) Theorizing the feast. In M. Dietler, and B. Hayden (eds.) *Feasts: Archaeological and Ethnographic Perspectives on Food, Politics, and Power*, 65–114. Smithsonian Institution Press, Washington, D.C.

Dobney, K. and Reilly, K. (1988) A method for recording archaeological animal bones: the use of diagnostic zones. *Circaea* 5(2), 79–96.

Dongoske, K. E. Martin, D. L. and Ferguson, T. J. (2000) Critique of the claim of cannibalism at Cowboy Wash. *American Antiquity* 65(1), 179–190.

Duday, H. (1998) Le charnier gaulois de Ribemont-sur-Ancre (Somme). *Etudes et Documents Fouilles 4, Les Celtes: Rites Funéraires en Gaule du Nord entre le VIᵉ et le 1ᵉʳ Siècle avant Jesus-Christ.* 113–119. Namur, Ministère de la Région Wallone.

Earle, T. (1987) Chiefdoms in archaeological and ethnohistorical perspective. *Annual Review of Anthropology* 16, 297–308.

Fagan, B. (2000) *The Little Ice Age: How Climate Made History 1300–1850.* New York, Basic Books.

Fernández-Jalvo, Y., Diez, J.C., Cáceres, I. and Rosell, J. (1999) Human cannibalism in the Early Pleistocene of Europe (Gran Dolina, Sierra de Atapuerca, Burgos, Spain). *Journal of Human Evolution* 37, 591–622.

Fiorato, V., Boylston, A. and Knüsel, C. J. (eds.) (2000) *Blood Red Roses: The Archaeology of a Mass Grave from Towton, A.D 1461.* Oxford, Oxbow Books.

Frayer, D.W. (1997) Ofnet: evidence for a Mesolithic massacre. In D.L. Martin and D. W. Frayer (eds.) *Troubled Times: Violence and Warfare in the Past*, 181–216. Amsterdam, Gordon and Breach Publishers.

Gardner, D. (1999) Anthropophagy, myth, and the subtle ways of ethnocentrism. In L. R. Goldman (ed.) *The Anthropology of Cannibalism*, 27–49. Westport, Connecticut and London, Bergin and Garvey.

Goldberg, P., Weiner, S., Bar-Yosef, O., Xu, Q. and Liu, J. (2001) Site formation processes at Zhoukoudian, China. *Journal of Human Evolution* 41(5), 483–530.

Goldman, L. R. (1999) From pot to polemic: uses and abuses of cannibalism. In L. R. Goldman (ed.) *The Anthropology of Cannibalism*, 1–26. Westport, Connecticut and London, Bergin and Garvey.

Graver, S., Sobolik, K. D. and Whittaker, J. (2002) Cannibalism or violent death alone? Human remains at a small Anasazi site. In W. D. Haglund and M. H. Sorg (eds.) *Advances in Forensic Taponomy: Method, Theory, and Archaeological Perspectives*, 309–320. Boca Raton (FL), CRC Press.

Grayson, D. K. (1990) Donner Party deaths: a demographic assessment. *Journal of Anthropological Research* 46(3), 223–242.

Haas, J. (1990) Warfare and the evolution of tribal polities in the prehistoric Southwest. In J. Haas (ed.) *The Anthropology of Warfare*, 171–189. Cambridge, Cambridge University Press.

Hamilakis, Y. (1998) Eating the dead; mortuary feasting and the political economy of the memory in the Bronze Age Aegean. In K. Branigan (ed.) *Cemetery and Society in the Aegean Bronze Age*, 115–132. Sheffield , Sheffield University Press.

Hamilakis, Y. and Konsolaki, E. (2004) Pigs for the gods: burnt animal sacrifices as embodied rituals at a Mycenaean sanctuary. *Oxford Journal of Archaeology* 23(2), 135–151.

Harner, M. (1977) The ecological basis for Aztec sacrifice. *American Ethnologist* 4, 117–135.

Harris, M. (1977) *Cannibals and Kings.* New York, Random House.

Hayden, B. (1990) Nimrods, piscators, pluckers, and planters: the emergence of food production. *Journal of Anthropological Archaeology* 9, 31–69.

Hayden, B. (1996) Feasting in prehistoric and traditional societies. In P. Wiessner and W. Shieffenhövel (eds.) *Food and the Status Quest*, 127–147. Providence and Oxford, Berghahn Books.

Herodotus (1987) *The History.* Translated by David Grene. Chicago, University of Chicago Press.

Hill, J. D. (1995) The pre-Roman Iron Age in Britain and Ireland: an overview. *Journal of World Prehistory* 9(1), 47–98.

Huntington, R. and Metcalf, P. (1991) *Celebrations of Death: The Anthropology of Mortuary Ritual.* Cambridge, Cambridge University Press.

Hurlbut, S.A. (2000) The taphonomy of cannibalism: a review of anthropogenic bone modification in the American Southwest. *International Journal of Osteoarchaeology* 10, 4–26.

Jamieson, J. B. (1983) An examination of prisoner-sacrifice and cannibalism at the St. Lawrence Iroquoian Roebuck site. *Canadian Journal of Archaeology* 7(2), 159–175.

Kantner, J. (1999) Anasazi mutilation and cannibalism in the American Southwest. In Goldman, L. (ed.) *The Anthropology of Cannibalism*, 75–104. Westport, Connecticut and London, Bergin and Garvey.

Keenleyside, A., Bertulli, M. and Fricke, H.C. (1997) The final days of the Franklin Expedition: new skeletal evidence. *Arctic* 50(1), 36–46.

Keesing, R. M. (1975) *Cultural Anthropology: A Contemporary Perspective* (Second Edition). Fort Worth (TX), Holt, Rhinehart, and Winston.

Knüsel, C. J. (2005) The physical evidence of warfare – subtle stigmata? In M. Parker Pearson and I. J. N. Thorpe (eds.) *Violence, Warfare, and Slavery*, 49–65. British Archaeological Reports, International Series 1374, Oxford, Archaeopress.

Knüsel, C. J. and Outram, A. K. (2004) Fragmentation: the zonation method applied to fragmented human remains from archaeological and forensic contexts. *Environmental Archaeology: The Journal of Human Palaeoecology* 9(1), 85–97.

Lambert, P. M., Billman, B. R. and Leonard, B. L. (2000a) Explaining variability in mutilated human bone assemblages from the American Southwest: a case study from the Southern Piedmont of Sleeping Ute Mountain, Colorado. *International Journal of Osteoarchaeology* 10, 49–64.

Lambert, P. M., Leonard, B. L., Billman, B. R., Marlar, R. A., Newman, M. E. and Reinhard, K. J. (2000b) Response to critique of the claim of cannibalism at Cowboy Wash. *American Antiquity* 65(2), 397–406.

LeBlanc, S. A. (1999) *Prehistoric Warfare in the American Southwest*. The University of Utah Press, Salt Lake City (UT).

Liston, M. A. and Baker, B. J. (1996) Reconstructing the massacre at Fort William Henry, New York. *International Journal of Osteoarchaeology* 6, 28–41.

Mafart, B., Pelletier, J.-P. and Fixot, M. (2004) Post-mortem ablation of the heart: a medieval funerary practice, a case observed at he cemetery of Gangobie Priory in the French Department of Alpes de Haute Provence. *International Journal of Osteoarchaeology* 14, 67–73.

Marlar, R.A., Leonard, B.L., Billman, B.R., Lambert, P.M. and Marlar, J.E. (2000) Biochemical evidence of cannibalism as a prehistoric Puebloan site in southwestern Colorado. *Nature* 407, 74–78.

Melbye, J. and Fairgrieve, S. I. (1994) A massacre and possible cannibalism in the Canadian Arctic: new evidence from the Saunaktuk site (NgTn-1). *Arctic Anthropology* 31(2), 57–77.

Murphy, E.M. and Mallory, J.P. (2000). Herodotus and the cannibals. *Antiquity* 74, 388–394.

Novak, S. 2000. Battle-related trauma. In V. Fiorato, A. Boylston, and C. J. Knüsel (eds), *Blood Red Roses: The Archaeology of a Mass Grave from Towton, AD 1461*, 90–102. Oxford: Oxbow Books.

Novak, S. A. and Kollman, D. D. (2000) Peri-mortem processing of human remains among the Great Basin Fremont. *International Journal of Osteoarchaeology* 10, 65–75.

Ogilvie, M.D. and Hilton, C.E. (2000) Ritualized violence in the Prehistoric American Southwest. *International Journal of Osteoarchaeology* 10, 27–48.

Olsen, S.L. and Shipman, P. (1994) Cutmarks and peri-mortem treatment of skeletal remains on the Northern Plains. In D. W. Owsley, and R. L. Jantz, (eds.) *Skeletal Biology of the Great Plains: Migration, Warfare, Health, and Subsistence*, 377–387. Washington, D.C., Smithsonian Institution Press.

Orschiedt, J. (1997) Beispiele für Sekundärbestattungen vom Jungpaläolithikum bis zum Neolithikum. *Ethnographisch-Archäologische Zeitshrift* 38, 325–345.

Outram, A. K. (1999) A comparison of paleo-Eskimo and Medieval Norse bone fat exploitation in Western Greenland. *Arctic Anthropology* 36(1–2), 103–117.

Outram, A. K. (2001) A new approach to identifying bone marrow and grease exploitation: why the indeterminate fragments should not be ignored. *Journal of Archaeological Science* 28, 401–410.

Outram, A. K. (2002) Bone fracture and within-bone nutrients: an experimentally based method for investigating levels of marrow extraction. In P. Miracle and N. Milner (eds.), *Consuming Passions and Patterns of Consumption*. 51–63. McDonald Institute Monograph Series, Cambridge.

Outram, A. K. (2003) Comparing levels of subsistence stress amongst Norse settlers in Iceland and Greenland using levels of bone fat exploitation as an indicator. *Environmental Archaeology: The Journal of Human Palaeoecology* 8, 119–128.

Outram, A. K. (2004) Applied models and indices vs. high resolution, observed data: detailed fracture and fragmentation analyses for the investigation of skeletal part abundance patterns. *Journal of Taphonomy* 2(3), 167–184.

Outram, A. K., Knüsel, C .J., Knight, S. and Harding, A. F. (2005) Understanding complex fragmented assemblages of human and animal remains: a fully integrated approach. *Journal of Archaeological Science,* 32(12), 1699–1710.

Owsley, D. W., Ubelaker, D. H., Houck, M. M., Sandness, K. L., Grant, W. E., Craig, E. A., Woltanski, T. J. and Peerwani, N. (1995) The role of forensic anthropology in the recovery and analysis of Branch Davidian Compound victims: techniques of analysis. *Journal of Forensic Sciences* 40(3), 341–348.

Parker Pearson, M. (1999) Food, sex and death: cosmologies in the British Iron Age with particular reference to East Yorkshire. *Cambridge Archaeological Journal* 9(1), 43–69.

Pickering, M. (1999) Consuming doubts: What people ate? Or what some people swallowed? In L. R. Goldman (ed.) *The Anthropology of Cannibalism*, 51–74. Westport, Connecticut and London, Bergin and Garvey.

Pickering, T. R., White, T. D. and Toth, N. (2000) Cutmarks on a Plio-Pleistocene hominid from Sterkfontein, South Africa. *American Journal of Physical Anthropology* 111, 579–584.

Pickering, T. R., Dominguez-Rodrigo, M., Egeland, C. P. and Brain, C.K. (2004) Beyond leopards: tooth marks and the contribution of multiple carnivore taxa to the accumulation of the Swartkrans Member 3 fossil assemblage. *Journal of Human Evolution* 46, 595–604.

Plummer, T. W. and Stanford, C. B. (2000) Analysis of a bone assemblage made by chimpanzees at Gombe National Park, Tanzania. *Journal of Human Evolution* 39, 345–365.

Rautman, A. E. and Fenton T. W. (2005) A case of historic cannibalism in the American West: implications for southwest archaeology. *American Antiquity* 70(2), 321–341.

Rumsey, A. (1999) The white man as cannibal in the New Guinea Highlands. In L. R. Goldman (ed.) *The Anthropology of Cannibalism*, 105–122. Westport, Connecticut and London, Bergin and Garvey.

Russell, M. D. (1987a) Bone breakage in the Krapina hominid collection. *American Journal of Physical Anthropology* 72, 373–379.

Russell, M. D. (1987b) Mortuary practices at the Krapina Neanderthal site. *American Journal of Physical Anthropology* 72, 381–397.

Sahlins, M. (1983) Raw women, cooked men, and other "great things" of the Fiji Islands. In P. Brown and D. Tuzin (eds.) *The Ethnography of Cannibalism*, 72–93. Washington, D.C., Society for Psychological Anthropology.

Sahlins, M. (1985) *Islands of History*. Chicago and London, University of Chicago Press.

Scott, D. D., Willey, P. and Connor, M. A. (2002) *They Died with Custer: Solders' Bones from the Battle of Little Bighorn.* Norman (OK), University of Oklahoma Press.

Shipman, P. and Rose, J. (1983) Early hominid hunting, butchering, and carcass processing behaviors: approaches to the fossil record. *Journal of Anthropological Archaeology* 10, 465–474.

Simon, J. J. K. (1992) Mortuary practices of the late Kachemak Tradition in southcentral Alaska: a perspective from the Crag Point Site, Kodiak Island. *Arctic Anthropology* 29(2), 130–149.

Simon, J. J. K. and Steffian, A. F. (1994) Cannibalism or complex mortuary behavior? In T. L. Bray and T. W. Killion (eds) *Reckoning with the Dead: The Larsen Bay Repatriation and the Smithsonian Institution,* 75–100. Smithsonian Institution Press, London.

Steadman, D. W., Antón, S. C. and Kirch, P. V. (2000) Ana Manuka: a prehistoric site on Mangaia, Cook Islands. *Antiquity* 74, 873–883.

Strathern, A. (1979) *Ongka: A Self-Account by a New Guinea Big-Man.* London, Duckworth.

Strathern, A. (1982) Witchcraft, greed, cannibalism, and death: some related themes from the New Guinea Highlands. In M. Bloch and J. Parry (eds.) *Death and the Regeneration of Life,* 111–133. Cambridge, Cambridge University Press.

Taylor, T. (2002) *The Buried Soul: How Humans Invented Death.* London, Fourth Estate.

Teschler-Nicola, M., Gerold, F., Bujatti-Narbeshuber, M. Prohaska, T., Latkoczy Ch., Stingeder, G. and Watkins, M. (1999) Evidence of genocide 7000 BP – Neolithic paradigm and geo-climatic reality. *Collegium Antropologicum* 23, 437–450.

Trinkaus, E. (1985) Cannibalism and burial at Krapina. *Journal of Human Evolution* 14, 203–216.

Turner, C. G. II (1993) Cannibalism in Chaco Canyon: the charnel pit excavated in 1926 at Small House ruin by Frank H. H. Roberts Jr. *American Journal of Physical Anthropology* 103, 1–22.

Turner, C. G. II and Turner, J. A. (1992) The first claim for cannibalism in the Southwest: Walter Hough's 1901 discovery at Canyon Butte Ruin 3, northeastern Arizona. *American Antiquity* 57(4), 661–682.

Turner, C. G. II and Turner, J. A. (1993) Taphonomic analysis of Anasazi skeletal remains from Largo-Gallina sites in northwestern New Mexico. *Journal for Anthropological Research* 49(2), 83–110.

Turner, C.G. II and Turner, J.A. (1995) Cannibalism in the prehistoric Southwest: occurrence, taphonomy, explanation and suggestions for standardized world definition. *Journal of Anthropological Science* 103, 1–22.

Turner, C.G. II and Turner, J.A. (1999) *Man Corn: Cannibalism and Violence in the American Southwest.* Salt Lake City (UT), University of Utah Press.

Tuzin, D. (1983) Cannibalism and Arapesh cosmology: a wartime incident with the Japanese. In P. Brown and D. Tuzin (eds.) *The Ethnography of Cannibalism,* 61–71. Washington, D.C., Society for Psychological Anthropology.

Tuzin, D. and Brown, P. (1983) Editor's preface. In P. Brown and D. Tuzin (eds.) *The Ethnography of Cannibalism,* 1–5. Washington, D.C., Society for Psychological Anthropology.

Ubelaker, D. H., Owsley, D. W., Houck, M. M., Craig, E., Grant, W., Woltanski, T., Fram, R., Sandness, K., and Peerwani, N. (1995) The role of forensic anthropology in the recovery and analysis of Branch Davidian Compound victims: recovery procedures and characteristics of the victims. *Journal of Forensic Sciences* 40(3), 335–340.

Ucko, P. J. (1969) Ethnography and archaeological interpretation of funerary remains. *World Archaeology* 1, 262–277.

Valentin, F. and Le Goff, I. (1998) La sépulture secondaire mésolithique de La Chaussée-Tirancourt: Fractures sur os frais ou os secs? *L'Anthropologie* 102, 91–95.

Verano, J. W. (1986) A Mass Burial of Mutilated Individuals at Pacatnamu. In C. B. Donnan and J. A. Cook (eds.). *The Pacatnamu Papers Vol.* 1.,117–138. University of California, Los Angeles, Museum of Cultural History.

Verano, J. W. (2001) The physical evidence of human sacrifice in Ancient Peru. In E.P. Benson and A.G. Cook (eds.) *Ritual Sacrifice in Ancient* Peru, 165–184. Austin (TX), University of Texas Press.

Villa, P. and Mahieu, E. (1991) Breakage patterns of human long bones. *Journal of Human Evolution* 21, 27–48.

Villa, P., Courtin, J., Helmer, D. (1988) Cannibalism in Old World prehistory. *Rivista di Antropologia (Roma)* LXVI, 47–64.

Villa, P., Bouville, C., Courtin, J., Helmer, D., Mahieu, E. Shipman, P., Belluomini, G. and Branca, M. (1986a) Cannibalism in the Neolithic. *Science* 233, 431–437.

Villa, P., Courtin, J., Helmer, D., Shipman, P., Bouville, C., and Mahieu, E. Belluomini, G. and Branca, M. (1986b) Un cas de cannibalisme au Néolithique: boucherie et rejet de restes humains et animaux dans la grotte de Fontbrégoua à Salernes (Var). *Gallia Préhistoire* 29, 143–171.

Wahl, J. and König, H. G. (1987) Anthropologische-traumatologische Untersuchung der menschlichen Skelettreste aus dem Bandkeramischen Massengrab bei Talheim, Kreis Heilbronn. *Fundberichte aus Baden-Württemberg,* 12, 65–193.

Walker, P. L. and Long, J. C. (1977) An experimental study of the morphological characteristics of tool marks. *American Antiquity* 42: 605–615.

Wheeler, R. E. M. (1943) *Maiden Castle, Dorset.* Oxford, Society of Antiquaries of London.

White, T. D. (1986) Cut marks on the Bodo cranium: a case of prehistoric defleshing. *American Journal of Physical Anthropology* 69, 503–509.

White, T. D. (1992) *Prehistoric Cannibalism at Mancos 5MTUMR-2346.* Princeton, (NJ), Princeton University Press.

White, T. D., and Toth, N. (1991) The faunal remains from Grotta Guattari: a taphonomic perspective. *Current Anthropology* 32, 118–124.

Whitley, M. (1943) Excavations at Chalbury Camp, Dorset, 1939. *Antiquaries Journal* 23, 98–121.

18.   Altering Identities: Body Modifications and the Pre-Columbian Maya

Pamela L. Geller

Introduction

Historically, body modifications have received ample attention in popular and scholarly literature. I would argue that this attention has been fraught with what are now seen as misrepresentations or denigrating attitudes. Descriptions of 'artificial cranial deformation' and 'dental mutilation' abound, shaping reception and understanding of rich, informative data sets. Tracing Western responses to modified bodies yields interesting insights. Comparison of modern investigators' descriptions and attitudes reveals little divergence from those of sixteenth and seventeenth-century chroniclers. As a result, complex and nuanced meanings encoded by practices of body modifications remain obscured.

To think about bodies and their transformation in a less ethnocentric light, the pre-Columbian Maya serve as an important case study. Maya peoples possessed a penchant for indelible body modifications. Fortunately for bioarchaeologists, Maya corporeal transformations possess observable, material dimensions. Buikstra (1997, 227) has noted, 'Although various explanations have been posited, ranging from social status to ethnic markers, we are still far from appreciating the reasons why the Maya chose to alter their appearance.' More than just an act of beautification or idiosyncratic behavior, Maya peoples' indelible body modifications speak to a connection between identity constitution and embodied experience. Society's molding of bodies, in both ritual and quotidian affairs, generates social identity, a forging of historical connections, aesthetic ideals, and future outlooks. Elaboration about practices involved in social identity construction is complemented by a discussion of practices for constructing self-identity. This second endeavour is indeed difficult for bioarchaeologists, since material and human remains are privileged in their work. Decidedly more phenomenological, reconstructing practices of self-identity constitution looks to sensual dimensions of modification, such as pain. Hence, the construction and reconstruction of identity, whether in public ritual venues or the individualised space of the body, possesses not just a conceptual, but material and corporeal dimensions.

A particularly salient example is the practice of dental modification. As a member of the Programme for Belize Archaeological Project (PfBAP), I joined other investigators in excavating burials containing dental remains, which were within and adjacent to the 250,000 acres owned by the Programme for Belize (PfB) in the Rio Bravo Conservation and Management Area (Fig. 18.1). Since its inception in 1992, the PfBAP has explored this previously little known and thickly forested area in northwestern Belize. Investigations have revealed dense settlement at sites ranging in size from major centers to house ruins. It is from these contexts that the materials discussed here derive. Moreover, as my perspective is a bioarchaeological one, dental data are better understood by also looking at mortuary contexts, individuals' osteobiographies, and ethnohistoric accounts.

The PfBAP burial sample consists of the remains of 132 individuals, who lived from the Late Preclassic to the Terminal Classic period [*c.*400 BC – AD 900]. The sample is composed of a cross-section of society; everyone from ruler to rural farmer is represented. Investigators have encountered the majority of burials in association with commoner and elite residences at 14 different sites. Maya peoples generally buried their deceased kin beneath or within their domestic structures; the individuals that comprise the sample are not an exception. From this configuration, we can recognize that Maya peoples literally lived with their ancestors, per McAnany (1995; see also Gillespie 2000, 2002). Just as manipulation of decedents' bodies facilitated transformation from liminal corpse to venerated ancestors, irreversible modification during life similarly signaled a shift in individuals' identities. As I will argue here, dental modification may have been carried out in the context of a rite of passage, and that associated pain and permanence may have signified an individual's transition from one identity to another.

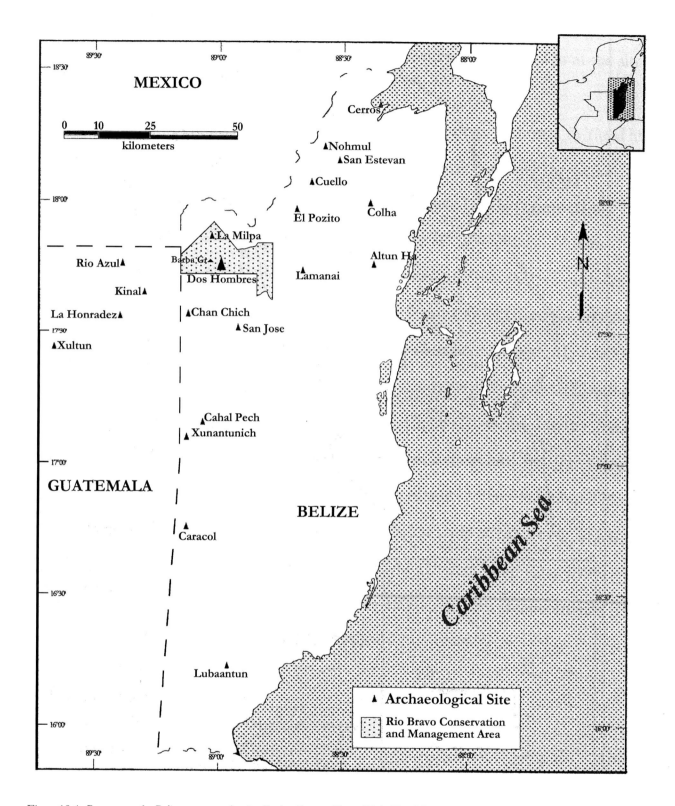

Figure 18.1. Programme for Belize property, showing Barba Group, Chan Chich, Dos Hombres, La Milpa, and adjacent sites (Reproduced courtesy of Brett Houk).

The modified body in western discourse

Sixteenth and seventeenth-century perceptions

Writings from the sixteenth and seventeenth centuries contain numerous reflections about the human body. Study of "Others'" bodies (*i.e.* native, non-Western bodies) grew out of Western medical tradition in which the "theatrical display" of bodies provided anatomists with the resources for dissection lessons as well as authoritative claims (Laqueur 1990, 74–75). As anatomical or native non-Western specimens, bodies and their mutability were objects of curiosity and ambivalence, if not outright aversion.

The writings of John Bulwer, a London physician who also developed an interest in rhetoric, psychology, and ethnology, serve as case in point. Woven through Bulwer's works is a fascination with the corporeal and its communicative capabilities. Body modifications as inscriptive practice provide the focus for his fourth and final work, *Anthropometamorphosis, man transform'd; or, The artificiall changeling* (1650). Written in the style of an armchair ethnography, the text provides a temporally and spatially sweeping consideration of the body's malleability, somewhat akin to a literary cabinet of curiosities. According to Bulwer, the natural body represented a flawless blueprint designed by God, and its "deformation" resulted from mental depravity and renunciation of Judeo-Christian beliefs. In fact, Bulwer viewed all alterations with equal distaste, whether as extreme as nose removal or inconsequential seeming as hair styling. Condemning English youths, effeminate gallants, and "cosmetic-ed" women for their corporeal transgressions, Bulwer nonetheless asserted that cultural modifications of flesh and bone, indeed crimes against God, were at their worst in the Americas.

Of course, historically contingent religious, political and ideological contexts are what framed Bulwer's secondary gleaning of corporeal inscriptions. *Anthropometamorphosis* emerged from an epoch of *conquistadores* and Cartesian thinkers. His work was born of the necessity to clarify and categorize burgeoning knowledge of the world's flora, fauna, geography, and people, which occurred during this 'Age of Discovery'. Admittedly, Bulwer does not represent seventeenth-century European society's sentiments indiscriminately. His voice did, however, resonate with literate and multi-lingual intellects dispersed throughout the continent (Campbell 1999, 15–16). The writings of Europeans chronicling the New World similarly find a place in this developing dialogue, as well.

During this time, vehement opposition to somatic alterations and differences delved into the longstanding issue of human constitution and nature. How to conceive of Amerindians – so dramatically different in form, style, custom, and belief – remained a continuing problem for missionaries, *conquistadores*, colonizers, and European recipients of information removed from first-hand experiences. European unease with religious incongruities went hand in glove with corporeal disparities – skin color, costumes, *and* permanent body modification. Chroniclers of the New World detailed the artificially changed bodies of native peoples as visibly distinct from God's intended, Christian design, the thread of which Bulwer picked up and entwined through his own treatise (*e.g.* Tozzer 1941; Cortés 1960; Diaz del Castillo 1963; Sahagún 1971). In trying to understand the 'Other', chroniclers in fact bred misunderstanding, which subsequently contributed to fallacious and denigrating representations of New World natives. As visual cues, corporeal alterations added further support to presumed savagery, technological failings, cultural inferiority, and Godless-ness. For missionaries in their quest to civilize and convert native peoples, the continuing presence of indelible body modifications justified their noble enterprise, and subsequent abolition of these marks highlighted their success.

Contemporary perception and perpetuation

Almost four centuries later negative perceptions and responses persist, further obscuring the complex meanings encoded in the puncturing of skin, the modifying of dentition, and the reshaping of cranial bones. Reactions to the recent resurgence of body modifications within contemporary Western society provide ample evidence of such attitudes.

In their investigations of body modifications, physical anthropologists are not exempt when it comes to disparaging attitudes, as evidenced by their invocation of value-laden language. While there are notable exceptions (*e.g.* Jacobi 2000; F. Saul 1972; F. Saul and J. Saul 1991; Havill *et al.* 1997; J. Saul and F. Saul 1997), many bioarchaeologists still commonly use phrases like 'artificial cranial deformation' and 'dental mutilation' (*e.g.* Owsley and Guerin 1982; Cocilovo and Garrett 1988; López Olivares 1997; Tiesler 1998; Alt *et al.* 1999; Costa-Junqueira 2001; Özbek 2001). While these terms are likely the result of historical convention, it is important to advocate usage of 'cranial shaping' and 'dental modification', as pointed out early on by Frank Saul (1972). Less ethnocentric descriptions lend themselves to productive interpretations of past modifiers' marks.

Furthermore, contemporary body modifiers are viewed with similar negative attitudes. Popular, medical, and scholarly sources level vehement opposition at countercultural 'modern primitives', who reference the styles and techniques of non-Western body modifiers in their own alterations. These sources often identify extreme modifications practiced by modern primitives as not only disfiguring, but symptomatic of latent psychological disorders (*e.g.* Favazza 1996; Koenig and Carnes 1999; Milner and Eichold 2001). As Bulwer espoused so vocally more than 350 years ago, the body is still conceived as a space whose boundaries should not be dissolved. Despite proclamation by 'modern primitives' that their alterations are designed to recreate the ideal, natural, beautiful, and primal body (Musafar 1996; Rosenblatt 1997), critics still assert that corporeal modification undermines the body's unity. Corporeal alterations remain visually discordant and unsettling to mainstream communities. The subtext of contemporary, disparaging responses mirrors Enlightenment attitudes mentioned earlier – corporeal modification undermines the body's integrity, giving rise to psychological imbalance and anti-social behavior.

Putting aside the suggestion of mental illness, countercultural reinterpretations of body modifications by 'modern primitives' are not without interpretive problems. First, conflation of these practices into a single corpus of bodily transformations fails to recognize often subtle historical shifts in artistry and meaning. Second, many modern primitives assert that body modifications are personal, thereby reinforcing creation and control of one's self-identity. However, Orlan, a French performance artist, who uses extreme body modifications as a key component in her work, recognizes indeed that the opposite is true:

> It's quite obvious that the majority of people who are into those things are liberating themselves from the dictates of a certain society, but in fact it all boils down to the same thing because they are conforming to the dictates of a smaller, mini-society. (Orlan in Ayers 2000, 182)

In fact, the increasing trendiness of body modifications, such as multiple piercings and tattoos, in Western society has demystified these corporeal alterations to a certain extent. In turn, these practices have in fact become more accessible and accepted by mainstream communities. Moreover, a certain degree of shock value provides an intrinsic motivation for modifications, as Orlan also recognizes and uses to her benefit. Extraordinary, seditious, and individualized performances downplay the fact that such practices and permanent marks may be quite prosaic and accepted when situated in their original cultural contexts. Finally, in their glossing of all native peoples as primitive and immutable (Rosenblatt 1997, 322), practitioners neglect or misconstrue the specific cultural meanings that underlie corporeal alterations.

As a counterpoint to the 'modern primitive' movement, I now reflect upon practitioners of plastic surgery. In the United States and Latin America, plastic surgeries, generally intrusive and bloody acts of corporeal transformation, are not regarded with similar derision, though very few extreme cases do provide exceptions (*e.g.* Michael Jackson). The linguistic usage of 'deformation', 'hazard', 'deviance', and 'mutilation', is not part of that domain. Instead, cosmetic surgeries are conceived of as acts of beautification, designed to produce bodies which appear seemingly natural, or unmarked by culture. In these instances, the corporeal ends are socially acceptable ones, regulated by an aesthetic ideology. In conducting ethnographic work at a plastic surgery center in the United States, Huss-Ashmore (2000, 27) has recognized that the aim of cosmetic surgery is to produce 'a new and better

person', and consequently, an internalized sense of self is realised on an exterior façade. She presents plastic surgery as a healing system within the field of medicine.

In irreversibly modifying the body to approximate a cultural, or counter-cultural ideal, how different are practitioners of cosmetic surgeries and 'modern primitives'? Many would argue that while the means of modification are similar, the ends are not. I, however, assert that the ends are more similar than most might feel comfortable admitting. Drawing from my discussion of 'modern primitives' and plastic surgery proponents, I have identified two significant dimensions of corporeal alteration, which I believe were also at issue for the pre-Columbian Maya. First, one important end of body modifications is to facilitate identity (re)constitution. Second, many, though not all, body modifications produce painful sensations. These characteristics are interrelated, and may further enlighten interpretations about case studies distanced in space and time, such as the pre-Columbian Maya and their practice of dental modification, as I now discuss.

The study of pre-Columbian Maya body modifications

Physical anthropologists' early scholarship centered on irreversible body modifications, especially those of the pre-Columbian Maya (Buikstra 1997, 224). However, mounting information about shaped crania and modified dentition led not to robust interpretations, but rather to the creation of enduring classificatory systems (*e.g.* Dembo and Imbelloni 1938; Dingwall 1931; Romero Molina 1951, 1952, 1960, 1965, 1970; Cifuentes Aguirre 1963). In fact, Maya bioarchaeologists still reference Romero Molina's taxonomic system for dental modification, and in this discussion, I do not take exception.

Referencing American dental collections housed at Mexico's Museo Nacional de Antropología, Romero Molina classified modifications according to design and location on the tooth (Fig. 18.2). Design distinctions included the following: engraving labial surfaces; inlaying labial surfaces with semi-precious stones, such as hematite, jade, and turquoise; and filing or removing incisal edges or corners. These designs could either be displayed singly or in simultaneous combinations. From his analysis of 1212 modified teeth, Romero Molina organized designs into seven types (A through G); within these types he numbered smaller sub-types. Altogether, he documented a total of 59 variants. While exceedingly useful, Romero Molina's categorisations are beginning to show their age; five decades of subsequent excavation and analysis have uncovered several dental modifications that do not fit neatly into these categories. Later, I discuss the exigency of regarding dental designs not as categories, but rather as single stages in a larger decorative process. Several Romero types seem to be foundational signs upon which modifiers elaborated. Examination of connections

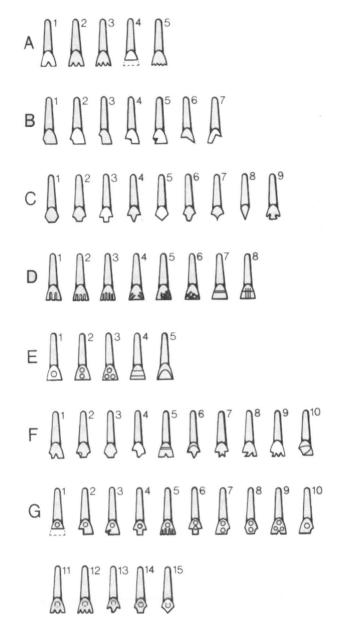

Figure 18.2. Romero Molina's classification of modified dentition (adapted from Romero Molina 1970, 51).

between designs facilitates understanding of the social processes that motivated modification.

While categorisation was invaluable for establishing basic evaluative criteria, analysed human remains were often not contextualised with respect to geography and chronology in early studies. Analysis of human remains generally occurred in settings far removed in time and space from excavations. *In situ* examination was a rarity, and skeletal analysts were provided with little background information about archaeological contexts and/or associations (but see Agrinier 1964; Stewart 1953). These lacunae were brought into sharp relief by emerging investigative interests in the 1960's. Spatial distribution of modification types was becoming an increasingly important concern (*e.g.* Romero Molina 1952, 1965; Comas 1969).

The study of deliberate corporeal transformation as an area of bioarchaeological concern has not fallen out of fashion. It has, however, remained quiescent. The vast majority of work is descriptive – an absorption with 'what' (type) and 'how' (process) (*e.g.* Havill *et al.* 1997). Suggestions as to 'why' modification was undertaken appear less frequently in the literature (though see López Olivares 1997). Past researchers have ventured tentative interpretations, such as beautification (Linné, 1940; Havill *et al.* 1997), markers of sex differences (Linné 1940), magical motivations (Linné 1940; Romero Molina 1951, 50–51), ethnic distinctions (Boas 1890; Dembo and Imbelloni 1938), occupational specialisation (Becker 1973), or elevated socioeconomic status (Romero Molina 1958; Comas 1969). This last explanation has had considerable longevity. Such an interpretation was not entirely unfounded, as archaeologists in the late-nineteenth and early-twentieth centuries were preoccupied with elite tombs, in which preservation was kinder to skeletal materials. Artistic representations portraying elites with elaborate body modifications provided further evidence that elevated social status dictated the alteration of bodies, indelible sumptuary laws as the case may be. However, an increase in excavations of commoner residences – from mid-twentieth century onward – necessitates rethinking representations of Maya body modifiers' identities and positions within society.

I consider the practice of dental modification as a means for constructing identities. As support, I look to individuals with dental modification who were excavated from graves associated with elite and commoner residences in PfB. Seeing that dental modifications make one aware of his or her body, I also argue that they afford ingress for discussing issues of embodiment in addition to the constitution of identity.

Dental modifications of the Maya

Unlike their Zapotec neighbors, pre-Columbian Maya portraiture rarely portrays individuals with mouths agape and dentition modified. Yet, from dental remains and historical documentation, we know that Maya peoples long practiced dental modification. At the site of Cuello in northwestern Belize, Saul and Saul (1997, 45–46) have uncovered the earliest known evidence of dental modification, a type of filing that dates to ca. 900 BC. Documented by Landa (Tozzer 1941, 125) at the time of Spanish conquest, the practice of modifying dentition occurred with less and less frequency following adamant Church prohibition (Havill *et al.* 1997, 103; Jacobi 2000, 175).

Burial data from northwestern Belize

The PfBAP burial sample serves as a case study in this discussion of dental modification. Of the sample's 132 individuals, the dentitions of 72 individuals were not sufficiently preserved to examine evidence for modification (Table 18.1). Unfortunately, preservation in the tropical Maya lowlands is very poor. Various taphonomic forces leave human remains in a highly fragmented and incomplete state. Teeth, the most durable component of the human body, also fall victim as root acids strip them of enamel. Moreover, the small size of teeth may prevent their archaeological recovery, as they go unnoticed in situ or slip through screens. With this being said, the number of modified teeth per individual may be the result of factors aside from those cultural activities that occurred during an individual's life.

Despite this, 60 individuals could be assessed for the presence or absence of dental modification. Twenty-six individuals possessed at least one modified tooth, and one individual displayed fully eight modified teeth (see Table 18.1). The majority of individuals modified their maxillary teeth, which are more visible than mandibular teeth when mouths are open. In the case of maxillary dentition, central incisors (N=27) were modified more often than were lateral incisors or canines (N=12 and N=13, respectively). There is also one individual with a modified premolar. Prevalence of designs on the visually prominent maxillary anterior teeth seems to be in keeping with the larger Maya pattern (Fastlicht ,1962; Havill *et al.*, 1997; Jacobi, 2000, 175).

Stylistically speaking, 16 different Romero types are evidenced on maxillary and mandibular teeth in the PfBAP sample (Table 18.2). I will discuss several of these types in greater detail later. There were three instances in which a modified tooth could have been categorised as two different types. Several individuals also displayed more than one type of modification. For example, one individual with a total of eight modified teeth had maxillary right and left mesial incisors and canines with Romero type B-2, maxillary right and left lateral incisors with Romero type A-4, and mandibular right and left mesial incisors with Romero type A-2.

With information about dental modification encountered at PfB sites in hand, I will make inferences about the PfBAP sample. Before proposing explanations for dental modification, I first consider pain as an intended effect of dental modification, and how the Maya may have made pain meaningful culturally. Discussion of the painful dimensions of dental modification is followed by demographic reconstruction. The 'whos' of dental modification are considered with respect to age, sex, 'ethnicity', and social position. For the PfBAP sample, individuals were aged and sexed using standard and well-

	No. of Individuals
Unknown	72
Dental modification absent	34
Represented by 6 teeth or more	30
Represented by 5 teeth or fewer	4
Dental modification present	26*
Mandibular modification	4
Maxillary modification	23
Total individuals in PfBAP sample	132

*Table 18.1. Occurrence of dental modification in PfBAP sample. *One individual had both maxillary and mandibular dental modification.*

Romero Types	Male*	Female*	Sex ?	Total
A-1	1			1
A-1 or B-7	1			1
A-2	1			1
A-4	4	1		5
B-2	1		1	2
B-2 or B-4			1	1
B-3	1			1
B-4	5	2		7
B-4 or B-5	1			1
B-5		2	2	4
B-?			1	1
C-3	1			1
C-5	1			1
E-1	3			3
F-1		1		1
F-4	2			2
F-9		1		1
G-3	1			1
G-15	1			1

*Table 18.2. Number of PfBAP individuals by sex with Romero types. *Male and Female are the sum of Male+Male? and Female+Female?, respectively.*

established techniques (*i.e.* Krogman and İşcan 1986, 51–52; Brooks and Suchey 1990; Saul and Saul 1991; Buikstra and Ubelaker 1994; White 2000). These data were correlated with information gleaned from mortuary contexts and materials, specifically grave types, locations, and materials, and goods, to make inferences about social relationships. I conclude with a metaphoric reckoning of the body as an alternative writing surface.

Dental modification and pain

By all accounts dental modification seems to be an exceedingly painful process, seeing that it involves the permanent dissolution of a corporeal boundary via filing, engraving, or drilling. In fact, altering dentition generates pain that is very real and experimentally replicable. In a recent conversation with my family dentist, Dr. Feinhals emphasized the excruciating pain that would result from all of the aforementioned dental procedures without modern day novocain or anesthesia. "It would hurt like hell," he said to me. And, judging from the discomfort incurred from my minor scraping of plaque build up, I believe him.

This is not to say that the pre-Columbian Maya had no effective analgesic against dental pain. Surrounding tropical environments contained abundant and readily available natural resources quite feasibly utilized for

brewing up pain relievers. In fact, Landa (Tozzer 1941, 198) recorded "a tree [*Thevetia peruviana*] whose milk is an especial medicine for curing teeth," though its direct application to modified dentition is not noted. Nonetheless, we all know from our own experiences at the dentist, technologically and medically savvy in comparison to the pre-Columbian Maya, that pain and discomfort typify filing, engraving, and drilling. Anesthesia and analgesics do not completely eliminate these sensations; they only dull them. Nonetheless, consideration of pain resulting from dental modifications has only received passing mention in the literature (Linné 1940, 8).

The experience of pain, especially as a result of intentional dental modification, raises some intriguing questions about its cultural construction and neurological transmission: Can we talk about physiological unity? Is pain primal? Or, are encounters with pain strictly mediated by culture and history? I would advance that certain occurrences produce pain regardless of one's cultural and historical circumstances; to name a few, there are childbirth, torture, circumcision, and – relevant for this discussion – dental modification. As Turner (1984, 38–39) states, 'The body is simultaneously an environment (part of nature) and a medium of the self (part of culture).' In other words, there exist universal physiological needs and responses, though ascribed symbols are often contingent upon culture and history. Moreover, psychiatric studies have demonstrated that pain threshold, the neurophysiologic detection of pain, does not vary cross culturally, but pain tolerance, which reflects behavioural responses to pain, is profoundly influenced by culture (*e.g.* Zatzick and Dimsdale 1990). Thus, pain presents a universal human sensation, though one that is channeled via specific cultural constructs.

In arguing for pain as culturally mediated, how did the Maya make the pain of tooth modification meaningful? I believe that modification of teeth figured into a process of becoming. I would suggest that the experience of pain during dental modification facilitated identity change. In the *Absent Body*, Leder (1990) has eloquently articulated that we are not really aware of our bodies unless they hurt or function improperly. Bodies are absent in their normal functioning. Pain brings individuals back into their bodies and transforms their experience of the world. Similarly, a shift in individuals' identities also changes how they experience and interact with the world. Thus, it is possible to argue that painful transformations of bodies provide the impetus for transformations of selves.

Admittedly, the experience of pain is a very personal one in that it allows for an exploration of one's self through the body (*e.g.* Honkasalo 2001). Yet, I also believe that painful body modifications, like dental alteration, were meant to be shared, either through empathy or simultaneous experience. Morinis (1985) has argued that pain produced in the moments of corporeal altering is central – not ancillary – to the successful enactment of becoming, as in the case of group initiation rituals. The importance of pain, whether experienced personally or as a product of empathy, is undeniable. In these instances, construction of pain becomes a joint venture, and corporeal inscriptions are experienced as a social body. 'Feeling someone's pain' becomes very appropriate in this situation, and a sense of belonging to a select group is fostered.

The dual occurrence of painful corporeal alteration and empathy figures prominently in non-Western rites associated with identity change. As numerous ethnographic cases detail (*e.g.* Blackwood and Danby 1955; Seeger 1975; Rubin ed., 1988; Kapchan 1993), it is often during rites of passage that changes are wrought to the body – foreskins are excised, nasal septa are pierced, body parts are tattooed, dentition is modified. The individual is emotionally, mentally, *and* physically stressed. Performative rites of passage reintegrate the individual from his or her liminal, disembodied state into a newly acquired identity. To complete the process of becoming, the individual is reintroduced into the community during the final stage replete with a newly constituted identity and changed body. And while painful memories fade, visible body modifications offer an enduring connection for participants and a permanent reminder for viewers. Permanent marks are iconic not only for unique cultural meanings encoded in, but also for pain generated by, transformative practices. Following from this, I now consider more closely the modified teeth of individuals in the PfBAP sample with respect to age, sex, ethnicity, and social status. Consideration of demography perhaps offers greater illumination about the connection between dental modification and identity constitution. Access to both dental and demographic dimensions of the pre-Columbian PfBAP populace draws on the continuing research under direction of Frank Saul and Julie Saul.

Demography and dentition

Because individuals' age ranges represent ages at death, rather than the age at which modifications occurred, I consider it only briefly in this discussion. It was neither possible to determine for individuals at what ages dental modifications occurred nor the ages at which additional modifications were made. However, all dental modifications were found on permanent, adult teeth (N=26 individuals, 26.8% of total number of adults in the

sample). Not one incidence of dental modification was identified on deciduous dentition. The youngest individual with dental modification of permanent teeth was 14–20 years at death. This age range was based upon dental development; the second mandibular molar had complete roots and slight wear, but the third molar had not erupted yet. Of the 97 adults in the PfBAP sample, 25 individuals (25.8%) did not have any signs of dental modification on their permanent teeth. Thus, there does not appear to be any significant difference between those who did have their teeth modified and those who did not. Although the sample is small, PfBAP evidence suggests that modification of teeth was perhaps linked to an identity that could occur only after an individual was socially perceived as a viable adult.

The second demographic dimension considered is variation according to sex. In the sixteenth century, Diego de Landa (in Tozzer 1941, 125) observed, 'The Indian woman of Yucatan are generally better looking than Spanish women and larger and well made…they had a custom of filing their teeth leaving them like the saw, and this they considered elegant.' He does not mention whether or not men modified their teeth. In the PfBAP sample, 71 individuals (53.8%) in the sample could be assessed as to sex. Table 18.3 summarizes PfBAP individuals by sex. The 71 sexed individuals include those with dental modification, those without dental modification, and those for whom it was unknown whether dental modification was present or absent.

Table 18.4 specifically deals with the 41 sexed individuals who could be assessed for the presence (N=22) or absence (N=19) of dental modification. Not included in Table 18.4 are four individuals with dental modification but unknown sex. Of those individuals who do not display dental modification, sex could not be determined in the case of 15 individuals, but 9 of them were immature individuals. Immature individuals are generally "designated unknown or uncertain as to sex because sexual dimorphism usually becomes distinct only in late adolescence" (Saul and Saul 1991, 135).

In the PfBAP sample, bodies sexed as males and females are both dentally modified. Recognizing that the sample is a small one, it seems that females were more likely to have their teeth modified than not, while males were just as likely to have their teeth modified as they

	F	F?	F+F?	M	M?	M+M?	?
N=	10	11	21	21	29	50	61
% of total (N=132)	7.5	(?)	15.9	15.9	(?)	37.9	46.2

Table 18.3. PfBAP individuals by sex.

	No. with dental modification	% of total sexed (N=71)	No. without dental modification	% of total sexed (N=71)
F	4	5.6	2	2.8
F?	2	(?)	0	(?)
F+F?	6	8.5	2	2.8
M	5	7.0	10	14.1
M?	11	(?)	7	(?)
M+M?	16	22.5	17	23.9

Table 18.4. PfBAP individuals by sex with and without dental modification.

were not. For the most part, the sample is too small to say whether or not certain dental designs were restricted to different sexes. The one exception is Romero E-1, which only occurred on elite males' dentition, as I will discuss later (see Table 18.2).

Past investigators have argued that dental modification marked ethnic differences, or, in the case of the more homogenous pre-Columbian Maya, community identity. If this was the case, I would expect to find specific types limited to certain sites. However, I found no evidence for this argument. Analysis of modified individuals' spatial distribution revealed that particular modification types did not appear to be site-specific for non-elite members of society. However, as I will discuss next in my consideration of social status, elite members of society from spatially distant sites did display similar types of dental modification.

Long thought to be, and popularly perpetuated as, a marker of social status, dental modification did in fact occur among all assessable individuals of elevated status in the PfBAP sample. However, as I will consider following my discussion of modified elite individuals, the teeth of commoners were also so marked. The distinction between elite and commoner was determined by conjunctive consideration of graves' types, goods, locations, and building materials, as well as information learned from human remains (Geller, 2004). Unlike traditional Maya studies of burials, I do not take socioeconomic status, predicated upon wealth with respect to grave goods, labour expenditure, or sacrificed human lives, as the primary or most interesting constituent of social identity (*e.g.* Rathje 1970; Welsh 1988; Krejci and Culbert 1992). Rather, a bioarchaeological approach is highly useful for considering the variable and vibrant lives of analysed decedents (*e.g.* Saul and Saul 1989; Fitzsimmons *et al.* 2003; Buikstra *et al.* 2004). Identity is interconnected with gender, age, occupation, religious affiliation, health status, and a host of additional factors that may or may not be relevant to a Maya case study.

PfBAP excavators encountered a total of four architecturally laborious tombs with a rich and varied array

of grave goods. These were located at spatially disparate sites in PfB (see Fig. 18.1). No teeth were recovered from the Barba Group rock-cut tomb and the occupant of the La Milpa tomb exhibited extreme ante-mortem tooth loss, as evidenced by an edentulous mandible.

In the case of individuals of elevated status with dental modification, the sample is admittedly a small one (N=3). Tombs housing dentally modified individuals were encountered at the sites of Chan Chich and Dos Hombres. The Chan Chich rock-cut tomb housing one individual dated to the Protoclassic (ca. AD 150–250), and was situated beneath the site's central platform. The Dos Hombres stone-lined tomb was Early Classic (ca. AD 250–550) in date, contained two individuals, and was encountered beneath the floor of an elite house group 100m to the southwest of the site's center. The Chan Chich tomb contained a single male with three modified, maxillary teeth – Romero G-15 on the right canine, Romero C-5 on the left canine, and Romero E-1 on the right lateral incisor (see Fig. 18.2). The right canine's and incisor's inserts were hematite. The Dos Hombres tomb housed the remains of two males?, both of whom displayed dental modification. These individuals both possessed Romero E-1 with hematite inlays on their maxillary teeth.

Individuals interred within these tombs were the sample's primary recipients of inlays, suggesting abidance of sumptuary laws and/or perhaps a stylistic sign of the times. There is, however, one exception, a Late Classic burial from Dos Hombres. The individual in question was in fact interred in a pit situated above (and later in time than) the elite house group's aforementioned stone-lined tomb. His maxillary canines both had a Romero G-3 design with hematite inserts, the singular example of this type in the sample. Despite his grave type, other mortuary data – grave location, grave goods, associated architectural features – and presumed familial ties suggest he was a socially prominent person.

When assessable, tomb individuals displayed an interesting pattern of modification, hinting that dental modification perhaps mark cumulative processes rather than single, discrete events. These individuals all have Romero E-1 type with hematite inlays, and they only appear on maxillary teeth. No one else in the entire PfBAP sample had this type of modification. Dos Hombres individuals exhibited no additional types. The Chan Chich individual, however, also displayed Romero G-15 and C-5 (see Fig. 18.2). Interestingly enough, Romero G-15 shares stylistic elements with Romero E-1 and Romero C-5. In both cases, Romero G-15 represents a more advanced stage of modification. After filing the incisal edges of the right and left canines into a point (Romero C-5), a circular hematite inlay was later inserted into the right canine (Romero G-15). It is also possible that the right canine was first inlaid, like the adjacent lateral incisor (Romero E-1), and subsequently its sides were filed into a point (Romero G-15). All other maxillary teeth that were present retained no traces of either dental filing or inlaying. Admittedly, we do not know the order in which these modifications were undertaken. However, stylistic overlap between these types possibly indicates that intricate dental modifications did not occur in one fell swoop. Conception of decorative types as works in progress, rather than static classificatory types, suggests that for some prominent individuals dental modification perhaps was an ongoing process and exercise in extension of one's pain threshold.

It is possible that addition of designs to a previously modified tooth signified promotion from one political or religious office to a more prestigious position. Sustenance of painful procedures, not once but twice, perhaps stressed the modified individual's worthiness, as evidenced by the occupant interred within the Chan Chich tomb. Irreversibility of dental modification provided a lasting image and reminder of moments of performative filing or inlaying. Sharing of stylistic types by these individuals perhaps signal a specific, restricted kind of identity, likely related to rulership and/or socio-religious prominence. Moreover, it is possible that females were excluded from such identity constitution, seeing that individuals displaying these distinctive types were males or possible males. Finally, specific dental types displayed by PfB's individuals may have linked them with similarly decorated and powerful others at spatially distant centers, such as Copan, Tikal, Nakbe, and Lubaantún (Hammond *et al.* 1975; Buikstra *et al.* 2004).

Findings in tombs indeed offer a point of contrast with the remainder of the PfBAP sample, which as I mentioned earlier contained both males and females with dental modification. As I now discuss, the grave types, locations, and dental designs of modified commoner males and females suggest they filled important positions within their communities, though perhaps not the larger society, like modified, elite individuals.

Non-elites and dental modification

As evidenced by the PfBAP sample, modification was not simply performed on the dentition of individuals worthy of tomb interment. Dentally modified individuals were also interred in other grave types, which included cists, pits, and simple graves. All of these graves were encountered in association with structures primarily residential in function. Further challenging the restriction of dental modification to individuals of high-status is the fact that grave goods were not recovered from the graves of eleven individuals in the sample. Although given the combined archaeological adversaries of humidity, insects, and burrowing animals, it is possible that grave goods were interred but failed to preserve.

The most prevalent dental design in the PfBAP sample corresponds to the Romero B category (Fig. 18.3). Teeth exhibiting Romero B types, the exception being Romero B-7, have notched lateral corners. Several researchers have deliberated over the connection between Sun God imagery and dentition with Romero B designs (Blom *et al.*, 1934, 10–11; Coe 1959, 136; Linné, 1940, 14). Notching the lateral corners of maxillary central incisors produces a "T"-shaped pattern similar to that sported by a stylized Sun God (Fig. 18.4). Houston and Taube (2000, 268) identify this design as the *ik* sign, which denotes wind, breath, and aroma. In the PfBAP sample, there are 11 individuals who have at least one tooth with Romero B designs. Lateral notching on both upper, central incisors occurs in 4 of these 11 individuals. With respect to sex,

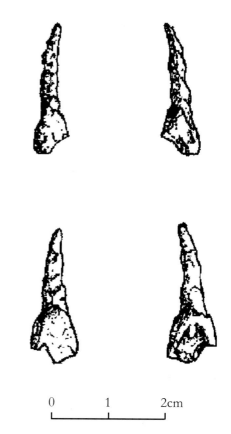

0   1   2cm

Figure 18.3. Some of examples of PfBAP teeth modified the Romero B style (Drawn by Jenifer Bryan).

Figure 18.4. Stylized Sun God sculpture from Copan. Notice the notched central incisors in the style of Romero B (Photograph taken by author).

both males and females displayed Romero B types. It is possible to infer that identities associated with dental modification were not contingent upon sexual differences.

I suggest that individuals with notched lateral incisors (particularly Romero B types), regardless of sex, were distinct and perhaps central figures within their communities, though perhaps not on par with tomb occupants. As mentioned earlier, not all individuals had their teeth modified, suggesting that certain select individuals within communities achieved specific social identities distinguishing them from other members that comprised the larger community. Despite the relative paucity of their mortuary materials, inasmuch as grave types, materials, and goods are concerned, dental modifications perhaps signaled their prominence. Selection of specific dental designs that alluded to the divine perhaps could have legitimated these individuals' standing within their communities.

Romero B designs, as well as other designs which involved filing, are also more accessible – technically, materially, and socially – than the Romero E, C, and G types worn by tomb occupants. Indeed, Maya peoples were most likely familiar with dental wear given their coarse diet. Drilling and inlaying of semi-precious stones, however, may have necessitated specialised training and access to limited resources. Thus, it is possible that similar to tomb occupants, endurance of painful modifications facilitated a shift in one's identity, but a shift in identity

that was less socially significant than those of elite individuals. This reconstitution of identity was visible on an exterior surface for all to see and empathise with, as well as suggested a more subtle realignment in one's sense of self.

Conclusion

Fortunately, for bioarchaeologists several varieties of intentional body modification remain conspicuous after millennia. In the case of the pre-Columbian Maya, dental remains retain the evidence of inlays and filings. In this discussion, I have argued that Maya dental modification represented an important cultural practice through which identities may have been reconstituted. Painful modifications suggest a subtler shift in one's sense of self, as an individual attempts to cohere their external surface and internal image. Refashioning an individual's body was also enacted according to socially acceptable norms that referenced culturally potent and widely understood symbols. Select modified individuals, perhaps prominent members of their respective communities, appropriated different designs and techniques at different levels of society, Romero E, C, and G types for individuals of elevated social positions and Romero B for commoner members of society. However, we do see similarities inasmuch as modifications were painful for all and only adults, or possibly individuals with newly acquired adult status, were modified. Ultimately, conceiving of body modifications as a means through which to reconstitute identity underscores the importance of considering modified bodies in a less ethnocentric light.

Acknowledgements

For the opportunity to participate in the PfBAP and permission to draw on its data, I thank Project Director Fred Valdez, who also served as a member of my dissertation committee. My four seasons in Belize prominently included apprenticeship to Frank Saul and Julie Saul, whom I also thank for permission to cite skeletal analyses from human remains whose study was under their direction. Critical comments by Miranda Stockett, Wendy Ashmore, and Jane Buikstra throughout the fomentation of these ideas significantly improved this manuscript, though I am responsible for any inconsistencies or inadequacies in the final product.

References

Agrinier, P. (1964) *The Archaeological Burials at Chiapa de Corzo and their Furniture.* Papers of the New World Archaeological Foundation no. 16, publ.12. Provo, Brigham Young University Press.

Alt, K. W., Parsche, F., Pahl, W. M. and Ziegelmayer, G. (1999) La deformación de la detadura como "decoración corporal": distribución, motivos y aspectos culturales. *Antropológicas* 15, 51–58.

Ayers, R. (2000) Serene and happy and distant: An interview with Orlan. In M. Featherstone (ed.) *Body Modification*, 171–84. SAGE Publications Ltd, London.

Becker, M. J. (1973) Archaeological evidence for occupational specialization among the Classic period Maya at Tikal, Guatemala. *American Antiquity* 38, 396–406.

Blackwood, B. and Danby, P. M. (1955) A study of artificial cranial deformation in New Britain. *Journal of the Royal Anthropological Institute of Great Britain and Ireland* 85(1/2), 173–191.

Blom, F. F., Grosjean, S. S. and H. Cummins (1934) Maya skull from the Uloa Valley, Republic of Honduras. *Tulane University Middle American Research Institute* 5, 1–24.

Boas, F. (1890) Cranium from Progreso, Yucatan. *Proceedings of the American Antiquarian Society* 6, 350–357.

Brooks, S. T. and Suchey J. M. (1990) Skeletal age determination based on the *Os Pubis*: A Comparison of the Acsadi-Nemeskeri and Suchey-Brooks methods. *Human Evolution* 5, 227–238.

Buikstra, J. E. (1997) Studying Maya bioarchaeology. In S. L. Whittington and D. M. Reed (eds.) *Bones of the Maya: Studies of Ancient Skeletons*, 221–228. Washington, D. C., Smithsonian Institution Press.

Buikstra, J. E. and Ubelaker, D. H. (1994) *Standards for Data Collection from Human Skeletal Remains*. Fayetteville, Arkansas Archaeological Survey Research Series No. 44.

Buikstra, J. E., Price, T. D., Wright, L. E., and Burton, J. A. (2004) Tombs from the Copan Acropolis: A life-history approach. In E. E. Bell, M. A. Canuto and R. J. Sharer (eds.) *Understanding Early Classic Copan*, 191–212. Philadelphia, PA, University of Pennsylvania Museum of Archaeology and Anthropology.

Bulwer, J. (1650) *Anthropometamorphosis: Man Transform'd; or, the ARTIFICIAL Changeling. Historically Presented, In the mad and cruel Gallantry, Foolish Bravery, ridiculous Beauty, Filthy Finenesse, and loathsome Lovelinesse of most NATIONS, Fashioning & altering their Bodies from the Mould intended by NATURE. With a VINDICATION of the Regular Beauty and Honesty of NATURE. AND An APPENDIX of the Pedigree of the ENGLISH GALLANT*. London, J. Hardesty.

Campbell, M. B. (1999) *Wonder & Science: Imagining Worlds in Early Modern Europe*. Ithaca, Cornell University Press.

Cifuentes Aguirre, O. (1963) *Odontología y Mutilaciones dentarias mayas*. Colección Editorial Universitaria no. 46. Guatemala, Editorial Universitaria.

Cocilovo, J. A. and Costa-Junqueira, M. A. (2001) La deformación artificial en el período Arcaíco de Arica. *Latin American Antiquity* 12(2), 203–214.

Coe, W. R. (1959) *Piedras Negras Archaeology: Artifacts, Caches, and Burials*. Philadelphia, The University Museum, University of Pennsylvania.

Columbus, C. (1960) *The Journal of Christopher Columbus*. New York, Clarkson N. Potter.

Comas, J. (1969) Algunos cráneos de la región maya. *Anales de Antropología* 6, 233–248.

Cortés, H. (1960) *Five letters, 1519–1526*. New York, Norton.

Dembo, A. and Imbelloni, J. (1938) *Deformaciones intencionales del cuerpo humana de carácter étnico*. Biblioteca Humanior, Argentina, Buenos Aires.

Díaz del Castillo, B. (1963) *The Conquest of New Spain*. New York, Penguin Putnam Inc.

Dingwall, E. J. (1931) *Artificial Cranial Deformation: A Contribution to the Study of Ethnic Mutilations*. London, John Bale, Sons & Danielsson, Ltd.

Fastlicht, S. (1962) Dental inlays and filing among the ancient Mayas.

Journal of the History of Medicine and Allied Sciences 17, 393–401.

Favazza, A. R. (1996) *Bodies under Siege: Self-mutilation and Body Modification in Culture and Psychiatry*. Baltimore, The John Hopkins University Press.

Fitzsimmons, J. L., Scherer, A., Houston, S. D., and Escobedo, H. L. (2003) Guardian of the acropolis: the sacred space of a royal burial at Piedras Negras, Guatemala. *Latin American Antiquity* 14(4), 449–468.

Garrett, J. (1988) Status, the warrior class, and artificial cranial deformation. In R.L. Blakely (ed.) *The King site: Continuity and contact in sixteenth-century Georgia*, 35–46. Athens, University of Georgia Press.

Geller, P. L. (2004) *Transforming Bodies, Transforming Identities: A Consideration of Pre-Columbian Maya Corporeal Beliefs and Practices*. Unpublished Ph.D. Thesis, Department of Anthropology, University of Pennsylvania, Philadelphia, PA.

Gillespie, S. (2000) Maya "nested houses": the ritual construction of place. In R.A. Joyce and S.D. Gillespie (eds.) *Beyond Kinship: Social and Material Reproduction in House Societies*, 135–60. Philadelphia, University of Pennsylvania Press.

Gillespie, S. (2002) Body and soul among the Maya: keeping the spirits in place. In H. Silverman and D.B. Small (eds.) *The Space and Place of Death*, 67–78. Washington, D.C., American Anthropological Association.

Havill, L. M., Warren, D. M., Jacobi, K. P., Gettelman, K. D., Colllins Cook, D. and Pyburn, K. A. (1997) Late Postclassic tooth filing at Chau Hiix and Tipu, Belize. In S. L. Whittington and D. M. Reed (eds.) *Bones of the Maya: Studies of Ancient Skeletons*, 89–104. Washington, D. C., Smithsonian Institution Press.

Honkasalo, M. L. (2001) Vicissitudes of pain and suffering: chronic pain and liminality. *Medical Anthropology* 19(4), 319–353.

Houston, S. D. and Taube, K. A. (2000) An archaeology of the senses: Perception and cultural expression in ancient Mesoamerica. *Cambridge Archaeological Journal* 10(2), 261–294.

Huss-Ashmore, R. (2000) "The Real Me": Therapeutic narrative in cosmetic surgery. *Expedition* 42(3), 26–37.

Jacobi, K. P. (2000) *Last Rites for the Tipu Maya: Genetic Structuring in a Colonial Cemetery*. Tuscaloosa, The University of Alabama Press.

Kapchan, D. A. (1993) Moroccan Women's Body Signs. In K. Young (ed.) *Bodylore*, 3–34. Knoxville, University of Tennessee Press.

Koenig, L. M. and Carnes, M. (1999) Body Piercing: Medical concerns with cutting edge fashion. *Journal of General Internal Medicine* 14(6), 379–385.

Krejci, E., and Culbert, T. P. (1995) Preclassic and Classic burials and caches in the Maya Lowlands. In N. K. Grube (ed.) *The Emergence of Lowland Maya Civilization: The Transition from the Preclassic to the Early Classic, a conference at Hildesheim, Germany, November 1992*, 103–116. Möckmühl, Germany, Verlag Anton Saurwein.

Krogman, W. M. and İşcan, M. Y. (1986) *The Human Skeleton in Forensic Medicine*. Springfield, Illinois, Charles C. Thomas Publisher.

Laqueur, T. W. (1990) *Making Sex: Body and Gender from the Greeks to Freud*. Cambridge, Harvard University Press.

Leder, D. (1990) *The Absent Body*. Chicago, University of Chicago Press.

Linné, S. (1940) Dental modification in aboriginal America. *Ethnos* 5, 2–28.

López Olivares, N. M. (1997) Cultural odontology: dental alterations from Petén, Guatemala. In S. L. Whittington and D. M. Reed (eds.) *Bones of the Maya: Studies of Ancient Skeletons*, 105–115.

Smithsonian Institution Press, Washington, D. C.

McAnany, P. A. (1995) *Living with the Ancestors*. Austin, University of Texas Press.

Milner, V. and Eichold II, B. H. (2001) Body piercing and tattooing perspectives. *Clinical Nursing Research* 10(4), 424–441.

Morinis, A. A. (1985) The ritual experience: pain and the transformation of consciousness in ordeals of initiation. *Ethos* 13, 150–174.

Musafar, F. (1996) Epilogue. In A. R. Favazza (ed.), *Bodies under Siege: Self-mutilation and Body Modification in Culture and Psychiatry*. Baltimore, The John Hopkins University Press.

Owsley D. W. and Guerin, B. L. (1982) Cranial deformation – a cultural practice of the 18th century Overhill Cherokee. *Journal of Cherokee Studies* 7(2), 79–81.

Özbek, M. (2001) Cranial deformation in a subadult sample from Degirmentepe (Chalcolithic, Turkey). *American Journal of Physical Anthropology* 115(3), 238–244.

Rathje, W. L. (1970) Socio-political implications of Lowland Maya burials: methodology and tentative hypothesis. *World Archaeology* 1:359–373.

Romero Molina, J. (1951) Las mutilaciones dentarias prehispanicas de America. In J. Romero Molina and S. Fastlicht (eds.) *El Arte de las Mutilaciones Dentarias*, 9–58. Mexico, Ediciones Mexicanas.

Romero Molina, J. (1952) Los patrones de la mutilación dentaria prehispánica. *Anales del Instituto Nacional de Antropología e Historia* 4, 177–221.

Romero Molina, J. (1958) *Mutilaciones Dentarias Prehispanicas de Mexico y America en General*. Mexico, Instituto Nacional de Antropologica e Historia.

Romero Molina, J. (1960) Ultimos hallazgos de mutilaciones dentarias de México. *Anales del Instituto Nacional de Antropología e Historia* 12, 151–215.

Romero Molina, J. (1965) Recientes adiciones a la colección de dientes mutilados. *Anales del Instituto Nacional de Antropología e Historia* 17, 199–256.

Romero Molina, J. (1970) Dental mutilation, trephination, and cranial deformation. In T. D. Stewart (ed.) *Handbook of Middle American Indians: Physical Anthropology*, 50–67. Austin, University of Texas Press.

Rosenblatt, D. (1997) The antisocial skin: structure, resistance, and "Modern Primitive" adornment in the United States. *Cultural Anthropology* 12(3), 287–334.

Rubin, A. (1988) *Marks of Civilization: Artistic Transformation of the Human Body*. Los Angeles, UCLA, Museum of Cultural History.

Sahagún, B. D. (1971) *A History of Ancient Mexico: Anthropological, Mythological and Social*. Detroit, Ethridge Books.

Saul, F. P. (1972) *The Human Skeletal Remains of Altar de Sacrificios: An Osteobiographic Analysis. Papers of the Peabody Museum of Archaeology and Ethnology, vol. 63, no. 2*. Cambridge, Massachusetts, Harvard University.

Saul, F. P. and Saul, J. M. (1989) Osteobiography: A Maya Example. In M. Y. Iscan and K. A. R. Kennedy (eds.) *Reconstruction of Life from the Skeleton*, 287–302. New York, Alan R. Liss, Inc.

Saul, F. P. and Saul, J. M. (1991) The Preclassic population of Cuello. In N. Hammond (ed.) *Cuello: An Early Maya Community in Belize*, 134–158. Cambridge, Cambridge University Press.

Saul, J. M. and Saul, F. P. (1997) The Preclassic skeletons from Cuello. In S.L. Whittington and D. M. Reed (eds.) *Bones of the Maya: Studies of Ancient Skeletons*, 181–195. Washington, D. C., Smithsonian Institute Press.

Seeger, A. (1975) The meaning of ornaments: A Suya example. *Ethnology* 14(3), 211–224.

Stewart, T. D. (1953) Skeletal Remains from Zaculeu, Guatemala. In R. B. Woodbury and A. S. Trik (eds.) *The Ruins of Zaculeu Guatemala*, vol. 1, 295–311. Richmond, The William Byrd Press.

Tiesler Blos, V. (1998) *La Costumbre de la Deformación Cefálica entre los Antiguos Mayas: Aspectos Morfológicos y Culturales*. Instituto Nacional de Antropología e Historia, México.

Tozzer, A. M. (1941) *Landa's Relación de las cosas de Yucatán*. Papers of the Peabody Museum of American Archaeology and Ethnology no. 18. Cambridge, Harvard University.

Turner, B. S. (1984) *The Body and Society: Explorations in Social Theory*. New York, Basil Blackwell Inc.

Welsh, W. B. M. (1988) *An Analysis of Classic Lowland Maya Burials*. Oxford, England, BAR International Series 409.

White, T. D. (2000) *Human Osteology*. San Diego, Academic Press.

Zatzick, D., and Dimsdale, J. E. (1990) Cultural variations in response to painful stimulus. *Psychosomatic Medicine* 52, 544–57.

19. The Living Dead and the Dead Living: Burials, Figurines and Social Performance in the European Mid Upper Palaeolithic

Paul B. Pettitt

Introduction

Funerary remains form one of the major datasets for reconstructing social beliefs and social organisation in prehistory. In addition to the potential light they shed upon society's views of the deceased, and what appropriate behaviour should mark their passing and subsequent commemoration, they also provide a window into wider issues of organisation and individual dress, symbolism and materiality. In view of Gamble's (1999) recent call for a social archaeology of the Palaeolithic, I attempt here a social interpretation of Mid Upper Palaeolithic burials and mortuary activity. Although these are not the first deliberate burials – they seem to have been practised, among other mortuary activity, by Neanderthals and early modern humans (*e.g.* Pettitt 2002 and references therein) – the Mid Upper Palaeolithic burials do represent our earliest evidence as yet for elaborate inhumations of selected individuals, accompanied by highly decorated clothing and exotic grave goods, and placed in meaningful locations. This is not to imply that burial was accorded to all and practised frequently in the Palaeolithic – as we shall see below it was probably restricted to individuals who were in some way 'special' – but the relative rarity of burial and therefore tangible mortuary data for the period of concern is informative in itself. In recent years, new analyses of the age, context, pathology and associations of the burials that have been revealed to archaeologists have dramatically improved our understanding of these, and may now, I believe, allow some tentative interpretations.

The origins of burial, which is often taken to represent one of the hallmarks of modern human behaviour, occurred during the Palaeolithic. Burial, however, was merely one physical act among many aspects of mortuary activity and interest in the dead corpse which probably evolved slowly over the course of human evolution from a generalised core of emotional and behavioural responses to death (Taylor 2002; Pettitt forthcoming). Gamble (1999, 404ff) has referred to burial as one example of a *detaching ritual*. I define *detachment* as the weakening of existing social bonds between the living and the dead and the potential development of new social bonds between the living and the newly-dead. This latter transformation may, for example, refer to perceived connections of some 'special' living individuals with the spirit realm, or newly-established incarnations of the dead with the spirit world. Whatever its specific form, detachment is a *process*, which may occur simply through the attrition of time, unembellished by any cultural acts, as with higher primates (*e.g.* Pettitt forthcoming). Alternatively, it may be governed by rules, embellished by ritual practice, material culture and the like, and so be viewed as a *detaching ritual* (Gamble 1999).

I shall argue here that the complex detaching rituals in place in the Upper Palaeolithic were firmly rooted in wider social issues tied up with individual specialisms, sex-based social roles, and an encultured landscape and cosmology in which liminality was central. In order to do this, I begin with some generalisations drawn from the anthropology of death. I shall focus on the European Mid Upper Palaeolithic (~30 to ~20 ka BP) wherein a number of body-centred behavioural innovations appear to have originated in modern human societies. While a number of general material traits are shared over vast areas of occupied Europe during this time, certainly enough to view this as a cultural uniformity, regional differences do occur. Thus, at least three major cultural areas may be detected across a mid-latitude European transect in this period. In the west, a tradition of cave and small open site occupation defines the Gravettian/Périgordian, a cultural grouping that may also be extended to include the (rare) British and Italian occurrences of this period; the Willendorfian/Pavlovian group of Austria, Slovakia and the Czech Republic, characterised by large open site aggregations (the German mid Upper Palaeolithic record may be seen as belonging to either of these groups); and the major river valley aggregations of the Russian Plain referred to as the Kostenki/Avdeevo group. An appropriate term for this unity, recognising as it does regional variation, is the Gravettian-Pavlovian/Willendorfian-Kostenki/Avdeevo technocomplex, which may be referred to by the acronym GPWKA (Roebroeks *et al.* 2000).

In this paper, I seek to unite two categories of tangible data, burials which are overwhelmingly male (the living dead), and humanoid figurines which are overwhelmingly female (the dead living). These occur alongside the appearance of hand-prints and stencils in cave art, which apart from numerous examples in France and Spain are also found in Italy's only painted cave of Upper Palaeolithic age, Grotta Paglicci (Mussi and Zampetti 1997), and a visually impressive ornamentation of the body with jewellery which, far from being random, appears to respect grammatical 'rules'. Although some humanoid depictions occur in the preceding European Aurignacian (see below), the record for these is far greater in the GPWKA and demands explanation. No convincing examples of elaborate burial (or burial at all for that matter) have yet been found for the Aurignacian. I argue here that this appearance and elaboration is not coincidental, and explore ways in which these material phenomena interacted. Meaningful patterns can, I suggest, be detected, and I interpret this as reflecting an elaboration of body-centred politics at this time. Thus I seek to link the bodies of the living and of the dead, albeit from funerary contexts.

The anthropology of death: a point of departure for the departed

Early attempts at an anthropology of death, notably the work of Robert Hertz (cited in Huntington and Metcalf 1979: see also Parker Pearson 1999), demonstrated that a number of societies do not see death as instantaneous. The notion of a blurring of distinctions between the living and the dead, or at least of continued intercession of the living into the world of the dead through which one may infer a meaningful coexistence, seems also to have been held through the classical and medieval periods (M. Carroll pers. comm.). The notion, therefore, of a fixed dichotomy between the living and the dead may well be restricted to the modern, scientifically informed and anti-superstitious world, *i.e.* a product of enlightenment thought.

A common theme to the 'liminal' position is the existence of a period of cosmological time in which the mortal is neither alive nor finally dead, which Hertz referred to as the 'intermediary' period. A final phase sees the individual 'reach' a more permanent status, which may take a myriad of forms, many of which, however, invoke

a continued role of the deceased in the world of the living (as, for example, an 'ancestor', 'spirit', 'god' or the like). I refer to the latter as the 'destination phase'. When the liminal phase is finally over and the destination phase is finally reached, funerary ritual is performed. It is clear, then, that detaching rituals may well encompass dying, liminal and destination phases, each of which will presumably have its own material and therefore archaeological signature. The presence of human relics on archaeological sites may attest to once-living individuals in their liminal and destinational phases; as they continue to possess social agency among the living I therefore refer to them as the 'living dead'. These processes need not be confined to the world of flesh and bone; culturally-produced artefacts of significant materials may possess their own social agency, interceding as if they too, had life of some sort – in effect the 'dead living'. Dying, liminality and destinations imply transformation, a notion that has received attention in the Palaeolithic literature of late (see below).

The ubiquity of liminal phases and transitional processes between the living and the dead, which are to a certain extend shared by the living bereaved (Huntington and Metcalf 1979, 65), renders this a plausible interpretative framework for approaching the prehistoric mortuary record. It must be admitted that it is difficult to test such a notion adequately, although one might predict archaeological correlates of these phases that particularly reflect the differing status of the body, transformational themes, and the like. Thus it is here that I seek to unite two broad phenomena of the Mid Upper Palaeolithic record, to suggest a complex cosmology firmly embedding transformation.

Mid Upper Palaeolithic GPWKA burials

Over 50 burials are known that may be convincingly associated with the GPWKA. They are an odd lot. Almost all that have been analysed in detail bear evidence of pathological conditions, occasionally severe (Table 19.1), and some inbreeding among buried individuals also exist (see below). These pathological conditions and inbreeding seem unlikely to reflect the health of Gravettian humans as a whole. Rather, this must suggest that the individuals who were accorded burial in the GPWKA were in some way marked out from the rest of society (Formicola *et al.* 2001). First, I undertake a brief survey of the general elements of the better-understood burials from west to east.

The GPWKA burials with secure chronology date to a relatively tight period of time within the GPWKA as a whole, namely between the 27th and 24th millennia BP (Fig. 19.1). Among these, there are a number of traits among grave goods which vary from region to region (Pettitt forthcoming) but emphasise the inclusion in graves of the bones of large, dangerous herbivores, ochre, elaborate decoration especially using shells, bone and ivory

Specimen	Pathological conditions
Goat Hole, Paviland ('Red Lady'), Wales partial skeleton	No pathological conditions observed.
Lagar Velho, Portugal	Minor traumatic injury to the left lateral radial diaphysis. Non-pathological hyper arctic body proportions.
Arene Candide 1 ('Il Principe'), Italy	Traumatic loss of left mandibular ramus and part of left clavicle, possibly caused by animal attack.
Baousso da Torre 2, Italy	
Barma del Caviglione, Italy	Fractured right radial diaphysis.
Grotta dei Fanciulli 4 (Grotte des Enfants), Italy	Asymmetrical hypertrophy possibly caused by nerve injury to upper limb.
Barma Grande 2, 3, 4 (triple burial), Italy	Considerable osteophytosis on vertebrae on all three individuals caused by degeneration of intervertebral discs. BG2: humeral asymmetry. *NB: indicators of genetic relatedness.*
Brno II (Francousca Street), Czech Republic	Periostitis of femur, ulna and humerus: considerable pain for some years.
Pavlov 1, Czech Republic	Neurocranial trauma.
Dolní Věstonice DV3	Pathologies to cranium (*e.g.* temporomandibular articulation & associated asymmetry due to traumatic loss of left mandibular condyle). Subchondral pits in weight-bearing articular regions.
Dolní Věstonice DV11/12 partial skeleton, Czech Republic	Trauma to frontal bone.
Dolní Věstonice DV13, 14 & 15 (triple burial), Czech Republic	DV15 (female?) bears abnormalities on diaphyses of femur, humerus, radius and ulna. Pathologically short left forearm. Curved spine [scoliosis?]: severely disabled. Dental abnormalities of positioning & number; enamel hypoplasia. = developmental difficulties. Traumatic injuries probably led to soft tissue pathologies, *e.g.* alopecia, cataracts &c. *NB: indicators of genetic relatedness.*
Dolní Věstonice DV16, Czech Republic	Scoliosis of spine, deformed right femur.
Sungir 3, Russia	Suite of developmental deformities, *e.g.* femoral bowing.

Table 19.1. Some pathological conditions among the better-studied GPWKA burials. Sources: Alt et al. (1997), Formicola (1989), Formicola and Buzhilova 2004, Formicola et al. (2001), Oliva 2000, Trinkaus and Jelinek (1997), Trinkaus et al. (2001). Trinkaus et al. (2002b).

beads and the teeth of carnivores (although the latter are totally absent in Italy), and the occasional blade of exotic stone. With few exceptions the buried individuals are overwhelmingly male, at least with examples where preservation of diagnostic elements such as pelves, crania and, to a lesser extent, long bone dimensions allow sex determination. Original determinations of the sex of the Grimaldi burials, for example, suggested that two-thirds were male, although Formicola's (1988a) reassessment has demonstrated that, of 13 individuals (eight single, one double, one triple burial) nine are male; one, possibly two female; and two, possibly three, unsexed. Similarly, of the

remains of some 36 humans at the early GPWKA (Pavlovian) sites of Dolní Věstonice I and II and Pavlov I, six near-complete skeletons derive from four burials (3 single, one triple) and of these, four are male, one or possibly two female (Trinkaus and Jelinek 1997; Formicola *et al.* 2001).

The 'Red Lady' of Paviland, actually a young adult male on the basis on body size and the morphology of the left *os coxae* (Trinkaus and Holliday 2000), was the first human fossil to be excavated, and was published the same year in which it was discovered (Buckland 1823). Buckland described the find as:

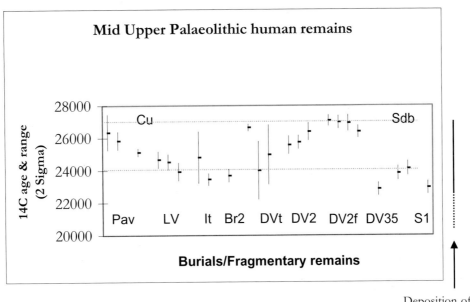

Deposition of female
figurines

Figure 19.1. Chronology of GPWKA burials. Key and sources:

Pav.   *Paviland 1 'Red Lady' (Aldhouse-Green and Pettitt 1998, Pettitt 2000)*

Cu.   *Cussac locus 1 (Aujolat* et al. *2002).*

LV.   *Lagar Velho, (Duarte* et al. *1999, Pettitt et al 2002).*

It.   *Left: Barma Grande 6 'Burnt burial' (Formicola et al. 2004). Right: Arene Candide 1 'Il Principe' (Pettitt* et al. *2003).*

Br2.   *Brno 2, (Pettitt and Trinkaus 2000).*

DVt   *Dolní Věstonice 2 DV13, 14, 15 (triple burial) (Klíma 1988, Alt* et al. *1997, Formicola* et al. *2001).*

DV2   *Dolní Věstonice 2 DV2 (Svoboda* et al. *2002).*

DV2f   *Dolní Věstonice 2 fragmentary human remains (dates of hearths) (Trinkaus and Jelínek 1997, Trinkaus* et al. *2000, 2001, Svoboda* et al. *2002).*

DV35   *Dolní Věstonice DV35 femur (Trinkaus* et al. *1999).*

Sdb   *Sungir' 2 & 3 (double burial) (Pettitt and Bader 2000).*

S1   *Sungir' 1 (adult) (Pettitt and Bader 2000).*

nearly the entire left side of a human female skeleton. [All bones were]…stained superficially with a dark brick-red colour, and enveloped by a coating of a kind of ruddle. The entire body must have been entirely surrounded or covered over at the time of its interment with this red substance. Close to that part of the thigh bone where the pocket is usually worn, I found laid together, and surrounded also by ruddle, about two handsfull of small shells of the nerita littoralis…at another part of the skeleton, viz. in contact with the ribs, I found forty or fifty fragments of small ivory rods nearly cylindrical, and varying in diameter from a quarter to three quarters of an inch, and from one to four inches in length. Rings made of the same ivory [were]…found with the rods. Both rods and rings were stained superficially with red and lay in the same red substance that enveloped the bones; they had evidently been buried at the same time with the woman (*ibid.* 87–9).

In addition to this, Buckland's plan and section of the cave (Fig. 19.2), shows clearly (with some poetic licence having added the right side and skull of the Red Lady) a mammoth cranium with intact tusks referred to in the text. Commenting on the finds of Buckland and his successor, Sollas, Garrod (1926), acting on a suggestion by Breuil, suggested that the cranium originally formed part of the ceremonial interment of the Red Lady. In addition, some limestone slabs may have been placed deliberately to delineate the head and feet of the burial (Aldhouse-Green 2000). The ochre staining is far stronger on the bones of the pelvis and lower limbs, suggesting a two-piece set of clothing, presumably leggings and parka, rather than a burial shroud (*ibid.*).

Any other associations and details of the burial are lost to us, but enough detail is recorded to gain a fair understanding of it, which occurred in a cave that was highly visible from a distance in the plain below and which seems to have seen only small-scale and intermittent occupation (Aldhouse-Green and Pettitt 1998). Most importantly, the Red Lady possesses a number of traits that unite GPWKA burials from Paviland to the northeast of Moscow. He was interred in a shallow grave, associated

Figure 19.2. Plan and section of the Goat Hole Cave, Paviland, Wales, from Buckland 1823, showing clearly the position of the 'Red Lady' and apparently associated mammoth cranium. Note top hat on excavator climbing ladder!

with the bones of a large herbivore, emplaced with enigmatic items of mammoth ivory, and was highly ornamented with ochred clothing which was also sewn with elaborate shell decoration. Given the location of the periwinkle shells – generally in the waist/pubic region, it is possible that these were sewn onto a loincloth.

The young child buried under a rockshelter at Lagar Velho in Portugal's Lapedo Valley has attracted attention as a possible Neanderthal/modern human hybrid (Duarte *et al.* 1999). This is unlikely, and also unfortunate, as it has distracted from the fact that this is an excellent, well-excavated and recorded example of a GPWKA burial which shares a number of traits with the Red Lady and other burials. The nature of the burial has been described in detail by Duarte (2002). A ~4/5-year-old child (age estimation based on dental development, ossification of the vertebrae, upper and lower limb epiphyses and pelvic morphology (Trinkaus *et al.* 2002a)) was laid in a shallow grave tucked away against the wall of the shelter, and the bones and grave fill were stained with red ochre. The act of burial seems to have been preceded by the burning of a *Pinus sylvestris* branch, a direct association with fire that is strikingly reminiscent of practises at Dolní Věstonice, Barma Grande and Sungir' (see below). As with the 'Red

Lady', at least one limestone block seems to have been placed over the burial, and grave goods include red deer pelves at each end of the body and rabbit vertebrae laid over one leg. In addition, the child appeared to have been wearing a headdress decorated with red deer canines and a *Littorina obtusata* shell was suspended around his/her neck.

A variation on the general traits of GPWKA burials is seen in the apparently unaccompanied remains of at least five individuals placed at three separate locations deep within Cussac Cave, France, for which only preliminary information has been published (Aujolat *et al.* 2002). In Locus 1, numerous cranial and postcranial bones in anatomical disorder, apparently deriving from one individual, were found under a limestone bloc beneath two bear hollows, apparently associated with ochre. At Locus 2, the near-complete skeleton of one adult was placed in an oval depression (another bear hollow?) by the cave wall, although with no signs of ochre. At Locus 3, the remains of at least three individuals were placed on a ledge near to a stalagmitic pillar. Intriguingly, while numerous postcranial remains were recovered, no cranial elements were found. A degree of ochre staining was found in this area. As only a preliminary publication has appeared to date, one must exercise caution in the interpretation of the Cussac remains, although the apparent association with bear hollows and ochre is intriguing. Speculatively, this may indicate a connection between the dead and hibernation. The placement of human remains in a cave is reminiscent of the emplacement of at least three adult males (an adult female and a neonate) in the Cro-Magnon rockshelter, Dordogne, now firmly dated to the earlier phases of the GPWKA (Henri-Gambier 2002). Together, these are suggestive of a French regional funerary variant on the GPWKA 'norm', involving the tucking away of human bodies in enclosed sites, albeit in the case of Cro-Magnon in an occupation context.

Italy has yielded a number of rich burials from the mid and later phases of the GPWKA; these comprise some 14 individuals (in 11 burials) in Liguria, and seven individuals (in five burials) from Apulia (Mussi 1986, 1988, 1995, 2001; Formicola 1988b, 1989; Mussi *et al.* 1989). There are examples of single, double and triple burials. Once again skeletal morphology indicates that most are male (Formicola 1988a, 1989): of three females, one was buried with a foetus/neonate (Santa Maria d'Agnano), another was apparently placed face down into the grave of an adult male (the double burial at the Grotta dei Fanciulli/ Grotte des Enfants) and a third (if sexing is correct) was found in the centre of the Barma Grande triple burial. Sex determination of the female skeletons in the Grotta dei Fanciulli double burial and the Barma Grande triple burial are believed to be unequivocal (based on the morphology of the pelvis and skull, together with metrical data) (Formicola 1988a).

These presumably reflect three very different social contexts of burial, given their variability. At Arene Candide in Liguria a young adult male was buried in a shallow grave rich in ochre (Fig. 19.3). He wore a headdress on to which were sewn red deer canines and hundreds of perforated shells (several species of the genera *Cardium, Cypraea, Cyclonassa* and *Purpura*), and was also accompanied by body ornamentation of *Cypraea* shells, mammoth ivory pendants, four batons of elk antler, three of which were elaborately incised, and had a 23cm long blade of exotic flint in his right hand. Furthermore, yellow ochre at his left neck may represent a cosmetic attempt to cover an injury – perhaps fatal (Mussi 1995, Pettitt *et al.* 2003). This elaborate ornamentation of the body with ochre, shells, deer teeth and beads of ivory, and inclusion in the grave-cuts of such exotic items as Vaucluse flint, is characteristic of all but the Baousso da Torre burial of an adult male (Mussi *et al.* 1989, 1995). In addition, most burials (with the exception of the Barma Grande triple burial) were located towards the walls of the caves and aligned along the cave's long axis (Mussi 1995). The elaborate body decoration of the Ligurian burials is arranged in 'zones', *i.e.* restricted to tight clusters at certain body parts (Fig. 19.4). This practice is shared by other burials, particularly those at Sungir' and is a trait also observable on a number of the 'venus' figurines (see

Figure 19.3. Arene Candide 'Il Principe'.

below). Of particular interest is the triple burial of Barma Grande (Formicola 1988b; Mussi 1988, 1995), which, if the identification of the central individual as female were correct, may closely parallel the triple burial of Dolní Věstonice (see below). The bodies were emplaced side by side in a grave pit and were covered with ochre. A bovid femur underlay the head of the central individual and all three individuals were elaborately ornamented with shells (*Cyclonassa* sp.), deer canines, ochred fish vertebrae and bone pendants. In addition, two individuals 'held' long blades of exotic flint, in all, very similar to the situation at Arene Candide. The presence of a rare squamous morphology on the frontal bone of all three individuals suggests that they may be genetically related, perhaps even exhibiting signs of inbreeding which has also been suggested for later Italian Epigravettian burials (Frayer *et al.* 1988). At Barma Grande, the BG6 burial of an adult male, also ornamented with *Cyclope neritea* shells, was originally interpreted as having been laid on the remains of a hearth, although it is now thought that the grave cutting simply disturbed the remains of a previous hearth and that the association is therefore fortuitous (M. Mussi *pers. comm.*; Formicola *et al.* 2004).

Moravia has yielded the remains of at least seven individuals whose remains are fragmentary, and five complete individuals in three burials from the GPWKA. Fragmentary human remains are numerous both at Dolní Věstonice and Pavlov. Contextually, the fragmentary human remains at Dolní Věstonice II do not differ from the general distribution of cultural remains, suggesting a

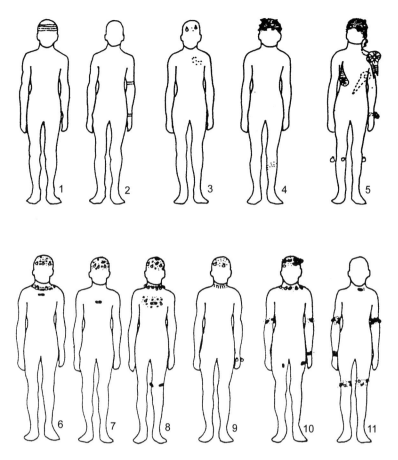

Figure 19.4. Schematic 'zoned' representation of body ornamentation on the Ligurian GPWKA burials, after Mussi (1995).
Key:
1. *Grotte des Enfants 6*
2. *Grotte des Enfants 5*
3. *Grotte des Enfants 4*
4. *Grotta del Caviglione 1*
5. *Grotta delle Arene Candide 1 'Il Principe')*
6. *Barma Grande 4*

7. *Barma Grande 3*
8. *Barma Grande 2*
9. *Barma Grande 5*
10. *Baousso da Torre 2*
11. *Baousso da Torre 1*

meaningful correlation between the two (Trinkaus *et al.* 2000). They mainly cluster in areas peripheral to the main activity areas (the west of the site), and are often associated with hearths, and therefore an association with fire seems apparent. The lack of carnivore gnawing marks suggests that these cannot all represent bodies that were originally buried and which have been subsequently disturbed, fragmented and dispersed post-depositionally. The integrity of spatial patterning among cultural debris furthermore suggests that large-scale geological activity (for example, downslope solifluxion) cannot be held to explain the fragmentary nature of these remains. The possibility remains, therefore, that these represent human body parts/bones which were defleshed and that had an association with fire and occurred on the periphery of the occupation areas. It is tempting to view these as powerful human relics, a conclusion that may pertain elsewhere, as with the association of an ochred human skull with the Sungir' adult male burial and the inclusion of an adult human femur in the double burial at the same site (see

below). If this is correct, it further blurs the distinction between the living and the dead, as relics are suggestive of participation of the dead in the world of the living. Human relics are 'ambiguous, betwixt and between' and may often 'mediate between the realms of living mortals and the afterlife' (Verpoorte, pers. comm.).

Near-complete skeletons from clear burial contexts in the Moravian settlements have understandably attracted more attention than the fragmentary remains. In addition to at least two single burials (DVIII female, DVXVI male) and the triple burial (DVXIII, XIV, XV) at Dolní Věstonice, and single burials at Brno Francouzská Street and Pavlov I, one must also consider the apparent mass grave of over 20 individuals at Předmostí, the remains from which are unfortunately now lost to science (Klima 1988, 1995; Oliva 2000; Pettitt and Trinkaus 2000; Svoboda 1988, 1991; Svoboda *et al.* 1996; Trinkaus and Jelínek 1997; Trinkaus *et al.* 2000, 200; Verpoorte 2001 and pers. comm.). The DVXIII-XV triple burial from Dolní Věstonice II consists of three extended individuals laid side-by-side, similar to that of Barma Grande, Italy. The outer two individuals were sexed as males while the central individual is a possible female. Sex determination of the central skeleton was made difficult because of in situ deformation of the pelvis (Formicola *et al.* 2001). Several rare osteological traits on all three individuals suggest that they were genetically related (Alt *et al.* 1997). Two were placed on their backs, the outer left individual (male) facing towards the individual in the centre (possible female) with his arm extended towards the central individual's pubic area, and a third skeleton (right outermost, from the viewer's perspective) lay on his stomach facing away from the other two. Both of the outer individuals' heads and upper torsos were stained with a thick mat of ochre suggestive of elaborate headgear, and their crania were encircled with pendants of arctic fox and wolf teeth and mammoth ivory pendants. On DVXIII (left male) these pendants were cemented in ochre, possibly indicative of a mask (Svoboda 1988). The female's pubic area was also ochred. A fire of spruce wood, several pieces of which appear to have been tools, was lit in the grave atop the individuals. The occurrence of all three young adults in the same grave, suggestive of one death event or at least very close deaths, and the remains of a wooden pole stuck deep into the hip of DVXIII, strongly suggests that at least one of these individuals was killed. In this light, Taylor (2002) has suggested that this might be an example of 'scapegoating' – the murder of certain individuals to atone for imbalances, account for disasters, etc. Alternatively, this may reflect internal fighting among young males perhaps in times of seasonal stress where the 'walkaway option' was not viable (Verpoorte pers. comm.), the deliberate murder of 'special' individuals, perhaps to keep power among the young or alter its nature, or may simply reflect complex social mechanics that we do not understand. If these individuals were all genetically related, their mortuary context is all the more intriguing. Although charcoal is, of course, ubiquitous on GPWKA occupation sites, particularly those in Moravia, and one must therefore be cautious, fire does seem to have been an important element of Moravian GPWKA mortuary ritual. The DVXVI adult male burial was also associated with a hearth towards which the body was faced (Svoboda 1988; Svoboda *et al.* 1996). Other small fires were lit in the shallow depression into which the grave was cut and the body laid. Charcoal was abundant in the Předmostí mass grave, suggesting the association of fire with the dead.

Ornamentation and ochring of the dead are again commonly found among the Moravian burials, and mammoth scapulae and other large bones were used to cover at least DVIII, Pavlov, Brno II and Předmostí. The DVXVI male burial wore four carnivore canines zonated as pairs in the pelvic area and at the elbow (Svoboda 1988), and the head and pelvic areas were ochred in a strikingly similar way to the triple burial. The Brno II adult male appears to have been buried in a shallow grave and

covered with a mammoth scapula (Oliva 2000; Pettitt and Trinkaus 2000). The remains were coloured with ochre, and over 600 fossil *Dentalium* shells were recovered from the skull area, again suggesting elaborately ornamented headgear. The considerable degrees of wear on these suggest that the headgear had a long use-life, rather than being simply funerary clothing. The remains of large animals, in this case a large number of rhinoceros ribs, a mammoth scapula and tusk, horse teeth, as well as enigmatic roundels of mammoth ivory and a 140mm wide ring of marl, were clearly associated with the burial. An associated mammoth ivory 'marionette' may be viewed in the context of the GPWKA figurines, although it is clearly male (Mussi pers. comm. and see below), and a worked and worn reindeer antler found with the burial has often been interpreted as a drum stick.

As the fragmentary human remains at Dolní Věstonice include an infant (DV36) and a child (DV17) we can rule out the possibility that it was just adolescents and adults that were buried – although one could argue that DV36 and DV17 never received an actual burial. Once again, the dominance of adolescent and adult males is apparent. In addition to the burials and possible human relics on the Moravian settlement sites, Svoboda (2000) has speculated that a further Moravian detaching ritual of the earlier and later Upper Palaeolithic may have involved the deposition of the dead through openings ('chimneys') into karstic cavities, as suggested by the human remains at Mladeč and Koněprusy caves, respectively. Such activity currently appears to have been lacking in the Mid Upper Palaeolithic.

The broadly GPWKA settlement site of Sungir', some 200km northeast of Moscow, Russia, has yielded three individuals in two burials and a number of more isolated human remains (N. Bader 1965; O. Bader 1998; Pettitt and Bader 2000). Sungir' 1 is an adult male in extended, supine position with hands placed over his pubis. The whole body was covered with ochre, and an association with fire is apparent. Numerous fox teeth and mammoth ivory beads were sewn onto his headgear. The clothing of this individual – apparently two separate layers – was elaborately ornamented with nearly 3000 beads of mammoth ivory, in a clearly zonated manner in which horizontal bands seem to have been the main decorative motif (Bader 1998). In addition, the male wore 25 armlets of mammoth ivory. The skull of a female, stained in ochre, was buried in close proximity to the male burial. The Sungir' 2 and 3 double burial was found ~3m from the adult burial. A clear grave cutting contained the bodies of two individuals each of late juvenile/early adolescent age and laid head to head. Although confident osteological sexing of infants and juveniles is problematic, Sungir' 2 has been identified as a male and Sungir' 3 as a female on the basis of pelvic morphology and DNA analysis (Formicola and Buzhilova 2004). Once again ochre was abundant in the graves and an association with fire is apparent. Sungir' 2 wore clothing decorated with nearly

5000 mammoth ivory beads again in, it seems, two layers of zonated horizontal bands including a loincloth or belt, headgear elaborated ornamented with ivory beads and fox teeth, an ivory pin at his throat probably fastening a cloak or other item of clothing, and a zoomorphic pendant worn around the neck. In addition he was accompanied by a 2.4m long enigmatic item usually described as a straightened mammoth tusk, and an associated carved openwork ivory disk, which may be a spear, or some kind of 'standard' or 'staff of power', and a large ivory sculpture of a mammoth below his left shoulder. To his left side, intriguingly, was placed an ochre-stuffed femur of a human adult, in a position that mirrors the placement of a bâton alongside the Sungir' 3 child. In my opinion, no better evidence than this – which I take to indicate the similar function of a human femur and a *bâton de commandement* – exists to suggest the possession of power by human remains in the GPWKA. 'Power' in this context referring to the social agency of the dead, which may have acted through these (possibly) metaphysically linked relics. The Sungir' 3 skeleton (possible female) had even richer associations. Again highly ochred and wearing layered clothing decorated in horizontal zones (of over 5000 beads), a beaded cap, ivory throat pin, although lacking fox teeth and chest pendant, Sungir' 3 was associated with the bâton already mentioned, several small spears of mammoth ivory to her side, and three ivory openwork discs again suggestive, in my opinion, of some item of power. Overall, several thousand person-hours of labour must have gone into the ornamentation of these two individuals.

Enough shared traits should now be apparent from this cursory survey of the main GPWKA burials. To summarise, the following traits seem apparent:

–   A concern with fire, either preceding the interment, atop it, or in its close proximity.
–   An association with the bones of large, dangerous animals, some possibly representing offerings of meat, but also using, for example, mammoth scapulae and other 'coverings'. Carnivores seem a close association in particular, usually by suspended teeth, although this varies regionally. (NB It is interesting to note that a later prehistorian may well interpret these as the remains of funerary (or ancestral) feasting. This remains a possibility. See also venus figurines below).
–   An association with enigmatic items of mammoth ivory.
–   Colouring of clothing/shrouds/headgear/masks with ochre.
–   Elaboration of clothing with shells, beads, teeth.
–   Elaboration of the head area, (*e.g.* bonnets, head-dresses, usually with considerable ornamentation).
–   Reference to the pubic region, either through ochring (*e.g.* Dolní Věstonice triple burial), shell/bead ornamentation (*e.g.* Dolní Věstonice DVXVI,

possibly Paviland) or hand placement (Sungir' 1, Dolní Věstonice triple burial).
–   Association with exotic lithics, usually placed by the head or held in the hands.
–   Possible use (and ochring) of fragmentary human body parts as relics, in Central and Eastern Europe (*e.g.* Dolní Věstonice, Sungir').
–   Placement of human remains in caves in Western and Central Europe.
–   Possible placing, on occasion, of limestone blocks over parts of the skeleton.

'Venus' figurines

Unequivocal depiction of the human form originates, although is rare, in the Aurignacian, for example with the bas-relief human outline on ivory from Geissenklösterle and the ivory 'lion anthropomorphs' (*löwenmenschen*) from the Höhlenstein-Stadel and Hohle Fels caves, Germany, and the 'dancing venus' carving on slate from Stratzing/Krems-Rehberg on the Galgenberg hill in Austria (Hahn 1982; 1993; Conard 2003). While Hahn (1986) has drawn attention to the apparent focus on fast and aggressive animals in Aurignacian art, the recent discovery of a carving of a water bird on ivory from a substantial habitation level at the Hohle Fels suggests that Aurignacian lion-anthropomorphs played a role in living contexts among a wider depiction of animals (Conard 2003). Some of the carvings may have adorned bodies, suggesting a primary role in display among the living, and of relevance here is the lustre observed by Hahn (1993, 235) on the raised parts of the Geissenklösterle bas-relief which may indicate that it was attached to clothing. Alternatively, they may have been carried in pouches or wrappings. In any case, apart from the suggestion that the Hohlenstein *löwenmensch* may have been cached in a cult site, a specific association of these figurines with funerary activity appears to be lacking.

Traditionally, interpretations of the mid Upper Palaeolithic 'venus' figurines have tended to emphasise the world of the living rather than of the dead. Here, I argue that, while there is undeniable evidence that some of them seem indeed to have been used in domestic settings, there is a strong correlation between these and contemporary burials across Europe. As Figure 19.5 reveals, in regions (plotted by country) where burials are found, figurines are generally found also. This cannot be explained as simply a sampling question relating to the size of the sample areas (*i.e.* countries) given that low figurine/burial frequencies are found in both smaller sample areas (Portugal, UK) and by far the largest (Siberia), in addition to large numbers being recovered from small sample areas (*e.g.* Moravia/Slovakia). Only two exceptions to this rule occur – Paviland and Lagar Velho. It has been suggested that three bone 'spatulae' from the Mid Upper Palaeolithic site of Paviland, which are without parallel in Western Europe, may be anthropomorphic

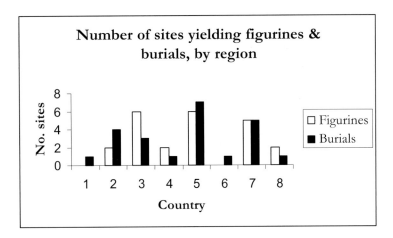

Figure 19.5. Occurrence of Mid Upper Palaeolithic (GPWKA) burials and figurines by country.
Key:

1. *UK (Paviland)*
2. *Pavlovian of Czech Republic & Slovakia (Dolni Věstonice, Brno, Pavlov, Petrkovice, Moravany)*
3. *France (Abri Pataud, Cussac, Brassempouy, Tursac, Sireuil, Lespugue, Monpazier).*
4. *Germany & Austria (Willendorf, Mainz Linsenburg, Mauern).*
5. *Italy (Barma Grande, Grotta del Principe/Grotte du Prince, Baousso da Tourre, Caviglione/Grotta de Cavillon, Grotta dei Fanciulli/ Grotte des enfants, Savignano, Paglicci, Arene Candide, Trasimeno, La Marmotta, Grotte delle Veneri).*
6. *Portugal (Lagar Velho).*
7. *Russian Plain (Kostenki 1 and 13, Avedeevo, Gagarino, Khotylevo II).*
8. *Siberia (Mal'ta, Buret').*

artefacts (Aldhouse-Green and Pettitt 1998). If these can be compared with the Eurasian 'Venuses' *sensu lato*, we may note that they are three radiocarbon millennia younger than the 'Red Lady'. In regions where burials have not been found (at least as yet) neither have figurines. Although this pattern varies at the site level (figurines are found without burials and *vice versa*) the trend does suggest that regional groups who made and deposited figurines tended also to bury some of the dead. As to what this means is obscure. Verpoorte (pers. comm.), for example, has suggested that this may relate to occupational intensity (and therefore convergent practises which may not be cosmologically linked). Given that this pattern appears to pertain over areas with different occupation modes (*e.g.* France, where occupation was centred on rockshelters) and the Czech Republic with major open sites, and that there is no demonstrable link between the length of duration of individual sites and the practice of burial or ritual, this may be unlikely. In any case, even if the practice of burial and the creation of female figurines is a factor of occupation intensity (*i.e.* the more intense, the greater the likelihood of each occurring) they still appear to be linked. Alternatively, I suggest as a working hypothesis that a cosmological link was apparent and it may be that a process of mutual exclusion was in operation. Perhaps it is informative that the only figurine actually buried with a (real) burial is male, *i.e.* the Brno II marionette (Mussi pers. comm.). This general correlation and overall similarities of bodily decoration on the two classes of data

(admittedly generalised over the whole GPWKA range), lead me to believe that the two were in some way interconnected, at least in death. While I do not argue, therefore, that the figurines themselves have a specific funerary function, I suggest that, viewed alongside the burials, they both blur the distinctions between the living and the dead, and were themselves on occasion the subject of mortuary activity. They, therefore, seem to have had their own 'lives' which terminated with death and its associated detaching rituals.

Although Duhard (1993) has rightly noted archaeologists' overemphasis on female, as opposed to male, figurines, where they are identifiable to sex, the overwhelming majority of carved human/humanoid figurines from the Mid Upper Palaeolithic are female. The notion that a number were male derives largely from an erroneous interpretation of the archaeology of Mal'ta and Buret', Siberia (Schlesier 2001), which has been dismissed by Soffer *et al.* (2001). The 'Venus' figurines were carved from mammoth ivory, and from soft stones such as steatite, marl and limestone. They emphasise breasts and hips/buttocks at the expense of the extremities of the lower limbs, upper limbs and heads, and often bear accentuated pubic triangles. There is usually no ambiguity that these are female. Early interpretations viewed them as examples of volt magic, perhaps functioning to raise fertility or to assist coping with the dangers of childbirth. Leroi-Gourhan (1968) suggested that, whatever their function, they respected a design grammar relating to structuralist principles that he also extended to cave art. Some have seen them as especially linked to pregnancy, although Rice (1981; supported by Duhard 1990, 1993) suggested, using ethnographic analogy, that they represent females at all stages of fertility, not just fertile and pregnant individuals, and speculated that they may rather have been a general symbol of womanhood. Gamble (1982) stressed their chronological coincidence with the climatic downturn towards the Last Glacial Maximum and stressed their role in social negotiation. McDermott (1996) suggested that some relate to self-expression among pregnant women, who were communicating through the figurines their personal experience of their own bodies, although this is difficult to maintain for most of the figurines. Verpoorte (2001), in a seminal analysis of the figurines from the Pavlovian sites of the Czech Republic, has suggested that they may not depict 'real' humans, but mythical human-*like* beings, perhaps ritually associated with fire and other animals given their contextual associations with hearths and zoomorphic figurines. This is interesting given the apparent association of isolated human remains and burials with hearths at Dolní Věstonice. Such a notion would accord well with the suggestions of Mussi *et al.* (2000), who see elements of transformation between humans and non-humans as a characteristic of the Ligurian figurines. If the interpretations of Verpoorte and Mussi *et al.* are correct, they underline the ambiguity between the living and the dead, or at least between the profane world and the spiritual. These and other hypotheses are understandably difficult to test, although the applicability of the figurines to numerous theories suggests that they may have been polysemous and their function in society may have differed through the course of their own use ('lives') or from region to region.

In reality, the figurines are highly complex stylistically, and Delporte (1993a) has illustrated how several regional groupings occur which map onto other archaeological variability within the GPWKA technocomplex. They often depict items of clothing such as simple hats, textile adornments such as belts and bands, or are coloured with ochre (Soffer *et al.* 2000). Some may have been hidden or short-lived, others on display (Soffer *et al.* 1993). It may be too simplistic to view them as possessing one function only, and may be best to see them as functioning variably with regional manifestations on a general theme.

Whatever the actual functions of the figurines, several generalisations may be made, in particular in relation to the largely male burials. Although apparently naked in the main, the 'clothing' that exists on the venuses appears to be 'zonated' in nature, and the horizontal bands above the breasts on, for example, Pavlov I, Kostenki I, Avdeevo, Gagarino and conceivably Mal'ta and Buret', are strikingly reminiscent of the banded shell ornamentation observed in some burials, notably Sungir'. Although faces are rare, probably because they are facing down (in this light Tim Taylor *pers. comm.* has made the interesting

comment that they may be in an attitude of submission), their heads appear elaborately coiffured, again striking chords with the elaborate head decoration and association of the heads in burials with grave goods. Furthermore, it is their depositional context which offers, in my opinion, the most convincing indications that dead males (in the main) and female (in the main) statuettes were subtly linked, at least when they came to be laid to rest.

As many figurines were excavated in the infancy of archaeology, contextual information is often lacking, and it has become dogmatic that the original context of most of the figurines is lost to us. An examination of the old literature, however, reveals that enough information is present for a number of figures to allow, in my opinion, some generalisations (Table 19.2). French figurines seem to have been tucked away in caves, as with Italian and German examples. In the Grimaldi sites it is interesting that most of the figurines came from the Grotte du Prince, from which came no burials, whereas only two (perhaps three) figurines came from the Barma Grande, which was rich in burials (Bolduc *et al.* 1996; Mussi *et al.* 2000; Mussi 2003). Perhaps an inverse association between burials and figurines was in operation there. In Moravia figurines such as the 'Black Venus' of Dolní Věstonice and others at the same site and at neighbouring Pavlov were found in domestic refuse associated with fire and other animal figurines (Verpoorte 2001), and in some sites such as Kostenki and Avdeevo in Russia, female figurines were placed in pits, which, to some, suggested that they were "goddesses" protecting stores or even themselves buried accompanied by grave offerings (Gvozdover 1995). They also have a close association with fire, for example at Kostenki 1 layer 1, where a number were found in close proximity to hearths (Iakovleva 2000). Similarly, at Mainz-Linsenburg, one figurine was recovered from a small hand-sized pit in proximity to a hearth, as shown in Figure 19.6 (Neeb and Schmidtgen 1922–4; Bosinski 2000). These associations parallel the burials, as outlined above. At the Siberian sites of Mal'ta and Buret', figurines were recovered from pits, sometimes lying on their backs and associated with animal bones and artefacts, and sometimes placed vertically facing hearths (Derev'anko *et al.* 1998). Such an association with fire is common, in fact, across Eurasia, which is highly reminiscent of the association of burials with fire in Central, Eastern and probably Western Europe. A number are ochred, especially those of mammoth ivory, which probably reflects their original association with ochre when deposited in their last resting place, as a number of well-excavated figurines demonstrate. Pit contexts are common in Central and Eastern Europe, and when figurines have been recovered from such contexts they have associations that are not dissimilar to those in male burials (*i.e.* bones of large and dangerous herbivores, enigmatic items of ivory and bone). I suggest that venuses recovered from pits were not subject to the clearing of domestic space winding up in rubbish pits, nor that they presided over storage pits, but that these pits

Site	Context	Condition
Grotte du Pape (Brassempouy)	1. Near the right (western) wall. 2. The right part of the cave. 4. Left part of the avenue, in mixed ashy deposit. 5 & 6. Near the entrance. 7. Left side of the avenue, near the entrance.	Mostly broken and/or attenuated.
Abri du Facteur (Tursac)	Peripheral to main activity, 1.5m from wall, in ochre-rich deposit.	Attenuated.
Grotte des Rideaux (Lespugue)	Deep in the cave, possibly in a central position (Mussi pers. comm.)	
Le Goulet de Cazelle (Sireuil)	No information available	Attenuated.
Monpazier	No information available	Attenuated.
Weinberg (Mauern)	Very close to the wall of a small canopy in front of several caves, in an ochre-rich deposit. Rich carbon and bone suggest probable association with fire.	Attenuated.
Mainz Linsenberg	Apparently in proximity to hearths, one in a small depression.	Highly fragmentary.
Willendorf II	Habitation horizon, association with hearth	Complete, ochred.
Savignano	Recovered by farmer from clay deposit: probably open dwelling site.	Attenuated. Some ochre staining.
Balzi Rossi: Barma Grande or 'Grotte du Tunnel'	No information available	2 or 3 figurines.
Balzi Rossi: Grotte du Prince (Montreal figurines)	No reliable information.	Most Grimaldi figurines. Attenuation common.
Petrkovice	Ditch at edge of dwelling.	Broken (2 figurines).
Dolní Věstonice	Generally in the centre of dwellings, usually in association with fire (*i.e.* in centre/periphery of hearths. Some with ochre staining.	Generally broken.
Pavlov I	Domestic contexts including dwellings	Highly fragmentary & attenuated
Brno 2 (Francouzká Ulice)	Partial, probably male 'marionette'	In burial, next to skull
Moravany	No information available	Broken.
Poliakov (Kostenki I)	Numerous figurines & isolated heads, generally found in 'storage' pits & stained with ochre. Various other contents of pits, *e.g.* large mammal bones including mammoth, red/yellow ochre, sand lenses, bone charcoal. One (limestone) in dwelling.	Usually broken (mainly decapitated). Note 20 isolated heads. Limestone figurine in hut broken into three pieces.
Avdeevo	>25 figurines, almost all in pits (singular, double, triple). Some evidence of placing & association. One in dwelling, others in cultural layer.	Almost always 'damaged'. Often broken. Highly fragmentary marl figurines in upper pit fills or cultural layer.
Gagarino	Usually in a niche in the wall of the dwellings or pits.	Almost all broken.
Khotylevo II	One in small pit (lying against wall) associated with mammoth bones, stylised figurine & 'pellets' like Kostenki & Avdeevo.	Generally broken & fragmentary.

Table 19.2. Depositional contexts of mid Upper Palaeolithic 'Venus' Figurines.
Sources: Bisson, M. S. and Bolduc, P. (1994), Bolduc et al. 1996, Clottes and Cérou (1970), Delporte (1993a. 1993b), Gamble (1992. & pers. comm.), Gvozdova (1995), Hoffecker (2002), Klima (1983), Mussi 1997, Mussi et al. (2000), Piette (1895), Praslov (1993), Soffer (1985), Verpoorte 2001, White & Bisson (1998). Attenuated = no complete sculpting of the entire body, usually a lack of presence of the lower legs and feet.

were *graves*. As to whether graves functioned in the GPWKA similarly to those today is another matter, but I suggest at least that the primary function of pits that have yielded venus figurines among other items was indeed to *contain the figurines* in the same way that GPWKA graves contained dead bodies. At Avdeevo, dating to the latest phases of the GPWKA, one may separate pits containing one, two and three figurines. Table 19.3 presents some of the Avdeevo figurine contexts. Associations are always with large herbivore bones and enigmatic organic items. The parallel with burials – single, double and triple – is apparent. I interpret these as burials, in the case of the double and triple forms presumably of figurines that were in some way 'related'.

To summarise, while there are regional stylistic variation in figurines, a number of traits, while not shared by every figurine, are remarkably common. These are:

– A concern with fire.
– An association with the bones of large, dangerous herbivores, possibly meat offerings
– An association with enigmatic items of bone and ivory.
– Possible placing of limestone blocks over deposited figurines.
– Colouring with ochre, or association with activity

using ochre.
– Elaboration of the body (apparently not clothing) with zonated ornamentation of organics, beads, *etc.*
– Apparent elaboration of the head area (*e.g.* with bonnets, hats).
– Occasional reference to the pubic area (*e.g.* through carving of the vulva).
– Placement in caves, or in excavated 'graves'.

Discussion

The generalisations about venus figurines reveals some striking similarities with the GPWKA burials. I appreciate that there are regional differences in this correlation; it is, for example, strongest in the Kostenki-Avdeevo region and perhaps weakest in Western Europe. Although, therefore, some of these traits are not shared by all figurines, when viewed as one data set I suggest that this pattern cannot be coincidental. The males and females are dressed similarly, generally deposited similarly, given similar associations and even co-occur geographically. Why are both associated with fire, with ochre, with dangerous animals or meat offerings apparently across their geographical range? Why are most of the human buried dead male, and most of the 'modelled dead' female?

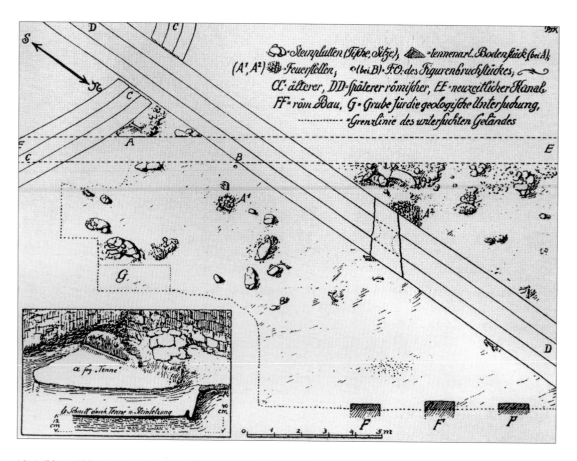

Figure 19.6. Plan of Mainz-Linsenburg after Neeb Schmidtgen 1922–24. Note small hearth (feuerstellen A¹) and figurine (B) in small pit approximately 1.5 metres from hearth.

Avdeevo figurines: >25 (10 mammoth ivory, 15 marl, chalk)

IVORY FIGURINES

Single burials

Figurine 3	Cultural layer	Damaged: 'several blows'
Figurine 4	Bottom of pit [Male?]	Damaged: head blow
Association: flint blades, adzes		
Figurine 5	Fragments, wall of pit	Damaged: highly fragmentary
Figurine 10	One fragment in pit house, one fragment in associated pit.	

Double burial

Figurine 1	Bottom of pit	Damaged head
Figurine 2	Bottom of pit (face down)	Damaged head, leg, back
Association: Decorated antler mattock.		

Triple burial

Figurine 6	Bottom of pit, face down	Damaged face, neck, legs
Figurine 7	Bottom of pit, on side (slid)	Back to back with...
Figurine 8	Bottom of pit, face down	Head opposite to Figure 7

Shallow dents on faces of all 3: not natural damage.
Association: 2 mammoth rib 'shovels', large ivory 'wand',
ivory imitation wolf metapodial, large flint blade.

MARL FIGURINES
Highly fragmentary
Found in cultural layer or in upper pit fills

'More than 300 small pits were opened on this site [Avd-N]. Judging by the intact
worked bone pieces, which were often found in them, they might be *storage pits.*'
(Gvozdover 1995, my emphasis).

Table 19.3. Venus figurines from Avdeevo (22,000 – 20,000 based on ^{14}C dates on Charcoal, after Gvozdover 1995). Interpreted as burials.

Perhaps Mussi's notions of transformation are relevant here, as with Verpoorte's notion that the figurines do not depict 'real' humans but imaginary, or part imaginary liminal beings. If the figurines represent humans that have been transformed into other beings, perhaps through the 'deaths' that are accorded detaching rituals, then the male humans were apparently undergoing transformation too. One cannot rule out the possibility that ochre was simply a form of colouring, although the ubiquitous association with fire might suggest that this is the agent of transformation, the phenomenon that links the living and the dead through its transformational properties. These observations certainly suggest that there was no fixed dichotomy between the 'living' and the 'dead': power was power and linked several states of being into a cosmo-logical whole involving males, females, dangerous animals, and enigmatic fossils and stones, burial, fire, and was marked by detaching rituals. Perhaps 'containment' in dark caves and below the ground, accompanied by other items of symbolic and powerful meaning, was the only way to dispose of such power.

The buried dead of the GPWKA presumably reflect a small subsection of Eurasian society in the Mid Upper Palaeolithic, probably one set of 'specialists' among many. Certainly, the degree of technical skill observable on lithic and organic tools suggests that other specialists existed at this time, and extending this argument to include indirect indications of fishing, trapping and hunting of large animals one might expect a panoply of specialists in this period. The connections between the buried dead and the figurines may reveal a shadowy glimpse of social and cosmological dynamics between the 27th and 24th millennia BP, which take us far further than simple dichotomies between the living and the dead. It is ironic that while new studies reveal more about this remote world, they serve to remind us of the little we understand of these peoples' lives. As Verpoorte (2001) has noted, as our understanding of the Mid Upper Palaeolithic progresses, it only serves '…to make the Upper Palaeolithic more questionable, more problematic…' Perhaps their power is still with us, these relics of a wild and undomesticated Europe, lingering, blurring, confusing.

Acknowledgements

I am grateful to Chris Knüsel and Rebecca Gowland for inviting me to speak at the BABAO session from which this publication arose, and for this opportunity to put my thoughts into print. I have greatly enjoyed collaborating with various colleagues in Europe and America on Mid Upper Palaeolithic burials, and I hope the references will draw attention to these people. Robin Dennell and John Hoffecker kindly drew my attention to aspects of the eastern Eurasian Mid Upper Palaeolithic record that I was unfamiliar with. Maureen Carroll kindly discussed notions of 'liminal' positions between the living and the dead in the classical and medieval periods. Stephen Aldhouse-Green, Margherita Mussi, and Alexander Verpoorte, who have all been generous with their thoughts and knowledge on these issues over the years, were kind enough to give the manuscript a close reading and offer incisive comments. Needless to say, faults, unsupported speculations and the like, are all mine. This is respectfully dedicated to the dead of the Upper Palaeolithic. If only they knew what thoughts would one day be spun about their distant lives.

References

Aldhouse-Green, S. H. R. (2000) Climate, Ceremony, Pilgrimage and Paviland: the 'Red Lady' in his palaeoecological and technoetic context. In Aldhouse-Green, S. H. R. (ed.) *Paviland Cave and the 'Red Lady': a Definitive Report.* 227–46. University of Wales College, Newport and National Museums and Galleries of Wales. Bristol, Western Academic and Specialist Press.

Aldhouse-Green, S. H. R. and Pettitt, P. B. (1998) Paviland Cave: contextualizing the Red Lady. *Antiquity* 72(278), 756–772.

Alt, K. W., Pichler, S., Vach, W., Klima, B., Vlček, E. and Sedmeiler, J. (1997) twenty-five thousand-year-old triple burial from Dolní Věstonice: an Ice Age family? *American Journal of Physical Anthropology* 102, 123–31.

Aujoulat, N., Geneste, J.-M., Archambeau, C., Delluc, M., Duday, H. and Henri-Gambier, D. 2002. La grotte ornée de Cussac: Le Buisson-de-Cadouin (Dordogne): premières observations. *Bulletin de la Société Préhistorique Française* 99(1), 129–37.

Bader, O. N. (1965) Nouvelles sépultures Paléolithiques en U.R.S.S. *Archéologie* 4, 61–4.

Bader, N. O. (1998) *Upper Palaeolithic Site Sungir' (Graves and Environment)* (in Russian). Moscow: Scientific World.

Bisson, M. S. and Bolduc, P. (1994) Previously undescribed figurines from the Grimaldi Caves. *Current Anthropology* 35(4), 458–68.

Bolduc, P., Cinq-Mars, J. and Mussi, M. (1996) Les figurines des Balzi Rossi (Italie): une collection perdue et retrouvée. *Bulletin de la Société Préhistorique de l'Ariège* LI, 15–53.

Bosinski, G. (2000) The period 30,000 to 20,000 BP in the Rhineland. In W. Roebroeks, M. Mussi, J. Svoboda and K. Fennema (eds.) *Hunters of the Golden Age: the Mid Upper Palaeolithic of Eurasia 30,000 – 20,000 BP,* 271–80. Leiden, University Press.

Buckland, W. (1823) *Reliquiae Diluvianae, or Observations on the Organic Remains contained in Caves, Fissures, and Diluvial Gravel and on Other Geological Phenomena, attesting the Action of an Universal Deluge.* London: John Murray.

Clottes, J. and Cérou, E. (1970) La Statuette féminine de Monpazier (Dordogne). *Bulletin de la Société Préhistorique Française* 67, 435–44.

Conard, N. J. (2003) Palaeolithic ivory sculptures from southwestern Germany and the origins of figurative art. *Nature* 426, 830–2.

Delporte, F. (1993a) Gravettian female figurines: a regional survey. In H. Knecht, A. Pike-Tay and R. White (eds.) *Before Lascaux: the Complex Record of the Early Upper Palaeolithic,* 243–57. Boca Raton, CRC Press.

Delporte, F. (1993b) *L'Image de la Femme dans l'Art Préhistorique.* Paris, Picard.

Derev'anko, A. P., Shimkin, D. B. and Powers, W. R. (1998) *The Paleolithic of Siberia: New Discoveries and Interpretations.* Urbana, University of Illinois Press.

Duarte, C. (2002) The burial taphonomy and ritual. In J. Zilhão and E. Trinkaus, (eds.) *Portrait of the Artist as a Child: the Gravettian Human Skeleton from the Abrigo do Lagar Velho and its Archeological Context,* 187–20.Lisbon, Ministéria da Cultura/Instituto Português de Arqueologia.

Duarte, C., Maurcio, J., Pettitt, P. B., Souto, P., Trinkaus, E. and Zilhao, J. (1999) An earlier Upper Palaeolithic human skeleton from the Abrigo do Lagar Velho (Portugal) and modern human emergence in Iberia. *Proceedings of the National Academy of Sciences (USA),* 96, 7604–9.

Duhard, J.-P. (1990) Les figurations humaines de Laugerie-Basse. *Paléo* 2, 217–28.

Duhard, J.-P. (1993) Upper Palaeolithic figures as a reflection of human morphology and social organisation. *Antiquity* 67, 83–91.

Formicola, V. (1988a) The male and the female in the Upper Palaeolithic burials from Grimaldi caves (Liguria, Italy). *Bulletin du Musée d'Anthropologie Préhistorique de Monaco* 31, 41–8.

Formicola, V. (1988b) The triplex burial of Barma Grande (Grimaldi, Italy). *Homo* 39(3), 130–43.

Formicola, V. (1989) The Upper Palaeolithic burials of Barma Grande, Italy. In Giacobini, G. (ed.) *Hominidae.* Milan, Jaca, 483–6.

Formicola, V. and Buzhilova, A. P. (2004) Double child burial from Sunghir (Russia): pathology and inferences for Upper Palaeolithic mortuary practices. *American Journal of Physical Anthropology* 124, 189–98.

Formicola, V., Pondrandolfi, A. and Svoboda, J. (2001) The Upper Palaeolithic triple burial of Dolní Věstonice: pathology and funerary behaviour. *American Journal of Physical Anthropology* 115, 372–9.

Formicola, V., Pettitt, P. B. and Del Luccese, A. (2004) A direct AMS radiocarbon date on the Barma Grande 6 Upper Palaeolithic skeleton. *Current Anthropology* 45(1), 114–18.

Frayer, D. W., Macchiareli, R. and Mussi, M. (1988) A case of dwarfism in the Italian late Upper Palaeolithic. *American Journal of Physical Anthropology* 75, 549–65.

Gamble, C. S. (1982) Interaction and alliance in Palaeolithic society. *Man* 17, 92–107.

Gamble, C. S. (1999) *The Palaeolithic Societies of Europe*. Cambridge, University Press.

Garrod, D. A. E. (1926) *The Upper Palaeolithic Age in Britain*. Oxford, Clarendon Press.

Gvozdover, M. (1995) *Art of the Mammoth Hunters: the Finds from Avdeevo*. Oxford, Oxbow.

Hahn, J. (1982) Demi-relief aurignacien en ivoire de la Grotte Geissenklösterle près d'Ulm (Allemagne Fédérale). *Bulletin de la Société Préhistorique Française* 79(3), 73–7.

Hahn, J. (1986) *Kraft und Aggression: Die Bottschaft der Eiszeitkunst im Aurignacien Süddeutschslands?* Tübingen: Archaeologica Venatoria 7.

Hahn, J. (1993) Aurignacian art in Central Europe. In H. Knecht, A. Pike-Tay and R. White (eds) *Before Lascaux: The Complex Record of the Early Upper Palaeolithic*, 229–41. Boca Raton, CRC Press,.

Henri-Gambier, D. (2002) Les fossils du Cro-Magnon (Les-Eyzies-de-Tayac, Dordogne): Nouvelles données sur leur position chronologique et leur attribution culturelle. *Bulletin et Mémoires de la Société Anthropologique de Paris* 14, 89–112.

Hillson, S. W. (2002) The dental age-at-death. In J. Zilhão and E. Trinkaus, (eds.) *Portrait of the Artist as a Child: the Gravettian Human Skeleton from the Abrigo do Lagar Velho and its Archeological Context*, 242–5. Lisbon, Ministéria da Cultura/Instituto Português de Arqueologia.

Hoffecker, J. F. (2002) *Desolate Landscapes: Ice Age Settlement in Eastern Europe*. New Brunswick, Rutgers University Press.

Huntington, R. and Metcalf, P. (1979) *Celebrations of Death: the Anthropology of Mortuary Ritual*. Cambridge, University Press.

Iakovleva, L. (2000) The Gravettian art of eastern Europe as exemplified in the figurative art of Kostenki 1. In W. Roebroeks, M. Mussi, J. Svoboda and K. Fennema (eds.) *Hunters of the Golden Age: the Mid Upper Palaeolithic of Eurasia 30,000 – 20,000 BP*, 125–33. Leiden, University Press.

Klima, B. (1983) Une nouvelle statuette Paléolithique à Dolní Věstonice. *Bulletin de la Société Préhistorique Française* 80, 176–8.

Klima, B. (1988) A triple burial from the Upper Palaeolithic of Dolní Věstonice, Czechoslovakia. *Journal of Human Evolution* 16, 831–35.

Klima, B. (1995) Dolní Věstonice II: ein Mammutjägerrastplatz und Seine Bestattungen. Liège, ERAUL 73.

Leroi-Gourhan, A. 1968. *The Art of Prehistoric Man in Western Europe*. London, Thames and Hudson.

McDermott, L. 1996. Self-representation in Upper Palaeolithic female figurines. *Current Anthropology* 37(2), 227–75.

Mussi, M. (1986) On the chronology of the burials found in the Grimaldi caves. *Antropologia Contemporanea* 9(2), 95–104.

Mussi, M. (1988) Continuite et discotinuie dans les practiques funeraires au Paleolithique: le cas de l'Italie. In O. Bar Yosef (ed.) *L'Homme de Neanderthal* Volume 5 *La Pensée*, 93–107. Liège, ERAUL 32.

Mussi, M. (1995) Rituels funeraires dans les sepultures Gravettiennes des Grottes de Grimaldi et de la Grotte delle Arene Candide: une mise au point. In M. Otte (ed.) *Nature et Culture*, 833–46. Liège, ERAUL 68.

Mussi, M. (1997) Die Rote von Mauern: la 'dame rouge' de Mauern revisitée. *Bulletin de la Société Préhistorique de l'Ariège* LII, 45–60.

Mussi, M. (2001) *Earliest Italy*. New York, Kluwer.

Mussi, M. (2003) East and south of the Alps: the MUP funerary and arstistic record of Italy and Moravia compared. In J. Svoboda and L. Sedláčková eds. (2003) *The Gravettian Along the Danube*, 252–269. Dolní Věstonice, Dolní Věstonice Studies Volume 11.

Mussi, M. and Zampetti, D. (1997) Carving, painting, engraving: problems with the earliest Italian design. In M. Conkey, O. Soffer, D. Stratmann, and N. G. Jablonski (eds.) *Beyond Art: Pleistocene Image and Symbol*, 217–38. San Francisco, Memoirs of the Californian Academy of Sciences.

Mussi, M., Cinq-Mars, J. and Bolduc, P. (2000) Echoes from the mammoth steppe: the case of the Balzi Rossi. In W. Roebroeks, M. Mussi, J. Svoboda, and K. Fennema (eds.) *Hunters of the Golden Age: the Mid Upper Palaeolithic of Eurasia 30,000 – 20,000 BP*, 105–24. Leiden, University Press.

Mussi, M., Frayer, D. W. and Macchiarelli, R. (1989) Les vivants et les morts. Les sepultures du Paleolithique Superieur en Italie et leur interpretation. In I. Hershkovitz (ed.) *People and Culture Change: Proceedings of the Second Symposium on Upper Palaeolithic, Mesolithic and Neolithic Populations of Europe and the Mediterranean Basin*, 435–58. Oxford, British Archaeological Reports International Series 508(i).

Neeb E. and Schmidtgen, O. 1922–1924. Eine altsteinzeitliche Freilandraststelle auf dem Linsenberg bei Mainz. *Mainzer Zeitschrift* 17–19, 108–112.

Oliva, M. (2000) The Brno II Upper Palaeolithic burial. In Roebroeks, W., Mussi, M., Svoboda, J. and Fennema, K. (eds.) *Hunters of the Golden Age: the Mid Upper Palaeolithic of Eurasia 30,000 – 20,000 BP*, 143–53. Leiden, University Press.

Parker Pearson, M. (1999) *The Archaeology of Death and Burial*. Stroud, Sutton.

Pettitt, P. B. (2000) Radiocarbon chronology, faunal turnover and human occupation at the Goat's Hole, Paviland. In Aldhouse-Green, S. (ed) *Paviland Cave and the 'Red Lady': a Definitive Report*, 63–71. University of Wales College, Newport and National Museums and Galleries of Wales. Bristol, Western Academic and Specialist Press.

Pettitt, P. B. (2002) The Neanderthal dead: exploring mortuary variability in Middle Palaeolithic Eurasia. *Before Farming* 1(1), 1–26. http://www.waspjournals.com/journals/beforefarming

Pettitt, P. B. (forthcoming) *The Palaeolithic Origins of Human Burial*. London, Routledge.

Pettitt, P. B. and Bader, O. N. (2000) Direct AMS Radiocarbon dates on the Sungir mid Upper Palaeolithic burials. *Antiquity* 74, 269–70.

Pettitt, P. B. and Trinkaus, E. (2000) Direct radiocarbon dating of the Brno 2 Gravettian human remains. *Anthropologie (Brno)* XXXVIII(2), 149–50.

Pettitt, P. B., van der Plicht, J., Bronk Ramsey, C., Monge Soares, A. and Zilhão, J. (2002) The radiocarbon chronology. In J. Zilhão and E. Trinkaus (eds.) *Portrait of the Artist as a Child: the Gravettian Human Skeleton from the Abrigo do Lagar Velho and its Archeological Context*, 132–8. Lisbon, Ministéria da Cultura/Instituto Português de Arqueologia.

Pettitt, P. B., Richards, M. P., Formicola, V. and Maggi, R. (2003) The Gravettian burial known as 'The Prince' ('Il Principe'): new evidence for his age and diet. *Antiquity* 77, 15–19.

Piette, E. (1895) La station de Brassempouy et les statuettes humaines de la période glyptique. *L'Anthropologie* VI, 129–152.

Praslov, N. (1993) Eine neue frauenstatuette aus Kalkstein von Kostenki I (Don, Russland). *Archäoligisches Korrespondenzblatt* 23, 165–73.

Rice, P. 1981. Prehistoric venuses: symbols of motherhood or womanhood? *Journal of Anthropological Research* 37, 402–14.

Roebroeks, W., Mussi, M., Svoboda, J. and Fennema, K. (eds.) (2000) *Hunters of the Golden Age: the Mid Upper Palaeolithic of Eurasia 30,000 – 20,000 BP.* Leiden, University Press.

Schlesier, K. H. (2001) More on the 'venus' figurines. *Current Anthropology* 42(3), 410.

Soffer, O. (1985) *The Upper Palaeolithic of the Central Russian Plain.* San Diego, Academic Press.

Soffer, O., Adovasio, J. M. and Hyland, D. C. 2000. The "Venus" Figurines: textiles, basketry, gender and status in the Upper Palaeolithic. *Current Anthropology* 41(4), 511–37.

Soffer, O., Adovasio, J. M. and Hyland, D. C. (2001) Reply to Schlesier. *Current Anthropology* 42(3), 410–13.

Soffer, O., Vandiver, P., Klíma, B. and Svoboda, J. (1993) The pyrotechnology of performance art: Moravian venuses and wolverines. In H. Knecht, A. Pike-Tay and R. White, (eds.) *Before Lascaux: the Complex Record of the Early Upper Palaeolithic,* 259–76. Boca Raton, CRC Press.

Svoboda, J. (1988) A new male burial from Dolní Věstonice. *Journal of Human Evolution* 16, 827–30.

Svoboda, J. (1991) Dolní Věstonice II Western Slope. Liège, ERAUL 54.

Svoboda, J. (2000) The depositional contexts of the Early Upper Palaeolithic human fossils from the Koněprusy (Zlatýkůn) and Mladeč caves, Czech Republic. *Journal of Human Evolution* 38, 523–36.

Svoboda, J., Ložek, V., and Vlček, E. (1996) *Hunters Between East and West: the Paleolithic of Moravia.* New York, Plenum.

Svoboda, J., van der Plicht, J. and Kuželka, V. (2002) Upper Palaeolithic and Mesolithic human fossils from Moravia and Bohemia (Czech Republic): some new ^{14}C dates. *Antiquity* 76, 957–61.

Taylor, T. (2002) The Buried Soul: How Humans Invented Death. London, Fourth Estate.

Trinkaus, E. and Holliday, T. (2000) The human remains from Paviland Cave. In Aldhouse-Green, S. (ed) Paviland Cave and the 'Red Lady': a Definitive Report, 141–204. University of Wales College, Newport and National Museums and Galleries of Wales. Bristol, Western Academic and Specialist Press.

Trinkaus, E., Holliday, T. W. and Brůžek, J. (2002a) The skeletal age-at-death. In J. Zilhão and E. Trinkaus, (eds.) *Portrait of the Artist as a Child: the Gravettian Human Skeleton from the Abrigo do Lagar Velho and its Archeological Context,* 246–51. Lisbon, Ministéria da Cultura/Instituto Português de Arqueologia.

Trinkaus, E. and Jelínek, J. (1997) Human remains from the Moravian Gravettian: the Dolní Věstonice 3 postcrania. Journal of Human Evolution 33, 33–82.

Trinkaus, E., Hillson, S. W. and Santos Coelho, J. M. (2002b) Palaeopathology. In J. Zilhão and E. Trinkaus, (eds.) *Portrait of the Artist as a Child: the Gravettian Human Skeleton from the Abrigo do Lagar Velho and its Archeological Context,* 489–95. Lisbon, Ministéria da Cultura/Instituto Português de Arqueologia.

Trinkaus, E., Jelinek, J. and Pettitt, P. B. (1999) Human remains from the Moravian Gravettian: the Dolní Věstonice 35 femoral diaphysis. *Anthropologie (Brno)* 37, 167–75.

Trinkaus, E., Svoboda, J., West, D. L., Sládek, V., Hillson, S., Drozdová, E. and Fišaková, M. (2000) Human remains from the Moravian Gravettian: morphology and taphonomy of isolated elements from the Dolní Věstonice II site. *Journal of Archaeological Science* 27, 1115–32.

Trinkaus, E., Formicola, V., Svoboda, J., Hillson, S. W. and Holliday, T. W. (2001) Dolní Věstonice 15: pathology and persistence in the Pavlovian. *Journal of Archaeological Science* 28, 1291–1308.

Verpoorte, A. (2001) *Places of Art, Traces of Fire. A Contextual Approach to Anthropomorphic Figurines in the Pavlovian (Central Europe, 29–24 kyr BP).* Leiden, Archaeological Studies of Leiden University 8.

White, R. and Bisson, M. (1998) Imagerie féminine du Paléolithique: l'apprt des nouvelles statuettes de Grimaldi. *Gallia Préhistoire* 40, 95–132.

Index